A Bloody and Barbarous God

A Bloody and Barbarous God

The Metaphysics of Cormac McCarthy

Petra Mundik

University of New Mexico Press \ Albuquerque

© 2016 by the University of New Mexico Press
All rights reserved. Published 2016
Printed in the United States of America

First paperback edition, 2021
Paperback ISBN: 978-0-8263-6334-3

Library of Congress Cataloging-in-Publication Data
Mundik, Petra, 1984–
  A bloody and barbarous god : the metaphysics of Cormac McCarthy / Petra Mundik.
    pages cm
  Includes bibliographical references and index.
  ISBN 978-0-8263-5670-3 (cloth : alk. paper) — ISBN 978-0-8263-5671-0 (electronic)
  1. McCarthy, Cormac, 1933– —Criticism and interpretation. 2. Metaphysics in literature.
  3. Good and evil in literature. 4. Apocalypse in literature. 5. Gnosticism in literature.
  6. Philosophy in literature. 7. Mysticism in literature. 8. Spirituality in literature. I. Title.
  II. Title: Metaphysics of Cormac McCarthy.
  PS3563.C337Z775 2016
  813'.54—dc23
                    2015025658

Cover photograph: *1853 San Acacio Mission Church San Luis Valley* courtesy of Wick Beavers
Book design: Catherine Leonardo
Composed in Minion Pro
Display is Clarendon LT Std

Contents

INTRODUCTION

"A Direct Apprehension of Reality": Cormac McCarthy and the Perennial Philosophy 1

CHAPTER 1

"Terra Damnata": The Anticosmic Mysticism of *Blood Meridian* 7

CHAPTER 2

"Suzerain of the Earth": Unravelling the Mystery of the Judge in *Blood Meridian* 31

CHAPTER 3

"Disciples of a New Faith": Satanic Parody in *Blood Meridian* 53

CHAPTER 4

"This Luminosity in Beings So Endarkened": Gnostic Soteriology in *Blood Meridian* 71

CHAPTER 5

"Diverging Equity": The Nature of Existence in *All the Pretty Horses* 101

CHAPTER 6

"All Was Fear and Marvel": Positive and Negative Epiphanies in *The Crossing*, Book 1 125

CHAPTER 7

"The Illusion of Proximity": Transcendence and Immanence in *The Crossing*, Book 2 141

CHAPTER 8

"Mourners in the Darkness": Blindness and Insight in *The Crossing*, Book 3 161

CHAPTER 9

"The Right and Godmade Sun": Destiny and Salvation in *The Crossing*, Book 4   179

CHAPTER 10

"Beauty and Loss Are One": Transience and Fate in *Cities of the Plain*   201

CHAPTER 11

"The Bloody and Barbarous God": Sin and Forgiveness in *Cities of the Plain*   217

CHAPTER 12

"That Man Who Is All Men": The Illusory and the Real in the Epilogue to the Border Trilogy   235

CHAPTER 13

"In All That Dark and All That Cold": Good and Evil in *No Country for Old Men*   259

CHAPTER 14

"All Things of Grace and Beauty": The Presence of the Sacred in *The Road*   287

NOTES   327

WORKS CITED   397

INDEX   413

Introduction

"A Direct Apprehension of Reality"

Cormac McCarthy and the Perennial Philosophy

■ Despite differing interpretations of McCarthy's fiction, most critics will agree that his writing demonstrates mystical strains. Though in his initial interpretation of McCarthy's early novels Vereen M. Bell classifies the novelist as a nihilist, four years later he has modified his views, conceding that, despite some nihilistic tendencies, "there can be no doubt that McCarthy is a genuine—if somehow secular—mystic" ("Between the Wish" 926). Edwin Arnold, however, had no doubts from the start about McCarthy's esoteric spirituality, arguing that he "is a mystic in the way his favorite writer Melville is a mystic, acknowledging and in fact honoring the majesty of the astounding and awful as well as of the simple and beautiful" ("Mosaic" 23). I believe that the presence of the "astounding and awful" in these novels forms much of the basis of the polarization in McCarthy criticism, precisely because it can be read as a nihilistic portrayal of the darker aspects of human existence or as a spiritual apprehension of the nature of evil.

In "Meeting McCarthy," Gary Wallace cites McCarthy's views on the subject of spirituality, recalling a conversation in which the reclusive novelist discussed his own spiritual experiences: "McCarthy commented that some cultures used drugs to enhance the spiritual experience, and that he had tried LSD before the drug was made illegal. He said that it had helped to open his eyes to these kinds of experiences." Wallace adds that McCarthy "said that he felt sorry for me because I was unable to grasp this concept of spiritual experience. He said that people all over the world, in every religion, were familiar with this experience. He asked if I'd ever read William James's *The Varieties of Religious Experience*. I had not. His attitude seemed to indicate that in this book were the answers to many of the questions posed during our evening discussion."[1] When Wallace admits to being "nonplussed" by these words, McCarthy tells him that he is simply talking about "Truth," which is what "writers must accomplish in their writing." When Wallace fails to understand what "Truth" is, McCarthy tells him that truth is simply "Truth" and "that the mystical experience is a direct apprehension of reality" (138). In the context of the conversation with Wallace, McCarthy seems to be referring to "reality" in the traditional, Platonic sense of the word, where the ultimate Reality is held to be the Good, or the Absolute. Huston Smith writes, "Atop being's hierarchy is the Form of the Good, the most real of the various grades of reality, the 'Good Itself.' Radically different from our everyday world, it can be described only through poetic images" (*Forgotten Truth* 5). I believe that McCarthy's novels are, to some extent, akin to these "poetic images," which strive toward a Platonic Reality. Such a reading seems to be supported by McCarthy's assertion that "Truth" is what writers must accomplish in their writing. Though McCarthy never directly attempts to describe the Good, he does adumbrate its presence in symbolic images of "the fire" and other such themes that will be discussed throughout this book, where I contend that his views of the mystical experience offering a glimpse of an ultimate "Truth" or spiritual Reality are in complete agreement with the major tenets of the Perennial Philosophy. Aldous Huxley neatly defines this term as follows: "*Philosophia Perennis*—the phrase was coined by Leibniz; but the thing—the metaphysic that recognizes a divine Reality substantial to the world of things and lives and minds; the psychology that finds in the soul something similar to, or even identical with, divine Reality; the ethic that places man's final end in the knowledge of the immanent and transcendent Ground of all being—the thing is immemorial and universal." According to Huxley, the Perennial Philosophy is the "Highest Common Factor" in all traditional religions and its subject matter is "the nature of eternal, spiritual Reality" (vii). McCarthy similarly believes that the spiritual experience, or a direct revelation of "Truth," is something with which "people all over the world, in every religion" are "familiar" (Wallace 138). This does not imply that every religious person is familiar with such an experience but rather that this experience is potentially accessible through every religion.

McCarthy's writing reveals a preoccupation not only with experiences of divine Reality but also with the question of evil. William Spencer argues that this is not only "a pervasive theme" in McCarthy's novels but "perhaps *the* issue of human existence that he is most interested in confronting in his fiction" (69). This preoccupation with evil, most often explored through depictions of violence, has given rise to many of the nihilistic readings of McCarthy's novels. Nevertheless, when such vivid descriptions of violence are combined with his interest in spiritual revelations and his portrayal of the created world as hostile to humanity, it becomes apparent that his world view also has much in common with Gnosticism, which is similarly characterized by a negative evaluation of the created world and a reliance on direct spiritual insight.

Before proceeding further, let me briefly outline the main tenets of the Gnostic belief system. Gnosticism emerged alongside Christianity between the first and third centuries CE, not so much as a heresy, but as a syncretic blending of many influences, including Christian, Hellenic, Babylonian, Egyptian, Iranian, Jewish, and even the Eastern traditions of Buddhism and Hinduism.[2] In *The Gnostic Religion*, Hans Jonas explains that according to Gnostic cosmology, the entire manifest cosmos "is the creation not of God but of some inferior principle" known as the *demiurge* (327). The demiurge rules over all that he has created, sometimes with the assistance of evil angels known as *archons*, while the real or alien God remains wholly "transcendent" (42). In the Gnostic genesis myth, flesh (*hyle*) and soul (*psyche*) were created by and belong to the demiurge, but "enclosed in the soul is the spirit," or *pneuma*, "a portion of the divine substance from beyond which has fallen into the world" (44). Thus, people are composed of both "mundane and extra-mundane" (44) principles and carry within them the potential for immanence as soul and flesh, or transcendence as pure spirit; "Duo sunt in homine" (Man has a twofold nature), as the medieval theologians put it.[3] According to Jonas,

> The radical nature of the dualism determines that of the doctrine of salvation. As alien as the transcendent God is to "this world" is the pneumatic self in the midst of it. The goal of gnostic striving is the release of the "inner man" from the bonds of the world and his return to his native realm of light. The necessary condition for this is that he *knows* about the transmundane God and about himself, that is, about his divine origin as well as his present situation, and accordingly also about the nature of the world which determines his situation. (44)

Knowledge of the true state of the cosmos and of the nature of the alien God is referred to as "gnosis" and, as Elaine Pagels explains in *The Gnostic*

Gospels, just as "those who claim to know nothing about ultimate reality are called agnostic (literally, 'not-knowing')" so "the person who does claim to know such things is called Gnostic ('knowing')" (xix). The possession of gnosis enables the spirit to become aware of its divine origins, escape from the created world, and reunite with the transcendent God. Although a vision of the cosmos as a terrible aberration may at first glance appear nihilistic, Gnosticism's primary concern is soteriological: salvation may be attained through gnosis.

Leo Daugherty recognizes this Gnostic vision in McCarthy's *Blood Meridian*, which he examines in his perceptive article "Gravers False and True: *Blood Meridian* as Gnostic Tragedy." Daugherty points out that while "most thoughtful people have looked at the world they lived in and asked, How did evil get into it?, the Gnostics have looked at the world and asked, How did *good* get into it?" He goes on to explain that for the Gnostics "evil was simply everything that *is*, with the exception of the bits of spirit emprisoned here," asserting that what the Gnostics saw is precisely "what we see in the world of *Blood Meridian*" (162). Though Daugherty was the first to offer an in-depth Gnostic reading of *Blood Meridian*, other critics have alluded to the Gnostic elements in McCarthy's fiction. Vereen Bell writes, "What with any other novelist would be a merely ornate style repeatedly seems to move us toward an epiphany, though only the kind that a seasoned gnostic might construe" (*Achievement* 132). Similarly, Sven Birkerts notes, "McCarthy has been, from the start, a writer with strong spiritual leanings. His orientation is Gnostic: he seems to view our endeavors here below as a violation of some original purity" (39). More recently, in *Reading the World: Cormac McCarthy's Tennessee Period*, Dianne Luce offers a Gnostic reading of McCarthy's earlier novel, *Outer Dark*.[4] Luce argues that *Outer Dark* "reflects McCarthy's awareness of Gnostic symbols, character types, and anticosmic attitudes and his extensive borrowing from or alluding to them in creating his own parable of spiritual alienation in the cosmic realm" (68). Harold Bloom also identifies a Gnostic trend running through the canonically valued works of American fiction in his influential *How to Read and Why*. Beginning with Melville's *Moby-Dick*, Bloom asks, "Just who is Melville's God, or the God of those who came after him: Faulkner, West, Pynchon, Cormac McCarthy?" Bloom's answer is that "Melville was not a Christian, and tended to identify with the ancient Gnostic heresy," and that "Faulkner is a kind of unknowing Gnostic," while "West, Pynchon, and McCarthy in their different ways are very knowing indeed" (237). Thus there is a critical consensus that Gnosticism informs McCarthy's writing. McCarthy's work provides numerous clues that point toward his conscious awareness of Gnosticism, the most overt of these occurring in *Suttree* (1979), where the protagonist watches construction workers, while the narrative voice describes them as "Gnostic workmen who would have down this shabby shapeshow that masks the higher world of form" (464). It is clear, then, that McCarthy is a "very knowing" Gnostic indeed, and there is evidence that he consciously draws inspiration from the symbols, allegories, and belief systems of this ancient religion.

I maintain that McCarthy's novels are enriched by a system of metaphysics that draws on the teachings of various esoteric traditions, namely, Gnosticism, Christian mysticism, and Buddhism. That is not to say that the novels do not draw their influences from other traditions—for example, Sufism, Hinduism, or Neoplatonism—but the necessarily limited scope of this book does not allow me to explore these other avenues of interpretation. All of the aforementioned traditions—including those not covered in this book—are located within the boundaries of the Perennial Philosophy, in that their subject matter is "the nature of eternal, spiritual Reality" (Huxley vii). Although Gnosticism stands at a slight angle to the other traditions, largely due to its "heretical" position, its emphasis on the primacy of personal experience and the soteriological importance of gnosis, or spiritual insight, is in line with the main tenets of the Perennial Philosophy.

I wish to clarify that I have focused on the later novels, partly due to the fact that a book offering close readings of McCarthy's entire oeuvre would be far too long, but mainly because I believe that they represent an important shift in interest on McCarthy's part, turning away from the wholly dark, Southern Gothic themes of his early period and becoming more metaphysically complex and spiritually affirmative. I refer to "the later novels" rather than "the Western novels" in order to include *The Road*, a work that I argue is the culmination of the world view that we see developing throughout the Western novels, despite the absence of a distinctly southwestern setting. Furthermore, I want to draw attention away from the Western motif, because, unlike the majority of writing on this subject, this book does not examine the sociopolitical and historical themes surrounding the southwestern region. Instead, I focus on McCarthy's metaphysics and theodicy, which, I contend, deal with the universal human condition, not just with human existence in the American Southwest.

I believe that McCarthy's writing yields to a method of exegetic reading that stretches back for centuries and is found in other cultures besides that of the West.[5] In this esoteric tradition, the literal meaning of the text conceals beneath its surface spiritual meanings available to the initiated reader, known in the West as the allegorical, the tropological, and the anagogical.[6] While McCarthy would certainly not lay claim to practicing the fourfold interpretation in all its complexity, he could justly characterize himself as one who subscribes to it at least in part. For, as I will argue throughout this book, there lies beneath the rich and complex surface of his writings a deeper meaning, overlooked by the great majority of his readers, which is as important to a full understanding of his work as the doctrines concealed beneath the surface are to the work of Blake or Dante. In the words of the great Tuscan poet,

> O voi ch'avete li 'ntelletti sani,
> mirate la dottrina che s'asconde
> sotto 'l velame de li versi strani.
> (O you who have sound intellects,
> consider the teaching that is hidden
> behind the veil of these strange verses.)
> (Alighieri, *Divine Comedy: Inferno*, canto IX, lines 61–63)

CHAPTER 1

"Terra Damnata"

The Anticosmic Mysticism of *Blood Meridian*

■ *Blood Meridian; or, The Evening Redness in the West*, Cormac McCarthy's first Western novel, follows the debaucheries of the historical Glanton gang as they murder, rape, and scalp their way across Mexico and the American Southwest of the 1850s. McCarthy's graphic portrayals of violence, set within surreal, nightmarish landscapes, convey a consistently anticosmic or world-rejecting attitude toward existence and creation. The marked absence of divine intervention in the face of extraordinary depravity suggests, at best, total divine indifference to human suffering, or at worst, the presence of a malevolent demiurge. McCarthy presents the reader with a vision of evil allowed to run rampant and unchecked; few novelists have attempted such a devastating portrayal of human brutality and cruelty. Although *Blood Meridian* does have a carefully researched historical setting, a reading that focuses solely on the conquest of the West as an imperialist process drastically limits the wider scope of the novel. In a review of *Blood Meridian* Tom Nolan writes, "McCarthy's screed is a theological purgative, an allegory on the nature of evil as timeless as Goya's hallucinations on war, monomaniacal in its conception and execution, it seeks and achieves the vertigo of insanity, the mad internal logic of a noon-time nightmare that refuses to end" (2). Nolan's identification of *Blood Meridian*'s "timeless" quality seems particularly pertinent, as the novel's exploration of evil extends beyond its specific spatiotemporal setting.

In *Blood Meridian*, evil is examined within the microcosm of individual human beings, as well as within the macrocosm of the manifest world. In his preoccupation with the problem of evil, McCarthy frequently employs Gnostic symbols and concepts, the most immediately apparent being the anticosmic depiction of hostile, hellish landscapes. Sam Smith defines the anticosmic position as a "belief that the material creation is inherently flawed and thus cannot be made suitable for any ideal purpose." Conversely, the procosmic position "views the natural world as created for and suited to the fulfillment of the eternal promises and purposes of God for man" (1). Gnosticism is clearly anticosmic in its insistence that "earthly material existence, like the world itself, is a product of the Demiurge and correspondingly is a sphere hostile to God, dominated by evil powers" (Rudolph 88). The narrative voice within *Blood Meridian* is markedly anticosmic, referring to the landscape as a "terra damnata of smoking slag" (61), a "godless quadrant cold and sterile" (293), "a purgatorial waste" where "nothing" moves "save carnivorous birds" (63), "a country where the rocks would cook the flesh from your hands and where other than rock nothing was" (138). This nightmare vision offers no relief and no hope of escape; journeys only take the traveler "into a land more hostile yet" (152). The landscape in *Blood Meridian* often evokes the imagery of T. S. Eliot's "The Waste Land." For example, "the rock trembled and sleared in the sun, rock and no water and the sandy trace and they kept watch for any green thing that might tell of water but there was not water" (62) recalls "What the Thunder Said": "Here is no water but only rock / Rock and no water and the sandy road" (lines 331–32). As in "The Waste Land," the desolate landscapes through which McCarthy's characters wander serve as symbolic projections of spiritual desolation.[1]

One of the most obscure allusions to the hostility of the created world is evoked through a passage that describes Glanton's gang sleeping "with their alien hearts beating in the sand like pilgrims exhausted upon the face of the planet Anareta, clutched to a nameless wheeling in the night" (46). Leo Daugherty interprets the reference to "Anareta" in the following way: "Anareta was believed in the Renaissance to be 'the planet which destroys life,' and 'violent deaths are caused' when the 'malifics' have agents in 'the anaretic place' (*OED* entry, 'anareta') . . . the implication is clearly that our own Earth is Anaretic" (163). McCarthy's evocative descriptions of malevolent landscapes, in which "death seem[s] the most prevalent feature" (48) can thus be read as Gnostic portrayals of a nightmarish, Anaretic world.

Even the sun in *Blood Meridian* is portrayed in a decidedly Gnostic fashion, signifying death and violence, rather than traditional notions of renewal and illumination.[2] McCarthy's trademark "bloodred" sunsets abound in *Blood Meridian*, establishing a clear connection between the sun and the numerous scenes of bloodshed that occur throughout the novel. The most fascinating references to the sun, however, are those that defamiliarize the celestial sphere entirely. For example, the sun is described as being "the color of steel" (15), immediately evoking weaponry, and hence violence, but also introducing an unexpected sensation of coldness. The revolting "urine-colored sun" that rises "blearily through panes of dust on a dim world" (47) is similarly unsettling. The most startling solar imagery, however, consists of the following: "The top of the sun rose out of nothing like the head of a great red phallus until it cleared the unseen rim and sat squat and pulsing and malevolent behind them" (44–45).[3] In *Blood Meridian*, McCarthy inverts the traditional, life-giving symbolism of the sun—hence the image of the phallus and all the subsequent connotations of procreation—and turns it into a symbol of cosmic malevolence. It is noteworthy that in this inversion of a concept upheld by the Platonist and Neo-Platonist philosophers of classical antiquity, for whom the sun was a visible manifestation of the "Good," McCarthy is following in the subversive footsteps of the Gnostic heretics.[4] As Hans Jonas explains, "Gnostic dualism comes as a new principle of meaning, appropriates the elements which it can use for its purposes, and subjects them to a radical reinterpretation" (260). Whereas for the classical mind, the seven "heavenly spheres"—namely the sun, the moon, Mercury, Venus, Mars, Jupiter, and Saturn—"had represented the divinity of the cosmos at its purest, they now most effectively separated it from the divine. Enclosing the created world, they made it a prison for those particles of divinity which had become entrapped in this system" (260–61). For the Gnostics, the heavenly spheres become a symbol of oppression, representing the barriers that surround the earth and keep the divine human spirit imprisoned within the manifest realm of matter. Jonas explains that even for pagan nature worshippers the sun occupied a many-faceted position, being at the same time "the god which dispenses light, warmth, life, growth . . . who victoriously rises out of night, puts to flight the winter, and renews nature" but who also brings "scorching, pestilence, and death" (257). The sun in *Blood Meridian* has been reduced to its wholly negative components, bringing pestilence in the form of a "heliotropic plague" of gold seekers, "itinerant degenerates bleeding westward" (78), who seem to be under the maleficent influence of the sun. Pestilence is also evoked through the image of the Dieguenos, who "watched each day for that thing to gather itself out of its terrible incubation in the house of the sun . . . and whether it be armies or plague or pestilence or something altogether unspeakable they waited with a strange equanimity" (300–301). The concept of the sun bringing disease is emphasized not only through direct references to "plague or pestilence" but also through the oblique reference to "incubation," as though the sun were hatching a bacterial menace.

The idea that the sun may bring "something altogether unspeakable" is emphasized throughout the novel. When the Glanton gang abandons a murdered Apache in the desert, they leave him to "scrutinize with his dying eyes the calamitous advance of the sun" (110), as though the progression of the sun across the sky marked the progress of some terrible catastrophe. The imagery of disaster and chaos is further developed in a passage that describes the sunset as the "red demise of that day" and "the distant pandemonium of the sun" (185). The sun in *Blood Meridian* is portrayed as a merciless devourer. Wandering in the desert, men with "burnedout eyes" grow "gaunted and lank under the white hot suns of those days" until they appear "like beings for whom the sun hungered" (248). Its indifference to human beings is made apparent in its ability to wipe out all trace of their violent deaths: "In the days to come the frail black rebuses of blood in those sands would crack and break and drift away so that in the circuit of few suns all trace of the destruction of these people would be erased ... and there would be nothing, nor ghost nor scribe, to tell to any pilgrim in his passing how it was that people had lived in this place and in this place died" (174). The sun in *Blood Meridian* is a bringer of death, not life. Such a description of a celestial body usually associated with the life-giving properties of light and warmth suggests that in McCarthy's narrative the Gnostic horror of existence extends well beyond our planet and includes the entire cosmos in its negative evaluation.

In keeping with the Gnostic penchant for theological subversion, McCarthy's portrayals of the sun invert not only the aforementioned classical philosophies but also Christian teachings. The Glanton gang stumbles across the remains of a group of scalped travelers, again described as "right pilgrims nameless among the stones with their terrible wounds." *Blood Meridian* is replete with "pilgrims" who never find their way to any kind of god and whose journeys lead straight to death. The dead, in "their wigs of dried blood," lie "gazing up with ape's eyes at brother sun now rising in the east" (153). Here, "brother sun" is a chillingly sarcastic reference to Saint Francis of Assisi's (1182–1226) "Laudes Creaturarum," or "Praise of the Creatures," also referred to as the "Canticle of the Sun":

> Be praisèd, O My Lord, by all Thy creatures!
> And chiefly by Monsignor Brother Sun,
> Whom in the day Thou lightenest for us;
> For fair is he and radiant with resplendence;
> And of Thee, Most High, beareth he the semblance.
> (lines 6–10)

The last two lines are most telling and McCarthy's implications are clear: if the sun bears the likeness of the creator God, what terrible things can we deduce about this deity's nature by examining the malevolent sun of *Blood Meridian*?

In *Blood Meridian*, as in Gnostic thought, the heavenly spheres are regarded as symbols of evil. Hans Jonas describes the Gnostic view of the cosmos in great detail:

> We can imagine with what feelings gnostic men must have looked up to the starry sky. How evil its brilliance must have looked to them, how alarming its vastness and the rigid immutability of its courses, how cruel its muteness! The music of the spheres was no longer heard, and the admiration for the perfect spherical form gave place to the terror of so much perfection directed at the enslavement of man. The pious wonderment with which earlier man had looked up to the higher regions of the universe became a feeling of oppression by the iron vault which keeps man exiled from his home beyond. (261)

The novel features numerous references to the starry sky, all of which are marked with a sense of dismay, fear, or loneliness: "The night sky lies so sprent with stars that there is scarcely space of black at all and they fall all night in bitter arcs and it is so that their numbers are no less" (15). Such descriptions evoke a sense of oppressive eternity, for no matter how many stars fall in their "bitter arcs," their numbers are never lessened. The oppressive quality of the cosmos is emphasized further when the stars are described as burning "with a lidless fixity" (213), as though they were unblinking eyes, fixed upon the world below in unceasing surveillance. The night sky is full of evil omens, such as the "pale green meteor" that "passed overhead and vanished silently in the void" (227). Even the "constellation of Cassiopeia" evokes a sense of cosmic malice, burning "like a witch's signature on the black face of the firmament" (256), as though the malevolent forces responsible for creation had signed their handiwork for all to see.

Much like the French mathematician and mystic Blaise Pascal (1623–1662), who wrote of "the terrifying immensity of the universe which surrounds me" (6), the Gnostics were dismayed by the spatial and temporal enormity of the cosmos, believing that "the vastness and multiplicity of the cosmic system expresses the degree to which man is removed from [the alien] God" (Jonas 43). Jonas explains that the "starry sky—which from Plato to the Stoics was the purest embodiment of reason in the cosmic hierarchy . . . and therefore the divine aspect of the sensible realm" became for the Gnostics "the fixed glare of alien power and necessity" (254). Furthermore, the night sky's "vastness, power, and perfection of order" no longer evoked "contemplation and imitation but aversion and revolt" (255). The narrative voice in *Blood Meridian* frequently evokes the enormity of the cosmos: "The sun when it rose caught the moon in the west so that they lay opposed to each other across the earth, the sun whitehot and the moon a pale replica, as if they were the ends of a common bore beyond whose terminals burned worlds past all reckoning" (86). These words suggest that not only does the universe extend forever outward to infinite numbers of other worlds, but this terrible infinitude also extends forever downward, albeit in more metaphysical sense, into "the awful darkness inside the world" (111). This apprehension of the terrible vastness of the created world is prevalent throughout McCarthy's work.[5]

Blood Meridian abounds in passages that evoke the terror of the void, featuring descriptions of "the vast world of sand and scrub shearing upward into the shoreless void" and "to the uttermost rebate of space" (50) or "staccato mountains bespoken blue and barren out of the void" (175) or the "ribbed frames of dead cattle" that lie "like the ruins of primitive boats upturned upon that shoreless void" (247).[6] Paul Oppenheimer explains that the "void" is a concept closely allied with cinematic portrayals of evil, especially in situations depicting the aftermath of evil actions: "Past the disaster lies not a horror but a blank, a nothing, a zero, a black hole. . . . The very physics of the universe, their natural laws, have devoured themselves, to leave a silent state of nil. The universe has performed itself into exhaustion, chaos, a word that to the Greeks who invented it meant not anarchy or disorder but a yawn, a gap, nothing" (7). In *Blood Meridian*, frenzied eruptions of violence leave only a "shoreless void" (247) in their wake.

Wandering lost through the wilderness, the kid contemplates a companion named Sproule and sees that "he was wounded in an enemy country far from home and although his eyes took in the alien stones about yet the greater void beyond seemed to swallow up his soul" (65).[7] This passage evokes a Gnostic despair at the terrible vastness of creation, which "swallows up" and imprisons the human spirit. It also emphasizes the Gnostic motif of alienation, which teaches that the divine spirit within us feels estranged among the "alien stones" of the created world. In fact, the idea that human beings are prisoners on earth is alluded to directly in *Blood Meridian* when the Glanton gang is referred to as "a patrol condemned to ride out some ancient curse" (151). Given the purgatorial wasteland that dominates the novel, this ancient curse seems to be manifest existence itself. Elsewhere, the horses of the Glanton gang are described as trudging "sullenly the alien ground," while "the round earth rolled beneath them silently milling the greater void wherein they were contained" (247). The passage not only emphasizes the alien nature of the created world but also locates this alienation within the greater context of the enormity of the cosmos.

The narrative voice then goes on to evoke the metaphysical complexity of this vision of alienation, in what is perhaps one of the most frequently cited passages within the novel: "In the neuter austerity of that terrain all phenomena were bequeathed a strange equality and no one thing nor spider nor stone nor blade of grass could put forth claim to precedence. The very clarity of these articles belied their familiarity, for the eye predicates the whole on some feature or part and here was nothing more luminous than another and nothing more enshadowed and in the optical democracy of such landscape all preference is made whimsical and a man and a rock become endowed with unguessed kinship" (247). The reader is presented with a reductionist vision in which inherent value and meaning have been leveled out so that it is no longer possible to say that human beings are in any way better or more significant than inanimate minerals. This "strange equality" is not to be mistaken for the transcendent state of unity described by the Perennial Philosophy, in which all phenomena appear equally unreal, or as manifestations of māyā (illusion). Frithjof Schuon explains that "the metaphysical doctrine of illusion is not just a solution of convenience which justifies bringing everything on the plane of phenomena to a single level" (67). He adds, "Metaphysical synthesis is not a physical levelling out" because "there is no true synthesis without discernment" (68). The description of the "optical democracy" in *Blood Meridian* is concerned with just such a physical leveling out.

René Guénon also addresses this concept of "levelling out" in *The Reign of Quantity*, a work that details the decline of the Perennial Philosophy in the modern world. Guénon writes that unity and uniformity are often mistaken for the same thing, but "the imposition of uniformity" actually leads "in a direction exactly opposite to that of true unity" (67). Guénon explains that the "uniformity, in order that it may be possible, presupposes beings deprived of all qualities and reduced to nothing more than simple numerical 'units'" (65). The "result of all efforts made to realize" such uniformity "can only be to rob beings more or less completely of their proper qualities" (66). He concludes by stating that all efforts at "levelling"—such as we witness in *Blood Meridian*'s optical democracy—"always work downwards... not only below the degree occupied by the most rudimentary of living beings, but also below that occupied ... [by] lifeless matter" (66–67). Hence, what we witness in *Blood Meridian* is a caricature of unity, in which a human being is not only reduced to the level of a spider, or a blade of grass, but in which all of these living things are placed on the same level as inanimate stones, thus completely obliterating the traditional hierarchical chain of being.

Looking at this passage in the context of McCarthy's entire oeuvre, with its metaphysical overtones and theological preoccupations, it is unlikely that this vision of "optical democracy" constitutes McCarthy's understanding of the world, at least as it is presented in his novels. Though it is difficult to prove that at the time of writing *Blood Meridian* McCarthy disapproved of such a reductionist view of living beings, his later work *The Sunset Limited* provides us with some interesting insights into his latest view on the matter. In this "novel in dramatic form," the character Black puts forward a view of humanity that is completely in line with the teachings of the Perennial Philosophy: "I would say that the thing we are talkin about is Jesus," says Black, "but it is Jesus understood as that gold at the bottom of the mine. He couldnt come down here and take the form of a man if that form was not done shaped to accommodate him" (95). The image of the "gold at the bottom of the mine" occurs in both Buddhist and Gnostic thought and "in both cases this is a simile for the divine spark in man" (Conze, *Further Buddhist Studies* 29). In *The Sunset Limited*, Black goes on to stress this divine essence within all human beings, even at the cost of sounding like a heretic: "And if I said that there aint no way for Jesus to be ever man without ever man bein Jesus then I believe that might be a pretty big heresy. But that's all right. It aint as big a heresy as sayin that a man aint all that much different from a rock. Which is how your view looks to me" (95). Here, man and rock do not share an unguessed kinship. Even the character White—a suicidal rationalist whose argument runs counter to Black's throughout the play—has to concede that a human being is higher than a rock: "It's not my view," he retorts. "I believe in the primacy of the intellect" (96). Thus the "optical democracy" passage in *Blood Meridian* puts forward a view that prevents human beings from seeking their full potential. As the traditions of the Perennial Philosophy, as well as the metaphysics underlying McCarthy's fiction, proclaim, no matter how blackened the human heart may be, a divine essence remains. Whether one considers humanity in spiritual or intellectual terms, the existence of the spirit or the mere presence of consciousness necessarily separates a human being from an inanimate stone. Thus the vision of "optical democracy" seems to arise out of the apparent perversities—in both thought and action—that constitute the depraved world of *Blood Meridian*, rather than being a nihilistic pronouncement on the essential meaninglessness of human existence.

Blood Meridian explores these aforementioned perversities in detail, arguing that human beings are born with an inherent potential for evil. When we are first introduced to the nameless protagonist of *Blood Meridian*, known only as "the kid," we are told: "He can neither read nor write and in him broods already a taste for mindless violence" (3). These words suggest that bloodlust lies at the very core of human nature; it is something that comes from within, not without. When the child grows into "the kid," he indulges his taste for violence in pub brawls with soldiers: "They fight with fists, with feet, with bottles or knives. All races, all breeds" (4). The narrative voice thus implicates the entire human race in this mad, violent struggle.

Human depravity is also discussed by a lone hermit who shelters the kid early in the novel. After showing the kid "some man's heart, dried and blackened," the hermit cradles "it in his palm as if he'd weigh it" (18). This strange action evokes an esoteric reference to the Egyptian Anubis, the jackal-headed god of the dead, who is thought to weigh the hearts of human beings after death to determine which is righteous and which corrupt.[8] Clearly the human heart does not pass the test, for the hermit announces, "A man's at odds to know his mind cause his mind is aught he has to know it with. He can know his heart, but he don't want to. Rightly so. Best not to look in there. It ain't the heart of a creature that is bound in the way that God has set for it" (19). Traditionally the heart was considered the seat of passions and desires, which must be overcome by rejecting earthly concerns and seeking refuge in spiritual pursuits. Buddhist sutras describe the heart as "the poisonous serpent... which is always breathing out the fire of the three poisons, bringing us agonies and sufferings" (qtd. in Conze, *Buddhist Scriptures* 142). Gnostic teachings also warn against the danger of letting oneself be ruled by one's heart, for the "evil powers" that rule the cosmos are "evident and active in [humanity's] passions and desires" (Rudolph 88). Similarly, Manichean doctrines teach, "Although man has Light within him, the Darkness made sure that he would perpetuate his enslavement by desire" (Smoley 57). These traditions, however, all stress the importance of self-knowledge. "Know Thyself" advised the Delphic Oracle, as did the Gnostic Gospels: "Let every man be watchful of himself. Whosoever is watchful of himself shall be saved from the devouring fire" (qtd. in Jonas 84). Thus the hermit's "rightly so" can be read sarcastically, for human beings would greatly benefit from knowing their own hearts, if only they had the courage to examine what lies within. In fact, in *The Achievement of Cormac McCarthy*, Vereen Bell argues that the hermit, with his pronouncements on humanity's willful ignorance of its own depravity, "comes closer to speaking the paraphrased theme of the novel than any other spokesman" (127). The narrative voice of *Blood Meridian* indirectly urges the reader to closely examine this blackened heart, already weighed and found wanting by the hermit. Nevertheless, it is worthwhile to note that the hermit attempts to rape or molest the kid when the latter falls asleep: "He woke sometime in the night with the hut in almost total darkness and the hermit bent over him and all but in his bed" (20). Thus the hypocritical, pederastic hermit must be included in the novel's negative evaluation of the human race.

As mentioned earlier, the terrifying "void" that constitutes the cosmos is a central metaphor in *Blood Meridian*, but the horror applies not only to the macrocosm of the solar system but also to the microcosm of the human being. Brady Harrison argues that in *Blood Meridian* the "void without speaks to the void said to lurk within the Western consciousness." He goes on to cite "Conrad's *Heart of Darkness* (1899) as the most famous example of the void within as the void without," because "the heart of darkness lurks as much in Kurtz, as Conrad presents it, as in the African jungle" (35). Extrapolating this idea to *Blood Meridian*, we could argue that "the secret dark of the earth's heart" (195) mirrors the awful darkness inside the heart of the human being. The various atrocities described in vivid detail throughout the novel confirm this view. On one occasion the Glanton gang attacks a village of peaceful elders, women, and children simply because their scalps are indistinguishable from those of the Apaches they were hired to kill. The men are depicted knee-deep in blood-red water, "hacking at the dying and decapitating those who knelt for mercy" (156), while others lie "coupled to the bludgeoned bodies of young women dead or dying on the beach" (157). Not content with the bounty collected for the scalps, the men also make belts and harnesses from the skins of the slain.

The Glanton gang is depicted in ways that evoke a primitive hunting clan. Its members appear as "a pack of viciouslooking humans . . . bearded, barbarous, clad in the skins of animals stitched up with thews and armed with weapons of every description . . . dangerous, filthy, brutal." Descriptions of the gang suggest cannibalism: "the trappings of their horses" are "fashioned out of human skin and their bridles woven up from human hair and decorated with human teeth," the riders themselves wear "scapulars or necklaces of dried and blackened human ears," and the entire procession is "like a visitation from some heathen land where they and others like them fed on human flesh" (78).[9] Being scalp hunters, the members of Glanton's gang do in fact feed on human flesh, albeit in an indirect sense, for they exchange the scalps for food and weapons and are therefore using human flesh as a form of currency.

The Glanton gang is often portrayed as having somehow regressed to a prehistoric level: "There was nothing about these arrivals to suggest even the discovery of the wheel" (232). For that matter, there was nothing to suggest even the invention of fire, or speech: "In darkness absolute the company sat among the rocks without fire or bread or camaraderie any more than banded apes. They crouched in silence eating raw meat . . . and they slept among the bones" (148). As they wander through the plains, they appear to predate speech itself: "Like beings provoked out of the absolute rock and set nameless and at no remove from their own loomings to wander ravenous and doomed and mute as gorgons shambling the brutal wastes of Gondwanaland in a time before nomenclature was and each was all" (172). The hyperbolic reference to Gondwanaland—a "supercontinent thought to have once existed in the southern hemisphere and to have broken up in Mesozoic or late Palæozoic times" (*Oxford English Dictionary Online*; hereafter cited as *OED*)—further emphasizes the notion that there is something primitive and regressive about the Glanton gang, as though they had not evolved beyond the level of the earliest life-forms.

Perhaps the most shocking aspect of *Blood Meridian* is that the narrative voice continually reminds the reader that there is nothing unique about the behavior of the Glanton gang. Bill Baines writes, "McCarthy's book focuses on cruelty, perhaps man's most apparent quality in the world the author creates. The book's inhumanity is not—as is often the case in Westerns—the cruelty of white to Indian or Indian to white, but the cruelty of human to human perennial to literature and to other affairs of mankind" (59). The novel is not solely preoccupied with the depravity of the Glanton gang but also features a lengthy description of a horde of Comanches attacking Captain White's gang of Filibusters. Piping on "flutes made from human bones" (52), the Comanches are depicted as "a horde from a hell more horrible yet than the brimstone land of christian reckoning, screeching and yammering and clothed in smoke like those vaporous beings in regions beyond right knowing where the eye wanders and the lip jerks and drools" (53). After the slaughter, "some of the savages" were "so slathered up with gore they might have rolled in it like dogs" and others "fell upon the dying and sodomized them with loud cries to their fellows" (54). Clearly, this is no ordinary Western and there are no "good guys" among these cowboys and Indians. The passage not only represents the hallucinogenic and nightmarish qualities of this vision but also suggests the quintessentially Gnostic idea that this world is already worse than any hell we could ever imagine. R. M. Grant explains, "Ultimately, the difference between Christian and Gnostic philosophical theology seems to lie in their attitudes toward the world. For any Gnostic the world is really hell" (150).

The world of *Blood Meridian* is drenched in violence and bloodshed and the enigmatic Judge Holden takes every opportunity to remind the Glanton gang that human life has always been this way.[10] While the scalp hunters sit among the ruins of a settlement of the Anasazi, the judge proclaims, "All progressions from a higher to a lower order are marked by ruins and mystery and a residue of nameless rage" (146). The judge claims that it is this "nameless rage" that shapes human history. The "nameless rage" evokes W. B. Yeats's poem "Meru," which describes how "man," "despite his terror, cannot cease," "Ravening, raging, and uprooting that he may come / Into the desolation of reality" (lines 4–7). The judge argues that history is cyclical, doomed to repeat itself in the rise and fall of civilization: "This you see here, these ruins wondered at by tribes of savages, do you think that this will be again? Aye. And again. With other people, with other sons" (147). Barcley Owens argues that "when Judge Holden gestures toward the Anasazi ruins and describes them as the end result of empire building, he prophesises America's future" (119). Indeed, this is the imagined future of the entire human race, which we will later see depicted in McCarthy's apocalyptic novel *The Road*.

The notion that a remarkable penchant for brutality dates back to the very beginnings of human history is demonstrated by McCarthy's epigraphic reference to the three-hundred-thousand-year-old skull, which "shows evidence of having been scalped." The reference, taken from a 13 June 1982 article in the *Yuma Daily Sun*, also serves as a reminder that much of the violence depicted in *Blood Meridian* is not the work of outlandish fiction but is grounded in historical reality. Harold Bloom makes this point in *How to Read and Why* when he writes, "None of [*Blood Meridian*'s] carnage is gratuitous or redundant; it belonged to the Mexico-Texas borderlands in 1849–50, which is where and when most of the novel is set" (255). Sadly, one does not need to look far to find other instances of carnage in the annals of human history.

The novel continually highlights humanity's potential for savagery by developing a metaphoric connection between human beings and wolves. "Wolves cull themselves, man" announces the judge. "What other creature could? And is the race of man not more predacious yet?" (147). *Blood Meridian*'s catalog of massacres, depravities, and atrocities provides evidence in the affirmative.[11] The judge's words recall those of Plautus (254–184 BCE) in *Asinaria*, "Lupus est homo homini," or "Man is a wolf to man" (2.4.88). The connection between wolf and man is maintained throughout the novel: "the hunters smiled among themselves" after hearing "the howling of a wolf" (117); the ex-priest-cum-scalp-hunter, Tobin, announces that he "would never shoot a wolf" and knows "other men of the same sentiments" (129); and at "night the wolves in the dark forests called to [the scalp hunters] as if they were friends to man" (188). The Glanton gang even functions like a wolf pack: "Although each man among them was discrete unto himself, conjoined they made a thing that had not been before and in that communal soul were wastes hardly reckonable more than those whited regions on old maps where monsters do live" (152). The collective sum of their brutality is greater than its individual components. Their "communal soul" becomes a magnified version of the darkness inside each man's heart, where one feels it is "best not to look" (19) for fear of what "monsters" one may find.[12]

Precisely because the suffering and cruelty inflicted by human beings against one another is so ubiquitous in *Blood Meridian*, it is easy to overlook the fact that nature itself is presented as being inherently cruel. Animals also injure and devour each other, as the following description of a "snakebit" horse demonstrates: "It had been bitten on the nose and its eyes bulged out of the shapeless head in a horror of agony and it tottered moaning toward the clustered horses of the company with its long misshapen muzzle swinging and drooling and its breath wheezing in the throttled pipes of its throat. The skin had split open along the bridge of its nose and the bone shone through pinkish white." The other horses show no compassion for the crazed animal; instead it frightens and infuriates them and it is clear that they would like to kill it: "A small mottled stallion ... struck at the thing twice and then turned and buried its teeth in its neck. Out of the mad horse's throat came a sound that brought the men to the door" (19). The suffering of the horse is as senseless as the suffering of the victims of Glanton's gang, and yet it is entirely natural. The novel establishes no dichotomous opposition between natural and moral evil, suggesting that the condition of all life on earth is one of violence, suffering, and brutality.

Blood Meridian presents the reader with a world in which everything devours everything else.[13] The novel is filled with such sights as a "howling wilderness" where "coyotes had dug up the dead and scattered their bones" (42), "three buzzards hobbl[ing] about on the picked bone carcass of some animal" (26), the stone floor of a church "heaped with the scalped and naked and partly eaten bodies of some forty souls" (60), and a village where "the dead were still in the streets and buzzards and pigs were feeding on them" (181). Men, too, partake in this devouring: "One of the mares had foaled in the desert and this frail form soon hung skewered on a paloverde pole over the raked coals while the Delawares passed among themselves a gourd containing the curdled milk taken from its stomach" (161). Toward the end of the novel the kid encounters a field of slain buffalo with "the meat rotting on the ground and the air whining with flies and the buzzards and ravens and the night a horror of snarling and feeding with the wolves half crazed and wallowing in the carrion" (317). The latter feeding frenzy recalls a scene from McCarthy's favorite novel, Herman Melville's *Moby-Dick*, where "thousands on thousands of sharks, swarming round the dead Leviathan, smackingly feasted on its fatness" (286).[14] Melville's words—"Consider, once more, the universal cannibalism of the sea; all whose creatures prey upon each other, carrying on eternal war since the world began" (270)—may well be extended to cover the wastelands of *Blood Meridian*.

Such a view of nature is distinctly Gnostic; as a Manichean text illustrates, it is the fate of all living creatures to be "cast into all things, to the teeth of panthers and elephants, devoured by them that devour, consumed by them that consume, eaten by the dogs, mingled and bound in all that is, imprisoned in the stench of darkness" (qtd. in Jonas 86–87). The German mystic and theologian Jacob Boehme (1575–1624) was also dismayed by this brutal aspect of existence and lamented, "Within all nature there is a continual wrestling, battling, and devouring, so that this world may truly be called a valley of sorrow, full of trouble, persecution, suffering, and labour" (qtd. in Hartmann 166–67). Boehme dealt with this theme in his *Six Theosophic Points*, writing that the essence of the "life of darkness"—mentioned in the epigraph to *Blood Meridian*—is "a perpetual stinging and breaking, each form being enemy to the other" (99) and that this behavior is also "seen among men and beasts" where "there is a biting, hating and striking, and an arrogant self-will, each wishing to rule over the other, to kill and devour the other, and elevate itself alone; also to trample upon everything with guile, wrath, malice and falsehood, and make itself lord" (104). Boehme's description of the "life of darkness" reads like a summary of the narrative action within *Blood Meridian*.

This anticosmic stance emerges organically from a vision of "nature, red in tooth and claw" (Tennyson, LVI, line 15). *Blood Meridian* demonstrates that not only are the living organisms on this planet subject to an endless cycle of devouring but they are also threatened by the hostile forces of nature. This is made apparent when the men ride past "parched beasts" that "had died with their necks stretched in agony in the sand and now upright and blind and lurching askew with scraps of blackened leather hanging from the fretwork of their ribs they leaned with their long mouths howling after the endless tandem suns that passed above them" (247). It is as though the very earth demands the blood of creatures. "This is a thirsty country," an old Mennonite announces early in the novel; a country that has soaked up the "blood of a thousand Christs" and still "nothing" has changed, or will ever change. The world is a "great stained altarstone" demanding constant blood sacrifice (102). As Vasily Grossman asks in *Life and Fate*, "Is it that life itself is evil?" (407).[15] According to the Gnostics, who "saw evil as something inherent in the material creation itself" (Pearson 106), the answer to the above question is a resounding "Yes!" And it is difficult to draw any other conclusion after reading through McCarthy's historically accurate world of *Blood Meridian*.

The Gnostics were not content with simply identifying the manifest world as evil but sought to explain why it was so, arriving at the conclusion that "the created order cannot be the product of the transcendent God but must have been created by a lower divine being" (Pearson 106). In most Gnostic myths, the demiurge created the cosmos after seeing a reflection of the divine light of the alien God. Hans Jonas writes, "It is with the help of the projected *image* of the divine *form* that the lower forces make the world or man, i.e., as an *imitation* of the divine original" (163). Jonas explains that this concept arises out of the "mythic idea of the substantiality of an image, reflection, or shadow as representing a real part of the original entity from which it has become detached" (162). These ideas can be traced back to Plato, who, in his famous allegory of the cave, saw "the entire manifest world as a pale image of a Reality and Light beyond the Cave of Shadows, the Cave in which the troglodytes are chained" (Wilber 323). The troglodytes are the unenlightened human beings who mistake the shadows of the manifest world for the ultimate Reality of the Ideal Forms. It is noteworthy that in *Blood Meridian* members of the Glanton gang are described as descending a mountain—in itself a movement evoking devolution rather than progress—"with their hands outheld before them and their shadows contorted on the broken terrain like creatures seeking their own forms" (65). Depicted as reaching out to "shadows" in the mistaken search for "forms," the men resemble "the troglodytes who worship the Shadows without seeing the Light" (Wilber 366). Descriptions of the Glanton gang in atavistic terms, as previously discussed, further emphasize its members' resemblance to Plato's troglodytes.

Though both the Gnostics and the Platonists spoke of the created world as a mere shadow of an Ideal Absolute, Hans Jonas explains that the crucial difference between these traditions "is that the former deplore the 'descent' by image-reflection as the cause of divine tragedy," while the latter "affirm it as the necessary and positive self-expression of the efficacy of the first source" (164). The Gnostics go as far as to describe the process of creation as an "imitation, illicit and blundering, of the divine by the lower powers" (202). Both traditions, however, stress the "vertical structure of this scale of unfolding, that is, the *downward* direction of all metaphysical generation which therefore cannot be but deterioration" (164). In other words, according to both the Gnostics and Platonists, created things are only an inferior imitation of a perfected original source. This idea is hinted at during a strange scene in *Blood Meridian* where the "lifeforms"—prisoners, guards, dogs, mules, and a fat priest—"all lightly shimmering in the heat," appear "like wonders much reduced. Rough likeness thrown up at hearsay after the things themselves had faded" (75). Here McCarthy offers a perspective on reality in which all "lifeforms" appear as mere shadows of the "things themselves," or as inferior imitations of the original divine source.

Shadows, along with their metaphysical and theological connotations of the darkness of evil, feature prominently in *Blood Meridian*. The narrative voice describes how the shadows "of the men and their mounts advanced elongate before them like strands of the night from which they'd ridden, like tentacles to bind them to the darkness yet to come" (45). Here the shadows seem to be residues of the night itself, binding the men to both literal and metaphorical darkness. Later, "horse and rider" appear "spanceled to their shadows on the snowblue ground" (152). To "spancel" is to "fetter or hobble" with "a short noosed rope" (*OED*), thus repeating the motif of humanity's imprisonment in fetters of darkness. In *Blood Meridian*, such imprisonment seems to be the fate of all created things; even the "stones of the desert" lie "in dark tethers of shadow" (227). In this anticosmic vision of the world, all things seem to be tainted by the very corporeality of their manifest existence.

The evil forces seem to possess an autonomous existence of their own; the shadows appear "austere and implacable like shapes capable of violating their covenant with the flesh that authored them and continuing autonomous across the naked rock without reference to sun or man or god" (139). So strong are these ties to the darkness that when "white" John Jackson rides in "black" John Jackson's shadow, the "black would check or start his horse to shake him off. As if the white man were in violation of his person." The shadow here is not just "the shape he stood from the sun," but it seems as though it "bore something of the man himself and in so doing lay imperilled" (81). The depraved men of Glanton's gang, utterly devoid of spiritual or even moral values, seem to embrace such evil as their natural element. They ride, "treading their thin and flaring shadows," until they cross "altogether into the darkness which so well became them" (163).[16] The men clearly feel at home surrounded by darkness with all its evil connotations.

The Gnostic idea that creation is flawed is discussed in *Blood Meridian* through the words of the hermit: "God made this world," he announces, "but he didnt make it to suit everybody, did he?" The kid agrees that he "can think of better places and better ways," instinctively feeling that there must be better worlds than this one. The hermit then goes on to ask, "Can ye make it be?," to which the kid replies, "No" (19). The hermit, here, seems to be arguing along the lines of Gottfried Wilhelm Leibniz's (1646–1716) "Best Possible World Theodicy," which "seeks to demonstrate that God cannot be blamed for the existence of evil in the world, since this world is the best of all possible worlds" (Peterson 92). Leibniz envisioned "God actualizing that possible world that contains the amount of evil necessary to make the world the best one on the whole" even if that entailed "bringing about a world that has a great many evils in it but evils of such kinds and arranged in such ways that they contribute to the world being the very best one possible" (Peterson 93). The hermit also speculates on the creation of humanity, arguing, "You can find meanness in the least of creatures, but when God made man the devil was at his elbow" (19). Though the hermit does not blame the creator directly, his words imply that the creation of human beings was influenced by the forces of evil.

The judge, on the other hand, implicates God directly, asking, "If God meant to interfere in the degeneracy of mankind would he not have done so by now?" (146). His words echo those of the Marquis de Sade (1740–1814), who argued that "true crimes against nature are impossible," because "the impulse to crime is natural" (Neiman 170). Hence, if "even evil has its own purpose" then "every crime you commit is a brick in the wall of providential design" (181). Sade's God asks, "Did not the perpetual miseries with which I inundate the universe convince you that I love only disorder, and that to please me one must emulate me?" (190). If the character of the creator can be gauged by the nature of his creation, then the depraved human beings and savagely hostile landscapes that abound in *Blood Meridian* point to a supremely indifferent or downright malevolent entity.[17] This idea has also been put forward by Christopher Douglas, who writes, "As with earlier Christian theologians, McCarthy believes that the details of creation can tell us something interesting about the character of the creator; but unlike them, McCarthy is not comforted by the evidence of design that he discerns in the universe. For McCarthy, that design is evidence of a no-longer benign creator whose dark purposes can be discerned in the awful silence of an empty landscape" (11). In *Blood Meridian*, divine silence points to Gnosticism rather than atheism, in that it does not signify the absence of a creator God, but rather the presence of a malicious demiurge.

A particularly telling scene within the novel explores the question of divine intervention via a description of the senseless deaths of travelers in the desert: "Far out on the desert to the north dustspouts rose wobbling and augured the earth and some said they'd heard of pilgrims borne aloft like dervishes in those mindless coils to be dropped broken and bleeding upon the desert again and there perhaps to watch the thing that had destroyed them lurch onward like some drunken djinn and resolve itself once more into the elements from which it sprang" (111). The reference to "pilgrims" immediately places this passage in a religious context, which is further emphasized by the addition of "dervishes"; a "dervish" being "a Muslim friar, who has taken vows of poverty and austere life . . . some of whom are known from their fantastic practices as *dancing* or *whirling*" (OED). Both "pilgrim" and "dervish" signify those who have set out in search of God, through either spatial or spiritual journeys, yet in *Blood Meridian* these seekers encounter only a senselessly maleficent force in the wilderness. Despite this apparent "mindlessness," the dustspout evokes a sense of hostile agency in its "lurching" away like a "djinn," which, according to Muslim demonology, is "an order of spirits lower than the angels, said to have the power of appearing in human and animal forms, and to exercise supernatural influence over men" (*OED*). It is noteworthy that in *Blood Meridian* the supernaturally evil Judge Holden is also described as "a great ponderous djinn" (96). The dustspouts may be "mindless," but the mindlessness of evil does not detract from its destructive efficacy; the dustspout moves with a certain sinister deliberation, lurching onward and then resolving itself into the elements.[18]

Apart from the dual reference to the Muslim faith in the usage of "dervish" and "djinn," the passage also evokes the biblical book of Job, reinforcing the connection to the three main Semitic religions—Judaism, Christianity, and Islam—all of which worship a lone creator deity. Unlike the voice of God that speaks "out of the whirlwind" (Job 38:1), McCarthy's narrator reminds us that "out of that whirlwind no voice spoke and the pilgrim lying in his broken bones may cry out and in his anguish he may rage, but rage at what?" (111). As previously argued, this terrible silence does not necessarily point to the nonexistence of a creator deity but might rather be read as an indication of his malevolent nature. Christopher Douglas also puts forward this argument, stating that *Blood Meridian*'s "reverse-agnosticism, that perhaps God *does* exist, is not a cause for hope for McCarthy, but a cause for terror. There are patterns of evil in our world. God's silence is no longer seen as indifference, but as the possibility of his malice" (12). The Marquis de Sade argued along the same lines, as paraphrased by Susan Neiman: "The alternative to God's absence is His presence. If He should be known by His works, what must we infer about His nature?" (188). What can we infer about the nature of a deity that leaves his pilgrims lying in their broken bones?

Blood Meridian very subtly questions the nature of the relationship between the God of the Semitic religions and his people. Although the novel is set in the nineteenth century, McCarthy is a contemporary writer writing for a contemporary audience. Thus the description of the "sun to the west" that "lay in a holocaust" cannot fail to evoke the atrocities committed against the Jewish people in Nazi concentration camps, even though the original meaning of the word "holocaust" is "a burnt offering." The following line—"where there rose a steady column" (105)—suggests the rising of a column of smoke, simultaneously evoking the smoke rising from the Nazi crematoriums and the pillar of smoke that Yahweh used to guide the children of Israel through the desert (Exodus 13:21). Even though this "steady column" is subsequently revealed to be composed of "small desert bats," smoke is again evoked through the "dust" that "was blowing down the void like the smoke of distant armies" (105). The narrative voice then announces that "here beyond men's judgements all covenants were brittle" (106). It is impossible to ignore the close proximity of the words "holocaust" and "covenant," the covenant being the agreement between Yahweh and the children of Israel, whereby they would be protected in exchange for their obedience and worship.

The Holocaust of the twentieth century was viewed by some Jewish scholars as a breaking of this covenant. In *Holocaust: Religious and Philosophical Implications*, David Weiss and Michael Berenbaum discuss this concept, writing, "The classic Judaic delineation of the relationship between God and the House of Israel is no longer tenable" because the "covenant that was, or the illusion of this covenant, has been abrogated in the German death camps." They argue that the survivors of the Holocaust must form "a new covenant, a unilateral, voluntary assertion by the House of Israel of the will to continue Jewish existence in the face of an indifferent, changeable, or non-existent deity" (71). Weiss and Berenbaum add that this is a problem not just for the Jewish people but for all individuals, because "the question to God, Why? is the same for the first child struck down in human history and for the last to perish in Auschwitz. That is the eternal confrontation of all men with God" (75). McCarthy alludes to these problems in *Blood Meridian* precisely because the novel is preoccupied with the question of human suffering and evil in the face of an indifferent, nonexistent, or, worst of all, malevolent deity.

Both the Gnostics and the Buddhists taught that suffering lies at the very core of the undesirable state that is existence, but, being soteriologically focused, both systems offered a way out. Furthermore, neither religion faced the Judeo-Christian problem of having to reconcile the evils of existence with the goodness of a creator God, presenting the path to salvation as a personal journey independent of divine intervention. Edward Conze explains that for the Gnostics and Buddhists, "salvation takes place through *gnosis* . . . or *jñāna*," respectively, both words approximating "spiritual insight." Conze adds that in "both cases ... insight into the origination and nature of the world liberates us from it" (*Further Buddhist Studies* 16–17). The Buddhists and the Gnostics arrived at similar conclusions as to what the nature of this world may be. The "Buddhist idea of *samsara* ... teaches that the world in which we live our daily lives is illusory" (Wagner and Flannery-Dailey 272). Similarly, the Gnostic Gospel of Truth states that "those who live in [the world] experience 'terror and confusion and instability and doubt and division,' being caught in 'many illusions'" (qtd. in Pagels, *Gnostic Gospels* 125). Moreover, the Buddha taught his followers that "all conditioned things are impermanent" and that everything in the manifest cosmos is "everchanging, doomed to destruction, quite unreliable, crumbling away however much we try to hold it" (Conze, *Buddhism* 16, 113). Likewise, Gnostic texts such as the Mandean Ginza stress the impermanent aspects of creation, claiming that the world "is a thing wholly without substance ... in which thou must place no trust.... All works pass away, take their end and are as if they had never been" (qtd. in Jonas 84). In both Buddhist and Gnostic traditions, insight into the nature of the world involves the realization that earthly existence is characterized by illusion and impermanence.

Impermanence and illusion also constitute the nature of the manifest world as revealed in *Blood Meridian*. For example, the violent lightning storms that persist throughout the novel illuminate "a land of some other order out there whose true geology was not stone but fear." The description of a landscape in which fear is more real than stone suggests a nightmare world, nightmarish in the sense that it is grounded in subjective perception rather than objective reality and is therefore ultimately illusory. Lightning lights up the "blue and barren" desert, revealing a "demon kingdom summoned up or changeling land that come the day would leave neither trace nor smoke nor ruin more than any troubling dream" (47). This "demon kingdom" or "changeling land" is reminiscent of the way that Gnostics or Buddhists perceived consensus reality, a collective nightmare born of ignorance and spiritual blindness. The Buddhist *Hridaya Prajñāpāramitā* (Heart Sutra of the Perfection of Wisdom) teaches that once enlightenment has been attained "everything that we can see around us" is revealed in its essential "emptiness" and disappears "like an insignificant dream" (qtd. in Conze, *Buddhism* 84–85). Similarly, the Gnostic Gospel of Truth teaches that the *pneumatics* (enlightened Gnostics) have "cast ignorance aside from them like sleep, not esteeming it as anything, nor do they esteem its works as solid things either, but they leave them behind like a dream in the night" (qtd. in

Wagner and Flannery-Dailey 268). As Hans Jonas explains, the "metaphor of sleep" serves "to discount the sensations of 'life here' as mere illusions and dreams, though nightmarish ones, which we are powerless to control" (70). In *Blood Meridian*, metaphors of nightmarish sleep, or hallucination, continue in descriptions such as that of the rising sun, in whose "eastern light the fires on the plain faded like an evil dream and the country lay bare and sparkling in the pure air" (205), or that of "the secular aloes blooming like phantasmagoria in a fever land" (163). These fevered visions and evil dreams emphasize the Gnostic insistence on the fundamental unreality and sinister nature of the manifest world.

Judge Holden seems to articulate this Buddhist-Gnostic vision of the illusory and sinister nature of the world when he tells the men, "Had you not seen it all from birth and thereby bled it of its strangeness it would appear to you for what it is, a hat trick in a medicine show, a fevered dream, a trance bepopulate with chimeras having neither analogue nor precedent, an itinerant carnival, a migratory tentshow whose ultimate destination after many a pitch in many a mudded field is unspeakable and calamitous beyond reckoning" (245). These words could have been taken right out of the Buddhist *Vajracchedikā Prajñāpāramitā* (Diamond Sutra of the Perfection of Wisdom):

> As stars, a fault of vision, as a lamp,
> A mock show, dew drops, or a bubble,
> A dream, a lightning flash, or cloud,
> So should one view what is conditioned.
> (qtd. in Conze, *Buddhist Wisdom Books* 67)

Like the judge's description of the world as a "medicine show" or "carnival," the *Diamond Sutra* describes the world as a "mock show," because "like a magical show it deceives, deludes and defrauds us" and "is false when compared with ultimate reality," (69) or Nirvāṇa. The trope of the world as a "medicine show" or an "itinerant carnival" is repeated throughout *Blood Meridian*. For example, a traveling troupe of "itinerant magicians" is described as "a set of right wanderfolk cast on this evil terrain" (89). The tribe of Yumas who massacre the Glanton gang watch the fire "as might some painted troupe of mimefolk" (276). Even Judge Holden, leading a naked "idiot" on a leash through the wilderness, seems like "some degenerate entrepreneur fleeing from a medicine show" (298). The repeated motif of the "migratory tentshow" emphasizes the Buddhist and Gnostic beliefs that the manifest world is both fraudulent and impermanent.

The judge's sermon about the nature of the world seems to draw upon other similes from the *Diamond Sutra*. For example, his description of the world as "a fevered dream" echoes the sutra's teachings that the world is like "a dream," because "only the enlightened are awake to reality. . . . Compared with their vision of true reality, our normal experience is that of a dream, unreal and not to be taken seriously" (Conze, *Buddhist Wisdom Books* 70). The judge's description of the world as a hallucinatory "trance bepopulate with chimeras"—one of the definitions of "chimera" being a "horrible and fear-inspiring phantasm" (*OED*)—evokes the sutra's reference to "a fault of vision," because "the world as it appears to the ignorant is like a hallucination which springs from an eye-disease" (Conze, *Buddhist Wisdom Books* 69). The judge's reference to the world as "itinerant" and "migratory" places emphasis on its essential impermanence. The *Diamond Sutra* also emphasizes the impermanent nature of existence, comparing the world to a "dewdrop" because of its evanescence and "a bubble" because "it can be enjoyed only for a moment" (Conze, *Buddhist Wisdom Books* 70) before bursting and revealing its inherent emptiness. Elsewhere, the judge claims that "this desert upon which so many have been broken . . . is vast . . . but it is also ultimately empty" (330), hinting at the idea that the manifest cosmos is ultimately a void.

Though Judge Holden does not posit the existence of anything other than his own hallucinatory void, he indirectly points to something beyond the supposed illusions of manifest existence. Dreams and hallucinations lack reality only in comparison to the full consciousness we experience in waking life. In other words, there would be no point in talking about the unreality of dreams if there were no waking life; dreams, in that case, would be our *only* reality. By this same logic, it makes no sense to talk about the unreality of manifest existence unless we are prepared to admit the existence of an actual reality. The Buddhists teach that the "world is like a dream," because "just as one perceives the lack of objectivity in the dream pictures after one has woken up, so the lack of objectivity in the perceptions of waking life is perceived by those who have been awakened by the knowledge of true reality" (Conze, *Buddhism* 168). For the Gnostics and Buddhists, "the crown of all . . . endeavour" is "an attempt to penetrate to the actual reality of things as they are in themselves" (Conze, *Buddhist Scriptures* 145). As McCarthy himself put it in an interview with Gary Wallace, "The mystical experience is a direct apprehension of reality" (138). This ultimate Reality is defined in both Buddhism and Gnosticism "as that which stands completely outside the sensory world of illusions and ignorance" (Conze, *Buddhism* 110). The "mystic is a realist" (Underhill 93), because a mystic's sole purpose is to strip away all the veils of illusion that obscure the ultimate Reality of the Absolute. Thus, by comparing the world to a "fevered dream," the judge is inadvertently pointing to the existence of an Absolute Reality that transcends the illusions and deceptions of the manifest cosmos. Such a view imbues the anticosmic vision within *Blood Meridian* with a minute fragment of hope; if the world as depicted in the novel is indeed an evil nightmare, then its bloodstained landscapes and frenzied acts of violence are ultimately only the products of a dream from which one may eventually awaken.

CHAPTER 2

"Suzerain of the Earth"

Unravelling the Mystery of the Judge in *Blood Meridian*

■ The nightmarish landscapes and orgiastic violence in *Blood Meridian* are presided over by the "vast abhorrence" (243) that is Judge Holden. The judge dominates the novel and, as the narrative voice informs us, is so "charged with meaning" that his "very portent renders [him] ambiguous" (282). It is, however, possible to glean something from this ambiguity and to come to a few conclusions regarding the judge's ontological status. Though the judge himself purports to scorn mysteries of a spiritual nature, claiming that the "mystery is that there is no mystery," the ex-priest Tobin insists that the judge is the greatest mystery of all: "Aye, said the expriest watching, his pipe cold in his teeth. And no mystery. As if he were no mystery himself, the bloody old hoodwinker" (252). The judge may indeed be a mystery, but mysteries do not necessarily have to remain unsolved; a close examination of the metaphysics underlying the novel may at least partially illuminate the enigmatic nature of the judge and unravel his more esoteric pronouncements.[1]

The narrative voice in *Blood Meridian* continually draws attention to the judge's otherness from the men around him, suggesting that he is no ordinary human being. Descriptions of the judge emphasize his deviation from the average human form: "He shone like the moon so pale he was and not a hair to be seen anywhere upon that vast corpus, not in any crevice nor in the great bores of his nose and not upon his chest nor in his ears nor any tuft at all above his eyes nor to the lids thereof" (168). This gigantic, hairless, albino man—who stands nearly seven feet tall and weighs around three hundred pounds—evokes the sinister whiteness and monstrosity of Moby-Dick; at one stage the judge is even described as a "pale and bloated manatee" (167) with a "pleated brow not unlike a dolphin's" (93). The judge's face appears "serene and strangely childlike" (6), which makes his depraved brutality all the more shocking. When the kid and the judge meet after twenty-eight years, the kid is now a forty-five-year-old man, but the judge "seemed little changed or none in all these years" (325), as though he had not aged at all.[2]

Textual evidence suggests that the judge is demonic. One of *Blood Meridian*'s epigraphs is a quote from Jacob Boehme's *Six Theosophic Points*: "It is not to be thought that the life of darkness is sunk in misery and lost as if in sorrowing. There is no sorrowing. For sorrow is a thing that is swallowed up in death, and death and dying are the very life of the darkness" (1). Taken out of context, this may seem to be a nihilistic and death-embracing celebration of humanity's penchant for evil, but such a reading is entirely misleading. In *Six Theosophic Points*, Boehme states that the "Life of Darkness" is "Wherein the Devils Dwell." Boehme explains that "we cannot, then, say of the devil that he sits in dejection, as if he were faint-hearted. There is no faint-heartedness in him," but only a desire "that his fierceness may become greater" (108). Thus the quotation does not apply to human existence—situated, as it is according to Christian doctrine, between heaven and hell, and between good and evil—but to the existence of "devils," wholly malevolent entities who, according to Boehme, dwell solely in the metaphorical darkness of evil.

The influence of Jacob Boehme's theosophy on McCarthy's novels is obvious, not only in this particular epigraphical reference but also through the fact that both men are preoccupied with the same theological themes regarding the nature of God, humanity, and evil. By choosing this exact quotation as an epigraph, McCarthy was not trying to convey the idea that human beings no longer suffer when they embrace an evil way of life. Rather, the epigraph evokes demonic entities who have turned away from the divine so completely that they no longer feel the pain of separation and rejoice in their own depravity, or as Boehme explains, "what with us on earth is sorrowing . . . is in the darkness power and joy" (*Six Theosophic Points* 102). According to Boehme, human beings may never turn completely away from the divine source, because it is an integral part of their being, whereas devils dwell entirely in "Darkness" and no longer yearn for the "Light." Human beings suffer and sorrow in the darkness, but the devils do not. In *Blood Meridian*, the only character always enjoying the game, dancing, fiddling, and "always smiling," even, as Barcley Owens points out, "when nobody knows the joke" (16), is the judge. By implication, the judge is no ordinary mortal but a demon incarnate, rejoicing in "the life of darkness."

It is quite appropriate, then, that Judge Holden also possesses attributes commonly associated with Judeo-Christian representations of the devil. As the ex-priest tells the kid, "That great hairless thing. You wouldn't think to look at him that he could outdance the devil himself now would ye? God the man is a dancer, you'll not take that away from him. And fiddle. He's the greatest fiddler I ever heard and that's an end on it" (123). It is noteworthy that "playing the fiddle . . . is thought to be a special accomplishment of the devil" (Puckett 553). When the judge first appears in the novel, a reverend sobs in dismay, "This is him. The devil. Here he stands" (7). Elsewhere he is described as "a great ponderous djinn" (96), which, according to Muslim demonology, places him among "an order of spirits lower than the angels" (*OED*). When he steps "through the fire," "the flames delivered him up as if he were in some way native to their element" (96), thus strengthening the connection between the judge and the flames of hell in popular Christian cosmology.

The judge is depicted in demonic vignettes throughout the novel. At night he squats on a sandstone ledge, "pale and naked," surrounded by bats that come "from some nether part of the world to stand on leather wings like dark satanic hummingbirds" (148). When the kid tells Tobin that he had seen the judge in Nacogdoches before he joined the gang, Tobin replies, "Every man in the company claims to have encountered that sootysouled rascal in some other place" (124). The judge seems ubiquitous and omnipresent, again evoking the albino monstrosity of Moby-Dick, who is described as being "not only ubiquitous, but immortal (for immortality is but ubiquity in time)" (Melville 184). Tobin's account of the gang's first encounter with the judge abounds in supernatural overtones, further developing the demonic connection. The ex-priest recalls how they "come upon the judge on his rock there in that wilderness by his single self," sitting in his trademark lotus position with his "legs crossed, smilin as we rode up. Like he'd been expecting us." Tobin adds that the judge "didnt even have a canteen" or a horse and "you couldnt tell where he'd come from" (125). It is clear that the judge is no ordinary mortal—how could a human being survive in the wilderness without a horse, water, or shelter?

In the novel, the judge appears just in time to strike a bargain with the desperate gang, who have run out of gunpowder and are being pursued by Indians. When he learns of their plight, the judge looks "about him with the greatest satisfaction in the world, as if everything had turned out just as he planned and the day could not have been finer" (126), suggesting that the meeting and even the gang's dire misfortunes have all somehow been orchestrated by the judge himself. It is of particular significance that the morning after the judge joins the gang it is discovered that "two men had deserted in the night and that made us down to twelve and the judge thirteen" (127). The gang of thirteen men functions as a dark parody of the Last Supper, at which Jesus and the twelve apostles numbered thirteen.[3] The number thirteen also has demonic connotations, as Satan "was said to be the 13th figure at witch's rites" (Tresidder 169). The implications are clear; the judge is the thirteenth figure in the Glanton gang, a position that links him either to Judas the betrayer or to Satan himself.

In exchange for being allowed to join the gang, the judge saves the men's lives by leading them to the edge of a volcano with a "weal of brimstone all about the rim of the caldron" (131). It is significant that "brimstone" evokes the traditional fire and brimstone of hell, while "caldron" suggests witchcraft. The judge transmutes the quintessentially satanic sulphur, charcoal, feces (bat guano), and urine into much-needed gunpowder, no doubt an allusion to Satan's invention of gunpowder and canons in John Milton's *Paradise Lost*.[4] John Sepich points out that "gunpowder is one of the Devil's more significant gifts to man" ("Bloody Dark Pastryman" 550) and that "Holden's gift of gunpowder has overtones of Mephistopheles' gift to Faust" (*Notes* 121). Tobin refers to this concoction as "a devil's batter by the stink of it" and identifies the judge as the "bloody dark pastryman himself" (132). Recalling the story of how their lives were saved, Tobin muses aloud, "The judge. Give the devil his due" (125), thus further emphasizing the judge's demonic nature.

Tobin tells the kid that a "secret Commerce" and a "terrible covenant" (126) were forged between Glanton and the judge that day. Such contracts are a typical feature of demonic encounters in myths and legends. Paul Oppenheimer writes that "the demonic figure cannot be encountered without the willingness to make the rash promise of the soul. One must invite his presence—he cannot come uninvited—and one must be prepared to surrender everything for the supernatural strength that he will provide" (19). In *Blood Meridian*, it is Glanton who decides to "invite" the judge's "presence." The other members of the gang seem wary of the newcomer and do not share Glanton's willingness to form a pact. Tobin recalls how "Davy wanted to leave him there. Didnt set well with his honor and it dont to this day."

Glanton, however, "just studied him," and afterward he and the judge "rode side by side and soon they was conversin like brothers" (126). When Glanton and most of his men lose their lives at the hands of the Yuma Indians, the covenant with the judge appears to be broken. It is noteworthy that the judge escapes the massacre completely unharmed. At this point, Tobin really begins to fear the judge and attempts to defend himself by "holding aloft a cross he'd fashioned out of the shins of a ram" (290), much like an exorcist.

The judge is clearly no ordinary mortal, but at times it is suggested that he is more of a god than a demon.[5] Sitting half-naked in front of the fire, the judge is described as a "great pale deity" (92). Later, the judge appears as a statue of some godlike being or idol. His eyes, like a sculpture's, are "empty slots" (147). Sitting on the ground with "his hands rested palm down upon his knees," the judge seems to be engaged in deep meditation (147). Rick Wallach argues that here the judge "incarnates the attributes of an oriental deity." Specifically, "the judge's poses suggest Shiva," whose "visage, like Holden's, is always serene amid the carnage he engenders" (128–29). The men seated around the judge grow wary of this meditative state, "so like an icon was he in his sitting that they grew cautious and spoke with circumspection among themselves as if they would not waken something that had better been left sleeping" (147). The implication is that the men grow fearful in the judge's presence, because they sense something otherworldly and malevolent.

The judge is situated somewhere between the demonic and the godlike, a position that corresponds to the Gnostic view of the god of this world. As Hans Jonas explains, the Gnostics believed that demons known as archons "collectively rule over the world" and "are also creators of the world, except where this role is reserved for their leader, who then has the name of *demiurge*" and "is often painted with the distorted features of the Old Testament God" (43–44). The human spirit is "a portion of the divine substance from beyond which has fallen into the world; and the archons created man for the express purpose of keeping it captive there" (44). The demiurge and his archons conceal the existence of the divine source, or the alien God, in order to keep human beings imprisoned in the cosmos. Thus Gnostic theology identifies the biblical God, Yahweh, as a demon, responsible not only for the creation of the world but also for the obscuration of divine Reality. By conflating the creator God and the devil into one entity, Gnostic theology creates a new kind of deity, whose simultaneously demonic and godlike characteristics are reflected in the multifaceted enigma that is Judge Holden.

In "Gravers False and True: *Blood Meridian* as Gnostic Tragedy," Leo Daugherty argues that "gnostic thought is central to Cormac McCarthy's *Blood Meridian*" (159) and perceptively identifies the judge as one of the Gnostic archons, or perhaps even the demiurge himself. Daugherty writes that like the "archons, Holden also possesses all the other characteristics of Yahweh as the Gnostics saw him: he is jealous, he is vengeful, he is wrathful, he is powerful and—most centrally—he possesses, and is possessed by, a will" (163). The "Earth is the judge's" (164), writes Daugherty, and, indeed, the judge is described as seeming "much satisfied with the world, as if his counsel had been sought at its creation" (140). Christopher Douglas draws attention to McCarthy's use of "as if," arguing that it "marks the failure of traditional realist language to evoke the larger theological design behind the events of the novel and the impossibility of linguistically imagining the design that McCarthy suspects must lurk behind the amoral nothingness of the world" (13). Thus, far from dismissing the judge's participation in the creation of the world as a hypothetical fantasy, McCarthy's "as if" actually gestures toward the ineffable and unutterable reality of this vision.

Sitting in a saloon, the judge is depicted "among every kind of man, herder and bullwhacker and drover and freighter and miner and hunter and soldier and pedlar and gambler and drifter and drunkard and thief," but though he "sat by them," he remained "alone as if he were some other sort of man entire" (325). Once again, we may apply Douglas's reading to McCarthy's characteristic usage of "as if," identifying it as a linguistic marker pointing to a "larger theological design" rather than a simple exercise in hypothetical rhetoric. Although the judge seems perfectly at home in the crazed, blood-soaked world of *Blood Meridian*, it is continually suggested that he is somehow not of this world. This is yet another of the judge's paradoxical attributes that can be resolved in the light of Gnostic thought. Gnostic texts often refer to the world as the "inn" in order to emphasize the concept that the pneuma lives in temporary exile from its true home. The archons can be thought of as "the 'fellow-dwellers of the inn' though their relation to it is not that of guests" (Jonas 56). Hence, just as the archons inhabit the realm of the manifest world without being human, the judge walks among men while being no ordinary mortal. Furthermore, the judge's existence is not limited to the so-called Wild West of the 1850s, for he was also "among the dregs of the earth in beggary a thousand years and he was among the scapegrace scions of eastern dynasties" (325). This suggests that the judge cannot be limited by time, place, or social hierarchy; his existence stretches back to distant times, distant lands, and infiltrates all levels of human society, from beggar to king.

Most disturbingly, the judge seems to possess no beginning and no end. In a fit of ether-induced delirium, the kid experiences a revelation regarding the judge's mysterious lack of origins: "Whoever would seek out his history through what unravelling of loins and ledgerbooks must stand at last darkened and dumb at the shore of a void without terminus or origin and whatever science he might bring to bear upon the dusty primal matter blowing down out of the millennia will discover no trace of any ultimate atavistic egg by which to reckon his commencing" (310). The kid's vision reveals that the origin of the judge cannot be uncovered through genealogy, nor scientific enquiry; any attempt to do so will only lead one back to the primordial void, the chaos that precedes the existence of the cosmos in the creation myths of countless traditions. Similarly, the judge has no final destination; in the final paragraph of the novel he is dancing an eternal dance, reminiscent of Shiva's cosmic dance of destruction: "He never sleeps, the judge. He is dancing, dancing. He says that he will never die" (335). Ordinary sleep is a minor prelude to the great sleep of death and the immortal judge is eternally wakeful.[6]

Harold Bloom comments on the judge's lack of origins in *How to Read and Why*, but he curiously argues against a Gnostic interpretation of the passage. Despite the fact that Bloom identifies McCarthy as a Gnostic—"Faulkner is a kind of unknowing Gnostic; West, Pynchon, and McCarthy in their different ways are very knowing indeed" (237)—and is prepared to admit that "McCarthy gives Judge Holden the powers and purposes of the bad angels or demiurges [sic] that the Gnostics called archons,"[7] he inexplicably goes on to insist that McCarthy is actually telling "us not to make such an identification," because "any 'system,' including the Gnostic one, will not divide the Judge back into his origins. The 'ultimate atavistic egg' will not be found" (*Modern Critical Views* 4). I agree with Bloom's assertion up to a point, namely that the supernatural nature of the judge is such that he surpasses the limitations of the human mind and thus cannot be limited to any one system of thought. Nevertheless, certain aspects of the judge's nature may be illuminated by references to the various spiritual and philosophical traditions that have attempted to address the problem of evil. This is the line of argument adopted by Steven Frye, who argues that the judge's purported lack of origins should not discourage us from interpreting the literary figure in the context of various systems and traditions, including, but not limited to, "Judeo-Christian cosmology and typology, scientific materialism with its often purely atheist implications, the continental philosophy of Friedrich Nietzsche, philosophical nihilism, and the fascinating conceptions of ancient Gnosticism." Frye argues that Judge Holden "is by no means a patchwork creation of competing philosophical configurations, but a distinctive artistic embodiment of darkness that stands apart but nevertheless draws on these various perspectives" (*Understanding Cormac McCarthy* 79). He adds that "it is perhaps more fruitful to consider that various notions of evil, literary or philosophical, partially illuminate rather than define his nature" (91). I would argue that although Gnosticism is not the definitive system through which one may arrive at an understanding of the judge, it is nevertheless a particularly useful one due to its preoccupation with the evil manifest in creation.[8]

Furthermore, McCarthy subtly alludes to the judge's connection with Gnostic archons in his esoteric subheading to chapter 15, "The Ogdoad" (204). The heading refers to a scene in which the Glanton gang stumbles upon eight decapitated heads arranged in a circle. "The heads were eight in number . . . and they formed a ring all facing outwards. Glanton and the judge circled them and the judge halted and stepped down and pushed over one of the heads with his boot" (220). According to *A Dictionary of Gnosticism*, the *ogdoad* (Greek for "group of eight") is the "eighth sphere, above the seven planetary spheres" and "may be considered to be the sphere of the fixed stars, but may also be associated with the home of Sophia [the Gnostic personification of wisdom], or the demiurge, or in simpler cosmologies the home of the true God" (A. Smith 177). According to these "simpler" Gnostic cosmologies, the cosmos is ruled by seven archons, whose kingdoms are hierarchically arranged in concentric circles around the manifest world. In what is known as the "Ascent of the Soul"—a teaching common to both Hermeticism and Gnosticism—the souls of the dead must pass through the *hebdomad* (Greek for "group of seven"). During this process "all passions and vices are given back to the various spheres from which they were derived in the soul's original descent." Afterward, the "'essential man' proceeds to the Ogdoad (Eighth) where he praises the Father with those who are there" (Pearson 279). In other words, the perfected spirit ascends to the "eighth realm," thereby returning to its divine source. By knocking over the eighth head, the judge reduces the ogdoad of the alien God to the hebdomad of the archons. If one considers the ogdoad to be the realm of the alien God, then the judge's action is symbolic of his denying transcendence to those who would seek to escape from the manifest world through spiritual development.[9]

The very title of "the judge" carries connotations of biblical judgement, a concept that strengthens his resemblance to the demiurge and the archons. Harold Bloom writes that Judge Holden "seems to judge the entire earth" and the name Holden "suggests a holding, presumably of sway over all he encounters" (*Modern Critical Views* 4). The judge seems to be obsessed with bringing every animate and inanimate thing in creation under his jurisdiction. When asked why he shoots and stuffs birds, catches butterflies, presses leaves and plants between the pages of his ledger book, and sketches artifacts—often destroying the originals after their image has been recorded—the judge replies, "Whatever in creation exists without my knowledge exists without my consent" (198). This statement would be absurd if uttered by a mortal man, but chilling if uttered by an archon bent on keeping all things imprisoned in the fetters of manifest existence.

This reading also illuminates the judge's desire to have "the existence of each last entity . . . routed out and made to stand naked before him," so he might be "suzerain of the earth." When asked what a suzerain is, the judge replies, "He is a special kind of keeper," one who "rules even where there are other rulers," because his "authority countermands local judgements" (198). Once again, the judge's emphasis on judgment links him significantly to a Gnostic portrayal of Yahweh. Similarly, his insistence that he be the supreme ruler recalls Yahweh's commandment: "Thou shalt have none other gods before me. . . . Thou shalt not bow down thyself unto them, nor serve them: for I the LORD thy God am a jealous God" (Deuteronomy 5:7, 9). As the Gnostics were quick to point out, Yahweh is actually unwittingly revealing the existence of another god, "For if there were no other one, of whom would he be jealous?" (qtd. in Pearson 66). Like Yahweh, the judge's insistence on being the sole ruler subtly suggests the existence of other "principalities," "powers," and "rulers of the darkness of this world" (Ephesians 6:12) with which he competes for supremacy.[10]

Most telling of all, however, are pronouncements the judge makes with his hands placed on the ground: "This is my claim, he said. And yet everywhere upon it are pockets of autonomous life. Autonomous. In order for it to be mine nothing must be permitted to occur upon it save by my dispensation" (199). Robert Jarrett explains that "dispensation . . . is a key term in evangelical Protestant theology, referring to the different covenants regulating the relations between Jehovah and man" (*Cormac McCarthy* 78). It is by such a "dispensation" that a "terrible covenant" (126) was formed between the mortal Glanton and the sinister, Yahweh-like Holden. Leo Daugherty also links this passage to Yahweh, arguing that "Judge Holden's power is not yet complete, since his will is not yet fulfilled in its passion for total domination" and that "this was also necessarily true of the Gnostic archons, just as it was true of the Old Testament Yahweh" (163). According to Gnostic thought, the demiurge and his archons must exercise their tyrannical rule in order to prevent the trapped fragments of the divine from returning to their source, for if all divine fragments were liberated, there would be nothing left to animate the dead matter of the cosmos. As Kurt Rudolph explains, "the powers which rule the world, the Archons ... try to impede the [spirit's] return in order to prevent the perfecting of the world of light and thus protract the world process" (172). The archons are powerless in exerting their dominion over those who possess gnosis, or what the judge calls "pockets of autonomous life." Thus the judge knows that he will never be suzerain of the cosmos unless he can keep every living thing imprisoned in the manifest realm.

The judge's megalomaniacal claims also connect him to the Buddhist Māra, the "Evil One" who "corresponds to Satan" and "is the Lord of this world and of this earth" (Conze, *Buddhism* 35). It is noteworthy that in the New Testament, Jesus also refers to Satan as "the Prince of this world" (John 14:30) and tells his disciples, "I pray not for the world" (John 17:9), presumably because the world belongs to Satan. Māra, like the Gnostic archons, wishes to keep all things imprisoned in saṃsāra (the manifest cosmos) so that he may rule over them. The Buddhist text *Buddhacarita* (The Acts of the Buddha) describes Māra as "one who hates the very thought of freedom" (qtd. in Conze, *Buddhism* 35). Such a description may also be applied to Judge Holden, who announces, "The freedom of birds is an insult to me. I'd have them all in zoos" (199). In Buddhist legends, Māra attempts to prevent Prince Gautama from attaining enlightenment. Knowing that the soon-to-be Buddha poses a threat to his archon-like dominion, Māra muses, "If [Gautama] should succeed in overcoming me, and could proclaim to the world the way to final beatitude, then my realm would be empty today." He then consoles himself with the fact that "so far he has not yet won the eye of full knowledge. He is still within my sphere of influence" (qtd. in Conze, *Buddhist Scriptures* 49). Māra feels that the created world is his domain and resents the "autonomous" existence of the Buddhas and Bodhisattvas who have broken free of his influence.[11]

Māra attempts to interrupt Gautama's meditation by contesting the future Buddha's right to the ground on which he is seated. Māra argues that he is the lord of this world and "claims therefore that the Bodhisattva, representing that which is beyond this world and irredeemably hostile to it, has no right even to the piece of ground on which he is seated in meditation" (Conze, *Buddhism* 35). Māra's tyrannical and possessive attitude toward his ground is strikingly similar to Judge Holden's behavior when he places "his hands on the ground" and announces, "This is my claim" (199). The judge's obsession with his "claim" is revealed again later in the novel when he confronts the kid, asking, "For even if you should have stood your ground . . . yet what ground was it?" (307). The implications are clear: the ground, whether literal or metaphorical, belongs to the judge. No resistance will be tolerated, no territory ceded.

The tyrannical judge, like the Gnostic archons or the Buddhist Māra, wants all created life to succumb to his will; "autonomous" life must not be permitted to exist. In Gnostic thought, the rule of the archons is viewed as "tyranny, and not providence," because it is an "unenlightened and therefore malignant force, proceeding from the spirit of self-assertive power, from the will to rule and coerce" (Jonas 254). This "tyrannical world-rule" is called *heimarmene*, the "universal Fate" that constitutes "the inexorable and hostile law of the universe" (Jonas 254). The judge seems to demonstrate the power of heimarmene by performing an uncanny coin trick by the fire. He first makes a coin circle the fire as if on "some subtle lead" and then throws it away into the night, where it vanishes, only to return again after some time with a "faint high droning" (247). He explains that the "arc of circling bodies is determined by the length of their tether," whether they are "moons, coins" or "men" (246). It is highly significant that the judge draws attention to "moons" and "men," because the Gnostics believed that heimarmene controlled the paths of heavenly bodies, as well as the individual destinies of human beings. For example, the Gnostic Apocryphon of John describes how the archons "caused *Heimarmene* to come into being, and with a measure, times and seasons they bound the gods of the heaven," that is, the stars and planets, "the angels, demons and men, that they might all be in its fetter and it be lord over them all: a plan wicked and perverse" (qtd. in Rudolph 106). The judge's coin trick is a metaphor for these inexorable forces, meant to show the members of Glanton's gang that heimarmene controls the paths of celestial bodies and the motions of earthly objects, as well as the individual destinies of human beings. The demonstration also serves as a reminder that in each case, the archon judge holds the tether.

Images of tethers, fetters, and puppets on strings abound in *Blood Meridian*. A "fortuneteller" who raises her head is described as "a blindfold mannequin raised awake by a string" (94). The kid, sleeping on his horse, resembles "a mounted marionette" (129). Indians "assemble upon the trembling drop of the eastern horizon like baleful marionettes" (278). When Toadvine and the Vandiemanlander ride south to catch up with the rest of the gang, they are described as being "trammelled to chords of rawest destiny" (154). Hans Jonas explains that in Gnostic texts, the "chain, bond, and knot are frequent symbols for the body" (63). The Gnostic Apocryphon of John features the following proclamation: "This is the fetter, this is the tomb of the creature of the body, which was put upon man as a fetter of matter" (qtd. in Rudolph 103). Manichean cosmogony describes the biblical Adam's lament upon finding his spirit trapped in a prison of flesh: "Woe, woe unto the shaper of my body, unto those who fettered my soul, and unto the rebels that enslaved me!" (qtd. in Jonas 87). Thus the repeated references to "fetters" in *Blood Meridian* are highly evocative not only of the constricting forces of heimarmene but also of the Gnostic belief that the spirit is trapped in the fetters of corporeal existence.[12]

In *Blood Meridian*, human beings are compared to clay dolls or mannequins; men are described as looking "like mud effigies" and Toadvine appears as "a great clay voodoo doll made animate and the kid looked like another" (8, 13). The notion that human beings are created from clay already exists in the Bible—for example, Job beseeches God to remember that "thou has made me as the clay" (Job 10:9) and Elihu tells Job, "I also am formed out of the clay" (Job 33:6)—but the Gnostics interpreted this creation myth as further evidence of the essential repulsiveness of matter. The *Ginza Rba*, a Mandean prayer book, commands humanity to "arise, arise" and "put off thy stinking body, thy garment of clay, the fetter, the bond" (qtd. in Jonas 85). The fact that the narrative voice in *Blood Meridian* compares human beings to clay dolls "made animate" not only evokes a Gnostic repulsion at the corporeality of flesh but also serves to rob the characters of their individual agency, suggesting that they are merely mindless automata controlled by the forces of heimarmene.

Blood Meridian also makes frequent references to forces of fate or destiny, suggesting that all human beings are bound to predetermined paths. When the Glanton gang stumbles upon a site where the tracks of murderers cross the tracks of unlucky travelers, the unlikelihood of the "convergence of such vectors in such a waste" leads the ex-priest to ask "if some might not see the hand of a cynical god conducting with what austerity and what mock surprise so lethal a congruence" (153). Tobin's "cynical god" behaves like the Gnostic demiurge, cruelly toying with creation for his own amusement. The passage suggests that both groups—victims and murderers—were blindly led down their respective paths by some unseen force, like pawns on a chessboard. The narrative voice describes another meeting of two groups of riders, "divided upon that midnight plain, each passing back the way the other had come, pursuing as all travelers must inversions without end upon other men's journeys" (121). The key word here is "must," implying that the travelers have no choice in this matter.

The idea that there is some other sentience orchestrating these events is suggested when the movements of men are described as being "beyond will or fate" and "under consignment to some third and other destiny" (96). The passage implies that human beings are not ruled by their own free will, nor by the mechanical cause-and-effect fate meted out by a deterministic cosmos, but rather by some "other," all-encompassing agency that rules over humanity. It is noteworthy that one of the less common meanings of the word "consignment" refers to "confinement within bounds by way of discipline or punishment" (*OED*). This "other destiny" that imprisons human beings is suggestive of the Gnostic concept of the universe as "a vast prison," where each archon acts as "a warder" (Jonas 43). The "other destiny" or "agency" is also evoked in a passage that describes the Glanton gang planning an attack "upon a band of peaceful Tiguas": "On the eve of that day they crouched about the fire where it hissed in a softly falling rain and they ran balls and cut patches as if the fate of the aborigines had been cast into shape by some other agency altogether. As if such destinies were prefigured in the very rock for those with eyes to read" (173). Once again, it is suggested that some "other agency"—a word that implies sentience—determines the courses and outcomes of human lives.

The idea that these destinies are predetermined is emphasized yet again when the Yuma Indians burn the remains of the massacred Glanton gang. Staring into the flames, the Yumas are depicted as "contemplating towns to come and the poor fanfare of trumpet and drum and the rude boards upon which their destinies were inscribed for these people were no less bound and indentured and they watched like the prefiguration of their own ends the carbonized skulls of their enemies incandescing before them bright as blood among the coals" (276). Not only are the Yumas aware that their paths will end in inevitable death, but they also sense that they are "bound and indentured," as though by some cosmic contract. This sense of being "bound" once again recalls the fetters of heimarmene that permeate the novel and leads us back to the archon judge, who always holds the tether. As the judge talks to a sergeant about the African origins of "Black John Jackson," his hands are described as "drafting with a marvellous dexterity the shapes of what varied paths conspired here in the ultimate authority of the extant . . . like strings drawn together through the eye of a ring" (85). The image of the converging strings serves as another metaphor for the fetters of heimarmene. When Jackson demands to know what is being said about him, the judge only smiles and tells him that it is "not necessary . . . that the principals here be in possession of the facts concerning their case, for their acts will ultimately accommodate history with or without their understanding." The judge argues that human beings will necessarily succumb to destinies beyond their control—to the "formal agenda of an absolute destiny" (85)—whether or not they are aware of the forces that bind them.

The judge is frequently depicted as the author of this "absolute destiny" (85), predetermining the paths of all individuals. When, near the end of the novel, the kid looks into the judge's "lashless pig's eyes," he can "read whole bodies of decisions not accountable to the courts of men" and finds "his own name . . . logged into the records as a thing already accomplished" (310).[13] At this final meeting in a saloon, the judge begins to taunt the kid with his preternatural knowledge of the arrangement of the cosmos, pointing "out various men in the room" and asking "if these men were here for a good time or if indeed they knew why they were here at all." The kid evades the questions, claiming, "Everybody dont have to have a reason to be someplace." "That's so," agrees the judge. "They do not have to have a reason. But order is not set aside because of their indifference." The judge seems to be implying that it makes no difference whether human beings behave as though they have free will or whether they allow themselves to be swept along by the tide of events. Either way, their lives are constrained by the order of the universe, that rigid harmony of the spheres that the Gnostics saw as heimarmene. When the kid does not reply, the judge rephrases his statement, explaining, "If it is so that they themselves have no reason and yet are indeed here must they not be here by reason of some other?" (328). Once again, the forces of heimarmene are referred to as the "other" order, recalling the novel's earlier evocations of the "other destiny" (96) and the "other agency" (173). Taunting the kid, whom he is about to murder, the judge asks, "And if this is so can you guess what that other might be?" "No," replies the kid, "Can you?" The judge doesn't need to guess, he already knows; his enigmatic reply, "I know him well" (328), is a gesture back toward himself, as he is "that other." In other words, Judge Holden seems to be the very personification of heimarmene.[14]

The judge goes on to repeat the argument that human beings do not need to be aware of heimarmene for it to have the power to shape their lives or for some higher sentience to use them as pawns in the cosmic game. Looking around the room, the judge announces, "This is an orchestration for an event. For a dance in fact. The participants will be apprised of their roles at the proper time. For now it is enough that they have arrived. As the dance is the thing with which we are concerned and contains complete within itself its own arrangements and history and finale there is no necessity that the dancers contain these things within themselves as well." The dance seems to be heimarmene itself, that terrible harmony of the cosmos, which, according to Gnostic thought, binds all created things. The judge adds that none of the men present "can finally comprehend the reason for his presence," but if he were, in fact, "to know he might well absent himself and you can see that that cannot be any part of the plan if plan there be" (329). In other words, if human beings were to understand the nature of the dance—that is, the nature of the cosmos as the Gnostics saw it—they might refuse to participate in existence.

This knowledge seems to be none other than gnosis, the possession of which "involves an experiential and intuitive perception of our true nature and origin." This, then, enables the Gnostic practitioner to escape "from the enslaving material prison of the world and the body into the upper regions of spirit" (Wagner and Flannery-Dailey 264). The importance of spiritual knowledge is also stressed in Buddhist thought, as the only means of freeing oneself from the prison of saṃsāra. Edward Conze writes, "Wisdom alone allows us to see . . . the workings of the unseen, impersonal, actually real cosmic forces which pervade the universe" (*Further Buddhist Studies* 38). Such liberation through knowledge, or spiritual insight, is exactly what the archons (or, in Buddhist legend, Māra) are trying to prevent. According to Gnostic soteriology, "the end of the world takes places when all that is spiritual (*pneumatic*) is shaped and perfected through knowledge (*gnosis*)" (Rudolph 196). Consequently, the archons necessarily "try to hinder the Gnostics' upward Journey," that is, the attainment of gnosis and the subsequent ascent from the prison of the manifest cosmos that such spiritual insight entails. Thus, if all the dancers should come to "comprehend the reason" for their presence at the dance, they would chose to "absent" themselves. There would be no dance to speak of and such an outcome is not a part of the judge's "plan."

The judge then goes on to tell the kid that human beings cannot avoid their destiny. Even if they were to glimpse the future and chose a different path, they would still arrive at the same destination: "Any man who could discover his own fate and elect therefore some opposite course could only come at last to that selfsame reckoning at the same appointed time" (330).[15] Continuing his musings on the subject of human will, the judge points to a random man in the saloon and reveals the nature of his existential trouble: "You know his opinion of the world. You can read it in his face, in his stance. Yet his complaint that a man's life is no bargain masks the actual case with him. Which is that men will not do as he wishes them to. Have never done, never will do" (330). The judge's words curiously echo the writing of Jacob Boehme, whose influence on *Blood Meridian* has already been established. Boehme writes that each human being's "life is a cause of trouble" precisely because of the multiplicity of contrary wills manifested in each individual, "for [life] exists in many different wills, each essence having a will of its own which may be put into action. Thus the life of man is its own enemy, one form fights the other, and this is the case not only in man, but in all creatures" (qtd. in Hartmann 318). The malevolent judge encourages men to exert their will over one another in perpetual conflict and is disgusted when they fail to do so. The judge tells the kid that the life of a man who fails to dominate others becomes "so balked about by difficulty and . . . so altered of its intended architecture that he is little more than a walking hovel hardly fit to house the human spirit at all" (330). The judge's words serve as an allusion to the Nietzschean concept of "will to power," which will be discussed later, but they also hint at the Gnostic teaching that the human spirit, "including the base and the humble, has divine origins . . . and stands higher than the whole [manifest] cosmos which in itself has no value" (Rudolph 267). According to the Gnostics, the archons imprisoned the divine spirit in the inferior material body, causing it to cry out, "Grief and woe I suffer in the body-garment into which they have transported and cast me" (qtd. in Jonas 461). Thus the

Gnostics would also agree with the judge's claim that the debased "hovel" of flesh is not fit to "house the human spirit."

The Gnostics viewed human nature as a triune composed of body, psyche, and spirit, believing that the spirit, or pneuma, was trapped not only within the prison of the human body, but also within the prison of the psyche. Kurt Rudolph explains, "Gnostic anthropology is therefore basically tripartite, although in distinction to similar contemporary conceptions a clear line is drawn between the material and the psychic and the spiritual part" (90). According to Gnostic teachings, human beings could be divided into three types based on their level of spiritual development. Those persons who were completely immersed in bodily, material existence were known as *hylics* or *choics*, meaning "earthly." Slightly higher up in this hierarchy were those dominated by mental processes associated with the mind or soul; such people were known as *psychics*, without the modern connotations of the word. Most valued were the pneumatics, or the "spiritual" persons who possessed gnosis and did not identify with their own bodies or psyches (Rudolph 92).

According to Gnostic teachings, hylic and psychic individuals remain under the dominion of the archons and are kept in a state of perpetual submission through the forces of heimarmene. Kurt Rudolph explains that the Gnostics placed a "negative judgement upon the whole of bodily and psychic existence," believing it to be "a product of evil powers" and arguing that "through this man is not only the object but also the subject of the activity of such powers" (92). Consequently, "only a small part of man (namely, the divine spark) can escape" this dominion (58). Thus it is in the archon judge's best interest to incite the human ego and to kindle the desire to physically dominate others, for such behavior emphasizes the psychic and hylic aspects of human existence. The judge's scorn for the random man in the saloon, representative of all humanity imprisoned under the thrall of archons, is that of an arrogant tyrant disgusted with the weakness and ignorance of his slaves. Taunting the kid, the judge asks, "Can he say, such a man, that there is no malign thing set against him? That there is no power and no force and no cause?" (330). The answer to the question, as the judge well knows, is "No, he cannot," for the judge himself is this "malign thing," this "power," "force," and "cause" set against every human being.

As previously mentioned, *Blood Meridian* is preoccupied with the Nietzschean question of the human "will," which is illuminated in a new light by the influence of the theosophical writings of Jacob Boehme. When the kid, still only a child, runs away from home, the narrative voice announces that "not again in all the world's turning will there be terrains so wild and barbarous to try whether the stuff of creation may be shaped to man's will or whether his own heart is not another kind of clay" (4–5). Though the "wild and barbarous" terrain is presented as being unique, the question put forward by the narrative voice is perennial: Can human beings shape the world according to their will, or are they shaped along with the world by forces beyond their control? Sitting among the ruins of the Anasazi, the judge illustrates this problem of human will by pointing to these ancient people's attempt to escape the fate of all civilizations, pronouncing that whoever "builds in stone seeks to alter the structure of the universe and so it was with these masons however primitive their works may seem to us." The Anasazi attempted to "shape the stuff of creation" to their will, but these "dead fathers" are all lost to the world and their "spirit is entombed" in the very "stone" through which they wished to take charge of their destinies (146).

Glanton takes up the challenge issued by the narrative voice at the beginning of the novel and attempts to shape "the stuff of creation" to his will, but in his determination to do so, he approaches the monomaniacal madness of Melville's Captain Ahab. Like the sailors in Ahab's crew, Tobin claims that he "always knew" that Glanton was "mad" (127). Sitting before the fire, the leader of the band of scalp hunters is described as ignoring any "portents" that he might see in the flames, for it was "much the same to him" whether they appeared or not, or whether "his history should run concomitant with men and nations, whether it should cease." This is because Glanton had "long forsworn all weighing of consequences and allowing as he did that men's destinies are given yet he usurped to contain within him all that he would ever be in the world and all that the world would be to him and be his charter written in the urstone itself he claimed agency and said so and he'd drive the remorseless sun on to its final endarkenment as if he'd ordered it all ages since" (243). These words echo those of Ahab, who in his determination to find the white whale, exclaims, "Talk not to me of blasphemy, man; I'd strike the sun if it insulted me" (Melville, *Moby-Dick* 167). Like Ahab, Glanton will claim personal agency even in the face of a predetermined destiny written on the "urstone" at the very beginning of creation, even if it means driving the sun—the very symbol of divine light—to its final demise.[16]

From a Gnostic perspective, Glanton's quest is doomed to fail, for no amount of willpower, determination, or violence against creation will free one from the fetters of heimarmene if one does not possess spiritual insight, the gnosis that is akin to the Buddhist state of enlightenment. According to the traditions that constitute the Perennial Philosophy, it is this very obsession with the will that keeps humanity from developing spiritually. As the great German mystic Meister Eckhart (1260–1327) taught, "Nought burns in hell but self will" (*Works* 48). Jacob Boehme also addressed the question of whether human will may be asserted against the whole of creation and argued that the human being does indeed have the potential for such rebellion, but only if, like Satan, one is willing to set oneself in opposition to the divine.

In *Jacob Boehme: Life and Doctrines*, Franz Hartmann explains that, according to Boehme, "Man's will and imagination have become perverted from their original state," because "man has surrounded himself by a world of will and imagination of his own" and "has therefore lost sight of God" (6). In Boehme's theosophy, the "devil" is equated with "spiritual will perverted" and "if it is perverted in a personal being, then will there be a personal devil" (Hartmann 152). Such a personal devil seems much like the demonic judge in *Blood Meridian*. Leo Daugherty notes that, much like the biblical God Yahweh, the judge "judges things simply according to the binary criterion of their being inside or outside his will" and "is enraged by any existence or any act outside that will" (163). The judge's monomaniacal obsession with the triumph of his own will recalls Boehme's description of the devils as possessing a perverted spiritual will.

Franz Hartmann's explanation of Boehme's theory of the way in which the will manifests and exhausts itself in all created things is reminiscent of McCarthy's oft-quoted "meridian" passage. Hartmann writes that, for Boehme, "the earth, like every other cosmic body, is a form of manifestation of will, and has a sensation of its own. Every part of the earth strives for the full enjoyment of the beneficent sun-rays, and when arriving at the meridian it would fain stand still, as if in mute adoration and worship of the glory of the celestial orb, but is pushed on by those parts that follow. Thus every part alternatively embraces the sunlight and sinks again into darkness once during the daily revolution of our planet" (168). *Blood Meridian* states that "in the affairs of men there is no waning and the noon of his expression signals the onset of night. His spirit is exhausted at the peak of its achievement. His meridian is at once his darkening and the evening of his day" (147). In both instances, the idea conveyed is that no matter how one may strive to achieve a state of permanence, transience is the very essence of existence. Death claims all created things, despite the monomaniacal willpower and demoniac rage of those who, like Glanton or Ahab, would attempt to oppose the irresistible forces of destiny that relentlessly drive human beings to their inevitable demise.

The very title of this novel—*Blood Meridian; or, The Evening Redness in the West*—emphasizes the theme of death as the most inexorable of fates. All over the world, the West has been seen as the cardinal point symbolic of death, due to its associations with sunset, darkness, and decline.[17] The "evening" of the title is not just the "evening of [humanity's] day" (147) but the evening of Western civilizations, following in the footsteps of the lost Anasazi. One of the epigraphs to *Blood Meridian*, taken from Paul Valéry's essay "The Yalu," describes the typical Westerner's response to the inevitability of death, as seen from an Eastern perspective: "Your ideas are terrifying and your hearts are faint. Your acts of pity and cruelty are absurd, committed with no calm, as if they were irresistible. Finally, you fear blood more and more. Blood and time" (1). Valéry's words suggest that these senseless acts of "pity and cruelty," committed with a demoniac rage "as if they were irresistible," stem from a fear of "blood"—that is, the vulnerability of mortal flesh—and "time," which is the very essence of transience, mutability, impermanence, and mortality.

This kind of behavior has been well documented by the psychiatrist Otto Rank, who wrote that "the death fear of the ego is lessened by the killing, the sacrifice, of the other; through the death of the other, one buys oneself free from the penalty of dying, of being killed" (130). Similarly, in his study of death denial, Ernest Becker argued that "only scapegoats can relieve one of his own stark death fear: 'I am threatened with death—let us kill plentifully'" (149). The demoniac violence that permeates the novel seems to be in accordance with Becker's insight that such behavior stems from a desperate rage against one's own mortality. Becker explains that the aim of such violence is to "deny one's lack of control over events, his powerlessness, his vagueness as a person in a mechanical world spinning into decay and death" (84). We witness this kind of behavior in the Glanton gang, who though all too eager to take the lives of others are terrified of losing their own.

When Sproule, already dying of consumption and nursing a gangrenous arm, is bitten by a vampire bat, he begins "gibbering hysterically," holds out "his bloodied hands as if in accusation," and emits "a howl" of "outrage" (66). Similarly, when the kid is ordered to shoot the wounded Shelby, the latter weeps and begs for his life, claiming that "this is a terrible place to die" (208). Recalling a time when the gang ran out of gunpowder and its members were threatened with certain death, Tobin describes how he "looked at the men" around him and saw how "the dignity was gone out of them" and "did not like to see them so" (131). Glanton, on the other hand, accepts death with a curious composure. Determined to claim agency even in the face of his destiny, he commands the Yuma chief standing over him to "hack away" (275), as though he were giving the order and thus were master of his own demise. Glanton paradoxically insists on claiming "agency" even while knowing "that men's destinies are given" (243). It is noteworthy that the circumstances of Glanton's death are revealed to him by a tarot reader earlier in the novel, thus revealing the futility of his struggle to be the master of a destiny that has already been predetermined by some "other agency." When Glanton draws "The Chariot" card reversed, the fortune-teller cries that she sees "the cart ... wheel-less in the dark river" (96). Among the subheadings in chapter 19, in which Glanton meets his death at the Yuma ferry crossing, are the enigmatic "Dawn on the River" and "Carts without Wheels," both of which echo the tarot reader's words. Thus, despite his Ahab-like attempts to control his destiny, Glanton's path is no different from the paths of all the other "moons," "coins," and "men," all of which are "determined by the length of their tether," or by those cosmic forces that the Gnostics saw as the heimarmene of the archons.

The only character within the novel who seems to have successfully transcended death and time is the demonic judge. The judge attempts to incite the kid to embrace the destructive, death-dealing rage of secretly terrified mortals, telling him, "You of all men are no stranger to that feeling, the emptiness and the despair. It is that which we take arms against, is it not? Is not blood the tempering agent in the mortar which bonds?" (329). The "emptiness and despair" come from the knowledge of one's mortality, against which human beings rage in vain. The judge seems to be offering the kid the same kind of covenant that he offered to Glanton: to sublimate one's fear of death in a frenzy of violence and to take control of death by becoming its agent.

Before the judge murders the kid, he taunts his victim with talk of death: "What do you think death is, man?" (329). He addresses the kid much like the Old Testament angels (whom the Gnostics regarded as archons) address human beings: "Understand, O man," says the Archangel Gabriel to Daniel (Daniel 8:15). The judge continues to ask questions that he knows the kid cannot answer: "Of whom do we speak when we speak of a man who was and is not? Are these blind riddles or are they not some part of every man's jurisdiction? What is death if not an agency? And whom does he intend toward?" The judge talks of death as though it were a sentient entity. When the kid refuses to answer the riddles, the judge offers a clue as to Death's identity by drawing attention to himself. "Look at me" (329), he says, as though offering an answer to his own riddles. Death's agency seems to be his own.

The judge's proclamations continue with these biblical overtones: "There is room on the stage for one beast and one alone. All others are destined for a night that is eternal and without name. One by one they will step down into the darkness before the footlamps." The "Beast" is among the titles given to Satan in Revelation and is thus a reference to the demonic judge himself, who, unlike ordinary human beings, is not destined for death. This reading is strengthened by the judge's claim that "there will be one there always who is a true dancer and can you guess who that might be?" The kid, guessing to whom the judge is referring, replies, "You aint nothing" (331). The judge seems to be something altogether beyond the ordinary comprehension of the mortal characters within the novel. He is the only "true dancer," like Shiva the Destroyer, whose dance "burns the world to ashes . . . at the end of each aeon" (Pereira 32). The shift into a strange, dreamlike register in the final paragraph of the novel captures the sinister, nightmarish qualities of the judge: "His feet are light and nimble. He never sleeps. He says that he will never die. He dances in light and in shadow and he is a great favorite. He never sleeps, the judge. He is dancing, dancing. He says that he will never die." The judge "throws back his head and laughs deep in his throat" in the knowledge that he is free from death and time (335).

The final paragraph of the novel emphasizes the immortality of the judge on several levels. Apart from the obvious proclamations "that he will never die," the fact that the judge never sleeps further emphasizes his freedom from death and time. As Jacob Boehme writes, "The image of God does not sleep. In it there is not time. With sleep, time became manifest in man. . . . Sleep signifies death and surrender" (qtd. in Hartmann 156). Thus the sleepless judge is not subject to death or time and will never surrender his "claim" (199) on this world. In "McCarthy Music," Jay Ellis points out that "all 334 preceding pages are mostly in the past tense. Suddenly we are in the continual present of a dangerous immortal" (166). The judge seems to be a composite of the Great Evil in all its guises, drawing on the traditions of the Judeo-Christian Satan, the Islamic djinns, the Hindu Shiva, the Buddhist Māra, a Gnostic archon, and a literary personification of Fate, Time, and Death itself.[18]

CHAPTER 3

"Disciples of a New Faith"

Satanic Parody in *Blood Meridian*

■ *Blood Meridian* is, in many ways, a study of the gradual paradigm shift that occurred during the era that Marshall Berman refers to as "Classical Modernity" (1789–1900). In the West, the Age of Modernity inaugurated the shift away from the mythico-magical apprehension of the world, dominated by the teachings of organized religion, toward the dominance of a rational and scientific world view. In *Forgotten Truth*, a study of the decline of the Perennial Philosophy, Huston Smith argues that the "final definition of modernity" is "an outlook in which this world, this ontological plane, is the only one that is genuinely countenanced and affirmed." Smith explains that although a world view dominated by reason can only satisfactorily deal with empirical reality, which is a level occupying "no more than a single ontological plane," it is continually challenging "the notion that other planes exist" (6). According to Smith, this denial of a world beyond the empirically quantifiable resulted in what Nietzsche referred to as the "death of God," for "if 'God' in principle requires more exalted quarters, the non-existence of such quarters entails his non-existence as well" (7). Modernity brought with it not only empiricism and reason, but also reductionism and nihilism. In *Blood Meridian*, McCarthy investigates the onset of this new age, as well as its metaphysical and spiritual consequences.[1]

The full title of the novel—*Blood Meridian; or, The Evening Redness in the West*—evokes a process of decline, suggesting that despite all celebrations of progress, the West has already reached its meridian, or peak, and is now beginning its descent. The idea is further developed by McCarthy's choice of a quote from Paul Valéry's essay "The Yalu" as an epigraph: "Your ideas are terrifying and your hearts are faint. Your acts of pity and cruelty are absurd, committed with no calm, as if they were irresistible. Finally, you fear blood more and more. Blood and time" (1). The speaker of these words, a Chinese scholar, criticizes Westerners for worshiping intelligence "as if it were an omnipotent beast." He goes on to say that a "man intoxicated" on intelligence "confuses his quick changes of heart with the imperceptible variation of real forms and enduring Beings" (Valéry 372). In its original context, the quote forms part of Valéry's critique of the West's obsession with reason and its abandonment of spiritual and contemplative modes of knowing; this critique may also be applied to the paradigm shift explored throughout *Blood Meridian*.

In *Blood Meridian*, the apparent decline of Western spirituality is signified through the repeated motifs of ruined churches, desecrated sacred sites, and broken icons. In the very first chapter, a "ratty canvas tent" that serves as a "nomadic house of God" collapses "like a huge and wounded medusa" (7). In the town of Bexar, the kid wakes in "the nave of a ruinous church" (26) and the "old church" at San José de Tumacacori is also "in ruins" (224). In a nameless church in a deserted village, the "altars" have "been hauled down and the tabernacle looted" (60). Other sacred sites are in a similar state of disarray. Glanton's men ride past "the ruinous walls" of a cemetery, with its "grounds strewn with bones and skulls and broken pots like some ancient ossuary" (175). Even the ex-priest-cum-scalp-hunter, Tobin, serves as a personification of a ruined church, "in his rags and his collar of blood" (293). Nearly all the churches encountered throughout the novel seem to be in a state of deterioration.

The novel is also replete with desecrated icons. "Saints in their niches" are "shorn of ears and noses," having been "shot up by the American troops trying their rifles" (26). "Primitive painted saints" hang "cocked on the walls as if an earthquake had visited" (60). A "dead Christ in a glass bier" lies "broken on the chancel floor" (60) and a "carved stone virgin" holds "in her arms a headless child" (27). A "crucified Apache" hangs from a "crosstree with its mouth gaped in a raw hole" (247). An "alter-christ"—McCarthy's pun on a penitent reenacting the crucifixion—has been "disembowelled" and lies dead "with the scraps of rope by which he had been bound still tied about his wrists and ankles" (315). In an echo of Nietzsche's "death of God," all these images of Christ depict death with no promise of resurrection.

Massacres of the penitent and the devout abound throughout the novel. "The remains of several bodies" and "one child" lie "along the back wall" of a ruined church (26). In a deserted village, the "stone floor" of a church is

"Disciples of a New Faith" ■ 55

"heaped" with the "scalped and naked and partly eaten bodies of some forty souls who'd barricaded themselves in this house of God against the heathen" and the "murdered" lie "in a great pool of their communal blood" (60). The reference to "communal blood" is, of course, a dark parody of communion wine, which transubstantiates into the blood of Christ during the Eucharist. Fleeing from the Glanton gang, helpless people are described "running toward the church where they knelt clutching the altar and from this refuge they were dragged howling one by one and one by one they were slain and scalped in the chancel floor" (181). Later in the novel, we encounter a "company of penitents" that "lay hacked and butchered among the stones in every attitude. Many lay about the fallen cross and some were mutilated and some were without heads" (315). The "fallen cross" serves as yet another example of a desecrated religious icon that signifies the decline of Western spirituality.

In *Blood Meridian*, carrion birds are often found in or around churches. "Three buzzards hobbled about on the picked bone carcass of some animal dead in the chancel," and in yet another ruined church, there are "buzzards squatting among the old carved wooden corbels" (26, 58). Furthermore, the novel features numerous passages in which vultures are compared to clergymen. Carrion birds are depicted "with their wings outstretched in attitudes of exhortation like dark little bishops" (59). Similarly, a headless body floating downriver is ridden by "a vulture standing between the shoulderblades in clerical black" (262). Vultures perch "among the niches in the carved facade hard by the figures of Christ and the apostles." Stretching their wings, the birds are described as "holding out their own dark vestments in postures of strange benevolence" (72). The word "vulture" may be used figuratively to refer to a "person of a vile and rapacious disposition" (*OED*). Thus the frequent comparisons made between vultures and clerics serve as a damning indictment of corruption within the hierarchy of the church.

In *Blood Meridian*, the decline of spirituality is accompanied by the ascendance of rationalism. The figure of the judge seems to embody Reason taken to a pathological degree. Such a phenomenon was witnessed during the French Revolution when a shrine to the goddess Reason was set up in Notre Dame and rationalism turned into a religious cult.[2] The judge's affiliations with reason, especially in the form of science, are emphasized continually in *Blood Meridian*. One of the subheadings to chapter 14 reads, "The Point of View for His Work as a Scientist," referring, of course, to the judge

(186). Numerous examples of this scientific "work" are documented throughout the novel. Tobin describes how, while the gang fled from a band of Indians, the "judge would stop to botanize and then ride to catch up. My hand to God. Pressing leaves in his book. Sure I never saw the equal to it and all the time the savages in plain view below us." Tobin adds that the judge would stay up all night "watchin the bats" and describes how he "would go up the side of the mountain and make notes in a little book and then he would come back down" (127). When the members of the Glanton gang come across "a great femur from some beast long extinct," the judge not only sketches it into his log but gives the men a lecture on paleontology: "They sat watching and putting to him such queries as they could conceive of. He answered them with care, amplifying their own questions for them, as if they might be apprentice scholars" (251). The judge is in a position of influence, from which he can instruct and manipulate the others.

Further examples of the judge's "work as a scientist" (186) abound. The judge continually sketches pictures of flora, fauna, and artifacts in his sketchbook, tirelessly documenting and analyzing the world around him. John Cant writes, "The judge traverses the landscape as did Lewis and Clark, those men of the Enlightenment who surveyed the interior at Jefferson's behest, recording all in their notebooks, from surveyed measurements to sketches of the flora" (169). Indeed, we are told that the judge "roamed through the ruinous kivas picking up small artifacts" and "sat upon a high wall and sketched in his book until the light failed" (139). At this point, the narrative voice suddenly changes register, announcing, "He is a draftsman as he is other things, well sufficient to the task" (140). This eerie comment serves a dual purpose: not only does it prompt the reader to wonder precisely what "other things" the otherworldly judge might be, but the narrator's unexpected switch to the present tense suggests that Judge Holden is not just a historical figure but something altogether more sinister, which continues to linger on into our own time. The judge is like no other character within the novel because he embodies far more than can be contained within the limitations of an individual personality. He seems to be, among other things, a sinister and parodic personification of the modern, scientific paradigm.[3]

At first glance, there may seem to be nothing unusual about the judge's interest in natural history, but when we consider his disturbing habit of destroying the original object once he has recorded it in his sketchbook, we begin to see McCarthy's parodic criticism of scientific practices carried to pathological extremes. When the judge finds a "footpiece from a suit of armor hammered out in a shop in Toledo three centuries before," he sketches it "in profile and in perspective, citing the dimensions in his neat script, making marginal notes." After carefully documenting the little artifact, he "studied it again and then he crushed it into a ball of foil and pitched it into the fire." He then "gathered up the other artifacts ... and cast them also into the fire" (140). Similarly, after "copying out" ancient pictographs found among the rocks, he takes "a piece of broken chert" and with it "he scapples away one of the designs, leaving no trace of it only a raw place on the stone where it had been" (173). When a "Tennessean named Webster" asks the judge about this odd behavior and "what he aims to do with those notes and sketches," the judge smiles mysteriously and replies that it is "his intention to expunge them from the memory of man" (140). Webster sensibly argues that "no man can put all the world in a book. No more than everything drawed in a book is so," but the judge paradoxically insists, "What is to be deviates no jot from the book wherein it's writ. How could it? It would be a false book and a false book is no book at all" (141). The judge's counter-intuitive argument gives primacy to the signifier while rejecting the original signified. By destroying the original object and leaving only the representation behind, the judge makes sure that no reality is *permitted* to exist outside the text. In other words, there is nothing left that may contradict the veracity of his "book," not even the dim "memory of man."

The judge's aim is not so much to understand the world but rather to subjugate it to his will. He claims that "only nature can enslave man and only when the existence of each last entity is routed out and made to stand naked before him will he be properly suzerain of the earth." He explains that a "suzerain" is "a special kind of keeper," who "rules even where there are other rulers" and whose "authority countermands local judgements" (198). The judge aims to become the sole author of the world, announcing that it is his "claim" and "nothing must be permitted to occur upon it save by [his] dispensation" (199). John Cant argues that the judge uses "the language of the accountant," which "expresses the notion of knowledge as power, of the earth as commodity" (170). Cant adds that this is "the language of quantity rather than value," because it offers the "false promise of progress through empirical investigation and the use of reason alone" (171). Ultimately, the judge will permit no interpretations or judgements to override his own pronouncements. The judge destroys the objects he has sketched because this gives him power over all that he has documented. When the original object is destroyed, all that remains is the judge's own interpretation of it.

Furthermore, by destroying the objects around him, the judge is reducing existence to a purely material level. After documenting the outward appearance of an object, the judge feels that he possesses that object in its entirety and can thus do away with the original. René Guénon explains that "the idea that there exist things that are purely 'material'" is an "outlook" that "can be regarded as indispensable in order to enable science to deal with its object, for if a contrary admission were made, science would at once be compelled to recognize that the real nature of its objects eludes it" (*Reign of Quantity* 212). According to this view, in order to understand the world, science must reduce everything to a quantifiable level. Huston Smith argues that this kind of reductionism is inherently violent: "The Western hunt for knowledge, analytic and objective to its core, has violence built into it. For to know analytically is to reduce the object of knowledge, however vital, however complex, to precisely this: an object" (*Forgotten Truth* 126). Elaborating on the theme of scientific violence, Smith writes, "To approach existence as if it were purely or even primarily physical and mathematical is to falsify it. The approach could end in smashing our planet, for if a hammer is the only tool one learns to use, it is tempting to regard everything as if it were a nail" (117). Smith's argument is especially pertinent to the bizarre actions of Judge Holden, who desires to document and control everything around him, even at the cost of destroying it.

Huston Smith argues that science in itself is beneficial to humanity when it remains its own empirical field, but "out of place, as an angel that has fallen, science turns demonic. It presumes to control too much and to disclose more reality than in fact it does" (*Forgotten Truth* 117). Smith makes a distinction between science and scientism, arguing, "Whereas science is positive, contenting itself with reporting what it discovers, scientism is negative. It goes beyond the actual findings of science to deny that other approaches to knowledge are valid and other truths true. In doing so it deserts science in favor of metaphysics—bad metaphysics, as it happens, for as the contention that there are no truths save those of science is not itself a scientific truth, in affirming it scientism contradicts itself. It also carries marks of a religion—a secular religion" (16) In other words, Smith argues that when science seeks to pronounce on matters that fall outside the scope of rational or empirical inquiry, it mutates into a scientistic pseudo-religion.

According to this argument, a purely rational and empirical world view results in a diminished outlook. Jacob Boehme, who witnessed the beginnings of the ascendance of science during the Renaissance, warned that those who embrace science and reject the spiritual aspects of existence "are devoid of understanding. They have a science, but no real knowledge. They have broken the mirror and are looking through spectacles" (qtd. in Hartmann 312). Boehme argues that "science cannot abolish faith in the all-seeing God, without worshipping in His place the blind intellect" (qtd. in Hartmann 35). According to this argument, when God is pronounced dead, Reason is worshipped in his stead. John Cant suggests that the "judge represents the endless futile quest of empirical reason to replace God" (174). The judge represents not only a shift away from the religious world view toward the scientistic but also the creation of an inverted pseudo-religion.

The idea that a pseudo-religion is being inaugurated by the judge is suggested throughout the novel. The narrative voice describes the judge "standing on the rise in silhouette against the evening sun like some great balden archimandrite. He was wrapped in a mantle of freeflowing cloth beneath which he was naked" (273). It is significant that an "archimandrite" is ecclesiastical Greek for the "superior of a monastery or convent, corresponding to the *abbot* in the Western Church" (*OED*). Recalling the judge's first mysterious address to the Glanton gang, the ex-priest Tobin claims, "It was like a sermon but it was no such sermon as any man of us had ever heard before." The religious overtones of the word "sermon" are compounded by the imagery of the "sunrise" of "many colours" and "the wind ... flappin the judge's old benjamin about him" (129), which, according to Schimpf, paint a scene reminiscent of "Charlton Heston as Moses on the mount reading the Ten Commandments, his scarf flapping in the wind" (22). The judge is continually portrayed as a priest or cult leader and the Glanton gang as his devotees.[4]

After hearing the judge's sermon, the members of the Glanton gang "follow behind him like the disciples of a new faith" (130). Tobin adds that when the judge distributed the gunpowder he had just created out of sulfur and bat guano, "he called us all about to fill our horns and flasks and we did, one by one, circling past him like communicants" (134). Riding through the rain, the members of the Glanton gang are described as "wardens of some dim sect sent forth to proselytize among the very beasts of the land" (187). After slaughtering and scalping a village of peaceful Tiguas, the Glanton gang bathe at a warm spring, where "they stripped and descended like acolytes into the water" (175). An "acolyte" is a "person who attends a priest and performs subordinate duties" (*OED*) and the bathing itself evokes a baptismal scene. Furthermore, the headless corpse of White John Jackson is described as "sitting like a murdered anchorite discalced in ashes and sark" (107). An "anchorite" is a "person who has withdrawn or secluded himself from the world," usually "for religious reasons" (*OED*). "Discalced" is a form of "discalceate," meaning "unshod" or "barefooted," specifically when "applied to certain orders of friars and nuns" (*OED*). "Sark" is an archaic term for a "shirt," or any "garment worn next the skin" (*OED*); an ash-covered sark suggests a hair shirt worn by medieval monks. Thus the description of the murdered gang member carries religious connotations. Indeed, all of the aforementioned scenes reinforce the idea that the Glanton gang members are the disciples of the judge's new religion.

Although the judge never explicitly offers up the worship of science or reason in place of God, he does endorse a behavior inextricably tied up with scientific progress, namely, war. Throughout human history, war has led to the development of new materials and technologies. Shane Schimpf argues that "the history of war is in part a history of the march of science wielded in the name of killing one's enemies ever more efficiently" (5). The judge offers up a lengthy oration on the subject of war and its importance in men's lives. He argues that humanity was created for the express purpose of waging war: "It makes no difference what men think of war, said the judge. War endures. As well ask men what they think of stone. War was always here. Before man was, war waited for him. The ultimate trade awaiting its ultimate practitioner" (248). The judge considers himself the ultimate practitioner of the ultimate trade. When asked about his other pursuits, namely, "What about all them notebooks and bones and stuff?" and whether they are not also his trade, the judge replies, "All other trades are contained in that of war" (249). John Sepich argues that the novel reads "like three hundred pages of grotesque evidence, derived from McCarthy's imagination, to support Judge Holden's claim that war and violence dominate men's lives" (*Notes* 1). The evidence in question is taken not only from McCarthy's imagination but also from human history. Indeed, in *Notes on "Blood Meridian,"* Sepich himself carefully documents the historical sources that McCarthy employs in the novel.

For the judge, war is not only the "ultimate trade" but also the "ultimate game."[5] As if in answer to humanity's anxiety over the purpose of its existence, the judge proclaims, "Men are born for games. Nothing else." He adds that "all games aspire to the condition of war for here that which is wagered swallows up game, player, all." The judge talks about war as though it were a manifestation of something sacred and divine. He explains the nature of war by giving the example of "two men at cards with nothing to wager save their lives." He argues that this enhances the game "to its ultimate state," in other words, the state that is also achieved by war. The judge explains that the situation created by war "admits no argument concerning the notion of fate," for the "selection of one man over another is a preference absolute and irrevocable and it is a dull man indeed who could reckon so profound a decision without agency or significance either one." Not only is the judge confirming the existence of fate, but he is also suggesting that there is an agency behind these seemingly random outcomes. According to the judge, "war is the truest form of divination," for it involves "the testing of one's will and the will of another within that larger will which because it binds them is therefore forced to select" (249). Again, the judge points to the existence of a "will" larger than that of either of the parties involved in the game; a sentience that is forced to choose which man will live and which man will die. The universe in *Blood Meridian* is depicted as a place utterly indifferent to human suffering, but the conditions created by war seem to "force" it to intervene in human affairs.

The idea that the conditions created by war—namely, the choosing of one life over another—involve a "divine" will is also explored in René Girard's *Violence and the Sacred*. According to Girard, "Chance embodies all the obvious characteristics of the sacred. Now it deals violently with man, now it showers him with gifts. Indeed, what is more capricious in its favors than Chance, more susceptible to those rapid reversals of temper that are invariably associated with the gods?" (314). Girard adds that, in primitive societies, "chance can always be trusted to reveal the truth, for it reflects the will of the divinity" (313). This divine will seems to be the "agency" and the "larger will" of which the judge speaks. Furthermore, the violent conditions of war serve to strengthen the sense of the sacred. Girard explains, "Violence strikes men as at once seductive and terrifying; never as a simple means to an end, but as an epiphany.... And violence promotes imbalance, tipping the scales of Destiny in one direction or another" (152). Both chance and violence—factors inherent in the conditions of war—are inextricably tied up with religious concepts of fate, destiny, and divine will.

When the judge speaks of the "agency" present in outcomes of life and death, he posits the existence of a god: "War is the ultimate game because war is at last a forcing of the unity of existence. War is god" (249). The judge worships "war" in its own right, and in doing so he moves beyond reason and into the realms of pseudo-religion. Knowing that he is invoking theology by proclaiming war as god, the judge turns to the ex-priest and asks, "But what says the priest?" Refusing to participate in the judge's sacrilege, Tobin replies, "The priest does not say." The judge will not be denied, retorting, "*Nihil dicit*" (250). Latin for "he says nothing." According to *Black's Law Dictionary*, "Judgment taken against party who withdraws his answer is *judgment nihil dicit*, which amounts to confession of cause of action stated, and carries with it, more strongly than judgment by default, admission of justice of plaintiff's case" (Black 1045). The judge uses legal jargon to manipulate the ex-priest's reply, arguing that by "not saying," "the priest has said" (250).

The judge points out that "the priest has put by the robes of his craft and taken up the tools of that higher calling which all men honor." Then, evoking the biblical defiance manifested by Satan, the judge proclaims that the "priest would be no godserver but a god himself" (250). Aldous Huxley explains that "for the Perennial Philosophy, good is the separate self's conformity to, and finally annihilation in, the divine Ground which gives it being; evil, the intensification of separateness, the refusal to know that the Ground exists" (184). Huxley adds, "Hell is total separation from God, and the devil is the will to that separation. Being rational and free, human beings are capable of being diabolic" (229). For all the traditions that make up the Perennial Philosophy, the sole purpose of spiritual development is to attain a state in which one ceases to be separate from the Absolute. Similarly, Jacob Boehme argues that "the devil mixed lies and truth together, and said to the first human beings that they would be like God" (qtd. in Hartmann 161). In this sense, the judge once again evokes the depiction of Satan in Genesis, who tempts human beings with the promise of godlike powers.

The judge tells his disciples that the worship of war is greater than the worship of God, because war gives human beings the godlike ability to decide who shall live and who shall die. Nevertheless, both callings require a form of worship and the judge claims that "men of god and men of war have strange affinities" (250). Still refusing to proclaim his allegiance to the judge's new religion, the ex-priest states, "I'll not secondsay you in your notions. . . . Don't ask it." The judge knows, however, that he has won the argument: "Ah Priest. . . . What could I ask of you that you've not already given?" (251). The judge knows that by turning his back on a spiritual life and embracing a life of violence and bloodshed, the ex-priest has inadvertently become his disciple.

The judge's new religion has obvious parallels to Nietzschean philosophy. According to the judge, "Moral law is an invention of mankind for the disenfranchisement of the powerful in favor of the weak. Historical law subverts it at every turn. A moral view can never be proven right or wrong by any ultimate test" (250).[6] In *Beyond Good and Evil*, Nietzsche argues that "those qualities which serve to make easier the existence of the suffering," most significantly "pity," are the products of an inferior "slave morality" (207). When one is a superior "Übermensch" (Superman), one need feel moral responsibility only "towards one's equals," for "beings of lower rank" are worthless and one may act toward them "as one wishes" or "as the heart dictates." In other words, Nietzsche believes the *Übermensch* to be "beyond good and evil" (205). Thus the judge is once again invoking a pseudo-religious philosophy that directly opposes the tenets of spiritual traditions, for pity—whether understood as Christian love and charity or Buddhist compassion—is upheld as one of the greatest virtues by both Western and Eastern religions.

A scalp hunter named Irving tries to disagree with the judge, arguing that "might does not make right" and that the "man that wins in some combat is not vindicated morally." The judge dismisses Irving's argument by insisting that he is talking about "higher" things, a statement that, once again, is indicative of a pseudo-religious philosophy. Though the judge admits that a "man falling dead in a duel is not thought thereby to be proven in error as to his views," he argues that the man's "very involvement in such a trial gives evidence of a new and broader view." According to the judge, a human being cannot make moral judgements because "his knowledge remains imperfect and however much he comes to value his judgements ultimately he must submit them before a higher court." This "higher court" sounds suspiciously like the court over which the biblical God presides on judgement day, yet, in a quintessentially satanic reversal, the judge's court rejects all moral, ethical, and spiritual guidelines. The judge explains, "Here are considerations of equity and rectitude and moral right rendered void and without warrant and here are the views of the litigants despised." Much like the seemingly random universe depicted in *Blood Meridian*, where the innocent might just as easily meet with a terrible death as the guilty, the judge's court is not concerned with seeking justice. In fact, the judge scorns the very idea of "right and wrong," arguing that "decisions of life and death, of what shall be and what shall not, beggar all questions of right. In elections of these magnitudes are all lesser ones subsumed, moral, spiritual, and natural"

(250). The judge elevates the death-dealing nature of war to a godlike status, thereby rejecting all that is "moral, spiritual, and natural" and embracing all that is depraved, profane, and perverted.

By categorizing the "spiritual" as "lesser," the judge directly opposes the teachings of all the traditions that make up the Perennial Philosophy. According to esoteric traditions, there is no level of existence higher than the spiritual. Although, as Huston Smith explains in *Forgotten Truth: The Primordial Tradition*, "higher" is a misleading term, because "higher levels are not literally elsewhere; they are removed only in the sense of being inaccessible to ordinary consciousness—invisible, for one thing" (21). Nevertheless, spiritual development is often described in terms of "transcendence" or "a mounting up, an attainment of a higher order of reality" (Underhill 203). René Guénon writes that any movement that "shuts out all 'transcendence'" also "shuts out all effective spirituality" (*Reign of Quantity* 288). In essence, by degrading all that is "spiritual," the judge also rejects transcendence and denies humanity any soteriological hope.

The satanic aspects of the judge are further emphasized through his numerous lies and contradictions, for the biblical devil is often depicted as the "father of lies." In the King James Bible, Jesus speaks of the devil (literally), claiming, "He was a murderer from the beginning, and abode not in the truth, because there is no truth in him. When he speaketh a lie, he speaketh of his own: for he is a liar, and the father of it" (John 8:44). In fact, the judge is portrayed as a liar right from the beginning of the novel. When we are first introduced to the judge, he interrupts a sermon to declare the Reverend Green "an imposter" (6) who is "not only illiterate, but is also wanted by the law" for various crimes, such as "violating" a "girl of eleven years . . . while actually clothed in the livery of his God" and "having congress with a goat" (7). Later the judge admits that he had "never laid eyes on the man before today. Never even heard of him" (8). Thus the reader is encouraged to recognize the judge as a liar right from the very beginning and to regard all his proclamations with skepticism.

Further lies and contradictions abound. Some are subtle, such as when the judge tells the scalp hunters "that our mother earth . . . was round like an egg and contained all good things within her." The judge's statement is immediately cast into suspicion by the sentence that follows: "Then he turned and led the horse he had been ridin across that terrain of black and glassy slag, treacherous to man and beast alike" (130). Clearly, the earth in *Blood Meridian* is not motherly and filled with goodness but hostile and treacherous to her children. Furthermore, the judge gives this speech before using the gifts of the "mother earth" to make deadly gunpowder, thereby heightening the sense of irony.

Other contradictions are more obvious. After watching the judge recording specimens in his ledger book, Toadvine insists that "no man can acquaint himself with everything on this earth." The judge replies, "The man who believes that the secrets of the world are forever hidden lives in mystery and fear. . . . But that man who sets himself the task of singling out the thread of order from the tapestry will by the decision alone have taken charge of the world and it is only by such taking charge that he will effect a way to dictate the terms of his own fate" (199). The judge argues that the world can be known in its entirety and that such knowledge can be used to control not only the world itself but one's fate in it. Later in the novel, however, the judge directly contradicts himself when he tells the scalp hunters, "Even in this world more things exist without our knowledge than with it and the order in creation which you see is that which you have put there, like a string in a maze, so that you shall not lose your way. For existence has its own order and that no man's mind can compass, that mind itself being but a fact among others" (245). According to the judge, human knowledge is only a tenuous "string" which is used to navigate the unfathomable maze that is the world. The judge now argues that, try as they might, human beings can never use their limited minds to understand the nature of existence.

The judge's views are in direct contradiction to the esoteric metaphysics expressed in McCarthy's other novels. For example, the scientist-judge is described as "breaking ore samples with a hammer . . . in whose organic lobations he purported to read news of the earth's origins" and "holding an extemporary lecture in geology to a small gathering who nodded and spat." Some of the men consider this lecture blasphemous and "quote him scripture to confound his orderings up of eons out of the ancient chaos and other apostate supposings." The judge merely smiles and dismisses the Bible by reminding the men, "Books lie" (116). It should be noted that the judge's statement is in direct contradiction to his later claim that "what is to be deviates no jot from the book wherein it's writ. How could it? It would be a false book and a false book is no book at all" (141). Nevertheless, the men argue, "God don't lie." Surprisingly, the judge agrees, "No. . . . He does not." Then, holding up "a chunk of rock," the judge proclaims that "these are his words. . . . He speaks in stones and trees, the bones of things."[7] The judge waits until the "squatters in their rags nodded among themselves and were soon reckoning him correct, this man of learning." In fact, he encourages them "until they were right proselytes of the new order"—yet another reference to the judge's pseudo-religion—and then he "laughs at them for fools" (116). The judge continually misleads the men around him and mocks those who fall for his lies. The very fact that the judge leads James Robert, the "imbecile," through the desert with "the idiot in its rawhide collar pulling at the lead" (298), has highly symbolic connotations, namely that the judge is the leader of the ignorant. According to Dianne Luce, "the judge's many lies, false accusations, and self-contradictions" are "meant to undermine . . . men's faith not in him but in their own moral sense" ("Ambiguities" 23). While the judge's lies do serve this purpose, their detrimental effects extend beyond the moral realm, for they also undermine any possibility of spiritual transcendence.[8]

In another such attempt to deny transcendence, the judge tells the men, "Your heart's desire is to be told some mystery. The mystery is that there is no mystery" (252). The statement is contradictory, for if it is a "mystery" that "there is no mystery," then the first half of the statement renders the second half meaningless. The judge's words parody the language of Zen riddles and parables known as koans, but whereas the purpose of koans is to "increase pressure in the trainee's mind until the structures of ordinary reason collapse completely, clearing the way for sudden intuition" (H. Smith, *Religions of Man* 147), the judge's riddles serve no such transcendent cause. Furthermore, the judge's claim is in direct contradiction to McCarthy's own belief that "our inability to see spiritual truth is the greatest mystery" (Wallace 138). When the judge moves away "into the darkness beyond the fire"—a location symbolic of his metaphysical position—his nihilistic statement is immediately contradicted by the ex-priest, who mutters, "As if he were no mystery himself, the bloody old hoodwinker" (252). Not only does the ex-priest identify the judge as a liar, but he also draws attention to the fact that the judge is a supernatural figure and thus one of the greatest mysteries within the novel.

An examination of the judge's incessant falsehoods also sheds light on one of the most mysterious passages within *Blood Meridian*, namely, the kid's hallucinatory dream of the "coldforger," or "a worker in metal . . . who worked with hammer and die, perhaps under some indictment and an exile from men's fires" (310). The concept of the exiled metalworker is a common one in various cultures. In his study *Violence and the Sacred*, René Girard explains that while "metal is a source of inestimable benefits" because it "facilitates domestic tasks and helps the community defend itself against outside enemies," its "advantages are not without a reverse side; all weapons, after all, are double-edged" (260). As a result, the metalworker is regarded with suspicion because he is "the master of a potent form of violence," "a slightly sinister figure," and "someone to be avoided." Hence, in many primitive societies, "his forge is relegated to the outskirts of the community" (261). Precisely because metalwork uses technological advancement to produce a variety of weapons, it is closely allied to both science and war. It is significant that these are the judge's main preoccupations and the substance of his pseudo-religion. René Guénon explains that the evil connotations of metalwork also stem from the fact that "from the traditional point of view metals and metallurgy are in direct relation with the 'subterranean fire,' the idea of which is associated in many respects with that of the 'infernal regions'" (*Reign of Quantity* 186). Thus McCarthy's "worker in metal" is linked to the satanic elements personified by the judge.[9] As the kid watches the coldforger in his dream, he notes how the "judge enshadowed him where he crouched at his trade." Not only does the coldforger work in the shadow of the judge—the shadow carrying further connotations of darkness and evil—but he also "seeks favor with the judge," thereby consciously courting the evil that the judge embodies (310).

The coldforger is also a "false moneyer," working with his "gravers and burins" and seeking to "render this residual specie current in the markets where men barter" 310). Just as the judge spreads falsehood and deceit, the coldforger spreads false currency. The dissemination of counterfeit currency represents the dissemination of the judge's pseudo-religion, the false coins being the false teachings. Furthermore, because false currency devalues legitimate currency, it becomes increasingly difficult to recognize genuine spiritual insight among all the pseudo-religious falsehoods. Edwin Arnold also points out that the "coldforger" is both "a deceiver (one who forges, imitates intending to defraud)" and "a maker (one who forges, creates)" ("Go to Sleep" 48). It is noteworthy that the coldforger has been depicted as "an artisan" (310), for this is precisely the meaning of "demiurge." The Greek *demiourgiōs* (δημιουργός) is derived from *demos* (people) and *ergon* (work), literally "people-worker," which may be translated as "skilled worker" or "artisan."[10] According to the Gnostic Apocryphon of John, the demiurge and his archons taught "people metallurgy and warfare" and led "them astray with many deceptions" (qtd. in Pearson 130). It is significant that in *Blood Meridian*, metallurgy and warfare are encapsulated in the figures of the coldforger and the judge, respectively, both of whom seek to deceive through either forgeries or lies.[11]

It is noteworthy that the New England transcendentalist philosopher Ralph Waldo Emerson (1803–1882) recalled a dream in which the different religious symbols of various traditions were also described in terms of currency. In the dream, Emerson conversed with a pundit, who told him that "the names of gods, as Jove, Apollo, Osiris, Vishnu, Odin . . . the sacred names of Western Europe and its colonies, as Jesus and the Holy Ghost . . . are like coins of different countries, adopted from local proximity or convenience, and getting their cipher from some forgotten accident, the name of a consul, or the whim of a goldsmith; but they all represent the value of corn, wool, and labor, and are readily convertible into each other, or into the coin of any new country" (qtd. in Christy 160). According to Emerson, the outward symbols of various spiritual traditions may vary, but they all represent a sacred truth and, like foreign currency, may be exchanged for coinage of equal value. The trouble with McCarthy's coldforger, however, is that he is flooding this market with counterfeits that possess no value. When accused of deceiving men with an uncanny coin trick, the judge is the first to admit, albeit only to taunt his accusers, "that there are coins and false coins" (246). Thus, just as a market flooded with counterfeit currency will inevitably collapse, the judge's pseudo-religion will also result in spiritual deterioration.

The coldforger is then described as "contriving from cold slag brute in the crucible a face that will pass" (310). The face on the coldforger's coinage is most probably that of the judge, the priest of the pseudo-religion, who presides over the forge and whose favor the coldforger seeks. The description of the coldforger's work carries sinister connotations; "contriving" suggests not only "manufacturing" but also "plotting" and "scheming." Similarly, the words "cold" and "brute" evoke an unfeeling cruelty, or the brutalization of that which was once refined. Furthermore, a "crucible" is associated with alchemy and carries overtones not only of the esoteric and the supernatural but also of transmutation.

The description of the coldforger's work also resonates with a passage in Evelyn Underhill's *Mysticism*, where she writes of how the mystics "ever seek, like the artists they are, some new and vital image which is not yet part of the debased currency of formal religion, and conserves its original power of stinging the imagination to more vivid life" (114). The coldforger's work is a dark parody of this process, for he seeks to contrive a new image, not to conserve the power of the original currency, but rather to debase it completely. The coldforger deceives humanity by "hammering out like his own conjectural destiny all through the night of his becoming some coinage for a dawn that would not be" (310). The connotations of a nonexistent dawn are particularly significant. With the triumph of light over darkness, dawn symbolizes salvation and illumination, but in working toward a dawn that will not be, the coldforger is in effect plunging the world into eternal night. This seems to be exactly what the judge desires, and this is why he presides over the coldforger's work. Earlier in the novel, the kid desired to know what exactly the judge was "judge of" (135), and now his question is finally answered; the narrative voice tells us, "Of this is the judge judge and the night does not end" (310). Namely, it is the judge's responsibility to oversee the production of the false currency, spreading confusion throughout the world and keeping humanity in a state of perpetual spiritual ignorance, or the "night" that "does not end." Hope remains, however, in the fact that if the face on the coins is one "that will pass," then perhaps the false teachings of the pseudo-religion may pass away also, suggesting that the future of the judge's reign is as "conjectural" as the coldforger's "destiny." Precisely because the text suggests that the judge's new religion will fail, Shane Schimpf believes that *Blood Meridian* is "ultimately nihilistic." He argues that "the new religion, the worship of science, is just as barren as the one it has replaced. God has failed in this new land, but science has not really succeeded either" (40). I believe, however, that *Blood Meridian* is concerned not so much with religion or science failing humanity but rather with modernity's failure to strike a balance between the spiritual and the rational, both of which have their place in human existence.

CHAPTER 4

"This Luminosity in Beings So Endarkened"

Gnostic Soteriology in *Blood Meridian*

■ While the most memorable character within *Blood Meridian* is undoubtedly the enigmatic Judge Holden, the role of chief protagonist belongs to the inscrutable kid, whose portentous birth and mysterious death mark the beginning and ending of the novel. The very first sentence of *Blood Meridian* literally draws the reader's attention to the protagonist, commanding us to "see the child" (3). The register of these words simultaneously evokes the simplicity of a child's storybook and the sonorous language of the Bible. The kid, however, makes an unlikely protagonist; not only does he remain nameless throughout the novel, but the reader is never made privy to the character's interior life. Furthermore, the narrative does not unfold from the kid's perspective and the novel contains many scenes that could not have been witnessed by the protagonist. Insight into the kid's mysterious nature may be gleaned only through the comments of other characters, the symbolic qualities of the landscape, or the metaphorical nature of certain scenes in which he plays a part.

The significance of the kid is emphasized when the narrative voice is suddenly interrupted by the words of the nameless child's equally nameless father: "Night of your birth. Thirty-three. The Leonids they were called. God how the stars did fall. I looked for blackness, holes in the heavens. The Dipper stove" (3). The Leonids are an annual meteor shower named after the constellation Leo, from which they appear to originate. Every thirty-three years "the earth passes through a particularly dense section of the Leonid stream," producing a stunningly prolific display. According to historical and astrological records, an exceptional display occurred in the year 1833, when "the sky came alive with Leonids." Observers "on the North American east coast saw a spectacular 50,000 to 200,000 meteors per hour, describing them as being like snow or rain" (Reynolds 44). Shane Schimpf notes that the 1833 Leonid meteors were so spectacular "that many interpreted them as a sign that the Apocalypse was at hand." Schimpf argues that the "religious connection" of this celestial event "brings to mind the second coming of Jesus" (60). In other words, the portentous circumstances surrounding the kid's birth suggest the arrival of a messianic figure.

Other critics have also commented on the significance of the Leonid shower within *Blood Meridian*. In "Yuman Belief Systems and Cormac McCarthy's *Blood Meridian*," Stacey Peebles refers to "a study entitled *Yuman Tribes of the Gila River*" in which "Leslie Spier notes that for some of the Yuma, the Leonid meteor shower of November 13, 1833, marks the beginning of recorded time." Peebles points out that "the kid, the novel's nominal if somewhat overshadowed protagonist, is born on the day the Quechan [Yuma] most likely began to keep time," arguing that this endows him with something akin to a "Christ-like significance" (233). The Native American Yumas, or the Quechan, figure prominently in *Blood Meridian*, especially in chapter 19, where they attack Glanton's gang of scalp hunters at the Yuma ferry crossing. Significantly, the kid is portrayed as one of the few survivors of this historically accurate massacre.

Furthermore, Elizabeth Andersen explains that the novel's opening line, "See the child" (3), "introduces the kid with a free translation of the Biblical phrase *ecce puer* ('behold the child'). Appearing in Isaiah 41:1, it alludes to a child who is raised from the dead in a story that has traditionally been read as a prefiguration of the miracles performed by Jesus, and of his own resurrection. As such, it has long been used as a counterpart to the New Testament's *ecce homo*, 'Behold the man,' the words of Pontius Pilate in presenting Jesus to the crowd demanding his execution (John 19:5)." According to Andersen, both *ecce homo* and *ecce puer* came to be used "as a familiar title for works of art and literature depicting the victims of injustice, poverty, death, and disease." In the nineteenth century, the period in which *Blood Meridian* is set, *ecce homo* "emerged as a popular title for philosophical essays exploring the human condition." Andersen argues that by "evoking this tradition, McCarthy presents the kid as an analogue of Christ and an Everyman figure whose progress in the novel represents every man's progress through life" (89). Thus the very first words of *Blood Meridian* command the reader to behold the kid's messianic significance.

Further suggestions of a messianic birth are evoked when the kid is described in grandiose terms: "All history present in that visage, the child the father of man" (3). The words are an allusion to William Wordsworth's "My Heart Leaps Up," which contains the lines

> The Child is the father of the Man;
> And I could wish my days to be
> Bound each to each by natural piety.
> (lines 7–9)

The same lines also appear as an epigraph to Wordsworth's "Ode: Intimations of Immortality from Recollections of Early Childhood." The lines are commonly interpreted as a reference to the inherent innocence and spiritual purity of childhood, as expressed in Christ's words, "Verily I say unto you, except ye be converted, and become as little children, ye shall not enter into the kingdom of heaven" (Matthew 18:3). The implication is that children quite naturally possess the meekness, piety, and goodness that an adult can attain only through spiritual discipline.

McCarthy's use of the allusion, however, is not without irony, for the Wordsworthian lines are immediately preceded by the observation that "he can neither read nor write and in him broods already a taste for mindless violence" (3). Edwin Arnold argues that "McCarthy's ironic play on Wordsworth is noteworthy, certainly, for it underscores not the child's 'natural piety' but the 'mindless violence' which overcomes it" ("Naming" 62). This mindless violence hardly conjures up images of Christlike meekness and instead forces the reader to reevaluate the veracity of Wordsworth's rather sentimental recollection of the innocence of childhood. If McCarthy's "child" already hungers for violence, what kind of "man" will he be "father" to? This reading may at first appear to undermine the idea that the kid is a messianic figure; however, the two readings are not incompatible. The contradiction may be resolved if we briefly reconsider some of the characteristics of the Gnostic myth of the savior.

In Gnostic thought, the savior is often depicted as a figure who allows himself to fall into the manifest world in order to liberate the fragments of the divine substance imprisoned here. According to Hans Jonas, the fall of the Gnostic savior is "an irremissible condition of his saving function" because "the parts of divinity lost to the darkness can be reached only down there in the depth in which they are swallowed up; and the power which holds them, that of the world, can be overcome only from within" (127). In some Gnostic myths, however, the savior "forgets that he is a stranger and gets lost . . . by succumbing to the lure of the alien world and becoming estranged from his own origin" (49). The lost savior must then himself receive the "call from without," or a message from the "transmundane" realm, reminding him of his own divine origins (74). Only then can the savior resume his soteriological function, which consists of imparting gnosis to the spirits still trapped in corporeal existence. Although the Gnostic savior is "a definitive divine figure," this "does not prevent him from undergoing in his own person the full force of human destiny, even to the extent that he the saviour himself has to be saved" (127). Jonas explains that "in the last analysis, he who comes is identical with him to whom he comes"; in other words, the savior is identical "with the life to be saved" (78). Hence the Salvator Salvatus, or "Saved Savior," serves "an active-passive double role" as a savior who requires salvation (79).[1]

The Gnostic myth of the savior resolves the perceived incompatibility between the messianic overtones surrounding the kid's birth and his depraved behavior. The falling stars that augur the kid's birth seem to symbolize the savior's descent from the transmundane to the material, while the kid's subsequent corruption suggests that he forgets his divine origins and falls under the evil spell of the world. It is noteworthy that the Gnostic savior is also referred to as the "Primal Man" or "Adam," in order to emphasize the concept that all the spirits imprisoned in the manifest world are essentially "part of his original substance. . . . so that he is actually present in every human soul, exiled, captive, stunned" (Jonas 128). *Blood Meridian* subtly hints at such a situation by describing how, as the kid "walks through the narrow streets," "whores call to him from the dark like souls in want" (5). From a Gnostic perspective, the scene suggests that the divine fragments imprisoned in the degraded flesh of whores recognize the savior and long to return to their source. Thus, if all human beings are a part of the savior's "original substance," then one may well regard the savior, or the original "Primal Man," as the father of man; McCarthy's description of "the child" as "the father of man" seems to echo this concept (3).

Although McCarthy draws attention to the fact that the kid has "a taste for mindless violence" (3), he also hints at the idea that something worthwhile lies dormant within. Captain White's man, who approaches the kid with the intention of recruiting him for an army of filibusters, recalls how his own life was turned around by the captain: "Set my feet in the path of righteousness. I'd done took to drinkin and whorin till hell wouldnt have me. He seen somethin in me worth savin and I see it in you" (30). The promise of potential salvation is highlighted by the fact that immediately before his conversation with Captain White's man, the kid strips off his clothes to bathe and wades "out into the river like some wholly wretched baptismal candidate" (27). The words of Captain White's man, along with the baptismal imagery, suggest that the kid somehow stands apart from the utterly depraved characters that populate the novel, even if it is only a case of potential, rather than actual, goodness. Whether the kid succeeds in awakening to his true nature is another matter, for, as I will later argue, the protagonist seems to depict a failed messianic figure rather than a genuine savior.

The kid, however, does seem dimly aware of his own distinction, which is made apparent when he voices his disgust with a comrade named Sproule. When Sproule is bitten by a vampire bat, he starts "gibbering hysterically" and lets out a "howl of such outrage as to stitch a caesura in the pulsebeat of the world" (66). "Caesura" refers to a "break, interruption" or "interval," while "pulsebeat" suggests the "rhythmical throbbing of the heart" (*OED*). In other words, Sproule's outrage is of such magnitude that he desires to shatter the vital rhythms of life itself. The kid responds by spitting "into the darkness of the space between them" (66). Spitting is a common component of "folk magic" in various cultures, where it serves as "a universal defence against the evil eye, bad luck, illness and witchcraft" (Guiley 325). Thus, by spitting between them, the kid seeks to distance himself from the maleficent effects of Sproule's destructive rage.

The fact that the space between the two men is described in terms of "darkness" suggests that the kid feels himself to be significantly other to Sproule; hence this "space" is metaphysical rather than spatial. The kid's disgust with Sproule is compounded by the following condemnation: "I know your kind. . . . What's wrong with you is wrong all the way through" (66). These words not only reject Sproule as being rotten to the core but also express the kid's own desire to keep his distance from this corruption.[2] Above all, the words serve to illustrate the fact that, despite his reticence and inscrutability, the kid does possess some semblance of a personal moral code, albeit a rudimentary one that still allows him to join a bloodthirsty gang of scalp hunters.

Though the kid finds himself among truly despicable characters when he joins the Glanton gang, he remains oddly aloof and disconnected from the frenzied violence that permeates the novel.[3] A striking example of the kid's strange otherness can be found in a description of his observing a distant battle: "He saw from that high rimland the collision of armies remote and silent upon the plain below.... He watched all this pass below him mute and ordered and senseless." Not only does the kid take no part in the action, but the description of the violence as "remote" and "silent," along with the kid's elevated vantage point, positions the character in an almost godlike state of detachment. Furthermore, the description of the changing light serves to imbue the kid with a strange numinosity while simultaneously plunging ordinary men into darkness: "The warring horsemen were gone in the sudden rush of dark that fell over the desert. All that land lay cold and blue and without definition and the sun shone solely on the high rocks where he stood" (213). Despite the fact that in *Blood Meridian* the sun is frequently portrayed as a maleficent entity, the novel nevertheless conforms to the traditional symbolic dichotomy according to which light is equated with good and darkness with evil.

It is significant that Jacob Boehme describes spiritual development in terms of symbolic light imagery, which is remarkably similar to the aforementioned scene in *Blood Meridian*: "It is well known that the light of the sun does not shine upon the earth because we desire it to shine, neither can we attract the sunlight to us. All we do is to step out of the darkness, or climb to the top of the mountain which rises above the clouds" (qtd. in Hartmann 46). The fact that the kid is the only one on whom the light shines suggests that he possesses a degree of spiritual development higher than that of the other men fighting in the depths of the darkness below. A similar scene of illumination occurs when the kid miraculously becomes the sole survivor of a bloody massacre: "With the darkness one soul rose wondrously from among the new slain dead and stole away in the moonlight" (55). Despite the fact that in this instance the source of illumination is the moon rather than the sun, the numinous quality remains. The very fact that the kid is referred to as a "soul," combined with the "wondrous" nature of his rising, imbues the passage with the air of sacred mystery.

The scene also features another trope frequently used as a metaphor for spiritual development, namely the concept of rebirth or resurrection. For example, Evelyn Underhill explains that "the state of negation and misery" described by St. John of the Cross as "The Dark Night of the Soul" is "the intervening period of chaos between the break-up of an old state of equilibrium and the establishment of the new," serving as a kind of "mystic death"

(286). Similarly, in *Aperçus sur l'initiation*, René Guénon writes, "Every change of state whatsoever is both a death and a birth, depending on the side it is envisaged from: death in relation to the antecedent state, birth in relation to the subsequent state" (182). He adds that initiation into a higher level of spiritual apprehension "is generally described as a 'second birth,' which in fact it is; but this 'second birth' necessarily implies death to the profane world" (183). Thus the kid's mysterious moonlight resurrection seems to suggest ascension into a higher state of spiritual apprehension. Unfortunately, the mysterious rebirth is not enough to liberate the kid from what Guénon calls the "profane world." Though the kid rises bathed in moonlight, he remains mired in the residue of the battle: "The ground where he'd lain was soaked with blood and with urine from the voided bladders of animals and he went forth stained and stinking like some reeking issue of the incarnate dam of war herself" (55). Blood and excrement are powerful symbols of corporeality, mortality, the frailty of the flesh, and from a Gnostic perspective, the undesirability of manifest existence. Thus the fact that the kid rises smeared with effluent suggests that his spiritual rebirth has not been entirely successful.

Nevertheless, *Blood Meridian* contains several scenes laden with esoteric symbolism suggesting the presence of the sacred, in which the kid features as the focal point. Separated from the rest of the Glanton gang, the kid comes across "a lone tree burning on the desert. A heraldic tree that the passing storm had left afire" (215). This eerie image immediately calls to mind the burning bush out of which an angel spoke to Moses: "And the angel of the Lord appeared unto him in a flame of fire out of the midst of a bush: and he looked, and, behold, the bush burned with fire, and the bush was not consumed" (Exodus 3.3). Though no divine voice speaks forth from this strange phenomenon, the vision is not without significance. The description of the tree as "heraldic" suggests the "action of announcing and ushering in with pomp and ceremony" (*OED*). Therefore the tree serves as a dramatic messenger or herald of some important message.

The spiritual significance of the scene is compounded by the description of the kid as the "solitary pilgrim drawn up before it" who "had travelled so far to be here" (215). It is noteworthy that the kid is also referred to in this way at the beginning of the novel, when he is described as "a pilgrim among others" (5). In its earlier usage, the word "pilgrim" refers to "a foreigner, an alien . . . a stranger" or "a person who experiences life as a sojourn, exile, or period of estrangement" (*OED*). It is significant that the Gnostics often describe the fallen spirit, or pneuma, as "a stranger who does not know the ways of the foreign land" and "wanders about lost" (Jonas 49). Later the meaning of "pilgrim" took on a more specifically religious context, signifying "a person travelling through life, *esp.* one who undertakes a course of spiritual development" (*OED*).[4] Both definitions place the kid in a distinctly Gnostic context of spiritual striving, exile, and alienation.

The numinosity of the burning tree is emphasized by the kid's posture. Ostensibly warming his hands by the fire, he adopts the gestures of religious supplication: "He knelt in the hot sand and held his numbed hands out." The presence of various desert animals also imbues the scene with a ceremonial quality: "All about in that circle attended companies of lesser auxiliaries routed forth into the inordinate day" (215). The circular arrangement of initiates goes back to the earliest forms of rites and ceremonies; hence the "magic circle," which "provides a sacred and purified space in which all rites, magical work and ceremonies are conducted" as well as acts "as a doorway to the world of the gods" (Guiley 219). The description of the animals as "lesser auxiliaries" suggests that they serve as assistants, subordinates, or lower-ranking initiates taking part in a sacred rite.

The animals are described as a "constellation of ignited eyes that edged the ring of light all bound in a precarious truce before this torch whose brightness had set back the stars in their sockets." The very laws of nature seem to have been temporarily set aside by this strange ceremony, as suggested by the fact that the light emitted by the burning tree awakens the animals into an "inordinate day," as well as by the "precarious truce" between creatures that would normally be "vicious" and "deadly" to one another.[5] Further strange inversions are created by the description of the animal eyes appearing like stars in their constellations, while the stars themselves suggest eyes "in their sockets." When the kid awakens in the morning, he finds that "all the creatures that had been at vigil with him in the night were gone" (215). In the ecclesiastic sense of the word, "vigil" refers to "an occasion of devotional watching or religious observance" (*OED*). Thus the description of the strange ceremony concludes on a note that once again emphasizes its spiritual significance.

The kid's participation in spiritually symbolic vignettes is not limited to the scene with the burning tree. Wandering through the wilderness, the kid stumbles upon the site of a massacre, with a "company of penitents" lying "hacked and butchered among the stones." As he gazes "at this desolate scene," he sees "alone and upright in a small niche in the rocks an old woman kneeling in a faded rebozo with her eyes cast down." Drawn toward the pious figure, the kid makes "his way among the corpses and [stands] before her," but she does "not look up." The woman's posture suggests that she is lost in prayer, seeking solace in her faith amid the terrible carnage. As the kid watches the praying woman, he notes that the "shawl that covered her head was much faded of its color yet it bore like a patent woven into the fabric the figures of stars and quartermoons and other insignia of a provenance unknown to him" (315). This description of the keeling woman evokes the Virgin Mary. In *Notes on "Blood Meridian,"* John Sepich points out that the "'stars and quartermoons' of her costume . . . resemble elements associated with Mary in Revelation 12:1 and in the painted depiction of Mary's appearance as Our Lady of Guadalupe" (123).[6] The book of Revelation features a mysterious "woman clothed with the sun, and the moon under her feet, and upon her head a crown of twelve stars" (12:1), whom theologians have identified as Mary. Furthermore, this "woman" is described as having "fled into the wilderness" (Revelation 12:6), thereby strengthening the connection between the biblical figure and McCarthy's praying penitent.

The kid treats the kneeling woman with reverence, speaking "to her in a low voice" such as one might use during confession. Indeed, the kid does confess, telling "her that he was an American and that he was a long way from the country of his birth and that he had no family and that he had traveled much and seen many things and had been at war and endured hardships" (315). Patrick Shaw argues that the kid "impulsively confesses to the penitent in rhetoric reminiscent of a questing Christian knight in thrall to the Holy Virgin" (110). In fact, it is not only the kid's rhetoric but also his posture that suggests a questing knight, for he kneels before the woman "on one knee." Furthermore, he holds his "rifle before him like a staff" (315), a staff being a common accessory of pilgrims and travelers, thereby further emphasizing the motif of the medieval quest.

After revealing who he is and what he has done, the kid attempts to redeem himself before the kneeling woman: "He told her that he would convey her to a safe place, some party of her countrypeople would welcome her and that she should join them for he could not leave her in this place or she would surely die." When she fails to respond, the kid adopts an uncharacteristically gentle tone by referring to the old woman as "Abuelita"—the affectionate, diminutive form of "grandmother"—and asking, "No puedes escucharme?" (Can't you hear me?). As though in mockery of the kid's gentleness and compassion, the woman reveals her devastating secret: "He reached into the little cove and touched her arm. She moved slightly, her whole body, light and rigid. She weighed nothing. She was just a dried shell and she had been dead in that place for years" (315). The metaphorical significance of this scene is almost overdetermined; the symbols and sacraments of exoteric religion have been revealed as inherently empty and devoid of meaning.

The rejection of the iconography of the Virgin Mary and the sacrament of confession carry Gnostic overtones. The Gnostics believed that it was pointless to look to the church for salvation, for salvation could come only from within, that is, through the internal development of gnosis, as opposed to the external blessings of organized religion. The unknown author of the Gospel of Philip criticizes "those who mistake religious language for a literal language, professing faith in God, in Christ, in the resurrection or the church, as if these were all 'things' external to themselves." The unknown writer argues that a genuine spiritual experience must involve an "internal transformation" (qtd. in Pagels, *Gnostic Gospels* 133, 134). Thus the Gnostics rejected the idea that one could turn to a divine interlocutrix, like the Virgin Mary, for salvation. For them such religious iconography was really nothing more than a "dried shell."

In *Blood Meridian*, the kid's realization that the "Madonna" is a mummified husk serves as a kind of negative epiphany, which seems to have a profound impact on his psyche. Patrick Shaw argues that the "kid's epiphanic miscalculation vis-à-vis the penitent mummy is literally momentous beyond words, for immediately thereafter he disappears for seventeen years" (110). The novel gives no account of the kid's mysterious disappearance, with chapter 22 ending with the negative epiphany and chapter 23 beginning, "In the late winter of eighteen seventy-eight . . ." (316). The kid's disappearance mirrors the seventeen-year absence of the biblical Jesus, whose childhood is depicted up to the age of thirteen, after which the New Testament gives no account of his whereabouts until his thirtieth year. This analogy further strengthens the kid's position as a messianic figure within the novel, albeit a failed one.

The kid's latter years are taken up with aimless wandering: "They were remote places for news that he traveled in and in those uncertain times men toasted the ascension of rulers already deposed and hailed the coronation of kings murdered and in their graves. Of such corporal histories even as these he bore no tidings and although it was the custom in that wilderness to stop with any traveller and exchange the news he seemed to travel with no news at all, as if the doings of the world were too slanderous for him to truck with, or perhaps too trivial" (312). The kid seems to have no interest in the affairs of the world and is even more alienated from "corporal histories" than were isolated nineteenth-century Americans in remote settlements. As previously discussed, the kid is portrayed as an outsider, a position that resonates meaningfully with Gnostic ideas regarding the spirit's experience in the manifest world. According to Gnostic thought, the pneuma "suffers the lot of the stranger who is lonely, unprotected, uncomprehended, and uncomprehending in a situation full of danger. Anguish and homesickness are a part of the stranger's lot" (Jonas 49). This sense of alienation is also expressed in the kid's words to the kneeling penitent: "He told her ... that he was a long way from the country of his birth and that he had no family" (315). Given the metaphorical nature of *Blood Meridian*, it is probable that this homesickness and loneliness reflect the kid's existential and spiritual positions, as well as his actual history.

The Gnostics believed that this sense of alienation is necessary if one wishes to escape from the prison of the cosmos: "The recollection of his own alienness, the recognition of his place of exile for what it is, is the first step back; the awakened homesickness is the beginning of the return" (Jonas 50). The kid's homesickness may well be interpreted as a desire for salvation, a thwarted longing clearly expressed in the episode with the kneeling penitent. Spiritual yearning is also conveyed through the fact that throughout his lonely years of wandering, the kid "had a bible that he'd found at the mining camps and he carried this book with him no word of which he could read." This attachment to the Bible signifies a longing for spiritual wisdom or gnosis, but such insight has clearly not been attained. In fact, during his years of lonely wandering, the kid appears to drift even further from his messianic role: "In his dark and frugal clothes some took him for a sort of preacher but he was no witness to them, neither of things at hand nor things to come, he least of any man" (312). The Bible offers the illiterate kid no more redemption that the empty shell of the kneeling Madonna figure.

A degree of hope remains in the fact that the kid clearly longs for deliverance and that he is capable of compassion. Although the kid's concern regarding the well-being of the kneeling penitent may seem incongruous, especially if considered in light of the fact that he has spent his youth slaughtering the innocent with a band of vicious scalp hunters, there is evidence within the narrative to suggest that the protagonist has always had within him this potential for compassionate behavior. This inclination to help others manifests itself during the Comanche attack on Captain White's army. Though struggling to refill his rifle in the heat of battle, the kid notices that a "man near him sat with an arrow hanging out of his neck." The kid's natural instinct is to help the man by reaching for "the bloody hoop-iron point," but then he notices that he is too late, for the man has "another arrow in his breast to the fletching" and is already "dead." It is noteworthy that the dead man is described as being "bent slightly as if in prayer" (53). Once again, a dead figure adopts the posture of a kneeling penitent, a detail that links this particular episode to the kid's future encounter with the "eldress in the rocks" (305).

The same urge toward compassion is evoked later when the kid joins the Glanton gang. The kid is the only member of the gang who volunteers to help the injured David Brown, who has "an arrow in his thigh, fletching and all, and none would touch it." Brown pleads with the other gang members for assistance, asking, "Will none of ye help a man?" but receives no reply (161). After watching Brown make an excruciatingly futile attempt at removing the arrow himself, the kid comes forward and says, "I'll try her." The kid bears down on the arrow until the point comes "through the flesh of the man's thigh," then cuts "away the bloody point deftly" and withdraws "the shaft from the man's leg." Brown praises the boy, calling him a "stout lad" and a "sawbones" (a slang term for "surgeon"). But later when the kid returns "to his own blanket," Tobin calls him a "fool," adding, "God will not love ye forever. . . . Don't you know he'd of took you with him? He'd of took you, boy. Like a bride to the altar" (162).[7] In other words, had the kid not been successful, Brown would certainly have killed him. Given, however, the kid's initial hesitance in offering to help Brown, coupled with the fact that he had been with the gang long enough to understand the nature of its members, it is obvious that he knew the risk that he was facing when he extracted the arrow. Thus the kid's willingness to risk his own life in order to assist a suffering man suggests that he possesses an essentially compassionate nature, a virtue that comes to the fore despite his involvement with a depraved band of scalp hunters.

The kid displays further signs of these compassionate tendencies when the Glanton gang find themselves pursued by the army of General Elias and are forced to abandon four wounded members who can no longer ride. Four healthy men are selected by lottery to carry out the mercy killings and the kid is among those chosen. Instead of shooting the man with a shattered hip, the kid sits with him while the other members of the gang ride away. When the kid looks at the wounded man, he sees that "Shelby was crying" (207). "You wont thank me if I let you off," warns the kid, mindful of the approaching army, but he leaves the choice up to Shelby, telling him, "If you want me just to leave you I will. . . . You'll have to say" (207–8). Though death at the kid's hands would be much easier than at the hands of his enemies, Shelby refuses to make the sensible choice. Consequently, the kid does not kill him. In a final act of compassion, the kid fills Shelby's water flask "from his own"—though water is desperately scarce—then mounts his horse, looks "back at the wounded man" (209), and rides away.

Similarly, after the gang attacks a peaceful settlement of Gileños and encounters some minor resistance, the Mexican Juan Miguel, or "McGill," as he is called, is "skewered through with a lance." Seeing a fellow gang member in trouble, the kid "approaches him," only to be held back by Glanton's command: "Get away from him." Glanton then promptly shoots McGill "through the head" (157). Although Glanton's action can be read as a mercy killing, the kid's first instinct is to help, even if only by comforting the fatally wounded man. Scenes such as these establish the kid as somehow at odds with the other, callous, gang members, for whom such a mercy killing has more to do with convenience than actual compassion. Shane Schimpf comments on the kid's compassionate nature, arguing, "He alone in the novel represents what is supposedly noble and good in man—our capacity to empathize with another person and show mercy." Schimpf argues that *Blood Meridian* is chiefly concerned with the paradigm shift from a religious world view to a scientific one and that the "paradigm that has become antiquated is the religious one—the paradigm embodied by the Kid" (3). In other words, Schimpf believes that the kid's compassion symbolizes the outmoded values of traditional religion, which are set against the ascending power of scientific rationalism, as embodied by Judge Holden.

Whether or not one employs the Manichean dualism of good vs. evil, it is clear that the kid and the judge are constantly portrayed in opposition to one another. This opposition is established in the inverse physical descriptions of the two antagonists. For example, the kid "is not big" but "has big wrists" and "big hands" (4), while the judge is "enormous" but his "hands" are "small" (6). More significantly, the kid's "face is curiously untouched behind the scars, the eyes oddly innocent" (4). Conversely, the judge's face is "serene strangely childlike" and he possesses "small and lashless pig's eyes" (6, 310). If the eyes are windows into the soul, then the kid's countenance suggests that beneath the scarred exterior he still possesses pure innocence, while the judge's appearance suggests the very opposite: although he has the face of a child, his eyes betray his swinelike nature.

The narrative voice continually emphasizes the idea that there is a mysterious enmity between the judge and the kid. Often they are depicted as simply watching each other, as though there is some unspoken animosity between them: "The kid was watching the judge. When the judge's eye fell upon him he took the cigar from between his teeth and smiled. Or he seemed to smile" (79). The fact that the judge only seems to smile suggests that he has simply bared his teeth at the kid, a primal act of predatory aggression.[8] There are several instances in the novel where the kid makes a point of standing up to the judge, even if only by demonstrating that he is not afraid of him. When the Glanton gang runs out of food and needs to slaughter a horse for its meat, the judge calls for someone to come hold the animal while he strikes its head with a rock. When no one responds to the judge's request, Tobin leans toward the kid and whispers, "Pay him no mind lad." The kid ignores the warning, rises, spits into the fire, eyes Tobin, and asks, "You think I'm afraid of him?" Then he turns and defiantly walks "out into the darkness where the judge waited" (219). The dark beyond the fire is both literal and metaphorical, symbolizing the darkness of evil. The kid boldly walks into the judge's evil realm without fear of being devoured and, for the time being, survives to tell the tale.

Similarly, in a symbolic gesture of defiance, the kid refuses to partake of the meat offered up by the judge, despite the fact that he must be starving. As the kid, Tobin, and Toadvine crouch "at the rim of the pit" above a natural well, the judge calls for them to "come down and share this meat" (282, 283). The very fact that the judge is calling them down into a "pit" has sinister, demonic connotations. Furthermore, the sharing of meat, as with the sharing of bread, suggests a form of communion, which the kid clearly rejects. "The kid had set one foot over the edge of the pit and now he drew it back" (284). Not only does the kid refuse to come forward, he actually draws farther away from the judge.[9]

Tobin once again warns the kid about the power of the judge when the three of them are alone in the desert. Not being able to kill the judge, whose sinister intentions toward the kid are now obvious, the kid manages to shoot the judge's horses. Hiding under the "boardlike hide of a dead ox," Tobin and the kid listen "to the judge calling to them." The judge first tries to come to a settlement over the dead horses using legalistic jargon: "He called out points of jurisprudence, he cited cases. He expounded upon those laws pertaining to property rights in beasts mansuete and he quoted from cases of attainder insofar as he reckoned them germane to the corruption of blood in the prior felonious owners of the horses now dead among the bones. Then he spoke of other things." The mysteriously unspecified "other things" fill Tobin with horror. "Dont listen," he tells the kid. The kid claims that he "aint listenin," but Tobin demands, "Stop your ears." Tobin plugs his own ears and then stares pleadingly at the kid. "His eyes were bright from the bloodloss and he was possessed of a great earnestness. Do it, he whispered. Do you think he speaks to me?" (293). Later the judge will confirm Tobin's fears by condemning the kid with the words "Hear me, man. I spoke in the desert for you and you only and you turned a deaf ear to me" (307). Clearly, whatever is being said by the judge is of a great seductive power. The entire scene suggests the temptation of Christ in the wilderness, as described in the Gospels of Matthew, Mark, and Luke: "Then was Jesus led up of the Spirit into the wilderness to be tempted of the devil" (Matthew 4:1). Tobin feels that he can resist the judge only if he blocks out his words, but the kid is once again prepared to boldly expose himself to evil without letting it overcome him.

The most interesting aspect of this desert encounter is that the kid does not kill the judge when given the chance, even though his own life is clearly in danger, as the judge has already shot and wounded Tobin. It seems odd that the kid, who has shown no prior hesitation in killing others in self-defense, should endanger his own life and the life of a friend by refusing to kill a hostile enemy, especially when he has a clear shot at a very large target. A clue to the interpretation of this strange scenario lies in the slightly surreal conversation between Tobin and the kid, which suggests that the judge is no ordinary human being and that killing such an entity is not a straightforward matter. When the kid states, "If I kill him we can take the horses," Tobin, who knows that the kid is a "deadeye" (281), replies, "You'll not kill him. Dont be a fool. Shoot the horses" (291). The kid clearly feels that Tobin knows what he is talking about, as he does not offer a counterargument in defense of his own impressive marksmanship. Later the kid tries to discuss the nature of the judge with Tobin, arguing, "He aint nothin. You told me so yourself. Men are made of the dust of the earth. You said it was no ... parable. That it was a naked fact and the judge was a man like all men." Tobin simply replies, "Face him down then. . . . Face him down if he is so" (297). Again, the kid's inexplicable reluctance to face down the judge indicates that he takes Tobin's warnings seriously.

The judge is fully aware of the kid's refusal to kill him and so calls for the young man to come out from his hiding place and join him: "The priest had led you to this, boy. I know you would not hide. I know that you've not the heart of a common assassin. I've passed before your gunsight twice this hour and will pass a third time. Why not show yourself?" (299). The fact that the judge gives the kid three opportunities to shoot endows the scene with mythical, specifically biblical overtones, reminiscent of Peter's denial of Jesus: "Before the cock crows thou shalt deny me thrice" (Matthew 26:34). In a sense, not shooting the judge is equivalent to denying him, for as Robert Jarrett argues, "The kid repudiates the use of violence to settle [his] quarrel with the judge. The judge interprets such acts as symbolic not of the kid's affiliation with but as his repudiation of the gang through his disavowal of its violence" (*Cormac McCarthy* 85). Indeed, when the kid refuses to respond, either by shooting or showing himself, the judge expresses his disappointment: "No assassin, called the judge. And no partisan either. There's a flawed place in the fabric of your heart. Do you think I could not know?" (299).[10] Once again, the judge's words recall the Bible, specifically Jesus's words to the "lukewarm" souls: "I know your works: you are neither cold nor hot. Would that you were cold or hot! So, because you are lukewarm, and neither cold nor hot, I will spew you out of my mouth" (John 3:15–16). Desiring either a loyal disciple or a worthy adversary, but finding neither, the judge accuses the kid of the same sin of neutrality.

We may regard the kid's lack of action not as an act of cowardice or indecision but as the most effective means of standing up to the judge. Were the kid to shoot, he would be acting as a disciple and succumbing to the judge's code of violence. Thus, much like Melville's Bartleby, the scrivener who opts out of the game of life, the kid replies to the judge's taunts with a silent "I would prefer not." It is interesting to note that Herman Melville, whose influence on McCarthy is apparent, wrote "Fragments of a Lost Gnostic Poem of the 12th Century" (1891), which contains the lines "Indolence is heaven's ally here, / And energy the child of hell" (lines 6–7). Melville's Gnostic poem puts forward the idea that to participate in the world is to cooperate with the demiurge, while complete withdrawal aids the spirit's return to the alien God. Seen in this light, Bartleby becomes a Gnostic hero, refusing to participate in the demiurge's game of manifest existence. Thus the kid's refusal to play the judge's game in the desert may be read as a form of Gnostic protest.

Though not strictly a Gnostic, Jacob Boehme placed such strong emphasis on the existence of evil within the cosmos that his writings are often mistaken for Gnosticism. Boehme argued along similar lines to Melville, claiming that the "more [evil] were resisted, the greater would be the fierceness; like a fire that is stirred, whereby it burns but the more" (*Six Theosophic Points* 100). Referring to this particular doctrine of Boehme's, Franz Hartmann writes, "Therefore no man can successfully resist the devil by fighting him on the same level, nor can anyone overcome temptations in the end except by rising above them" (109). According to Boehme, passive resistance is the best weapon against evil, for if one attempts to fight the devil one will only end up playing according to the rules of his game and thereby falling under his influence. This is precisely the attitude adopted by the kid when he refuses to engage with the judge in the desert. Thus the kid's refusal to shoot the judge is a greater display of enmity than participating in an act of violent retribution.

This theory is confirmed by the fact that the judge seems to be disappointed by the kid's refusal to kill him. At their next meeting following the desert encounter, the judge acknowledges the enmity between them by speaking of it in typically sonorous terms: "Our animosities were formed and waiting before we two met. Yet even so you could have changed it all" (307). Similarly, at their final meeting he tells the kid, "I recognized you when I first saw you and yet you were a disappointment to me. Then and now" (328). These words suggest that the kid was destined to stand in opposition to the judge, a concept foreshadowed by the description of the kid's messianic birth at the beginning of the novel. Nevertheless, the judge seems to believe that the kid could have forsaken his messianic role and become his disciple. "Dont you know that I'd have loved you like a son?" he asks (306), revealing his thwarted desire to mold the kid in his own image.

The idea that the kid's destiny is somewhat ambivalent, in that it is dependent on his either accepting or rejecting the judge, is subtly hinted at by the repeated motif of the Four of Cups tarot card. Earlier in the novel, the kid notices "a gypsy card that was the four of cups" pinned to a wall of an abandoned shack and later draws the "quarto de copas" from a gypsy fortune-teller (59, 94). John Sepich points out that "McCarthy has twice associated the kid with a card whose symbol suggests a divided heart" (*Notes* 107). According to standard interpretations of the tarot, the card augurs a time of "dissatisfaction" and "re-evaluation" of one's way of life (Peach 52). As the kid examines the card, he turns it "upside down" and therefore slightly alters its meaning (94); reversed, the card represents a time of "satiety and excess" (Peach 52). Either reading suggests that the kid feels a deep-seated discontent with his life in the Glanton gang, a feeling that prevents him from becoming a wholehearted disciple of the judge. When the kid draws the card from the fortune-teller's pack, the judge watches him intently. "The judge was laughing silently. He bent slightly the better to see the kid. The kid looked at Tobin and at David Brown and he looked at Glanton himself but they were none laughing" (94). The description of the judge's gesture may call to mind the words of the ravenous wolf of the "Little Red Riding Hood" fairy tale—"All the better to see you with, my dear"—and all the sinister connotations thereof. Furthermore, the judge's laughter suggests that he is the only one who comprehends the relevance of the card.

The judge condemns the kid for his divided heart and for his failure to become a true disciple: "You came forward, he said, to take part in a work. But you were a witness against yourself. You sat in judgement on your own deeds. You put your own allowances before the judgements of history and you broke with the body of which you were pledged a part and poisoned it in all its enterprise" (307). For the judge, it does not seem to matter that the kid collected scalps like the rest of the gang members; what matters is that he felt a twinge of compassion as he did so. "You alone were mutinous," claims the judge. "You alone reserved in your soul some corner of clemency for the heathen" (299).[11] The judge does not condemn the kid for failing to participate in the violent actions of the Glanton gang; he accuses the kid simply of having a conscience.

In the words of the judge, "It was required of no man to give more than he possessed nor was any man's share compared to another's. Only each was called upon to empty out his heart into the common and one did not. Can you tell me who that one was?" The kid refuses to accept the judge's accusations and, defiant as always, replies, "It was you. . . . You were the one" (307). According to the judge, the kid fails the gang by refusing to participate wholeheartedly and by always withholding a part of himself. Stacey Peebles argues that the kid withholds the very part that makes him a messianic figure in the novel: "The small part of the kid that held back from complete, orgiastic, communal destruction with the Glanton gang—perhaps the same part that through Quechan mythology figures him as an icon of human history, or humanity—is odious and damning in the judge's eyes" ("Yuman Belief Systems" 239). In Gnostic terms, this part corresponds to the pneuma, or the "immaterial divine spark imprisoned in a material body," which "is as alien to the world as is the transcendent God" (Pearson 13). Precisely because this fragment of the divine essence does not belong to the manifest world, it falls outside the jurisdiction of the archon-judge and thus cannot be manipulated by him.

It is worth mentioning that the concept of the divine "spark" constitutes a running theme throughout *Blood Meridian*. Even when the sparks in question are the literal sparks of a campfire, the writing contains metaphysical overtones that point to further layers of meaning. Consider, for example, the following description of a dying fire: "The wind blew in the night and fanned the last smoldering billets and drove forth the last fragile race of sparks fugitive as flintstrikings in the unanimous dark of the world" (185). The description of the sparks as "fugitive" suggests that they are escaped prisoners, a concept evocative of the Gnostic belief that the spirit is a divine spark imprisoned in matter. Furthermore, the "unanimous dark" through which the sparks travel suggests the "realm of darkness" that is, for the Gnostics, the manifest cosmos, as opposed to "the divine realm of light" (Jonas 42) from whence the sparks originate. The concept of the divine spark is evoked yet again when the men throw their lice-ridden clothes into a fire: "The filthy hides of which they'd divested themselves smoked and stank and blackened in the flames and the red sparks rose like the souls of the small life they'd harboured" (240). According to Manichean teachings, the imprisoned "particles of light are to be found" not only in human beings but also in "plants" and "animals" (presumably this includes lice) and even within "water" (Rudolph 338).[12] Thus the imagery of the ascending sparks in the lice-burning scene seems to symbolize the Gnostic fragments of the divine leaving the prison of the manifest world.

Further analogies between the spark and the Gnostic fragments of the divine are made when, undressing in the dark, the men find themselves surrounded by the eerie phenomenon of Saint Elmo's fire:

> Then one by one they began to divest themselves of their outer clothes ... and one by one they propagated about themselves a great crackling of sparks and each man was seen to wear a shroud of palest fire. Their arms aloft pulling at their clothes were luminous and each obscure soul was enveloped in audible shapes of light as if it had always been so. The mare at the far end of the stable snorted and shied at this luminosity in beings so endarkened and the little horse turned and hid his face in the web of his dam's flank. (222)

Once again, the words "spark" and "soul" appear in close proximity, alongside the mention of death evoked through the reference to a "shroud." The passage also suggests that the "luminosity" of the divine is present even in the most depraved human beings. According to Irenaeus's account of Gnostic beliefs, the divine spark within human beings was compared to "gold sunk in filth," which "will not lose its beauty but preserve its own nature, and the filth will be unable to impair the gold" (Jonas 271). In other words, even when the spark, or pneuma, is plunged into the darkness of material existence, it maintains its divine nature.[13]

The idea that all human beings, no matter how depraved, contain the divine spark within them is suggested when the members of the Glanton gang are depicted seated around the fire: "They watched the fire which does contain within it something of men themselves inasmuch as they are less without it and are divided from their origins and are exiles. For each fire is all fires, the first fire and the last ever to be" (244). Fire here seems to be symbolizing the Gnostic concept of the pneuma. As has already been established, Gnostic thought teaches that the spirit, trapped in the material realm, is "divided from" its divine "origins" and dwells in a state of "exile."[14] Furthermore, because every pneuma, or spirit, is identical in essence to the divine source from whence it originates, it can be said that each spirit is all spirits. The passage above also bears a marked resemblance to the writings of Jacob Boehme: "Now all the qualities are made to burn by the kindled fire, and the fire is fed by them; but this fire is only one and not many. This fire is the true Son of God Himself, who is continuing to be born from eternity to eternity" (qtd. in Hartmann 87). This rather esoteric quote comes from Boehme's *Aurora*, which contains an exposition on the nature of the universe and its relation to the divine, or "The Seven Properties or Qualities of Eternal Nature."[15] According to Franz Hartmann, Boehme felt he could write about the "spiritual processes taking place in the universe" because "the spirit of man is one and universal, and he who knows his own divine self knows the whole of the universe" (71). We can see how Boehme's insistence on the fact that "the spirit of man is one" is echoed in the narrative voice in *Blood Meridian*, which claims that "each fire is all fires" (244).

In his Gnostic analysis of the novel, Leo Daugherty argues that the kid is significant to the extent that he "feels the 'spark of the alien divine' within him through the call of what seems to be conscience. He thus 'awakens' a bit, attaining in the process a will outside the will of his murdering . . . subculture and the archon who runs it." In other words, the kid refuses to give himself wholly to the judge and is able to maintain some semblance of resistance, if not so much in his actions, then at least in spirit.[16] Daugherty argues that the kid cannot effectively defend himself against the judge, because even though the "kid has 'awakened' . . . he is not progressed sufficiently in wisdom much beyond mere awakening and thus has no chance at survival" (164). That is to say, the kid is not a fully enlightened Gnostic and thus cannot escape the prison of the manifest cosmos that is the judge's domain. I believe, however, that the fact that the judge singles the kid out from the other members of the gang suggests that his spiritual awakening is significant enough to earn the judge's wrath.

In a typically Gnostic reinterpretation of a biblical theme, the judge condemns the kid in the words of Yahweh; as Tim Parrish states, the judge "seems to be playing God . . . to the kid-as-supplicant" (37). Just before he takes the kid's life, he proclaims, "This night thy soul may be required of thee" (327), echoing the biblical God's words to the rich man in Luke 12:20: "Thou fool, this night thy soul shall be required of thee: then whose shall these things be, which thou hast provided?" After voicing this sinister warning in the form of a biblical allusion and then stating that the kid has proven to be a "disappointment," the judge seems to offer the kid one last chance to join him: "Even so at the last I find you here with me." The kid, however, rejects the judge's offer, stating, "I aint with you" (328). The kid pays with his life for this final denial of the judge. After taking leave of the judge and then visiting a whore, the kid steps outside and looks up at the night sky. "Stars were falling across the sky myriad and random, speeding along brief vectors from their origins in night to their destinies in dust and nothingness. . . . He looked again at the silent tracks of the stars where they died over the darkened hills" (333). The stars, which travel to their deaths along predetermined paths, foreshadow the kid's impending and inevitable death. It is significant that, like his birth, the kid's death is augured by stellar phenomena. Commenting on the significance of this synchronicity, Stacey Peebles once again draws attention to the kid's mythological significance within the novel: "Like his birth during the Leonids, a meteor shower of cultural significance to the Yuman Indians, here his death is also marked by falling stars, another important signifier for the Quechan. The kid's life is bookended and emphasized by these semiotic markers." Peebles argues that although the kid may appear to be "an ignorant, aimless wanderer," his birth and death are "resonant with [Quechan] beliefs and therefore representational."[17] Thus "the kid is a necessary and important component in this mythological and ideological standoff with the judge" ("Yuman Belief Systems" 242). In other words, the kid is a sufficiently significant player in the cosmic game that both his entry into and his departure from the world do not go unnoticed or unheralded.

The exact nature of the kid's death remains a disturbing mystery. As the kid walks toward the jakes, he finds that "the judge was seated upon the closet. He was naked and he rose up smiling and gathered him in his arms against his immense and terrible flesh and shot the wooden barlatch home behind him" (333). This is the last we ever hear of the kid. When two men later walk down to the jakes, they encounter a third man urinating who warns them, "I wouldnt go in there if I was you." One of the men asks if there is "somebody in there?" The urinating man simply repeats, "I wouldn't go in." The men ignore the warning and one of them opens the door only to exclaim, "Good God almighty." When his companion asks, "What is it?" the man does not answer (334). John Cant comments on the fact that "despite McCarthy's propensity for making us 'see' all the action and his complete lack of squeamishness in depicting the endless catalogue of outrage that constitutes the novel, we do not 'see' the kid's fate." In a novel where the most horrific scenes of violence are depicted in unflinching detail, the fact that the kid's death is censored and left to the imagination makes it all the more horrific. Cant also argues that "McCarthy does not wish to show us this event since its full meaning is metaphorical" (173). While I agree with Cant's emphasis on the metaphorical nature of the event, I believe that we can still hazard a guess as to the kid's ultimate fate by extrapolating some of the novel's earlier events. The very fact that the hardened men of the so-called Wild West respond with such horror to what they see in the jakes suggests that the kid underwent a taboo-breaking ordeal that somehow exceeded the level of violence and depravity common to that society. Sodomy would certainly qualify as taboo breaking, but the visual signifiers of the aftermath would not be immediately obvious to casual observers. I propose instead that the judge cannibalized the kid, to a lesser or greater extent, and then regurgitated his flesh, for the remains of such a scene would no doubt inspire disgust and horror in even the most jaded of outlaws, no matter how desensitized they had become to the sight of ordinary dismemberments and disfigurations.

There is much evidence to support what Sara Spurgeon calls the "cannibalistic perversions" (90) of the judge. When we are first introduced to the Glanton gang, they are described as "a visitation from some heathen land where they and others like them fed on human flesh," and "foremost among them," like the head cannibal, "rode the judge" (78–79). Later in the novel, the body of a "halfbreed boy" is discovered "lying face down naked in one of the cubicles. Scattered about on the clay were great numbers of old bones. As if he like others before him had stumbled upon a place where something inimical lived." This "inimical" thing is no doubt the judge, who is seen "standing in the gently steaming quiet picking his teeth with a thorn as if he had just eaten" (118). Spurgeon argues that in this instance "the judge rapes and cannibalizes [the boy], absorbs his essence and emerges renewed" (95), and I believe that a similar fate befalls the kid. The very fact that the "halfbreed boy" is found in a "cubicle" links the setting of this particular scene of cannibalization to the kid's death in "the jakes." Furthermore, there is reason to suspect that the judge did not merely devour the kid's flesh but also proceeded to regurgitate the meal. The threat of such an act was foreshadowed by the judge's earlier condemnation of the kid for being "no assassin. ... And no partisan either" (299), words that recall Jesus's threatening promise to the "lukewarm" souls: "So, because you are lukewarm, and neither cold nor hot, I will spew you out of my mouth" (John 3:15–6). It is likely, then, that the judge similarly spewed the kid out of his mouth for being a lukewarm soul.

If the judge and the kid represent two antithetical positions within the novel, then it can be assumed that the hideous death of the kid signifies the triumph of the judge's paradigm. From a Gnostic perspective, this suggests the triumph of evil over the tiny fragment of divinity lying dormant within the kid. Many of the Gnostic sects, however, believed in reincarnation and taught that the pneuma was eternal and could never truly be destroyed.[18] For the fully enlightened Gnostics, death meant a final release from the manifest cosmos, while those who were still plagued by ignorance were thrust back into the world, life after life, until they too attained gnosis and escaped from the prison of existence. Thus, from a Gnostic perspective, the kid's death does not necessarily signify an ultimate failure.

In fact, the kid's death actually evokes a recurring trope in Gnostic, specifically Manichean, allegories, namely that of the "Sacrifice and Adulteration of the Soul" (Jonas 219), which involves the Primal Man, or the Salvator Salvatus, being devoured by one of the evil entities that rules over the manifest world. According to Jonas, the "devouring has also an effect on the devourer," because "the devoured substance acts like a soothing poison" that either satisfies or dulls the devourer's appetite. It is noteworthy that "some versions [of the myth] make the Primal Man not so much be defeated, as in anticipation of the effect voluntarily give himself to be devoured by the Darkness" (219). Jonas explains that "by this sacrificial means the furor of the Darkness is actually 'appeased'" (120). In *Blood Meridian*, the kid's final moments suggest that he meets his death with a certain resignation. Dianne Luce similarly points out that although the kid "appears passive, he goes to embrace his fate as if to a suicide—for he clearly expects to die. As he approaches the saloon he turns in silent farewell to the world and his life" ("Ambiguities" 41). Thus the kid's death may be a form of sacrifice intended to temporarily appease the wrath of the judge. Steven Frye, for example, argues that the kid's death "becomes a measured victory that echoes Christ's death on the cross, at least insofar as he is destroyed but never internally defeated, and he stands as an example of moral rectitude and heroism in the face of omnipresent evil" (*Understanding Cormac McCarthy* 90). Such a sacrificial role not only would justify the portentous omens surrounding the kid's birth and death but also would shed light on the judge's fascination with the kid, as well as the judge's claim that he "recognized" the kid when he first saw him (328).

Yet despite the kid's sacrifice, the judge seems triumphant at the end of the novel: "His feet are light and nimble. He never sleeps. He says that he will never die. He dances in light and in shadow and he is a great favorite. He never sleeps, the judge. He is dancing, dancing. He says that he will never die" (335). Steven Frye argues "that in spite of the kid's resistance, the world remains the judge's domain, a place in which heroic resolve and moral rectitude must inevitably end in death" (*Understanding Cormac McCarthy* 90). It seems that if the kid was a messiah, then he was indeed a failed one, for evil in the form of the judge continues its cosmic dance, with no respite and no terminus. Nevertheless, even though the novel proper ends with the death of the kid and the judge in celebratory dance, we must look to the epilogue for the final word on the struggle between good and evil.

The epilogue marks a change into a heightened, poetic register, signified not only by the italicized font but also by the esoteric symbolism that abounds within the strange scene. "*In the dawn there is a man progressing over the plain by means of holes which he is making in the ground. He uses an implement with two handles and he chucks it into the hole and he enkindles the stone in the hole with steel hole by hole striking the fire out of the rock which God has put there*" (337). On the surface level, this passage can be interpreted quite prosaically. For example, John Sepich argues that "the novel's epilogue is literally a description of digging postholes using a throw-down tool" and thus serves as a depiction of a historically significant "step toward the fencing of open range" (*Notes* 66). Similarly, Christopher Campbell explains, "Anyone who has ever labored with just such an '*implement*' in moderately rocky soil will recognize the sparks which fly with each plunge of the tool" (40). Nevertheless, the densely symbolic quality of McCarthy's prose suggests that there is more to the epilogue than can be gleaned from a literal interpretation, no matter how factually accurate such an interpretation may be.

When interviewed on the subject of *Blood Meridian*, Harold Bloom rejected the literal reading of the passage as "a very bad interpretation." According to Bloom, "That two-handed implement is, as I say, doing one thing and one thing only: it is striking fire which has been put into the rock, clearly a Promethean motif" (qtd. in Josyph 214). Hans Jonas explains that the Gnostics favored the Promethean motif for its antinomian themes because Prometheus, as Zeus's "challenger and victim," represented the Gnostic "'spiritual' man whose loyalty is not to the god of this world but to the transcendent one beyond" (Jonas 97). Leo Daugherty writes that it was precisely *Blood Meridian*'s epilogue that led to his first glimpses of "the novel's Gnostic, and perhaps even specifically Manichean, features" (168). Daugherty identifies the "*man progressing over the plain*" as "the revealer or 'revelator' of the divine, working to free spirit from matter—the pneumatic (albeit corporeal) messenger, in possession of gnosis, who is in service to the good, 'alien God'" (169). The Gnostic revelator of the divine is none other than the Salvator Salvatus, who "awakens the spirit from its earthly slumber, and imparts to it the saving knowledge" (Jonas 45). The Gnostics believed that "the saviour does not come just once into the world but . . . from the beginning of time he wanders in different forms through history, himself exiled in the world, and revealing himself ever anew until, with his gathering-in complete, he can be released from his cosmic mission" (Jonas 79). Thus the figure in the epilogue seems to be another incarnation of the Gnostic savior, one who has responded adequately to the call of gnosis and reached his soteriological potential.[19]

From a Gnostic perspective, the fact that the man in the epilogue is described as "*striking the fire out of the rock which God has put there*" suggests that he is freeing sparks of the divine fire trapped in matter, or rock, by the god of this world, the demiurge. Conversely, the passage may be interpreted in light of the more subtle Syrian-Egyptian strains of Gnosticism, which claim that the divine spark was not imprisoned by evil forces but that there was "a voluntary element in the downward movement of the divine" (Jonas 63). In this case, the reference to "God" may be read as a reference to the original divine substance, or the alien God. Evelyn Underhill points out that "fire imagery has seemed to many of the mystics a peculiarly exact and suggestive symbol of the transcendent state which they are struggling to describe" (421). For example, Ralph Waldo Emerson employs this imagery in "The Poet," where he writes, "We were put in our bodies, as fire is put into a pan to be carried about" (92). Similarly, Jacob Boehme writes of "the fire of the soul" that is "illuminated by the divine light" (qtd. in Hartmann 18). Thus the fire in *Blood Meridian*'s epilogue seems to be "that uncreated and energizing Fire" (Underhill 421) that symbolizes the spirit as well as the Absolute.[20]

It is also significant that the image of fire emerging out of the rock appears in the apocryphal Gospel of Thomas, which is often regarded as a Gnostic text. When the other disciples want to know what three secret sayings Jesus had imparted to Thomas, the latter replies, "If I tell you one of the sayings he spoke to me, you will pick up rocks and stone me and fire will come out of the rocks and consume you" (qtd. in Barnstone and Meyer 48). The concept of the enkindled fire as a symbol of spiritual awakening throws light on the judge's earlier reference to the kid as "Young Blasarius" (94). According to Shane Schimpf, the term appears in *Black's Law Dictionary* and refers to "an incendiary," or one who starts fires (148). On a literal level, the judge refers to the kid in this way because the latter helped Toadvine set fire to a hotel at the beginning of the novel. On a more symbolic level, however, the nickname alludes to the kid's messianic potential for "*striking the fire out of the rock.*"

The epilogue continues with the words "*on the plain behind him are the wanderers in search of bones and those who do not search*" (337). John Sepich argues that the mysterious "*wanderers*" are bone pickers in search of buffalo bones, explaining, "When the use of bone phosphorous for agricultural fertilizer was discovered in the nineteenth century, buffalo skeletons became significant commodities in the economy of the West" (*Notes* 67). Though historically valid, such an interpretation does not explain the presence of "*those who do not search.*" Harold Bloom takes the argument against a literal interpretation even further, arguing that the lone figure is "clearly contrasted with creatures who are either ghoulish human beings, if they *are* human beings, or already are, in fact, shades, looking for bones for whatever nourishment that might bring about" and adds that he "cannot see that as any kind of allegory of anything that has happened to the American West" (qtd. in Josyph 214). If, however, one looks at the passage as a Gnostic parable rather than a historical one, one may go some way toward illuminating the meaning of those who are "*in search of bones*" and "*those who do not search.*" The distinction drawn between the two different kinds of "*wanderers*" suggests that those who have not attained gnosis can be divided into those who search for answers in the wrong places and those who do not search at all.

From a Gnostic perspective, those who wander the barren plain "*in search of bones*" may be interpreted as those whose spiritual progress has been hindered by their preoccupation with the relics and testimonies of dead prophets and saints. According to the Gnostic Gospel of Thomas, Jesus rebuked his disciples for their preference for the "secondhand testimony" of dead prophets over the "primacy of immediate experience," stating, "You have ignored the one living in your presence and have spoken only of the dead" (qtd. in Pagels, *Gnostic Gospels* 145). Julian II, the last pagan emperor of Rome, also condemned the Galileans (Christians) for precisely this obsession with death: "You have filled the whole world with tombs and sepulchres, and yet in your scriptures it is nowhere said that you must grovel among tombs and pay them honour" (qtd. in Wright 414). Conversely, "*those who do not search*" are, according to Gnostic thought, the "unenlightened people" who believe they can "find fulfilment in family life, sexual relationships, business, politics, ordinary employment or leisure," whereas the true Gnostics "rejected this belief as illusion" (Pagels, *Gnostic Gospels* 145). Thus, from a Gnostic perspective, "*those who do not search*" are even less spiritually awakened than those who seek for answers in dry bones.

As Harold Bloom points out, the crowd of wanderers is "clearly contrasted" with the figure of the solitary man. While the man is depicted as "*progressing over the plain*" with the decisive determination of one who has a goal, the wanderers "*move haltingly in the light like mechanisms whose movements are monitored with escapement and pallet*" (337). These halting, mechanical movements suggest a complete lack of personal agency. Furthermore, Shane Schimpf argues that the "*escapement and pallet*" serve as "a reference to clocks and their mechanism," which is "a clear echoing of the idea of an orderly universe that can be fully described and controlled" (45).[21] The concept of an orderly, clockwork universe suggests the Gnostic belief in the inexorable forces of fate known as heimarmene. According to Gnostic teachings, heimarmene determines the motion of the entire cosmos, from the celestial spheres to the lowliest organism, thereby turning it into "a prison from which there is no escape." Only the attainment of gnosis "opens up a way on which man (strictly only a small part of man, namely the divine spark) can escape" (Rudolph 58). From a Gnostic perspective, the difference between the lone man and the wanderers is that the former is no longer controlled by heimarmene, while the latter are still its hapless puppets. Buddhism also "distinguishes two classes of people," namely, the "saints," who "alone are truly alive," and the "common worldlings," who, much like McCarthy's wanderers, "just vegetate along in a sort of dull and aimless bewilderment" (Conze, *Buddhist Wisdom Books* 38). As in Gnosticism, the difference between the two types of people in Buddhism is a direct result of spiritual development, or lack thereof.

The halting movement of the wanderers makes them *"appear"* to be *"restrained by a prudence or reflectiveness,"* but this is only an illusion and *"has no inner reality"* (337). "Reflectiveness" is synonymous with "thoughtfulness" or "contemplativeness" (*OED*) and therefore is a state of mind associated with meditation and spiritual practice. The wanderers only appear to possess insight into their situation, when in reality they move like sleepwalkers. Buddhism teaches that "only the enlightened are awake to reality as it is; compared with their vision of true reality, our normal experience is that of a dream, unreal and not to be taken seriously" (Conze, *Buddhist Wisdom Books* 38). Similarly, the fully awakened Gnostic "comes to understand that the material world is a dream" (Wagner and Flannery-Dailey 282). From both a Buddhist and a Gnostic perspective, only the lone figure *"progressing over the plain"* can be said to be fully awakened, fully aware, and thus in control of his destiny; the wanderers are mere cogs in the unrelentingly deterministic machine that is the manifest cosmos.

The wanderers *"cross in their progress one by one that track of holes that runs to the rim of the visible ground,"* seemingly seeking *"a validation of sequence and causality as if each round and perfect hole owed its existence to the one before it"* (337). They cannot comprehend the mystery of the path that lies before them, misunderstanding its nature and its cause. What is essentially the work of the savior or divine messenger, they mistake for a natural occurrence that has arisen quite simply and organically out of itself. The passage seems to be suggesting that the ordinary worldlings are incapable of recognizing the miracle of the saints, saviors, and Bodhisattvas, even if their works lie right before their eyes.[22]

Many critics, however, feel that the epilogue offers no redemption whatsoever and see *Blood Meridian* as a wholly nihilistic novel. Michael Carragher, for example, writes, "We look to the epilogue to find a bone-strewn plain [with] a man apparently sowing war.... No, there is no salvation; we are all damned to hell" (20). Similarly, Steven Shaviro argues, "We are called to no responsibility, and we may lay claim to no transcendence. *Blood Meridian* is not a salvation narrative; we can be rescued neither by faith nor by works nor by grace," concluding, "It is useless to look for ulterior, redemptive meanings" (148). Edwin Arnold, however, insists that there is "always the possibility of grace and redemption even in the darkest of [McCarthy's] tales" ("Naming" 46). Furthermore, Harold Bloom, along with Leo Daugherty, is among the few to argue that this "man striking fire in the rock at dawn is an opposing figure" who, to some extent, counteracts the evil of the judge. Bloom concludes that the "Judge never sleeps, and perhaps will never die, but a new Prometheus may be rising to go up against him" (*Modern Critical Views* 7). Like Arnold, Bloom, and Daugherty, I argue that despite the fact that the kid fails in his messianic role, and that the seemingly immortal judge continues his Shiva-like dance of destruction, the lone figure of the epilogue saves *Blood Meridian* from unrelenting nihilism. The Gnostic savior does not abandon "*that prairie upon which are the bones and the gatherers of bones and those who do not gather. He strikes fire in the hole and draws out his steel. Then they all move on again*" (337). These are the words with which *Blood Meridian* concludes. We are not left with the judge's eternal dance of war, violence, and spiritual death but rather with the unconquered solitary figure, slowly working toward his goal of freeing the divine element from the prison of manifest existence.

CHAPTER 5

"Diverging Equity"
The Nature of Existence in *All the Pretty Horses*

■ The first volume of Cormac McCarthy's Border Trilogy, *All the Pretty Horses*, may seem like a deviation from the brutally grim preoccupations of *Blood Meridian*, but despite the introduction of some rather uncharacteristic elements—namely a wholly sympathetic protagonist, a Quixotic quest, and a passionate love story—the novel is still very much informed by McCarthy's darkly anticosmic metaphysics. *All the Pretty Horses* traces John Grady Cole's painful initiation into an awareness of evil, suffering, and death, an apprehension of what the narrative voice constantly refers to as the "terrible truth" of the world. The title itself subtly foreshadows the darkness inherent in the novel. Taken from a lullaby in which a child is promised, "When you wake, you shall have, / All the pretty little horses," the words evoke a sense of childlike innocence, such as one expects to find in a fairy tale. Those familiar with the lullaby, however, will know that it also contains a very grim stanza:

> Way down yonder, down in the meadow,
> There's a poor wee little lamby.
> The bees and the butterflies pickin' at its eyes,
> The poor wee thing cried for her mammy.[1]

These lines provide a clue to the novel's true preoccupations, namely the ways in which suffering, death, and evil, whether man-made or natural, permeate all forms of existence.

Indeed, the narrative opens with what may well be John Grady's first encounter with death; staring at his dead grandfather in an open casket, the young boy's silent horror at this confronting vision is conveyed through the repetition of the words "That was not sleeping. That was not sleeping." After viewing his grandfather's body, John Grady walks "out on the prairie" and stands "holding his hat like some supplicant to the darkness over them all," as though pleading with the darkness to be merciful (3). The observation of death is subsequently echoed in John Grady's Hamlet-like contemplation of "an old horseskull in the brush.... Frail and brittle. Bleached white paper.... The muted run of sand in the brainbox when he turned it" (6). The horse skull functions as a memento mori, a reminder of the frailty and mutability of all living things. The irrevocable passage of time is evoked by the description of sand pouring through the skull, as though John Grady had turned over an hourglass. Precisely because horses represent all that is beautiful and life-affirming within the novel, the horse skull also serves as an "Et in Arcadia ego" motif, reminding the reader that not even paradise is free from death.

Themes of transience and death are also encapsulated in what is perhaps one of the most haunting passages in the novel, John Grady's vision of the ghostly Comanche tribe: "The shadows were long and the ancient road was shaped before him like a dream of the past where the painted ponies and their riders of that lost nation came down out of the north with their faces chalked and their long hair plaited." The description of this vision blurs the boundaries between illusion and reality. Though the riders are only apparitions, John Grady can actually hear "the low chant of their travelling song," as though the past has temporarily broken through into the present. The vision of the "nation and ghost of nation passing in a soft chorale" evokes a terrible sense of loss and serves as another memento mori, although this time on a much larger scale. The Comanches' passing "across that mineral waste to darkness ... lost to all history and all remembrance" foreshadows the fate of all nations and eventually the entire human race, as depicted in McCarthy's *The Road*.[2] Their "transitory and violent lives" encapsulate the nature of human existence as depicted throughout McCarthy's novels. Finally, despite this reminder of mortality, violence, and suffering, we are told that the Comanches bear the truth of their lives "like a grail," an image that suggests that there is some profoundly spiritual aspect to human existence. It is precisely this tension between the violent, death-seeking drive, represented by the image of the warriors "armed for war which was their life," and the redemptive, life-affirming principle, represented by the "women with children at their breast," that is explored throughout the novel (5).

When John Grady rides out to the place where he sees the apparitions, the sun is described as "blood red and elliptic under the reefs of bloodred cloud before him." Furthermore, the Comanches are "pledged in blood and redeemable in blood only" (5). The symbolic and descriptive references to blood make up a pervasive theme in McCarthy's fiction. The evocation of blood in descriptions of the natural landscape not only suggests that bloodshed and suffering are an inherent part of existence but also serves to reinforce the constant presence of death. The use of blood imagery, however, is not wholly negative. As John Cant explains, blood "is a recurring emblem" in McCarthy's work "and signifies both life and death, each defined in relation to its inescapable other." Cant also points out that the inherent vitality of McCarthy's blood imagery is expressed through the concept of "ardentheartedness," described in *All the Pretty Horses* in terms of John Grady's love of horses: "What he loved in horses was what he loved in men, the blood and the heat of the blood that ran them. All his reverence and all his fondness and all the leanings of his life were for the ardenthearted and they would always be so and never be otherwise" (6). In McCarthy's novels, blood stands not only for violence, suffering, and bloodshed but also for the sacred, life-affirming bond between all living things.[3] The passage seems to suggest that even though human beings have "pledged" their lives to bloodshed, they may yet be "redeemed" by the fact that the same red blood runs through the entire human race.

The apparition of the Comanches evokes in John Grady a deep nostalgia for an unrealistically romanticized way of life. This longing prompts the young protagonist to set out on a quest to find what can only be described as a nonexistent fantasy world. Several critics have commented on the ways in which *All the Pretty Horses* contains elements of the heroic romance or the chivalric quest. John Cant, for example, writes that the novel addresses a "romantic myth" because the "armed horseman on his mythic quest is a figure of Arthurian romance" and the "forbidden love of John Grady and Alejandra, a betrayal of the master of the mythic realm, reflects Lancelot and Guinevere" (181). Apart from the parallels between John Grady's quest and the Arthurian romance, *All the Pretty Horses* also alludes to three other famously romantic expeditions: the legend of the lost city of El Dorado, Herman Melville's *The Encantadas*, and Miguel de Cervantes's *The Ingenious Hidalgo Don Quixote of La Mancha*. Significantly, all three of these stories tell of a quest that either is hopeless or ends in despair, foreshadowing John Grady's rite of passage from his naïve idealism to a more realistic but much darker apprehension of existence.

The first of these literary allusions occurs in book 1, when John Grady and Rawlins first set out on their adventure. Riding through the dark night, the boys spot something shining in the distance. Rawlins asks, "What's them lights?" and John Grady jokingly replies, "I'd make it Eldorado" (32). El Dorado (the golden one) is the fabled city of gold often used as a metaphor for the Holy Grail, or any other lofty goal at the end of a difficult quest. El Dorado, however, is also a figure of speech for some unattainable prize or impossible search, as in Edgar Allan Poe's poem of the same name.[4] The motif of the unattainable prize is represented in *All the Pretty Horses* by the fact that John Grady's desire for an idyllic cowboy existence, in which he marries his first true love and inherits her father's picturesque ranch, is revealed to be an impossible dream. It is also significant that John Grady, Rawlins, and Blevins first encounter human evil and corruption in the form of the Mexican captain in the pueblo of Encantada, a direct allusion to Melville's series of sketches on the Galapagos Islands entitled *The Encantadas*, or the "Enchanted Isles." The first of these sketches contains an epigraph taken from Spenser's *The Fairie Queene*, describing "The Wandering Islands," which "have oft drawne many a wandering wight / Into most deadly daunger and distressed plight" (II.xii.11). The literary allusion emphasizes the motif of the doomed romantic quest that ends in despair because the goal is revealed to be illusory or unattainable. Finally, McCarthy makes both direct and indirect allusions to the tale of Don Quixote. The first of these occurs early on in the novel, when the boys pass by the "wreckage of an old wooden windmill fallen among rocks," and again when they water their horses under an old "windmill that creaked slowly in the wind" (23, 42). The most direct reference occurs in book 2, when Don Héctor addresses John Grady as though he were Quixote: "Beware gentle knight. There is no greater monster than reason" (146).[5] John Grady's identification with the deluded hero marks his quest as hopelessly quixotic.

The temporarily successful completion of the romantic quest occurs in book 2, which opens with a description of Don Héctor's hacienda as a vision of a pristine Edenic paradise: "The grasslands lay in a deep violet haze and to the west thin flights of waterfowl were moving north before the sunset in the deep red galleries under the cloudbanks like schoolfish in a burning sea and on the foreland plain they saw the vaqueros driving cattle before them through a gauze of golden dust" (93). McCarthy's vivid use of colors—violet, red, and gold—combined with descriptions of grasslands, cloudbanks, waterfowl, and cattle and even the evocation of marine imagery suggest an image of unspoiled paradise. This is further enhanced by descriptions of the hacienda's "natural springs," "clear streams," and "shallow lakes or lagunas. In the lakes and in the streams were species of fish not known elsewhere on earth and birds and lizards and other forms of life as well all long relict here for the desert stretched away on every side" (97). Not surprisingly, John Grady tells Rawlins that he would like to stay in this enchanted place "about a hundred years" (96). The hacienda is portrayed as a kind of oasis, a walled garden, or a magical land of plenty set apart from the barren wilderness and desolation that surround it. In *Symbols and Their Meanings*, Jack Tresidder explains that "the garden became a symbol of paradise—notably in the arid landscapes of Egypt and Persia—because it provided a foretaste of the joys of immortality." Furthermore, the "sealed fruitfulness of the enclosed garden became a Christian symbol of the Virgin Mary, often depicted in a garden setting" (74). The full name of the Hacienda de Nuestra Señora de la Purísima Concepción (The ranch of Our Lady of the Immaculate Conception) emphasizes the aforementioned symbolism.

During his stay at the hacienda, John Grady encounters not only the beauty of nature but also the delights of sensual pleasure through his encounters with the beautiful Alejandra. When John Grady first makes love to her, she is linked to the moon and to the dark waters, both ancient symbols of the feminine principle: "She was so pale in the lake she seemed to be burning. Like foxfire in a darkened wood. That burned cold. Like the moon that burned cold. Her black hair floating on the water about her, falling and floating on the water" (141).[6] Book 2 seems to deal explicitly with John Grady's initiation into sensuality. Buddhadasa Bhikkhu explains that according to Buddhist thought, "all the trouble and chaos in the world has its origin in sensuality," and that "if all suffering is to be eliminated, sensual attachment has to be done away with completely." It is noteworthy, then, that Alejandra not only initiates John Grady into sensuality but also seems to be the novel's chief personification of sorrow. When she first comes to John Grady's bed, he sees "in her face and in her figure something he'd never seen before and the name of that thing was sorrow" (140). When he meets her again later in the novel, she smiles "and in her eyes was the sadness he'd first seen the night she came to his room and he knew that while he was contained in that sadness he was not the whole of it" (248–49). Later, when John Grady again looks into her eyes, he realizes that "he'd never seen despair before. He thought he had, but he had not" (251).

Thus, in strikingly Buddhist fashion, the figure of Alejandra symbolizes both sensual attachment and suffering.

According to Buddhist thought, attachment can only lead to suffering, because "everything here is impermanent, everchanging, doomed to destruction, quite unreliable, crumbling away however much we try to hold it" (Conze, *Buddhism* 113). Indeed, John Grady's idyllic existence at the hacienda proves to be short-lived. Even among all the beauty and delight that life can offer, John Grady is subtly reminded of the ephemeral nature of existence. He watches Alejandra "coming down out of the mountains riding very stately and erect out of a rainsquall building to the north and the dark clouds towering above her... until the rain caught up with her and shrouded her figure away in that wild summer landscape: real horse, real rider, real land and sky and yet a dream withal" (131).[7] The description of Alejandra suggests that the reality we take for granted is only a kind of dream, an idea that goes back to the Hindu and Buddhist concept of Śaṃsāra (the manifest world) being only māyā (illusion).

Buddhism teaches that though the beauty of the world holds a glittering fascination, it does not reveal the true nature of existence, which is suffering, or *duḥkha*: "'Sorrow is' is the first of the four noble truths of the Buddha" (Dutt 71). In *The Religions of Man*, Huston Smith elaborates on this Buddhist teaching: "Beneath the neon dazzle is darkness. At the core—not of reality, we must remember, but of human life—is misery" (110). When John Grady encounters Alejandra later in the novel, after undergoing much suffering of his own, he finds her beauty incongruous: "As she walked toward him her beauty seemed to him a thing altogether improbable. A presence unaccountable in this place or any place at all" (248). In Buddhist terms, John Grady begins to see past the distracting beauty of the world and glimpses the darkness at the core of human existence. Similarly, when John Grady returns to the hacienda with his newfound understanding of suffering, he no longer sees it as a simple paradise but is confronted with a memento mori image of death and mutability. As he rides toward the ranch, he encounters buzzards "feeding on a dead colt" and stops to contemplate "the poor form stretched in the tainted grass eyeless and naked" (225). Like the horse skull John Grady contemplates after this grandfather's funeral, the dead colt serves as a timely reminder that even horses—symbols of all that is good and beautiful within the novel—are subject to the ravages of death and decay.

Horses also play a vital role in revealing subtle truths about existence, as presented within the novel. Although John Grady's encounters with horses at the hacienda form a part of the paradise motif, they also offer insight into the devastating effect that an individual's insistence on building up a separate ego has on the world around him or her and ultimately on his or her own existence. According to Buddhist thought, *tanha*, or "the desire to pull apart from the rest of life and seek fulfilment through those bottled-up segments of being we call our selves" (H. Smith, *Religions of Man* 14), is, along with sensual attachment, one of the chief causes of *duḥkha* (suffering).[8] Horses in the novel are presented as free from tanha until they encounter human beings. The vaquero Luis tells John Grady that "the horse shares a common soul" and "that among men there was no such communion as among horses" (111). The sixteen wild horses that John Grady and Rawlins break over the course of four days are described as "coming to reckon slowly with the remorselessness of this rendering of their fluid and collective selves into that condition of separate and helpless paralysis which seemed to be among them like a creeping plague" (105). The use of words such as "paralysis" and "plague" suggest illness and infection, as though the tanha of human beings has come to dwell within the horses like a virus or a parasite.

A similar concept of infection, or rather possession, is evoked when the "voice of the breaker" is described as "the voice of some God come to inhabit them" (105).[9] Later, John Grady dreams of "horses wild on the mesa who'd never seen a man afoot and who knew nothing of him or his life yet in whose souls he would come to reside forever" (118). When the job of breaking the wild horses is finally completed, "all communion among them [is] broken" (105). The horses sense this change and "the animals whinnied to one another in the dark and answered back as if some one among their number were missing, or some thing" (107). The missing thing is, of course, the loss of communion; the horses' collective selves have been "broken" and replaced by an alienating sense of separateness.

Although the idea that the world hides a dark truth is foreshadowed constantly throughout the novel—whether through Alejandra's suffering or in the horses' painful loss of unity—the nature of this truth is fully revealed to John Grady only in book 3. Suddenly, the hero, who should have won the girl and lived happily ever after, is evicted from the fairy-tale paradise of the hacienda and thrust into the depths of hell in Saltillo prison. Gail Morrison writes that the "hell in the prison . . . is Blakean in its divisions and also reminiscent of Melville in the malevolent and omnipotent presence of evil" (182). Furthermore, the novel presents that hell not as an aberration but, in McCarthy's typically Gnostic fashion, as the true nature of the world. According to the Gnostic thought that permeates McCarthy's fiction, the entire manifest cosmos is a "world of darkness, utterly full of evil" (Jonas 57). William James, whose work McCarthy recommends (Wallace 138), writes that the "evil facts" of life "are a genuine portion of reality; and they may after all be the best key to life's significance, and possibly the only opener of our eyes to the deepest levels of truth" (James 124). Dianne Luce aptly describes John Grady's journey as "an initiation into evil," adding that afterward he comes to understand that "he inhabits a mysteriously fallen world and is a part of it" ("When You Wake" 162). Thus, as a dreamer harshly awakened from a romantic reverie, John Grady stands blinking in the cold light of reality, encapsulated in the microcosm of the Saltillo prison.

The young protagonist also receives a lesson on the nature of evil from Perez, "a prisoner of means" who tells John Grady that, unlike the American, the Mexican realizes that evil is not the quality of any particular thing but that it has its own separate existence (184). Perez claims that the Mexican "knows where good and evil have their home," explaining, "There can be in a man some evil. But we dont think it is his own evil. Where did he get it? How did he come to claim it? No. Evil is a true thing in Mexico. It goes about on its own legs. Maybe some day it will come to visit you. Maybe it already has." John Grady agrees that this might be so with a simple "Maybe" (195). This is not the orthodox Catholic understanding of evil, described by Saint Augustine as *privatio boni* (privation of good) and thus conceived of as a mere absence.[10] Opposed to this is the Gnostic view of evil, in which the inherent "negativity of the concept 'cosmos' is not merely that of the absence of divine values in the universe: its combination with such terms as 'darkness,' 'death,' 'ignorance,' and 'evil' shows it to be possessed of a counter-quality of its own" (Jonas 252). The evil of which Perez speaks is closer to the Gnostic view in that it is presented as a palpable force in its own right. John Grady encounters such evil when he is forced to kill a hired "cuchillero" in a knife fight. Although he first recognizes evil only in the other man, whose eyes contain a "whole malign history burning cold and remote and black" and who appears to him as "some dark and reedy homunculous bent upon inhabiting him," John Grady soon recognizes the evil within himself (200).[11] A few days after the fight, he examines his reflection in a lunch tray, studying "the face that peered dimly out of the warped steel like some maimed and raging djinn enconjured there" (207), as though the evil within the *cuchillero* has really come to inhabit him.

The thoroughly Gnostic idea that the cosmos is permeated with evil is emphasized throughout the novel by the recurring presence of an evil "thing," which seems to have burrowed into the very heart of creation. John Grady encounters it in the prison in the form of "some brooding and malignant life slumbering in the darkened cages they passed" (181). Afterward he refers to it as "the pain of the world" and imagines it as "some formless parasitic being seeking out the warmth of human souls wherein to incubate" (256). Its sinister manifestations can also be found in descriptions throughout the novel, such as that of the "boil of dust . . . roiling slowly in the starlight like something enormous uncoiling out of the earth" (125). McCarthy's portrayal of evil is reminiscent of the view expressed by the Jesuit cleric Pierre Teilhard de Chardin, who made the heretical observation that evil "inevitably seeps out through every nook and cranny, through every joint and sinew" of the universe (311). There is something organic about this malignant presence; evil in McCarthy's fiction seems to grow out of the very core of the earth, as though it were a seed planted deep in the earth, or a larva in a cocoon.

Although John Grady gains awareness of this "thing" only after his experience in prison, its presence is already evoked by the narrative voice in book 1, where it is described as "something imperfect and malformed lodged in the heart of being. A thing smirking deep in the eyes of grace itself like a gorgon in an autumn pool" (71). Eventually, the loss of Alejandra opens John Grady up to a visitation from this parasitic thing: "He saw very clearly how all his life led only to this moment and all after led nowhere at all. He felt something cold and soulless enter him like another being and he imagined that it smiled malignly and he had no reason to believe that it would ever leave" (254). It is this very thing that will drive John Grady to his death in *Cities of the Plain*, the final volume of the Border Trilogy. John Cant describes this process as "the fate of the inverted romantic" and argues that the "thing" that enters John Grady is the "disillusioned nihilism that turns his 'ardentheartedness' towards the pursuit of death" (190). In other words, the life-affirming Eros he once felt toward Alejandra has been replaced by the death-seeking Thanatos characteristic of negative romanticism.[12]

The process taking place within John Grady also operates on a subconscious level, manifesting itself through the changed nature of his dreams of horses. When John Grady is first thrown into prison, his dream of running "among the horses" reveals that he still longs for the lost paradise and consequently for life itself, however idealistic such a view of life may be:

> That night he dreamt of horses in a field on a high plain where the spring rains had brought up the grass and the wildflowers out of the ground and the flowers ran all blue and yellow far as the eye could see and in the dream he was among the horses running and in the dream he himself could run with the horses and they coursed the young mares and fillies over the plain where their rich bay and their rich chestnut colors shone in the sun and the young colts ran with their dams and trampled down the flowers in a haze of pollen that hung in the sun like powdered gold and they ran he and the horses out along the high mesas where the ground resounded under their running hooves and they flowed and changed and ran and their manes and tails blew off of them like spume and there was nothing else at all in that high world and they moved all of them in a resonance that was like a music among them and they were none of them afraid horse nor colt nor mare and they ran in that resonance which is the world itself and which cannot be spoken but only praised. (162)

John Grady's dream is not only a deeply moving and visually sumptuous celebration of the natural world but also an evocation of a sense of the divine. Within the dream, John Grady finds himself in total harmony with the horses and with the world itself. Edwin Arnold points out that McCarthy's use of the word "resonance" "refers to the intensification or enrichment of a sound or feeling. In physics, it describes the effect one vibrating body has on another body: the movement of the first is translated to the second so that both bodies come to move together" ("Go to Sleep" 53). On a spiritual level, harmonized vibrations suggest the Hindu concept of the divine cosmic "vibration manifesting as the sound 'OM'" (Maheshwarananda 15). Thus the word and all its connotations enhance the sense of perfect harmony that permeates the dream.

This is a view of the world as John Grady would like it to be, containing no fear, nor darkness, nor suffering, nor loss. The dream world is composed only of light and beauty, bringing with it a profound sense of communion with the natural world and an apprehension of the sacred, which is described as a resonance "which cannot be spoken but only praised" (162). The notion of the sacred as something that cannot be readily articulated through everyday speech is one of the major tenets of the Perennial Philosophy. Praise succeeds where speech cannot, because praise is a form of prayer, or contemplation, and thus adequate to the sacred experience. Citing one of McCarthy's favorite books, *The Varieties of Religious Experience*, Evelyn Underhill explains that "William James considered 'ineffability' and 'noetic quality' to be the constant characteristics of the contemplative experience. Those who have seen are quite convinced: those who have not seen, can never be told. There is no certitude to equal the mystic's certitude: no impotence more complete than that which falls on those who try to communicate it" (331). This concept of the sacred goes far beyond the jurisdiction of the church, as Don Héctor points out: "What is sacred is sacred. The powers of the priest are more limited than people suppose" (144). Like the evil of which Perez speaks, the sacred as conceived by Don Héctor is something that exists in its own right, beyond the limitations imposed on it by the rites of organized religion or the artificial constructions of language.

The novel does not necessarily imply that the vision of the world in John Grady's dream is a false one, but only that it is an incomplete picture that ignores the darkness inherent in creation. After the malign "thing" enters John Grady and his apprehension of the world changes, his dreams of horses take on a darker, though still revelatory, quality:

> In his sleep he could hear the horses stepping among the rocks and he could hear them drink from the shallow pools in the dark where the rocks lay smooth and rectilinear as the stones of ancient ruins and the water from their muzzles dripped and rang like water dripping in a well and in his sleep he dreamt of horses and the horses in his dream moved gravely among the tilted stones like horses come upon an antique site where some ordering of the world had failed and if anything had been written on the stones the weathers had taken it away again and the horses were wary and moved with great circumspection carrying in their blood as they did the recollection of this and other places where horses once had been and would be again. Finally what he saw in his dream was that the order in the horse's heart was more durable for it was written in a place where no rain could erase it. (280)

Gone are the ecstatic, wild horses of the earlier dream; these wary horses do not run but move "gravely" through darkness and the dripping of water. The golden sunlight, the high plains, and the wildflowers have been replaced by shallow pools, stones, and rocks, evoking ancient ruins whose inscriptions have been eroded by the weather. Edwin Arnold argues that this second dream reveals "a more mature acceptance of the tragic nature of the world" ("Go to Sleep" 56). John Grady comes to understand that the things of this world are as transient as the writing on the stones that the weathers have eroded. Nevertheless, a sense of permanence and eternity is evoked through the "order" within the horse's heart. The dream suggests that the horses, and by implication all living things, possess a harmonious and transcendent spirit that can never be destroyed by any force of this world.

John Grady's apprehension of the darkness of the world is revealed gradually through a series of revelations. While most of these revelations stem from events that happen to him in person, some are revealed through the secondhand experience of Duena Alfonsa, who is described by Gail Morrison as "a sphinx-like voice of moral authority at the novel's philosophical center" (182). Alfonsa presents John Grady with two metaphors that attempt to explain the role of personal agency in the universe. The first of these is the example of "a tossed coin that was at one time a slug in a mint and of the coiner who took that slug from the tray and placed it in the die in one of two ways and from whose act all else followed." The coiner is depicted as "peering with his poor eyes through dingy glasses at the blind tablets of metal before him. Making his selection. Perhaps hesitating a moment. While the fates of what unknown worlds to come hang in the balance." Alfonsa explains the idea behind this metaphor, claiming that "the responsibility for a decision could never be abandoned to a blind agency but could only be relegated to human decisions more and more remote from their consequences" (231). Although this portrayal of a blindly deterministic chain reaction may at first appear to be a refutation of any notion of divine agency, the concept of the coiner must be considered in the context of McCarthy's work, for only by doing so can we begin to understand the full significance of what this figure represents.

The image of the coiner, busy at his trade, is reminiscent of the "false moneyer" in *Blood Meridian*, who similarly "crouches at his trade," "hammering out like his own conjectural destiny all through the night of his becoming some coinage for a dawn that would not be" (310). Like Alfonsa's coiner, *Blood Meridian*'s moneyer or "coldforger" seems to be producing coins that will have a profound effect upon the course of the world, although in this instance in the purely negative sense of an eventuality that will *not* come to be.[13] It is noteworthy that to "coin" means to "make, devise, produce," or to "form, fashion, or convert into" (*OED*), thus "coiner" can also be synonymous for "creator," a concept that immediately calls to mind the Gnostic demiurge. In *All the Pretty Horses*, the work of McCarthy's sinister artisan is also evoked in the description of an approaching storm: "Shrouded in the black thunderheads the distant lightning glowed mutely like welding seen through foundry smoke. As if repairs were under way at some flawed place in the iron dark of the world" (67). The references to "welding," "foundry," "smoke," "repairs," and "iron" all suggest the demiurgical coldforger. Furthermore, the idea of a "flawed place in the iron dark of the world" carries Gnostic connotations, suggesting that there is something fundamentally wrong with creation.

Alfonsa goes on to add that sometimes she believes that "we are all like that myopic coiner at his press, taking the blind slugs one by one from the tray, all of us bent so jealously at our work, determined that not even chaos be outside our own making" (241). These words evoke a similar passage from *The Crossing*, in which the God of this world is also described as an artisan, this time a weaver "much occupied" in weaving "that tapestry that was the world," so that "not chaos itself lay outside that matrix" (149).[14] It is significant that the weaver god is deafened by the noise of his loom—"Spoken to He did not answer. Called to did not hear" (149)—just as Alfonsa's "myopic coiner" is partially blinded by his trade. In Gnostic thought, metaphors of deafness and blindness are frequently used to signify an absence of gnosis, hence the demiurge is often referred to as the "blind god" or the "god of the blind" (Pearson 107).

Like McCarthy's weaver and coiner, who are determined that even chaos should be under their jurisdiction, the Gnostic demiurge was believed to exert tremendous power over the manifest cosmos by ensnaring all created things through the laws of heimarmene. Hans Jonas describes heimarmene as an "unenlightened and therefore malignant force, proceeding from the spirit of self-assertive power, from the will to rule and coerce. The mindlessness of this will is the spirit of the world, which bears no relation to understanding and love. The laws of the universe are the laws of this rule, and not of divine wisdom" (227–28). It is noteworthy that when John Grady contemplates what he calls "the pain of the world," which seeks out "human souls wherein to incubate," he comes to the realization that it is "mindless and so had no way to know the limits of those souls and what he feared was that there might be no limits" (257). John Grady's mindless "pain of the world" recalls the Gnostic concept of the mindless "spirit of the world," incapable of either love or compassion.[15]

The only way in which the Gnostics could reconcile the evil they saw in the world with the existence of a creator God was to deny that such a God could possibly contain all three of the qualities that he is credited with in the Judeo-Christian religions, namely omniscience, omnipotence, and benevolence. Logic dictates that an omniscient being would always be *aware* of evil, an omnipotent being would always be *capable* of eliminating evil, and a benevolent being would always *want* to eliminate evil; thus the creator God must be lacking one or more of these qualities. Modern theologians refer to this dilemma as the paradox or "problem of evil" (Adams and Adams 3). Some Gnostic schools, such as Iranian Gnosticism, or Manichaeism, avoided this paradox by insisting on "the dualism of two opposed principles," thus portraying the demiurge as a being devoid of benevolence. The Syrian-Egyptian, or Valentinian, Gnostics, however, attempted "the more ambitious task of deriving dualism itself" and tried to explain how the current cosmic predicament arose "from the one and undivided source of being," or, in simpler terms, how evil could have emerged from good. The latter schools favored the argument that the demiurge's faults "derive from his own ignorance" rather than his intrinsically evil nature, thereby solving the paradox of evil by eliminating omniscience as a quality of the creator God (Jonas 237). Alfonsa seems keenly aware of the paradox of evil and tells John Grady that in her youth she denied the existence of God altogether, refusing "to believe in a God who could permit such injustice as I saw in a world of his own making" (232). It is clear, however, that her views changed with time and she has come to understand that "what is constant in history is greed and foolishness and a love of blood and this is a thing that even God—who knows all that can be known—seems powerless to change" (239). Thus Alfonsa seems to be advocating the view that God is omniscient, and presumably benevolent, but seems to lack the omnipotence necessary to combat evil.

Alfonsa, however, does not speak for McCarthy himself, nor for the narrative voice in the novel, which seems to hint at the presence of a malevolent deity that does not wish to alleviate senseless suffering or prevent gratuitous evil. According to Michael Peterson, a "gratuitous evil . . . is a state of affairs that is not necessary (either logically or causally) to the attainment of a greater good or to the prevention of an evil equally bad or worse" (74). Although certain theodicies, notably Alvin Plantiga's "Free Will Defence," argue that a benevolent, omnipotent, and omniscient creator God might still allow evil to exist because "there is no way for God to create creatures capable of moral good without thereby creating creatures capable of moral evil" (Peterson 35), such theories do not account for the existence of the horrendous and seemingly unnecessary evils apparent in the natural world.[16] A memorable passage that encapsulates this problem occurs relatively early in the novel, when the boys ride past "a stand of roadside cholla against which small birds had been driven by the storm and there impaled. Gray nameless birds espaliered in attitudes of stillborn flight or hanging loosely in their feathers. Some of them were still alive and they twisted on their spines as the horses passed and raised their heads and cried out but the horsemen rode on" (73).[17] Steven Frye argues that the "scene centers on an image of death and suffering, forcing the travelers to witness the dark possibilities omnipresent always in the wilderness" (*Understanding Cormac McCarthy* 120). The disturbing image of the impaled birds illustrates not only the senselessness of natural evil but also its unsettlingly commonplace nature; after all, the horseman ride on without so much as a second glance.

Much like Alfonsa, John Grady finds that his attitude toward the God of this world changes with experience. In the early stages of their journey, Rawlins asks, "You think God looks out for people?" and John Grady replies, "Yeah. I guess He does. You?" Rawlins then goes on to make a rather naïve affirmation of his faith in such a God: "Yeah. I do. Way the world is. Somebody can wake up and sneeze somewhere in Arkansas or some damn place and before you're done there's wars and ruination and all hell. You don't know what's going to happen. I'd say He'd just about got to. I don't believe we'd make it a day otherwise" (92). This statement, though meant sincerely by Rawlins, unintentionally demonstrates the absurdity of such a belief and must be read ironically in the full context of the novel. The idea that a sneeze can lead to "wars and ruination and all hell" is reminiscent of the "Butterfly Effect," or "the effect of a very small change in the initial conditions of a system which makes a significant difference to the outcome" (Knowles 112), and actually suggests pure chaos theory rather than a universe carefully ruled by a benevolent God. Indeed, the very mindlessness and destructive nature of such an arrangement evokes the Gnostic concept of heimarmene.

Rawlins seems to be forgetting that the "way the world is" is likely to be the way God made it. More importantly, if this God was capable of creating such a dangerous and chaotic world, what evidence is there that he has any intention of "looking out for people"? John Grady seems to arrive at an understanding of this after his experience in jail. When Rawlins asks, "You ever pray?" John Grady replies, "Yeah. Sometimes. I guess I got kindly out of the habit" (214). Similarly, when the captain asks, "Are you no afraid of God?" John Grady replies, "I got no reason to be afraid of God. I've even got a bone or two to pick with Him" (272). The hardships John Grady has endured have not brought him closer to the creator of this world; rather, like the Gnostic heretics, he has begun to suspect that the entity responsible for creating such a place is not likely to answer requests to alleviate suffering.

Apart from discussing the nature of God, Alfonsa also presents John Grady with another metaphor for the forces of fate. Once again, heimarmene is hinted at through Alfonsa's description of the world as "a puppet show" in which the puppet strings "terminate in the hands of yet other puppets, themselves with their own strings which trace upward in turn, and so on." She draws attention to the sinister nature of this arrangement when she states, "In my own life I saw these strings whose origins were endless enact the deaths of great men in violence and madness. Enact the ruin of a nation" (231). The concept of endlessly entangled puppet strings suggests a cosmos in which free will cannot exist. If the actions of each entity are determined by the actions of another, and so on for all eternity, what hope does anyone have in carving out their own path? In fact, if we read *All the Pretty Horses* carefully enough, we see that John Grady's death in *Cities of the Plain* has already been predetermined. Alejandra tells John Grady, "I saw you dead in a dream," adding, "They carried you through the streets of a city I'd never seen. It was dawn. The children were praying. Lloraba tu madre. Con más razón tu puta. [Your mother was weeping. With more reason your whore]." John Grady doesn't understand the full meaning of this vision and, thinking that she is referring to herself as his whore, tells her, "Dont say that. You cant say that" (252). Of course, Alejandra is referring to Magdalena and describing John Grady's death exactly as it will occur in *Cities of the Plain*. Prophecies that come true despite warnings suggest a world ruled by heimarmene, in which human beings have no more control over their own destiny than the tangled multitude of puppets have over their movements.

During her long conversation with John Grady, Alfonsa succinctly summarizes one of the main themes of the novel, stating, "In the end we all come to be cured of our sentiments. Those whom life does not cure death will. The world is quite ruthless in selecting between the dream and the reality, even where we will not. Between the wish and the thing the world lies waiting"

(238). Her words echo lines of T. S. Eliot's "The Hollow Men," a poem that represents the disenchanted spirit of the modernist movement:

> Between the idea
> And the reality
> Between the motion
> And the act
> Falls the Shadow
> (lines 72–76)

All the Pretty Horses can also be read as a narrative of gradual disenchantment, in the light of John Grady's gradual progress "from innocence into experience" (Morrison 178), which can be viewed as life's attempts to "cure" him of his "sentiments."[18] Most of the revelations regarding the nature of the world come to John Grady during and after his experience in Saltillo prison. Back on the "outside," he struggles to make sense of what he thought he knew about the world before he set out on his journey and what he has come to learn about it after enduring various ordeals.

While most of John Grady's life lessons take place in book 3, he is too busy trying to survive to understand their significance. It is only in book 4 that John Grady finds time to contemplate the significance of what he has been through. A particularly poignant moment of contemplation occurs when he shoots a doe. The vision of the dying animal holds great symbolic resonance, reminding John Grady of the suffering for which he considers himself responsible: "He thought about the captain and he wondered if he were alive and he thought about Blevins."[19] In particular, the doe's "warm and wet" eyes remind John Grady of Alejandra and he recalls "the first time he ever saw her passing along the ciénaga road in the evening with the horse still wet from her riding it in the lake and he remembered the birds and the cattle standing in the grass and the horses on the mesa." This memory of lost paradise contrasts sharply with the landscape in which he now finds himself, in which the "dark" sky, the "cold wind," and the "dying light" evoke a terrible sense of transience and loss. John Grady watches as the "cold blue cast" of the changing light, which mirrors the slow process of death, begins to turn "the doe's eyes to but one thing more of things she lay among in that darkening landscape. Grass and blood. Blood and stone. Stone and the dark medallions that the first flat drops of rain caused upon them" (282). Death here is presented in a very ambivalent light. On the one hand, the doe seems to be returning to the earth and becoming one with the landscape, suggesting reintegration rather than mere decay. On the other hand, the fact that the doe's eyes have become a mere "thing" among "things" suggests that the spirit has left the body, leaving only an inanimate shell behind.

The doe's death serves as a reminder of impermanence and mortality, prompting John Grady to recall painful memories of Alejandra and "the sadness he'd first seen in the slopes of her shoulders which he'd presumed to understand and of which he knew nothing." The fact that John Grady realizes that he had only "presumed" to understand Alejandra's suffering suggests that he has progressed in wisdom, because he is now able to see the deficiency in his earlier view. The suffering experienced by John Grady has not only deepened his understanding of Alejandra's "sadness" but has left him feeling estranged from the world around him: "He felt a loneliness he'd not known since he was a child and he felt wholly alien to the world although he loved it still" (282). It is significant that the concept of alienation, or the "alien life," is, according to Hans Jonas, the "primary symbol of Gnosticism" (52). Jonas notes that for the Gnostics, "the word 'alien' (and its equivalents) has its own symbolic significance as an expression of an elemental human experience" (49). Simply to claim that John Grady becomes alienated, however, does not capture the full complexity of his position. Instead of rejecting the world like a seasoned Gnostic, John Grady remains in a state of tension, caught between his love of the world and his alienation from it.

Nevertheless, John Grady begins to suspect "that in the beauty of the world were hid a secret" (288). This secret is revealed in an epiphanic moment, during which John Grady comes to understand that "the world's heart beat at some terrible cost and that the world's pain and its beauty moved in relationship of diverging equity and that in this headlong deficit the blood of multitudes might ultimately be exacted for the vision of a single flower" (282). McCarthy's careful choice of words, namely "diverging" rather than "divergent," implies not only that the relationship between beauty and pain is not in balance but, more importantly, that the scales will grow more and more unbalanced with time. Thus the "headlong deficit" and the "terrible cost" will only grow larger and larger until the world reaches a point of no return. McCarthy presents us with such an outcome in *The Road*, where the scale has finally tipped completely in favor of pain, and beauty has disappeared almost entirely from the world. Though the balance between beauty and pain still remains in John Grady's heart while he watches the dying doe, the "diverging equity" pulls him toward darkness and despair, while the life-affirming force grows weaker and weaker.

The idea that the world hides a dark secret has been alluded to from the very beginning of the novel, when John Grady's father stands "looking over the country with those sunken eyes as if the world out there had been altered or made suspect by what he'd seen of it elsewhere. As if he might never see it right again. Or worse did see it right at last. See it as it had always been, would forever be" (23). These words suggest that the atrocities John Grady's father had experienced in the Goshee POW camp are not the anomalies but rather the realities of existence. John Grady's apprehension of the world becomes similarly altered by his own experiences in Saltillo prison, and the terrible truth is foreshadowed in a dream he has while recovering from the prison knife fight: "He slept and when he woke he'd dreamt of the dead standing about in their bones and the dark sockets of their eyes that were indeed without speculation bottomed in the void wherein lay a terrible intelligence common to all but of which none would speak" (205). In the dream, the dead already know the dark secret of the world and John Grady has begun to suspect what it might be.

Alfonsa articulates her own version of the dark secret when she tells John Grady about the impoverished Mexican children she saw in her youth: "They lost their childhood overnight and they had no youth. They became very serious. As if some terrible truth had been visited upon them. Some terrible vision. At a certain point in their lives they were sobered in an instant and I was puzzled by this but of course I could not know what it was that they saw. What it was that they knew" (232). Alfonsa's own terrible experiences during the Mexican Revolution would later teach her the secret of the children's knowledge. Even a proprietor in a café, a nameless and minor character, reaffirms this dark world view when, watching a wedding taking place in the street, he says "that it was good that God kept the truths of life from the young as they were starting out or else they'd have no heart to start at all" (284). The proprietor's words reinforce the idea that the world hides a dark secret, which one comes to understand only after undergoing much suffering.

All the Pretty Horses draws to an end in the same way that it began, with John Grady's solitary contemplation of death. We can witness the effects of his changed apprehension of the world by comparing his response to the death of his grandfather with his response to the death of a woman who has been like an "abuela," or grandmother, to him. While his grandfather's death turned John Grady into a "supplicant" to the darkness, pleading with the world to show benevolence, his reaction to his abuela's death is quite different. As he stands over the abuela's grave, he feels that the world "seemed to care nothing for the old or the young or rich or dark or pale or he and she. Nothing for their struggles, nothing for their names. Nothing for the living or the dead" (301).[20] John Grady no longer expects the world to be fair, kind, or merciful, having learned that the "mindless" spirit of the world is indifferent to human suffering.

Blood imagery also links the ending with the early pages of the novel, in which John Grady first rides out into a "bloodred" sunset and encounters the ghosts of the Comanches. The presence of something numinous and sacred is depicted in the final paragraph of the novel through vivid descriptions of the landscape: "The desert he rode was red and red the dust he raised.... In the evening a wind came up and reddened all the sky before him.... The bloodred dust blew down out of the sun.... He rode with the sun coppering his face and the red wind blowing out of the west." Blood serves not only as a reminder of the violent and painful nature of the world but also of the interconnectedness and vitality of all living things. John Grady is presented with a powerful vision of "a solitary bull rolling in the dust against the bloodred sunset like an animal in sacrificial torment" (302). On one level, this arresting image serves as a reminder that the potential for bloodshed, violence, and suffering is an ever-present condition of existence and that "nature is as incomprehensibly appalling as it is lovely and bountiful" (Huxley 190). The "small desert birds" that fly "chittering among the dry bracken" (302) reinforce this idea by evoking the earlier image of these small birds painfully impaled on cactus spines.

The concept of sacrifice, however, also suggests a reverence for the sacred and a surrendering of the material to the transcendent. While the "First Noble Truth" of the Buddha teaches that "the totality of human life in its usual condition is steeped in suffering" (H. Smith, *Religions of Man* 113), the interiorization of this teaching is also the first step toward enlightenment. Suffering can either lead to despair or teach one to face existence with equanimity and compassion for all suffering things. These two approaches to suffering are rather paradoxically voiced by Alfonsa, who at first rather cynically tells John Grady, "It is not my experience that life's difficulties make people more charitable." He replies, "I guess it depends on the people" (229), suggesting that the truth might be otherwise. Later, however, Alfonsa recalls the words of the revolutionary Gustavo, who told her that "the closest bonds we will ever know are bonds of grief. The deepest community one of sorrow" (238). The very idea that all living things suffer can lead to a deep sense of interconnectedness and a realization that to be alive is to participate in a "community of sorrow."

John Grady encounters this profound sense of interconnectedness through his relationship with horses. When he is shot in the leg earlier in the novel, he experiences a similar sense of communion with Blevins's horse: "He found he was breathing in rhythm with the horse as if some part of the horse were within him breathing and then he descended into some deeper collusion for which he had not even a name" (266). The final passage reaffirms the redemptive quality of such unity. The novel ends with the words "and the horse and rider and horse passed on and their long shadows passed in tandem like the shadow of a single being. Passed and paled into the darkening land, the world to come" (302). On the one hand, this image evokes a terrible sense of loss, much like the image of the ghostly Comanches at the beginning of the novel. In fact, Edwin Arnold argues, "since John Grady is moving toward death (and also toward legend) throughout the trilogy, this is an apt and appropriate conclusion" ("Go to Sleep" 50). On the other hand, the image of the horse and rider moving like "a single being" also evokes a profound sense of communion. Thus the novel's ending evokes a Wordsworthian

> sense sublime
> Of something far more deeply interfused
> Whose dwelling is the light of setting suns.
> ....
> A motion and a spirit, that impels
> All thinking things, all objects of all thought,
> And rolls through all things.
> ("Tintern Abbey," lines 95–97, 100–103)

The sacred and redemptive communion between horse and rider somewhat mitigates the sense of transience and loss simultaneously evoked by the ending.

Throughout the novel, horses have represented a life-affirming principle that keeps John Grady from falling into nihilistic despair, despite his initiation into the dark secret of the world. Evelyn Underhill writes that the "horrors of nihilism . . . can only be escaped . . . by a trust in man's innate but strictly irrational instinct for that Real 'above all reason, beyond all thought' towards which at its best moments his spirit tends" (15). Timothy P. Caron argues that for John Grady "the horse embodies all that is good and noble within this world" and that "even in a world as coldly cruel as the one that John Grady Cole inhabits, he does find some transcendence, some hope for something pure and uncompromised and beautiful" (164, 166). In Buddhist terms, horses provide John Grady with temporary release from the illusion of the separate, isolated ego; or, as Huston Smith explains, "When we are selfless we are free" (*Religions of Man* 114). William James argues that a feeling of unity is central to the religious experience. After discussing various case studies, James concludes that "the only thing" that the variety of religious experience "unequivocally testifies to is that we can experience union with *something* larger than ourselves and in that union find our greatest peace" (380). Thus when John Grady's being merges with that of the horse, they are both freed from the pain of solitary existence.

The ending also sheds light on a mysterious passage evoked early in the novel when the boys first set out for their journey: "They heard somewhere in that tenantless night a bell that tolled and ceased where no bell was" (30). Although these words initially appear rather strange, when read in light of the novel's ending they seem to be a clear allusion to John Donne's famous sermon: "No man is an island entire of itself; every man is a piece of the continent, a part of the main. . . . Any man's death diminishes me, because I am involved in mankind. And therefore never send to know for whom the bell tolls; it tolls for thee" (243). It is precisely through such knowledge that one may finally arrive at an apprehension of what Gustavo called the "community . . . of sorrow" (238). The fact that the narrative thwarts the happy ending one would normally expect from a romantic quest serves to enhance John Grady's understanding of the world. Mark Busby argues that "each McCarthy novel takes a representative young boy's initiatory experience through a border crossing and turns the experience upside down so that the expected initiation is thwarted and seemingly denied. But ironically, it is through the denied experience that a young man is initiated into a more profound understanding than the expected initiation could have offered" ("Into the Darkening Land" 231). It is this newfound wisdom, rather than a traditional happily-ever-after scenario, that serves as the hero's prize. Thus the tolling of the symbolic bell at the beginning of the novel foreshadows not only John Grady's forthcoming initiation into the darkness of a world permeated by death but also his realization that a profound interconnectedness runs through all living things. Despite the fact that John Grady comes to learn the terrible secret of the world, he does not succumb to nihilistic despair, and the novel ends with a sense that there exists some sacred, redemptive quality that stands against the overbearing darkness.

CHAPTER **6**

"All Was Fear and Marvel"

Positive and Negative Epiphanies in *The Crossing*, Book 1

■ Replete with spiritual and philosophical insights, *The Crossing* is divided into four books, each of which contains a cryptic parable. These parables, composed of enigmatic warnings and lessons, are narrated by four mysterious anchorites: a dying man, an ex-priest, a blind man, and a gypsy. The first of these anchorites, the dying Don Arnulfo, teaches the young protagonist, Billy Parham, about the impossibility of truly knowing something through a study of its outward form and hints at a different, more spiritual way of knowing. The first book is dominated not only by Don Arnulfo's lesson but also by the potent symbol of the wolf, a totem animal that initiates Billy into an apprehension of the sacred interconnectedness between all living things. In the first book of *The Crossing*, the wolf serves the same narrative function as the horse in *All the Pretty Horses*; both animals represent a numinous quality that may be ascertained only through a direct spiritual experience, or an epiphany. The wolf and all that it represents within the novel also serves to reinforce the lesson taught by Don Arnulfo.

The symbolic significance of the wolf is evoked in the very first page of the novel when Billy wakes in the middle of the night "to hear wolves in the low hills to the west of the house" (1). Drawn from his bed, he steps outside to witness a haunting, epiphanic vision of the wolves: "Running on the plain harrying the antelope and the antelope moved like phantoms in the snow and circled and wheeled and the dry powder blew about them in the cold moonlight and their breath smoked palely in the cold as if they burned with some inner fire and the wolves twisted and turned and leapt in a silence such that they seemed of another world entire" (4). The whole passage is imbued with esoteric significance; the antelope burn with an "inner fire" reminiscent of the spark of the divine, which, according to Manichean doctrines is also "bound up in plant and animal life" (Pearson 303). The wolves, possessing a transcendent quality, appear as though they belong to "another world" or some sacred realm, wholly removed from the mundane and workaday. Later in the novel, Billy will again experience this proximity to the sacred, mesmerized by a she-wolf's eyes that burn "like gatelamps to another world. A world burning on the shore of an unknowable void" (74). Billy watches "seven" wolves—their very number is mythologically resonant[1]—pass "within twenty feet of where he lay. . . . They stood with their ears cocked. . . . They were looking at him. He did not breathe. They did not breathe. They stood. They turned and quietly trotted on" (4–5). Here Billy's affinity with the wolves is established by the mutual acceptance and silent acknowledgement of each other's presence: "He could feel the presence of their knowing that was electric in the air" (4). McCarthy's description of the wolf pack is imbued with a numinous quality that cannot be explained by a mere literal, realistic interpretation of the experience. Similarly, Billy cannot relate such an experience to anyone else: "He never told anybody" (5), though whether this is due to a failure of language or a desire to keep the vision a secret is not clear.

Apart from an introduction to the sacred nature of the wolf, the opening pages of *The Crossing* are also concerned with darker, though no less sacred, aspects of existence. René Girard argues that the term "sacred" "encompasses the maleficent as well as the beneficent" phenomena, explaining that the Latin *sacer* is "sometimes translated 'sacred,' sometimes 'accursed'" (257). Thus the narrative voice within *The Crossing* also reveals negative epiphanies in which the dual threats of evil and disaster are ominously foreshadowed, as in the following passage: "The darkness that passed over them came in a sudden breath of cold and stillness and passed on. As if the darkness had a soul itself that was the sun's assassin hurrying to the west as once men did believe, as they may believe again" (73). These words suggest that the world is heading toward cyclical destruction, so that human beings will once again come to believe in the myths of their ancestors.[2] Furthermore, the darkness—an ancient symbol of evil and ignorance—behaves as an entity, evoking the palpable presence of something sentient and maleficent.

In McCarthy's novels heavenly bodies possess an ambivalent nature, sometimes representing the light of spiritual wisdom and at other times evoking a Gnostic horror of the enormity and tyranny of the universe. The descent of night is frequently associated with evil and foreboding and, in the following passage from *The Crossing*, even the moonlight carries sinister connotations: "The light of the unrisen moon lying in a sulphur haze over the valley to the east. He watched while the light ran out along the edges of the desert prairie and the dome of the moon rose out of the ground white and fat and membranous" (9).[3] McCarthy's depictions of planets, stars, and moons often recall the Gnostic belief that these heavenly bodies are the tyrannical "'gods of corruption' who enslave mankind and expose them to the unavoidable becoming and passing away" (Rudolph 86). References to the creation of the world within *The Crossing* reinforce the Gnostic world view that creation is "not an event planned in the scheme of Life but a violence done to it and to the divine order" (Jonas 64). Illuminated by the sun, the mountains look as though they were "new born out of the hand of some improvident god who'd perhaps not even puzzled out a use for them" (31). McCarthy's "improvident god," who creates mountains without reason or foresight, suggests the "blind and arrogant" demiurge, who creates the world in "fault and ignorance" (Jonas xxxi).

Further negative epiphanies are revealed through disturbing and nightmarish dreams. Billy's younger brother, Boyd, describes a recurring dream vision of an apocalyptic event: "There was a big fire out on the dry lake. . . . These people were burnin. The lake was on fire and they was burnin up" (35). Boyd also describes his terrible sense of foreboding: "I had this feelin that somethin bad was goin to happen" (36). This dream vision evokes the Buddhist "Fire Sermon," in which "the whole living world" appears to the Buddha "like a house on fire, blazing with the flames of death, disease, and old age" (Conze, *Buddhist Scriptures* 106). Various Buddhist sutras describe how the Buddha "sees beings inflamed by the fire of birth . . . cooked, scorched, and tormented by it; and he sees how they have to endure many kinds of suffering" (Conze, *Buddhist Scriptures* 208). Thus, from the Buddhist perspective, Boyd's dream might be a symbolic vision of the way things actually are, rather than a prescient vision of things to come.[4]

Billy also experiences darkly epiphanic dreams dominated by a sense of foreboding and failure: "In the dream a messenger had come in off the plains from the south with something writ upon a ledgerscrap but he could not read it. He looked at the messenger but that face was obscured in shadow and featureless and he knew that the messenger was messenger alone and could tell him nothing of the news he bore" (83). The "ledgerscrap" carried by the messenger is reminiscent of a fragment of the Akashic records, "a theosophical concept referring to the archiving of all world events and personal experiences—of all the thoughts and deeds that have ever taken [and will take] place on Earth." These records "may be 'read' only when the reader is in a special altered state of consciousness," and it is supposed to be "possible to tap the akashic records during dreams" (Lewis 23). In the dream, Billy is not able to read the akashic letters and thus cannot know what fate awaits him.[5]

The darker aspects of existence are further emphasized by a negative evaluation of human nature. The wolf "dreams of man and has so dreamt in running dreams a hundred thousand years or more. Dreams of that malignant lesser god come pale and naked and alien to slaughter all his clan and kind and rout them from their house" (17). The idea that the wolf might dream of human beings suggests that the image of "man" has the same darkly symbolic status in the wolf's imagination as the wolf has always had in our myths and legends. This new perspective extends a Gnostic mistrust of the demiurgic "malignant lesser god," applying humanity's fear of God to the wolf's fear of humanity.[6] The horrors unleashed by human beings are captured in the pathetic fallacy of the description of the wolf traps, which "lay all undisturbed beneath the snow with their jaws agape like steel trolls silent and mindless and blind" (36). The fact that human beings invent such torturous instruments in order to subjugate their fellow creatures suggests that the wolves are correct in their perception of humanity's destructive nature.[7]

When Billy's father sets the wolf traps, he looks like "a man bent at fixing himself someway in the world. Bent on trying by arc or chord the space between his being and the world that was. If there be such a space. If it be knowable" (22). In *The Crossing*, the human being is depicted as a creature that wishes to set itself apart from the rest of creation. Billy's father tries to establish his own space, much like the heretic depicted later in the novel who wishes to "assess boundaries and metes. See that lines were drawn and respected" (151). According to Buddhist thought, the desire to create "such a space" stems from a mistaken belief in the existence of an individual ego. Edward Conze explains that the "fact of individuality disappears with the belief in it, since it is no more than a gratuitous imagination" and when this false belief "ceases to exist, the result is Nirvana—the goal of Buddhism" (*Buddhism* 14). If there is no separate self, then there can be no such "space between"; thus the father's attempts at "fixing himself . . . in the world" are, from a Buddhist perspective, ultimately futile.

These various dreams, epiphanies, and visions, whether numinous or sinister, are later framed by Don Arnulfo's meditations on the nature of the wolf and of the world itself. Don Arnulfo acts as the first of *The Crossing*'s various anchorites and his advice to Billy constitutes the first parable within the novel. The woman who looks after Don Arnulfo claims that he is a *brujo*, a warlock, who "thinks he knows better than the priest . . . thinks he knows better than God" (48), a description reminiscent of the Gnostic pneumatics, who likewise believed that they knew "better" than the demiurge. In Gnostic thought, "a deep contempt" was "displayed towards the biblical God of creation and his government of the world" (Rudolph 79). The authority of the church and the hierarchy of the clergy were similarly mistrusted, as the Gnostics believed that "obedience to the clerical hierarchy requires believers to submit themselves to 'blind guides' whose authority comes from the malevolent creator" (Pagels, *Gnostic Gospels* 111). Instead, great emphasis was placed on personal, spiritual wisdom. Hans Jonas explains that the "very concept of a saving power of gnosis as such, surpassed that of mere faith" (286). Similarly, Kurt Rudolph writes that, for the Gnostics, "faith plays only a provisional role" compared with direct "knowledge" (76). Don Arnulfo's caretaker cannot comprehend a spirituality based on knowledge rather than on blind faith and, as Billy leaves the premises, she calls out after him, "La fe. . . . La fe es todo" (The faith. . . . The faith is everything) (49). Even though Don Arnulfo will later claim, "Yo ne sé nada. Esto es la verdad" (I know nothing. This is the truth) (47), his insight into his own limitations is indicative of great wisdom, because only a fool believes that he knows everything.

Steven Frye emphasizes the importance of Billy's encounter with Don Arnulfo, arguing that the old man "initiates Billy's epistemic quest, a journey during which Billy makes or discovers meaning in the events that he witnesses and receives insight into a divine order by means of the stories he hears from other witnesses" ("Cormac McCarthy's 'World in Its Making'" 52). Don Arnulfo advises Billy that "el lobo es una cosa incognoscible. . . . Lo que se tiene en la trampa no es mas que dientes y forro. El lobo propio no se puede conocer. Lobo o lo que sabe el lobo. Tan como preguntar lo que saben las piedras. Los arboles. El mundo." (The wolf is an unknowable thing, that which one has in the trap is no more than teeth and fur. One cannot know the true wolf. Wolf or what the wolf knows. It's like asking what the stones know. The trees. The world.) (45). Don Arnulfo displays a Gnostic mistrust of corporeality, arguing that outward forms—or what he refers to as "teeth and fur"—do not constitute the true essence of the wolf.[8] He extends this argument to include the world itself, which he believes is an "unknowable thing," at least in the sense that it cannot be grasped through conventional reason. He goes on to tell Billy that the "wolf is like the copo de nieve," or "snowflake," explaining, "You catch the snowflake but when you look in your hand you dont have it no more. Maybe you see his dechado [design]. But before you see it it is gone. If you want to see it you have to see it on its own ground. If you catch it you lose it. And where it goes there is no coming back from. Not even God can bring it back" (46). On a literal level, Don Arnulfo is saying that the wolf can only be truly observed in its natural environment, because capturing the wolf robs it of the essential quality of its wild freedom.[9] On a more esoteric level, however, Don Arnulfo is talking about the impossibility of truly knowing something through a study of its outward form, because the very the essence of the thing—its spirit—cannot be studied, or apprehended empirically.

Don Arnulfo then goes on to talk about the impermanent and illusory nature of the manifest world and all things in it: "Escuchame joven [Listen to me, young one], the old man wheezed. If you could breathe a breath so strong you could blow out the wolf. Like you blow out the copo. Like you blow out the fire from the candela. The wolf is made the way the world is made. You cannot touch the world. You cannot hold it in your hand for it is made of breath only" (46). These words recall the Buddhist sutras, which teach that the "things of this samsaric world are all illusion, like a dream," like "mists on a lake, clouds across a southern sky, spray blown by wind above sea." "Where'er one looks, where is their substance?" the sutras ask, advising one to "meditate on their illusion" and not to "seize on them as truth" (qtd. in Conze, *Buddhist Scriptures* 91–92). The advice given by Don Arnulfo resembles the advice given by the sutras, as both stress the mutability, transience, and above all, the illusory nature of all manifest things.[10] Don Arnulfo's words may also be interpreted to mean that the true reality, that which lies beyond the material realm of things that we can indeed "touch" and "hold" physically, is made of spirit; for the Greek word "pneuma" ($\pi\nu\varepsilon\tilde{\upsilon}\mu\alpha$) means both "wind and breath," as well as "spirit, soul, or life force" (*OED*).

When Billy asks how he is to catch the wolf given these circumstances, Don Arnulfo tells him that he "should find that place where acts of God and those of man are of a piece. Where they cannot be distinguished" (47). In the words of Meister Eckhart, this is a place, or state, where "God and I are one in process" (*Works* 132). In such a state, there is no longer any distinction between the self and the Absolute. In Hindu terms, as explained by Śaṅkara, "Brahman [Absolute] is real, the world is illusory; and the individual soul is Brahman itself and no other" (qtd. in Bishop 286). According to this view, nothing stands outside the nonduality of the Absolute and to realize that one is the Absolute is to realize that everything is One. In other words, Don Arnulfo is telling Billy to become one with the wolf, so that there is no longer any sense of separation between subject and object, the self and the other. When Billy asks where he can find such a place, Don Arnulfo explains "that it was not a question of finding such a place but rather of knowing it when it presented itself" (47).[11] These words suggest that this place cannot be found via a spatial journey but can only be arrived at through the cultivation of spiritual insight.

Don Arnulfo then tells Billy that the wolf understands sacred rites more clearly than most human beings ever can: "He said that men believe the blood of the slain to be of no consequence but that the wolf knows better. He said that the wolf is a being of great order and that it knows what men do not: that there is no order in the world save that which death has put there." According to Don Arnulfo, human beings try to superimpose their own order on the universe, indulging in fantasies of control and personal agency, forgetting that death always has the final say. He adds that "men drink the blood of God yet they do not understand the seriousness of what they do" (45). Don Arnulfo insists that ceremonies such as the drinking of the blood of Christ during Holy Communion—which in itself carries overtones of ancient rites performed with the blood of a sacrificial victim—are utterly meaningless and empty if they are performed without a profound apprehension of what they actually represent.[12]

Don Arnulfo argues that though human beings may "wish to be serious" when they perform these blood rites and ceremonies, "they do not understand how to be so." He explains, "Between their acts and their ceremonies lies the world and in this world the storms blow and the trees twist in the wind and all the animals that God has made go to and fro yet this world men do not see. They see the acts of their own hands or they see that which they name and call out to one another but the world between them is invisible to them" (46).[13] According to Don Arnulfo, most human beings have become so alienated from spiritual reality that they can see only the "acts of their own hands" or "that which they name"; that is, they can experience reality only on a physical or mental level, remaining ignorant of the spiritual world. They cannot physically touch or rationally interiorize the divine, because it is ineffable. They mistake the symbol for the thing itself and consequently have no direct, unmediated experience of the sacred aspects of existence, as the wolf does.

Associating the inherently predatory nature of the wolf with aspects of the sacred may initially appear counterintuitive; however, the apparent contradictions disappear if we once again consider René Girard's ideas on the subject. According to Girard, the "sacred consists of all those forces whose dominance over man increases or seems to increase in proportion to man's efforts to master them" and "violence" constitutes the very "heart and soul of the sacred" (31). Like Don Arnulfo, Girard places special emphasis on the sacred quality of blood, arguing that "blood serves to illustrate the notion that the same substance can stain or cleanse, contaminate or purify, drive men to fury and murder or appease their anger and restore them to life" (37). In other words, bloodshed depends on the context in which it is spilled. While senseless conflict can "infect" the community by creating an "unlimited propagation" (30) of retributive violence, blood spilled in a sacrificial ceremony can lead to a "sacrificial catharsis," which "prevents the spread of violence by keeping vengeance in check" (18). This idea is actually articulated in book 4 of *The Crossing*, when Billy's confrontation with a drunken revolutionary leads the narrative voice to make the observation that the "ends of all ceremony are but to avert bloodshed" (359). According to the narrative voice in *The Crossing*, the wolves apprehend this sacred significance of blood through the ritual of the hunt, preferring to kill only those animals that are capable of participating in this ancient sacrament: "The wolves in that country had been killing cattle for a long time but the ignorance of the animals was a puzzle to them. The cows bellowing and bleeding and stumbling through the mountain meadows with their shovel feet and their confusion, bawling and floundering through the fences and dragging posts and wires behind. The ranchers said they brutalized the cattle in a way they did not the wild game. As if the cows evoked in them some anger. As if they were offended by some violation of an old order. Old ceremonies. Old protocols" (25).[14] The human trapper also fails to participate in the sacrament of the hunt and in the wolf's eyes is a "god insatiable whom no ceding could appease nor any measure of blood" (17). The wolves see human beings as incapable of comprehending the blood offerings meant to subdue their terrible wrath.

When Billy looks into the eyes of the she-wolf, he sees "a world burning on the shore of an unknowable void. A world construed out of blood and blood's alcahest and blood in its core and in its integument because it was that nothing save blood had power to resonate against that void which threatened hourly to devour it" (73).[15] As a hunter, the wolf understands the dual functions of blood as described by Girard; for those whose lives are immersed in bloodshed, blood is simultaneously a source of violent death and of life-giving vitality. Watching the wolf feed, Billy wonders whether "the living blood with which it slaked its throat" had "a different taste to the thick iron tincture of his own. Or to the blood of God" (52). Later he tastes the blood of the dead wolf and finds that it tastes "no different than his own" (125). Unlike the men criticized by Don Arnulfo, Billy is able to understand the "seriousness" of such a sacrament. Billy's realization is reminiscent of Ralph Waldo Emerson's proclamation that "one blood rolls uninterruptedly an endless circulation through all men, as the water of the globe is all one sea, and truly seen, its tide is one" ("Over-Soul" 74). In McCarthy's novels, the fact that the same red blood flows through all human beings and animals functions as a symbol of their essential, spiritual unity.

Billy experiences a form of communion between himself and the wolf even before he tastes her blood. Looking into her eyes, he sees "no despair but only that same reckonless deep of loneliness that cored the world to its heart" (105).[16] Billy's identification with the wolf is compounded by the overwhelming empathy and compassion he experiences after watching the wolf's noble fight to the death.[17] The revelation is conveyed through a poignant and lyrical passage, which reads like poetry in prose:

> He squatted over the wolf and touched her fur. He touched the cold and perfect teeth. The eye turned to the fire gave back no light and he closed it with his thumb and sat by her and put his hand upon her bloodied forehead and closed his own eyes that he could see her running in the mountains, running in the starlight where the grass was wet and the sun's coming as yet had not undone the rich matrix of creatures passed in the night before her. Deer and hare and dove and groundvole all richly empaneled on the air for her delight, all nations of the possible world ordained by God of which she was one among and not separate from. Where she ran the cries of the coyotes clapped shut as if a door had been closed upon them and all was fear and marvel. He took up her stiff head out of the leaves and held it or he reached to hold what cannot be held, what already ran among the

mountains at once terrible and of a great beauty, like flowers that feed on flesh. What blood and bone are made of but can themselves not make on any altar nor by any wound of war. What we may well believe has power to cut and shape and hollow out the dark form of the world surely if wind can, if rain can. But which cannot be held never be held and is no flower but is swift and a huntress and the wind itself is in terror of it and the world cannot lose it. (127)[18]

The sacred qualities of the wolf, in the Girardian sense, are again emphasized by the juxtaposition of "fear and marvel" and a "terrible...beauty" of Yeatsian proportions ("Easter, 1916," line 16). Billy's shamanic epiphany recalls Rudolf Otto's description of the experience of *das Heilige* (the Sacred), characterized by "the feeling of terror" and "religious fear before the fascinating mystery" (qtd. in Eliade 9–10). William James, whose work McCarthy cites in his interview with Gary Wallace (138), also refers to the religious experience in such terms, arguing that "it is still in these richer animistic and dramatic aspects that religion delights to dwell. It is the terror and beauty of phenomena, the 'promise' of the dawn and of the rainbow, the 'voice' of the thunder, the 'gentleness' of the summer rain, the 'sublimity' of the stars, and not the physical laws which these things follow, by which the religious mind still continues to be most impressed" (James 362). Billy's contemplation of the dead wolf triggers an exalted vision of "the rich matrix" of all living creatures, of which he too is "one among and not separate from" (127).[19] The experience again recalls the works of Ralph Waldo Emerson, who wrote, "I am nothing; I see all; the currents of the universal Being circulate through me; I am part and parcel of God" ("Nature" 311). According to Evelyn Underhill, in certain moments of outward contemplation such as that practiced by the nature mystics, an individual may be made aware of "the deep and primal life which he shares with all creation" and "the barrier between human and non-human life, which makes man a stranger on earth as well as in heaven, is done away. Life now whispers to his life: all things are his intimates, and respond to his fraternal sympathy" (260). In fact, Underhill cites the case of Saint Francis of Assisi and his "brother Wolf" (261) as an example of just such a communion, a story reminiscent of the relationship between Billy and the she-wolf.[20]

It is the spirit of the wolf that Billy tries to reach out to as he holds the dead animal, but in vain because it is that which "cannot be held never be held." It is spirit itself—the spirit that resides in all things—that inspires such "fear and marvel." Spirit has the power to "hollow out the dark form of the world" (127) because it is, according to various traditions, the divine light that shines forth from the darkness. According to the Gnostic Gospels, for example, when "the cosmos" is "deprived of [this] element of light, it will come to an end" (Jonas 46). Here we also find a turning away from the narrative voice's earlier insistence that blood can redeem and toward a realization that "what blood and bone are made of" is spirit itself and thus spirit is what they "can themselves not make on any altar nor by any wound of war" (127). In other words, the narrative voice now suggests that whether spilled in senseless violence or religious sacrifice, blood does *not* have the power to "resonate" against the "void," as previously asserted. It may be sacred—in the Girardian sense—and it may serve as a reminder of the interconnectedness of all living things, but ultimately, it has no existence without spirit, which is the ground of that sacred communion of which blood is only a symbol.

Billy's apprehension of unity is only a fleeting vision, which fades with the wolf's departing spirit, leaving Billy with a heavy burden of sorrow, loss, and guilt over the wolf's death. "Afterwards," writes Edwin Arnold, "as is often the case after such a shattering revelation, Billy finds his common existence repugnant, cold, and all too hard" ("Go to Sleep" 62). After burying the wolf, Billy wanders through a wasteland in which "there was nothing about but the wind and the silence" (134). Barcley Owens describes this as "an ascetic period of atonement" during which Billy becomes "gaunt like a supplicant monk who has taken a vow of primitivism" (89). Like a Neolithic hunter, Billy whittles "a bow from a holly limb" and "arrows from cane." Shooting down a hawk, he goes out in search of the body but finds only "a single drop of blood that had dried on the rocks and darkened in the wind and nothing more" (129). Making "a cut in the heel of his hand with his knife," Billy watches "the slow blood dropping on the stone," over the blood of the hawk (130). Dianne Luce interprets this as "a gesture that affirms his brotherhood with the predator on the altar of the world itself" ("Vanishing World" 187). Barcley Owens also sees the ritual nature of Billy's action, which he describes as "a redemptive revitalization, a divine state of madness, mutilating his body in a ritual shedding of blood, cutting his hand with a knife, re-enacting Christ's stigmata" (89). It is clear that Billy has not forgotten the wisdom imparted by Don Arnulfo and the insight gathered from his own experiences. Unlike those who "do not understand the seriousness of what they do" (45), Billy has learned to regard the blood of all creatures with due reverence, knowing that every drop he spills might as well be his own.

The death of the wolf, however, hangs over Billy like a curse and something seems to have gone awry with the very rhythms of nature. Sitting on his "horse on a promontory overlooking the Bavispe River," Billy is bewildered to find that "the river was running backwards. That or the sun was setting in the east behind him" (130).[21] Billy's withdrawal from the world of human beings is not only an attempt to find absolution for the personal guilt he feels over the death of the wolf but also a desire to distance himself from his fellow "malignant lesser god[s]" (17), whom he holds responsible for so much death and destruction. This period of solitary asceticism, however, brings no escape from the guilt and sorrow. On the contrary, the loss of the wolf leaves a permanent scar on Billy's psyche, and throughout his wanderings he moves ever closer to an anticosmic view of existence: "In that wild high country he'd lie in the cold and the dark and listen to the wind and watch the last embers of his fire at their dying and the red crazings in the woodcoals where they broke along their unguessed gridlines. As if in the trying of the wood were elicited hidden geometries and their orders which could only stand fully revealed, such is the way of the world, in darkness and ashes" (130).[22] As Billy gazes into the dying flames, he sees patterns in which the nature of the world is "fully revealed" and comes to understand that once the glittering veneer is removed, the world moves in "darkness and ashes." Such a view is shared by the Buddhist sutras, which teach that "suffering is the lot of everyone, everywhere and all the time; therefore, my friend, do not hanker after the glittering objects of this world! And, once this hankering is extinct in you, then you will clearly see that this entire world of the living can be said to be on fire" (qtd. in Conze, *Buddhist Scriptures* 111). Billy's experience opens him up to a darker view of the world, heightening his awareness of the suffering and impermanence inherent in mortal existence.

The impermanence of the world, along with the transient lives of its inhabitants, is further emphasized by Billy's contemplation of ancient pictographs depicting "men and animals and suns and moons as well as other representations that seemed to have no referent in the world although they once may have." Later, the creators of these images will appear before Billy in a dream, as flesh devouring "wild men" whose "teeth were filed to points. . . . They gathered around him and warned him of their work before they even set about it" (135).[23] Billy wakes in fright and imagines them still out there in the dark: "Chiseling in stone with stones those semblances of the living world they'd have endure and the world dead at their hands" (135–36).

Attempting to preserve an image of their world even while they destroy it with their own hands, Billy's dream figures are representative of the tragedy of the human race. Looking "out over the country to the east," Billy contemplates the land where "priests had passed and soldiers passed and the missions fallen into mud... all of it waiting like a dream for the world to come to be, world to pass" (135). The dream is a common motif in the Buddhist sutras, which compare this world to "a mass of foam, a bubble, a mirage, a dream, a magical show" (qtd. in Conze, *Buddhism* 133). According to Billy's dream vision, nothing can triumph against impermanence; whether men of God or men of war, everyone and everything eventually vanishes into the "mud" of the earth.

Billy's period of lonely wandering culminates in a strange encounter with a shaman, who seems preternaturally aware of the darkness inherent in the young boy's outlook. The shaman refers to the boy as a "huérfano" (orphan). Billy protests against this title, but the shaman insists, "Eres, he said. Eres huérfano." (You are. . . . You are an orphan.) (134). The authenticity of the shaman's insight is confirmed by the fact that he knows that Billy's parents have been killed, though Billy does not yet consciously know it himself. Not long before this encounter, however, Billy has had a disturbing dream that, unbeknownst to him, announced his father's death. In the dream, the father is "lost in the desert"; in "the dying light of the day" he stands "looking toward the west where the sun had gone and where the wind was rising out of the darkness" (112). The dream is full of foreboding, for the lost man, the setting sun, the western cardinal point, and the approaching darkness are all ancient omens and symbols of death.

The landscape is similarly charged with meaning: "The small sands in that waste was all there was for the wind to move and it moved with a constant migratory seething upon itself. As if in its ultimate granulation the world sought some stay against its own eternal wheeling," as though the world itself were desperately seeking a state of permanence or respite from the endless cycles of creation and destruction. Billy sees that his father's eyes contemplate "the cold and the dark and the silence" with "a terrible equanimity" (112), recalling John Grady's father in *All the Pretty Horses*, who looks out over the country "as if he might never see it right again. Or worse did see it right at last. See it as it had always been, would forever be" (23). Both fathers, though one belongs to a dream and the other to waking life, seem to arrive at a final apprehension of the world as a place of darkness, impermanence, and suffering. According to Buddhist thought, "This world, i.e. everything conditioned and impermanent, is emphatically regarded as wholly ill, as wholly pervaded with suffering" (Conze, *Buddhism* 21). Billy's dream ends as all is "swallowed up" in the darkness and "in the silence he heard somewhere a solitary bell that tolled and ceased and then he woke" (112). The bell, of course, tolls for his father, but also for himself. Similarly, in *All the Pretty Horses*, John Grady also hears "somewhere in that tenantless night a bell that tolled and ceased where no bell was" (30). These nonexistent bells draw the reader's mind to John Donne's famous sermon that states, "Never send to know for whom the bell tolls; it tolls for thee" (243), and serve as reminders of mortality, but also unity.

The shaman reinforces the dream's message, not only confirming the father's death but warning Billy against the growing sense of alienation that has cut him off from other human beings. He tells Billy to "cease his wanderings and make for himself some place in the world because to wander in this way would become for him a passion and by this passion he would become estranged from men and so ultimately from himself." The shaman tries to teach Billy that to possess insight into living beings is to possess insight into the world itself, explaining that "the world could only be known as it existed in men's hearts. For while it seemed a place which contained men it was in reality a place contained within them and therefore to know it one must look there and come to know those hearts and to do this one must live with men and not simply pass among them" (134). The shaman seems to be expounding a variation of the "Mind-only" teachings of Yogacara Buddhism, according to which the "external world is really Mind-itself" and "the basis of all illusions consists in that we regard the objectifications of our own mind as a world independent of that mind, which is really its source and substance." The Yogacarins argue that "the root of all evil must lie in our proclivity to see anything as separated from, or as external to, that inmost self, in the way of an object. In reality all things and thoughts are but *Mind-only*" (Conze, *Buddhism* 167–68). In Buddhist terms, the manifest world is māyā, because it exists only in the imperfect perception of the sentient beings still trapped in samsaric existence; for enlightened beings, only Nirvāṇa, or the Absolute, is real.

The shaman urges Billy to develop a more compassionate approach to his fellow human beings, insisting that "while the huérfano might feel that he no longer belonged among men he must set this feeling aside for he contained within him a largeness of spirit which men could see and that men would wish to know him and that the world would need him even as he needed the world for they were one" (134). The shaman tries to teach Billy that although he may feel alienated from others, he must not forget that he is connected to them. The Buddhists—especially those of the Mahayana—also put great emphasis on the necessity of treating all living things with limitless compassion. Buddhist teachings encourage one to exercise compassion daily, and the "essential purpose of these exercises consists in reducing the boundary lines between oneself and other people" (Conze, *Buddhism* 102). The shaman insists that Billy must not withdraw from others, because all humanity is essentially one.

Before Billy takes his leave, the shaman imparts a final piece of wisdom regarding the fact that Billy would be needed by the world: "Lastly he said that while this itself was a good thing like all good things it was also a danger" (134). The danger lies in the fact that an active involvement in the world may leave one mired in material concerns and stunt one's spiritual development, which is one of the reasons that monks and nuns in various traditions withdraw themselves from ordinary society. On the other hand, withdrawal from the world may result in alienation, leaving one feeling disconnected from the fundamental unity of all things. Aldous Huxley describes "the path of spirituality" as "a knife-edge between abysses. On one side is the danger of mere rejection and escape, on the other side the danger of mere acceptance and enjoyment of things which should only be used as instruments or symbols" (72). The Buddhist scriptures warn of similar dangers:

> He who clings to the Void
> And neglects Compassion,
> Does not reach the highest stage.
> But he who practices only Compassion
> Does not gain release from toils of existence.
> He, however, who is strong in practice of both,
> Remains neither in Samsara nor in Nirvana.
> (qtd. in Conze, *Buddhist Scriptures* 179)

In other words, those capable of cultivating both wisdom and compassion will become Bodhisattvas, no longer immersed in samsaric existence but refusing to enter Nirvāṇa until all other beings have achieved enlightenment. According to Edward Conze, the "Bodhisattva would be a man who does not only set himself free, but who is also skilful in devising means for bringing out and maturing the latent seeds of enlightenment in others"

(*Buddhism* 129). Sensing what the Buddhists call Bodhicitta—or the desire to develop spiritually in order to help sentient beings—in Billy's "largeness of spirit," the shaman warns him against the dangers of wandering too close to the twin abysses of selfish wisdom and ignorant compassion.

The shaman argues that the world needs those with spiritual insight and that such people should not withdraw entirely from the world; however, they must also be careful not to succumb to the world's deceptive pleasures, distractions, and manifold illusions. His words confirm Don Arnulfo's earlier intimations regarding the illusory nature of the manifest world, revealing that what we perceive as external reality is really a state of mind, contained entirely within us. Although the shaman hints, in his own words, that all is māyā, his vision of the world is grounded in a profound sense of union. He tries to remind Billy that despite the illusory nature of the external world, there exists a fundamental unity that pervades all living things. Thus the shaman's words reinforce the theme of spiritual unity and the essential oneness between all living things, which Billy experienced upon touching the dead wolf, while simultaneously warning of the dangers faced by those who venture out on a spiritual path.

CHAPTER 7

"The Illusion of Proximity"

Transcendence and Immanence in *The Crossing*, Book 2

■ While *The Crossing* is the heart of the Border Trilogy, the tale told by the ex-priest is the heart of *The Crossing*. Replete with esoteric insight, the ex-priest's narrative explores not only the nature of God, humanity, and the world but also the complex interrelationship between these concepts. Precisely because all of McCarthy's fiction is, to a lesser or greater extent, preoccupied with such theological and metaphysical questions, the ex-priest's tale may serve as a kind of Rosetta Stone, decoding some of the novelist's more enigmatic metaphysics. Though numerous critics have commented on the ex-priest's story, most focus on the importance of storytelling itself and only a few venture into theological concerns.[1] Foremost among the latter is Edwin Arnold, who outlines the influences of Jacob Boehme on the novel as a whole. Arnold argues, "The essence of the priest's tale is that man cannot reason with God, cannot require balance or justice or even understanding" and must come to the realization that God is "all-encompassing" ("McCarthy and the Sacred" 225). While I agree with Arnold's claim that the ex-priest comes to apprehend the all-encompassing nature of the divine, I believe that the ex-priest's tale presents two different kinds of God, namely, a lower-order creator of the cosmos and an ineffable Absolute. Hence the ex-priest's tale may be illuminated by Gnostic teachings, which maintain such a distinction between the demiurgical creator and the transcendent alien God.

The ex-priest begins the tale by recounting his unsuccessful attempt to reconcile his Christian faith in the biblical God with the apparent senselessness of natural disasters and the suffering and destruction they leave in their wake. Recalling the days before his apostasy, the ex-priest describes how he had originally sought to find a theologically and theistically satisfying explanation for the problematic existence of natural evil. In his early days, the priest tried to intuit the reasons behind God's "miracles of destruction" (142), such as the earthquake that devastated the town and in particular the church of Huisiachepic. Wishing to maintain his belief in the omnipotence and benevolence of the biblical God, the young priest believed that such natural evils must be the will of God as punishments for the moral evils of human beings. Otherwise, if natural disasters were out of God's control, he would not possess full omnipotence, and if the suffering they inflicted was undeserved, God could not be called benevolent.

The ex-priest explains that in his youth, he was "seeking evidence for the hand of God in the world," having "come to believe that hand a wrathful one." When the Bible speaks of the wrath of God, it insists that such wrath is not capricious cruelty but simply deserved punishment. In light of such claims, the young priest could not bring himself to believe that God "would destroy his own church without reason." Searching the rubble, he tried to find "evidence of something suitably unspeakable such that He might be goaded into raising his hand against it. Something in the rubble. In the dirt. Under the vigas. Something dark." But he found "nothing" except the humble remains of the innocent dead: "A doll. A dish. A bone" (142). In fact, the earthquake left behind only "a great crack in the mountain wall across the river like an enormous laugh" (145), as though something were mocking the young priest's faith in the goodness of God.

The ex-priest then tells Billy that he had been wrong to search for a material "thing" among the rubble: "What was here to be found was not a thing. Things separate from their stories have no meaning. They are only shapes. . . . When their meaning has become lost to us they no longer have even a name." In other words, the ex-priest now understands that spiritual insight cannot be arrived at through a preoccupation with the material objects of this world. Instead, he puts forward the idea that meaning lies in the stories we tell about the world or the myths and parables we have devised to explain the nature of existence: "The story on the other hand can never be lost from its place in the world for it is that place" (143). The story here seems to suggest something like the Jungian archetypes, which cannot be lost because they emerge out of the collective unconscious of the human psyche and tend to reappear time and time again in different cultures, different times, and different forms. According to Carl Gustav Jung (1875–1961), these "collective representations" emanate "from primeval dreams and creative fantasies" and the "archetype is a tendency to form such representations as a motif—representations that can vary a great deal in detail without losing their basic pattern" (*Man and His Symbols* 55, 67). The same explanation also applies to the ex-priest's insistence that all stories are "one story only, for there is only one to tell" (143). These words hint at the concept of an essential unity underlying human existence.

The ex-priest then expounds the theory that the manifest world is ultimately illusory, for "this world also which seems to us a thing of stone and flower and blood is not a thing at all but is a tale. And all in it is a tale and each tale the sum of all lesser tales and yet these also are the selfsame tale and contain as well all else within them" (143). The ex-priest's vision of the manifest world as a tale conforms to the Hindu and Buddhist doctrine that saṃsāra is made up of māyā. Edward Conze explains that "the enormous quantity of matter that we perceive around us, compared with the trembling little flicker of spiritual insight that we perceive within us, seems to tell strongly in favour of a materialistic outlook in life. But if we look more closely, then we discover that there is no bulk of matter at all, but only thoughts and words. . . . These material things have their roots in our own minds, and it is there that they can be uprooted" (*Buddhist Wisdom Books* 65). The Buddhist idea that the material world is rooted in our own minds corresponds to the ex-priest's idea that consensus reality is a tale that we tell ourselves and each other.

The concept of essential unity, which runs throughout the Border Trilogy, is emphasized in the ex-priest's insistence that "whether in Caborca or in Huisiachepic or in whatever other place by whatever other name or by no name at all I say again all tales are one" (143). This idea has been put forward by Ralph Waldo Emerson in his 1836 essay "Nature," where he argues, "So intimate is this Unity, that it is easily seen, it lies under the undermost garment of Nature, and betrays its source in Universal Spirit" (320). Francis Elamanamadathil interprets this passage as meaning that "the multiplicity of the world is based on one spirit" (22). Such intuitions into the essential unity of apparent multiplicity seem to underlie the ex-priest's repeated insistence that all tales, "rightly heard," are one (143).

The ex-priest then introduces a tale within a tale, describing the life of a man who gradually became a heretic and whose desperate desire to come to terms with his own understanding of God had a profound impact on the ex-priest's own spiritual development. This man suffered the loss of his son in another earthquake, much like the one that first shook the young priest's faith. This senseless death impelled the man to see the world as a much darker place; the ex-priest describes the man's new perspective in markedly Buddhist-Gnostic terms: "Such a man is like a dreamer who wakes from a dream of grief to a greater sorrow yet" (146).[2] Both Buddhist and Gnostic texts often use the metaphor of waking from a dream to describe the attainment of enlightenment or gnosis, respectively. According to Edward Conze, the Buddha "is one who is awake all the time, and in Sanskrit the root BUDH denotes both *to wake up* and *to know*" (*Buddhism* 139). Similarly, according to Gnostic thought, the human being "is not only imprisoned but is 'asleep'" and "only a 'call' from outside can 'awaken' him . . . i.e. drive out his ignorance" (Rudolph 119). These traditions insist that because the manifest world is only an illusion, the reality we take for granted is like a dream and we continually delude ourselves about the true nature of existence.

The man wakes to "a greater sorrow" because he has inadvertently come to realize something akin to the "First Noble Truth" of the Buddha, namely that existence is suffering, or duḥkha. According to Huston Smith, duḥkha is the "pain that seeps at some level into all finite existence. The word's most constructive overtones suggest themselves when we discover that it is used in Pali to refer to an axle which is off-center with respect to its wheel, also to a bone which has slipped out of socket" (*Religions of Man* 111). This definition of duḥkha is consistent with the ex-priest's claim that, for the man in his tale, the "pin has been pulled from the axis of the universe" (146). In both cases, the imagery of dislocation suggests that there is something fundamentally awry with the cosmos.

The man finds that "all that he loves is now become a torment to him" (146) because he has come to understand the impermanence of all created things. The transience of existence is emphasized by the ex-priest's response to Billy's claim that he is "just passin through": "Myself also . . . I am the same" (141). Later the ex-priest reminds Billy, "Life is a memory, then it is nothing" (145). According to the Buddhist sutras, "impermanence" is one of the three "marks" or features of saṃsāra and one of the causes of suffering. Buddhism teaches that "all conditioned things are marred by having three 'marks,' i.e. by being impermanent, 'ill' and 'alien to our true self'" (Conze, *Thirty Years* 210). During his quest to achieve enlightenment, the Gautama Buddha said, "When I consider the impermanence of everything in this world, then I can find no delight in it" (qtd. in Conze, *Buddhist Scriptures* 40). The Buddhists believe that the attainment of Nirvāṇa consists of "the extinction of all desire" (Conze, *Selected Sayings* 18) and only then are we free from "the torment" that the man in the ex-priest's tale feels at the thought of having to lose all that he loves.

McCarthy's newly awakened man does not know where to turn for spiritual guidance; the church he once believed in lies both literally and metaphorically "in pieces on the ground" and he feels that "in the darkened chancel within him" the "ground" of his faith has "also shifted, also cracked ... was also a ruin." Thus, he becomes "a heretic" (147) and his heresy takes on Gnostic overtones. The ex-priest explains, "It was never that this man ceased to believe in God. No. It was rather that he came to believe terrible things of Him" (148). In other words, the heretic does not lose his faith in the biblical God; rather, he comes to see him as a malevolent entity. Like the heretic, the Gnostics never ceased to believe in the biblical creator. Instead, they too came to believe terrible things of him, portraying him "as a lower and hostile being" and referring to him as the "accursed God" (Rudolph 139).

The ex-priest explains that "naught save sorrow could bring a man to such a view of things." For the Gnostics and Buddhists, sorrow, or the interiorization of the idea that existence is deeply undesirable, has the power to bring an individual to a new "view of things." From the vantage point of this new perspective, the heretic sees that the "very ground under his feet is composted with the blood of the ancients" (148). This is also a view expressed by the cultural anthropologist and existentialist Ernest Becker: "Creation is a nightmare spectacular taking place on a planet that has been soaked for hundreds of millions of years in the blood of its creatures. The soberest conclusion that we could make about what has actually been taking place on the planet for about three billion years is that it is being turned into a vast pit of fertilizer" (282–83). The French poet, playwright, and novelist Alfred de Vigny (1797–1863) evokes the same vision of the world in his poem, "La maison du berger." "Notre sang dans son onde et nos morts sous son herbe / Nourrissant de leurs sucs la racine des bois" (Our blood in her waves and our dead beneath her grass / Nourishing with their juices the root of the woods). The heretic becomes increasingly convinced that existence is permeated with suffering and finds himself plagued by the awareness that death senselessly consumes generation after generation.

No longer able to trust in the goodness of the biblical God, the heretic begins to apprehend a sinister force at work in the world. He sees "that every act soon eluded the grasp of its propagator to be swept away in a clamorous tide of unforeseen consequence. He believed that in the world was another agenda, another order, and with this power lay whatever brief he may have held" (147). As the heretic watches passers-by in the street, he becomes "convinced that those aims and purposes with which they imagine their movements to be invested are in reality but a means by which to describe them. He believes that their movements are the subject of larger movements in patterns unknown to them, and these in turn to others." The ex-priest tells Billy that the heretic "finds no comfort in these speculations I can tell you" (148). As in *Blood Meridian*, references to these patterns of "another order" evoke the Gnostic concept of heimarmene, which binds the paths of all of things, including the lives of human beings and the orbits of the heavenly bodies. Hans Jonas writes, "In its physical aspect this rule is the law of nature; in its psychical aspect, which includes for instance the institution and enforcements of the Mosaic Law, it aims at the enslavement of man" (44). The heretic begins to believe that the concepts of free will and agency are illusory and that human beings are really the helpless puppets of the sinister, unforeseeable forces of the universe, as ruled by a malevolent, vengeful demiurge.

The ex-priest reveals that "in his heart this man had already begun to plot against God but he did not know it yet. He would not know it until he began to dream of Him" (148). Highly charged with symbolic meaning, the heretic's troubling dreams offer a glimpse of the world artificer at work: "In his dreams God was much occupied. Spoken to He did not answer. Called to did not hear. The man could see Him bent at his work.... Weaving the world. In his hands it flowed out of nothing and in his hands it vanished into nothing again. Endlessly. Endlessly." The motifs of the heretic's dream appear to be overtly Gnostic; the demiurgical weaver is concerned chiefly with the endless construction and destruction of the cosmos and totally indifferent to the pleas and calls of a suffering man.[3] The weaver god is sinister, obsessed with the task of controlling his creation, and ultimately "a slave to his own selfordinated duties" and thus not truly omnipotent, or truly Absolute. Obsessed with control, he utilizes the powers of heimarmene and possesses "a fathomless capacity to bend all to an inscrutable purpose."[4] The heretic sees that he is a mere thread in the terrible scheme of things and that "somewhere in that tapestry that was the world in its making and in its unmaking was a thread that was he." Realizing that he is only a tiny, powerless cog trapped in a vast, inscrutable, fathomless machine, the heretic wakes from his dreams "weeping" in despair (149).

McCarthy's demiurge, deafened by the noise of his loom, is a direct reference to the weaver god in Herman Melville's *Moby-Dick*, a novel permeated with Gnostic, specifically Manichean, symbols and concepts. Melville's demiurge appears in chapter 102, "A Bower in the Arsacides": "The weaver-god, he weaves; and by that weaving he is deafened, that he hears no mortal voice; and by that humming, we, too, who look on the loom are deafened; and only when we escape it shall we hear the thousand voices that speak through it" (427). Both McCarthy's and Melville's interpretations of the demiurge stress the fact that he deafens and silences both himself and those who wish to listen and understand; in other words, he not only lacks gnosis but tries to prevent others from attaining it too.[5] Melville claims that we will only hear the voices that call to us when we escape from the weaver god's influence. According to Hans Jonas, the Gnostics believed that the demiurge had purposely created the "noise of the world" in order "to drown out the 'call of Life'" (73), the call that wakes the pneuma, slumbering in its material prison, and guides it back to its divine origins; distancing ourselves from the noise of the world allows us to hear the divine call.

As a form of protest against the forces of destiny to which he believes we are all subject, the heretic moves into the ruined church of Caborca, which literally stands on three legs, under the shadow of a domed roof that might cave in at any moment. In a sense, we all live under such a roof, constantly subject to forces beyond our control, uncertain of the impending hour of our deaths.[6] Under this perilous roof, the heretic studies the Bible: "From time to time in his circling he'd pause and hold his book aloft and thump at a page with his finger and address his God at large" (150). The heretic's reading of the Bible is reminiscent of William Blake's (1757–1827) subversive reinterpretation of the scriptures. In "The Everlasting Gospel," Blake writes, "Both read the Bible day and night, But thou read'st black where I read white" (526). It is noteworthy that in his comprehensive study of Gnosticism, Stephan Hoeller refers to Blake as a "Gnostic poet of the early nineteenth-century" (26). The heretic reads the Bible against the grain, like a Gnostic seeking to reveal the true nature of the demiurge: "He'd become something like a barrister. He pored over the record not for the honor and glory of his Maker but rather to find against Him. To seek out in nice subtleties some darker nature. False favors. Small deceptions. Promises forsaken or a hand too quickly raised. To make cause against him, you see" (153). The heretic seeks incriminating evidence within the Bible itself, presumably reading verses that show the creator's terrifying wrath.

The heretic begins to conduct a lawsuit against the creator of this world. The "lawsuit concerning the world" is a common feature in the Gnostic

Gospels, where the spirit demands to know who is accountable for "the existence of the world as such and for its own exile here: that is, it asks the great 'Why?'" (Jonas 88). The spirit is instructed to "conduct your lawsuit, and be victorious (in it), speak and gain a favourable hearing" (qtd. in Rudolph 183). The heretic has "no plans for forgetting the injustices of his past life. The ten thousand insults. The catalog of woes. He had the mind of the injured party, you see. Nothing was lost on him" (155).[7] He puts the demiurge on trial because he desires personal agency and wants to "strike up some colindancia with his Maker. Assess boundaries and metes. See that lines were drawn and respected." From a Gnostic perspective, by establishing his own boundaries the heretic hopes to claim his own space outside of the demiurge's matrix and thereby escape the forces of heimarmene. The ex-priest explains that such a thing is not possible while one is still trapped within the bounds of manifest existence, because the "boundaries of the world are those of God's devising. With God there can be no reckoning. With what would one bargain?" (151). In other words, the manifest world belongs to the creator and there is no space here that may be claimed as one's own. From a subtler Buddhist perspective, creating boundaries is an exercise in futility, because it merely reinforces the misleading concept of the separate ego, which alienates the individual from all other life on earth.

While essentially demonstrating the beginnings of Gnostic thought, the heretic can see only the imperfect creator of this world and not the transcendent alien god of Gnostic theology. By his own retrospective estimates, the priest too once possessed only a misguided view of God, similarly conflating the creator with the Absolute.[8] The townspeople of Caborca call for the young priest to speak to the heretic, to "this misguided man of the nature of God and of the spirit and the will and of the meaning of grace in men's lives." The young priest's dogmatic words about the goodness of the biblical creator send the heretic into an incensed rage: "This old man raised his book aloft and shouted at the priest. You know nothing. This is what he shouted. You know nothing." The heretic's words trouble the young priest: "The conviction with which the old man spoke had jarred his heart and he weighed the old man's words and was troubled because of course the old man's words were true ones. And if the old man knew that then what else must he know?" (151). As a result, the young priest begins to question his own faith.

As the ex-priest explains to Billy, both men, at this point in their spiritual development, were still "heretics to the bone" (151) in that neither of them had arrived at a spiritually sound understanding of God. The young priest's mistaken views lay in his pantheistic tendencies: "He carried within himself a great reverence for the world, this priest. He heard the voice of the Deity in the murmur of the wind in the trees. Even the stones were sacred" (152). Pantheism is the "theory that God is immanent in or identical with the universe," while panentheism is the "belief that God encompasses and interpenetrates the universe but at the same time is greater than and independent of it" (*OED*). Aldous Huxley argues that in order to practice panentheism and avoid pantheism, "nature, though loved and heeded as a teacher," must only be "used as a means to God, not enjoyed as though she were God" (69). Thus, according to the ex-priest, his old belief that God is composed of the imperfect, illusory world of form—or, in other words, that this world is not an emanation of God, but rather God itself—was just as mistaken as the heretic's inability to apprehend the divine Absolute above and beyond the demiurgic creator.

The ex-priest assures Billy that he now knows that he had been mistaken in his early pantheistic approach and describes how he eventually arrived at the realization that God does not "whisper through the trees," or, in other words, that he is not identical with creation. The ex-priest adds that there can be no mistaking an experience of the divine: "His voice is not to be mistaken. When men hear it they fall to their knees and their souls are riven and they cry out to Him" (152). The ex-priest's description of the effects of the divine voice calls to mind the Gnostic concept of the "Call from Without," which occurs when the "transmundane penetrates the enclosure of the world and makes itself heard therein as a call. . . . It is the 'call of Life' or 'of the great Life,' which is equivalent to the breaking of light into the darkness" (Jonas 74). A Gnostic Mandean poem describes the response of those who hear the call:

> From the day when we heard thy word
> . . . .
> All our days we shall not forget thee
> not one hour let thee from our hearts.
> For our hearts shall not grow blind,
> these souls shall not be held back.
> (qtd. in Jonas 89–90)

According to Gnostic thought, the pneuma, trapped within the body and psyche, hears the beckoning call of the alien God and longs to return to its divine origins.

The ex-priest explains that when human beings hear the divine call "there is no fear in them but only that wildness of heart that springs from such longing and they cry out to stay his presence" (152). The concept of "longing," whether for a return to the alien God or the attainment of Nirvāṇa, is common to both Gnostic and Buddhist teachings. Stephan Hoeller writes that for the Gnostics, a "certain painful, often indistinct, longing for something greater, more meaningful, and more enduring than can be experienced in earthly embodiment is the beginning of the undoing of this great separation" (12). Edward Conze describes a similar longing from a Buddhist perspective, in which "a longing for the Absolute makes itself felt, and attentions shift more and more towards that which is not of this world, towards the Unconditioned, which does not share in the faults of the conditioned" (*Selected Sayings* 17). The ex-priest claims that "while godless men may live well enough in exile those to whom He has spoken can contemplate no life without Him but only darkness and despair" (152). In other words, when one comes to momentarily apprehend the Absolute, the agony of returning to a state of separation from the divine becomes unbearable. According to such a view, the manifest world is revealed to be permeated with "darkness and despair" and the spiritual seeker comes to view earthly existence as a form of exile or imprisonment, or at the very least an undesirable and imperfect state of being.

Speaking of his earlier self, the ex-priest tells Billy that "as with all priests his mind had become clouded by the illusion of its proximity to God" (155). The ex-priest explains that during his early pantheistic approach to the world he "stood in mortal peril and knew it not," because to "see God everywhere is to see Him nowhere" (152, 153). Frithjof Schuon identifies the dangers of such a pantheistic search for God, asking, "How can one attempt to 'see God,' who is invisible and infinite, in what is visible and finite without the risk of deluding oneself or falling into error, or without giving the idea a meaning so vague that the words lose all significance?" (106). According to Buddhist and Gnostic thought, nature can often blind us with its very materiality, making us forget that it is all illusion: "Maya has the two functions of concealing the real and projecting the unreal. The multiplicity of the world veils the real from us," or to put it more succinctly, "Maya is the world and it conceals the Brahman [the Absolute]" (Elamanamadathil 28). Stephan

Hoeller explains this identical concept as it is found in Gnosticism: "The created world, including a major portion of the human mind, is seen as evil by the Gnostics primarily because it distracts consciousness away from knowledge of the Divine" (16). Thus, for both traditions, nature, and indeed our own thought processes, can block our apprehension of higher, spiritual concepts. The priest had originally erred in mistaking the impermanent, illusory, manifest world for the Absolute itself, as well as being lulled into a sense of self-satisfied complacency by the fact that he was following the conventional religious path of priesthood.

The ex-priest rejects his earlier belief in a God that whispers through the trees and insists that "trees and stones are no part of it" (152). In other words, the manifest world is illusory and impermanent and thus not God. But how are we to reconcile this denial of the world with the concept that there can be nothing other to or separate from the Absolute? Frithjof Schuon writes, "One cannot say that God is this tree, nor that this tree is God, but one can say that the tree is, in a certain respect, not 'other than God,' or that, not being non-existent, it cannot not be God in any fashion" (110). Ultimately, both Buddhist and Gnostic texts argue that to grasp the concept of the Absolute intellectually is impossible and to attempt to do so only leads to error and confusion. In his study of Buddhist nature poetry, J. D. Frodsham explains, "Study of the Buddhist scriptures can lead at the best to but a partial and intellectual understanding of the Truth. Truth itself can only be experienced: for this abyss between Being and Non-being—'the state of mirror-like voidness'—can be crossed by no bridges built by faith or intellect" (*Murmuring Stream* 35). Instead, one must possess spiritual insight, which, according to the Perennial Philosophy, can be attained only through a direct experience of divine Reality.

The priest, in his youth, makes the error of trying to understand God, or the Absolute, intellectually: "The priest in the very generosity of his spirit stood in mortal peril and knew it not. He believed in a boundless God without center or circumference" (153). It is clear that the priest is well-read in theological concepts, because the circle/circumference analogy is a very popular definition in the writings of the many mystics. Evelyn Underhill explains the concept in the following way: "To say that God is Infinite is to say that He may be apprehended and described in an infinity of ways. That Circle whose centre is anywhere and whose circumference is nowhere, may be approached from every angle with a certainty of being found" (238). Technically, the young priest was not incorrect in applying such a description to the Absolute; the problem lies in the fact that "by this very formlessness he'd sought to make God manageable" (153). Buddhist texts do their best to avoid making the Absolute "manageable" by refusing to associate Nirvāṇa with anything found in samsaric existence. Edward Conze writes that Buddhism "wishes jealously to guard the transcendence of the Absolute, and to avoid the danger of misconceptions which arise if the same name which applies to something found in this world is also given to what is absolutely different from the world—as when Christians call God a *person*" (*Buddhism* 166).[9] According to this line of thought, the Absolute is, in fact, everywhere in the sense that nothing is separate from it, but to mistake the manifest world, or rather to mistake the very illusion that veils the Reality of the Absolute from us, for the Absolute itself, is to arrive at a spiritual dead end.

Much like the priest in his early days, the heretic also tries to make the divine manageable, albeit in a slightly different but equally misguided way. While the ex-priest believes himself to have originally erred in trying to view the illusion that conceals the divine as the divine itself, he believes that the heretic errs not only in conflating the creator deity and the Absolute into one entity but, more subtly, in reducing this conflated entity into an inherently paradoxical personal God. A personal God can be related to as though he were, in effect, a person and must necessarily possess subjective individuality. Thus a personal God cannot simultaneously be both a subject and an object because such a position would collapse all notions of individual personality. Paradoxically, however, the personal God must also be infinite and limitless in order to be considered a God, or, as the heretic believed, "It was true that He did indeed contain all else within Him . . . else He were no God at all" (156). Nothing must be allowed to stand entirely outside God's will; otherwise the believer would veer away from a monotheistic apprehension of God and into heretical dualism. How, then, to reconcile the individuality of a personal God with the belief that there exists nothing that can be other to God? Logically, God cannot be personal and unlimited, and this is precisely why Ralph Waldo Emerson wrote, "I deny personality to God because it is too little, not too much" (qtd. in Christy 80). The heretic, however, rejects Emerson's position and tries to comprehend a God that has both a personal and a limitless nature. Thus he necessarily comes up against a paradox and begins "to see in God a terrible tragedy. That the existence of the Deity lay imperiled for want of this simple thing. That for God there could be no witness. Nothing against which He terminated. Nothing by way of which his being could be announced to Him. Nothing to stand apart from and to say I am this and that is other. Where that is I am not." The heretic approaches "madness" in his vain attempts to reconcile the contradictory elements of his understanding of God (154).

The various traditions of the Perennial Philosophy, as well as the Gnostics, saw that the only way out of this double bind is to cast away all notions of a divine personality. Edward Conze, referring to the Buddhist concept of Nirvāṇa, writes, "The Absolute alone is not dependent on anything else; it is ultimately real. Any relative thing is functionally dependent on other things, and can exist, and be conceived, only in and through its relations with other things. By itself it is nothing, it has no separate inward reality" (*Buddhism* 134). Similarly, commenting on Emerson's denial of a personal God, Arthur Christy explains that, according to the New England transcendentalist, "God could not exist . . . as other objects exist, a unit in an indefinite multiplicity of objects, distinct from them all as they are distinct from each other, each knowable. To think of God thus was to bring him down to the level of the finite" (81). Huston Smith explains, "Only persons who sense *themselves* to be not finally real—*anatta*, no-self—will sense the same of the God of theism. And for them it does not matter that in the last analysis God is not the kind of God who loves them [i.e., a personal God], for at this level there is no 'them' to be loved" (*Forgotten Truth* 52). According to the Perennial Philosophy, one can never "witness" the Absolute, because to apprehend it is to become it. In fact, once the Absolute is apprehended the concept of a personal self vanishes also, as in the Buddhist doctrine of *anatta* (no self).

Incapable of differentiating between the personality of the creator and the ultimate nature of the Absolute, the heretic becomes obsessed with the concept of acting as a witness to God's existence. Recalling his own miraculous survival of two earthquakes, he comes to wonder whether "God had preserved him not once but twice out of the ruins of the earth solely in order to raise up a witness against Himself?" Like Job, the heretic feels that he has been chosen for some divine purpose, yet, unlike Job, he refuses to be subservient to the deity responsible for this election.[10] Thus the heretic begins to experience even more "contradictions in his position," for if "men were the drones he imagined them to be then had he not rather been appointed to take up his brief by the very Being against whom it was directed?" (154). To rephrase the heretic's question in Gnostic terms, if human beings are enslaved by heimarmene and controlled entirely by a malevolent demiurge, then is anyone ever truly capable of rebellion against their creator, unless it be by the demiurge's own choosing? Though the heretic has a dim apprehension of the limitless nature of the Absolute, he continues to apply this boundlessness to the malevolent caprice of a personal demiurge. Thus, when the still-unenlightened priest comes back to once again "declaim to the old man concerning the goodness of God," the heretic responds with his old misotheistic fury: "The old man clapped his hands to his ears . . . and began to scrabble up stones from the rubble and to pelt the priest with them and so drove him away" (155–56). Utterly dismayed by his own terrible apprehension of God, the heretic falls ill, stops eating, and lies down to die.

Weakened by his illness, the heretic enters into a three-day period of silent meditation during which "he spoke to no one. Not even to God" (155). During this time, he develops an even keener apprehension of the enormity of the creator's power and comes to believe that "the God of the universe was yet more terrible than men reckoned. He could not be eluded nor yet set aside nor circumscribed about" (156). Though, from a Gnostic perspective, the heretic continues to conflate the individual malevolence of the demiurge with the all-encompassing nature of the Absolute, he also arrives at a deeper understanding of the interconnectedness of spirit, not just among all living things but between all things and God, however troubling his apprehension of God may be. When the priest visits again in "three days' time" the heretic takes "the priest's hand in his own and he bade the priest look at their joined hands and he said see the likeness. This flesh is but a memento, yet it tells the true. Ultimately every man's path is every other's. There are no separate journeys for there are no separate men to make them. All men are one and there is no other tale to tell" (156–57). The heretic's words recall the writings of Ralph Waldo Emerson: "There is one mind common to all individual men. Every man is an inlet to the same and to all of the same" ("History" 3); or, "The heart and soul of all men being one, the bitterness of *his* and *mine* ceases. He is mine. I am my brother and my brother is me" ("Compensation" 33). The heretic reminds the priest of the essential unity of the human race and, indeed, all life. This is precisely what Emerson is referring to in "The Over-Soul" when he writes, "We live in succession, in division, in parts, in particles. Meantime within man is the soul of the whole; the wise silence; the universal beauty, to which every part and particle is equally related; the external One" (68). This is different from the pantheistic concept that all of nature is divine. Rather, the heretic teaches the priest that all things are divine because, when stripped of their illusory components—or their "flesh," which is only a "memento"—they are revealed as the pure Reality of spirit, one with each other and, ultimately, one with the Absolute.

Such a statement is in marked contrast to the heretic's earlier desire to strike up a *colindancia* with God, claiming that "what we seek is the worthy adversary. For we strike out to fall flailing through demons of wire and crepe and we long for something of substance to oppose us. . . . Otherwise there were no boundaries to our own being and we too must extend our claims until we lose all definition. Until we must be swallowed up at last by the very void to which we wished to stand opposed" (153). It seems that the heretic has come to accept that there are, in fact, no boundaries—not between one being and another, and not between any being and the Absolute. According to such thought, there can never be anything of genuine substance to oppose us, because all things are one; or as Emerson writes, "The act of seeing and the thing seen, the seer and the spectacle, the subject and the object, are one" ("Over-Soul" 68). Thus, in coming to believe that there are "no separate men," the heretic no longer strives to define the boundaries of his own being.

The heretic admits that he has also changed his mind about God: "At his dying he had told the priest that he'd been wrong in his every reckoning of God and yet had come at last to an understanding of Him anyway" (157). These words are reminiscent of those uttered by various Buddhists, Gnostics, and mystics, who all refuse to define or describe any aspect of the Absolute, except its very ineffability. Edward Conze writes, "As far as the Absolute itself is concerned, nothing can be said about it at all, nor can anything be done about it. . . . Any idea we form about the Absolute is ipso facto false" (*Buddhism* 112). The Gnostic *Secret Book of John* also laments the failure of language when faced with the alien God: "What shall I say to thee concerning him, the inconceivable?" (qtd. in Rudolph 64). In effect, our language, created to deal with the tangible concepts and realities of the manifest world, cannot adequately express or describe a direct apprehension of the ineffable Absolute.[11]

Uncomprehending, the young priest mistakes the heretic's statement for confession and begins "the words of absolution," but the old man "seized his arm midway in its crossing there in the still air by his deathbedside and stayed him with his eyes" (157). Like all Gnostics, the heretic does not want absolution because he does not believe he is at fault. While according to Christian thought the "flaws and evils of earthly life are considered the consequence of [the] Fall," the "Gnostics do not hold that any kind of sin, including that of Adam and Eve, is powerful enough to cause the degradation of the entire manifest world" (Hoeller 14). Instead, they believe that "the world is flawed because it was created in a flawed manner" (63). Only a "salvific change in consciousness" (15) can bring about redemption and it is ultimately up to the individual to pursue the path of gnosis or enlightenment; forgiveness will not bring about salvation. Furthermore, the heretic's dying words to the priest—"Save yourself, he hissed. Save yourself. Then he died" (157)—echo the final words of the Buddha: "Work out your own salvation with diligence" (qtd. in Conze, *Buddhism* 16). The heretic dies like "a man going on a journey" (157), and it is significant that Gnostic texts often describe death, or "escape from the entanglements of earthly existence," as "the heavenly journey of the soul" (Rudolph 171). Thus the account of the heretic's death evokes both Gnostic and Buddhist themes.

The ex-priest tries to explain how he arrived at his own final apprehension of the Absolute, insisting that it was in fact the encounter with the heretic that triggered his own quest for spiritual insight. Recalling the effects of this encounter, the ex-priest describes how his "soul [was] forever changed, forever wrenched about in the road it was intended upon and set instead upon a road heretofore unknown to it" (158). The ex-priest claims that his own belief system was profoundly altered by his exposure to the heretical views. At first, the young priest felt that he had "no answers to the questions the old messenger had brought"; however, he eventually came to realize "that they were not the old pensioner's queries at all but his own" (157). The heretic struggled to apprehend the true nature of God, and by witnessing that struggle the young priest was eventually able to abandon conventional priesthood and to experience his own apprehension of the divine. Though the heretic possessed only questions, he prompted the young priest to seek for answers. In other words, the heretic served as a catalyst for the young priest's spiritual development. "In the end what the priest came to believe was that the truth may often be carried about by those who themselves remain all unaware of it. They bear that which has weight and substance and yet for them has no name whereby it may be evoked or called forth." Thus when another, such as the young priest, comes across this "very thing" or is able to recognize the validity of the heretic's questions and seek his own answers, he "will have in his possession that elusive freedom which men seek with such unending desperation" (157). In other words, the ex-priest believes that spiritual wisdom may be imparted by those who do not even know they possess it themselves or, if they do know, have no means of articulating the ineffable.

The young priest's search for the answers to the heretic's questions is, from a Gnostic perspective, the pursuit of gnosis, which eventually enabled him to "recognize that which is buried in our hearts and is never truly lost to us nor ever can be.... It is this which we long for and are afraid to seek and which alone can save us" (153). In Gnostic terminology, the pneuma seeks freedom from the bondage of heimarmene, but such liberation may be arrived at only through the attainment of spiritual wisdom, which enables the pneuma to return to its divine origins. This wisdom, whether the Gnostic gnosis or the Buddhist *jñāna*, possesses a soteriological function in that it is simultaneously a form of knowledge and a saving grace. Edward Conze explains, "Salvation takes place through *gnosis* or *jñāna*, and nothing else can finally achieve it.... In both cases the mere insight into the origination and nature of the world liberates us from it, and effects some kind of reunion with the transcendental One, which is identical with our true Self" (*Further Buddhist Studies* 16–7). In Gnostic terms, what is sought but "never truly lost" is the spirit's recollection of its own divine nature, and this knowledge is at once liberating and salvific.

Abandoning the views held by conventional Christianity, the young priest finally arrived at his own understanding of the divine and thus became the "ex-priest." The ex-priest's apprehension is presented as being even more profound than the heretic's, because the ex-priest came to see "what the anchorite could not. That God needs no witness." The ex-priest tells Billy, "The truth is rather that if there were no God then there could be no witness for there could be no identity to the world but only each man's opinion of it" (158). According to the Perennial Philosophy, the Absolute needs no witness because it *is* the ultimate witness to all things. Ken Wilber explains that the Absolute is "the pure Witness that itself is never witnessed—is never an object—but contains all objects within itself" (227–28). Following this line of thought, any notions of multiplicity or separation from the Absolute arise out of misguided perceptions, for if the Absolute is All, then nothing can ever stand apart from it and nothing can ever act as a witness to it. As mentioned earlier, the Absolute is called the nondual because, "in the perfect gnosis, all dualities are abolished, the object does not differ from the subject" (Conze, *Buddhism* 134). Hence the Absolute can be experienced only when there is no longer any distinction between the self and other. In the words of Meister Eckhart, "If I am to know God directly, I must become completely He and He I: so that this He and this I become and are one I" (qtd. in Underhill 420).[12] According to the Perennial Philosophy, one experiences the Absolute when one becomes It.

At the very end of his story, the ex-priest reveals what he has come to believe not only about the nature of God but also about the nature of the world. He explains that the manifest world is ultimately illusory: "Stones themselves are made of air" (158). Edward Conze writes that in Buddhist thought, "the highest insight is reached when everything appears as sheer hallucination" (*Buddhism* 168). The Buddhists call Nirvāṇa the "ultimate reality" and define it as "that which stands completely outside the sensory world of illusions and ignorance" (110). The ex-priest adds that "what [stones] have power to crush never lived." In other words, all that is impermanent and susceptible to destruction (that is, the empirical world of matter and form) is nothing but illusion, while that which is real, enduring, and truly alive (the spirit) can never be destroyed. The ex-priest concludes that "in the end we shall all of us be only what we have made of God" (158). His words imply that death strips us of all our worldly achievements and possessions, so that all that remains is what we have invested in our spiritual development.

The ex-priest understands the spiritual dangers of language and tells Billy that even to speak of that which is essentially ineffable is to commit heresy: "The heretic's first act is to name his brother. So that he may step free of him." He adds that "to God every man is a heretic" (158), presumably because "every man" considers himself to be a separate entity, other to his brother and other to the Absolute. The ex-priest believes such notions to be heretical, because the Absolute can have no "other" to stand opposed to it.[13] Meister Eckhart argued that the essence of all sin and heresy is "neither libido nor cupiditas but selfhood, that is, the self-centeredness of the ego, 'I,' 'me,' 'mine,' etc. This is not egoism in the ethical sense of self-seeking at the expense of other men, but it is the self-sufficiency of the creature set over against God" (qtd. in Otto 124). According to Meister Eckhart, this sinful "self-sufficiency" is what drives individuals to identify their fellow human beings as other to themselves. This label of "otherness" is then extended to all things, even to the Absolute itself, so that the human self stands completely alone, cherishing a deluded belief in a separate ego. Furthermore, language functions quite well on the level of ordinary, everyday experiences but leads one astray when one tries to describe spiritual Reality, by creating a false sense of distinction, duality, and separation. In the words of Meister Eckhart, "Why dost thou prate of God? Whatever thou sayest of Him is untrue" (qtd. in Huxley 125). Thus the ex-priest believes that "every word we speak is a vanity" (158), because the Absolute is beyond language and can never be described, only apprehended directly.

The ex-priest claims that "every breath taken that does not bless is an affront" (158). His words suggest that every action that distracts one from the pursuit of spiritual insight is born of ignorance and is thus harmful. According to Buddhist thought, "ignorance (*avidyā*) is the root evil," because it misdirects "our attention towards a manufactured world of our own making" and "conceals the true reality to which wisdom, the highest form of gnosis, alone can penetrate." This view is shared by Gnostic teachings, which "declare ignorance to be the basic fault which has alienated us from true reality" (Conze, *Further Buddhist Studies* 17). Gnosis, or enlightenment, is the only meaningful pursuit, because everything else is, soteriologically speaking, futile.

The ex-priest summarizes his apprehension of the ultimate Reality of the Absolute in the elegantly succinct phrase "For nothing is real save his grace" (158). This idea forms the basis of the various traditions of the Perennial Philosophy; for example, in Buddhism, Nirvāṇa is described as "the real Truth and the supreme Reality" (Conze, *Buddhism* 40). Edward Conze points that "when we compare the attributes of the Godhead as they are understood by the more mystical tradition of Christian thought, with those of Nirvana, we find almost no difference at all" (*Buddhism* 39). Rachel Wagner and Frances Flannery-Dailey put forward a similar argument: "According to the world views of both Gnostic Christianity and Buddhism . . . the realization of true reality involves complete freedom from entrapment in the material realm and offers peace of mind" (282). The ex-priest's words are in accordance with the Perennial Philosophy in that they point to the existence of an ultimate, spiritual Reality.

Thus the ex-priest's tale concludes with a vision of existence that echoes both Buddhist and Gnostic thought, in that only the divine can be considered ultimately Real. According to the ex-priest, the true reality of our own existence is located in our identification with the divine, and this necessitates the rejection of the belief in a separate ego. The manifest world of sense and form—what the ex-priest refers to as the world of trees and the stones—is rejected as misleading and illusory. As these are the last words assigned to the ex-priest, we can assume that this is the single most important aspect of his final apprehension of spiritual Reality and, as such, informs the metaphysical and spiritual concept of the divine Absolute that runs throughout McCarthy's work.

CHAPTER 8

"Mourners in the Darkness"
Blindness and Insight in *The Crossing*, Book 3

■ Book 3 of *The Crossing* concerns the blind man, an archetypal blind seer much like Tiresias, whose parable is permeated with Gnostic references to the light of wisdom and the darkness of ignorance.[1] Much like the anchorites encountered in the preceding pages of the novel, namely Don Arnulfo and the ex-priest, the blind man presents a view of existence that echoes the main tenets of the Perennial Philosophy, but with darkly Gnostic overtones. His story explores the idea that the multifarious distractions of the visible world may blind human beings to the true nature of existence, concealing the ultimate Reality of the divine behind the veil of illusion identified as the manifest world. The blind man posits an inverse relationship between physical and spiritual blindness, arguing that the possession of the former may free one from the latter.

The theme of "blindness" is first introduced by a "Primadonna," who emerges from a troupe of traveling actors to tell Billy, "Perhaps it is true that nothing is hidden. Yet many do not wish to see what lies before them in plain sight. You will see" (230). These words foreshadow the approaching conversation with the blind man, during which Billy will indeed be made to "see," whether he wishes to or not. Seeking hospitality later in the novel, Billy stumbles across the blind man's house quite by chance and is invited in by the man's wife. The blind man recounts the story of how he had once been a Mexican revolutionary and had his eyes literally sucked out of their sockets by a sadistic German officer. Billy eats a dinner of hard-boiled eggs while listening to the blind man's tale, an unconventional meal curiously not dissimilar to eyeballs. As is the case with all of McCarthy's storytellers, the conversation—or rather monologue, as Billy does not talk a great deal—soon takes a turn toward metaphysics and mysticism. In fact, the description of this horrific event is permeated by references that seem to reflect Gnostic teachings.[2] The German is referred to as the "architect of his [the blind man's] darkness, the thief of his light" (277).[3] The Gnostics would not have hesitated to apply such a description to the demiurge, whom they regarded as the architect of this "world of darkness" (Jonas 57). In Gnostic teaching, darkness is associated with ignorance and corporeality, whereas light is associated with spirituality and wisdom, or gnosis; for example, Gnostic texts constantly refer to "the light of gnosis in contrast to the earthly darkness" (Hoeller 217). Thus the demiurge and his archons may also be described as "thieves of light" in that they keep the pneuma imprisoned in matter by obstructing the light of gnosis.

Indeed, many other esoteric traditions connect darkness with ignorance and evil and light with spiritual wisdom and divinity. Consider, for instance, Saint John's pronouncement "and the light shineth in darkness; and the darkness comprehended it not" (John 1:5). In *The Crossing*, the metaphorical significance of light is emphasized by the description of the "deeper fire" burning in the blind man's empty eye sockets.[4] In fact, the blind man is depicted with "red holes in his skull" that "glowed like lamps" (277), as though there were a source of light buried deep within him. Such a description is evocative of the Gnostic concept of the pneuma, "a portion of the divine substance" (Jonas 44) trapped within the darkness of the manifest world. In fact, Gnostic texts frequently referred to the pneuma as the "spark" to emphasize its status as a fragment of the divine light.

The German officer robs the blind man of the light of the visible world but is not able to extinguish the inner light of gnosis burning within him. In fact, without his eyes to distract him, the blind man is able to "see" the world in a new light, and what he sees fills him with despair: "Despair was in him like a lodger. Like a parasite that had turned out his very being from its abode and taken up the shape of that space within him where it once had been" (278).[5] Edward Conze argues that the "overwhelming majority of people cannot live joyfully without adopting some kind of ostrich attitude to life," because "for most of us life would be intolerable if we could see it as it is" (*Buddhism* 44–45). Thus most human beings would reject the blind man's newfound apprehension of the world as unduly pessimistic. Precisely because no one else seems to share his new understanding, the blind man's suffering is exacerbated by a terrible sense of alienation: "His thoughts were that other than wind and rain nothing would ever come again to touch him out of that estrangement that was the world. Not in love, not in enmity" (279). Unable to bear the weight of such isolation, he attempts to drown himself in a river but is thwarted by the fact that the "water came but to his knees" (280). As he sits down in the shallow stream, he hears "a bell that tolled slowly three times and ceased" (281). This would not be a remarkable occurrence, were it not for the fact that when he questions a passerby, he is told "that there was no church. That there was nothing at all anywhere in sight" (282). The mysterious tolling of this nonexistent bell, a common theme throughout the Border Trilogy, evokes John Donne's sermon—"never send to know for whom the bell tolls; it tolls for thee"—and thus serves not only as a memento mori but also as a reminder of the apparent interconnectedness between all human beings.[6] In the midst of his loneliness and despair, the blind man is subtly reminded that he is not the only being singled out for such anguish but that all his fellow creatures share in this suffering and mortality, even if they are not always consciously aware of these darker aspects of existence.

The conversation between the blind man and the passerby explores another common theme in *The Crossing*, namely the cosmic illusion that the Buddhists and Hindus call māyā. Edward Conze explains that Buddhist texts compare the world to a "magical illusion," because "it is deceptive" and "one mistakes it for what it is not. It is not genuine, and as a magical trick it should not be treated too seriously" (*Buddhism* 173). The blind man discusses the impermanent and illusory nature of the world, telling the passerby "that the world and all in it had become to him a rumour. A suspicion" (282). Once again, the reader is presented with the idea that the world we take for granted as unproblematically "real" is actually insubstantial and misleading, so that without the organs of sight all that remains is "rumour" and "suspicion."[7] The passerby's reply to the blind man's statement is profound: "Si el mundo es ilusión la perdida del mundo es ilusión también" (If the world is an illusion, the loss of the world is also an illusion)" (282–83). In other words, one cannot lose that which was only the product of mistaken perception. Thus, as the passerby argues, the blind man has not lost something external to himself; rather he has lost only the illusions created by his sense perceptions. The passerby's words suggest that now, without his eyes to deceive him, the blind man can arrive at a more spiritually accurate apprehension of the world.

The blind man's reply to the passerby is that it is not the loss of sense perceptions that dismays him but precisely this new apprehension of the world. Unaffected by the multifarious distractions afforded by sight, the blind man claims that he can finally "see" into the dark core of existence: "He said that the world in which he made his way was very different from what men suppose and in fact was scarcely world at all. He said that to close one's eyes told nothing. Any more than sleeping told of death. He said that it was not a matter of illusion or no illusion. He spoke of the broad dryland barrial and the river and the road and the mountains beyond and the blue sky over them as entertainments to keep the world at bay, the true and ageless world" (283). This reference to the "true and ageless world" echoes Jacob Boehme's description of the "true and abiding realities" that are to be found "behind the Laws and Forces of Nature," that is, beyond "the material world of the senses" (Martensen 110). The blind man repeats his thoughts in Spanish, emphasizing the fact that these words apply to all human beings, not just to the blind: "En este viaje el mundo visible es no mas que un distraimiento. Para los ciegos y para todos los hombres." (On this voyage the visible world is no more than a distraction. For those that are blind and for all men.) (292). While he does not deny that the world is illusory and "scarcely world at all," the blind man is not interested in the nature of the illusion. Rather, he has come to believe that the beauty of the manifest world continually distracts us from the pursuit of an enduring ultimate Reality.[8] Buddhism teaches that in order to apprehend "ultimate reality," we must "learn to check our insatiable desire for sights" and sounds, and only then can we "learn to prevent our mind or thoughts or heart from becoming entranced with the objects which our senses meet" (Conze, *Buddhism* 99). The Buddhist Tripitaka continually refers to the manifest world as a glittering trap, claiming that "man finds himself standing in the fairground of the sensory world, fascinated by its brightness" (qtd. in Conze, *Buddhist Scriptures* 107). According to Buddhist teachings, one must not allow oneself to be distracted by this fairground, because "suffering is the lot of everyone, everywhere and all the time; therefore, my friend, do not hanker after the glittering objects of this world! And, once this hankering is extinct in you, then you will clearly see that this entire world of the living can be said to be on fire" (111). The concept of the visible world as a place of distraction that blinds the individual to spiritual insight is not particular to Buddhist thought; the Gnostics also believed that the material world conceals the pneuma and blocks out the light of gnosis. The Gnostic Gospels warn of "the deceptive arts (the 'snares' and 'traps') of the archons" (Rudolph 117), or, in other words, the distracting illusions conjured by the malevolent entities responsible for creating the material world.

The blind man believes that the ultimate Reality of the divine cannot be found among the distracting illusions of the visible world. "Ultimamente sabemos que no podemos ver el buen Dios. Vamos escuchando. Me entiendes, joven? Debemos escuchar." (Ultimately we know that we cannot see the good God. We go listening. Do you understand me, young one? We should listen.) (292).[9] The blind man's insistence on the importance of listening calls to mind the Gnostic concept of the "call from beyond" (Jonas 74). The Gnostics used the metaphor of the "call of awakening" (71) to describe sudden epiphanic apprehensions of a higher spiritual Reality. It is particularly noteworthy that, much like the blind man, the Gnostic Gospels describe the call of the divine as that which "cannot be seen but must be heard" (74–75). Similarly, Aldous Huxley states that "in the various expositions of the Perennial Philosophy . . . liberation might be defined as the process of waking up out of the nonsense, nightmares and illusory pleasures of what is ordinarily called real life into the awareness of eternity" (163). Therefore, when the blind man asks if Billy is awake—"Esta despierto, el joven?" (284)—he might subtly be inquiring into the boy's level of spiritual development, as well as his state of consciousness.

The blind man believes that his loss of sight has freed him from the glittering trap of the world and allowed him to arrive at various esoteric insights previously inaccessible to him. One such intuition addresses the relationship between individual consciousness and the external world. The blind man explains "that men with eyes may select what they wish to see but for the blind the world appears of its own will. He said that for the blind everything was abruptly at hand, that nothing ever announced its approach. Origins and destinations became but rumours. To move is to abut against the world. Sit quietly and it vanishes" (291). In other words, the blind man argues that the world is not endowed with the tangibility and continuity that we take for granted; rather, it is we who imbue it with these qualities through our acts of perception and consciousness. Like the shaman in book 1, the blind man puts forward an idea of the world that echoes the teachings of the Buddhist school of Yogacara, according to which the "external world is really Mind itself" and the "highest insight is reached when everything appears as sheer hallucination" (Conze, *Buddhism* 168). It appears that the blind man has already reached such an insight, sensing that the world "vanishes" when we "sit still," that is, when we do not actively perceive it.

The blind man tells Billy "that in his blindness he had indeed lost himself and all memory of himself yet he had found in the deepest dark of that loss that there also was a ground and there one must begin" (291–92). Evelyn Underhill seems to be referring such an experience when she describes how, "by a deliberate inattention to the messages of the senses, such as that which is induced by contemplation, the mystic can bring the ground of the soul ... within the area of consciousness. ... Thus becoming unaware of his usual and largely fictitious 'external world,' another and more substantial set of perceptions, which never have their chance under normal conditions, rise to the surface" (55). Underhill explains that the cultivation of this state leads to the "discovery of that Absolute in the 'ground' or spiritual principle of the self" (113). William James alludes to such an experience, arguing that there is "in the human consciousness a sense of reality, a feeling of objective presence, a perception of what we may call 'something there,' more deep and more general than any of the special and particular 'sense' by which the current psychology supposes existent realities to be originally revealed" (49). Edward Conze writes about this idea from a Buddhist perspective, explaining that there is "a point in ourselves at which we touch that ultimate reality" (*Buddhism* 110). Huston Smith explains that this concept is common to all the traditions of the Perennial Philosophy and summarizes it in the following way: "Within man, the best lies deepest; it is basic, fundamental, the ground of his being" (*Forgotten Truth* 20). Thus the blind man's words suggest that only after having discovered such a "ground" within the "deepest" reaches of himself could he "begin" his spiritual journey.

From a Buddhist perspective, blindness might free one from the distractions generated by māyā, the cosmic illusion. The blind man feels that he is finally able to see the world as it really is, to experience the truth of existence. Dianne Luce also argues that the blind man is "compensated" for the loss of his eyes "with a truer perception of the world itself" ("Vanishing World" 167). When the blind man says, "Ese mundo es un mundo frágil. Ultimamente lo que vine a ver era más durable. Más verdadero." (This world is a fragile world. What I have seen lately was stronger. Truer.) (291), he is referring to what he regards as the spiritual truth of the ultimate Reality. When Billy asks the blind man's wife if their story is a true one, the blind man "broke in to say that indeed the tale was a true one. He said that they had no desire to entertain him nor yet even to instruct him. He said that it was their whole bent only to tell what was true and that otherwise they had no purpose at all" (284). This seems to be the very same conception of a single, ultimate "Truth" to which McCarthy alludes during the Wallace interview.[10]

The blind man goes on to explain what his blindness has taught him about the nature of the world: "He said that the light of the world was in men's eyes only for the world itself moved in eternal darkness and darkness was its true nature and true condition" (283). On one hand, this is literally true—the earth does move through the vast darkness of space—but it is also a metaphysical and spiritual statement echoing the Gnostic belief that the manifest world is ultimately a dark and evil place. In Gnostic thought, the alien God is known as the "King of Light," whose world is "a world of splendour and of light without darkness," while the manifest cosmos of the demiurge is "the world of darkness, utterly full of evil" (Jonas 57). The Gnostics associated darkness with the evil they saw as inherent in the created world. "Physically," darkness stood for "matter," or the "body," which was seen as the prison of the divine spirit. "Psychologically," darkness represented "ignorance or forgetfulness" of one's divine origins (Rudolph 58). Thus, for the Gnostics, darkness served as the perfect symbol for all the levels of existence within the manifest world, namely, the physical and the psychological, as opposed the spiritual.

The blind man's words also resonate with the writings of Jacob Boehme, whose *Six Theosophic Points* McCarthy cites in an epigraph to *Blood Meridian*. Although not strictly a Gnostic, Boehme nevertheless "saw a dark principle in all the primary sources of existence, more deeply than he saw existence itself" (Berdyaev xiii).[11] Boehme associated the material world with darkness and evil, claiming that "the realm of matter and darkness is the realm of anguish, contention, and suffering; the realm of the Spirit is the kingdom of light, joy, peace, and happiness" (qtd. in Hartmann 18). According to Hans Martensen, Boehme believed that "this flesh of ours, our gross corporeity . . . is subjected, like the whole physical world, to heaviness and darkness, corruption and death, and in which, in ignorance of the glory which encircles us, we move, as it were, with closed eyes and sealed ears" (110). Like the blind man, Boehme believed that the light of the divine was obscured by the darkness of the corporeal world.

The blind man insists that this world is a realm of darkness, telling Billy "that in darkness it turned with perfect cohesion in all its parts but that there was naught there to see" (283). This "perfect cohesion" is reminiscent of the previously discussed Gnostic concept of heimarmene, which, according to the Apocryphon of John, binds "the gods of the heaven," or the heavenly bodies, as well as "men," so "that they might all be in its fetter and it be lord over them all" (qtd. in Rudolph 106). The blind man argues that the world is "sentient to its core" (283), suggesting that although the cosmic forces of fate or destiny may seem impersonal, they are in fact controlled by a maleficent sentience. This sentience suggests the Gnostic demiurge, who, along with his archons, "caused *Heimarmene* to come into being" (Rudolph 106). The blind man adds that the world was "secret and black beyond men's imagining and that its nature did not reside in what could be seen or not seen" (283). Again, these words recall Gnostic descriptions of the "whole world system" as "the prison" or "the dark place," utterly permeated with "death, deception" and "wickedness" (Rudolph 109, 69). The blind man confesses that these terrible insights into the nature of the cosmos are "things he'd long suspected" (284) and that his blindness only confirmed his darkest fears.

Continuing his tale, the blind man remembers how his "dreams were a torment to him and yet he would not wish them away," explaining "that as the memory of the world must fade so must it fade in his dreams until soon or late he feared that he would have darkness absolute and no shadow of the world that was."[12] The blind man confesses "that he feared what that darkness held for he believed that the world hid more than it revealed" (289). Convinced that the distractions of the visible world are what keep the dark truths hidden from us, the blind man fears that as he begins to lose even the memory of those distractions, he will have to penetrate even deeper into the terrible secrets of that darkness. The blind man is more conscious of evil than any other anchorite encountered in *The Crossing*, presumably because he is no longer subject to the distracting beauty of the world.[13]

In response to the blind man's words, Billy wonders whether evil is a natural state of existence or whether it arises only in extreme situations. He asks the blind man "if such men as had stole his eyes were only products of the war," but the blind man replies that "since war itself was their doing that could hardly be the case." In other words, the blind man believes that evil is not a mere response to suffering but its very essence and cause. To emphasize his belief that the world is permeated with evil, the blind man reminds Billy, "Etienda que ya existe ogro. Este chupador de ojos. Él y otros como él. Ellos no han desaparecido del mundo. Y nunca lo haran." (Understand that that ogre still exists. That sucker of eyes. He and others like him. They have not disappeared from the world. And they never will) (290). Earlier in the conversation, the blind man's wife had tried to argue that since the days of the blinding, "Y mucho ha cambiado. Y a pesar de eso todo es lo mismo."

(Much has changed. And despite that everything is the same.) The blind man, however, disagrees: "He said that on the contrary nothing had changed and all was different. The world was new each day for God so made it daily. Yet it contained within it all the evils as before, no more, no less" (278).[14] The blind man believes that this is the way the world always was and always will be and, in truly Gnostic fashion, he assigns the responsibility for the "evils" of the world to the creator.

The blind man recounts not only his own story but also that of his wife, as she too has had much cause to contemplate the existence of evil in the world. The blind man explains that when his wife was only a young girl, she witnessed the execution of her father and two brothers among a group of "rebel sympathizers" (285). Not knowing what to do, the girl found herself sitting in a church at midnight, unburdening her sorrows to a sympathetic *sepulturero*, or cemetery sexton, who offered the following words of consolation: "He said that while one would like to say that God will punish those who do such things and that people often speak in just this way it was his experience that God could not be spoken for and that men with wicked histories often enjoyed lives of comfort and that they died in peace and were buried with honor" (288). The sepulturero's words reveal the lack of divine justice in the world by drawing attention to the seemingly senseless suffering of the innocent and the undeserved prosperity of the guilty.

Though his words may at first appear Gnostic, the sepulturero shies away from such heretical thinking by arguing that without such injustice, true virtue and genuine goodness could not actually exist. He explains "that the notion that evil is seldom rewarded was greatly overspoken for if there were no advantage to it then men would shun it and how could virtue then be attached to its repudiation?" (288). The sepulturero's argument is based on the premise that precisely because evil behavior is so lucrative, to shun it engenders great moral, ethical, and spiritual value. Immanuel Kant (1724–1804) raised much the same point when he argued that a "morally transparent world would preclude the possibility of morality" (qtd. in Neiman 68). In other words, if there were indeed a clear connection between evil behavior and misfortune, people would avoid committing evil deeds simply to avoid punishment. Conversely, people would behave virtuously only to reap the guaranteed rewards and not for the sake of virtue itself. Billy questions the validity of this argument, asking whether the advice "which the sepulturero had given to the girl in the church had been false advice." The blind man replies that "the sepulturero might presume to speak of a darkness of which he had no knowledge, for had he such knowledge he could not then be a sepulturero" (292). In other words, if the sepulturero could see the world as the blind man sees it, he could no longer go on serving the exoteric church but would become a heretic, like the blind man himself.

The blind man explains his own views, stating "that even the sepulturero would understand that every tale was a tale of dark and light and would perhaps not have it otherwise. Yet there was still a further order to the narrative and it was a thing of which men do not speak" (292). Beginning with a clear Manichean reference to the powers of good and evil—"dark and light"—the blind man elaborates on this simple dualism by insisting that the relationship between good and evil is, in fact, far more complex. The blind man's words may be illuminated by reference to the two major Gnostic systems, namely, the pure dualism of the Manicheans and the more sophisticated qualified nondualism of the Valentinians. Hans Jonas explains that the main difference between these two systems lies in their approach to the origins of and relationship between good and evil. Jonas writes that, according to the straightforward dualism of the Manichean school of thought, "the two realms as such exist side by side completely unconnected. . . . For the Darkness is what it is destined to be, and left to itself it fulfills its nature as the Light fulfills its own." In contrast to this, the qualified nondualism of the Valentinian system "lets a downward movement start in the Light itself and thus makes it responsible for the given dualism" (211–12). Essentially, there is nothing "other" to the Light, because "the origin of darkness, and thereby of the dualistic rift of being" is placed "*within* the godhead itself" (174). In other words, even the seemingly dualistic rift between good and evil has its origins within the nondual Absolute.[15] The blind man seems to be advocating qualified nondualism when he speaks of the "further order" to the apparent division between good and evil.

The blind man then goes on to explain the relationship between order and disorder and their respective connections to good and evil, arguing that "while the order which the righteous seek is never righteousness itself but is only order, the disorder of evil is in fact the thing itself" (293). In other words, the blind man believes that while disorder is always the manifestation of evil and thus evil itself, order is not the manifestation of righteousness or righteousness itself but simply "order." Conversely, both classical philosophy and Christian thought associated "order" with good and "disorder" with evil. A typical example of such thought can be found in George Meredith's poem "Lucifer in Starlight" (1883), which describes Satan's attempt to fly up to heaven: "On a starred night Prince Lucifer uprose. / Tired of his dark dominion" (lines 1–2). But he is prevented from invading heaven by the very power of divine order:

> He reached a middle height, and at the stars,
> Which are the brain of heaven, he looked, and sank.
> Around the ancient track marched, rank on rank,
> The army of unalterable law.
> (lines 11–14)

It is precisely this kind of thinking that the blind man warns against, emphasizing that mere order must not be imbued with any inherent virtue. In fact, the Gnostic concept of heimarmene illustrates a system in which evil harnesses order to further its own ends. Hans Jonas explains that for the Gnostics,

> That universe has none of the venerability of the Greek *cosmos*.... Yet it is still a *cosmos*, an order—but order with a vengeance, alien to man's aspirations.... Far from being chaos, the creation of the demiurge, unenlightened as it is, is still a system of law. But cosmic law, once worshipped as the expression of a reason with which man's reason can communicate in the act of cognition, is now seen only in its aspect of compulsion which thwarts man's freedom. The cosmic *logos* of the Stoics, which was identified with providence, is replaced by *heimarmene*, oppressive cosmic fate. (328)

In other words, where the Christians and Hellenists saw harmony and providence, the Gnostics saw only tyranny and thus refused to assign any virtue to the apparent order of what they saw as an essentially cruel and tyrannical cosmos. The blind man's attitude toward order is closer to the Gnostic view in that he refuses to ascribe a positive evaluation to the concept.

The blind man argues that most human beings do not realize that while "the righteous are hampered at every turn by their ignorance of evil," "to the evil all is plain, light and dark alike." Thus, according to the blind man, the righteous who remain ignorant of evil do so at their own peril, behaving like very small children who try to hide themselves by covering their own eyes. Further dangers arise when one tries to justify the righteousness of certain behavior simply because it is orderly. The blind man warns that one who seeks "to impose order and lineage upon things which rightly have none . . . will call upon the world itself to testify as to the truth of what are in fact but his desires." In other words, if human beings try to justify their actions by enforcing order—a tactic used by all totalitarian regimes—they will find ways to create totally arbitrary moral systems in which "right" and "wrong" lose their status as objective absolutes and are reduced to purely subjective whims. One guilty of such behavior "may seek to indemnify his words with blood for by now he will have discovered that words pale and lose their savor while pain is always new" (293). Ultimately, such human beings will end up justifying their fraudulent righteousness through bloodshed, as the countless ideologically laden atrocities that human beings have committed against each other throughout the course of history will testify all too clearly.[16]

When Billy asks whether such "knowledge were a special knowledge only to the blind," the blind man replies "that it was not" and goes on to explain "that most men were in their lives like the carpenter whose work went so slowly for the dullness of his tools that he had not time to sharpen them" (292). The "dullness" here is an obvious reference to a lack of insight. According to the blind man, most human beings allow themselves to be distracted by their sense perceptions, cluttering up their lives with inconsequential trivialities so that they have neither the time nor the inclination for spiritual development. The blind man tells Billy that "the picture of the world is all the world men know and this picture of the world is perilous," explaining that eyesight, or "that which was given him to help him make his way in the world has power also to blind him to the way where his true path lies" (293). It is important at this stage to distinguish between two kinds of blindness, namely the physical and the spiritual. The blind man is physically blind but possesses spiritual insight. His words serve as a warning to those who have the use of their eyes but are spiritually blind.

The idea that the eyes can blind and that the manifest world deceives is a common theme in the Perennial Philosophy and indeed within McCarthy's fiction.[17] In her study of mysticism, Evelyn Underhill explains that many practitioners of esoteric traditions agree that we cannot apprehend divine Reality through our senses, because "this sense-world, this seemingly real external universe—though it may be useful and valid in other respects—cannot be *the* external world, but only the Self's projected picture of it. . . . The evidence of the senses, then, cannot be accepted as evidence of the nature of ultimate reality" (6). According to Underhill, "Transcendental matters are, for most of us, always beyond the margin;

because most of us have given up our whole consciousness to the occupation of the senses, and permitted them to construct there a universe in which we are contented to remain." Underhill imparts much the same warning as the blind man when she concludes that although the senses are "useful servants," they make "dangerous guides" (56). In keeping with the theme of blindness, Edward Conze, in his commentary on the Buddhist sutras, writes, "To the Spirit in us all external and internal objects—imaginary, false, sham supports—are obstacles, obstructions to vision, impediments to the free flow of transcendental wisdom. Our eyes blind, our ears deafen, our intellects stupefy us" (*Buddhist Wisdom Books* 96). The same idea can be found in a Hermetic Gnostic text that describes how the material body is the "enemy whom you have put on [as] a robe, who drags you by the throat downwards . . . so that you may not look up and see the beauty of the truth and the good that lies therein." This enemy "makes insensitive the organs of sense . . . blocking them with much matter and filling them with filthy desire, so that you neither hear what you ought to hear nor see what you ought to see" (qtd. in Rudolph 114). Buddhists also associate such blindness and ignorance with evil, as Edward Conze explains: "Buddhism teaches that *ignorance* (*avidyā*) is the root evil and the starting point of the chain of causation. This ignorance is in part blindness to the true facts of existence, and in part a self-deception which, misdirecting our attention towards a manufactured world of our own making, conceals the true reality" (*Further Buddhist Studies* 17). It is significant that *avidyā* (ignorance) is derived from the root word *vid* (to see); hence, *a-vidyā* literally translates to "not seeing." Buddhist sutras warn that "sense-pleasures are impermanent, deceptive, trivial" and "ruinous" (Conze, *Buddhist Scriptures* 108). McCarthy's blind man claims that the world that man "imagines to be the ciborium of godlike things will come to naught but dust before him" (293). His words recall Buddhist warnings against attachment to the impermanent and deceptive world of the senses.

In effect, physical blindness prompted the blind man to develop spiritual insight, forcing him to realize that he had been spiritually blind before the German officer sucked out his eyes. When, in the early days of his blindness, a woman passing him on the road had "asked him had he always been blind," the newly blinded man had contemplated her question and "after a while" he came to the realization "that yes he had" (279). The blind man claims that the realization that he had "always been blind" applies to all human beings still deceived by the illusions of manifest existence. Jacob Boehme expressed a similar feeling when he wrote, "By my own powers I am as blind as the next man and can do nothing, but through the Spirit of God, my own inborn spirit pierces all things—though not always with enough perseverance" (qtd. in Berdyaev vii). Like the blind man, Boehme believed that although our eyes are blind to the ultimate divine Reality, the spirit within us sees very clearly, but only if it is trained to do so through "perseverance," or spiritual development. The Buddhist sutras similarly criticize the spiritual blindness and ignorance of unenlightened human beings, claiming that "greed and delusion obscure their sight, and they are blind from birth" (Conze, *Buddhist Scriptures* 50). Much like Boehme and the blind man, Buddhism teaches that spiritual perseverance, or meditation, results in "the eye of faith and the eye of wisdom replacing the eyes of the body" (Conze, *Buddhism* 25). The Buddhist sutras claim that it is possible to cultivate spiritual insight by turning away from the manifest illusions of the visible world; in the blind man's case, this process was facilitated by his physical blindness.

The blind man tells Billy, "Somos dolientes en la oscuridad. Todos nosotros. Me entiendes? Los que pueden ver, los que no pueden." (We are mourners in the darkness. All of us. Do you understand me? Those who can see, those who cannot.) (293). The blind man's message echoes the First Noble Truth of the Buddha: all existence is suffering. Huston Smith explains that, according to Buddhist thought, suffering "seeps at some level into all finite existence," and precisely because existence is finite and all its joys must eventually end, "even pleasure is but gilded pain" (*Religions of Man* 110). The blind man's choice of the word "mourners" serves as a reminder that we are all marked by the certainty of death. The impermanence of existence is further emphasized by the blind man's next piece of advice: "Lo que debemos entender . . . es que ultimamente todo es polvo. Todo lo que podemos tocar. Todo lo que podemos ver." (What we should understand . . . is that finally everything is dust. All we can touch. All we can see.) (293). The reference to "dust" alludes to the Anglican burial service, "ashes to ashes, dust to dust," a phrase based on a line from Genesis 3:19: "Dust thou art, and unto dust thou shalt return." According to the blind man, none of the sensual experiences of the manifest world possess any permanence or stability and all are marked by entropy and death.

After delivering this rather grim sermon, the blind man says an astonishing thing: "En esto tenemos la evidencia más profunda de la justicia, de la misericordia. En esto vemos la benición más grande de Dios." (In this we have evidence more profound than justice, than mercy. In this we see the greatest blessing of God.) (293). At first glance, these words don't seem to make any sense; why should we be grateful for the impermanence of all that we know and love? The blind man's words puzzle Billy and he asks "why this was such a blessing." The answer, the blind man's final statement in the novel, is esoteric and profound: "The blind man did not answer and did not answer and then at last he said that because what can be touched falls into dust there can be no mistaking those things for real. At best they are only tracings where the real has been. Perhaps they are not even that. Perhaps they are no more than obstacles to be negotiated in the ultimate sightlessness of the world" (294). The blind man argues that although the world is composed of manifest illusion, which serves to distract us from the divine Reality, these distractions are only Platonic "tracings where the real has been"; hence there can be no mistaking them for Truth. These "obstacles," once "negotiated," lead to the ultimate Reality of the Absolute. In the words of Plotinus: "The objects of earthly loves are mortal, hurtful and loves of shadows that change and pass, for these are not what we really love, not the Good that we are really in search of" (qtd. in Perry 113). The blind man's words are similar to Huston Smith's description of the relationship between the Absolute, or "Being," and the manifest world: "We cannot presume that Being in its infinity bears more than a trace of resemblance to the being we encounter in rocks or mountains or waterfalls" (*Forgotten Truth* 55). The blind man's unconventional optimism in the face of impermanence is also reminiscent of the Buddhist approach. Edward Conze explains that "the Buddhist doctrine of universal suffering" reflects "itself in a doctrine of cheerful countenance. . . . This world may be a vale of tears, but there is joy in shedding its burden" (*Buddhism* 21). According to the blind man, the manifest world may be a place of darkness, but it is also only "dust," which falls to nothing like "an insubstantial pageant, faded" (Shakespeare, *Tempest* 4.1.155). Although the blind man presents a stark vision of the illusory and transient nature of the world, he finds hope in the face of its very impermanence.

After hearing the blind man's story, Billy's own perception of reality continues to darken, though it is not clear whether this is due to the lessons learned from the various anchorites or as a response to his own experiences of terrible misfortune, for which he blames himself, namely, his failure to save the wolf and the death of his parents. It is probably a mixture of both, with the anchorites' parables serving as a metaphysical framework for the narrative structure of the novel. Bidding farewell to the blind man and his wife, Billy tracks down his severely wounded brother, Boyd, who in turn asks Billy to bring the Mexican girl with whom he has fallen in love to his bedside. As Billy sets out to fetch the unnamed girl, he has time to contemplate some of the darkness described by the blind man. Lying "on the cooling earth" and watching the stars, Billy studies "those worlds sprawled in their pale ignitions upon the nameless night" and tries "to speak to God about his brother." We are not told whether he succeeds, but the fact that "after a while he slept ... and woke from a troubling dream and could not sleep again" (295) suggests that his attempt to find comfort in God was unsatisfactory. The presence of the cold, incomprehensibly distant and innumerable worlds in the night sky, combined with the failed attempt to speak to an unresponsive God, creates a scene of dismal alienation and terrible loneliness. Billy reveals more about his relationship with the God of this world when he converses with the Mexican girl, who believes "that God looked after everything and that one could no more evade his care than evade his judgment," adding "that even the wicked could not escape his love." Billy watches her, quietly, and then admits "that he himself had no such idea of God and that he'd pretty much given up praying to Him" (325). Billy seems to have lost faith in the idea that an omniscient, omnipotent, and benevolent God looks after this world.

Further glimpses into the darkness of Billy's interior life are revealed through the grim descriptions of the landscape that falls under his gaze, as though he were projecting his own despair onto the inanimate objects around him. Billy looks "east to see if there were any trace of dawn graying over the country but there was only the darkness and stars." The absence of dawn signifies the absence of light and hence the absence of hope; only the enormity and darkness of space, with its cold and distant stars, remains. Prodding the ashes of a dying fire with a stick, Billy finds that the "few red coals that turned up in fire's black heart seemed secret and improbable. Like the eyes of things disturbed that had best be left alone" (325). The "fire's black heart" may just as well refer to the black heart of the cosmos, which the blind man had come to apprehend.[18]

When Boyd runs away with the Mexican girl, leaving his brother completely alone, Billy suddenly becomes aware of the "enmity of the world," which "was newly plain to him that day and cold and inameliorate as it must be to all who have no longer cause except themselves to stand against it" (331). Billy's negative epiphany appears to be of a similar nature to that particular variety of existential crisis that purportedly precedes the Kierkegaardian leap of faith: "It is then that you catch yourself by yourself, just for a moment, against the background of a kind of nothingness all around you, and with a gnawing sense of your powerlessness, your utter helplessness in the face of this astonishing fact that you are there at all" (Conze, *Buddhism* 23). This is the vision of the world that the blind man has been trying to convey, yet it took the bitterness of a brother's betrayal to make Billy fully aware of the validity of the blind man's insight. Unfortunately, Billy's despair is not alleviated by an apprehension of what the blind man calls the "Good God." Although Billy is sufficiently aware of the dark aspects of the world to accept what is essentially the First Noble Truth of the Buddha—that existence is suffering—he is unable to see beyond this devastating vision and thus cannot fathom the soteriological potential of the blind man's gnosis. The blind man's ability to see beyond the darkness of the manifest world, as depicted in McCarthy's works, forms the basis of his conviction that he can see further and more clearly than those who, like Billy, still possess the physical faculties of sight yet lack the clarity of spiritual insight.

CHAPTER 9

"The Right and Godmade Sun"
Destiny and Salvation in *The Crossing*, Book 4

■ Though all four books of *The Crossing* contain meditations on the certainty of death, the illusory nature of time, and the inexorability of fate, these preoccupations are brought sharply into focus in the fourth and final book. In the last quarter of the novel, Billy journeys with his dead brother's bones, holds a strange conversation with a band of gypsies transporting a disintegrating airplane, has a devastating encounter with a hideously crippled dog, and experiences a chillingly epiphanic double sunrise, which concludes the novel. As in the preceding pages of *The Crossing*, many of McCarthy's allusions, symbolic images, and metaphysical themes draw on various spiritual traditions, including the Judeo-Christian religions, Eastern philosophy, and mysticism, as well as apocryphal, Gnostic texts.

Early in book 4, Billy Parham is confronted by an aggressively inebriated Mexican revolutionary, whose "black eyes in their redrimmed cups were sullen and depthless. Like lead slag poured into borings to seal away something virulent or predacious" (357). The description of the sinister element in the drunken man's eyes suggests the work of the demiurgic "artisan" in *Blood Meridian*: the sinister "coldforger" who works "under some indictment and in exile from men's fires," busy "contriving from cold slag brute in the crucible a face that will pass" (310). When Billy sees the bullet scars in the drunken man's chest, he comes to realize that "what he saw was that the only manifest artifact of the history of this negligible republic . . . that had the least authority or meaning or claim to substance was seated before him in the sallow light of this cantina and all else from men's lips or from men's pens would require that it be *beat out hot all over again upon the anvil* of its own enactment before it could even qualify as a lie" (363; italics mine). This passage further evokes the work of *Blood Meridian*'s demiurgic coldforger, "hammering out like his own conjectural destiny all through the night of his becoming some coinage for a dawn that would not be" (310). In all the cases cited above, the narrative voice seems to be alluding to the apparent presence of the sinister creator of this world and his interminable task of forging the course of individual destinies.

In book 4, the inexorable forces of fate are evoked time and time again, along with the implications such forces might have for free will. For example, as Billy faces down the violent drunk, he feels "a sense that some part of his arrival in this place was not only known but ordained" (363), as though the event had been orchestrated by an agency other than his own. Similarly, when Billy joins a funeral party and sits down to eat, he watches how the "mourners wished one another that they profit from their meal and then all of it ground away in the history of its own repetition and he could hear those antecedent ceremonies dropping somewhere like wooden blocks into their slots. Like tumblers in a lock or like the wooden gearteeth in old machinery slipping one by one into the mortices cut in the cogwheel rolling up to meet them" (374). The image of this relentless machine evokes the Gnostic view of heimarmene as the "diabolic invention" (Jonas 205) of the demiurge and his archons. In *The Crossing*, even seemingly insignificant occurrences in the natural world are depicted as having been preordained; cranes that fly overhead are described as having "their metal eyes grooved to the pathways which God has chosen for them to follow" (388). "God," here, seems to refer to the demiurge, whose will transforms the birds into mechanical automata with "metal eyes," rather than living creatures possessing free will.

The idea that all events have been preordained and that the paths of human beings have also been "chosen for them" is emphasized throughout Billy's conversation with a fortune-teller who reads his palm.[1] When Billy asks her what she has seen, she only shakes her head sadly and refuses to reveal what the future holds. Her reluctance to reveal the truth to Billy is later explained by Quijada, the Yaqui Indian, who asks a rhetorical question: "If people knew the story of their lives how many would then elect to live them?" (387).[2] Billy, rightly suspecting that the fortune-teller has foreseen something inauspicious, asks her "if there were no good news at all" (368). She replies only "that he would live a long life," but "con mucha tristeza" (with much sorrow). Then, echoing the First Noble Truth of the Buddha, which teaches that existence is suffering, she adds "that there was no life without sadness" (369). When Billy presses her to reveal what she has seen, she explains "that whatever she had seen could not be helped be it good or bad and that he would come to know it all in God's good time" (368), thereby affirming the idea of predestination, which informs book 4 of *The Crossing*.

The notion that all has been preordained and that one cannot avoid one's destiny is further emphasized by the fact that the fortune-teller foresees the events of the final volume of the Border Trilogy, *Cities of the Plain*. When Billy asks for news of his brother, Boyd, the fortune-teller replies, "Veo dos hermanos. Uno ha muerto." (I see two brothers. One has died.) When Billy tries to tell her that she is mistaken, "that he had a sister who had died," the fortune-teller shakes her head and insists that she is referring to a "hermano" (brother), "uno que vie, uno que ha muerto" (one is living, one has died) (369). At first glance, it may appear that the fortune-teller is referring to Boyd and suggesting that there was another Parham boy who died before Billy and Boyd were born. This is not the case, however, because as the narrative later reveals, Boyd is already dead. The fortune-teller is actually referring to Boyd as the dead brother and to John Grady Cole as the living one.

It is impossible to make sense of the fortune-teller's words until one reads about Billy's fate in *Cities of the Plain*. In the final volume of the Border Trilogy, Billy and John Grady will become as close as brothers, until they too are parted by death, and Billy will indeed lead a long life filled with much sorrow. It seems that Billy is already subconsciously aware of his fate, catching a glimpse of John Grady's death in a dream in which he "knelt in the rain in a darkened city and he held his dying brother in his arms but he could not see his face and he could not say his name."[3] When he wakes, we are told, "He knew he feared the world to come for in it were already written certainties no man would wish for" (325). The reference to the "world to come" subtly links the dream with the ending of *All the Pretty Horses*, in which John Grady rides out "into the darkening land, the world to come" (302), both passages emphasizing the inevitability of future events.

The theme of predestination is also explored when Billy encounters a rider whom he recognizes as one of the thwarted rapists of Boyd's girlfriend. This unlikely meeting raises questions of whether such events are part of a cosmic pattern or merely random chance.[4] Billy and the man discuss this problem openly, further elaborating on the theme of predestination, or heimarmene, which persists throughout book 4. The man raises the notion that the paths of all human beings have been laid down for them at birth and that the mere act of living carries one toward an unavoidable destiny. "He said that men believe death's elections to be a thing inscrutable yet every act invites the act which follows and to the extent that men put one foot before the other they are accomplices in their own deaths as in all such facts of destiny." The man adds "that while men may meet with death in strange and obscure places which they might well have avoided it was more correct to say that no matter how hidden or crooked the path to their destruction yet they would seek it out" (379). He explains that there is no deviating from such a path, for even when we imagine that we are acting freely, our choices—no matter how random they might seem—have already been predetermined by our destiny.

The inverse of this argument will later be put forward by Quijada, who tells Billy, "People speak about what is in store. But there is nothing in store. The day is made of what has come before. The world itself must be surprised at the shape of that which appears. Perhaps even God" (387). Billy voices his own opinion on the matter, arguing that it makes no difference to the individual whether his life has been preordained or whether he is in fact the master of his own destiny: "He said that whether a man's life was writ in a book someplace or whether it took its form from day by day was one and the same for it had but one reality and that was the living of it. He said that while it was true that men shape their own lives it was also true that they could have no shape other for what then would that shape be?" (379–80). Billy reasons that, in the first hypothetical case, human beings merely believe that they are acting out of free will, when they are in fact following a preordained path; in the second case, they carve out their own paths, but either way, the belief in free will remains. Billy seems to be arguing that we must live *as though* we possess free will; whether or not we actually do is ultimately of no consequence to us, at least not from our individual perspectives.

After looking forward to the ending of the Border Trilogy, the narrative then takes a retrospective view, presenting scenes that seem to hark back to McCarthy's first Western novel, *Blood Meridian*. When Billy arrives at the town of San Buenaventura in search of his brother's bones, he halts his horse and looks "out over this desolation" and at "the evening light failing in the west" (388). As he watches the sun setting, he feels that the "desolation of that place was a thing exquisite" (389). The landscape evokes the "purgatorial waste" (63) of *Blood Meridian*, where the kid also looks "about at this desolate scene" (315). When Billy walks into a church, he finds that "in that half fugitive light knelt a solitary figure bent at prayer. . . . He bent and touched the kneeling figure on the arm. Senora, he said" (389). This scene is reminiscent of the kid's encounter with the kneeling penitent in *Blood Meridian*:

"He saw alone and upright in a small niche in the rocks an old woman kneeling in a faded rebozo with her eyes cast down.... He spoke to her in a low voice.... Abuelita, he said.... He reached into the little cove and touched her arm." Of course, while the kid finds that the woman is only "a dried shell," who "had been dead in that place for years" (315), Billy's encounter proves much less macabre, though also spiritually disappointing. The woman talks to Billy and tells him "that she only prayed. She said that she left it to God as to how the prayers would be apportioned. She prayed for all. She would pray for him" (390). Though her universal, limitless compassion is deeply admirable, it seems to be lost on the deaf ears of the indifferent demiurgic deity who presides over the Border Trilogy and indeed over all of McCarthy's works.

Billy's response indicates a degree of disillusionment with the God of this world; he feels that he "knew her well enough, this old woman of Mexico, her sons long dead in that blood and violence which her prayers and her prostrations seemed powerless to appease. Her frail form was a constant in that land, her silent anguishings." He sees how her prayers have been powerless to prevent suffering, to keep back "the night," which "harbored a millennial dread" and "fed upon the children still." Yet he also wonders "what worse wastes of war and torment and despair the old woman's constancy might not have stayed." He sees "her small figure bent and mumbling, her crone's hands clutching her beads of fruitseed. Unmoving, austere, implacable. Before such a God" (390). It seems that the God of this world, as presented in McCarthy's fiction, displays no desire to alleviate human or animal suffering. The indifference of this God is further emphasized during Billy's quest to return Boyd's bones to American soil. The divine presence manifests itself as "the old gods of that country," who watch Billy indifferently, "tracing his progress over the darkened ground. Perhaps logging his name into their ancient daybook of vanities" (393). When Boyd's disinterred corpse is thrown on the ground by a band of robbers, Billy sees his dead brother "lying there with his caven face turned up and clutching himself like some fragile being fraught with cold in that indifferent dawn" (395). The passage implies that the cold and indifferent sky houses an equally cold and indifferent deity.

After his death, Boyd frequently appears in Billy's dreams, hinting at a spiritual dimension of existence that persists after death: "In the dream he knew that Boyd was dead and that the subject of his being so must be approached with a certain caution for that which was circumspect in life must be doubly so in death and he'd no way to know what word or gesture might subtract him back again into that nothingness out of which he'd come." When Billy finally "did ask him what it was like to be dead Boyd only smiled and looked away and would not answer" (400).[5] This chilling visitation from the dead boy contributes to the recurring themes of transience, mortality, and loss that permeate the entire Border Trilogy. To emphasize this point, Billy meets a man who speaks "as one who seemed to understand that death was the condition of existence and life but an emanation thereof" (379). The man's words echo the Buddhist attitude toward death, as explained by Edward Conze: "Dying, like becoming, or like coming to birth, is really a continuous process, going on steadily all the time.... Death is not to be regarded as a unique catastrophe which happens when one existence comes to an end, but it takes place all the time within that existence" (*Thirty Years* 96). Elsewhere Conze explains that, according to Buddhist thought, life "is bound up with death and inseparable from it" and that "birth" itself "is the cause of death," because "we start dying the moment we are born" (*Buddhism* 23). Gnosticism also equates life with death, utilizing "'death' as a symbol of the world as such" and teaching that the manifest cosmos is "a world of death without eternal life, a world in which the good things perish and plans come to naught" (Jonas 59, 58). Thus both the Buddhists and Gnostics believed that the opposite of death is not earthly life—which is just an "emanation" of death—but total liberation from manifest existence.

Themes of death and transience are further explored in the final parable delivered by the leader of a band of gypsies who stop to help Billy's injured horse. The gypsies have with them the husk of an old airplane, a symbolic parallel to Boyd's remains that Billy is carrying back across the border to America. The gypsy recounts the tale of how he and his men were hired by the father of a dead pilot to recover the remains of his son's airplane from the mountains. In keeping with the theme of heimarmene that pervades book 4, the gypsy presents his own views regarding the machinations of destiny. He tells Billy that a "seeress" had "tried to warn them back" from their quest to retrieve the plane and though he "had weighed the woman's words," he eventually dismissed the warning because "he knew what she did not." The gypsy explains that, unlike the seeress, he knew "that if a dream can tell the future it can also thwart that future. For God will not permit that we shall know what is to come." According to the gypsy, the very act of divining the future causes that future to take an alternate course. He goes on to explain that "those who by some sorcery or by some dream might come to pierce the veil that lies so darkly over all that is before them may serve by just that vision to cause that God should wrench the world from its heading and set it upon another course altogether" (407). The gypsy's portrayal of God, though not explicitly condemnatory, possesses certain Gnostic overtones that evoke the capricious demiurge rather than the benevolent, loving God of Christianity. For example, the Apocryphon of John, a Gnostic text that offers a subversive reinterpretation of the creation myth in Genesis, describes how the demiurge "enshrouded man's perceptions with a veil and made him heavy with unperceptiveness—as he said himself through the prophet (*Isaiah* 6:10): 'I will make heavy the ears of their hearts, that they may not understand and may not see'" (qtd. in Jonas 93). The gypsy's description of a God who places a dark veil over humanity's knowledge of what heimarmene holds in store evokes the behavior of the demiurge, who, according to the Gnostics, similarly obscures the light of gnosis and plunges creation into the darkness of ignorance in order to dull our perceptions and confuse our insights.

Further Gnostic overtones are revealed in the gypsy's description of a drowned corpse that he and his men saw in the mountains, carried along by the flooded river "like a pale enormous fish." The decomposing body is described as "some incubus or mannequin," as though it has been reanimated by some strange entity, or unseen force.[6] The gypsy recalls how the drowned man "circled once facedown in the froth of the eddywater beneath them as if he were looking for something on the river's floor and then he was sucked away downriver to continue his journey." Viewed in light of the earlier conversations regarding destiny and predetermination, it appears that not even a corpse is free from the forces of heimarmene but must continue along the path laid out for it by sinister cosmic forces. The gypsy's vivid descriptions of the decomposing body reveal the horrors of the flesh: "His clothes were gone and much of his skin and all but the faintest nap of hair upon his skull all scrubbed away by his passage over the river rocks. In his circling in the froth he moved all loosely and disjointed as if there were no bones in him." The gypsy describes how he and the other men were afforded a glimpse of the drowned man's skeletal and muscular structure, along with his internal organs: "They could see bones and ligaments and they could see the tables of his smallribs and through the leached and abraded skin the darker shapes of organs within." He recalls how "when he passed beneath them they could see revealed in him that of which men were made that had better been kept from them" (409). The gypsy's words suggest that to see the internal organs of a fellow human being is a disturbing reminder that we are composed of meat and subject to the inevitability of death and decay.

The Gnostics regarded all bodies, even those of the living, as corpses designed to trap the pneuma, which has been "buried in the body as if in a tomb and a sepulchre" (Jonas 190). For example, the Apocryphon of John regards the body as "the tomb," "which was put upon man as a fetter of matter (Gr. *hyle*)" (qtd. in Jonas 103). Such aversion to the human form is not restricted to Gnosticism but also occurs in the Buddhist tradition, in which "the monk is urged to visit cemeteries or burial grounds in order to see what his body is really like in the varying stages of decomposition" (Conze, *Buddhism* 98). Buddhist sutras regard the body with the same revulsion evoked by the image of the drowned man: "A damp skin hides it, but it is a wound, large, with nine openings / All around it oozes impure and evil-smelling matter" (qtd. in Conze, *Buddhist Scriptures* 160). Edward Conze explains that certain Buddhists cultivate a sense of revulsion toward the body and all its functions, for "when we see how precarious the body is, how exposed to all sorts of dangers and frailties, how repulsive in its essential function, then we should feel shame and horror at the conditions in which our divine Self had landed itself" (*Buddhism* 98). Thus, according to Buddhist thought, "that of which men were made" might be unpleasant to look at, but it had not "better [be] kept from them." On the contrary, Buddhism teaches that human beings should meditate on the horror of the flesh in order to seek release from the bodies in which they have been reborn.

The gypsy then goes on to explain that their quest was complicated by the fact that there were actually two identical airplanes, both stranded in the mountains, with no way to tell which belonged to the son of the grieving father. He explains that "if the airplane which their client has paid to be freighted out of the wilderness and brought to the border were in fact not the machine in which the son has died then its close resemblance to that machine is hardly a thing in its favor but is rather one more twist in the warp of the world for the deceiving of men" (405). The words "twist" and "warp" once again evoke the work of the demiurgic weaver god. This reading is strengthened by the reference to "the deceiving of men," for the Gnostics believed that the demiurge and his archons "lead them [human beings] astray with many deceptions" (Pearson 130). Recounting the dilemma of the two planes prompts the gypsy to contemplate the authenticity and significance of relics from the past. He tells Billy that a "false authority clung to what persisted," claiming that the historical artifact "could never speak for that which perished but could only parade its own arrogance. It pretended symbol and summation of the vanished world but was neither" (410, 411). These words imply that although the father desired the airplane as a memento of his lost son, no object can ever stand in for or even adequately represent that which was lost. The gypsy adds "that in any case the past was little more than a dream and its force in the world was greatly exaggerated" (411). The description of the past as a dream echoes the insights of various mystics, for whom "the things of our common-sense world" similarly "appear delusive, deceptive, remote and dreamlike" (Conze, *Buddhism* 110). Thus the gypsy's words serve as a warning to Billy not to become attached to relics of the past, nor to any of the transient objects of this world.

The gypsy explains that "the world was made new each day and it was only men's clinging to its vanished husks that could make of that world one husk more" (411).[7] The gypsy's vision of constant renewal stresses the importance of living in the present instead of looking back to the past. Buddhist sutras also place emphasis on the immediate present, or the eternal now, explaining that we imbue our lives with a false sense of history and continuity, when in reality "we die all the time, from moment to moment, and what is really there is a perpetual succession of extremely shortlived events" (Conze, *Thirty Years* 96). This is precisely why the "heart of Zen training lies in introducing the eternal into the now" (H. Smith, *Religions of Man* 150). Although the gypsy's comments about "vanished husks" are made in reference to the shell of the damaged airplane, the comment is also relevant to the futility of Billy's macabre quest to bury his brother in American soil. Billy mistakenly associates his brother's remains with the memory of his brother. Mere bones, however, possess a "false authority" and can never restore the essence of the living Boyd; they simply reduce him to the level of the artifact he left behind, namely, a dried "husk" of bones and dust.[8]

As is often the case in *The Crossing*, the most important lesson of the tale is imparted in Spanish: "La cáscara no es la cosa" (The husk is not the thing) (411). The gypsy warns Billy against mistaking the outward form, or symbol, for the thing itself.[9] Gary Wallace cites McCarthy's views on this very subject, recalling a conversation in which McCarthy "said that the religious experience is always described through the symbols of a particular culture and thus is somewhat misrepresented by them." McCarthy adds "that those who have not had a religious experience cannot comprehend it through second-hand accounts," precisely because "the mystical experience is a direct apprehension of reality, unmediated by symbol" (138). It is noteworthy that in *The Varieties of Religious Experience*, a work recommended by McCarthy (Wallace 138), William James similarly argues, "Knowledge about a thing is not the thing itself" (354). The idea of direct experience is central to the Perennial Philosophy and, according to Frederick Streng, "To live authentically human beings must know and actualize 'the nature of things.' This is the centuries-long claim of religious seers and philosophers in Eastern and Western cultures. For people to live out their fullest potential they need to awaken to the deepest reality in existence" (371). This is precisely why "the crown of all Buddhist endeavour ... is an attempt to penetrate to the actual reality of things as they are in themselves" (Conze, *Buddhist Scriptures* 145). Thus the gypsy's words—"the husk is not the thing"—not only apply to the physical "husks" of the airplane and Boyd's remains but hint at the very inadequacy of secondhand symbols, whether words or images, in the face of direct experience.

These ideas regarding the primacy of direct experience and the limitations of language are also explored when Quijada tells Billy that the "world has no name" and goes on to explain that the "names of the ceros and the sierras and the deserts exist only on maps. We name them that we do not lose our way. Yet it was because the way was lost to us already that we have made those names. The world cannot be lost. We are the ones. And it is because these names and these coordinates are our own naming that they cannot save us. That they cannot find for us the way again" (387). Quijada's words recall Gnostic metaphors of the spirit trapped in the manifest world, depicted as a traveler who cannot find his way back home and "wanders about lost" (Jonas 49). Like Quijada, the Gnostics were also wary of the false authority of names. The Gospel of Philip claims that the "names of this world belong to error; they have been introduced by the archons ... to lead men astray" (qtd. in Jonas 62). The writer of the gospel concludes that "all earthly language is inadequate" (63), in that it cannot convey the ineffable essence of the alien God.

The various traditions of the Perennial Philosophy all comment on the inadequacy of language when it comes to spiritual experience. In fact, the very "word 'mystic' derives from the Greek root *mu*, meaning silent or mute ... and by derivation unutterable" (H. Smith, *Forgotten Truth* 110). Attempted descriptions of the divine often resort to the apophatic Via Negativa, or negative theology, speaking only in terms of what the Absolute is *not* and very often negating even those negative statements. Huston Smith explains precisely why the Absolute cannot be defined by mere words: "The Infinite cannot be defined positively because definitions compare: either they liken what they define to something or they distinguish it from something.... But the Infinite is all-inclusive, so there is nothing other than it to which it *can* be likened" (*Forgotten Truth* 55). Smith also discusses the futility of attempts to convey that which can only be experienced directly with reference to a Sufi formulation which distinguishes "between the Lore of Certainty, the Eye of Certainty, and the Truth of Certainty, the first being likened to hearing about fire, the second to seeing fire, and the third to being burned by fire" (88). A complete understanding of the latter can be arrived at only through direct experience; no symbol or description can ever convey the full, physical sensation of burning. The Sufis believe that while this holds true for the experience of fire, which we may at least look at and talk about, it is infinitely truer when it comes to experiencing the Absolute, which is both unseen and unutterable. The Buddhist sutras are similarly wary of the traps of language and warn that "The denying of reality is the asserting of it / And the asserting of emptiness is the denying of it" (qtd. in Conze, *Buddhist Scriptures* 172). Both the gypsy's and Quijada's reverence for "the thing" itself and the resulting mistrust of all symbols, representations, or attempts to replace the signified with the signifier echoes the dismay that many of the world's great mystics have felt at the inadequacy of language.

The gypsy extrapolates these ideas to include artifacts, mementos, and even memories, arguing that all are mere representations and can never restore the lost lives they seek to immortalize. While contemplating old photographs of complete strangers, the gypsy had come "to see that as the kinfolk in their fading stills could have no value save in another's heart so it was with that heart also in another's in a terrible and endless attrition and of any other value there was none." He adds that precisely because "the husk is not the thing," every "representation" is "an idol" and "every likeness a heresy."[10] The gypsy goes on to explore the reasons why people take photographs of themselves and each other, explaining that through these "images they had thought to find some small immortality but oblivion cannot be appeased" (413). According to the gypsy, the only earthly immortality we may hope to attain is to live on in the memories of others, but we entrust the memories of our existence to the hearts of other mortals; those who remember us also disappear from the world and take their memories with them. The gypsy claims that "we seek some witness but the world will not provide one" (411), arguing that without a permanent witness to remember our existence, our mementos, photographs, and artifacts become empty signifiers.[11] He explains that his people have internalized the necessary impermanence of all attachments "and this was why they were men of the road" (413).

The Buddhist sutras also stress that impermanence is inherent in all human relationships and that our mortal and therefore brief attachments to friends and family are "like meetings of dream friends, like travellers sharing food with strangers" (qtd. in Conze, *Buddhist Scriptures* 91). It is noteworthy that *The Crossing* itself is permeated with such transitory human relationships that last only for the duration of a single evening, or a single meal, such as those that Billy forms with Don Arnulfo, the ex-priest, the blind man, and finally with the gypsy himself. Returning to the pervading theme of death, the gypsy claims that this too is a source of great misunderstanding, arising out of our failure to see the world as it really is. The gypsy explains that "what men do not understand is that what the dead have quit is itself no world but is also only the picture of the world in men's hearts" (143).[12] This assertion is in agreement with the Mind-only teachings of Yogacara Buddhism, as discussed in previous chapters, according to which "the basis of all illusions consists in that we regard the objectifications of our own mind as a world independent of that mind, which is really its source and substance" (Conze, *Buddhism* 167–68). From a Buddhist perspective, death itself is merely a product of the cosmic illusion, or māyā.

The gypsy then goes on to discuss his ideas regarding ultimate Reality: "He said that the world cannot be quit for it is eternal in whatever form as are all things within it" (413). The gypsy's words are very much in line with the Perennial Philosophy; as Ken Wilber explains, "When all things are nothing but God, there are then no things, and no God, but only *this*. No objects, no subjects, only *this*. No entering this state, no leaving it; it is absolutely and eternally and always already the case" (309). According to this theory, there can be no "quitting" the eternity of the Absolute, because, as Huston Smith explains, it is "unbounded" and "undifferentiated." "Unbounded," because "a boundary would limit it and contradict its infinity" and "undifferentiated, because differentiation implies distinction and thereby in some respect separation." Smith adds that the notion of "separation" or "distance" from the Absolute is valid only symbolically, in that, spiritually speaking, "distance symbolizes ignorance epistemologically and privation affectively" (*Forgotten Truth* 57). If, as Meister Eckhart proclaimed, "God is all and is one. All things become nothing but God" (qtd. in Wilber 309), then all things are one in the ultimate Reality of the Absolute and the "world cannot be quit" because nothing is other to anything else. As with the traditions of the Perennial Philosophy, the gypsy believes that death is only an illusion, born out of the idea that there exists an external world somehow other to ourselves, when, according to the gypsy's view of reality, the manifest world we perceive is unreal, arising out of our own mistaken perceptions.

The gypsy argues that there exists an ultimate Reality, which is timeless, infinite, and eternal. He argues, therefore, that our concept of linear time is misguided in that it arises out of our inability to see ourselves as one with the Absolute: "Pensamos ... que somos las víctimas del tiempo. En realidad la vía del mundo no es fijada en ningún lugar. Cómo sería posible? Nosotros mismos somos nuestra propia jornada. Y por eso somos el tiempo también." (We think that we are the victims of time. In reality the way of the world is not fixed in any place. How could this be possible? We ourselves are our own journey. And for this we are time as well.) (413).[13] The gypsy's words are once again reminiscent of the Perennial Philosophy, which teaches that the "universe is an everlasting succession of events; but its ground ... is the timeless now of the divine spirit" (Huxley 184). Similarly, Rudolph Otto explains that according to the Perennial Philosophy, "multiplicity in space and time is superimposed upon the one unique and by nature uniform Being, because of our seeing only in *Avidya*" (225), "avidyā" being Sanskrit for not-seeing, or seeing in error. Buddhism also teaches that enlightened beings step out of the limitations of both space and time by becoming "identical with the Absolute," or in other words, "with the sum total of existence, with the totality of all things at all times" (Conze, *Thirty Years* 60). Like the gypsy, the Perennial Philosophy insists that the human perception of linear time is false, because, according to the logic of nondualism, there is no separate self and all is timeless. The gypsy argues that "we are time as well," because he believes that we superimpose the concepts of linear time on our existence, when, ultimately, we are timeless and therefore time itself. "Somos lo mismo" (We are the same), insists the gypsy, emphasizing the theme of spiritual unity that runs throughout *The Crossing*. He then adds a series of adjectives—"Fugitivo. Inescrutable. Desapíadado." (Fugitive. Inscrutable. Unpitied.) (413)—that give his pronouncement a distinctively Gnostic air. "Fugitive" suggests the Gnostic concept of the pneuma, being "that which stems from elsewhere and does not belong here," suffering "anguish and homesickness." "Inscrutable" expands on this theme by evoking the Gnostic description of the pneuma as a "stranger who is lonely, unprotected, *uncomprehended*, and *uncomprehending* in a situation full of danger" (Jonas 49;

italics mine). "Inscrutable," however, also points to the ineffable nature of the alien God and by extension the pneuma itself. "Unpitied" evokes the description of the "pitiless sky, which no longer inspires worshipful confidence" (Jonas 255). The gypsy's description of our existential and spiritual situation echoes the Gnostic vision of the human plight in a hostile but ultimately illusory cosmos.

After the gypsies take their leave, Billy experiences a series of distinctly Gnostic revelations. The first of these occurs when Billy sees how "the nacre bowl of the moon sat swaged into the reefs of cloud like a candled skull" (416). This vision of foreboding recalls the Gnostic horror at the perceived evil of the night sky: "How evil its brilliance must have looked to them, how alarming its vastness and the rigid immutability of its courses, how cruel its muteness!" (Jonas 261). The "candled skull" also evokes death and the sinister connotations of occult rituals, in which such candles may be used. On a more subtle level, the image suggests the Gnostic concept of the divine spark trapped within matter, reminiscent of the "inner fire" burning within the antelopes in book 1 of *The Crossing* and the "deeper fire" burning in the blind man's empty eye sockets in book 3 (4, 277).[14]

This nighttime vision is followed by a dream that seems to signify the human plight from a Gnostic perspective. In this dream, Billy sees "God's pilgrims laboring upon a darkened verge in the last of the twilight of that day" (421). As discussed previously, the word "pilgrim," especially in its early usage, can refer to "a foreigner, an alien" or "a stranger" (*OED*), a quintessentially Gnostic metaphor for the pneuma's position in the manifest cosmos. Furthermore, the "laboring" of these pilgrims evokes the toiling of Adam and Eve after their expulsion from the Garden of Eden. The God of Genesis, whom the Gnostics equated with the demiurge, tells Adam, "In the sweat of thy face shalt thou eat bread, till thou return unto the ground" (Genesis 3:19). The pilgrims "seemed to be returning from some deep enterprise that was not of war nor were they yet in flight but rather seemed coming from some labor to which perhaps these and all other things stood subjugate" (421). Again, the reference to labor evokes the toil of earthly existence, but now it becomes clear that the pilgrims do not labor freely but are enslaved, or "subjugate." As has already been established, the Gnostics believed that both the soul and the body were "a product of evil powers" and through this man was "not only the object but also the subject of the activity of such powers" (Rudolph 88). Alternatively, as Hans Jonas explains, "Through his body and his soul man is a part of the world and subjected to *heimarmene*" (44). Thus subjugation evokes the Gnostic concept of heimarmene, which enslaves the pilgrims "and all other things" within the manifest cosmos.

In the dream, Billy looks "to see if he could tell by the nature of their implements what it was they had been about but they carried none and they toiled on in silence against a sky that was darkening all around and then they were gone" (421). The fact that the pilgrims toil "against" the "darkening" sky suggests that they work in opposition to the forces of darkness.[15] Billy cannot follow them to the "place where they were going," because it is separated from him by "a dark arroyo" (421), an image that suggests the domain of the dead; an underworld usually separated from the realm of the living by a dark river, such as the Styx, which runs through Hades in Greek mythology. The Spanish word "arroyo" is derived from the Late Latin "arrugius," meaning a "gold mine" or an "underground passage" (*OED*). It is interesting that both Gnostic and Buddhist texts use gold as a metaphor for the divine potential within living things. Edward Conze compares a Gnostic text that reads, "As gold sunk in filth will not lose its beauty but preserve its own nature, and the filth will be unable to impair the gold, etc.," with the Buddhist Ratnagotravibhaga: "Supposing that gold belonging to a man on his travels had fallen into a place full of stinking dirt. As it is indestructible by nature, it would stay there for many hundreds of years" (qtd. in *Further Buddhist Studies* 29). Conze concludes that "in both cases this is a simile for the divine spark in man" (29). Thus Billy may have had a symbolic Gnostic vision of the human plight; the dream pilgrims are subjugated by heimarmene, struggling for spiritual insight against the encroaching darkness, only to fail and disappear into the underworld, where the living cannot follow. When Billy wakes "in the round darkness," he feels "that something had indeed passed in the desert night and he was awake a long time but he had no sense that it would ever return again" (421), evoking a sense of missed opportunity, or a failure to understand the significance of that which has been revealed to him.

Homeless and utterly alone, Billy drifts aimlessly for months, occasionally settling down to work "for the Carrizozo's and for the GS's" and then leaving for "no reason he could name" (422). The narrative voice covers this period of lonely wandering in a few abrupt sentences, slowing down the pace only as Billy approaches the final, darkly epiphanic revelation that concludes the novel. Sheltering from a storm in an abandoned building, Billy is approached not by the usual mysterious anchorite come to impart wisdom but by a wretched dog, both heart-wrenching and nauseating in its suffering: "It was an old dog gone gray about the muzzle and it was horribly crippled in its hindquarters and its head was askew someway on its body and it moved grotesquely." The narrative voice refers to the dog as an "illjoined thing," immediately evoking the presence of an entity responsible for the joining. This concept is further developed by a description of the dog as being "so scarred and broken that it might have been patched up out of parts of dogs by demented vivisectionists" (423). These "demented vivisectionists" bring to mind the Gnostic archons who assist the demiurge in the process of creation.[16] According to the Gnostic reinterpretation of Genesis in the Apocryphon of John: "Yaldabaoth (the demiurge) . . . then says to the authorities with him, 'Come, let us create a man according to the image of God and according to our likeness, that his image may become a light for us'" (qtd. in Pearson 116). The archons' abortive attempt at the creation of a human being results in a creature as wretched as the dog of *The Crossing*. The first human "could not stand erect because of the powerlessness of the angels, but crept like a worm" (Pearson 116). Similarly, the crippled dog is so deformed that it can only "crab sideways" (423).

Billy's experience with the wretched dog is a darkly distorted reflection of his encounter with the noble wolf in book 1 of *The Crossing*. The image of the decrepit dog, hobbling hideously toward the abandoned building, is in stark contrast to the image of the swift wolf "running in the mountains, running in the starlight," where all was "fear and marvel" (127). The unsettling disparity between these two images that frame the novel serves as a reminder that "nature is as incomprehensibly appalling as it is lovely and bountiful" (Huxley 190). Hailed as the "repository of ten thousand indignities and the harbinger of God knew what" (424), the dog serves not only as a reminder of the Buddhist teaching that existence is suffering but also as an evil omen of further suffering to come.

The description of the dog also calls to mind a saying from the *Dao De Jing*: "Heaven and Earth are not benevolent; / They treat the ten thousand things like straw dogs" (qtd. in Needham and Ling 48). Joseph Needham and Wang Ling explain that straw dogs were "part of the ancient sacrificial ritual (replacing earlier sacrificial victims)" (48). Precisely because Buddhism, like Taoism, teaches that nature is not benevolent and all unenlightened sentient beings are marked by duḥkha (suffering), Buddhist sutras stress the importance of cultivating compassion for all sentient beings: "Even as a mother watches over and protects her child, so with a boundless mind should one cherish all living beings, radiating friendliness over the entire world, above, below, and all around without limit" (qtd. in Conze, *Buddhist Scriptures* 186). Yet while the wolf inspired awe, respect, and compassion in Billy, the crippled dog inspires only horror, disgust, and anger. Both animals are in equal need of compassionate aid, and if the dog was sent to Billy as a test, it is a test that Billy fails spectacularly. Instead of offering the dog shelter, Billy cruelly chases it away, throwing rocks and a "length of pipe," which "went clanging and skittering up the road behind the dog and the dog howled again and began to run, hobbling brokenly on its twisted legs with the strange head agoggle on its neck." As the dog runs away it emits a series of anguished howls, "a terrible sound. Something not of this earth. As if some awful composite of grief had broken though from the preterite world" (424). The fleeing dog evokes a terrible sense of despair, as though all the past, or "preterite," misfortunes of the novel—Billy's failure to save the wolf, the murder of his parents, Boyd's death, and the stories of the heretic, the ex-priest, the blind man, and the numerous minor characters who voice their individual narratives of suffering, loss, and despair—were somehow gathered up into one devastating totality, captured in the image of a hideously crippled dog, a "composite of grief," senselessly cast out into the cold, the rain, and the dark. It is also worth noting that the word "preterite" may also be used in a theological sense, in reference to a "person not elected to salvation by God" (*OED*). Thus the "preterite world" may, in fact, be not only the world of the past but the entire corporeal cosmos, which will never be redeemed and where only freedom from manifest existence offers soteriological hope.

The dog vanishes into the night "on its stricken legs and as it went it howled again and again in its heart's despair until it was gone from all sight and all sound in the night's onset" (424–25). Gone, too, is Billy's chance to redeem the sense of guilt he feels over all his failed enterprises through one simple act of compassion. Billy, however, realizes the significance of this missed opportunity only when it is too late. Waking from sleep in the abandoned barn, Billy walks out into the eerie "white light of the desert noon," soon finding himself bewildered and disoriented by the fact that what he had assumed to be the light of the midday sun is rapidly "drawing away along the edges of the world" and changing back into night. The confusion, despair, and hopelessness of this scene are emphasized, metaphorically, by the repeated descriptions of the "fading light" and "darkening shapes of cloud." The light of the sun, the symbol of illumination, enlightenment, and gnosis, has turned out to be false and fleeting, fading away to be replaced by a pall of hopeless dark. The "road which lay before" turns "yet more dark and darkening still where it ran on to the east and where there was no sun and there was no dawn and when he looked again toward the north the light was drawing away faster and that noon in which he'd woke was now become an alien dusk and now an alien dark" (425). There is no dawn, no redemption, no salvation, and no hope. The "alien dark" evokes Gnostic overtones; as Hans Jonas explains, "'alien' is a constant attribution of the 'Life' that by its nature is alien to this world and under certain conditions alien within it" (49). Jonas adds, "As alien as the transcendent God is to 'this world' is the pneumatic self in the midst of it" (44). Thus the Gnostics believed that if we are indeed children of light and our pneuma is alien to the world, then, conversely, the darkness of the world is also alien to our pneuma and one can speak of the "alien dark" in relation to the light that is our home.

It is important to point out that the false light that Billy has witnessed is not only symbolic or metaphorical but also an actual historical event with terrifying implications for the entire human race and indeed for all life on earth. While McCarthy gives no explanation for the disturbing phenomenon, Alex Hunt provides compelling evidence that "the account of this double sunrise parallels actual accounts of the Trinity Test, the first successful detonation of a nuclear device" (31), which took place at the White Sands test site, Trinity, New Mexico, at 5:29:45 a.m. on 16 July 1945. This scientific explanation, however, does not in any way diminish the darkly epiphanic quality of this vision and, as Edwin Arnold points out, Billy's witnessing of the Trinity Test is "an apocalyptic event, one of both terror and truth" ("Go to Sleep" 62). It now becomes clear that the deformed dog was, in fact, a "harbinger" of the countless mutations, deformities, and horrifying illnesses that, in due time, would be inflicted on living things by the fallout from this man-made radiation.

The Crossing is symmetrical in that it is framed by two diametrically opposed yet profoundly epiphanic experiences. The first of these occurs in book 1, when Billy apprehends the interconnectedness of all living things through a vision of the dead wolf's spirit "running in the starlight" among "the rich matrix of creatures" and "all nations of the possible world ordained by God of which she was one among and not separate from" (127). The second epiphany, revealed through an apocalyptic vision of the false atomic sunrise and the devastating darkness that ensues, results in an inverse apprehension of a profound alienation that seems to underlie human existence.[17] Overwhelmed by the hopeless darkness closing in all around him, Billy feels a sudden bitter sense of regret over his callous treatment of the dog and tries to call the animal back in a futile attempt to share the burden of suffering and to extend the same compassion to the wretched animal as he had once shown to the wolf. "He called and called. Standing in that inexplicable darkness. Where there was no sound anywhere save only the wind" (425–26). The desire to act compassionately comes too late; the dog does not return, leaving Billy alone in a state of desolate alienation. The "inexplicable darkness," while a literal description of the physical setting, is also a metaphor for the very nature of existence as Billy has come to understand it. This is especially true of the Gnostic world view, in which the "darkness has embodied its whole essence and power in this world, which now therefore is *the* world of darkness" (Jonas 57). Billy sinks down by the side of the road, buries his face in his hands, and weeps for all that he has lost: "After a while he sat in the road. He took off his hat and placed it on the tarmac before him and he bowed his head and held his face in his hands and wept" (426). This experience seems to be a culmination of all the darkness and suffering that Billy has encountered throughout the novel.

The Crossing, however, is not without hope. The novel ends on a complex note of despair tinged with redemptive potential: "He sat there for a long time and after a while the east did gray and after a while the right and godmade sun did rise, once again, for all and without distinction" (426). Although the false sunrise dashed the promise of illumination and renewal, thrusting Billy back into the darkness that he has come to believe is the true state of the manifest world, the light of the real sun, with all its connotations of illumination and enlightenment, does eventually return, offering the possibility of salvation to all. Edward Conze writes that both Gnostic and Buddhist texts "place a great emphasis on Light" (*Further Buddhist Studies* 27), or *phos* and *aloka*, respectively. The Buddhist sage Nagasena (c. 150 BCE) describes spiritual wisdom as being "like a lamp which a man would take into a dark house," and the Buddha himself spoke of enlightenment as that state in which "the light of gnosis has dispelled the darkness of ignorance" (qtd. in Conze, *Buddhist Scriptures* 155, 62). In his study of Buddhism, Huston Smith writes that "as the stars go out in deference to the morning sun, so individual awareness will be eclipsed in the blazing light of total awareness" (*Religions of Man* 131). The Gnostic Apocryphon of John refers to the alien God as the "immeasurable light which is pure, holy and immaculate" (qtd. in Wagner and Flannery-Dailey 263). Visible light, in particular the light of the sun, has long been associated with spiritual insight in various traditions.

There is, however, a problematic aspect to this reading: McCarthy's description of the sun as "godmade" raises the question "*Which* God?" Is this a reference to the imperfect demiurge responsible for creating the darkness of the cosmos or to the transcendent Absolute from whence the light of gnosis emanates? Dianne Luce prefers the former reading, arguing that, when it comes to Gnosticism and by extension McCarthy's fiction, "seldom if ever is the sun presented unambiguously as a metaphor for spiritual vision or divine illumination" (*Reading the World* 78). Luce's interpretation of the ending of *The Crossing* is as follows: "The gnostic sun glares upon the just and the unjust, and the death-force is ubiquitous and eternal" (90–91). While I agree that McCarthy does occasionally portray the sun in a sinister manner, most notably in *Blood Meridian*, where the sun is described as "a great red phallus . . . squat and pulsing and malevolent" (44), Luce's reading is not one that can be applied indiscriminately to all the "suns" in McCarthy's fiction. For example, in *Suttree* the sun illuminates the otherworldly water bearer when he gives the protagonist a drink from the waters of life. When Suttree looks at this redeeming, life-affirming figure, he sees "the pale gold hair that lay along the sunburned arms of the waterbearer like new wheat" (471). More significantly, *The Road* depicts a dark and depraved world, totally devoid of light and all that light represents, save for the fragile spark of metaphorical "fire" that the boy and the father carry with them. Here the narrative voice mourns "the banished sun," which "circles the earth like a grieving mother with a lamp" (32). The father, waking "in the black and freezing waste out of softly colored worlds of human love, the songs of birds, the sun" (272), can only dream of what has been lost.

The sun at the end of *The Crossing* has more in common with these benevolent, life-giving portrayals of sunlight then with the malevolent "phallus" of *Blood Meridian*, and even the usage of "godmade" begins to make sense when one looks closely at Gnostic, specifically Manichean, attitudes toward the sun. Dianne Luce agrees that "McCarthy's lack of narrative interest in tracing the failure in the Divine would seem to support Leo Daugherty's claim that the author drew more from the Manichean version of gnosticism than the Valentinian (Syrian-Egyptian)" (*Reading the World* 68). According to Kurt Rudolph, Manichaeism was the most popular form of Gnosticism, so widespread that it "can be regarded as one of the four world religions," along with "Buddhism, Christianity and Islam" (327). Rudolph explains that the Manichean texts show a "positive evaluation of the sun and moon," referring to the transcendent alien God as the "God of the realm of light" whose "abode is the sun" (337). Thus the "godmade sun" in *The Crossing*, especially when read in the full redemptive context of a sunrise that dispels the darkness and the rain, seems to be an emanation of the alien God and a symbol of spiritual enlightenment, rather than the work of an ignorant and malevolent creator demiurge.[18]

Edwin Arnold also argues for the redemptive potential of the sunrise that concludes *The Crossing*, pointing out that "McCarthy ends the book with a paraphrase of Matthew 5:45, taken from Christ's Sermon on the Mount" ("McCarthy and the Sacred" 233). The sermon reads, "That ye may be the children of your Father which is in heaven; for he maketh his sun to rise on the evil and on the good, and sendeth rain on the just and the unjust." Arnold explains, "This is Christ's description of the common grace of God, offered 'without distinction' to all" (233). The idea that all sentient beings are capable of attaining salvation is common to all traditions of the Perennial Philosophy. Evelyn Underhill explains that "the germs of that same transcendent life, the spring of the amazing energy which enables the great mystic to rise to freedom and dominate the world, is latent in all of us; an integral part of our humanity" (445). Buddhism, for example, teaches that "not only are all beings alike in that they dislike suffering, but they are also capable of enlightenment"; therefore, "each of them is a potential Buddha" (Conze, *Thirty Years* 56). In Gnostic eschatology, the pneuma within every human being is identical in substance with the alien God. To explain this concept, Elaine Pagels cites the first-century quasi-Gnostic Simon Magus, who "claimed that each human being is a dwelling place, 'and that in him dwells an infinite power . . . the root of the universe.' But since that infinite power exists in two modes, one actual, the other potential, so this infinite power 'exists in a latent condition in everyone,' but 'potentially, not actually'" (*Gnostic Gospels* 135). Thus *The Crossing* ends on a hopeful note, the sunrise serving as a reminder that although the manifest world as depicted in the novel may be a place of darkness, soteriological hope may be found in the light that shines "for all and without distinction" (426). From a Gnostic perspective, the fact that "the right and godmade sun" rises again suggests that the light of gnosis continues to penetrate the darkness of the manifest world, offering its promise of enlightenment and salvation to every sentient being.

CHAPTER 10

"Beauty and Loss Are One"

Transience and Fate in *Cities of the Plain*

■ The third installment of the Border Trilogy, *Cities of the Plain*, unites the protagonists of *All the Pretty Horses* and *The Crossing*. In the final volume, John Grady's ill-fated love for a Mexican prostitute is a reenactment of his equally ill-fated love for a Mexican aristocrat in *All the Pretty Horses*, while Billy Parham's failure to prevent John Grady's death echoes his failure to prevent his brother's death in *The Crossing*. *Cities of the Plain* is permeated with a sense of futility, as both protagonists engage in unsuccessful attempts to redeem themselves, or to recover that which they lost in the first two novels, only to find that they are powerless to control the inexorable forces of fate that seem to shape their lives. Reading *Cities of the Plain* leaves one with a feeling of déjà vu, which may be attributed to the fact that, rather confusingly, the last novel of the trilogy was actually written first. According to Richard Woodward's interview with McCarthy, when *All the Pretty Horses* was published, "the third part" of the trilogy had already "existed for more than 10 years as a screenplay" (28). Thus *Cities of the Plain* contains the rough outlines of the characters and plotlines that would later be expanded and deepened in *All the Pretty Horses* and *The Crossing*. The text's origins as a screenplay and its subsequent conversion into a novel—a reversal of the usual process—account for the predominance of action and dialogue over the vivid imagery and prose poetry one normally encounters in McCarthy's novels. It also explains the different quality of the prose, which seems rather stark in comparison to the rest of the trilogy, lacking the aesthetic quality and passionate intensity of *All the Pretty Horses*, as well as the numinosity and otherworldliness of *The Crossing*. One could argue, however, that the starkness of the writing is really a form a laconic subtlety and that the novel still deserves careful reading and close examination.

Cities of the Plain possesses many themes and concepts characteristic of the rest of the trilogy. The ubiquitous trope of the blood-red sky, for example, is maintained in *Cities of the Plain*, which features descriptions such as the following: "the sky over the mountains behind them was blood red" (29) and "the sky to the west blood red where the sun had gone and the small dark birds blowing down before the storm" (232). In the second example, themes of violence and suffering are evoked not only through the blood imagery but also through references to the "small dark birds" and "the storm," which recall a description in *All the Pretty Horses* of "a stand of roadside cholla against which small birds had been driven by the storm and there impaled" (73). The allusion to this scene of senseless agony not only serves as a commentary on the cruelty of nature but also ominously foreshadows the terrible fate awaiting the characters of the Border Trilogy. In fact, when John Grady rides to his fatal and fated knife fight with the Mexican pimp, Eduardo, the scene is described as "dark and windy and starless and cold and the sacaton grass along the creek thrashed in the wind and the small bare trees he passed hummed like wires" (233). Here the relentless wind seems to be driving the protagonist toward his inescapable destiny, while the trees that hum like taut wires compound the tension of the moment. John Grady and Magdalena will both find themselves propelled by inexorable forces toward a painful end, much like the little birds blown onto cactus spines.

The suffering of animals is a recurring theme throughout the Border Trilogy and indeed throughout McCarthy's work, being present even in his first novel, *The Orchard Keeper*.[1] In *Cities of the Plain*, the reader is confronted with an image of a dead calf that had "been eaten to the bones and the bones had been dragged about over the ground. The ribcage lay with its curved tines upturned on the gravel plain like some great carnivorous plant brooding in the barren dawn" (158).[2] The idea seems to be that nature itself is carnivorous; whether directly or indirectly, all the creatures of the natural world devour the flesh of others and are in turn devoured; even plants feed on the fertilizer created by decaying flesh.

Violence, cruelty, and death also figure in a disturbing anecdote about jackrabbits, narrated in a darkly comic manner by a relatively minor character, Troy. During a nighttime drive with Billy, Troy runs over a jackrabbit, which makes "a soft thud under the truck" (20). For Troy, the incident brings to mind another nighttime drive some time ago, when "there was all these jackrabbits in the road. They'd set there and freeze in the lights." Troy states that he did not think much of the roadkill at the time and continued to drive throughout the night until he pulled into a "filling station . . . just about daybreak." He then recalls how a woman caught a glimpse of the car and "commenced to holler like she was bein murdered" (21). Troy explains that at first he "didn't know what had happened," until he "got around to the front of the car" and saw that "it was just packed completely full of jackrabbit heads. . . . There was a hundred of em jammed in there and the front of the car the car bumper and all just covered with blood and rabbit guts . . . they was all lookin out, eyes all crazy lookin. Teeth sideways. Grinnin." So appalling was the carnage that Troy admits he "came damn near hollerin" himself (21–22). The anecdote bears no direct relevance to the plot and thus serves a symbolic rather than a narrative function. The ghastly visage of decapitated jackrabbit heads evokes senseless suffering inflicted not through conscious cruelty but rather through sheer carelessness. In this sense, the absurd deaths of the jackrabbits symbolize what is represented in the novel as humanity's equally senseless suffering in an apparently indifferent universe.

Another significant instance of animal suffering occurs when John Grady and Billy hunt down a pack of wild dogs. In the first two books of the trilogy, both protagonists display remarkably compassionate behavior toward animals, respectively horses and wolves. In *Cities of the Plain*, however, the two protagonists cull the wild dogs with such unnecessary cruelty that one wonders whether one is reading about the same characters encountered in the first two volumes. This is particularly true of Billy, who seems to have learned nothing from the terrible sense of regret he felt at his mistreatment of the crippled dog at the end of *The Crossing*. During the dog-hunting scene in *Cities of the Plain*, Billy and John Grady rope the same dog, causing it to rise up "suddenly from the ground in a headlong flight taut between the two ropes and the ropes resonated a single dull note and then the dog exploded." The dog's head goes "cartwheeling," while its body slams "to the ground with a dull thud." The "blood that burst in the air before them" is described as "bright and unexpected as an apparition. Something evoked out of nothing and wholly unaccountable" (167). The use of "unexpected" and "unaccountable" perfectly captures this sudden spectacle of violent brutality. Edwin Arnold argues, "Although it is a great action episode, described and paced with all of McCarthy's controlled artistry, the almost unconscious brutality of the characters makes us confront their motive to violence as effectively as anything in *Blood Meridian*" ("Last of the Trilogy" 226). Truly, this is behavior one would expect from the Glanton gang rather than from the otherwise sympathetic protagonists of the Border Trilogy.

If we are to assume that the depiction of the dog hunt is something other than a failure to maintain coherent character development, we can only read it as McCarthy's comment on humanity's latent potential for evil. The dog-hunting scene serves to illustrate the point that even the most admirable characters within McCarthy's fiction are capable of gratuitously violent and unnecessarily callous acts. Though the boys never express regret for this cruelty—other than the laconic "goddamn" and "son of a bitch" (169)—they later return to the site and rescue the orphaned pups, an action more in line with the compassionate behavior displayed in the earlier volumes of the trilogy. It is noteworthy, however, that it is John Grady who takes the initiative for the rescue mission, while Billy—who is no longer the boy who showed such remarkable concern for the wolf in *The Crossing*—offers his assistance with exasperated reluctance.

The suffering that permeates *Cities of the Plain* is presented as a universal experience affecting all living things. References to violent histories and senseless bloodshed abound in the Border Trilogy; the final volume is no exception. John Wegner argues that "these novels cry out against the meaninglessness of war and the repetitive historical patterns that create war, arguing that war will simply bury man in the clay that much faster" (78). In *Cities of the Plain*, for example, the elderly Mr. Johnson describes the "terrible things" he saw during the Mexican Revolution, namely, "executions against the mud walls sprayed with new blood over the dried black of the old . . . and the corpses stacked in the streets or piled into the woodenwheeled carretas trundling over the cobbles or over the dirt roads to the nameless graves" (64). He recalls the "thousands who went to war in the only suit they owned" and "the endless riding of horses to their deaths bearing flags or banners or the tentlike tapestries painted with portraits of the Virgin carried on poles into battle as if the mother of God herself were authoress of all that calamity and mayhem and madness" (65).[3] Furthermore, it should be noted that the ironic "as if" in Mr. Johnson's statement nevertheless resonates with a certain truth, for organized religion has indeed been responsible for much of the "mayhem and madness" in human history.

One of the persistent themes within McCarthy's fiction is that cultures and civilizations must inevitably destroy themselves through this very "mayhem and madness" (65).[4] When John Grady asks Mr. Johnson, "What's the news?" the elderly man shakes his head and replies, "Wars and rumours of wars" (61). This is a direct quote from the New Testament on the events that will come to pass before the end of the world: "And ye shall hear of wars and rumours of wars: see that ye be not troubled: for all these things must come to pass, but the end is not yet" (Matthew 24:6). This biblical allusion strengthens the link between the proliferation of war and the annihilation of the human race on earth. The very title of *Cities of the Plain* is significant in that it alludes to the biblical cities of Sodom and Gomorrah, whose inhabitants were so corrupted that Yahweh only saw fit to exterminate them. Erik Hage argues that "this allusion suits McCarthy's larger enterprise in the trilogy—i.e., deliberating on the inevitable ebb and flow of civilizations caught up in the bloody epochs that constitute history" (59). In other words, the reference to the biblical cities of the plain serves as yet another example of a civilization destroyed as a result of humanity's depravity.

The theme of vanished civilizations is also evoked through descriptions of ancient pictographs. Though such imagery is utilized in almost all of McCarthy's novels, it seems especially pervasive in *Cities of the Plain*, where descriptions of "old shamans and the ledgerless arcana" abound (171).[5] John Grady rests in a rocky outcrop with "ancient pictographs among the rocks, engravings of animals and moons and men and lost hieroglyphics whose meanings no man would ever know" (49). The sense of loss is especially poignant here; the sacred mysteries of this ancient civilization have vanished forever, leaving only empty symbols in their wake. Later in the novel, Billy and John Grady pass "under pictographs upon the rimland boulders that bore images of hunter and shaman and meetingfires and desert sheep all picked into the rock a thousand years and more. They passed beneath a band of dancers holding hands like paper figures scissored out by children and stencilled on the stone" (165). These pictographs evoke the vast passage of time, the enormity of which eclipses the insignificant flicker of individual human existence. McCarthy uses the pictographs as a scaling device, placing the contemporary setting within the wider perspective of the history of the human race, which in itself is only a tiny segment of the geological history of the earth.

When the men of McGovern's ranch go hunting, they are described as sitting "against a rock bluff high in the Franklins with a fire before them that heeled in the wind and their figures cast up upon the rocks behind them enshadowed the petroglyphs carved there by other hunters a thousand years before" (87). The petroglyphs serve as a sort of memento mori for the modern hunters, who are destined for the same oblivion as those ancient men who have been dead a thousand years. Indeed, McCarthy's preoccupation with the transience of human life, on both an individual and a collective scale, is discussed in his interview with David Kushner for *Rolling Stone*. Kushner writes that McCarthy's "immersion in science has left him with an admittedly pessimistic worldview; he sees human life on the planet as temporary, and he's sensitized to the degree at which we are accelerating this fate through violence and neglect" (43). The culmination of this apocalyptic vision is realized in McCarthy's *The Road*, but it is a theme that is present, to a greater or lesser extent, throughout his entire oeuvre. The downfall of our civilization is subtly alluded to at the end of *Cities of the Plain*, when the aged Billy, resting under an overpass, sees how "the pale and naked concrete pillars of an east-west onramp stood beyond the truck, curving away, clustered and rising without capital or pediment like the ruins of some older order standing in the dusk" (289). The image serves as an ominous foreshadowing of the future, reminding the reader that our present civilization must one day fade away like all those that came before it, leaving only the ruins of concrete, as the ancient civilizations have left only the ruins of stone.[6]

This shadow of inevitable extinction points to the ephemeral nature of all life; in fact, the entire Border Trilogy is permeated with themes evoking the transience of existence. Susan Kollin argues that the very title of the final volume stems from a sense of nostalgia, "referring readers to the lamentable fate of Lot's wife, who looked back with longing on 'the cities of the plain' in the nineteenth chapter of Genesis," and adds that the "trilogy itself features characters who are likewise brought down by a similar desire, the yearning for experiences that are no longer available" (583). Edwin Arnold writes, "There is a great sense of regret and loss in McCarthy's writing" and "a realization that nothing lasts except loneliness and pain" ("Last of the Trilogy" 240). According to Arnold, John Grady's relationship with Magdalena is, to some extent, "a determined attempt to reenact and make right his failed romance with Alejandra," while "Billy's reluctant assistance is also an effort to redeem the past, specifically his inability, as he maintains, to care properly for his brother" (236–37). Hence, in *Cities of the Plain*, the actions of both John Grady and Billy are motivated by a desire to reclaim what they have lost in the first two volumes of the Border Trilogy.

Older characters within the novel, however, understand that it is impossible to resurrect the past, or even to hold on to the present, and counsel John

Grady against such futile attempts. The blind maestro warns the young man "that those things we most desire to hold in our hearts are often taken from us while that which we would put away seems often by that very wish to become endowed with unsuspected powers of endurance" (193). The maestro's words recall those of the Buddha: "To be conjoined with what one dislikes means suffering. To be disjoined from what one likes is suffering" (qtd. in Conze, *Buddhism* 43). Though the blind man does not know about the failed love affair with Alejandra, his words seem especially pertinent to John Grady's situation: "How frail is the memory of loved ones. . . . How those voices and those memories grow faint and faint until what was flesh and blood is no more than an echo and shadow. In the end perhaps not even that" (193). The maestro claims that we cannot hope to hold on to the memory of the past, because even the ephemeral recollections of what has been lost eventually become so faded and so distorted that in the end we are left with nothing approximating the original.

Mr. Johnson also warns John Grady that "there's hard lessons in this world." When the young man asks, "What's the hardest?" Mr. Johnson replies, "I don't know. Maybe it's just that when things are gone they're gone. They aint comin back" (126). Buddhist sutras similarly emphasize the idea that "everything, whether stationary or movable, is bound to perish in the end" (Conze, *Buddhist Scriptures* 63). Though Mr. Johnson's words can be applied to all facets of life, they are especially true of the loss of loved ones, and it is likely that he is thinking of the death of his daughter as he utters them. The narrative voice informs us that in Mr. Johnson's "time the country had gone from the oil lamp and the horse and buggy to jet planes and the atomic bomb but that wasnt what confused him. It was the fact that his daughter was dead that he couldnt get the hang of" (106). It is clear that even at the end of his long life, Mr. Johnson has still not come to terms with what he considers to be the hardest of life's lessons.

John Grady also struggles with this lesson throughout the novel, refusing to accept that the past is lost forever. John Scaggs argues that "John Grady's desire to recover what has been lost . . . is clear throughout the novel, and is echoed in even the smallest actions" (75). Scaggs cites the example of John Grady swirling the coffee grounds at the bottom of his cup and then swirling "them the other way as if he'd put them back the way they'd been" (*Cities of the Plain* 138) and argues, "It is clear that he has not learned, and never will, what Mr. Johnson considers to be the 'hardest lesson in this world'" (Scaggs 75).[7] The scene with the coffee cup serves as a reminder that one has as much chance of resurrecting the past as one has of swirling coffee grounds back into their original configuration.

As in every one of McCarthy's novels, the landscape in *Cities of the Plain* is highly symbolic, serving as yet another reminder of impermanence and extinction. Much of the novel is set on a drought-ridden ranch where the "wind in the flue" moans "with a long dry sound" (32). John Cant argues that the novel "is set within a landscape of death" (224). In a description of an apocalyptic landscape worthy of *Blood Meridian* or *The Road*, the narrative voice describes "the limits of the city where the roads died in the desert in sand washes and garbage dumps, out to the white perimeters at midday where smoke from the trashfires burned along the horizon like the signature of vandal hordes come in off the inscrutable wastes beyond" (213). Even the inanimate "roads" meet their death in the hostile void of the desert. The evocation of "vandal hordes" suggests the fall of Rome, recapitulating the theme of lost civilizations that permeates the novel.

The urban setting within the novel is continually portrayed as sordid and sinister, echoing McCarthy's depictions of Knoxville in *Suttree*.[8] *Cities of the Plain* features various descriptions of urban squalor that stand in stark contrast to the idyllic pastoral scenes encountered in the first two volumes of the trilogy: "They passed the old abandoned municipal buildings. Rusted watertanks in a yard strewn with trashpapers the wind had left" (140). Steven Frye argues that in the aforementioned passage, "dissipation, exploitation, and decline is rendered fully, at times explicitly evoking the wasteland iconography of T. S. Eliot's poem" (*Understanding Cormac McCarthy* 225). Edwin Arnold also argues that the novel's focus on the urban landscape renders it "the most claustrophobic and the darkest ... book in the trilogy, and at times it harkens to the hellish netherworld conjured up so expertly in *Outer Dark*, *Child of God*, and parts of *Suttree*" ("Last of the Trilogy" 235). The depiction of the earthly realm as a "hellish netherworld" is in accord with the Gnostic world view, which holds "an unequivocally negative evaluation of the visible world together with its creator" (Rudolph 60); this "negative evaluation" also informs much of McCarthy's fiction.

As in Gnosticism, McCarthy's anticosmic vision posits the presence of a sinister agency behind the existence of the hostile world. Often this is quite subtle, as in the description of the tracks of the street trolleys that run over the bridge connecting Juárez to El Paso, which are depicted as being "embedded in the bridge like great surgical clamps binding those disparate and fragile worlds" (7). The image of surgical clamps not only is evocative of pain and violence done to the body but also suggests the presence of a surgeon. The figure of this mysterious, sinister practitioner makes up a running theme throughout McCarthy's fiction, in which surgery is associated with the workings of a hostile creator God. In *Suttree* this is evoked through the symbolic, hallucinatory figures of the "surgeons" (86) and "brainsurgeon" (188), who correspond to the equally symbolic "demented vivisectionists" (423) of *The Crossing* and the "barbarous surgeons" (167) of *Blood Meridian*.

As in Gnostic thought, McCarthy's demiurgical figure is often portrayed as either the orchestrator or personification of heimarmene, the cosmic forces of fate to which all other characters are subject. According to Gnostic thought, as one gains gnosis, one comes to the realization that "the self . . . is not really its own, but is rather the involuntary executor of cosmic designs" (Jonas 329). This appears to be the case in the Border Trilogy, in which the characters seem to travel along predestined paths without any power to change the course of their destinies. As I have argued in preceding chapters, the future that awaits John Grady in *Cities of the Plain* can already be glimpsed in *All the Pretty Horses*. When John Grady wakes from drunken sleep in the first novel of the trilogy, he remembers "things from the night of whose reality he was uncertain." Among these recollections is "a vacant field in a city in the rain and in the field a wooden crate" (255). This is an exact description of the scene of his death in *Cities of the Plain*, "the farther corner of the lot where behind the wall was a clubhouse made from packing-crates" (256). The fact that this premonition is located in the first book of the trilogy conveys a deterministic sense of inevitability. In other words, John Grady's dream reveals that the chain reaction of events resulting in his death had been set in motion long before he even met Magdalena.

The question of personal agency versus orchestrated destiny is one that informs the entire Border Trilogy: Do we have free will or are we mere puppets in the hands of cosmic forces? In *Cities of the Plain*, John Grady frequently expresses views that suggest the latter, claiming, "There's some things you don't decide. Decidin had nothin to do with it" (121). Later the young man thinks "about his life and how little of it he could ever have foreseen and he wondered for all his will and all his intent how much of it was his own doing" (207). Before continuing on to the epilogue, the novel proper ends with the words "all continued on to their appointed places which as some believe were chosen long ago even to the beginning of the world" (262). The idea that human beings are driven along by the tide of destiny is also expressed by the maestro, who argues, "Men imagine that the choices before them are theirs to make. But we are free to act only upon what is given." According to the maestro, "Each act in this world from which there can be no turning back has before it another, and it another yet. In a vast endless net. . . . Choice is lost in the maze of generations and each act in that maze is itself an enslavement for it voids every alternative and binds one ever more tightly into the constraints that make a life." These words portray a deterministic world in which each apparent choice is determined by the one before it, and ultimately, there is no choice at all.[9] The maestro goes on to claim, "Our plans are predicated upon a future unknown to us. The world takes its form hourly by a weighing of things at hand, and while we may seek to puzzle out that form we have no way to do so" (195). The maestro believes that we cannot see the path that lies before us because it changes continually according to an ever-shifting tide of events.

In spite of the maestro's claims that the future cannot be known, various characters within the Border Trilogy experience accurate premonitions of their fate. As has already been mentioned, John Grady's death is foreseen by Alejandra in *All the Pretty Horses*, who sees him "dead in a dream," "carried . . . through the streets of a city I'd never seen. It was dawn. The children were praying" (252). Billy also has a prophetic dream about John Grady's death in *The Crossing*: "He knelt in the rain in a darkened city and he held his dying brother in his arms" (325). This is exactly what comes to pass in *Cities of the Plain*, when "in the gray Monday dawn a procession of school children" watch Billy "coming up the street all dark with blood bearing in his arms the dead body of his friend" (261). The fact that Billy dreamed of John Grady's death even before he knew of his existence suggests that it was inevitable, having been predetermined long before the events leading up to it were set in motion.

Similarly, John Grady and Magdalena both foresee their own and each other's deaths. John Grady has a prophetic and symbolically dense dream about Magdalena's death, in which he sees a "raw wooden stage trimmed like a fairground float" in "a room so cold his breath smoked," where "tourists sat in chairs with operaglasses hanging from their necks while waiters took their orders for drinks. When the lights dimmed the master of ceremonies strode onto the boards and doffed his hat and bowed and smiled and held up his whitegloved hands" (103). It is noteworthy that the theatrical symbolism of John Grady's dream, and its subsequent connotations of deception and illusion, evokes the Gnostic vision of the cosmos as a false reality created by "the deceptive arts" of the demiurge and his archons (Rudolph 117). This theatrical metaphor also occurs in Buddhist sutras; for example, the Prajñāpāramitā teaches that the world is like "a magical show" in that it "deceives, deludes and defrauds us, and it is false, when measured by what we slowly learn about ultimate reality" (Conze, *Selected Sayings* 19).[10] These theatrical metaphors suggest that the reality of the manifest world is as unreliable, deceptive, and transient as the false reality created on the stage, while simultaneously pointing to a higher Reality beyond the realms of the cosmic theater.

The description of the audience as "tourists" perfectly captures the Gnostic evaluation of humanity's position in the cosmos as travelers in a "foreign land" (Jonas 49). The fact that the audience members place orders for drinks suggests the Gnostic metaphor of spiritual drunkenness, which teaches that the ordinary human being is "drunken" and that only the cultivation of gnosis can "make him 'sober,' i.e. drive out his ignorance" (Rudolph 119). Similarly, Hans Jonas explains that in Gnostic thought, the "ignorance of drunkenness is the soul's ignorance of itself, its origin, and its situation in the alien world" (71). Thus not only are the audience members deceived by the theatrical performance, but they willingly dull their insight with the "wine of ignorance" (Jonas 71). The waiters who serve the drinks may be understood as the archons whose purpose it is "to lead men astray" (Rudolph 63), while the master of ceremonies might represent the creator and orchestrator of the cosmos—the demiurge himself.

John Grady's dream continues with a description of the wings of the stage, where "the alcahuete ['accomplice,' referring to Tiburcio] stood smoking and behind him milled a great confusion of obscene carnival folk," the detailed descriptions of which recall the grotesquely carnivalesque hallucinations depicted in McCarthy's *Suttree*.[11] The "obscene" folk include "painted whores with their breasts exposed, a fat woman in black leather with a whip, a pair of youths in ecclesiastical robes. A priest, a procuress, a goat with gilded horns," and "pale young debauchees with rouged cheeks and blackened eyes" (103–4). The scene evokes the Gnostic metaphor of the "orgiastic feast prepared by the world for the seduction of man" (Jonas 71). Hans Jonas explains, "The lust for the things of this world in general may take on many forms, and by all of them the soul is turned away from its true goal and kept under the spell of its alien abode" (71). Thus, from a Gnostic perspective, the orgiastic feast symbolizes the sensual appeal of the world, which distracts human beings from spiritual pursuits; in John Grady's dream, the "obscene carnival folk" seem to be preparing such a feast for the drunken audience.

John Grady's vision of Magdalena's death literally takes center stage within his dream: "At the center of all a young girl in a white gauze dress who lay upon a pallet-board like a sacrificial virgin. Arranged about her are artificial flowers that appear in their varied pale and pastel colors to be faded from the sun. As if perhaps replevined from some desert grave" (104).[12] The reference to the "grave," in conjunction with the funereal flowers surrounding the dream figure, imbues the scene with the unmistakable presence of death. The dream clearly foreshadows the image of Magdalena lying on her "coolingboard" (229) in the morgue. The theme of mortality is evoked even more subtly when the music begins—"Some ancient rondel, faintly martial"—only to fade away again "until only the whisper of the stylus remains, the periodic click like a misset metronome, a clock, a portent. A measure of something periodic and otherwise silent and vastly patient which only darkness could accommodate" (104). The periodic clicking symbolizes the ticking of a clock and thus the inevitable passage of time, bringing the "silent and vastly patient" specter of death closer with every measured stroke.[13] It is noteworthy that the images of the clock mechanism also evoke Newton's clockwork universe, with all its implied determinism.

The very fact that this symbolically dense passage is only a dream is in itself significant, as both the Buddhist and Gnostic traditions are chiefly concerned with "the problem of sleeping in ignorance in a dream world" (Wagner and Flannery-Dailey 259) and both regard the attainment of spiritual insight as an "awakening" (Conze, *Further Buddhist Studies* 29). John Grady, however, does not wake immediately but enters into another dream: "When he woke it was not from this dream but from another and the pathway from dream to dream was lost to him." In the second dream, he finds himself "alone in some bleak landscape where the wind blew without abatement and where the presence of those who had gone before still lingered on in the darkness about." The bleakness, the darkness, and the supernatural wind all evoke Hades, the classical realm of the dead. Furthermore, John Grady's wandering in the footsteps of "those who had gone before" suggests that he will soon be joining them. Even after he awakens, he can still hear voices calling to him: "Their voices carried back to him, or perhaps the echo of those voices. He lay listening" (104). In reality, the "voices" are revealed to be nothing more than a sleepwalking Mr. Johnson, but even he appears to be one of the departed shades, resembling "the ghost of some ancient waddy" (105). Thus the entire dream sequence is permeated with symbols of death.

Just before she has an epileptic fit, Magdalena experiences a vision of her own death that is strikingly similar to John Grady's prophetic dream. John Grady's dream occurs in "a room so cold his breath smoked" and Magdalena's vision is also set "in a cold white room" (103, 225); in both cases the cold is clearly evocative of death. Similarly, while John Grady dreams of "a young girl in a white dress who lay upon a pallet-board," Magdalena sees "herself on a cold white table" (104, 225). John Grady dreams of "painted whores" and Magdalena sees "whores and whores' handmaids many in number and all crying out to her" (103, 225). John Grady's dream consists of a theater performance centered around the "sacrificial virgin," and Magdalena's vision also suggests performative arts when she sees herself sitting "upright on the table" and throwing "back her head as if she would cry out or as if she would sing. Like some young diva remanded to a madhouse. No sound came" (104, 225). It is noteworthy that when Billy dreams of the dead Magdalena, she is similarly unable to make a sound: "He had a dream in which the dead girl came to him hiding her throat with her hand. She was covered with blood and she tried to speak but she could not" (257). She cannot sing or scream because her vocal cords were severed when her throat was slit. Thus Magdalena's prophetic vision reveals not only her death but also the way in which she is to be murdered.

Magdalena also experiences a subtle premonition regarding John Grady's death when she sees "pallbearers carrying upon their shoulders a flower-strewn pallet. Wreathed among those flowers the pale face of a young man newly dead" (207). Although this is an actual funeral procession and not a vision, it still serves as a sinister omen, especially in light of the fact that she sees the corpse of the young man after her final meeting with John Grady. The pallbearers are followed by a cart bearing the young man's coffin: "The cart rattled past and the spoked wheels diced slowly . . . and the long skeins of light in the street broken in the turning spokes and the shadows of the horses tramping upright and oblique before the oblong shadows of the wheels shaping over the stones and turning and turning" (208). The circular movements of the cart's wheels not only trigger Magdalena's epilepsy but also serve as another reminder of the clockwork universe, much like the periodic ticking in John Grady's dream.

Barcley Owens argues that in the Border Trilogy, the "circle motif" as portrayed by the turning cart wheels "represents chosen paths as closed orbits." He goes on to explain that "the clocklike circle of the sun and moon arching across the dome of the sky have long suggested celestial eternity.

However, McCarthy uses circle images to indicate the inscribed birth and death of each individual" (110). Owens points out that "even the straight shafts of light are caught and broken in the brutal fate of the wheels' circling" (111). Similarly, John Scaggs argues that in McCarthy's fiction, "clocks" are depicted "as threatening," explaining that "circular symbols and movement in the novel, therefore, suggest not eternity, but rather, quite the opposite: the inevitability of death, and the connection between clocks and death is evident in the description of the funeral that Magdalena witnesses" (79). This connection is also evident in a description within the novel of "the faultless chronicling of the ancient clockworks in the hallway and the ancient silence of the desert in the darkness about" (178). Barcley Owens argues, "The clock's loud ticking at night is the sound of time passing, regulated and parcelled into small, discrete units. The ticking, like the hands of the clock sweeping around in circles, is immutable fate, a future already decided" (111). These portents of inescapable destiny imbue the deaths of both protagonists with a fatalistic inevitability.

After losing Magdalena, John Grady rides away from the ranch to meet his death. Looking back at the house and his friends for one last time, he can "see them all at supper through the rainbleared glass of the kitchen window. ... He thought it was like seeing these people in some other time before he'd ever come to the ranch. Or they were like people in some other house of whose lives and histories he knew nothing. Mostly they all just seemed to be waiting for things to be a way they'd never be again" (233–34). Not only has he become utterly estranged from his old life, but he knows that things cannot remain the same for anyone; the irrevocable flux of time rushes ever onward toward the certainty of death. The novel is permeated with such reminders of mortality: Soccoro, the cook at the ranch, returns from mass "bearing on her forehead in ash the thumbprint of the priest placed there that morning to remind her of her mortality. As if she had any thought other." "Nothin's forever," Mac claims when he learns of Billy's decision to leave the ranch after John Grady's death, implying that Billy may return to his old job if he ever changes his mind. Mac's words, however, remind Billy that he will never see John Grady again and he replies, "Some things are." "Yeah. Some things are" (263), agrees the widowed Mac, who knows the permanence of loss all too well. In *Cities of the Plain*, loss itself seems to be the only thing that promises any kind of permanence.

For John Grady, however, transience and loss do not carry an entirely negative connotation. Though we are never made privy to a direct, word-for-word transcript of John Grady's thoughts, the narrative voice does offer rare glimpses into the protagonist's inner life, during which the impressions made upon the young man's mind are revealed to us through heightened poetic language. One such instance occurs the morning after John Grady's first night with Magdalena, when he passes a stranger in the street: "The man smiled at him a sly smile. As if they knew a secret between them, these two. Something of age and youth and their claims and the justices of those claims. And of the claims upon them. The world past, the world to come. Their common transiencies. Above all a knowing deep in the bone that beauty and loss are one" (71). The passage is both moving and profound, evoking the fragility and transience of life. It is significant that "the world to come" is also the last phrase in *All the Pretty Horses*, which ends with the iconic image of John Grady riding into the sunset: "Passed and paled into the darkening land, the world to come" (302). At the end of *All the Pretty Horses*, the Native Americans gaze at John Grady riding away: "They stood and watched him pass and watched him vanish upon that landscape solely because he was passing. Solely because he would vanish" (301). The image of horse and rider disappearing into the fading light is presented as being beautiful and poignant precisely because it is transient. The world that awaits John Grady in *Cities of the Plain* is indeed a darkening one, and the "sly smile" of the stranger seems to hint at the sinister nature of this fate. The passage suggests that destiny is unavoidable and that it has already made its claims upon both men and indeed on all human beings. Yet the two men seem to share the belief that impermanence intensifies the beauty of this ephemeral world, rendering it all the more poignant, fragile, and exquisite precisely because they both know, "deep in the bone," that it cannot last.[14]

In the words of W. B. Yeats, "Man is in love and loves what vanishes, / What more is there to say?" ("Nineteen Hundred and Nineteen," lines 42–43). And yet, in spite of Yeats's injunction, there is more to say, especially from the perspective of the Perennial Philosophy. McCarthy's equation of beauty with loss is not simply an aesthetic appreciation of the poignant loveliness of ephemerality but also a spiritual epiphany. According to the blind man of *The Crossing*, this very transience is a "blessing," because if that which "can be touched falls into dust," then "there can be no mistaking those things for real" (249). His words are in accordance with the Perennial Philosophy, which teaches that "the world is a passing show . . . a flitting panorama like the clouds. Whatever has name and form must change and vanish. It is only that immortal Truth, Spirit or God, that nameless, formless, birthless and deathless Reality—with which we are one—that never changes and ever exists" (Swami Ramdas qtd. in Perry 108). According to a Sufi aphorism, "When the heart weeps for what it has lost, the spirit laughs for what it has found" (qtd. in Huxley 106). The fact that John Grady's knowledge that "beauty and loss are one" is described as a "secret" hints at the esoteric nature of this realization. As such, it is neither a purely aesthetic appreciation of the ephemeral nor an exercise in despair, but rather an apprehension of the essential impermanence of worldly existence and therefore of immense spiritual value.

CHAPTER 11

"The Bloody and Barbarous God"

Sin and Forgiveness in *Cities of the Plain*

■ In *Cities of the Plain* the biblical God is depicted in a decidedly Gnostic fashion, portrayed as possessing a desire for sacrificial victims and accused of a callous indifference to human suffering. Some references to the nature of God are quite subtle, such as when John Grady tells Billy that all one can do in life is "just try and use your best judgement and that's about it." Billy replies, "Yeah. Well. The world dont know nothin bout your judgment." John Grady agrees: "I know it. It's worse than that, even. It dont care" (219).[1] Although John Grady's accusations of indifference are directed at the rather vague concept of "the world," they also necessarily implicate the creator responsible for this state of things. In fact, the indifference of the biblical God is addressed directly by Eduardo when he asks Magdalena, "A quién te rezas?" (To whom do you pray?) "A Dios" (To God), Magdalena replies. "Quién responde?" (Who answers?) he asks. "Nadie" (Nobody), she confesses. "Nadie," repeats Eduardo (183), drawing the reader's attention to divine silence in the face of human suffering, a recurring theme that runs throughout *Cities of the Plain* and, indeed, throughout all of McCarthy's works.

Eduardo's condemnation of the Christian God is remarkably Gnostic. He warns Magdalena that she is a "fool" to "trust" the other prostitutes, "for they would eat her flesh if they thought it would ... cleanse their souls in the sight of the bloody and barbarous god to whom they prayed" (213). Eduardo's words evoke the "bloody and barbarous" crucifixion, which forms the central image of Christianity. In *Answer to Job*, Carl Gustav Jung pointed out the problematic nature of the fact that Christianity is centered on a tale of human sacrifice by asking, "What is supposed to be demonstrated by this gruesome and archaic sacrifice of the son? God's love, perhaps? Or his implacability?" (92). Jung concluded that "one should keep before one's eyes the strange fact that the God of goodness is so unforgiving that he can only be appeased by a human sacrifice!" (111). Elizabeth Andersen addresses the theme of the sacrificed savior in McCarthy's novels, arguing that "McCarthy consistently depicts a world where better men embrace the role of Christ—committed to delivering their fellow man from bondage and enslavement—but where all such efforts will be punished by a monstrous god who is himself a slave to fate, enmeshed in a vast web of cause and effect in which any apparent free choice proves part of an inscrutable, deterministic pattern" (4). This theme of human sacrifice is emphasized yet again by the blind maestro, who tells a tale of how one man used his son to avenge himself on his enemy and then pointedly reminds John Grady that "it would not be the first time that a father sacrificed a son" (194). His words not only are an unmistakable reference to the crucifixion, as depicted in the New Testament, but also subtly hint at the idea that the Son was sacrificed to appease the wrath of his own Father.

Furthermore, Eduardo's damning reference to the eating of flesh and the cleansing of souls evokes the ritual of the Catholic Eucharist, in which participants partake of the *literal* flesh of Christ. According to the Roman Catholic Church, the bread and wine of the Eucharist literally change into the body and blood of Jesus Christ through the process of transubstantiation (Latin, *transsubstantiatio*). The change is said to take place in substance but is not made visible, or accessible, to any of the five senses: "The Real Presence is evinced, positively, by showing the necessity of the literal sense of these words, and negatively, by refuting the figurative interpretations" (Pohle n.p.). Eduardo's words are confirmed by the actions of the whores, who seem to be reenacting a sacrificial ritual with Magdalena as the victim. When Magdalena suffers a fit—"the girl bowed and thrashed and then went rigid with her eyes white"—the women crowd around her, performing various ceremonial actions: "one pushed forward with a statue of the Virgin and raised it above the bed," "some of them were chanting and some were blessing themselves," some "brought little figures from their rooms and votive shrines of gilt and painted plaster and some were at lighting candles." Though these actions appear conventionally pious, the true nature of their interest in the girl is betrayed when they notice that her mouth is bleeding: "Some of the whores came forward and dipped their handkerchiefs in the blood as if to wipe it away but they hid the handkerchiefs on their persons to take away with them and the girl's mouth continued to bleed" (72). Instead of helping the girl, they treat her like a sacrificial victim whose blood has magical properties.

In *Cities of the Plain*, the God of this world is portrayed not only as "bloody and barbarous" but also as unforgiving and implacable. John Grady and Magdalena find themselves incapable of prayer, despite the fact that they are both in desperate need of benevolent divine intervention. When the blind maestro asks John Grady why he does not pray to God, the young man initial replies, "I don't know" (197). "You don't believe in Him?" asks the maestro, but John Grady insists, "It's not that." "It is that the girl is a mujerzuela [whore]?" the maestro persists, to which John Grady replies, "I don't know. Maybe" (198). John Grady reluctantly admits to harboring the feeling that the God of the Bible is more judgmental than merciful and will not be willing to intercede on behalf of a prostitute. Furthermore, his reluctance to pray subtly implies that he believes that even to ask God for such a thing would be obscurely wrong. The maestro seems to share this view, revealing the real reason behind his insistence that John Grady "pray to God" when he states, "Your love has no friends. You think that it does but it does not. None. Perhaps not even God" (197, 199). The maestro's words imply that he believes that the young man should pray for himself, so that he might see the error of his love for a prostitute, rather than that he should pray for help in rescuing Magdalena from the whorehouse.

Magdalena reveals that she too is unable to pray when, at their final meeting, she tells John Grady "that she had tried to pray for them but that she could not." "Porqué no?" (Why not?), asks John Grady, echoing his earlier dialogue with the maestro. Magdalena replies, "No sé. Creí que Dios no me oiría." (I don't know. I thought that God would not hear me.) John Grady reassures her, "El oirá. Reza el domingo. Dile que es importante." (He will hear. Pray on Sunday. Tell him it's important.) (205), but his words sound hollow in light of his own inability to pray. Later that evening, Magdalena asks John Grady, "Quiero saber . . . si crees hay perdón de pecados" (I want to know . . . if you think sins are pardoned). John Grady contemplates her question, thinking "about what he believed and what he did not believe. After a while he said that he believed in God even if he was doubtful of men's claims to know God's mind. But that a God unable to forgive was no God at all" (206). There are two different ways in which one can interpret John Grady's statement; the first, as argued by Kim McMurty, is that "John Grady determines that he believes in a God who is merciful" (155). Such an interpretation, however, does not explain why both John Grady and Magdalena find themselves incapable of praying to what they believe is a merciful deity. The second possible interpretation of John Grady's hesitant and rather noncommittal reply to the Catholic Magdalena's question suggests that he believes that the merciful nature of the God of this world is a highly contestable claim. John Grady may be reflecting on the harshness of some traditional Catholic dogmas, such as the idea that the "torments of the damned shall last forever and ever" and that the "pains of hell are essentially immutable," there being "no temporary intermissions or passing alleviations" for condemned sinners, or the belief in the existence of an eternal "limbo of infants (*limbus parvulorum*)," where children "who die in original sin alone, and without personal mortal sin, are confined and undergo some kind of punishment" (Hontheim n.p.). It seems that John Grady believes that although there is a God as depicted in the Bible, his implacable and pitiless nature makes him unworthy of the divine title.

Magdalena continues to question John Grady on the subject of God's forgiveness: "Cualquier pecado?" (Whatever the sin?) John Grady replies, "Cualquier. Sí." (Whatever. Yes.)[2] "Sin excepción de nada?" (Without any exceptions?), she persists. His reply is, "Con la excepción de desesperación. . . . Para eso no hay remedio." (With the exception of suicide/desperation. For this there is no pardon/remedy.) (206). The fact that John Grady doubts his own words is revealed toward the end of the novel. As John Grady slowly bleeds to death after killing the pimp, he reveals his fears and misgivings about Magdalena's chances of receiving divine forgiveness. He tells Billy, "I thought about God forgivin people and I thought about if I could ask God to forgive me for killin that son of a bitch because you and me both know I aint sorry for it and I reckon this sounds ignorant but I didnt want to be forgiven if she wasn't." Clearly, if John Grady doubts that Magdalena was forgiven for being a prostitute, then he must believe that the Christian God is unable to forgive and therefore is no true God at all. "I thought maybe she wouldn't go to heaven," he explains, adding, "I didnt want to do or be nothin that she wasnt like goin to heaven or anything like that" (259). John Grady rejects the biblical God in favor of Magdalena, refusing to repent for his sins and forsaking even heaven itself in order to be with her after death.

Although John Grady does utter a short prayer shortly before death—"Help me, he said. If you think I'm worth it. Amen" (257)—his call for help remains unanswered. Such divine indifference in the face of human suffering is exactly what we have come to expect of McCarthy's misotheistic portrayal of the creator. Furthermore, the sincerity of John Grady's unanswered prayer for divine intervention is brought into question when he confesses to Billy that the murder of Magdalena had sapped his will to live: "Bud when I seen her layin there I didn't care to live no more. I knew my life was over. It come almost as a relief to me" (259). Even prior to this confession, characters within the novel recognize the presence of a sublimated death wish, or Thanatos, in John Grady.[3] Billy first comments on this when John Grady reveals his plans to purchase Magdalena from her pimp: "You're in a dangerous frame of mind, son" (120). Eduardo himself states that John Grady "wishes nothing so fondly as to throw himself into the grave of a dead whore" (250). Later Eduardo claims, "In his dying perhaps the suitor will see that it was his hunger for mysteries that has undone him. Whores. Superstition. Finally death. For that is what has brought you here. That is what you were seeking." As if to fulfil John Grady's death-seeking wish, he passes his knife blade "before him in that slow scythelike gesture" (253), evoking the traditional representation of Death as a cloaked figure carrying a scythe for reaping human souls. Even before the knife fight begins, Eduardo gives John Grady one last chance to "change [his] mind.... Go back. Choose life" (248). For John Grady, however, the choice has already been made.

When the blind man states, "A man is always right to pursue the thing he loves," John Grady asks, "No matter even if it kills him?" The maestro replies, "I think so. Yes. No matter even that" (199), and John Grady's silence reads like an affirmation of this assertion. Before the young man rides out to the fatal confrontation, he looks back at the little cabin that he had been renovating for Magdalena: "He'd left the lamp burning in the cabin and the softly lit window looked warm and inviting. Or it would have to other eyes. For himself he was done with all that and after he'd crossed the creek and taken the road he had to take he did not look back again" (233). John Grady turns his back on the warm light of life and rides out into the darkness of death.

It may be argued that Thanatos began to possess John Grady not with the death of Magdalena in *Cities of the Plain* but rather with Alejandra's rejection in *All the Pretty Horses* and that it has therefore been the driving force behind the young man's foolhardy actions throughout the final volume of the trilogy.[4] A previously discussed passage in *All the Pretty Horses* describes the very moment that John Grady turns away from Eros and embraces Thanatos. This moment occurs immediately after Alejandra's rejection: "He saw very clearly how all his life led only to this moment and all after led nowhere at all. He felt something cold and soulless enter him like another being and he imagined that it smiled malignly and he had no reason to believe that it would ever leave" (254). This "cold and soulless" thing propels John Grady toward his own death throughout *Cities of the Plain*. As implied by Billy, John Grady's falling in love with an epileptic Mexican prostitute and then attempting to abduct her from under the jealous gaze of a murderous pimp was not only insane, but suicidal.

John Grady's death essentially amounts to suicide, for he willingly exposes his already shredded abdomen to Eduardo's blade so that he may drive his own knife through the bottom of the pimp's jaw and up into his brain. John Grady's final strike results in immediate death for Eduardo, but his own wounds are just as fatal. As previously discussed, the argument for suicide is compounded by John Grady's own admission that he "didn't care to live anymore" and that the realization that his "life was over" came "as a relief" (259). It is particularly significant that John Grady felt such suicidal urges given his own belief that the biblical God could forgive any sin, "Con la excepción de desesperación" (With the exception of suicide/desperation) (206).[5] Magdalena does not contradict John Grady's statement and yet she herself displays suicidal tendencies when she insists "that there was always a choice, even if that choice was death" (102). Both characters' inclinations toward suicide may shed further light on the reason why John Grady and Magdalena refuse to pray to a God they know will not forgive their death seeking. By embracing death when love proves impossible, these archetypal lovers reject not only the indifferent world but also its merciless creator.

In *Cities of the Plain*, the focus placed on the lack of divine forgiveness for sins motivated by love and committed by essentially sympathetic protagonists is indicative of a Gnostic shifting of the burden of blame from the human to the divine. According to Hans Jonas, there is "one simple criterion" for determining "what is 'Christian' (orthodox) or 'gnostic' (heretical)" and that is to ask "whether the *guilt* is . . . human or divine" (307). McCarthy seems to be employing this typically Gnostic inversion through the very title of *Cities of the Plain*. Erik Hage argues that "even when McCarthy seems to adopt traditional Christian heterodoxy, as in titling the final Border Trilogy book *Cities of the Plain*—after the cities of Sodom and Gomorrah—he still subverts things: Instead of the cities being destroyed because of the hopelessly corrupted humanity (as in the biblical telling), the cities El Paso and Juárez thrive, while the hopelessly 'good' John Grady Cole is stabbed to death by a pimp in an alleyway in Juárez" (88). In *Cities of the Plain*, sin is equated with this divine injustice and not with any misguided notions of guilt that the heroic John Grady and the pious Magdalena might harbor. When Billy discovers that John Grady has bled to death, he gathers his dead friend into his arms and, weeping bitterly, calls "out to the broken day" and "to God to see what was before his eyes. Look at this, he called. Do you see? Do you see?" (261). In decidedly Gnostic fashion, Billy turns in bitter accusation against the God that he holds responsible not only for the creation of this flawed world but also for orchestrating the tragic events that take place within it.

It is highly significant that Magdalena's name and occupation serve as a direct reference to Mary Magdalene of the New Testament. The link between Magdalena and Magdalene is strengthened by the emphasis McCarthy places on the name. When Magdalena first tells John Grady her name, "She looked down. As if the sound of her name were troubling to her." Obviously aware of the name's connection with prostitution, John Grady is rather incredulous and asks, "Es su nombre de pila?" (That's your given name?) She replies, "Si. Por supuesto." (Yes. Of course.) But he persists, "No es su nombre ... su nombre professional?" (It's not your ... your professional name?) Magdalena is shocked and puts "her hand to her mouth," then insists, "No. Es mi nombre propio." (No. It's my proper name.) (67). Apart from demonstrating the clash between Magdalena's Hispanic and John Grady's Anglophone cultures and their different attitudes toward the propriety of bestowing biblical given names, such as Jesus and Magdalena, the main purpose of this dialogue is to draw the reader's attention to the significance of Magdalena's name and its subsequent connotations.

The biblical Magdalene is traditionally interpreted as a prostitute who repents of her sins and becomes a follower of Jesus. In *Cities of the Plain*, however, Magdalena is "sold at the age of thirteen to settle a gambling debt" and runs away "to a convent for protection," only to be sold back to her owner. "The procurer himself appeared on the convent steps the following morning and in the pure light of day paid money into the hand of the mother superior and took the girl away again" (139). In other words, the biblical Magdalene is a degraded woman who turns to the church and finds redemption, while McCarthy's Magdalena is an innocent girl who also turns to the church but finds only degradation: Holy Mother Church sells her back into bondage. The fact that McCarthy's Magdalena is portrayed not as a sinner but rather as one who has been sinned against carries Gnostic connotations. As has already been established, the Gnostics objected vehemently to the Christian obsession with human sin and divine forgiveness. For the

Gnostics, the original sin was the act of creation itself; thus the demiurgical creator was guilty of having sinned against humanity. "Adam is not the sinner, but the victim of archontic persecution" (Jonas 307). Thus, according to Gnostic thought, the condition of human beings on earth was not that of sinners but rather that of victims who, like Magdalena, had been sinned against.

Furthermore, contrary to the books of the New Testament, Gnostic apocryphal gospels regard Mary Magdalene "as the most important female disciple of Jesus" (A. Smith 155). For example, the Dialogue of the Savior identifies her as "one of the three disciples ... who enter into dialogue with Jesus and she is described as 'a woman who understood completely'" (156). According to the Gospel of Philip, Mary Magdalene was Jesus's "companion (*koinōnos*)" and he "loved her more than all of his disciples because she was more receptive to his teachings" (qtd. in Pearson 178). Similarly, in the Gospel of Mary her position is "especially favoured by Christ" and she is presented as "the person responsible for passing on the esoteric teachings of the Savior" (Pearson 251). The Gnostics, who were always more concerned with ignorance than with sin, placed great emphasis on Mary Magdalene's spiritual wisdom, rather than on her repentance and subsequent redemption. Considering McCarthy's fondness for the heretical inversions of biblical themes, it would make sense to interpret the significance of Magdalena's name in reference to Apocryphal texts, rather than those of the New Testament. Therefore, her name suggests not a repentant sinner—for she is an innocent who has been sinned against by those who sold her into a life of prostitution against her will—but rather one who possesses keen spiritual insight.

Magdalena's position within the novel as an innocent girl trapped in a whorehouse evokes another Gnostic figure, namely that of Sophia Prunikos. While Mary Magdalene is the whore who is turned into a saint—at least, according to the New Testament—Sophia is the divine being who is turned into a whore. Sophia (Greek, "wisdom") is a "pivotal figure in the Gnostic myth, representing the imprisonment of the soul"—or, more accurately, the spirit—"in the world of matter" (A. Smith 232). This motif is also evident in the *Exegesis of the Soul*, "a work of Christian Gnosticism that describes the journey of the soul from fall to redemption. The soul is a female figure who falls into prostitution" and suffers many ordeals until she is able to return to her divine source (A. Smith 90). Despite her life of hardship and degradation, Sophia remains essentially divine; the brothel cannot taint her. In

Cities of the Plain, Magdalena is portrayed in much the same light, maintaining her essential purity and goodness despite the evil that surrounds her. Various markers within the text point to Magdalena's innocence and purity. Magdalena wears a blue dress (219), and blue is also the color that John Grady paints the little cottage that he renovates in the hope that she will come to live there as his wife. Traditionally, blue has been associated with the Virgin Mary and thus carries with it all the connotations of feminine spirituality, as embodied by the Catholic version of the Magna Mater.

The narrative voice continually places emphasis on Magdalena's youthful innocence.[6] When John Grady first sees her, she is described as a "young girl of no more than seventeen and perhaps younger ... sitting on the arm of the sofa with her hands cupped in her lap and her eyes cast down ... like a schoolgirl" (6). Later she is described as sitting "upright alone on the dark velvet couch with her hands composed in her lap like a debutante" (85). Her body language has none of the shameless brazenness associated with stereotypical prostitutes but is startlingly demure, graceful, and introverted. When she undresses before John Grady, she behaves modestly and rather virginally, carefully laying her "dress across a chair," stepping "naked into the bed," and then pulling "the satin quilt to her chin." Indeed, even the tender love scene between the young couple is described without any overt eroticism: "Then she leaned and kissed him. In the dawn he held her while she slept and he had no need to ask her anything at all" (70). The narrative voice effectively leaves out all descriptions of sensuality, thereby emphasizing the essentially spiritual nature of their love. The fact that John Grady no longer feels a need to question her suggests that the two lovers have reached a perfect understanding.

Furthermore, Magdalena has a keen moral and ethical sense, which has not been corrupted by her association with the underworld of Juárez. When John Grady first speaks to her, he asks her if she remembers him from an earlier encounter during which he simply watched her across the room. At first she shakes her head, but only a few moments later she confesses "that it was a lie that she did not remember him." He reassures her "that she had not really lied," because "she'd only shook her head, but she shook her head again and said that these were the worst lies of all" (68). For Magdalena, a denial of truth, no matter how trivial, is simply unacceptable. Just before they make love, she asks him if he is married. When he replies by asking why she wishes to know, she explains "that it would be a worse sin if he were married." The fact that years of prostitution have not dulled her awareness of adultery as a sin shows a truly remarkable adherence to a moral code. Of course, on another level, Magdalena's question also betrays the fact that she has already fallen in love with him. John Grady gently teases her by asking whether "that was really why she wished to know," but she only says "that he wished to know too much" (70) and then kisses him on the mouth, an act supposedly eschewed by prostitutes.

Descriptions of Magdalena also emphasize her otherness from the world around her. Escaping from a hospital ward after an epileptic fit, Magdalena is depicted as "some tattered phantom routed out of the ordinal dark and hounded briefly through the visible world to vanish again into the history of men's dreams" (210). The description suggests that her presence in the physical world is as transient and ephemeral as that of a ghostly visitation. Furthermore, when John Grady sees her across the room, she looks "small and lost," sitting "with her eyes closed . . . listening to the music" (66–67). This portrayal not only evokes pity but also illustrates her desire to escape to a higher realm; she shuts out her surroundings by closing her eyes and allowing the beautiful music of "a string trio" to transport her elsewhere (66). Magdalena's ability to shut out the world is a two-way process; she can stop herself from looking out at the world, but she can also stop the world from looking in on her. When Eduardo tells her to "look at him," she obeys, but she possesses the "power to cause those dark and hooded eyes of hers to go opaque. So that the visible depth in them was lost or shrouded. So that they hid the world within" (182). Magdalena keeps an essential part of herself protected by keeping it hidden from the world.

The depiction of Magdalena as "lost" echoes an earlier passage within the novel, in which Troy talks about his dead brother: "I think he was just lost. This world was never made for him. He'd outlived it before he could walk" (28). Such feelings of alienation are typical of the Gnostic depiction of humanity's existential position within the cosmos. Edward Conze writes that this feeling of spiritual alienation is encountered in various religions, experienced by those who "believe that man is a spirit ill at ease, a soul fallen from heaven, a stranger on this earth. His task is to regain the state of perfection which was his before he fell into this world" (*Buddhism* 22). Magdalena is not at home in this world; she is "lost" like a stranger who does not know the way. Magdalena's alienation is best conveyed by the words of the blind maestro, who tells John Grady, "My belief is that she is at best a visitor. At best. She does not belong here. Among us." Assuming that he refers to the brothel, John Grady replies, "Yessir. I know she dont belong here." "No," insists the blind man, "I do not mean in this house. I mean here. Among us" (81). Like the blind man in *The Crossing*, the maestro possesses profound metaphysical and spiritual insight; the "eye of wisdom" having replaced "the eyes of the body" (Conze, *Buddhism* 25).[7] The blind man's insistence on Magdalena's status as a "visitor" is another revelation of her essentially spiritual nature. Gnosticism teaches that "the recognition of [the] place of exile for what it is, is the first step back; the awakened homesickness is the beginning of the return" (Jonas 50). In other words, according to Gnostic thought, even the vaguest feeling of estrangement from the world stems from an awareness of one's divine origins, however dim such awareness may initially be, and is thus an essential step on the path to spiritual liberation.

The spirit's alienation from the created world is also evoked in the description of the death of John Grady. The separation between the spiritual and the corporeal modes of existence is suggested through John Grady's sensation of leaving his own body: "Holding himself close so that he not escape from himself for he felt it over and over, that lightness that he took for his soul and which stood so tentatively at the door of his corporeal self" (256). The portrayal of John Grady's departing soul as "some light-footed animal that stood testing the air at the open door of a cage" (256–57) implies that the spiritual self has been imprisoned by the "cage" of the body. This elevation of the spirit above the body is in line with the Gnostic view, which teaches that the "inner human self" is "an immaterial divine spark imprisoned in a material body" and that it is "as alien to the world as is the transcendent God" (Pearson 13). Furthermore, John Grady is described as slowly bleeding to death in an "alien land" (257). These words apply to Mexico, but they also hint at a profounder alienation that extends outward to include all of creation.

Magdalena's epilepsy is also described with a direct reference to the spirit; just before she experiences an epileptic fit, Magdalena feels a "cold pneuma come upon her" (183). It is noteworthy that McCarthy chooses a noun so charged with esoterically spiritual meaning to describe epilepsy. As has already been established, pneuma may refer to "spirit, soul, or life force," as it does in Gnostic theology. In the context of Magdalena's Catholic faith, however, pneuma refers to the "breath of God" or "the Holy Spirit" (*OED*). Since Magdalena's so-called pneuma descends upon her rather than being an intrinsic part of her, we must define the word in the Christian sense as a visitation from the Holy Spirit. Eduardo accuses Magdalena of believing that the "cold pneuma" is a sign of God's grace: "Nada. Sí. Pero piensas que has traido una dispensa especial a esta casa? Que Dios te ha escogido?" (But do you think you have carried a special dispensation to this house? That God has chosen you?) Magdalena denies this, claiming, "Nunca creí tal cosa." (I have never thought such a thing.) (213). Eduardo, however, knows there are others who do, as he tells John Grady during their duel: "You are like the whores from the campo, farmboy. To believe that craziness is sacred. A special grace. A special touch. A partaking of the godhead.... But what does this say of God?" (251). Eduardo's question may be interpreted in two distinct ways. The first is that Magdalena's illness has nothing to do with the biblical God, but if this is so, why does the narrative voice describe the epileptic fit in terms of a divine visitation? The second possible interpretation is that the "cold pneuma" is really the "breath of God" and that this "special grace," therefore, reveals something of God's nature.

What, then, does the "cold pneuma" say of the nature of the God of this world as depicted in the novel? The very description of the "breath of God" as "cold" carries connotations of unfeeling cruelty and death. The divine is normally symbolized by solar imagery of life-giving fire, warmth, and light, whereas "cold" suggests the opposite spectrum of lifeless darkness and ice. Evelyn Underhill comments on the significance of light as a symbol of the divine: "The illuminatives seem to assure us that its apparently symbolic name is really descriptive: that they do experience a kind of radiance, a flooding of the personality with new light. A new sun rises above the horizon, and transfigures their twilit world" (249).[8] The sinister nature of McCarthy's depiction of the biblical God is further compounded by the description of Magdalena in thrall to this divine visitation, "bowed in the bed and raging as if some incubus were upon her" (72), an incubus being a "feigned evil spirit or demon ... supposed to descend upon persons in their sleep, and especially to seek carnal intercourse with women" (*OED*). "Incubus" is used not only to describe the Holy Spirit in demonic terms but also in conjunction with the malevolent Tiburcio. When Magdalena suffers an epileptic fit, he watches her like an "incubus of uncertain proclivity." The associations with demonic rape are strengthened by the fact that he bends "over her slightly" and touches her inappropriately: he "aped imperfectly with his pale and tapered hands those ministrations of the healing arts that he had seen or heard of or as he imagined them to be" (183). The word "ape" is significant in that Satan is often referred to as "the ape of God" (Guénon, *Reign of Quantity* 238). Thus Tiburcio's dark parody of the "laying of the hands"—a type of healing practiced by Jesus in the Bible—takes on decisively satanic overtones.

Cities of the Plain is permeated with references to the kind of evil one normally encounters in myths, legends, and fairy tales, namely, demons, witches, and sorcery. As Eduardo severs the fascia of John Grady's stomach muscles, he taunts the boy, "Perhaps he will see the truth at last in his own intestines. As do the old brujos of the campo" (252). Eduardo is referring to haruspication, which is "divining from the entrails of animals, especially from the liver," and also anthropomancy, which is the "inspection of entrails from human victims of sacrifice" (Buckland 241).[9] The divination is carried out by "brujos," which translates to male witches or sorcerers. Sorcery is also referred to in a description of John Grady holding a mare that is being impregnated by a stallion: "John Grady stood holding all of this before him on a twisted tether like a child holding by a string some struggling and gasping chimera invoked by sorcery out of the void into the astonished dayworld" (75). In this instance "chimera" may be defined as an "incongruous union or medley," but the word also evokes the "fabled fire-breathing monster of Greek mythology, with a lion's head, a goat's body, and a serpent's tail" (*OED*). Similarly, Magdalena's epilepsy is referred to as "the dormant sorcerer within" (225). The reference to sorcery, combined with the presence of characters whose villainy borders on the supernatural, not only serves to strengthen the fairy-tale motif within the novel but also imbues the narrative with a mythic quality that takes it beyond the realms of realism and into something approximating a parable.

The supernatural quality of this evil does not detract from its power but rather imbues the villains of the novel with an otherworldly quality.[10] For example, the old *criada* who works at the White Lake brothel is often depicted as a one-eyed crone with "stringy hair" (238) who "hiss[es]" (73, 100, 101, 221) rather than speaks and carries "a short length of broomstick" (72) to which she ties her keys. Considering how obvious the link is between witches and broomsticks, it is noteworthy that the narrative voice refers to this "piece of broomhandle" (220) on more than one occasion, thereby emphasizing the criada's status as the traditional villainess in fairy tales. On several occasions she is described as a fairy-tale witch, especially in association with Magdalena. Looking into the mirror while the criada brushes her hair and tells her that she will marry a rich man, Magdalena appears as "some maid in a fable spurning the offerings of the hag which do conceal within them unspoken covenants of corruption" (101). Later

Magdalena steals away from the brothel in the small hours of the morning with "the crone holding her hand like a child's" (220). Such descriptions not only emphasize the criada's sinister nature but also serve to contrast against, and therefore highlight, Magdalena's purity, innocence, and goodness.

The novel reads like a fairy tale, albeit a very dark one; the intense but ultimately ill-fated love between John Grady and Magdalena evokes the leitmotif of the star-crossed lovers of countless myths and legends.[11] Allusions to fairy tales occur throughout the narrative; in a direct reference to "Cinderella," for example, the whores wear "shoes of glass or gold" (66). Elsewhere, the criada tells Magdalena that she looks like a "princesa" (princess) and that she will "marry a great rich man and live in a fine house and have beautiful children" (101)—in other words, live happily ever after. Charles Bailey argues that because Magdalena hails "from the whorehouse named the White Lake" she can be identified as the Arthurian "Lady of the Lake." Bailey also states that Magdalena represents the "courtly lady" whose plight is made all the "more desperate by the horrors of the world that entraps her" ("Last Stage" 297). If Magdalena is the fairy-tale princess in need of rescue, then John Grady is clearly the heroic knight. Bleeding profusely after the knife fight, John Grady utilizes the language of fairy tales in order to convince a young boy to help him hide from the police: "He told him that he was a great filero [knife fighter] and that he had just killed an evil man" (256).[12] Bailey argues that when "John Grady rises to become a filero . . . he becomes the 'expert wielder of the knife blade.' Metaphorically, he becomes the swordsman, the fencer, the knight" ("Last Stage" 297). In this sense, *Cities of the Plain* is a modern retelling of an archetypal myth of heroic rescue.

The treachery of evil characters is another fairy-tale motif; one cannot make a deal with the devil without there being some catch or betrayal. This proves particularly true in *Cities of the Plain*. Even as she facilitates Magdalena's escape, the criada is described as "some powdered stepdam from a storybook. Some ragged conspiratress gesturing upon the boards" (220). The associations with conspiracy and betrayal are evoked again in descriptions of the criada's blinking with "only the one eye closed. So that she appeared to be winking in some suggestive complicity" (101). Elsewhere she is depicted as closing and opening her one good eye "in a huge and obscene wink" (237). The portrayal of the criada as conspiring villainess is justified, for she informs her son, Tiburcio, about Magdalena's plans to run away with John Grady and ultimately it is this betrayal that dooms the young lovers to separation and death.

Of course, the real villains of the story are Eduardo and Tiburcio, who respectively order and carry out the brutal murder of Magdalena. Billy's first encounter with Tiburcio seems almost supernatural. "When he looked in the backbar glass the alcahuete was standing at his left elbow like Lucifer" (129). Eduardo, too, evokes satanic connotations. Steven Frye describes the character as "an otherworldly incarnation of evil as amoral as he is seemingly indomitable" (*Understanding Cormac McCarthy* 137). During the knife fight, he "arches his back like a cat" and also "twists like a falling cat" (248, 251); these descriptions of his feline agility, along with his sleek black hair that shines "blue in the light," suggest the unlucky omen of the black cat, an animal traditionally associated with witches and devil worship.[13] As Eduardo evades John Grady's knife thrusts, his "shadow on the wall of the warehouse looks like some dark conductor raising his baton to commence" (248). His shadow seems to reveal his true nature; as the conductor of the orchestra, he is the orchestrator of the events and subsequently of the evil fate that befalls John Grady and Magdalena. Furthermore, Eduardo appears as yet another manifestation of McCarthy's "demented surgeon," who often represents the creator of this world, when he states, "Here is my plan. A medical transplant. To put the suitor's mind inside his thigh" (250). He then proceeds to carve his initial "the letter E in the flesh of [John Grady's] thigh" (252). Similarly, when Eduardo passes "the blade back and forth like a shuttle through a loom," (253) he evokes McCarthy's depiction of the demiurgical weaver god of *The Crossing*.

Toward the end of the fight, Eduardo asks John Grady a strange question: "Do you know what my name is, farmboy? Do you even know my name?" (253). It should be quite obvious to Eduardo that John Grady learned his name when he first became interested in Magdalena, not to mention the fact that earlier in the novel, when Billy goes to speak to Eduardo on John Grady's behalf, he asks for him by name: "I wanted to see Eduardo" (129). It is clear, then, that Eduardo's question is not literal but rhetorical and thus a metaphoric way of asking whether John Grady understands the nature of the man he has engaged in a duel to the death. It is also noteworthy that according to many traditions, to know someone's true or secret name is to have power over them, a belief reflected in fairy tales such as "Rumpelstiltskin." April DeConick explains that in ancient times it was "very important" for people to know the "secret magical name" of any particular demon, "because the name to them was power to control that demon" (221). Eduardo's rhetorical question, then, suggests that John Grady is powerless in the face of a nameless and demonic enemy.

Like the devil in fairy tales, Eduardo has a way with words; his speech is just as damaging to John Grady's psyche as his knife thrusts are to his body. Paul Oppenheimer argues that the demonic is often represented in the form of "deceptive, obscene, tritely eloquent, and jargonistic speech pouring out of a fiendish manipulator" (6). The most obvious instance of this in McCarthy's fiction can be found in the terrifying figure of Judge Holden, but Eduardo serves much the same purpose, though on a much smaller scale. The destructive power of his speech is evident not only during the knife fight, as I will go on to discuss, but also in an earlier scene when Eduardo confronts Magdalena about her love for John Grady:

> He spoke in reasoned tones the words of a reasonable man. The more reasonably he spoke the colder the wind in the hollow of her heart. At each juncture in her case he paused to give her space in which to speak but she did not speak and her silence only led inexorably to the next succeeding charge until that structure which was composed of nothing but the spoken word and which should have passed on in its very utterance and left no trace or residue or shadow in the living world, that bodiless structure stood in the room a ponderable being and within its phantom corpus was contained her life. (212)

Eduardo's words seem to create a sinister entity, as though he were a magician summoning a demon to carry out his bidding.

While John Grady fights and dies in stoic silence, much like the wolf in *The Crossing*, Eduardo engages in a contemptuous monologue, dismissing John Grady as just another one of the "suitors" and "farmboys" of "whom there can be no end." Eduardo claims that such young men "drift down out of your leprous paradise seeking a thing now extinct among them. A thing for which perhaps they no longer even have a name. Being farmboys of course the first place they think to look is in a whorehouse" (249). This lost "thing" seems to be an experience of the sacred, which has become increasingly difficult to find in a modern world progressively dominated by a strictly rational outlook.[14] According to Mircea Eliade, "Modern man has desacralized his world and assumed a profane existence" and "desacralization pervades the entire experience of the nonreligious man of modern societies." Eliade argues that as a result, "modern man finds it increasingly difficult to rediscover the existential dimensions of religious man in the archaic societies" (13). Eliade concludes "that for the nonreligious men of the modern age, the cosmos has become opaque, inert, mute; it transmits no message, it holds no cipher" (178). Vince Brewton also argues, "What Eduardo means by this nameless 'thing' is of course the McCarthean mystery of existence, and the search for an answer to this mystery forms a thread that runs throughout his entire work" (81). According to Eduardo, American boys view Mexico as a place of sacred mystery, where they hope to find that which has vanished from their own largely profane and secular lives.

Eduardo implies that because the "farmboys" are uneducated and simple-minded, they attempt to find meaning and fulfillment in the sensuality of a whorehouse. Eduardo mocks John Grady's search for some ineffable mystery, because he does not believe that such a thing can be found on either side of the border; for him, there isn't anything other than the "ordinary" world. He tells John Grady that "the Mexican world is a world of adornment only and underneath it is very plain indeed. While. . . . your world totters upon an unspoken labyrinth of questions" (253). Eduardo claims that Mexico only appears to offer the lost seeker answers to these questions, but beneath the gilded veneer is the same old "ordinary" world that John Grady flees from.

Eduardo's outlook is fundamentally nihilistic; he not only mocks John Grady's quest for the sacred but denies its very existence: "You cannot bear that the world be ordinary. That it contain nothing save what stands before one" (253). His words echo those of Judge Holden in *Blood Meridian*, who announces, "Your heart's desire is to be told some mystery. The mystery is that there is no mystery" (252). Both Eduardo and Holden reveal a hyper-rationalistic, materialistic, and reductionist approach to the world. René Guénon argues that those who embrace such an outlook "claim to exclude all 'mystery' from the world as they see it, in the name of a science and a philosophy characterized as 'rational'" (*Reign of Quantity* 110). Similarly, Huston Smith argues that though the purely scientific outlook "occupies no more than a single ontological plane," it continually "challenges by implication the notion that other planes exist" (*Forgotten Truth* 6). For Eduardo, only that which can be empirically measured and rationally apprehended is deemed to exist, while more intuitive, or spiritual, modes of knowing are ridiculed.

Vince Brewton argues that "the novels of the Trilogy propose an alternative to the Judge's [and by extension, Eduardo's] nihilism" (81). In *All the*

Pretty Horses, for example, John Grady encounters the ineffable aspects of the sacred through his communion with horses: "He found he was breathing in rhythm with the horse as if some part of the horse were within him breathing and then he descended into some deeper collusion for which he had not even a name" (266).[15] In *Cities of the Plain*, his love for Magdalena becomes the new gateway for the sacred experience: "He gathered her black hair in his hand and spread it across his chest like a blessing" (70). The wolf serves a similar function for Billy in *The Crossing*: "When the flames came up her eyes burned out there like gatelamps to another world" (73). Nick Monk argues that the young protagonists of the Border Trilogy seek the very mystery denied by Eduardo and Judge Holden: "In women, wolves, and horses lie the metonymic figurations of antimodernity. Residing in their ineffability is the antidote to the all-consuming rational determinism embodied in Judge Holden and embedded in the Eurocentric modernity from which McCarthy's heroes are in flight. McCarthy's wanderers desire union with this ineffability; in so doing they seek a mystery in life that defies rational explanation" (93). Although Monk's analysis is concerned with modernity rather than the Perennial Philosophy, his summary of the ineffable experiences that stand against the rational determinism of McCarthy's sinister characters is pertinent to my argument.

John Grady is able to refute Eduardo's claims because he knows from personal experience that there is something other than the ordinary world. The young man does not engage in a verbal contest, he simply puts an end to the outpouring of words by driving his knife through Eduardo's jaw. "He brought the knife up underhand from the knee and slammed it home and staggered back. He heard the clack of the Mexican's teeth as his jaw clapped shut" (254). John Grady's decisive knife thrust is a refutation of Eduardo's nihilism and an affirmation of there being something greater than "what stands before one" (253). Despite the fact that the protagonist meets his death, the novel does not end on a pessimistic note. The silencing of Eduardo reaffirms the transcendent mystery of the sacred; whether it resides in the beauty of wolves and horses, the communion between all living creatures, or the love felt for another being, John Grady seems to understand that it is something worth dying for.

CHAPTER 12

"That Man Who Is All Men"
The Illusory and the Real in the Epilogue to the Border Trilogy

■ The epilogue to *Cities of the Plain* is, stylistically and thematically, so far removed from the novel proper that it reads more like a separate short story. Throughout the actual novel, the chief protagonist is John Grady Cole and the narrative is focused on his unfortunate love affair with Magdalena; the epilogue, however, is set almost fifty years after the death of John Grady and thus the role of protagonist shifts to the aged Billy Parham. Edwin Arnold describes it as "a dream narrative, with Billy Parham as the primary dreamer" ("Go to Sleep" 64). Furthermore, while the novel proper is largely a realist text, the epilogue contains overtones of the surreal and the mythic, as well as taking on the didactic role of a parable.[1] In spite of its separation from the novel, the epilogue casts its dreamlike, otherworldly influence back over the chapters that precede it and indeed over the first two installments of the Border Trilogy. This view is also put forward by Erik Hage, who writes that the "full philosophical burden" of the epilogue "must be weighed against the entire trilogy" (62). When viewed in this light, the epilogue no longer appears as an odd attempt at giving closure to the action of *Cities of the Plain* but rather can be seen as the culmination of the philosophical, metaphysical, and spiritual concerns raised throughout the Border Trilogy.

The very beginning of the epilogue maintains the realist style of the novel in its description of Billy Parham's departure from the ranch. The realism, however, is suddenly subverted by a passage that sweeps the reader headlong into a torrent of passing years, bringing the narrative forward by half a century in a single paragraph: "He rode out in the dark long before daylight and he rode the sun up and he rode it down again. In the oncoming years a terrible drought struck west Texas. He moved on. There was no work in that country anywhere. Pasture gates stood open and sand drifted in the roads and after a few years it was rare to see stock of any kind and he rode on. Days of the world. Years of the world. Till he was old" (264). The description of drought, aridity, decline, and the relentless passage of time evokes the central metaphor of transience and death that pervades all of McCarthy's works.

This preoccupation with death continues in the description of Billy's dreams, in which the dead appear to him as silent visitors, a motif that runs throughout the Border Trilogy. In one such dream, Billy's dead brother Boyd appears "in the room with him but would not speak for all that he called out to him" (290). Billy also dreams of "his sister dead seventy years": "He saw her so clearly. Nothing had changed, nothing faded. . . . When she passed the house he knew that she would never enter there again nor would he see her ever again and in his sleep he called out to her but she did not turn or answer him but only passed on down that empty road in infinite sadness and infinite loss" (265–66). Billy's visions of the dead bring no comfort or reassurance of life after death, only a devastating reminder of the heartbreak of separation and the permanence of loss.

Billy yearns to join the dead; sitting under an overpass, he sees a strange figure approaching and for a brief moment believes that it is death come to claim him. "I thought at first you might be somebody else," he says when he sees that it is only an ordinary, human drifter. When the man wants to know for whom he has been mistaken, Billy replies, "Just somebody. Somebody I sort of been expectin. I thought I caught a glimpse of him once or twice these past few days. I aint never got all that good a look at him." The stranger asks, "What does he look like?" and Billy replies, "I dont know. I guess more and more he looks like a friend." The man guesses the answer to the riddle: "You thought I was death," and Billy confesses that he had "considered the possibility." Billy shares his crackers with the stranger and the two men discuss death over this meager meal. "Qué clase de hombre comparta sus galletas con la muerte?" (What kind of man shares his crackers with death?) asks the traveler. Billy replies, "What kind of death would eat them?" The man explains, "In Mexico on certain days of the calendar it is the custom to set a place at the table for death. . . . He has a big appetite" (267). He implies that death devours every living thing and its appetite is never satiated. The man wonders whether death would regard "a few crackers" as "an insult" but then speculates that "perhaps in his egalitarian way death weighed the gifts of men by their own lights and that in death's eyes the offerings of the poor were the equal of any." "Like God," states Billy. "Yes. Like God," the man agrees (268). The startling comparison between God and the personification of death carries heretical connotations because traditionally the God of the Bible is equated with life: "For the wages of sin is death; but the gift of God is eternal life" (Romans 6:23). According to Gnostic teachings, however, the "whole world system," along with its creator, is described as "darkness," "death," "deception," "wickedness," and "the fullness of evil" (Rudolph 69). Furthermore, one of the many names given by the Gnostics to the demiurge is "Sammael," which "is the name traditionally given to the 'angel of death' in Jewish tradition" (Pearson 107). Thus the equation of the God of this world with death is a remarkably Gnostic one.

The conversation reaches greater metaphysical profundity when Billy asks, "Where do we go when we die?" and the man replies, "I dont know. . . . Where are we now?" (268). Such questioning is typical of both the Buddhist and Gnostic traditions. In the *Excerpta ex Theodoto*, Theodotus the Valentinian Gnostic (ca. 140–160) wrote, "Not Baptism alone sets us free, but gnosis," that is, knowledge of "who we were, what we have become; where we were, whereinto we have been thrown; wither we hasten, whence we are redeemed; what is birth and what rebirth" (qtd. in Conze, *Further Buddhist Studies* 17). Edward Conze writes that Buddhism, too, aims to dispel the "misconceptions on precisely the points enumerated in the Valentinian statement. In both cases the mere insight into the origination and nature of the world liberates us from it" (*Further Buddhist Studies* 17). The man's reply to Billy's question implies that we cannot know where we are going if we do not know where we are, nor can we hope to escape from a place through which we wander in lost confusion.

The man reveals that in order to better understand where he was and where he was going, he had attempted to draw a map of his life: "In the middle of my life, he said, I drew the path of it upon a map and I studied it a long time. I tried to see the pattern that it made upon the earth because I thought that if I could see that pattern and identify the form of it then I would know better how to continue. I would know what my path must be. I would see into the future of my life" (268). The storyteller's words, "in the middle of my life," recall those of Dante Alighieri (1265–1321):

> Nel mezzo del cammin di nostra vita
> Mi ritrovai per una selva oscura
> Ché la diritta via era smarrita
> (In the midway of this our mortal life
> I found me in a gloomy wood
> Gone from the path direct)
> (*Divine Comedy: Inferno*, canto I, lines 1–2)

The allusion to Dante's *Divine Comedy*, in conjunction with the creation of a map, places the storyteller's tale in the context of a spiritual journey. The storyteller finds, however, that mapping the future of one's life proves more difficult than he had anticipated. He explains that the map "looked like different things" and there "were different perspectives one could take," adding that "at first I saw a face but then I turned it and looked at it other ways and when I turned it back the face was gone. Nor could I find it again" (269). Rather than revealing a clearly discernible path, the map yields ephemeral patterns and images, which shift continually depending on the perspective of the viewer.

When Billy asks, "How did you know that it was the middle of your life?" the man replies, "I had a dream. That was why I drew the map" (269). He then goes on to recount a strange dream of a traveler who "came to a place in the mountains where certain pilgrims used to gather in the long ago." As previously argued, motifs of travel and pilgrimage evoke the Gnostic vision of humanity's situation in the cosmos. The place of pilgrimage in the man's dream is a sacrificial altar: "And on the face of that rock there were yet to be seen the stains of blood from those who'd been slaughtered upon it to appease the gods" (270). The evaluation of divine powers as bloodthirsty is also quintessentially Gnostic, echoing the belief that the demiurge "delights in blood" (Jonas 94).

The goodness of the God of this world is questioned—albeit very subtly—through the traveler's inability to comprehend the danger of "the bloodstained altarstone which the weathers of the sierra and the sierra's storms had these millennia been impotent to cleanse" (270). The storyteller explains that "there [the traveler] elected to pass the night, such is the recklessness of those whom God has been so good as to shield from their just share of adversity in this world" (270–71). Although this statement may at first glance appear sincere in its gratitude to the God of this world, such a reading is subverted by two points. First, the fact that the traveler had been largely shielded from the unpleasant realities of human existence causes him to behave recklessly; ignorance—from a Gnostic point of view—is neither a blessing nor a virtue. Second, if the "share of adversity" that God had withheld from the traveler was indeed his "just share," then God's decision to spare this particular individual while allowing others to suffer seems morally arbitrary and cannot be the work of a "just" entity.

Billy interrupts the tale to ask the storyteller, "Who was the traveler? . . . Was it you?" The man replies, "I dont think so. But then if we do not know ourselves in the waking world what chance in dreams?" (271). Gnostic soteriology places great emphasis on the need to remove such ignorance of the self. Birger Pearson explains, "In Gnosticism knowledge of [the alien God] and knowledge of the self are two sides of the same coin, for the true human self is of divine origin, and salvation ultimately involves a return to the divine world from which it came" (12). Pearson argues that "Gnosticism in general can be defined as a religion of self-realization" (335). Kurt Rudolph also writes, "It is the act of self-recognition which introduces the 'deliverance' from the situation encountered and guarantees man salvation. For this reason the famous Delphic slogan 'Know Thyself' is popular also in Gnosis" (113). Thus, according to Gnostic thought, the fact that "we do not know ourselves" is precisely what keeps us imprisoned in the manifest cosmos.

The man goes on to explain his beliefs: "I think the self of you in dreams or out is only that which you elect to see. I'm guessing every man is more than he supposes" (271). In other words, the man argues that most human beings are incapable of accurately perceiving the complex nature of the self. The man's words suggest that there is more to ourselves than we imagine, whether in dreams or in waking life; his implications hint at a higher aspect of the self beyond that of our everyday experiences. For the Gnostics, this hidden self was the pneuma; Elaine Pagels explains that to "know oneself, at the deepest level"—that is, at the pneumatic or spiritual level—"is simultaneously to know [the alien] God; this is the secret of gnosis" (*Gnostic Gospels* xix). For example, the Gnostic-Christian Gospel of Thomas teaches, "When you come to know yourselves, then you will be known, and you will realize that you are the sons of the living Father. But if you will not know yourselves, then you dwell in poverty, and it is you who are that poverty" (qtd. in Pagels, *Gnostic Gospels* 129). The same view is put forward by the Perennial Philosophy, according to which "only the mystic can be called a whole man, since in others half the powers of the self always sleep" (Underhill 63). Thus, according to these teachings, while every ordinary human being is, as

McCarthy's storyteller insists, "more than he supposes," the mystic is a fully realized being.

The storyteller claims that "it is difficult to stand outside of one's desires and see things of their own volition." Billy tries to deflate this statement by adopting the argument of the empiricists, saying, "I think you just see whatever's in front of you," but the man disagrees: "I dont think that" (269). According to the man, we are blind not only to our true selves but also to the true nature of the world around us, the latter blindness arising out of the former.[2] In her study of mysticism, Evelyn Underhill writes, "We do not know ourselves; hence we do not know the true character of our senses and instincts; hence attribute wrong values to their suggestions and declarations concerning our relation to the external world." Much like McCarthy's storyteller, Underhill explains that humanity's inability to see clearly arises out of "false desires and false thoughts," through which "man has built up for himself a false universe" or "a little cave of illusion for each separate soul." Consequently, the "deliberate getting out of the cave must be for every mystic, as it was for Plato's prisoners, the first step in the individual hunt for reality" (199). Similarly, "the Buddhist idea of *samsara* ... teaches that the world in which we live our daily lives is illusory, constructed from the sensory projections formulated from our own desires" (Wagner and Flannery-Dailey 272). According to these teachings and McCarthy's storyteller, ordinary human beings are so blinded by their own ignorance and desire that they cannot perceive anything other than the constructions of their own limited surface-consciousness; thus the *ding an sich*—the "thing in itself"—continually escapes them.

It is later revealed that Billy truly cannot see what is in front of him. Looking out onto the darkened desert, he sees "one of the ancient spanish missions of that country but when he studied it again he saw that it was the round white dome of a radar tracking station." Beyond the illusory Spanish mission, he thinks he sees "a row of figures struggling and clamouring silently in the wind. They appeared to be dressed in robes and some among them fell down in their struggling and rose to flail again. . . . He called to them but his shout was carried away on the wind and in any case they were too far to hear him." In the morning he realizes that they "were only rags of plastic wrapping hanging from a fence where the wind had blown them" (289). Apart from drawing attention to the unreliable testimony of our senses, the scene also serves to highlight Billy's inability to find redemption through traditional religion. Christian iconography, symbolized by the

Spanish mission and the robed pilgrims, vanishes in the light of day, revealing a disenchanted modern landscape consisting of a radar tracking station and torn plastic wrapping, a world dominated by technology and devoid of spiritual significance.

The storyteller utilizes the motif of the dream within a dream to further destabilize the ground upon which humanity rests its comprehension of consensus reality. As the traveler in the storyteller's dream falls asleep upon the altar stone, he begins to dream his own dream, a secondary dream within the primary dream of the storyteller. The storyteller poses some searching questions regarding the ontological status of this secondary dream: "Let us say that the events which took place were a dream of this man whose own reality remains conjectural. How assess the world of that conjectural mind? And what with him is sleep and what is waking? How comes he to own a world of night at all? Things need a ground to stand upon. As every soul requires a body. A dream within a dream makes other claims than what a man might suppose." Billy replies by speculating that a "dream inside a dream might not be a dream" and the storyteller agrees that one has "to consider the possibility" (272–73). The storyteller's words suggest that if a dream may not be a dream, then waking life might not be waking life; if "things need a ground to stand upon," then upon what ground stands our apprehension of consensus reality? To extend the argument, what is there to assure us that we are not experiencing a shared dream within the dream of some creator deity?

Both Buddhism and Gnosticism, alongside the other traditions of the Perennial Philosophy, insist that what we take for granted as consensus reality is only a shared dream or mass delusion. Edward Conze explains that according to Buddhism, "The world is like a dream. A dream is merely an awareness of ideas; the corresponding objects are not really there. Just as one perceives the lack of objectivity in the dream pictures after one has woken up, so the lack of objectivity in the perceptions of waking life is perceived by those who have been awakened by the knowledge of true reality" (*Buddhism* 168). Similarly, Hans Jonas writes that in Gnostic texts, "the metaphor of sleep may equally serve to discount the sensations of 'life here' as mere illusions and dreams, though nightmarish ones, which we are powerless to control" (71). Ralph Waldo Emerson also specifically utilized the motif of the dream within a dream, writing, "Life is itself a bubble and a scepticism and a sleep within a sleep" ("Experience" 107) and "There are as many pillows of illusion as flakes in a snow-storm. We wake from one dream into another dream" ("Illusions" 569). McCarthy's epilogue to *Cities of the Plain* calls reality into question by constructing such "pillows of illusion" in a multilayered dream narrative.

Edwin Arnold argues that the implications of this narrative are even more complex than we may first suppose, explaining that the "complication provided by the 'dream-within-a-dream' structure of the stranger's tale is further complicated by the possibility that Billy may be dreaming the stranger himself and thus also the stranger's dream and the dream imbedded in that dream" ("Go to Sleep" 66). After all, Billy encounters the stranger soon after waking from a dream of "his sister dead seventy years," and we have no way of knowing whether he has in fact experienced a false awakening. Furthermore, as he watches the "gray light" of dawn, he recalls a vision of cranes "asleep in a flooded field in Mexico in a dawn long ago . . . gray figures aligned in rows like hooded monks at prayer." It is immediately after this dreamlike escape into reverie that he sees "another such as he sitting also solitary and alone" (265). It is quite possible that this nameless stranger of "no determinable age" might be a figure in Billy's dream (267). Edwin Arnold goes on to argue that "McCarthy, as author, is himself 'dreaming' Billy and the stranger and all that comes between them" ("Go to Sleep" 66). The traveler's dream is only the product of his mind, but he himself is only the mind product of the storyteller, who is possibly the mind product of Billy, who is the mind product of McCarthy, who presumably might only be the mind product of an entity on yet another ontological plane, and so on ad infinitum. "Dream delivers us to dream and there is no end of illusion," writes Ralph Waldo Emerson ("Poet" 103). The situation evokes an infinite regress, forcing the reader to question his or her own ontological status.

The storyteller insists that the traveler in his dream is possessed of a separate existence, or rather, that the traveler's existence is as valid as the storyteller's own. The storyteller tells Billy that "the dreams of this man were his own dreams. They were distinct from my dream. In my dream the man was lying on his stone asleep." Billy remains unconvinced, replying, "You still could have made them up. . . . It's like the picture of your life in that map. . . . Es un dibujo nada más. [It's nothing more than a drawing.] It aint your life. A picture aint a thing. It's just a picture."[3] It seems unlikely that Billy's pronouncement indicates a Platonic mistrust of representations as inferior replicas of the Absolute; rather, his world view suggests faith in the empirical reality of rational materialism. In response to Billy's oversimplification of the nature of reality, the storyteller asks some searching questions: "But what is your life? Can you see it? It vanishes at its own appearance. Moment by moment.... When you look at the world is there a point in time when the seen becomes the remembered? How are they separate?" (273). The storyteller seems to be implying that "the seen" differs from "the remembered" only through the subjective perception of the observer and that, objectively, the past is no less real than the present.[4]

The storyteller believes in the autonomy of his dream traveler's existence: "My traveler sleeps a troubled dream. Shall I wake him? The proprietary claims of the dreamer upon the dreamt have their limits. I cannot rob the traveler of his autonomy lest he vanish altogether" (274). John Cant writes, "The dreamer who dreams of a dreamer occupies a position analogous to that of the writer who must enter into the world of his creation as though it had a life of its own" (232). Similarly, Edwin Arnold argues that this "may be read as a deliberate meditation on the nature of artistic creation, the responsibilities and limitations of the creator, and the independence of that which is created" ("Last of the Trilogy" 239). Such a reading may be extended into the realms of theodicy to question the "responsibilities and limitations" of the creator God and the extent of humanity's autonomy. The main concern of theodicy is the paradox of evil, namely, that an omnipotent and benevolent creator God should be both able and willing to eliminate evil, yet evil persists, therefore the creator of this world cannot be both omnipotent and benevolent. While heretics such as the Gnostics support this conclusion, Christian theologians, such as Saint Augustine or, more recently, Alvin Plantiga, have used the so-called Free Will Defence to make an argument for the essential goodness of the creator God. The argument runs as follows: "God, of course, can create free creatures, but then he cannot *cause* or *determine* that they only perform right actions. Doing this would pre-empt their significant freedom. Hence, there is no way for God to create creatures capable of moral good without thereby creating creatures capable of moral evil. Conversely, God cannot eliminate the possibility of moral evil without eliminating the possibility of moral good" (Peterson 35). Thus the "power of an omnipotent God is limited by the freedom he confers upon his creatures" (41). Supposedly the God of this world considers our autonomy to be worth our consequent suffering. McCarthy's storyteller makes the same assumption when he refuses to wake his traveler from a nightmare lest he rob him of his autonomy.

The storyteller's argument for the separate ontological existence of dream figures is based on the fact that these entities behave unpredictably: "Had I created him as God makes men how then would I not know what he would say before he ever spoke? Or how he'd move before he did? In a dream we dont know what's coming. We are surprised" (285). The storyteller's statement implies that the creator God knows exactly how we will behave from the moment he creates us. This is a form of determinism, according to which we all follow the paths foreseen by the creator and no alternate actions are possible. Kim McMurty attempts to reconcile the storyteller's words with Christian thought, arguing, "The vagrant examines the difficult dilemma of free will versus predestination . . . and explains that although humans have free will to make choices, there is really only one choice to make, the choice that is made, which was predestined from the beginning of time" (155–56). Unfortunately, this explanation amounts to a logical impossibility, as the very concept of having a choice necessitates that there be more than one path to choose from. The logical extrapolation of this position is that it is wrong of God to punish human beings for their sins, because there was never a possibility of their acting otherwise. The storyteller argues that "this traveler also has a life and there is a direction to that life. . . . You may say that he has no substance and therefore no history but my view is that whatever he may be or of whatever made he cannot exist without a history. And the ground of that history is not different from yours of mine" (274). The storyteller's words urge Billy to consider the concept that he shares his ontological status with a dream figure. Of course, if we consider the fact that Billy, the storyteller, and the traveler are really characters in a novel then all three figures are literally on the same ontological plane, existing only as creations of McCarthy's imagination. Indirectly, the narrative also urges the reader to consider the possibility that our existence is as tenuous and illusory as that of the characters in the novel.

This is precisely the claim made by the Buddhist doctrine of anatta (no self), which teaches that "nothing in reality corresponds to such words or ideas as 'I,' 'mine,' 'belonging,' etc. In other words, the self is not a fact" and the "highest insight is reached when everything appears as sheer hallucination" (Conze, *Buddhism* 21, 168). The ultimate goal of Buddhism is to reach a state in which the "self becomes extinct" so that only "the Absolute remains" (114). The storyteller evokes these ideas by questioning the nature of the conscious and the subconscious mind: "Can a man be so hid from himself? And if so who is hid? And from whom?" (285). The storyteller's words recall those of Sri Ramana Maharshi, who would habitually answer the questions of his disciples with questions of his own: "Who is asking this question?" and "Who is this 'I' and what is its source?" (73). The implication of Sri Ramana Maharshi's words is that if we do not comprehend the nature of ourselves, we will not be able to comprehend the nature of the Absolute. McCarthy's storyteller asks similar questions in order to destabilize the concept of a stable and separate ego.

The storyteller then reveals the details of his traveler's dream. He tells Billy that in the dream the traveler was "afraid," while he himself was "only curious." When Billy asks, "You were not in the dream," the storyteller replies, "No" (276). It is noteworthy that the storyteller is made privy to the dream of a dream character without ever becoming a participant in this secondary dream. In this respect he mirrors the function of the reader, who experiences the narrative action without being on the same ontological plane as the fictional characters. The storyteller recounts how the traveler was "surprised to see descending down through the rocky arroyos a troupe of men bearing torches in the rain and singing some low chant or prayer as they came." The surreal strangeness of this vision is emphasized by a description of the leader of the procession, who "carried a sceptre on the head of which was his own likeness and the likeness carried also such a sceptre in miniature and this sceptre too in what we must imagine to be some unknown infinitude of alternate being and likeness" (275). The scepter is an embodiment of infinite regress and thus of infinity itself.[5]

When the procession reaches the traveler, he notices that they are carrying a litter upon which "lay a young girl with eyes closed and hands crossed upon her breasts as if in death" (279). This scene recalls John Grady's dream earlier in the novel, in which he sees "a young girl in white gauze dress who lay upon a pallet-board like a sacrificial virgin" (103). Three of the men step forward and silently offer the dreamer a cup, which he solemnly accepts: "He took it in both hands with the same gravity with which it had been offered and raised it to his lips and drank" (279). Immediately he finds that "all was taken from him so that he was like a child again and a great peace settled upon him." Although at first glance this appears to be a positive experience, the result is that "his fears abated to the point that he would become accomplice in a blood ceremony that was then and is now an affront to God" (280). In other words, by losing all fear and becoming like a child, the traveler seems to have also lost his moral discernment and is no longer able to distinguish between good and evil. The storyteller's claim that a "blood ceremony" is "an affront to God" reads like a criticism of the Catholic Eucharist, a rite in which participants partake of wine that they believe has been transubstantiated into the literal blood of Christ.[6] It is noteworthy that McCarthy chose to use the word "accomplice" rather than "participant," for the former evokes a negative moral judgment, whereas the latter is relatively neutral.

The storyteller explains that when the traveler drank the potion, it "caused him to forget. . . . He forgot the pain of his life. Nor did he understand the penalty for doing so" (280). After giving the traveler the potion, the strange men seem "to be waiting for him to come to some decision. To tell them something perhaps" (282). Despite the forgetting of his own sorrows, or perhaps precisely because he is no longer distracted by the details of his own life and the selfish concerns of the ego, the traveler apprehends something sinister in the very nature of the world: "He thought he saw in the world's silence a great conspiracy and he knew that he himself must then be a part of that conspiracy" (283). The traveler's realization recalls that of the heretic in *The Crossing*. The traveler in *Cities of the Plain* suspects that "the world's silence" conceals "a great conspiracy" (283), while the heretic dreams of a similarly silent and sinister creator God: "In his dreams God was much occupied. Spoken to He did not answer. Called to did not hear" (149). Furthermore, the traveler begins to suspect "that he himself must then be a part of that conspiracy" (283), while the heretic comes to realize that he is a thread within the creator God's terrible tapestry: "Somewhere in that tapestry that was the world in its making and in its unmaking was a thread that was he" (149). The concept of a cosmic conspiracy is a thoroughly Gnostic one; the Gnostics viewed humanity's existential situation as arising directly out of the "conspiracy of the world" (Jonas 73). Gnostic texts teach that the archons, or rulers of this world, have "as their collaborator 'fate' (*heimarmene*)"; note that the concept of conspiracy is implied by the use of the word "collaborator." "Man" himself is a part of this conspiracy, owing to the fact that "through his body and his soul man is a part of the world and subjected to the *heimarmene*" (44). Thus, for the Gnostics, the cosmic conspiracy consists not only of the belief that humanity is kept in ignorance of its divine origins but also of the idea that the entire cosmos is controlled like clockwork by the oppressive forces of heimarmene.

The storyteller goes on to explain that if the traveler "had any revelation it was this: that he was repository to this knowing which he came to solely by his abandonment of every former view" (283).[7] The intensely personal nature of the traveler's revelation suggests the solitary path of gnosis. Elaine Pagels writes that the Gnostics placed great emphasis on "the primacy of immediate experience," refusing to "accept on faith what others said, except as a provisional measure, until one found one's own path" (*Gnostic Gospels* 145). Thus, like McCarthy's traveler, those who found gnosis could also be described as a "repository" to their own "knowing," having achieved spiritual insight by abandoning "every former view." The various traditions of the Perennial Philosophy distinguish ordinary knowledge of the world from spiritual knowledge of the Absolute. Rudolph Otto writes, "The soul has something within it, a spark of supersensual knowledge that is never quenched. But there is also another knowledge in our souls, which is directed toward outward objects: namely knowledge of the sense and the understanding: this hides that other knowledge from us" (35). In other words, Otto argues that when we, like McCarthy's traveler, abandon our ordinary knowledge of the world, we clear the way for a different kind of knowing.

After the revelation, the traveler refuses to articulate his newfound knowledge: "He turned to his captors and he said: I will tell you nothing.... That is what he said and that is all he said" (282). Both the Eastern and Western traditions of the Perennial Philosophy stress that the Absolute can be experienced directly but never described or articulated. In his comparative study of the writings of two of the greatest mystics of Christianity and Hinduism, Rudolph Otto cites Meister Eckhart's claim that "God is inexpressible and he has no name," pointing out that the "Bhagavad Gita says the same" (Otto 79). Margaret Smith explains that "the word 'Mysticism' itself comes down to us from the Greeks and is derived from a root meaning 'to close.' The mystic was one who had been initiated into the esoteric knowledge of Divine things, and upon whom laid the necessity of keeping silence concerning his sacred knowledge" (20). Thus the traveler's sudden refusal to speak, despite his earlier complicity in willingly drinking the potion, suggests that he has had an experience of the ineffable.

The storyteller explains that when the traveler refused to speak, the men "led him to the stone and laid him down upon it and they raised up the girl from her pallet and led her forward." The girl then "leaned and kissed him and stepped away and then the archatron came forward with his sword and raised it in his two hands above him and clove the traveler's head from his body" (283).[8] This sacrificial rite is best illuminated by the theories of René Girard's *Violence and the Sacred*.[9] According to Girard, "the sacrificial process prevents the spread of violence by keeping vengeance in check," and thus "sacrifice is primarily an act of violence without the risk of vengeance" (18, 13). By participating in a sacrificial rite, "society is seeking to deflect upon a relatively indifferent victim, a 'sacrificeable' victim, the violence that would otherwise be vented on its own members" (4). Girard explains that the most "sacrificeable" victims are strangers, or "creatures who do not and have never belonged to the community" (270) and that the "surrogate victim—or, more simply, the final victim—inevitably appears as a being who submits to violence without provoking a reprisal" (86). In this sense, we can view the figure of Jesus Christ as the ultimate "sacrificeable" victim, whose tortured death on the cross remains to this day a symbol of Christian redemption. Marvin Meyer writes that "one of the pieces of furniture in most every church around is the altar. And while nobody usually gets sacrificed on that altar these days, it is a reminder that this idea of sacrifice is very much a part of mainstream Christian tradition to the present day" (190). Girard's points also apply to the dream traveler, who is not only an outsider but also submits to the violence done to him without engaging in a reciprocal attack.

At the instant of the deathblow, the traveler "woke from his dream and sat shivering with cold and fright" (283). When he looks up at the night sky, he finds that the "heavens which he had been invited to scrutinize by his executioners now wore a different look."[10] The traveler feels that the "order of his life seemed altered in midstride. Some haltstitch in the workings of things" (285).[11] The presence of a "haltstitch" has Gnostic connotations, suggesting the imperfect creation of the weaver god, as depicted in *The Crossing*. The traveler's new apprehension of the stars can be read as a shift into a Gnostic perception of the world, in which "the stellar firmament becomes now the symbol of all that is terrifying to man in the towering factness of the universe" (Jonas 225). Looking up, the traveler sees that "those heavens in whose forms men see commensurate destinies cognate to their own now seemed to pulse with a reckless energy. As if in their turning things had come uncottered, uncalendered. He thought that there might even be some timefault in the record" (285–86). For the traveler, the heavens no longer appear as the reliable and benevolent keepers of time and destiny but rather appear as a flawed mechanical system, which, like the Gnostic concept of heimarmene, has absolutely no concern for the suffering engendered by its machinations. The traveler senses "the world unravelling at his feet" and "a terrible darkness looming" (286). The word "unravelling" once again evokes the work of the weaver-God, suggesting that his creation is beginning to lose its power over the traveler.[12]

The storyteller explains that "for escaping from the world's dream of him this is at once his penalty and his reward" (283). This statement suggests the

Gnostic idea that the world benumbs and intoxicates us and that the pursuit of gnosis results in an "awakening from the state of unconsciousness ('ignorance') . . . that reveals to man his situation, hitherto hidden from him, and causes an outburst of dread and despair" (Jonas 69). This awakening also serves a soteriological function and is thus the ultimate goal of all Gnostic striving: "Joy to the man who has rediscovered himself and awakened!" states the Gospel of Truth (qtd. in Jonas 88). According to Gnostic thought, to awaken to the horror of existence incurs a terrifying "penalty" yet also contains within itself the "reward" of spiritual liberation.[13] The traveler in the epilogue seems to have experienced precisely such an awakening. In Buddhist terms, he arrives at an understanding of the First Noble Truth of the Buddha, namely, that existence is duḥkha (suffering)—a view that accords with the anticosmic position of the Gnostics. As has already been mentioned, the word "duḥkha" suggests "an axle which is off-center with respect to its wheel, also to a bone which has slipped out of socket" (H. Smith, *Religions of Man* 111). This is exactly what the dream traveler feels when he gets the impression that "in their turning things had become uncottered" (285).[14] The metaphor seems to hold something of a universal appeal, as we find similar references to cosmic dislocation in W. B. Yeats's "The Second Coming": "Things fall apart / The center cannot hold," as well as in Shakespeare's *Hamlet*: "The times are out of joint" (1.5.186–90). Thus the traveler comes to see creation as fundamentally unharmonious.

McCarthy's storyteller presents a complex view of a cosmos seemingly ruled by deterministic forces, which may nevertheless be transcended on an inner level. He explains that while the "events of the waking world . . . are forced upon us," it "falls to us to weigh and sort and order these events." Therefore, "it is we who assemble the story which is us. Each man is the bard of his own existence" (283). Even so, we can only "call forth the world which God has formed and that world only." According to the storyteller, we cannot control the events of this world, for they remain under the jurisdiction of the creator God, but we can at least control our responses to them; it is up to us whether the adversities we face enlighten or embitter us, break us or make us stronger. Having discussed what he believes to be our only potential for free will, the storyteller shifts his focus back to the forces of destiny, telling Billy that "this life of yours by which you set such store" is not "your doing, however you may choose to tell it. Its shape was forced in the void at the onset." His words imply that although we like to tell ourselves that we have shaped the course of our lives and chosen our own paths, he believes that in actuality we are controlled by destiny. The storyteller argues that "all talk of what might otherwise have been is senseless for there is no otherwise. ... The probability of the actual is absolute. That we have no power to guess it out beforehand makes it no less certain. That we may imagine alternate histories means nothing at all" (285). He goes on to explain, "Our decisions do not have some alternative. We may contemplate a choice but we pursue one path only" (286).[15] According to the storyteller, the fact that we can imagine alternate outcomes gives us the impression that we possess free will, but this is only an illusion, because the "template for the world and all in it was drawn up long ago" (287). In other words, our paths have been predetermined from the very beginning of creation. The storyteller's words evoke a view of the world akin to the Gnostic vision of a cosmos ruled by the forces of heimarmene.

Toward the end of the dream, the storyteller and the traveler find themselves on the same ontological plane and together they walk through a landscape of desolation: "We walked out in the dawn and there was an encampment on the plains below from which no smoke rose for all that it was cold and we went down to that place but all was abandoned there." Everywhere around them, they observe the relics of a vanished civilization: "There were huts of skin staked out upon the rocky ground with slagiron pikes and within these huts were remnants of old meals untouched and cold upon cold plates of clay" (287). The deserted huts also contain "stores of primitive and antique arms," "robes sewn up from the skins of northern animals," "and rawhide trunks," containing "old accounts and ledger books and records of the history of that vanished folk, the path they had followed in the world and their reckonings of the cost of that journey" (287–88). All of these images are in keeping with the themes of transience and death that permeate the novel. The ledger books, with their careful records of each individual's journey through the world, evoke the theme of inescapable destiny. Whatever the costs of their individual journeys, all human beings end up as "a skeleton of old sepia bones," which the traveler and the storyteller find "sewn up in a leather shroud" (288); death is the place where all paths converge.

The focus of the conversation shifts from the metaphysical to the spiritual when the storyteller tells Billy, "This life of yours is not a picture of the world. It is the world itself and it is composed not of bone or dream or time but of worship. Nothing else can contain it. Nothing else be by it contained" (287).[16] The storyteller's words echo those of Plotinus (ca. 204/5–270 CE):

"Each being contains in itself the whole intelligible world. Therefore All is everywhere. Each is there All, and All is each" (qtd. in Huxley 5). The storyteller seems to be reiterating the essential doctrine of the Perennial Philosophy, namely that the "only Reality" is "that immaterial and final Being, which some philosophers call the Absolute, and most theologians call God" (Underhill 5). According to the Perennial Philosophy, this ultimate Reality is identical to the spiritual self, to "this life of yours" that already contains within it the totality of "the world itself." Thus the storyteller's words stress the idea that the ultimate Reality cannot be described in terms of the material world of sense perception represented by "bone," nor the psychological realm of mental activity symbolized by "dream," nor the temporal processes of "time," but only through the spiritual practice of "worship."

The storyteller speaks of the Absolute in terms of its utter transcendence and ineffability: "The thing that is sought is altogether other. However it may be construed within men's dreams or by their acts it will never make a fit" (287). This view accords with "the theological idea of Divine Transcendence," which stresses "the total and incommunicable difference *in kind* between the Divine and everything else.... God is the Unconditioned, the Wholly Other for whom we have no words" (Underhill 337). According to such a view, the Absolute is *"ganz anders"* or "radically other" (H. Smith, *Forgotten Truth* 19), and we find the same approach in descriptions of the Brahman (Absolute) in Hinduism, expressed by the words *"neti neti* (not so, not so)" (Huxley 33). This does not contradict the claim that the spiritual self is identical with the Absolute, or the Atman with the Brahman, because the Perennial Philosophy also teaches that ultimately, "multiplicity is resolved into Unity: a unity with which the perceiving self is merged" (338). The storyteller claims that the ultimate Reality cannot be described nor "construed within men's dreams," only apprehended through direct experience.

The storyteller goes on to explain, "These dreams and these acts" through which human beings seek to reach the Absolute "are driven by a terrible hunger" (287).[17] This is the experience of what William James called the "sick soul," described by Evelyn Underhill as "the mood of the penitent; of the utter humility which, appalled by the sharp contrast between itself and the Perfect which it contemplates, can only 'cry out of the depths'" (98–99). The storyteller then makes a rather cryptic pronouncement, claiming that these dreams and acts "seek to meet a need which they can never satisfy, and for that we must be grateful" (287). He believes that we should be grateful for the fact that the earthly acts and wish-fulfilling dreams by which we seek to satisfy our longing for the Absolute cannot fulfil our spiritual hunger. In other words, the storyteller tells Billy that if we could satiate that "terrible hunger" with earthly distractions, we should no longer strive for the Absolute.[18]

The dream becomes stranger still when the storyteller describes how he and the traveler "walked together through all that desolation and all that abandonment and I asked him if the people were away at some calling but he said that they were not." The conversation intensifies the eerie presence of death and emphasizes the poignant transience of human existence. The storyteller asks the traveler to tell him "what had happened" to the people, but he receives a strange reply: "I have been here before. So have you" (288). This feeling of déjà vu also occurs earlier in the dream, when the traveler first meets the procession of men and feels that "strange as was their appearance and the mission they seemed bent upon yet they were also oddly familiar. As if he'd seen all this somewhere before" (279). These cryptic pronouncements suggest either a recurring dream or the dim recollection of a previous life.[19]

The theme of cyclical repetition is brought up again when the storyteller states, "Like the traveler, all I had forsaken I would come upon again." When Billy asks what it was that he had forsaken, the storyteller replies in haunting, poetic diction: "The immappable world of our journey. A pass in the mountains. A bloodstained stone. The marks of steel upon it. Names carved in the corrosible lime among stone fishes and ancient shells. Things dim and dimming. The dry sea floor. The tools of migrant hunters. The dreams enchased upon the blades of them. The peregrine bones of a prophet. The silence. The gradual extinction of rain. The coming of night" (288). These words summarize the content of the dream exactly as it would appear to the dreamer upon awakening, fading away into fragmentary and disconnected images and impressions. More significantly, they evoke the entire history of human existence, our sacrificial rites, endless wars, futile attempts at immortality, and inevitable extinction, along with the entire past and future history of the planet. Jacqueline Scoones offers an interesting interpretation of the storyteller's last words, arguing that "the final phrases progressively emptied of sound, motion, and light, reverse the act of creation. A cycle ends" (149). The passage ends with an apocalyptic vision of death, aridity, silence, and darkness.[20]

The storyteller reminds Billy, "This desert about us was once a vast sea" and asks, "Can such a thing vanish? Of what are seas made? Or I? Or you?"

(286). The vast desert about them is, of course, made of the calcified particles of the vanished sea—the bones of fish, coral, shells—ground down into sand. The remains of human beings undergo much the same "sea change," breaking down into the elements from which this entire world is composed.[21] The implication is that nothing truly vanishes; everything is simply broken down into its component elements and transformed into another configuration of energy and matter. Thus there are several possible interpretations of the storyteller's claim that "the world of our fathers resides within us. Ten thousand generations and more" (281). First, we may read this pronouncement quite literally, in that our physical bodies are indeed composed of the world that came before us; our bodies contain the same carbon atoms as the bodies of the early carbon-based life-forms on this planet.

On a more metaphysical level, the statement may be understood in terms of Carl Jung's theory of the collective subconscious, to which all human beings supposedly have access, especially in their dreams. The latter interpretation seems more pertinent, as the storyteller explains that we share the "world of our fathers" through our dreams: "At the core of our life is the history of which it is composed and in that core are no idioms but only the act of knowing and it is this we share in dreams and out" (281). Edwin Arnold also argues that "the stranger Billy meets in the epilogue to *Cities of the Plain* appears to speak to the idea of inherited collective knowledge" ("Go to Sleep" 40). It is likely, however, that the storyteller's words hint at something even higher than the collective subconscious, because the emphasis placed on the primacy of the "act of knowing" suggests gnosis. Furthermore, this direct "act of knowing" is reminiscent of McCarthy's own description of the mystical experience being a "direct apprehension of reality, unmediated by symbol" (Wallace 138), that is, not transmitted through the idiom of speech or through any mode of representation.

The storyteller claims that this "act of knowing" is not limited by human conceptions of time and history, occurring "before the first man spoke and after the last is silenced forever" (281). From the point of view of the Perennial Philosophy, these words suggest an experience of divine eternity outside the temporal constraints of individual mortality. Aldous Huxley writes, "The universe is an everlasting succession of events; but its ground, according to the Perennial Philosophy, is the timeless now of the divine spirit" (184). Huxley explains that the "body is always in time" but "the spirit is always timeless" (187) and that the ultimate spiritual goal is to "pass out of time and into eternity" (51). Plotinus described this as a state in which the spirit "neither sees, nor distinguishes by seeing, nor imagines that there are two things" and "the perceiver" becomes "one with the thing perceived" (Underhill 372). According to the Perennial Philosophy, when the spirit becomes one with the Absolute through the direct "act of knowing," it becomes aware of its own eternal and infinite nature; as a result, the concepts of "self" and "other" and all such dualities are completely dissolved.

The storyteller demonstrates this essential oneness; holding out his hand "palm out," he instructs Billy to do the same and then asks, "You see the likeness?" (287). Billy concedes that he does.[22] Edwin Arnold argues that in McCarthy's fiction, hands "serve as a major trope. . . . they represent the shared humanity of all peoples and illustrate McCarthy's insistence on the idea that we are all one" ("Go to Sleep" 71). When the storyteller first asks Billy to hold out his hand, Billy wants to know whether "this is a pledge of some kind." The storyteller replies, "No. You are pledged already. You always were" (287). Arnold explores the full implications of this statement, arguing, "A pledge is both an oath, a promise, and the person who takes that oath, who agrees to serve as surrogate, even as hostage, in the place of another" ("Mosaic" 185). The words evoke not only the content of the storyteller's dream, in which the traveler acts as a surrogate sacrificial victim, but also the religious connotations of a savior come to redeem others. The storyteller claims that "every man's death is a standing in for every other" (288). It is noteworthy that in *The Crossing* Billy encounters another man who also tells him "that for every man that death selects another is reprieved" (379). The storyteller goes on to argue, "And since death comes to all there is no way to abate the fear of it except to love that man who stands for us. We are not waiting for his history to be written. He passed here long ago. That man who is all men and who stands in the dock for us until our own time come and we must stand for him" (288). In this version of the savior myth, the sacrificial surrogate may be any human being, precisely because all of humanity is one.

As previously discussed, Kurt Rudolph explains that Gnosticism is characterized by the "*Urmensch*" or "*Anthropos*" myth, that is, the myth of the God-man, which teaches that there exists a "close relationship or kinship of nature between the highest God and the inner core of man" (92). Thus the idea that the savior and the saved "are of one nature" is "fundamental to gnostic soteriology" (122), because by achieving liberation from the manifest cosmos, the Gnostic literally "becomes God" (191). By suggesting that the roles of the savior and the saved are interchangeable, the storyteller's words evoke the Gnostic concept of the Salvator Salvatus, or Saved Savior. The storyteller departs with this message of unity, leaving Billy to spend the night alone "in a concrete tile by the highwayside," sitting "in the round mouth of the tile like a man in a bell" (289). The image of the bell seems to be a reference to "for whom the bell tolls," suggesting that since all beings are one, then the death of any other individual is also our own death. In the words of John Donne, "never send to know for whom the bell tolls; it tolls for thee" (243). As discussed in previous chapters, the tolling of a bell is a motif that reoccurs throughout the Border Trilogy.[23] These nonexistent and therefore metaphorical bells serve as a reminder of Donne's sermon regarding the essential unity and shared mortality of all beings.

Billy continues with his solitary wandering, but the imagery of drought-ridden desolation and industrial squalor is somewhat alleviated by his encounter with a "spring beneath a cottonwood." There he finds "a tin cup on a stob," which he takes down and holds with something akin to reverence. "He'd not seen a cup at a spring in years and he held it in both hands as had thousands before him unknown to him yet joined in sacrament. He dipped the cup into the water and raised it cool and dripping to his mouth" (290). The Gnostics made frequent use of the symbolic significance of the sacrament of water, the "idea of the 'water of life'" being "a symbol of illuminating knowledge, which was depicted ritually by a drink of water" (Rudolph 230). In McCarthy's fiction, the cup of pure water seems to signify a partaking of the "waters of life," or what the Gnostics referred to as "living water," an act that alleviates—at least temporarily—the spiritual drought and existential anguish experienced by the protagonist.[24]

The bleakness of Billy's solitary and impoverished existence is also alleviated by a simple act of human kindness when, in "the fall of that year when the cold weather came," he is "taken in by a family" consisting of a mother, father, and two children (290). Waking from a disturbing dream in which his dead brother Boyd "was in the room" but "would not speak," Billy finds the mother, Betty, "sitting on his bed with her hand on his shoulder." Having heard Billy calling out Boyd's name in his sleep, Betty asks about the lost brother and Billy gives her a brief account of the tale told in *The Crossing*: "We run off to Mexico together. When we was kids. When our folks died," adding, "I'd give about anything to see him one more time." Betty comforts him by "patting his hand," thereby reaffirming the symbolic significance of human hands as representative of the essential unity of all humanity. Billy's hand is described as "gnarled, ropescarred, speckled from the sun and the years of it.

The ropy veins that bound them to his heart. There was map enough for men to read. There God's plenty of signs and wonders to make a landscape. To make a world" (291).[25] The map of life that the storyteller tried in vain to draw has been etched out on Billy's hand through the simple act of living out the journey of his life. Billy feels unworthy of such kindness and protests, "I'm not what you think I am. I aint nothin. I dont know why you put up with me," but Betty replies, "Well, Mr Parham, I know who you are. And I do know why. You go to sleep now. I'll see you in the morning" (292). Billy's laconic reply, "Yes mam," serves not only as an expression of acquiescence but also as an indirect affirmation of the truth of Betty's statement. Edwin Arnold argues that the novel ends with Billy's being "blessed and perhaps finally justified by the touch of [Betty's] hand and the kindness of her heart" ("Go to Sleep" 67). Such simple acts of kindness, generosity, and hospitality stand against the terrible enormity of evil depicted in McCarthy's works.

As previously discussed, McCarthy's portrayal of the balance of good and evil recalls Vasily Grossman's epic work *Life and Fate*, in which one of the characters discusses the importance of "private kindness of one individual towards another," arguing that "human history is not the battle of good struggling to overcome evil. It is a battle fought by a great evil struggling to crush a small kernel of human kindness" (409–10). The Gnostics, despite their overt dualism, held a similar view of the cosmic situation; as Hans Jonas explains, their teachings placed great "emphasis on the fellowship of man as the only realm of kinship left, united not only by the community of origin but also by the community of the situation of aliens in the world" (264). For the Gnostics, the manifest cosmos was utterly permeated by evil, against which stood only the fragmented sparks of the divine located deep inside each human being.

Though there is no evidence that McCarthy has ever read *Life and Fate*, it is noteworthy that some of McCarthy's striking images and metaphors may also be found in Grossman's work. Consider the following passage on the presence of "goodness" in the world: "When Christianity clothed it in the teachings of the Church Fathers, it began to fade; its kernel became a husk. It remains potent only while it is dumb and senseless, hidden in the living darkness of the human heart—before it becomes a tool or commodity in the hands of preachers, before its crude ore is forged into the gilt coins of holiness" (Grossman 409). The passage not only suggests the insistence of the gypsy in *The Crossing* that "the husk is not the thing" (411) but also evokes the "false moneyer" in *Blood Meridian*, who is busily "hammering

... some coinage for a dawn that would not be" (310). An overt criticism of the traditional Christian church, along with a Manichean fascination with good and evil, forms a major theme in the works of both writers. Despite McCarthy's preoccupation with the power of evil, it is the simple act of a compassionate woman that concludes the Border Trilogy and leaves the reader with a lingering impression of the power of ordinary human kindness, which is like that "little candle" that "throws its beams" out into the vast darkness of an iniquitous world.[26]

CHAPTER 13

"In All That Dark and All That Cold"

Good and Evil in *No Country for Old Men*

■ In its preoccupation with the existence of evil, *No Country for Old Men* maintains the metaphysical tradition established in Cormac McCarthy's prior works. The novel explores evil not only as a specific sociohistorical problem, located within the violence of the drug trade between Texas and Mexico in the 1980s, but also as a universal spiritual struggle. The burden of the metaphysical speculation is borne by the monologues of the aging sheriff Ed Tom Bell, who shares the role of protagonist with the unfortunate Llewelyn Moss, the young man whose life changes irrevocably after the discovery of a suitcase filled with drug money. The reader is confronted with a representation of evil in the opening pages of the novel, with Sheriff Bell's recollection of a nineteen-year-old boy who was sentenced to death for killing a fourteen-year-old girl. Bell visits the boy before the execution and is disturbed to learn that the killing was not "a crime of passion," as reported by the papers, but a premeditated and cold-blooded act of sadism: "And he told me that he had been plannin to kill somebody for about as long as he could remember. Said that if they turned him out he'd do it again. Said he knew he was goin to hell.... I really believe that he knew he was goin to be in hell in fifteen minutes. I believe that. And I've thought about that a lot." The boy's belief in hell troubles the sheriff and he wonders about the spiritual implications of the boy's actions: "What do you say to a man that by his own admission has no soul? Why would you say anything? I've thought about it a good deal" (3). Were the boy a nihilist, one could argue that he did not believe in the spiritual consequences of his crime, but the conviction with which he talks about hell, even while paradoxically denying the existence of the soul, suggests that he subscribes to at least some version of Christianity, or more likely to Satanism, and has willingly chosen to embrace evil.[1]

Bell wonders about the nature of the evil he perceives in the boy, suspecting that he may be dealing with something new: "I thought I'd never seen a person like that and it got me to wonderin if maybe he was some new kind." Bell adds that the boy "wasn't nothin compared to what was comin down the pike" (3), a comment that foreshadows the arrival of the professional hitman and "psychopathic killer" Anton Chigurh (141). This view is shared by Sheriff Lamar, who, after finding his deputy brutally garroted by Chigurh, states, "I just have this feelin we're looking at something we really aint never even seen before." Bell agrees: "I got the same feelin" (46). Torbert, Bell's deputy, finds himself similarly perplexed by the violence of the drug traffickers, asking, "Who the hell are these people?" (79). Bell's reply once again expresses the suspicion that they are dealing with something unprecedented: "I dont know. I used to say they were the same ones we've always had to deal with. Same ones my grandaddy had to deal with. Back then they was rustlin cattle. Now they're runnin dope. But I dont know as that's true no more. I'm like you. I aint sure we've seen these people before. Their kind. I dont know what to do about em even. If you killed em all they'd have to build an annex on to hell" (79). Bell's tongue-in-cheek quip about the expansion of hell reveals a certain loss of faith in the ordered cosmos of traditional Christianity; if Satan keeps expanding his realm, where does this leave the balance between good and evil? According to Bell, the violence and suffering caused by the drug trade is a manifestation of the triumph of evil: "I think if you were Satan and you were settin around tryin to think up somethin that would just bring the human race to its knees what you would probably come up with is narcotics. Maybe he did." Although the reference to Satan is hypothetical, when pressed about his belief in such an entity, Bell admits that the existence of Satan "explains a lot of things that otherwise dont have no explanation. Or not to me they dont" (219). Bell's views echo those of Horace, as expressed in the latter's *Odes and Epodes*: "Aetas parentum peior avis tulit nos nequiores, mox daturos progeniem vitiosiorem" (Our father's age ignobler than our grandsires bore us yet more depraved; and we in turn shall leave a race more vicious than ourselves) (3.6.46–48). The idea that the modern world is facing a new kind of evil runs counter to ideas expressed in McCarthy's earlier novels, which are generally populated by characters who believe that the world has always been an evil place.[2]

Critics often cite the historically accurate violence depicted in McCarthy's *Blood Meridian* to argue the case that Bell is strangely unaware of the violent history of the Southwest. Erik Hage argues that "Bell's view seems to veer from McCarthy's ... for his borderlands novels place humanity on a historical continuum" (35). Hage argues that in *No Country for Old Men*, "drug-trafficking has replaced the Glanton gang as the new marauding evil of the Southwest" (34) but insists that this "new evil" is "just as pervasive and unharnessed as past evils—and one ultimately rooted in human nature" (121). David Cremean similarly argues that "one of Bell's shortcomings is a naïveté about, or at least a disconnection from, the meaning of the history of the region. Though he mentions its bloody past, he nevertheless believes it cannot compare to what he is witnessing now" (26). The puzzling thing about Bell's pronouncements, however, is that they don't seem to stem from an ignorance or misunderstanding of history. On the contrary, Bell seems completely aware of the extent of the historical violence of the Southwest, evoking scenes right out of *Blood Meridian* when he graphically describes the early settlers' "wive[s] and children" being "killed and scalped and gutted like fish" (195). Bell's Uncle Ellis also recounts the violent history of their own family, describing how Uncle Mac "was shot down on his own porch" and how his widow "buried him herself. Diggin in that hard caliche" (270). Such conversations serve to emphasize that Bell is all too aware that "this country has a strange kind of history and a damned bloody one too" and yet, despite this awareness, he continues to insist that the world is facing a "new kind" of evil (284, 3).[3]

David Cremean maintains that Bell is an unreliable narrator, arguing that "despite the sympathy with which McCarthy portrays Bell, his knack for homiletic utterances suggests that the sheriff can, and possible should, be viewed as unreliable in his judgments" (23). Although I agree that Bell is prone to "homiletic utterances," I do not believe that this is enough evidence to conclude that Bell is an unreliable narrator. On the contrary, I find it significant that McCarthy made similar "utterances" during his interview with David Kushner:

> If I wrote about violence in an exaggerated way, it was looking at a future that I imagined would be a lot more violent.... And it is. Can you remember twenty years ago having beheadings on TV? I can't.... I'm not one of those conspiracy guys, but the world is in a very unstable situation. If you were to take thoughtful people on, say, January 1st, 1900, and tell them what

the twentieth century was going to look like, they'd say, Are you shitting me? . . . I think about John [his son] all the time and what the world's going to be like. . . . It's going to be a very troubled place. (47)

I am not suggesting that Bell and McCarthy are interchangeable, nor am I conflating the artist with his creation, but the fact that McCarthy seems to agree with Bell's pessimistic appraisals of the world suggests that arguments presented in Bell's monologues are to be regarded seriously and not read against the grain as satirical or parodic passages.[4] If we can establish Bell's position as genuine and sincere, then we can better understand the world as it is represented within the novel.

The premise that the novel is informed by Bell's pessimism is borne out by its very title, which is not merely an allusion to W. B. Yeats's poem "Sailing to Byzantium" but carries with it far broader connotations of Yeats's own world view. The essence of Bell's negative evaluation of the world—"things to come. Things losing shape. Taking you with them" (127)—can be summed up by lines from Yeats's "The Second Coming": "Things fall apart; the centre cannot hold; / Mere anarchy is loosed upon the world" (lines 3–4). The sinister Anton Chigurh expresses the exact inverse of this sentiment, claiming that "things have fallen into place" (173). Bell confesses that his belief system is crumbling away: "I'm bein asked to stand for somethin that I dont have the same belief in it I once did. Asked to believe in somethin I might not hold with the way I once did" (296), while Chigurh holds on to "principles that transcend money or drugs" (153), explaining that "I have only one way to live. It doesnt allow for special cases" (295). Thus Yeats's lament that "The best lack all conviction, while the worst / Are full of passionate intensity" ("Second Coming" lines 7–8) is echoed in the world views of Bell and Chigurh, respectively.

Jim Welsh also argues that *No Country for Old Men* draws on the wider context of Yeats's work, suggesting that "Chigurh would seem to be the very personification of the Antichrist, that slouching 'rough beast' of Yeats's 1919 poem 'The Second Coming'" (74). A subtle clue linking Chigurh to this apocalyptic theme is the emphasis placed on the number 117.[5] The young protagonist Llewelyn Moss is killed outside his motel room, "standin in front of 117" (237). The number of the room is brought up again when Bell returns to the crime scene and walks "up to the door at 117" (243). When Chigurh breaks into the house where Moss's wife, Carla Jean, is staying, he notes that "the green diode numerals on the radio put the time at 1:17" (202).

The appearance of the number on the digital clock suggests a Bible verse. *No Country for Old Men* provides a further clue by drawing attention to Revelation, the only book of the Bible referenced within the novel. Bell mentions that his wife, Loretta, had "been readin St John. The Revelations" (305). Bell makes another reference to Revelation when he reveals that "I wake up sometimes way in the night and I know as certain as death that there aint nothin short of second comin of Christ that can slow this train" (159). Thus the novel makes a rather esoteric reference to a specific Bible verse: "And when I saw him, I fell at his feet as dead. And he laid his right hand upon me, saying unto me, Fear not; I am the first and the last" (Revelation 1:17). The words read like a reverse-order description of the way Chigurh murders his victims with his trademark weapon, the stun gun used for killing cattle.

Like the figure in Revelation, who is Christ in the Second Coming, Chigurh convinces his victim to "fear not," by driving a police car and impersonating a police officer: "Sir would you mind stepping out of the vehicle?" He then places his right "hand on the man's head like faith healer. The pneumatic hiss and click of the plunger sounded like a door closing." The scene ends like the Bible verse begins, with the dead man falling "soundlessly to the ground" (7). The satanic reversal and parody of a religious rite is conveyed not only through the reference to faith healing but also through the use of the word "pneumatic," which suggests pneuma, or spirit, and thus carries connotations of spirituality. By linking Chigurh to the figure in Revelation, the novel creates an evil, parodic version of the Second Coming, much like Yeats's poem of the same name, which asks, "And what rough beast, its hour come round at last / Slouches towards Bethlehem to be born?" (lines 21–2). Welsh identifies further connections between McCarthy's novel and Yeats's poetry, pointing out that the allusion to "Sailing to Byzantium" also evokes Yeats's "Byzantium," in which descriptions of the "supernatural" figure, "an image, man or shade, / Shade more than man, more image than a shade" (9–10) evoke similar descriptions of Chigurh as a "ghost" (248, 299).

During one of his internal monologues, Bell states that Chigurh is "a ghost. But he's out there," and he voices the same idea to a county prosecutor: "He's pretty much a ghost" (248, 299). When the prosecutor asks for clarification, "Is he pretty much or is he one?," Bell replies, "No, he's out there. I wish he wasn't. But he is." The prosecutor interprets this to mean that Chigurh is a real man: "He nodded. I guess if he was a ghost you wouldn't have to worry about him." Bell agrees during the course of the conversation, "I said that was right," but his internal monologue reveals that he has "thought about it since" and come to a slightly different conclusion: "I think the answer to this question is that when you encounter certain things in the world, the evidence for certain things, you realize that you have come upon somethin that you may very well not be equal to and I think that this is one of them things. When you've said that its real and not just in your head I'm not all that sure what it is you have said" (299). It is clear that Bell feels outmatched by Chigurh, but this interpretation does not account for all the nuances of the passage. The repeated reference to "certain things" suggests the presence of something ineffable and beyond the scope of Bell's lifetime of experience as a sheriff. Bell seems to be arguing that just because Chigurh is "real," that is, truly "out there" and not just in his own "head," does not entirely invalidate the possibility that he has encountered a supernatural evil.[6]

Bell describes Chigurh in apocalyptic terms in his first internal monologue, insisting, "Somewhere out there is a true and living prophet of destruction and I dont want to confront him. I know he's real. I have seen his work. I walked in front of those eyes once. I won't do it again. I won't push my chips forward and stand up and go out to meet him." These words appear to be a confession of weakness or cowardice, but Bell insists, "It aint just bein older. I wish that it was. I cant say that it's even what you are willin to do. Because I always knew that you had to be willin to die to even do this job." Bell is not afraid of physical injury or death, but he is afraid of Chigurh. Indeed, he goes on to explain that "I think it is more like what you are willin to become. And I think a man would have to put his soul at hazard. And I wont do that. I think now that maybe I never would" (3). His fear is clearly not physical but spiritual; Bell is afraid that an encounter with evil will jeopardize his soul. Bell's refusal to fight Chigurh seems to stem from the idea that engaging with evil, even to fight it, will only result in strengthening it.[7] For example, the Hermetic philosopher René Guénon claimed that "unfortunately it sometimes so happens that people who imagine that they are fighting the devil, whatever their particular notion of the devil may be, are thus turned, without the least suspicion of the fact on their part, into his best servants" (*Reign of Quantity* 248). Similarly, theosophist Franz Hartmann argues that "no man can successfully resist the devil by fighting him on the same level" (109). At the end of the novel, Bell confesses that he aims "to quit and a good part of it is just knowin that I wont be called on to hunt this man. I reckon he's a man" (282). These words emphasize his doubt over whether or not Chigurh actually is a human being; otherwise Bell wouldn't feel the need to bring the subject into question, not even to reinforce it.

The idea that Chigurh is no ordinary human being is hinted at throughout the novel. "They say the eyes are windows to the soul," says Bell, reflecting on the eyes of the nineteen-year-old murderer. "I dont know what them eyes was the windows to and I guess I'd as soon not know. But there is another view of the world out there and other eyes to see it and that's where this is goin." These "other eyes" seem to be a reference to Chigurh, the new evil "comin down the pike" (3). It is significant that Chigurh's eyes are described as "blue as lapis. At once glistening and totally opaque. Like wet stones" (56). Their cold, stonelike opacity makes it impossible to determine what kind of soul, if any, they conceal. When the other chief protagonist, Llewelyn Moss, first encounters Chigurh, he is also struck by the strange "blue eyes. Serene. Dark hair. Something about him faintly exotic. Beyond Moss's experience" (112). Chigurh remains an indefinable mystery to everyone he encounters. Linda Woodson argues that he "exists outside of society and is of indeterminate origin and purpose" ("You Are the Battleground" 6). When another sheriff describes Chigurh as "a goddamned homicidal lunatic," Bell disagrees: "Yeah. I dont think he's a lunatic though." But when asked, "Well what would you call him?" Bell replies, "I dont know" (192). Carson Wells, a hitman and former lieutenant colonel in the Vietnam War, understands that there is something about Chigurh that surpasses the ordinary: "He's a peculiar man. You could even say that he has principles. Principles that transcend money or drugs or anything like that" (153). No character within the novel seems entirely adequate to the challenge of understanding the nature of Chigurh's existence, though some, like Wells, come closer than others.

Chigurh's divergence from ordinary human behavior is apparent even in the most mundane of activities. While recovering from his wounds in a motel over the course of five days, he watches television in a disconcertingly peculiar manner: "He kept the television on and he sat up in bed watching it and he never changed channels. He watched whatever came on. He watched soap operas and the news and talk shows" (165). His behavior is similarly odd when he breaks into Carla Jean's house: "He emptied her bureau drawers out onto the bed and sat sorting through her things, holding up from time to time some item and studying it in the bluish light from the yardlamp. A plastic hairbrush. A cheap fairground bracelet. Weighing these things in his hand like a medium who might thereby divine some fact concerning the owner" (204). The reference to psychic mediumship evokes a sense of the paranormal. This nuance is strengthened by the fact that Chigurh's studying of Carla Jean's inconsequential trinkets is reminiscent of the strange behavior of *Blood Meridian*'s suspiciously supernatural Judge Holden, who also studies "small artifacts" (139).

Although Chigurh's actions are not overtly paranormal, he does display extraordinary feats of strength and endurance that often border on the superhuman. He seems largely impervious to stimuli such as cold: "Chigurh stood there a long time. It was cold out on the barrial and he had no jacket but he didnt seem to notice" (60). He remains equally unaffected by physical exertion: "Chigurh limped up the seventeen flights of concrete steps . . . breathing no harder than if he'd just got up out of a chair" (198). Even more impressive is his remarkably high pain threshold, evidenced by the manner in which he disinfects his own gunshot wound: "Other than a light beading of sweat on his forehead there was little evidence that his labors had cost him anything at all" (164). A boy who witnesses Chigurh's involvement in a serious car accident informs Sheriff Bell that "there was a bone stickin out under the skin on his arm and he didnt pay no more attention to it than nothing" (292). This stoicism persists even in the face of death. Finding himself at the wrong end of a gun, Chigurh seems "oddly untroubled. As if this were all part of his day" (112). On one level, Chigurh may be read as the personification of metaphysical evil and death, but the complexity of his character extends beyond allegorical representation.[8]

Jay Ellis argues that Chigurh "is more complex than just a figure of pure evil," because he "functions not only as an executioner, but also as a Socratic figure who, when he has time, engages in extended dialogue intended to help his victims see what they could not before see, that their past actions, in conjunction with chance events, have determined their fated end at his hands" ("Do You See?" 96). Ellis points out that Chigurh "increasingly acts out his part in Socratic dialogue through *No Country for Old Men*" and that "the words 'understand' or 'understood' occur at least 23 times in this novel" (101). The reader first encounters the Socratic side of Chigurh during his tense confrontation with a hapless gas station owner. Rather than killing the owner outright, Chigurh insists that the increasingly uneasy man "call" the result of a coin toss. Chigurh displays some of his peculiar "principles" (153) when he announces, "You need to call it. . . . I cant call it for you. It wouldnt be fair. It wouldnt even be right. Just call it." The man hesitates, wanting "to know what it is we're callin here," arguing that he "didnt put nothing up."

Chigurh insists, "Yes you did. You've been putting it up your whole life. You just didnt know it" (56). Chigurh wants the station owner to see that he has spent his entire life making seemingly inconsequential decisions, all of which have led to this chilling encounter with death. To illustrate this point, Chigurh tells the man that the date on the coin is "nineteen fifty-eight," and therefore the coin has "been traveling twenty-two years to get here. And now it's here. And I'm here" (56). The coin, too, has its individual destiny and the situation in the gas station represents something akin to Thomas Hardy's "The Convergence of the Twain," a poem that describes the "intimate welding" of the individual destinies of the *Titanic* and the iceberg. The station owner and the coin are depicted as having similarly converging paths that culminate in a shared destiny, although the entire event is set on a much less majestic scale than that of Hardy's tragedy.[9]

According to Chigurh, however, the path of a coin is no less important than the path of an iceberg or a great ocean liner. After the man, who still doesn't quite understand what is taking place, calls "heads" and wins his life on the coin toss, Chigurh hands him the "lucky coin" and warns, "Dont put it in your pocket. You wont know which one it is." Chigurh believes that the particular coin used in this game of chance is imbued with a significance that necessitates that it be kept separate from other coins. He explains, "Anything can be an instrument.... Small things. Things you wouldnt even notice. They pass from hand to hand. People dont pay attention. And then one day there's an accounting. And after that nothing is the same. Well, you say. It's just a coin. For instance. Nothing special there. What could that be the instrument of? You see the problem. To separate the act from the thing. As if the parts of some moment in history might be interchangeable with the parts of some other moment. How could that be?" (57). According to Chigurh, the coin is an instrument of fate. The people who encountered it during its twenty-two-year journey had no idea that the way in which they handled it and the places where they spent it would one day determine whether a man lives or dies; they were unwitting participants in a chain reaction of unforeseeable events. Chigurh claims that people remain unaware of the far-reaching consequences triggered by seemingly insignificant events until they are confronted with the day of reckoning. Such a view of the cosmos is in keeping with the Gnostic concept of heimarmene, that "inexorable and hostile law of the universe" (Jonas 254) that was believed to control the paths of all earthly phenomena, including the individual destinies of human beings.[10] Furthermore, Chigurh believes that there is no sense in distinguishing the object from the event. In other words, the man's life was won in a coin toss with one particular coin and no other. All the other coins in the world were following their own individual paths and fulfilling their separate destinies, as was every other object and entity.[11] This is why Chigurh insists that the station owner must keep the "lucky coin" separate from the others.

Chigurh again adopts the Socratic method in his final encounter with his fellow hitman Carson Wells. Although Wells isn't given the privilege of a coin toss, Chigurh nevertheless engages in an incisive dialogue with his victim. While holding Wells at gunpoint, Chigurh asks, "If the rule you followed led you to this of what use was the rule?" When Wells replies, "I don't know what you're talking about," Chigurh elaborates: "I'm talking about your life. In which now everything can be seen at once." Knowing that the moment of death has arrived, Chigurh wants Wells to examine the path that led him here, claiming that the present situation "calls past events into question" (175). Even though Chigurh admits that he and Wells are in the "same line of work," he finds it necessary to distance himself from the other hitman: "You think I'm like you. That it's just greed. But I'm not like you. I live a simple life" (177). This distinction between the two hired assassins suggests that Chigurh transcends mere criminality. The "simple life" he leads imbues him with the ascetic austerity of a monk pledged to evil, a satanic reversal of traditional, spiritual roles hinted at by other descriptions of Chigurh as a "faith healer" and a "prophet of destruction" (7, 3). In his study of the portrayal of evil in literature and cinema, Paul Oppenheimer points out that evil often "begins in criminality" but then "surpasses criminality, and finally, by comparison with criminality, overwhelms and belittles it, causing it to seem oddly cumbersome and even childish" (21). Chigurh lives by a different "rule," not motivated by the usual spectrum of human desires and thus remaining largely inscrutable.

It is significant that Wells is given a premonition of his own death exactly three days before it takes place. While examining the damage caused by a shootout between Chigurh and Moss at the Eagle Pass motel, Wells notices "two bulletholes in the windowglass" of a "second floor level" apartment across the street. After knocking on the door and receiving no answer, Wells lets himself in and finds the corpse of an old woman: "She'd been shot through the forehead and had tilted forward leaving part of the back of her skull and a good bit of dried brainmatter stuck to the slat of the rocker behind her. . . . A second shot had marked a date on a calendar on the wall behind her that was three days hence" (147). The path of the stray bullet converges with the path of the unsuspecting woman, much as Chigurh's coin converges with the equally unsuspecting gas station owner earlier in the novel. The woman's death reminds Wells of the inexorable machinations of fate: "Not what you had in mind at all, was it darling?" he asks (148). Wells correctly interprets the mark on the calendar as a portent of the day of his own impending death.

During the final encounter, he tells Chigurh, "By the old woman's calendar I've got three more minutes. Well the hell with it. I think I saw all this coming a long time ago. Almost like a dream. Déjà vu." Wells's words reveal that he had a vision of his own death long before he saw the calendar. Nevertheless, the question posed by Chigurh, namely, "How did you let yourself get in this situation?" suggest that it was still within Wells's power to make different choices, live by a different "rule," and thereby change his fate. Chigurh encourages Wells to engage in a final moment of self-reflection: "I thought you might want to explain yourself. . . . Not to me. To yourself" (178). Chigurh's questions seem to be directing Wells toward something akin to the existentialist concept of authentic existence, which, though "not clearly defined by the existentialists . . . implies an attitude of sincerity and honesty and the absence of self-deception" (de Silva 1). Furthermore, it is a mode of existence based on "a realization that one is what one makes oneself by one's acts" (Manser 20). It is worth mentioning that Sheriff Bell strives for the same realization: "It's a life's work to see yourself for what you really are and even then you might be wrong. And that is somethin I dont want to be wrong about" (295). Despite the fact that Bell and Chigurh are diametrically opposed in a Manichean battle between good and evil, respectively, both men insist on the importance of authentic existence arrived at through knowledge of the self.

Existentialist themes are also apparent in Chigurh's attempts to make his victims come to terms with the inevitability of death. He accuses Wells of believing that he can keep death at bay: "You think that as long as you keep looking at me you can put it off." Wells denies thinking such a thing, but Chigurh insists, "Yes you do. You should admit your situation. There would be more dignity in it. I'm trying to help you" (176). Behind the "existential preoccupation with the theme of death" is the belief that "living authentically is living constantly in its presence, for then alone can we attain 'freedom in the face of death'" (Dutt 80). When Wells accuses Chigurh of thinking that he is "outside of everything" and reminds him that he is "not outside of death," Chigurh replies, "It doesnt mean to me what it does to you" (177). The reply can be read in two ways, the surface reading being that Chigurh has adopted an existentialist approach to death. More subtly, however, the words hint at the idea that Chigurh is no ordinary mortal and may perhaps be Death itself, albeit a modern version that carries a pneumatic stun-bolt gun instead of the traditional scythe.

Wells grows weary of the conversation, announcing, "I'm not interested in your opinions. . . . Just do it. You goddamned psychopath. Do it and goddamn you to hell." Despite the verbal command, Wells's body language suggests that he is not quite ready: "He closed his eyes and he turned his head and he raised one hand to fend away what could not be fended away. Chigurh shot him in the face" (177). Although there is some discrepancy between Wells's words and his reaction to the shot, the fact that Wells commands it enables him to reclaim a certain degree of control over his fate, however insignificant it may appear. Furthermore, McCarthy makes a point of informing the reader that the "new day was still a minute away" (178), thereby emphasizing the fact that the old woman's calendar was not entirely accurate. The fact that, by asking Chigurh to shoot him a minute early, Wells refuses to die on the prophesied day suggests that even within a universe ruled by seemingly inexorable forces of fate, minute degrees of free will and personal agency remain.

The third and final Socratic dialogue takes place when Chigurh fulfils his promise to kill Carla Jean should Moss fail to deliver the stolen suitcase of money. Chigurh displays his infamous "principles" when he explains the situation to Carla Jean, insisting that he has to kill her because he gave his "word" to her husband. Carla Jean cannot understand his reasoning, insisting, "He's dead. My husband is dead." Chigurh explains that this does not make the slightest difference: "Yes. But my word is not dead. Nothing can change that" (255). He even apologizes for what he is about to do, repeating "I'm sorry" three times throughout their conversation (256, 258, 259). Naturally, Carla Jean feels that she does not deserve to die: "I dont know what I ever done, she said. I truly dont." Chigurh nods, as though to agree about her innocence, but his reply indicates otherwise: "Probably you do, he said. There's a reason for everything" (256). It is interesting that when Sheriff Bell learns of Carla Jean's death, he reflects, "I believe that whatever you do in your life it will get back to you. If you live long enough it will. And I can think of no reason in the world for that no-good to of killed that girl" (282). In an ironic twist, Bell's musings on what amounts to karmic retribution actually paraphrase the exact explanation that Chigurh gives for his obligation to kill Carla Jean. Chigurh offers Carla Jean his trademark coin toss, a privilege not granted to Wells. Like the gas station owner, Carla Jean calls heads, but the coin toss results in tails.

Chigurh apologizes for the third and final time, but Carla Jean refuses to accept that he is truly sorry: "The coin didnt have no say. It was just you." Chigurh disagrees: "I had no say in the matter. Every moment in your life is a turning and every one a choosing. Somewhere you made a choice. All followed to this. The accounting is scrupulous. The shape is drawn. No line can be erased. I had no belief in your ability to move a coin to your bidding. How could you? A person's path through the world seldom changes and even more seldom will it change abruptly. And the shape of your path was visible from the beginning" (258). Carla Jean herself seems to believe that certain things are predetermined. Earlier in the novel she recounts the story of how her relationship with Moss was heralded by a premonition she experienced in a waking dream or a state of altered consciousness:

> Anyway, the night before I went down there I had this dream. Or it was like a dream. I think I was still half awake. But it come to me in this dream or whatever it was that if I went down there that he would find me. At the Wal-Mart. I didnt know who he was or what his name was or what he looked like. I just knew that I'd know him when I seen him. I kept a calendar and marked the days. Like when you're in jail. I mean I aint never been in jail, but like you would probably. And on the ninety-ninth day he walked in and he asked me where sportin goods was at and it was him. And I told him where it was at and he looked at me and went on. And directly he come back and he read my nametag and he said my name and he looked at me and he said: What time do you get off? And that was all she wrote. There was no question in my mind. Not then, not now, not ever. (131–32)

The fact that their meeting seems inevitable turns sinister once one realizes that Carla Jean's marriage to Moss leads directly to her death at the hands of Chigurh.[12]

As previously argued, Chigurh's world view contains elements of existentialist philosophy, which, broadly speaking, aims "to make every man aware of what he is and to make the full responsibility of his existence rest on him, responsibility not merely for himself individually but for all men, in the inter-subjective world" (Dutt 47–48). Chigurh's philosophy, however, does not offer quite the same degree of individual agency. Although he maintains that our actions determine our paths, he also argues that once a series of events is set in motion, we remain powerless to change our destiny.[13] Such a view is more in line with the Hindu and Buddhist belief that "karma takes its course and the consequences of acts can never be annulled" (Conze, *Thirty Years* 46). Even the seemingly deterministic concept of karma, however, allows for the existence of free will. Huston Smith explains, "Though the orderliness of the world sees to it that up to a point acts will be followed by predictable consequences, these consequences never shackle man's will or determine completely what he must do. Man remains a free agent, always at liberty to do something to effect his destiny" (*Religions of Man* 129). Chigurh proposes a similar view of the universe governed by an ostensibly deterministic chain of causation, which nevertheless leaves room for the existence of a modicum of free will.

It is significant that Chigurh believes that Carla Jean's fate was already sealed, hence the coin toss was utterly futile: "Yet even though I could have told you how all of this would end I thought it not too much to ask that you have a final glimpse of hope in the world to lift your heart before the shroud drops, the darkness. Do you see?" (258). Linda Woodson argues that Chigurh uses the coin toss as it was used in "Roman society . . . as a way of revealing already determined fate" ("You Are the Battleground" 7). Furthermore, he seems certain of what this determined fate will be, even before he tosses the coin. This prescient knowledge of the outcome of the coin toss serves as another signifier of Chigurh's supernatural status. Carla Jean refuses to accept that he must kill her, sobbing, "You dont have to. . . . You dont. You dont" (259). Chigurh continues the Socratic dialogue in an attempt to make her "understand" his "principles": "You're asking that I make myself vulnerable and that I can never do. I have only one way to live. It doesnt allow for special cases. A coin toss perhaps. In this case to small purpose. Most people dont believe that there can be such a person. You can see what a problem that must be for them. How to prevail over that which you refuse to acknowledge the existence of. Do you understand?" (259–60). These words serve as another subtle reminder of Chigurh's otherness from ordinary human beings. Many ordinary people have "only one way to live" and follow a strict moral, political, or religious code, often blindly and unremittingly. In other words, the reality of such fundamentalists does not beggar belief, nor should anyone have any trouble acknowledging their existence. Rather, Chigurh seems to be alluding to Charles Baudelaire's maxim "The finest trick of the devil is to persuade you that he does not exist."[14] In order for Chigurh's words to make any sense, we have to read the passage as a gesture toward Chigurh's position within the novel as, among other things, a personification of metaphysical evil and death. A reading of Chigurh as death personified offers clarification of his penultimate words to Carla Jean: "When I came into your life your life was over. It had a beginning, a middle, and an end. This is the end. You can say that things could have turned out differently. That they could have been some other way. But what does that mean? They are not some other way. They are this way. You're asking that I second say the world. Do you see?" Carla Jean has no reason to reply in the affirmative, as it is quite obvious that he is going to shoot her no matter what she does, and yet her final words are: "Yes. . . . I do. I truly do." Her reply evokes the wedding rite, as though she has accepted her consummation with death. Chigurh replies, "Good. . . . That's good." "Then he shot her" (260). Chigurh kills Carla Jean only after he receives clear confirmation from her that she has "seen" and "understood" what he is and why she must die.

We witness a similar scene when Chigurh approaches a wounded man "lying in a spreading pool of blood." "Help me," the man asks, but Chigurh merely takes out his pistol and looks "into the man's eyes." When the wounded man averts his gaze, Chigurh insists, "Dont look away. I want you to look at me." The man obeys: "He looked at Chigurh. . . . Chigurh shot him through the forehead and then stood watching. Watching the capillaries break up in his eyes. . . . Watching his own image degrade in that squandered world" (122).[15] Apart from wishing to make the man "see" the inevitability of his death, much as he did with Carla Jean, Chigurh also wants to lock eyes with the dying man in order to watch all the signs of life draining out of his eyes. He watches the dying man with the same disconnected curiosity with which he inspected Carla Jean's hairbrush (204), as though he were an alien observing human life with scientific detachment.

According to Jay Ellis, by shooting his victims in the forehead, Chigurh is "imprinting in them a symbolic third eye—a visual representation of the enlightenment on matters of chance and destiny that he sometimes provides in a brief pre-murder Socratic dialogue" ("Fetish and Collapse" 137). I believe, however, that the symbol of the third eye is used ironically, as Chigurh imparts a perverted version of everything associated with the Hindu and Buddhist concept of enlightenment.[16] In particular, enlightenment is traditionally described in terms of light: "Here the Bodhisattvas win full enlightenment, and then they take away all the darkness and gloom ... from beings who for so long have been ... overcome by darkness, and they illuminate them through wisdom" (Conze, *Selected Sayings* 38). Chigurh's teachings, however, bring only darkness; the wounded man watches "the new day paling all about," but after he is imprinted with the symbolic third eye, we see the "light receding" from his dying eyes (122). Furthermore, enlightenment is associated with awakening—"Buddha" literally means the "Awakened One" (H. Smith, *Religions of Man* 90)—but Chigurh's victims fall into an eternal sleep. When Chigurh's gunshot sends Wells sprawling across the bed on which he had been sitting, "He lay half headless on the bed with his arms outflung" (178). Most significantly, enlightenment frees one from the cycle of death and rebirth: "The aim of Buddhism, like that of many other religions, is to gain immortality, a deathless life. The Buddha, after he had become enlightened, claimed to have opened up the doors to the Undying" (Conze, *Buddhism* 23). Chigurh, on the other hand, is an agent of death, if not Death itself.

Chigurh's sinister role as a "prophet of destruction" (3) who bestows false enlightenment on his victims calls to mind *Blood Meridian*'s Judge Holden, who is frequently portrayed as an evil priest proselytizing on the worship of war as God. Chigurh and Holden also share a penchant for lengthy oratory on questions of free will and personal agency in a largely deterministic universe, although Holden's speeches tend to be more articulate than Chigurh's. At times both Holden and Chigurh resemble sinister versions of the biblical Yahweh or the Gnostic demiurge. Simone Pétrement writes that "what the Gnostics blamed in the Demiurge, that is, the power that for them dominated and symbolized the world, was that it wished to be God and even to be *the only God*" (9). This exact accusation could also be made against both Holden and Chigurh; the former explicitly declares his intention to become the supreme "suzerain of the earth" (198), while the less extravagant Chigurh is content to merely "model himself after God," despite the fact that he is a "nonbeliever" (256). Both Holden and Chigurh display the demiurge's wrath, judgment, and pretensions to godlike power. If Judge Holden is to be read as the Gnostic demiurge, or at least a high-ranking archon, then Chigurh might well be a lower-order archon. Whatever the case, both characters seem to occupy a position among the "principalities," "powers," and "rulers of the darkness of this world" described in Ephesians 6:12.[17]

It is noteworthy that *No Country for Old Men* incorporates a subtle allusion to Yahweh's jealousy—"Thou shalt have no other gods before me"

(Exodus 20:3)—a characteristic that the Gnostics referred to as the "pride of the demiurge," indicative of his "ignorance, perversity, and conceit" (Jonas 295). The allusion occurs during a scene in which Sheriff Bell quietly contemplates the desert landscape: "The raw rock mountains shadowed in the late sun and to the east the shimmering abscissa of the desert plains under a sky where raincurtains hung dark as soot all along the quadrant. That god lives in silence who has scoured the following land with salt and ash" (45). The passage is striking in that it features a rare instance of the sonorous, biblical language that is found throughout *Blood Meridian* and *The Crossing* but is almost entirely absent from *No Country for Old Men*. The words seem to be a reference to Deuteronomy, which describes the renewal of the covenant between Yahweh and the children of Israel, forbidding the worship of "other gods" (29:26). Yahweh threatens to blight the land of those who forsake the covenant: "And that the whole land thereof is brimstone, and salt, and burning, that it is not sown, nor beareth, nor any grass groweth therein" (Deuteronomy 29:23). The biblical allusion in *No Country for Old Men* seems to be suggesting that the demiurgical Yahweh has blighted the land and withdrawn into silence because the covenant has been broken.

The silence of God is addressed directly later in the novel, during a conversation between Bell and Uncle Ellis. The latter blames himself for God's silence, confessing, "I always thought when I got older that God would sort of come into my life in some way. He didnt. I dont blame him. If I was him I'd have the same opinion about me that he does" (267). Uncle Ellis tries and fails to reconcile his faith with the suffering experienced by his own family, in particular the death of his older brother, Harold, who was killed in the First World War: "I dont know what sense any of it makes either. You know that gospel song? We'll understand it all by and by? That takes a lot of faith. You think about him goin over there and dyin in a ditch somewhere. Seventeen years old. You tell me. Because I damn sure dont know" (268). The difficult task of reconciling the existence of senseless suffering and evil with the existence of an omnipotent, omniscient, and benevolent God is the central problem of theodicy.[18]

William Rowe explains the reasoning behind the evidential problem of evil in three propositions, the first being that "there exist instances of intense suffering which an omnipotent, omniscient being could have prevented without thereby losing some greater good or permitting some evil equally bad or worse." The second proposition follows, that "an omniscient, wholly good being would prevent the occurrence of any intense suffering it could, unless it could not do so without thereby losing some greater good or permitting some evil equally bad or worse." Therefore "there does not exist an omnipotent, omniscient, wholly good being" (127). Bell and Ellis address these problems of theodicy during their discussion, but neither arrives at an atheistic position. Bell responds to Ellis's crisis of faith by jokingly asking, "You aint turned infidel have you Uncle Ellis?" Uncle Ellis reaffirms his belief in God, claiming, "No. No. Nothin like that." Bell's thoughts return to his own fears about a "new kind" of evil unleashed on the world, prompting him to ask, "Do you think God knows what's happenin?" Uncle Ellis states, "I expect he does." "You think he can stop it?" asks Bell; "No, I don't," claims Ellis (269). Essentially, Ellis is not a theist in the "narrow sense," as "someone who believes in the existence of an omnipotent, omniscient, eternal, supremely good being who created the world," but only in the broad sense, as "someone who believes in the existences of some sort of divine being or divine reality" (Rowe 126). In other words, the only way Ellis can reconcile the existence of suffering with the existence of God is to deny God's omnipotence.

Ellis also finds a way to come to terms with the fact that God has not spoken to him: "You'd think a man that had waited eighty some odd years on God to come into his life, well, you'd think he'd come. If he didnt you'd still have to figure that he knew what he was doin. I dont know what other description of God you could have" (283). It is interesting that Ellis can't imagine a God who lacks omniscience, arguing that a God who didn't know "what he was doin" would not fulfill the "description of God," yet he seems to accept the concept of a God who lacks the power to control "what's happenin" (269). Furthermore, Ellis maintains his faith in God's benevolence even in the face of the baffling divine silence in his own life, arguing that "those he has spoken to are the ones that must of needed it the worst" (283). In short, Ellis believes in a benevolent, all-knowing entity that is nevertheless incapable of eliminating the fundamental existence of evil. We find such an understanding of good and evil, or God and the Devil, in the Manichean belief system, in which "the two realms . . . exist side by side completely unconnected, and the Light, far from considering the existence of Darkness as a challenge, wants nothing but the separateness" (Jonas 211). Ellis's faith seems to rest on a Manichean foundation, without his being aware of it.[19]

Gnostic, specifically Manichean, tendencies can also be seen in Bell's belief system, specifically in his ideas regarding the positive presence of evil. When questioned about whether he believes in Satan, Bell explains, "I guess as a boy I did. Come the middle years my belief I reckon had waned somewhat. Now I'm startin to lean back the other way" (219). Bell's belief in the existence of Satan appears to fall within the boundaries of conventional Christianity, until Bell confesses that this renewed belief in Satan has not been matched by a renewed faith in God. Reflecting on the strength of his wife's faith, Bell muses, "I wish I had her ease about things. The world I've seen has not made me a spiritual person. Not like her" (303). Despite his lack of conviction, Bell remains grateful for the blessings in his life, chiefly for his marriage to Loretta: "I dont recall that I ever give the good Lord all that much cause to smile on me. But he did" (91). Although it is clear that he has not become an atheist or a materialist, Bell's experience of evil has complicated his Christian faith.

Bell displays further Manichean tendencies during a conversation with a county prosecutor. Finding himself troubled by the moral ambiguity of the legal profession, Bell recalls how another "lawyer one time told me that in law school they try and teach you not to worry about right and wrong but just follow the law and I said I wasnt so sure about that." The county prosecutor, however, says "that he pretty much had to agree with the lawyer. He said that if you dont follow the law right and wrong wont save you." Bell admits that he "can see the sense of" this view but adds that "it dont change the way I think" (298). Despite his waning faith and his self-professed inability to become a "spiritual person" (303), Bell's Manichean clarity regarding "right and wrong," or good and evil, is essentially spiritual rather than moral. This is made evident by the fact that immediately afterward, Bell asks the county prosecutor "if he knew who Mammon was." The prosecutor is taken aback: "You mean like in God and Mammon? . . . I cant say as I do. I know it's in the bible. Is it the devil?" Bell replies, "I dont know. I'm goin to look it up. I got a feelin I ought to know who it is" (298). "Mammon" refers to an "inordinate desire for wealth or possessions, personified as a devil or demonic agent" and "regarded as a false god or an evil influence" (*OED*). For example, the New Testament warns that a life of worldly preoccupations and acquisitions is incompatible with spiritual development: "No man can serve two masters. . . . Ye cannot serve God and Mammon" (Matthew 6:24). Thus Bell's reference to Mammon in the face of the prosecutor's moral ambiguity demonstrates a rejection of worldly pursuits, which are equated with evil.

Although Bell sees the world as being ruled by Mammon, he remains open to the possibility of transcendence, believing in the power of ordinary human kindness to stand against the violence and evil that he sees around him. The objective correlative of what Bell yearns for is contained in the remembered image of a stone water trough he encountered while fighting in France during the Second World War: "I don't know how long it had been there. A hundred years. Two hundred. You could see the chisel marks in the stone. It was hewed out of solid rock."[20] The sturdy trough had not only survived centuries of history but promised to survive centuries into the future. Bell explains that he "got to thinkin about the man that done that... this man had set down with a hammer and a chisel and carved out a stone water trough to last ten thousand years. Why was that? What was it that he had faith in? It wasnt that nothin would change. Which is what you might think, I suppose. He had to know bettern that" (307). For Bell, who shares Yeats's apocalyptic world view, the water trough is a symbol of that which endures when "things fall apart" and the "centre cannot hold." The fact that the trough was designed to be continually renewed by rainwater and therefore stays "pretty much full" is significant, because it continues to serve its purpose even after the house by which it stood is "blown to pieces" (307).

On a metaphysical level, the trough serves as a receptacle for the "living water" referred to throughout the Bible. In the Old Testament, for example, Jeremiah laments, "For my people have committed two evils; they have forsaken me the fountain of living waters, and hewed them out cisterns, broken cisterns, that can hold no water" (Jeremiah 2:13). John Wesley's notes on the verse explain that the reference to "living waters" is a "metaphor taken from springs, called living, because they never cease, or intermit; such had God's care and kindness been over them." Wesley explains that the cisterns represent "all other supports, that are trusted to besides God, are but broken vessels" (368). In Gnostic, specifically Mandean, scriptures, we find similar references to "living water" as "flowing water, which is of sublime origin and flows in streams," the "opposite" being "stagnant water and the troubled waters of the sea" (Jonas 97–98). The trough admired by Bell, however, is not a broken cistern nor a pool of stagnant water but a sturdy, reliable, and enduring source of living water, perpetually renewed by the rain.

The trough not only promises to endure even when civilizations crumble but also offers the sacrament of living water to whatever creature, whether human or animal, encounters it in the present or the distant future.[21] Thus the trough serves as a testament to the foresight, compassion, and kindness of the anonymous stonemason who painstakingly chiseled it out of solid rock, not to immortalize his own ego but to provide something useful for the benefit of other living beings. Bell admires the creator of this enduring artifact, reflecting that there must have been "some sort of promise in his heart. And I dont have no intentions of carvin a stone water trough. But I would like to be able to make that kind of promise. I think that's what I would like most of all" (308). In the New Testament, the living water becomes a symbol of Christ: "He that believeth on me, as the scripture hath said, out of his belly shall flow rivers of living water" (John 7:38). John Wesley explicates the verse to mean that "whosoever doth come to him by faith, his inmost soul shall be filled with living water . . . which shall likewise flow from him to others" (209). The living water provided by the trough seems to have made a deep, spiritual impression on Bell, because he carries the memory of it with him for the rest of his life. Unfortunately, although Bell has the desire "to make that kind of promise" (308), he doesn't know how to create something as meaningful and enduring.

It is worth mentioning that Bell believes in something even more enduring than chiseled stone, namely the concept of an eternal truth:

> The stories gets passed on and the truth gets passed over. As the sayin goes. Which I reckon some would take as meanin that the truth cant compete. But I dont believe that. I think that when the lies are all told and forgot the truth will be there yet. It dont move about from place to place and it dont change from time to time. You cant corrupt it any more than you can salt salt. You cant corrupt it because that's what it is. It's the thing you're talking about. I've heard it compared to the rock—maybe in the bible—and I wouldnt disagree with that. But it'll be here even when the rock is gone. (123)

Although Bell is, in his own way, a Christian, the "truth" that he is referring to is not only what he regards as the truth of the Gospel but also the concept of truth as universal, objective, and eternal, unaffected by relativism, subjectivity, or fashionable philosophies.[22] Bell's belief in an uncomplicated, essential truth, something "simple enough for a child to understand" (249), echoes McCarthy's own reply to the question "What is truth?," with his insistence that truth is always simply "Truth" (Wallace 138). Bell's understanding of truth as something that endures even when the rock crumbles away suggests that he views truth as something spiritual and transcendent that will survive even when the material world fades into oblivion. For Bell, truth outlasts even the stone water trough and its sacrament of living water.

No Country for Old Men is framed by two references to water sacraments; Bell's reflection on the water trough occurs toward the very end of the novel, and it is significant that water also plays an important role at the novel's beginning, namely in Moss's foolhardy yet compassionate decision to bring water to a dying Mexican drug dealer. When the injured man first asks for water, "Agua, cuate.... Agua, por dios," Moss curtly rebuffs him: "I aint got no water" (12, 13). Later that night, when Moss wakes from his sleep and quenches his own thirst with a drink of water, he finds that his conscience bothers him: "Then he just stood there holding the jar with the water beading cold on the glass, looking out the window and down the highway toward the lights. He stood there a long time." He thinks about the Mexican, wondering, "Are you dead out there? he said. Hell no, you aint dead" (23). Moss makes up his mind to return to the site of the failed drug deal in order to bring water to the dying man: "He took an empty gallon jug from under the sink and started filling it at the tap." It is clear that Moss is aware of the danger of his returning to the scene of the crime, especially in light of the fact that he is now in possession of the stolen drug money. When Carla Jean wakes and demands to know where he is going at one o'clock in the morning, Moss replies, "I'm fixin to go do somethin dumbern hell but I'm going anyways. If I dont come back tell Mother I love her" (24). When the baffled Carla Jean reminds him that his mother is dead, Moss quips, "Well I'll tell her myself then," revealing that he has considered the possibility that this act of charity might result in his own death. As Moss cautiously makes his way to site of the shootout, he questions whether it is worthwhile risking his own life: "For a Mexican dopedealer. Yeah. Well. Everybody is somethin" (26). Moss's conclusion carries two nuances of meaning, the first being that everyone is a sinner, the second being that everyone is worthwhile. The first reading suggests that it is wrong to dismiss someone as undeserving of life just because he is a drug dealer, since everyone is guilty of "something." The second reading suggests that even a "Mexican dopedealer" is still a worthwhile human being, because every life is precious. It is likely that both nuances of meaning operate in Moss's final decision to risk his life to save a complete stranger.

Unfortunately, when Moss arrives at the scene, he finds that the Mexican has been "shot through the head." When he tries to go back to his truck, he notices "someone standing beside it" and knows that he has been seen by whoever is searching for the missing suitcase of cash. He repeatedly curses his own stupidity: "You dumb-ass, he said. Here you are. Too dumb to live.

... There is no description of a fool, he said, that you fail to satisfy. Now you're going to die" (27). Although it seems painfully ironic that Moss's moment of compassion sets off a chain reaction that results not only in his own death but also in the death of Carla Jean, the irony is somewhat mitigated by the fact that the stolen suitcase of money contained a transmitting device, which would presumably have allowed the hitmen, Wells and Chigurh, to find Moss even if he had not returned to the scene of the shootout. In fact, Wells reminds Moss that the "transponder" is "not the only way [Chigurh] has of finding you" (152). Thus we may argue that Moss's mistake lay in his taking the drug money in the first place, not in his compassionate desire to bring water to a dying man.[23]

Whether or not Moss's futile action directly resulted in his own death does not detract from the fact that he was motivated by pure compassion. Moss's compulsion to bring water to a complete stranger falls within the category of "senseless kindness" described by Vasily Grossman in *Life and Fate*, as the "private kindness of one individual towards another; a petty, thoughtless kindness; an unwitnessed kindness. Something we would call senseless kindness." Grossman illustrates the concept of this "everyday human kindness" with various examples: "The kindness of an old woman carrying a piece of bread to a prisoner, the kindness of a soldier allowing a wounded enemy to drink from his water-flask, the kindness of youth towards age, the kindness of peasant hiding an old Jew in his loft. The kindness of a prison guard who risks his own liberty to pass on letters written by a prisoner not to his ideological comrades, but to his wife and mother" (407). According to Grossman, the very "powerlessness of kindness, of senseless kindness, is the secret of its immortality. It can never be conquered. The more stupid, the more senseless, the more helpless it may seem, the vaster it is" (410). Sheriff Bell admires this quality of kindness in his wife, Loretta, who brings home-cooked meals to the county jail: "They get fresh garden stuff a good part of the year. Good cornbread. Soupbeans. She's been known to fix em hamburgers and french fries" (159). The beneficial effects of Loretta's kindness become apparent in due time: "We've had em to come back even years later and they'd be married and doin good. Bring their wives. Bring their kids even. They didnt come back to see me. I've seen em to introduce their wives or their sweethearts and then just go to bawlin. Grown men. That had done some pretty bad things. She knew what she was doin. She always did" (159–60). Although Loretta's behavior provides an obvious example of how seemingly senseless acts of kindness may generate further good later on, the positive consequences of kindness are not its sole purpose; an act of kindness is valuable in itself as a form of rebellion against evil. Even though Moss's attempt to save the Mexican proved futile, his senseless kindness allowed compassion and charity to triumph over greed and selfishness, if only momentarily.[24]

Bell doesn't see the same kindness within himself, largely due to the fact that he has spent his entire adult life tormented by survivor's guilt: "I wont talk about the war neither. I was supposed to be a war hero and I lost a whole squad of men. Got decorated for it. They died and I got a medal. I dont even need to know what you think about that. There aint a day that I dont remember it" (196). Precisely because he is unable to forgive himself, and thus can't see the essential goodness of his own character, he projects all that is best within him onto the memory of his dead daughter: "I like talkin to her. Call it superstition or whatever you want. I know that over the years I have give her the heart I always wanted for myself and that's all right. That's why I listen to her. I know I'll always get the best from her. It don't get mixed up with my own ignorance or my own meanness" (285). David Cremean argues that the "daughter archetypally represents Bell's own Teiresian "feminine side, in Jungian terms his anima, his own inner, mystical voice" (30n7). Bell's daughter seems to be an essential part of Bell himself, rather than a separate entity external to him. In other words, Bell does have a spiritual side, which seems more subtle and esoteric than the well-meaning, but rather literal-minded, exoteric, and conventional Christianity of his wife.

The spiritual, perhaps even mystical, side of Bell is most evident in the poignant dream he has about his dead father:

> It was like we was both back in older times and I was on horseback goin through the mountains of a night. Goin through this pass in the mountains. It was cold and there was snow on the ground and he rode past me and kept on goin. Never said nothin. He just rode on past and he had this blanket wrapped around him and he had his head down and when he rode past I seen he was carryin fire in a horn the way people used to do and I could see the horn from the light inside of it. About the color of the moon. And in the dream I know that he was goin on ahead and that he was fixing to make a fire somewhere out there in all that dark and all that cold and I knew that whenever I got there he would be there. And then I woke up. (309)

The most striking image within Bell's dream is that of the fire in the numinous, moon-colored horn, being carried ahead to illuminate the darkness. David Cremean writes that the horn itself is spiritually evocative, "suggesting the horned moon associated with the Virgin Mary and with various other mythical archetypes" (25). The fire itself is of utmost significance, fire being a pervasive symbolic theme in McCarthy's fiction, as I have demonstrated in earlier chapters. McCarthy's fire imagery is grounded in overtly Gnostic concepts of the spirit, "*pneuma*" or "spark," as "a portion of the divine substance from beyond which has fallen into the world" (Jonas 44). Fire is also one of the "basic symbols" (Berdyaev xxiv) in the writings of Jacob Boehme, whose influence on McCarthy has been established in my previous chapters on *Blood Meridian*. Boehme writes that "if the divine eternal light is received in the soul, it kindles a fire therein which illuminates the whole substance of the soul" (qtd. in Hartmann 19). Fire imagery is not restricted to Gnosticism or Boehme's theosophy but appears in the various mystical traditions that make up the Perennial Philosophy: "Mysticism assumes that . . . there is within every living soul a divine spark, that seeks re-union with the Eternal Flame" (M. Smith 21). The image of Bell's father forging a path through the mountains evokes analogies of spiritual development frequently used to describe the way in which the spiritual journeys of individual mystics serve as a guide to the rest of humanity. Evelyn Underhill describes the mystics of the past in precisely such terms: "The mystics, expert mountaineers, go before him: and show him, if he cares to learn, the way to freedom, to reality, to peace" (448). Bell's dream father seems to be acting as such a guide, promising to light his son's path on his spiritual journey through the symbolic darkness of the manifest world.

The fire in the horn also serves as an allusion to W. B. Yeats's poem "Sailing to Byzantium," in which the "sages" are summoned to "come from the holy fire" and "perne in a gyre" (line 19). In *A Vision*, Yeats envisioned various "ages" through which the world traveled in eternal recurrence, one age declining as another age dawned. "The Second Coming" in effect describes the decline of one age and the terrible birth of a new one, a concept that McCarthy's also explores via the apocalyptic themes in *No Country for Old Men*. For Yeats, the cyclical nature of time is symbolized by conical spinning wheels, or gyres: "For simplicity of representation the gyre is drawn as a cone. Sometimes the cone represents the individual soul, and that soul's history—these things are inseparable—sometimes general life" (*A Vision* 104). It is significant that the conical horn in Bell's dream bears a markedly similar appearance to Yeats's gyre, while the fire within the horn evokes the "holy fire" in which the sages of Byzantium stand. Thus Bell's dream echoes the transcendence offered to the traveler in the concluding stanzas of "Sailing to Byzantium," when the holy fire purifies the man:

> Consume my heart away; sick with desire
> And fastened to a dying animal
> It knows not what it is; and gather me
> Into the artifice of eternity
> (lines 21–24)

The poem concludes by evoking Hindu and Buddhist beliefs that teach that the "perception of reality that is based upon sensory experience, ignorance, and desire keeps humans locked in illusion until they are able to recognize the false nature of reality and relinquish their mistaken sense of identity" (Wagner and Flannery-Dailey 273). In other words, the "holy fire" in Yeats's poem burns away the obstacles to enlightenment created by desire, by the sensual attachments of the body or the "dying animal," and by the ignorance of the self, which "knows not what it is." The "artifice of eternity" seems to be Nirvana itself, "the state in which the faggots of private desire have been completely consumed and everything that restricts the boundless life has died" (H. Smith, *Religions of Man* 125). The fire in Bell's dream seems to offer similar spiritual purification, while the horn resembles the gyre and the figure of the dream father serves as the sage, or spiritual guide.[25]

We find another significant Buddhist motif in Bell's explanation of why he decided to become a "lawman": "There was always some part of me that wanted to be in charge. Pretty much insisted on it. Wanted people to listen to what I had to say. But there was a part of me too that just wanted to pull everybody back in the boat. If I've tried to cultivate anything it's been that" (295). Beneath Bell's superficial craving for power lies a genuine desire to save other human beings. The concept of pulling people "back in the boat" evokes Buddhist metaphors of the spiritual journey as "a voyage across the river of life, a transport from the common-sense shore of nonenlightenment, spiritual ignorance, desire, and death, to the far-flung bank of wisdom which brings liberation from this prevailing bondage" (H. Smith, *Religions of Man* 153). According to Edward Conze, "the Buddhist doctrine, or Dharma . . . is conceived as a raft, or a ship, which carries us across the ocean of this world of suffering to a 'Beyond,' to salvation, to Nirvana" (*Thirty Years* 48). The

Buddhas and Bodhisattvas try to pull everyone into the boat, just as Sheriff Bell wishes to do: "The world is carried away in distress on the flooded river of suffering, which the foam of disease oversprays, which has old age for its surge and rushes along with the violent rush of death: across this river he will ferry the world with the mighty boat of gnosis" (Conze, *Buddhist Scriptures* 36). Although Bell lacks spiritual clarity and conviction and is therefore no savior, his wish to keep others safe stems from a foundation of compassion. It is no coincidence that his very name evokes the motif of "the bell," an allusion to John Donne's sermon that runs throughout the Border Trilogy, serving as a reminder of the interconnectedness of human beings: "And therefore never send to know for whom the bell tolls; it tolls for thee" (243). Thus, despite the themes of violence, evil, and inexorable fate, *No Country for Old Men* ends on a compassionate note, with the twin promises of redemption and transcendence. Simple acts of kindness and compassion endure in the evil world of the novel, eternal like the sacred fire in the father's horn or the living water in the stonemason's trough.[26]

CHAPTER 14

"All Things of Grace and Beauty"

The Presence of the Sacred in *The Road*

■ The nightmarish world of Cormac McCarthy's postapocalyptic novel *The Road* is the logical extreme of the world view presented in his earlier works, a culmination of moral and natural evil, violence, suffering, darkness, and despair, but with just enough hope and goodness to imbue the pages with a hint of soteriological potential. *The Road* depicts the aftermath of an unspecified disaster, most likely a meteorite strike, which has blotted out the sun with ash and wiped out almost all life on earth, except for a handful of human beings.[1] The narrative follows the journey of two survivors, a nameless man and his only child, as they trek to warmer coastal regions through a hostile wasteland, threatened by starvation, freezing temperatures, and roaming bands of cannibals. As though to overtly link *The Road* to his earlier works, McCarthy begins the novel with words that immediately evoke the closing passage of his preceding novel, *No Country for Old Men*. The opening sentence of *The Road*, which describes the father waking from a dream and watching over his son—"When he woke in the woods in the dark and the cold of the night he'd reach out to touch the child sleeping beside him" (3)—echoes the closing passage of *No Country for Old Men*, which describes another son, Sheriff Bell, waking from a dream about his own father watching over him: "And in the dream I knew that he was goin on ahead and that he was fixing to make a fire somewhere out there in all that dark and all that cold and I knew that whenever I got there he would be there. And then I woke up" (309). As I will later discuss at length, the central image of Bell's dream, namely the carrying of the fire through the darkness, also serves as a trope throughout *The Road*, with the fire symbolizing the aforementioned hope, goodness, and the promise of spiritual illumination.

The fact that *The Road* opens with its protagonist finding himself in a dark wood also evokes the opening of Dante's Alighieri's *Inferno*: "Mi ritrovai per una selva oscura / Ché la diritta via era smarrita" (I found me in a gloomy wood / Gone from the path direct) (*Divine Comedy: Inferno*, canto I, lines 2–3).[2] The allusion to the *Divine Comedy* places *The Road* in the tradition of the spiritual quest or pilgrimage. Harold Bloom writes that the "journey of the man and boy through a hellish landscape toward some promise of salvation mirrors the journey taken by the poet Dante and the ghost of the Roman poet Virgil in Dante's epic poem" (*Bloom's Guides* 23). Even though the father and son journey through the ash-strewn wasteland with the practical purpose of finding warmer weather near the coast, the very namelessness of the protagonists gestures toward a metaphorical rather than a strictly literal interpretation of their progress. The argument for a metaphorical, or even allegorical, reading is strengthened by the narrative's genre-defying lack of disclosure on the nature of the apocalyptic disaster. The reader is simply informed that "the clocks stopped at 1:17. A long shear of light and then a series of low concussions" (52). The degree of attention given to the seemingly insignificant detail of the clocks stands in sharp contrast to the elusiveness regarding the disaster in question, thereby implying that the numbers on the clock hold some symbolic import. Several critics have argued that the numbers point to Revelation 1:17 and the second coming of Christ: "And when I saw him, I fell at his feet as dead. And he laid his right hand upon me, saying unto me, Fear not; I am the first and the last."[3] The allusion to Revelation may explain why the narrative does not dwell on the sociological or ecological aspects of the disaster; rather, the novel's chief concern lies with the spiritual connotations of apocalypse as a disclosure of divine truth.

The aftermath of the apocalyptic disaster triggers precisely such a revelation for the main protagonist: "He walked out in the gray light and stood and he saw for a brief moment the absolute truth of the world. The cold relentless circling of the intestate earth. Darkness implacable. The blind dogs of the sun in their running. The crushing black vacuum of the universe" (130). The man's dark epiphany is presented in no uncertain terms as the "absolute truth," that is, not truth applicable only to this particular postapocalyptic scenario but the ultimate truth of existence.[4] As I have previously argued, McCarthy uses the word "truth" in the most straightforward and unproblematic sense of the word; in McCarthy's novels, as in his interview with Gary Wallace, truth *is* "Truth" (Wallace 138). It should come as no surprise that the "absolute truth" revealed to the man is described in terms that suggest the Gnostic concept of heimarmene, a negative evaluation of the harmony of the cosmos. Hans Jonas explains that "the concept of divine order, so central to classical thought, the music of the spheres etc.—in Gnosticism becomes a negative, fearful, deterministic thing" (250). For a brief moment, the man becomes aware of the terrifying enormity of a cosmos ruled by the "cold," "relentless," and "implacable" law of heimarmene.[5]

The presence of heimarmene is again evoked when the man tries to remain "upright" in the "sightless and impenetrable" darkness: "Upright to what? Something nameless in the night, lode or matrix. To which he and the stars were common satellites. Like the great pendulum in its rotunda scribing through the long day movements of the universe of which you may say it knows nothing and yet know it must" (15). The great pendulum is a reference to Foucault's pendulum, an experiment that "provides a clear and convincing demonstration of the rotation of the earth" (Somerville 40). The motion of the pendulum corresponds to the rotation of the earth, but the earth follows a predetermined path, as do all the stars and, by implication, the man himself. As I have explained in earlier chapters, the Gnostics believed that heimarmene controlled the "times and seasons" and the "gods of the heaven," that is, the stars and the planets, as well as the individual destinies of "angels, demons and men" (Rudolph 106). In *The Road*, the man, the earth, and the stars are all portrayed as "common satellites," subject to a force or sentience that remains sinisterly "nameless in the night."[6]

Gnostic themes are also apparent in McCarthy's frequent use of the word "alien" to describe the interrelationship between the sun, the earth, and living beings, the "Alien Life" being a "primary symbol of Gnosticism" and alienation "an expression of an elemental human experience" (Jonas 51, 49). At their spiritual core, human beings are regarded as being "alien to this world," because the pneuma "stems from elsewhere and does not belong here" (Jonas 49). Both the man and the child are described as "alien" at different points in the novel. The boy, with his "candlecoloured skin" and "great staring eyes" has "the look of an alien" (129). Later, the man feels that "he was himself an alien. A being from a planet that no longer existed" (154). If human beings are, on a spiritual level, alien to the world, then the world is also alien to them, "like a foreign land where [the pneuma] is far from home" (Jonas 49). Throughout the novel, the man and the child journey to the coast, but once they reach their long-awaited goal they find only "the desolation of some alien sea breaking on the shores of a world unheard of" (215). In *The Road*, the entire cosmos seems to be in a state of alienation; each new day is marked by the "alien sun commencing its cold transit" (178). The alien sun is an ambiguous concept, suggesting one of two possible interpretations. Either it is to be read in the same manner as the alien sea, that is, as belonging to the manifest cosmos and thus alien to the pneuma or it may be read in the Manichean sense, as an "agent of salvation" and a visible symbol of the "pure Light" of the Absolute, or alien God (Jonas 123, 233). The first possible interpretation is supported by a passage in which the man looks out at the ocean, contemplating what lies on the opposite shore: "And perhaps beyond those shrouded swells another man did walk with another child on the dead gray sands. Slept but a sea apart on another beach among the bitter ashes of the world or stood in their rags lost to the same indifferent sun" (219). Here the sun is portrayed as an indifferent god, unmoved by the plight of human suffering. The sun in *The Road*, however, is also described in purely beneficent terms, circling "the earth like a grieving mother with a lamp" (32). Such a description of the sun is in accord with the Manichean idea that the sun functions as a "protective escort" for the pneuma after the death of the body, transmitting "the Light to the Light above it in the world of praise" (Jonas 225, 233). The image of the sun as a grieving mother with a lamp suggests this protective and guiding function, as found in Manichaeism. Furthermore, the evocation of a mother's grief for her lost children can be read as a Gnostic metaphor for the situation of the pneuma as a child lost in the world and far from its true home.

The apocalypse brings about multiple revelations regarding the nature of existence. Although most of these can be explained in Gnostic terms, to do so would be to limit their full interpretive potential. As in earlier works, McCarthy draws on a variety of esoteric traditions to construct the metaphysics of *The Road*. For example, revelations regarding the transient and illusory nature of the created world, which abound throughout the novel, evoke the Hindu and Buddhist concept that saṃsāra (the manifest world) is made of māyā (illusion). The man contemplates these themes while recalling the "first years" after the disaster: "Creedless shells of men tottering down the causeways like migrants in a feverland. The frailty of everything revealed at last" (28). It is significant that the words "migrants" and "feverland" echo a prophetic proclamation made by the supernatural judge in *Blood Meridian*, who describes the world as "a fevered dream . . . a migratory tentshow whose ultimate destination . . . is unspeakable and calamitous beyond reckoning" (245). Both the man and the judge refer to fever and migration, words that respectively suggest hallucination and impermanence and correspond to Buddhist evaluations of existence. The *Diamond Sutra*, for example, states that the world is "a dream, unreal and not to be taken seriously," appearing "to the ignorant like a hallucination" (Conze, *Buddhist Wisdom Books* 70). Furthermore, Buddhist sutras frequently describe the world as "unsubstantial and frail, like a water bubble" (Conze, *Buddhist Scriptures* 112). It took no less than a disaster of global proportions for the "absolute truth" (130) of existence to be "revealed at last" (28) to the man in *The Road*, but *Blood Meridian*'s eerily omniscient judge did not need to experience an apocalypse in order to see the world "for what it is" (245).

From his postapocalyptic perspective, the man is able to reflect not only on the impermanence of existence but also on the ephemeral and trivial pursuits of what was once known as ordinary, everyday life. Looking at old newspapers printed before the disaster, he is struck by the "curious news. The quaint concerns" (28). The newspapers serve as silent testimony to the way in which human beings were content, in the words of Ernest Becker, to "tranquillize themselves with the trivial" (178). In his comparative study of existentialism and Buddhism, Padmasiri de Silva argues that "man is distracted by the petty concerns of daily life. . . . By this immersion and entanglement with the concerns and objects of everyday life, one's understanding is darkened by gossip, curiosity and mundane concerns" (53). The apocalypse in *The Road* annihilates these petty concerns and trivialities, bringing the man into stark confrontation with the very core of existence. Objects that were once crucial to the business of living have become devalued and faintly absurd: "Coins everywhere in the ash" (23).[7] After carrying "his billfold about till it wore a cornershaped hole in his trousers," the man becomes aware of the sheer uselessness of this obsolete item. He examines the contents: "Some money, credit cards. His driver's license. A picture of his wife. He spread everything out on the blacktop." These once-treasured symbols of financial affluence and social conformity suddenly appear to him as "gaming cards," pieces of a game no longer played. Although the picture of his wife holds more meaning than the other paraphernalia, evidenced by the fact that he "sat holding the photograph" for some time, even this is eventually discarded: "Then he laid it down in the road also and then he stood and they went on" (51). The man seems to realize that it is pointless to cling to the empty signifiers of an irretrievable past.[8]

Rummaging through "the charred ruins of a library," the man senses that the shelves have been "tipped over" as an expression of "some rage at the lies arranged in their thousands row on row." The nature of these lies is never articulated directly, but it is likely that the man is reflecting on the fact that the very existence of the books was based on the false assumption that there would always be a future: "He'd not have thought the value of the smallest thing predicated on a world to come. It surprised him. That the space which these things occupied was itself an expectation. He let the book fall and took a last look around and made his way out into the cold gray light" (187). The act of stepping out into the light seems to symbolize an illuminating experience; the man is able to see the old world in a new light, but this light is "cold" and "gray," suggesting that his newly found vision reveals a stark and painful reality.[9] This experience of reality is grounded in an awareness of impermanence; the man looks around and sees only "borrowed time and borrowed world and borrowed eyes with which to sorrow it" (130). Watching his beloved son sleeping, the man contemplates how "all things of grace and beauty such that one holds them to one's heart have a common provenance in pain. Their birth in grief and ashes" (54).[10] He sees the world as being "sustained by a breath, trembling and brief," and wishes, "If only my heart were stone" (11). The man seems keenly aware that everything we hold dear is ultimately a source of pain, because we are doomed to lose it in the end.

This view echoes the First Noble Truth of the Buddha, which teaches that suffering, or duḥkha, is "a universal characteristic of all *samsāric* existence, along with impermanence" (de Silva 33). It is noteworthy that the man's vision of "everything uncoupled from its shoring. Unsupported in the ashen air" (11) evokes one of the definitions of duḥkha as "an axle which is off-center with respect to its wheel" or "a bone which has slipped out of socket" (H. Smith, *Religions of Man* 111).[11] The *Samyutta Nikāya* states, "What is impermanent (*annicam*), that is suffering (*duḥkha*)." To exist is to suffer the ills of "birth, decay, disease, death, sorrow, lamentation, pain, grief," and "despair" (qtd. in H. Smith, *Religions of Man* 111). Buddhism encourages such reflections on impermanence and suffering because, as Padmasiri de Silva explains, "The contemplation of the miseries of the world . . . can be an invigorating experience which acts as a spur to the development of insight and understanding" (55). The man makes a conscious effort to face reality, not only in waking life but even in his dreams: "He said the right dreams for a man in peril were dreams of peril and all else was the call of languor and death" (18). Despite their painful nature, the man values the negative epiphanies revealed by the apocalypse, reminding himself that "when your dreams are of some world that never was or some world that never will be and you are happy again then you will have given up" (189). In other words, he believes that happiness is attainable only through delusion and ignorance.

The man's contemplation of impermanence is inextricably linked to his awareness of the certainty of death, a state of mind encouraged by Buddhism and existentialism alike. Padmasiri de Silva argues that, "though the Buddhist concept of *duḥkha* is wider than the existentialist concept of suffering, the existentialist's call 'back to authentic existence' is certainly rooted in the sense of tragedy that surrounds the day-to-day existence of man. They cite the view of Heidegger that the only way to achieve authentic existence, 'is to treat one's life as a progress towards death'" (39). Buddhist sutras teach that "not even for a moment should you rely on life going on, for Time, like a hidden tiger, lies in wait to slay the unsuspecting" (Conze, *Buddhist Scriptures* 112). The situation in *The Road* brings death to the fore, integrating it into the everyday experiences of the man and the boy. The two protagonists encounter death on a nearly daily basis during the course of their journey, coming across sights such as "a metal trashdump where someone had once tried to burn bodies. The charred meat and bones under the damp ash might have been anonymous save for the shapes of the skulls" (150). The postapocalyptic landscape is filled with corpses: "Human bodies. Sprawled in every attitude. Dried and shrunken in their rotted clothes" (47). Although the pages of the novel are already permeated with grotesque descriptions of death, McCarthy conjures up equally horrifying scenes of death from the preapocalyptic world. The man recalls "those disinterred dead from his childhood that had been relocated to accommodate a highway. Many had died in a cholera epidemic and they'd been buried in haste in wooden boxes and the boxes were rotting and falling open. The dead came to light lying on their sides with their legs drawn up and some lay on their stomachs. The dull green antique coppers spilled from out the tills of their eyesockets onto the stained and rotted coffin floors" (213–14). The horror is compounded by the fact that some of the corpses lie in unconventional positions, suggesting that they had been buried alive. Even the novel's descriptions of the postapocalyptic dead are linked back to images of death from human history: "The mummified dead everywhere. The flesh cloven along the bones, the ligaments dried to tug and taut as wires. Shrivelled and drawn like latterday bogfolk" (24). These references to decomposing cholera victims and mummified bog bodies serve as a reminder that death is not unique to the postapocalyptic world of *The Road* but a horrific certainty that has awaited all living beings since the beginning of time.

The fact that the man in *The Road* is suffering from an unspecified terminal illness drives the inevitability of death home with stark urgency: "At night when he woke coughing he'd sit up with his hand pushed over his head against the blackness. Like a man waking in a grave" (213). It is noteworthy that this passage links the man back to the hastily buried cholera victims writhing about in their premature graves. Although the man tries to conceal his illness from his son, he is painfully aware of his own mortality: "Every day is a lie.... But you are dying. That is not a lie" (236). The man personifies death, reminding himself that "he is coming to steal my eyes. To seal my mouth with dirt" (261). Such visualizations of death as a thief and murderer are encouraged by Buddhist sutras: "How can we ever feel secure from death, when from the womb onwards it follows us like a murderer with his sword raised to kill us?" (Conze, *Buddhist Scriptures* 112). Linda Woodson argues that *The Road* "dismantles those human creations designed to avoid the truth of death, that which is created as a hold against death's inevitability and a desire for immortality" ("Mapping *The Road*" 92). The extreme situation portrayed in *The Road* reveals one of the universal truths of the human condition, namely the absolute certainty of physical death.

Born after the apocalypse, the man's son has only ever known a corpse-strewn world and, as a result, has become strangely accustomed to mortality, regarding scenes of death with subdued equanimity. The father and son come across the ghastly aftermath of a raging fire, which has melted the road and left the bodies of fleeing victims half submerged in the tarmac: "They picked their way among the mummified figures. The black skin stretched upon the bones and their faces split and shrunken on their skulls. Like victims of some ghastly envacuuming." The man is afraid that the scene will traumatize the boy: "Take my hand, he said. I dont think you should see this." The boy is clearly familiar with such a situation: "What you put in your head is there forever?" he asks, seemingly repeating the father's words from an earlier conversation. The father confirms that this is so, but the boy replies, "It's okay Papa.... They're already there." The father insists, "I dont want you to look," but the boy calmly assures him that "they'll still be there" (190–91). Later in the novel the father comes to accept the boy's argument, no longer bidding him to look away. While exploring a beach, the father finds "an ancient corpse rising and falling among the driftwood. He wished he could hide it from the boy but the boy was right. What was there to hide?" (236). This attitude toward death is in line with Buddhist thought, which teaches that "one should face the fact of death" and "reflect on its meaning" (de Silva 36). The child shows extraordinary maturity in his acceptance of death and the father eventually accepts the wisdom of this approach.

Just because the boy is calm in the face of death does not mean that he is unmoved by scenes of suffering; quite on the contrary, he displays a remarkably compassionate heart. When father and son pass a man who has been struck by lightning, the boy repeatedly asks, "Can we help him? Papa?" while the man insists, "There's nothing to be done for him." The situation reduces the boy to tears: "The boy was crying. He kept looking back.... The burned man had fallen over and at that distance you couldnt even tell what it was" (50). Other such scenes abound throughout the novel. When the boy thinks he sees another little boy across the street, he calls out to him, despite the fact that such noise might attract danger. The father scolds him for his recklessness, but the son is concerned only with the welfare of the other child: "What if that little boy doesnt have anybody to take care of him? he said. What if he doesnt have a papa?... I'm afraid for that little boy.... We should go get him, Papa. We could get him and take him with us.... And I'd give that little boy half of my food.... He was crying again. What about the little boy? he sobbed. What about the little boy?" (85–86). Despite the fact that the child seems to have come to terms with death, he has not become desensitized to the suffering of others, often weeping for their plight as though it were his own. According to Buddhist teachings, "as our capacity for compassion grows, it widens the field of the sorrow which we feel as our own" (Conze, *Buddhism* 46). Buddhism also teaches that compassion reduces "the boundary lines between oneself and other people" (Conze, *Buddhism* 102). The child seems to be the very embodiment of such compassion; while the father is fixated on their own survival, the boy continually tries to help others, even if such aid proves detrimental to his own well-being. The boy extends his moral code even to a stray dog, which the father views only as a potential source of food in a time of desperate starvation. When the father tires to capture the animal with "a noose of wire," the boy begins "to cry and to beg for the dog's life" until the father promises that he will "not hurt the dog" (87). Despite the fact that many other survivors have resorted to cannibalism, the two protagonists refuse to eat human flesh. Although this position is depicted as something they both ostensibly agree on, the fact that the boy keeps asking his father, "We wouldnt ever eat anybody, would we?" (126)

suggests that he carries doubts about his father's commitment to their moral code and needs to hear regular affirmations to ease his anxiety. The boy requires frequent reassurance that they are "still the good guys" and "always will be" (77), because he values moral, ethical, and spiritual goodness over mere physical survival.

The boy is not only intensely compassionate but also profoundly forgiving, begging his father not to punish a thief who tried to steal the shopping cart with their meager possessions and rations of food. The man refuses to listen to the boy, forcing the thief to strip naked at gunpoint, telling him, "I'm going to leave you the way you left us" (257). The father's injustice is apparent in the fact that the thief did not literally steal the clothes off their back, nor was he going to leave them naked in the freezing wasteland. The boy is devastated, both by the plight of the thief and by his own father's behavior, looking back in tears "at the nude and slatlike creature standing there in the road shivering and hugging himself. . . . The boy kept looking back and when he could no longer see him he stopped and then he just sat down in the road sobbing." Trying to make his father see things from the other man's point of view, the boy insists, "He was just hungry, Papa. He's going to die. . . . He's so scared, Papa" (258). The father finally acquiesces to the boy's pleas and agrees to return the clothes, but by then it is too late: "They wheeled the tottering cart back up the road and stood there in the cold and the gathering dark and called but no one came" (259).[12] In the end, they leave the thief's "shoes and clothes in the road" with "a rock on top of them" and continue their journey. The father tries to lessen his guilt by evading responsibility for the thief's plight, claiming that he "wasnt going to kill him." The boy's reply, "But we did kill him" (260), is startling in its maturity; not only is he aware of the causal relationship between the mistreatment of the thief and his inevitable death—something the father refuses to articulate—but, in his tactful usage of the word "we," he avoids laying the entire burden of blame on his father's already troubled conscience.[13]

The child's moral integrity is all the more striking given the fact that he has only ever known the postapocalyptic world of dog-eat-dog survivalism. Susan Tyburski argues that the "boy's natural impulse to reach out, and be merciful, to other human survivors shines like a beacon in this demonic world, and is only enhanced by the surrounding atrocities" (126). Although the man has given the boy a moral upbringing, telling him "old stories of courage and justice" (41), the boy feels that the father's actions often fall short of the standards set by the storytelling, pointing out that "in the stories we're always helping people and we dont help people" (268). The boy's heightened moral sense far exceeds that of the man, suggesting that it is something that cannot be acquired but must come from within. This is precisely what Cormac McCarthy argues in an interview in the *Wall Street Journal*: "I don't think goodness is something that you learn. If you're left adrift in the world to learn goodness from it, you would be in trouble" (qtd. in Jurgensen 113).[14] McCarthy's ideas seem to be in accordance with the Gnostic conviction that there is "something fundamentally wrong with the world" (Barnstone and Meyer 2). Despite their negative evaluation of the created world, the Gnostics maintained that "a spark of transcendent knowledge, wisdom, and light persists within people who are in the know" (Barnstone and Meyer 3). Hans Jonas explains that the Gnostics saw in the world "a mixture of light and darkness, yet with a preponderance of darkness," so that the world's "main substance is darkness, its foreign admixture, light" (57). The boy in *The Road* seems to embody this foreign admixture of goodness in a thoroughly evil world.

In McCarthy's novels, most notably in *Blood Meridian*, the world is frequently depicted as an evil place. This concept is fully extrapolated in *The Road*, where the world is portrayed as a hellish realm, in line with the Gnostic belief that this "world is really hell" (Grant 150). Throughout the novel, father and son struggle through a nightmarish underworld: "The secular winds drove them in howling clouds of ash to find shelter where they could . . . the noon sky black as the cellars of hell" (177). It is noteworthy that the winds are described as "secular," that is, "belonging to the present or visible world as distinguished from the eternal or spiritual world" (*OED*). This suggests Gnostic rather than Platonic dualism, because the visible world is not merely inferior when compared to the spiritual realm but downright malevolent. It is not only the landscape that has become hellish but also its inhabitants. During a potentially life-threatening encounter with a cannibal, the father regards the other man with disgust and hatred: "My brother at last. The reptilian calculations in those cold and shifting eyes. The gray and rotting teeth. Claggy with human flesh. Who has made of the world a lie every word" (75). The presence of the demonic is suggested not only through the cold, reptilian quality of the other man's eyes but also through the accusation of his having turned the world into a lie; in the Bible, Satan is regarded as the "Father of Lies," "for he is a liar, and the father of it" (John 8:44). The father's reference to the other man as his brother is an allusion to Ralph Waldo Emerson's words: "I am my brother and my brother is me"

("Compensation" 33). The line can be read as bitter irony but also as a painful admission of the potential for evil latent within human beings; after all, the father ends up killing the other man, albeit to protect his son.

This latent evil is brought to the fore by the conditions of the postapocalyptic world. Father and son continually encounter atrocities such as "a charred human infant headless and gutted and blackening on the spit" (198), or a cellar filled with human beings who are gradually being eaten alive by their captors: "Huddled against the back wall were naked people, male and female, all trying to hide, shielding their faces with their hands. On the mattress lay a man with his legs gone to the hip and the stumps of them blackened and burnt" (111). The world in *The Road* is populated by "men who would eat your children in front of your eyes and the cities themselves held by cores of blackened looters who tunnelled among the ruins and crawled from the rubble white of tooth and eye carrying charred and anonymous tins of food in nylon nets like shoppers in the commissaries of hell" (181). The reference to a "commissary," a store for "issuing or selling articles to people engaged in a particular type of work" (*OED*), suggests, symbolically, that these men live in hell and carry out the devil's work. The man recalls the first year following the apocalypse, remembering the "fires on the ridges and deranged chanting. The screams of the murdered. By day the dead impaled on spikes along the road" (33).[15] These memories vaguely hint at the "bloodcults" responsible for carrying out these satanic-sounding rituals (16).

Reflecting on the impaled heads of the murdered, the man wonders, "What had they done? He thought that in the history of the world it might be that there was more punishment than crime but he took small comfort from it" (33). The man does not have any reason to believe that the "bloodcults" are carrying out some kind of vigilante justice—they kill people in order to eat them—thus his doubt seems to be directed toward cosmic rather than human justice. These reflections on punishment both evoke and contradict the words of Arthur Schopenhauer, who wrote, "If we could lay all the misery of the world in one pan of the scales, and all the guilt in the other, the pointer would surely show them to be in equilibrium" (qtd. in Neiman 199). Although Schopenhauer was an atheist and thus his philosophy is clearly not a Christian one, it nevertheless evokes a balanced cosmos in which humanity is justly punished for its crimes. This corresponds to the Judeo-Christian concept of a cosmos ruled by a perfectly just creator God, who dispenses richly deserved divine punishment to the sinful human race; for example, "he is the Rock, his work is perfect: for all his ways are judgment: a God of truth and without iniquity, just and right is he" (Deuteronomy 32:4). The man in *The Road* rejects such a vision of the cosmos, believing that crime and punishment, or sin and retribution, are not in balance.

The fact that the man takes "no comfort" from these thoughts subtly suggests that there is actually a degree of comfort to be found in such musings but that he refuses to console himself in this way. The potential comfort can perhaps be found in the thought that the punishments meted out by the cosmos outweigh the crimes committed by the human race, a Gnostic view that finds fault within the design of the cosmos itself and thus somewhat mitigates the extent of human guilt. That is not to say that the human beings are not capable of evil; quite to the contrary, Gnostic teachings stress humanity's potential for evil and, as I have already argued, so does the man in *The Road*. The point made by the Gnostics is that the blame for this evil lies not with the human beings but within the flawed cosmos itself, which is viewed as "a demonic system" (Jonas 281). Gnosticism denies the existence of "original sin" or "guilt of the human soul," blaming the "dubious character of the soul and the profound moral helplessness of man on the cosmic situation as such" (Jonas 196, 281). As I have explained in earlier chapters, according to Gnostic thought, the human soul or psyche, as distinct from the spirit or pneuma, is "no less than his body an effluence of the cosmic powers and therefore as an instrument of their dominion over his true but submerged self" (Jonas 269). The very fact that the disaster in *The Road* remains unspecified leaves open the very likely possibility that it was the result of natural rather than moral evil, that is, a meteorite strike rather than nuclear war. In this sense, the evil depicted in the novel possesses Gnostic overtones, precisely because it emerges out of the arrangement of the cosmos rather than stemming from human error.

As in Gnostic thought, the theodicy of *The Road* hints at the existence of an indifferent or downright malevolent deity responsible for the creation of a flawed world. The creator God remains absent throughout the novel, but this absence is not so much a signifier of nonexistence as it is of divine indifference. The biblical cadences of McCarthy's prose hint at the possibility that this "barren, silent, godless" (4) world has been abandoned by its creator, rather than never having had a creator in the first place. The narrator's gaze seems to search for this absent God, expanding from an aerial to a galactic view but revealing only desolation and alienation: "Out on the roads the pilgrims sank down and fell over and died and the bleak and shrouded earth went trundling past the sun and returned again as trackless and as unremarked as the path of any nameless sisterworld in the ancient dark beyond" (181). The image of the dying planet traveling through the cold, dark enormity of space evokes a Gnostic horror of the "vastness and multiplicity of the cosmic system" (Jonas 43). More significantly, the fact that the earth is "unremarked" hints, however subtly, at the potential existence of an uninterested or distracted observer.

The man addresses this divine observer not in prayer but in accusation: "Are you there? he whispered. Will I see you at the last? Have you a neck by which to throttle you? Have you a heart? Damn you eternally have you a soul? Oh God, he whispered. Oh God" (11–12).[16] Such angry tirades against the God of this world are common in Gnostic texts. For example, in the Manichean version of the Genesis myth, Adam resents his own existence, crying, "Woe, woe unto the shaper of my body" (qtd. in Jonas 87). The despairing words of the man in *The Road* are reminiscent of Christ's death cry on the cross, "Eli, Eli, lama sabachthani? . . . My God, my God, why hast thou forsaken me?" (Matthew 27:46), but they also serve as an allusion to the suffering of Job, who similarly asks God, "Hast thou eyes of flesh? Or seest thou as man seeth?" (Job 10:4). The man's association with Job is reinforced later in the novel when he contemplates the possibility that he may have to kill his own child in order to spare him from a worse death at the hands of cannibals: "Can you do it? When the time comes? When the time comes there will be no time. Now is the time. Curse God and die" (114). In the Bible the words "curse God and die" are uttered by Job's wife, when she finds him sitting "among the ashes" (Job 2:9, 2:8). In *The Road*, the man's wife offers similarly demoralizing advice, arguing that it is better to take their own lives than to continue their hopeless struggle for survival: "As for me my only hope is for eternal nothingness and I hope it with all my heart" (57). Further biblical parallels may be found between the father's moral struggle over the potential mercy killing of his own son and the story of Abraham being commanded to sacrifice Isaac. However, as Todd Shy argues, *The Road* presents a "darker version" of this tale: "The father, like Abraham, packs a weapon, but here both father and son may be sacrificed before an inscrutable, destructive god" (39). Throughout the novel, the man's relationship with the God of this world is defined through biblical allusions, all of which feature human despair in the face of divine injustice, but, unlike his biblical counterparts, the man does not experience any reconciliation with his creator.

The man's anger at the demiurge is rendered painfully ironic by the recollection of a beautiful night he spent camping on the beach with his wife, before the disaster destroyed the world: "When he went back to the fire he knelt and smoothed her hair as she slept and he said if he were God he would have made the world just so and no different" (219). The man's proclamation is most probably an inverted allusion to the words of Alfonso X, king of Castile in 1252, who announced, "If I had been of God's counsel at the Creation, many things would have been ordered better" (qtd. in Neiman 15).[17] Unlike King Alfonso, who was able to see beyond the surface trappings of his own comfortable life, the man in *The Road* believes that the world is perfect simply because he is momentarily happy. He gives no thought to the senseless suffering of others, which obviously existed even before the apocalyptic disaster, through the countless wars, famines, diseases, and natural disasters that have plagued the human race since the beginning of history. This memory, revealed after the reader has been subject to the horrors of the novel, serves as a glimpse into the man's ignorant naïveté, before the apocalypse opened his eyes to the darkly Gnostic "truth of the world" (130).

One of the more obscure references to God occurs when the man contemplates "the silence. The salitter drying from the earth" (261). A few critics have commented on the origins of the word *salitter* in the writings of Jacob Boehme, whose likely influence on McCarthy has already been discussed in previous chapters.[18] In Boehme's cosmogony, salitter represents "the embodiment of the total force of the divinity, the compendium of all forces operating in nature and in the human psyche" (Principe and Weeks 53). Furthermore, salitter functions as "the vehicle for God's power," preserving "the order of the cosmos," acting as "the matrix of all forces," and holding the world together in its entirety" (Principe and Weeks 54–55). Read in light of this basic definition, the reference to salitter in *The Road* suggests that the divine power is being withdrawn from creation, resulting in the unmaking of the world. Such a reading may seem at odds with Gnostic thought, which does not hold the true God responsible for creation, but the apparent contradictions are resolved by a closer examination of the concept of salitter, especially as it is described in Boehme's *Aurora*, the very text from which McCarthy selected the epigraph to *Blood Meridian*.

In *Aurora*, Boehme "draws an important distinction between two types of *Salitter*, one celestial and the other earthly; the former is pure and clear, the latter is dark, stinking and poisonous. . . . Boehme's 'earthly, stinking' *Salitter* is only a material reflection, a crude copy, striving to imitate the immaterial 'celestial, pure' *Salitter*" (Principe and Weeks 56–7). In this sense, the "heavenly-earthly duality of *Salitter* recalls the double existence of objects in the Platonic doctrine of Ideas" (Principe and Weeks 56). Thus the reference to salitter in *The Road* does not run counter to the Gnostic world view, which similarly teaches that the "demiurge is only an inferior image of the transcendent Father" (Pearson 161), or alien God, and that creation itself "is based . . . upon a misrepresentation of the image of the divine" (Barnstone and Meyer 111). According to a Sethian Gnostic text, when the demiurge created the cosmos, he made "an image in place of an image and a form in place of a form" (Barnstone and Meyer 111). Furthermore, Boehme does not posit a complete duality between the pure heavenly realm and the corrupted earthly realm but argues, much like the Gnostics, that an uncorrupted spark of divinity remains in the innermost nature of manifest creation: "But thou must not think that nature was thus corrupted and kindled even to the innermost ground, but only the outermost birth or geniture; but the innermost . . . retained its own right to itself, seeing the kindled devil could not reach into it" (*Aurora* 289). According to Boehme, the Last Judgment will bring about a permanent separation of good and evil, when "the total or universal God will separate the evil from the good, and set the good again in the meek, mild and pleasant delight, as it was before the horrible kindling of the devil, and will give that which is fierce or wrathful to king Lucifer for an everlasting habitation" (*Aurora* 149). Given that *The Road* describes the end of the world, or at least the end of life as we know it, the reference to salitter must be interpreted in light of Boehme's Last Judgment. Thus the fact that the salitter is drying from the earth may actually be a blessing of sorts, suggesting that all that is good and divine is being separated from all that is evil and corrupt.

If the manifest world is indeed evil and corrupt, as Boehme and the Gnostics argued, then its destruction in *The Road* can be read as an unmaking, a reversal of error and a return to the state of wholeness and perfection before the rupture of creation. The Gnostics viewed not only the end of the world in this light but also individual death, arguing that "it is the birth process in reverse: everything that was by chance contributed by the planetary spheres to the creation of the human body will be surrendered back to them, until the spiritual or divine element returns to God pure and undefiled" (Rudolph 186). The man in *The Road* senses something of this when he distances himself from his own suffering and regards the process of dissolution with detached curiosity: "Perhaps in the world's destruction it would be possible at last to see how it was made. Oceans, mountains. The ponderous counterspectacle of things ceasing to be. The sweeping waste, hydroptic and coldly secular. The silence" (274). It is noteworthy that the wasteland left behind after the unmaking of the world is "coldly secular," as opposed to spiritual, once again suggesting the drying up of the divine salitter. This theme is also subtly emphasized by the presence of the obsolete word "hydroptic," an erroneous form of "hydropic," referring to "dropsy," which is "a morbid condition characterized by the accumulation of watery fluid in the serous cavities or the connective tissue of the body" (*OED*). Figuratively, "hydropic" can also refer to any "insatiable thirst or craving" (*OED*). The fact that McCarthy chose the erroneous form "hyrdroptic" rather than "hydropic" is significant in itself, given that the word also appears in its erroneous form in Robert Browning's "A Grammarian's Funeral," where it refers to a "soul-hydroptic with a sacred thirst" (line 95). Thus McCarthy's use of the word suggests that the drying up of the divine salitter has left the world thirsting for the sacred.

There are other instances in the novel when the man transcends his personal misery and faces the end of the world with strangely serene composure: "He'd had this feeling before, beyond the numbness and the dull despair." This particular feeling of calm detachment is brought about by a contemplation of the way in which everything he thought he knew about reality is slowly being stripped away: "The world shrinking down about a raw core of parsible entities. The names of birds. Things to eat" (89). "Parsible" here appears to be an alternate spelling of "parsable," which in its extended use refers to something that can be "examined or analysed minutely" (*OED*). In simple terms, as the signified fades from existence, it takes with it the corresponding signifier. This "shrinking down" of the world in *The Road* extends beyond physical objects and their linguistic markers to include abstract concepts and belief systems, "the names of things one believed to be true. More fragile than he would have thought" (89). The "frailty of everything," which the apocalypse has "revealed at last" (28), applies not only to the impermanence of the tangible world but also to the insubstantial nature of the various ideologies that humanity has built up around itself. This is not an entirely undesirable phenomenon, especially when considered in light of the Gnostic Gospel of Philip, which teaches that "the names of earthly things are illusory. We stray from the real to the unreal. If you hear the word 'god,' you miss the real and hear the unreal. Father, son, holy spirit, life, light, resurrection, church. These words are not real. They are unreal but refer to the real, and are heard in the world. They fool us. If those names were in the eternal realm, they would never be heard on earth. They were not assigned to us here. Their end dwells in the eternal realm" (qtd. in Barnstone and Meyer 261). According to this Gnostic argument, words not only refer to earthly things but are themselves earthly things because they are found in the manifest world. Therefore, when our earthly languages attempt to describe the ultimate Reality of the alien God, which by its very nature is ineffable and inexpressible, they only lead to confusion. The Gnostics warn that when people hear the word "God" they think they have understood something of spiritual Reality, not realizing that the word itself has grounded them in earthly reality; gnosis can be gained only by direct, personal experience and not via language.

Most significantly, the man in *The Road* feels that even the "sacred idiom" is "shorn of its referents and so of its reality. Drawing down like something trying to preserve the heat. In time to wink out forever" (89).[19] The use of "sacred" suggests that McCarthy is not referring to the "idiom" in the linguistic sense but rather in the theological sense, meaning "a property of Christ as either human or divine" (*OED*). In the theology of the Incarnation, this is referred to as Communicatio Idiomatum, or "Communication of Idioms," meaning that "the properties of the Divine Word can be ascribed to the man Christ, and that the properties of the man Christ can be predicated of the Word" (Maas n.p.). In other words, "he Who is the Word of God on account of His eternal generation is also the subject of human properties; and He Who is the man Christ on account of having assumed human nature is the subject of Divine attributes" (Maas n.p.). The fading of the sacred idiom therefore suggests a Gnostic rejection of the Christian doctrine that only Jesus Christ is simultaneously both human and divine. This doctrine is refuted in the heretical Gospel of Thomas, which claims that ordinary human beings are always capable of attaining states of divinity: "You saw the Spirit, you became the Spirit. You saw Christ, you became Christ. You saw the Father, you became the Father." According to the Gospel of Thomas, whoever attains gnosis becomes "no longer a Christian, but a Christ" (qtd. in Pagels, *Gnostic Gospels* 134). The father in *The Road* senses the divinity in his own child, claiming that "if he is not the word of God God never spoke" (5). According to the New Testament, God created the world out of the Word, or the sacred Logos: "In the beginning was the Word, and the Word was with God, and the Word was God" (John 1:1). The Logos is also identified as Jesus Christ: "And the Word was made flesh, and dwelt among us, (and we beheld his glory, the glory as of the only begotten of the Father,) full of grace and truth" (John 1:14). In McCarthy's novel, the father rejects the traditional sacred idiom by proclaiming his own son as the divine Logos, thereby advocating, whether consciously or otherwise, for the Gnostic Christianity of the apocryphal Gospel of Thomas.[20]

In *The Road*, the child is often referred to in terms that suggest a divine nature; for example, the father describes his son's head as a "golden chalice, good to house a god" (75). The "chalice" refers to the "cup in which the wine is administered in the celebration of the eucharist" (*OED*) and therefore the container for the blood of Christ. "Chalice" also suggests "grail," as in the Holy Grail or Saint Grail, which, according to medieval legend, was "the platter used by Jesus at the Last Supper, in which Joseph of Arimathea received his blood at the cross" (*OED*). It is noteworthy, however, that the father refers to the boy's head as being fit for "*a* god" rather than simply "God," thereby moving away from the monotheism of traditional Christianity toward a more open definition of divinity. It is highly significant that McCarthy's working title for *The Road* was originally *The Grail* (Cormac McCarthy Papers, Texas State University–San Marcos, box 91).[21] If the boy is indeed the Holy Grail, then the sacred blood he carries is his own, rather than that of Christ. The child is again described as a receptacle for divinity when the father sees him "glowing in that waste like a tabernacle" (273). A "tabernacle" may refer to several things; in the Old Testament it is the "dwelling-place of Jehovah, or of God," but it may also refer to the "ornamented receptacle for the pyx containing the consecrated host," that is, the body of Christ (*OED*). The word may also be applied to any "place of worship distinguished in some way from a church," or even the "human body regarded as the temporary abode of the soul or of life" (*OED*). When read in light of the fact that the Christian themes and symbols throughout *The Road* have a tendency to evoke apocryphal rather than conventional texts, the reference to "tabernacle" calls for a wider definition of the word, suggesting that the boy's body is a vessel for his own divine spirit. This concept is explored in the works of Boehme, who argues that "the true Christian has his church within his soul. . . . This church is with him and in him wherever he goes, and he is always in his church" (qtd. in Hartmann 9). Despite some discrepancies between the different schools of Gnosticism, most Gnostic teachings share the "view that the divine light is hidden within us and we can find it, we don't have to go through a church" (Pagels, "Elaine Pagels on Understanding Gnosticism" 146). In fact, the child in *The Road* seems to be emitting this divine light when he is described as "glowing" in the wasteland (273).

Despite the fact that many schools of Gnosticism maintain that the divine light is to be found within all human beings, and in Manichaeism even within plants and animals, this teaching does not entirely eliminate the need for a savior. As I have explained in the preceding chapters, the Gnostic savior is "identical with him to whom he comes," that is, "with the life to be saved" (Jonas 78). This means not only that those who require salvation already possess the divine light but also that the savior was originally in the same position as those who are to be saved and therefore is in need of salvation himself. This idea appears in the Gospel of Thomas, where Jesus teaches his disciples that "whoever drinks from my mouth will become like me. I myself shall become that person, and the hidden things will be revealed to that one" (qtd. in Barnstone and Meyer 68). According to Gnostic teachings, the savior serves the function of a "revealer," one who "discloses knowledge that frees and awakens people, and that helps them recall who they are" (Barnstone and Meyer 4). The child in *The Road* seems to embrace this role in a memorable interchange between father and son. When the father tells his son, "You're not the one who has to worry about everything," the child replies, "I am the one" (259). According to Allen Josephs, the "proclamation 'I am' is among the strongest phrases in the Old and New Testaments, the latter inevitably an echo of God's pronouncements to Moses: 'I AM THAT I AM' (Exodus 3:14)" (25). Josephs cites further examples of similar proclamations made by Jesus in the New Testament: "I am the way, the truth and the light" (John 14:6); "I am the door of the sheep" (John 10:7); "I am the good shepherd" (John 10:11); "I am the light of the world" (John 8:12); "I am the alpha and the omega" (Revelation 1:8). Josephs argues that the child offers "to take responsibility ... in unmistakably religious language" (26). There is no doubt that McCarthy has always been adept at depicting authentic dialogue, but the sonorous, biblical connotations of the proclamation "I am the one" seem strange coming from the mouth of a little boy. If the boy's words were meant to be read purely as insistence on the fact that he is "the one who has to worry about everything," then surely his reply would have been formulated in a manner that replicated the casual speech patterns of a child, for example, "Yes I am." It seems likely, then, that the child's words function on both levels, indicating his readiness to take up moral responsibility as well as spiritual leadership.

Erik Hage argues that "if the boy is a messianic figure, he is one that is disconnected and adrift from all ecclesiastical forms; for all religions, all cultural structures, and all evidence of the world that housed such beliefs has been obliterated" (52). Hage's argument seems especially pertinent in light of a scene in which the boy catches a snowflake in his hand and watches it "expire there like the last host of christendom" (16). The "host" refers to the "bread consecrated in the Eucharist, regarded as the body of Christ sacrificially offered" (*OED*). Therefore the scene not only suggests the demise of traditional Christianity but also hints at the very ephemerality of religious symbols. As I have discussed in earlier chapters, McCarthy told Gary Wallace that "the mystical experience is a direct apprehension of reality, unmediated by symbol" (Wallace 138). Even though the postapocalyptic world of *The Road* has been shorn of all the surface trappings of organized, exoteric religion, the potential for personal, esoteric spirituality remains undiminished. Such a scenario appears advantageous when viewed from a Gnostic perspective, as Gnosticism emphasizes the preeminence of direct spiritual experience, which is seen as offering "the ultimate criterion of truth, taking precedence over all secondhand testimony and all tradition— even gnostic tradition!" (Pagels, *Gnostic Gospels* 25). Gnosticism teaches that to "know oneself" allows one "to know god directly, without any need for the mediation of rabbis, priests, bishops, imams, or other religious officials" (Barnstone and Meyer 1). This is true even of the Gnostic savior, who is successful only insofar as he can aid others in attaining this knowledge of their own divine selves, or the pneuma, which leads to knowledge of the Absolute.

The father in *The Road* does not need a specific religious context in which to situate the perceived divinity of his son: "There were times when he sat watching the boy sleep that he would begin to sob uncontrollably but it wasn't about death. He wasn't sure what it was about but he thought it was about beauty or goodness. Things that he'd no longer any way to think about at all" (129). The man does not analyze these abstract, intellectual categories of goodness and beauty; rather he apprehends the sacred directly, almost somatically, its overwhelming power transcending language and finding expression in his tears.[22] When the father washes "a dead man's brains" out of his child's hair, he feels that his task is "like some ancient anointing. So be it. Evoke the forms. Where you've nothing else construct ceremonies out of the air and breathe upon them" (74). "Anointing" refers to the "application of oil, as a sign of consecration to a sacred office" (*OED*); thus the father's ceremony marks his son as the "Anointed One" or the Messiah. The evocation of forms can be read in a theological as well as a philosophical sense. The former refers to an essential element of any sacrament, which "is said to consist of *matter* (as the water in baptism, the bread and wine in the

Eucharist) and *form*, which is furnished by certain essential formulary words" (*OED*). In an anointing, matter consists of the oil and form refers to the ceremonial words uttered during the ritual; the father in *The Road* lacks both these elements but constructs his own ceremony nevertheless. The reference to the father breathing upon the forms echoes the creation myth in Genesis, in which God forms "man out of the dust of the ground" and breathes "into his nostrils the breath of life" (2:7). The connection between breath and spirit is encapsulated in the etymology of pneuma, which is derived from the Greek πνεῦμα (wind, breath), meaning "spirit, soul, or life force," as it does in Gnostic teachings, or "the spirit of God" in the Bible (*OED*). In the philosophical sense, "the forms" refers to Plato's theory of forms or ideas, which is concerned with "the permanent reality which makes a thing what it is, in contrast with the particulars which are finite and subject to change" ("Form"). According to this theory, everything in the manifest world is only an imperfect copy or shadow of the transcendent and eternal realm of Forms. The father in *The Road* is able to evoke the Absolute Forms, even when the transient things of this world have vanished from existence.

All of these readings, whether theological or philosophical, point to the idea that there exists some eternal, transcendent, spiritual Absolute. When the father looks at his numinous son, he feels that "this blessing is no less real for being shorn of its ground" (31). Thus, even when the material world crumbles away, along with the external trappings of religion, the divine Absolute remains accessible to the human spirit. As the man lies dying, he contemplates his son and concludes, "There is no prophet in the earth's long chronicle who's not honored here today" (277). The father's apprehension of his son's divine, messianic nature is described in terms that evoke the transcendent unity of religions, as posited by the Perennial Philosophy. Aldous Huxley writes, "The doctrine that God can be incarnated in human form is found in most of the principal historic expositions of the Perennial Philosophy—in Hinduism, in Mahayana Buddhism, in Christianity and in the Mohammedanism of the Sufis, by whom the Prophet was equated with the eternal Logos" (50). The child in *The Road* seems to be a literary representation of the belief that the "Logos passes out of eternity into time for no other purpose than to assist the beings, whose bodily form he takes, to pass out of time and into eternity" (Huxley 51). The father seems to address all the spiritual seekers of the world when he declares, "Whatever form you spoke of you were right" (277). Martin Lings posits a similar argument in his study of the transcendent unity of religions, claiming that "this unity transcends the differences between the religions without in any way denying those same differences on their own level.... Thus, Christianity is very clearly different from Islam or Buddhism qua form; but it is one with them qua essence (or qua perennial philosophy)" (xv). In the novel, the man acknowledges the differences between religions by referring to their different forms—namely, the different representations of the messianic figure—while at the same time maintaining their essential unity by proclaiming them all "right."

The man's faith in the messianic nature of his son seems to be confirmed just before his death, when he experiences a sustained vision of the child bathed in an otherworldly light: "He watched him come through the grass and kneel with the cup of water he'd fetched. There was light all about him ... and when he moved the light moved with him" (277).[23] Light functions as a visible symbol of spirituality, divinity, and grace in countless traditions. For example, in "The Over-Soul," Ralph Waldo Emerson writes, "From within or from behind, a light shines through us upon things and makes us aware that we are nothing, but the light is all" (689). Similarly, Rudolph Otto notes that both Śaṅkara and Meister Eckhart refer to the spiritual self in terms of luminosity: "We have to know and liberate this self which is purely spiritual and gives forth its own light. This inward being is for Śaṅkara the atman, for Eckhart the spirit" (79). Randall Wilhelm, in the notes to his article on the use of still life imagery within *The Road*, points out that "the 'God as Light' maxim would hold true, for instance, in Christian theological terms as well as for the Semitic deity Baal, the Egyptian deity Ra, and the Persian deity Ahura Mazda, among others" (144n13). References to divine light are especially prevalent in the Gospel of Thomas, which states, "There is light within a man of light, and he lights the whole world. If he does not shine, there is darkness" (qtd. in Barnstone and Meyer 51). The child in *The Road* seems to be precisely such a man of light, illuminating the darkness of the world with his inherent goodness. The father becomes fully aware of his son's otherworldly radiance when the child acts as a water bearer, water being a widespread component of sacramental rites and a symbol of the purifying nature of divine grace.[24] In Sethian and Mandean Gnosticism, the "water of life" is a "symbol of illuminating knowledge, which was depicted ritually by a drink of water" (Rudolph 230). The Sethians and Mandeans both practiced a form of baptism in which "the cup of living water" became the "means whereby one partakes of immortality" (Rudolph 227). It is noteworthy, therefore, that the divine child brings the dying man this Gnostic symbol of immortality, suggesting that the body dies, but the spirit endures.

The child in *The Road* is associated with all the traditional markers of divinity; namely, beauty, goodness, compassion, forgiveness, the grail, the tabernacle, the ceremony of anointing, otherworldly light, sacramental water, and, most frequently and memorably, a hidden, spiritual fire that is referred to throughout the novel. Rudolph Otto identifies these markers in the various traditions of the Perennial Philosophy, explaining that "figures of fire, of life, light, truth and knowledge, of the water of life, of the spikenard outpoured, of the divine seed and the indwelling χάρις [grace]" signify the "indwelling Kingdom of God," which is identical with the "Spirit," and with "the Godhead itself" (131–32). As the man approaches death, the frightened child seeks reassurance regarding the existence of the fire:

> Is it real? The fire?
> Yes it is.
> Where is it? I dont know where it is.
> Yes you do. It's inside you. It was always there. I can see it. (279)

The father's reply connects the fire with the divine light that he sees emanating from his son. Jacob Boehme frequently refers to fire and light as essential symbols of the sacred: "If the divine eternal light is received in the soul, it kindles a fire therein which illuminates the whole substance of the soul, so that the latter becomes luminous, and a mirror, or eye, in which the light of God is reflected" (qtd. in Hartmann 19). Similar imagery can be found in the Gnostic Gospel of Philip, which states, "Light is fire. I am not referring to flame, which has no form, but to another kind of fire, whose appearance is white, which is luminous and beautiful" (qtd. in Barnstone and Meyer 277). The father's words also reflect the Gnostic belief that "the divine light is hidden within us" (Pagels, *Gnostic Gospels* 146), an idea succinctly expressed in the Gospel of Thomas when Jesus instructs his disciples that "the kingdom is inside you" (qtd. in Barnstone and Meyer 45). In the same gospel, Jesus proclaims, "I am the fire that blazes. Whoever is near me is near fire" (qtd. in Barnstone and Meyer 64). The fire that the man and the child carry throughout the novel seems to signify precisely such an indwelling grace.[25]

At various intervals during their journey, father and son recite an affirmation confirming their roles as the "good guys" and the fire carriers:

> Because we're the good guys.
> Yes.
> And we're carrying the fire.
> And we're carrying the fire. Yes. (120)

Both father and son agree that they are not the only ones carrying the fire. While sitting on the beach and wondering what lies on the opposite shore, the man suggests, "Maybe there's a father and his little boy and they're sitting on the beach." The boy asks, "And they could be carrying the fire too?" and the father replies, "They could be. Yes" (216). The fact that the role of fire carriers is not exclusive to the protagonists corresponds to the Gnostic idea, as expounded by the first-century quasi-Gnostic Simon Magus, that "each human being is a dwelling place" and "in him dwells an infinite power ... the root of the universe," synonymous with the divine spark (qtd. in Pagels, *Gnostic Gospels* 135). While "this infinite power is contained potentially in all humans," it remains latent unless it is "fully formed, presumably by gnosis" (Pearson 32). Thus what seems to distinguish the child sharply from the other human beings in the novel, at least in the eyes of the father, is that his divine potential has been fully actualized.

While it is important to distinguish between the metaphorical fire that the father and son carry throughout the novel and the apocalyptic fire that destroys the world, they are not necessarily incompatible symbols when regarded from a Gnostic perspective. Although the destructive, maleficent force of the apocalyptic fire sets it apart from the numinous, beneficent fire that illuminates the child, there is nonetheless a sense that the fiery destruction of creation signifies a Gnostic triumph over the corporeal world. Harold Bloom puts forward a similar argument, suggesting that the fire "evokes the Hasidic belief that worldly things and beings are 'shards' in which sparks of the original divine substance lie trapped, awaiting release. Ironically, the motif also evokes the fire of the apocalypse that altered the world, as if to suggest that in the fiery ruination of the world, the few shards of divine fire (embodied in the mutual and absolute love of the father and the son) have been revealed" (*Bloom's Guides* 31). The man watches a "forest fire ... making its way along the tinder-box ridges above them, flaring and shimmering against the overcast like the northern lights." Even though the fire is destructive, it is depicted as beautiful, captivating, and even numinous: "Cold as it was he stood there a long time. The color of it moved something in him long forgotten. Make a list. Recite a litany. Remember" (31). According to

Valentinian Gnosticism, the end of days will take place "when all that is spiritual (pneumatic) is shaped and perfected through knowledge (gnosis). ... Then the fire that is hidden in the world will blaze forth and burn: when it has consumed all matter it will be consumed with it and pass into nonexistence" (Rudolph 196). The Valentinians also differentiated between the spiritual fire, which is to be liberated, and the earthly fire, which will be annihilated with the rest of creation.

In Gnostic texts such as *The Revelation of Adam*, descriptions of the apocalypse portray a scenario similar to what we see depicted in McCarthy's novel: "Then fire and sulfur and asphalt are cast upon those people, and fire and blinding mist come over those realms, and the eyes of the powers of the luminaries are darkened," meaning that the light of the sun and moon will be blocked out, as in *The Road*, "and the inhabitants of the realms cannot see in those days" (qtd. in Barnstone and Meyer 184). In the novel, father and son come across analogous scenes of fire and asphalt: "A mile on and they began to come upon the dead. Figures half mired in the blacktop, clutching themselves, mouths howling. . . . Passing them in silence down that silent corridor through the drifting ash where they struggled forever in the road's coagulate" (190–91).[26] This appalling spectacle is foreshadowed on the preceding page of the novel when the man recalls a horrific childhood memory of snakes being set alight by a group of men: "As they were mute there were no screams of pain and the men watched them burn and writhe and blacken in just such silence themselves" (189). The silent agony of the burning snakes mirrors the silently howling mouths of the burned corpses; in both cases, the spectators regard the suffering in silence themselves. Such descriptions of fiery agony occur throughout the Buddhist sutras, in which the Buddha sees the entire universe as being "aflame with the fire of a vast mass of physical and mental suffering" (Conze, *Buddhist Scriptures* 208). The similarities between the father's memory of the burning snakes and his encounter with burned human corpses serves as a reminder that such suffering is not something unprecedented that has been brought about by the apocalypse but rather an inherent fact of existence plaguing all life-forms.

Ironically, the men in *The Road* commit the evil act of burning the snakes out of a misguided attempt to combat evil itself: "The men poured gasoline on them and burned them alive, having no remedy for evil but only the image of it as they conceived it to be" (189). The snake-burning passage in *The Road* reverses the biblical role of the serpent; far from leading humanity into temptation and sin, the snakes become innocent victims of human ignorance. In this sense, the passage signals a rejection of traditional Judeo-Christian ideas about original sin in favor of something closer to the Buddhist and Gnostic belief that "ignorance, not sin" is "the source of all evil" (H. Smith, *Religions of Man* 122). In *The Road*, the snakes serve as symbols of illumination, crawling "across the floor of the grotto to illuminate its darker recesses" (189). Both Gnostic and Buddhist "systems are fond of Serpents (*nagas*) as beings connected with wisdom" (Conze, *Further Buddhist Studies* 27). Gnostic texts, such as the *Hypostasis of the Archons*, feature a "remarkable revision of the Genesis account," referring to the serpent as "the instructor, because it knows and teaches about knowledge" (qtd. in Barnstone and Meyer 167). Hans Jonas explains the role of the serpent in certain Gnostic teachings: "Since it is the serpent that persuades Adam and Eve to taste of the fruit of knowledge and thereby disobey their Creator, it came in a whole group of systems to represent the 'pneumatic' principle from beyond counteracting the designs of the Demiurge, and thus could become as much a symbol of the powers of redemption as the biblical God had been degraded to a symbol of cosmic oppression" (93). In some schools of Gnostic thought, Jesus is seen as a "particular incarnation of the 'general serpent'" (Jonas 93). It is significant that the child in *The Road* is also associated with serpents. When the man watches him "stoke the flames," he describes him as "God's own firedrake" (29). The choice of the word "firedrake" is noteworthy, as the word "dragon" is derived from the Greek δράκων (*drakōn*), which, according to Liddell and Scott's "δράκων": *A Greek-English Lexicon*, could also mean "snake" or "serpent." According to the same source, the word is probably derived "from the verb δέρκομαι (*derkomai*)," or "I see clearly." Thus this association with the serpent further identifies the child as a Gnostic savior.

The child's ability to "see clearly" is hinted at throughout the novel. The man surveys the landscape and sees "nothing," but the child is able to spot the "palest wisp" of smoke (76). Even more significant is the child's instant recognition of his own reflection, especially when contrasted with father's momentary confusion: "They came upon themselves in a mirror and he almost raised the pistol. It's us, Papa, the boy whispered. It's us" (132). Such scenes operate on both a literal and figurative level, suggesting that the child has not only superior eyesight but also superior insight. The mirror scene in particular calls to mind the Delphic maxim "γνῶθι σεαυτόν" (*gnōthi seauton*), or "know thyself," which is also "the key-note of all Indian philosophy, not excluding the Buddhist and Jaina *Darsanas*" (Dutt 61). The same formula is used in Gnostic thought, especially in the Gospel of Thomas when Jesus proclaims that "he who has known himself has already come to knowledge concerning the depth of the All" (qtd. in Rudolph 113). Gnosticism teaches that "to attain this knowledge—to become a Gnostic—is to know oneself, god, and everything. . . . To know oneself truly is to attain this mystical knowledge, and to attain this mystical knowledge is to know oneself truly" (Barnstone and Meyers 8). Conversely, "self-ignorance is also a form of self-destruction" (Pagels, *Gnostic Gospels* 126). It is noteworthy that the father is prepared to shoot his own image, destroying himself both symbolically and literally by wasting the last remaining bullet in the pistol. The act of seeing clearly, with all its Platonic connotations of perceiving and understanding Absolute Reality, is depicted as being of paramount importance. The dying man asks the child not to set up their tent because "he didn't want anything covering him. . . . He wanted to be able to see" (277). His wish is granted and what he sees is a beatific vision of his son bathed in divine light.

The influence of Platonism is also apparent in the two cave dreams that frame the narrative. Alex Hunt and Martin Jacobsen argue that these dreams "allude to Plato's 'Allegory of the Cave,' in which the concept of progressive illumination emerges through the story of prisoners chained in a cave and allowed to see only shadows" (157). In the allegory of the cave, Plato "describes the ordeal necessary for the soul's ascent from shadowy illusion to enlightenment." The allegory features several levels of awareness: "Those chained to the wall of shadows are imprisoned in the shadowy world of imagination and illusion; those loose within the cave occupy the 'common sense' world of perception and informed opinion; those struggling through the passageway to the surface are acquiring knowledge through reason; the rich surface world of warmth and sunlight is the highest level of Reality directly grasped by pure Intelligence" (Soccio 141). At the beginning of the novel, the man wakes from a dream in which "he had wandered in a cave where the child led him by the hand." This places the child at a higher level of awareness; whereas the man merely wanders, the child leads. The dream differs from Plato's allegory in that the man and child carry their own light, which plays "over the wet flowstone walls" (3). The fact that these cave dwellers use their own guiding light suggests the Gnostic "doctrine of redemption," which "centres upon the restoration to its origin of this divine spark of light" (Rudolph 91). The fire that the man and the child carry throughout the novel, which can be read as the divine spark of illuminating gnosis, is also the source of the light they carry through the dream cave.

Further Gnostic themes within the cave dreams can be discerned in the description of the man and child as "pilgrims in a fable swallowed up and lost among the inward parts of some granitic beast" (3). As I have previously argued, the word "pilgrim" has obvious religious connotations but can also refer to "a foreigner, an alien," or "a stranger" (*OED*), a definition that suggests the Gnostic concept of the "alien-life," as well as the description of the pneuma as a "stranger who does not know the ways of the foreign land" (Jonas 49). The concept of the man and child being "swallowed up" conveys the Gnostic belief that "the parts of divinity lost to the darkness can be reached only down there in the depth in which they are swallowed up" (Jonas 127). The metaphor of being swallowed alive also emphasizes the idea of not belonging in one's environment, hence "to come from outside" and "to get out" are "standard phrases in Gnostic literature" (Jonas 55). The bowels of the "granitic beast" evoke Gnostic descriptions of "the labyrinthine aspect of the world," where the pneuma "loses its way and wanders about" (Jonas 52). Although the first dream of the cave functions as a clear allusion to Plato's allegory, it simultaneously conveys a Gnostic portrayal of humanity's situation as prisoners in the manifest world.

As the man and the child make their way through the cave, they find "deep stone flues where the water dripped and sang. Tolling in the silence the minutes of the earth and the hours and the days of it and the years without cease" (3).[27] These words convey the relentless passage of time, a concept that for the Gnostics inspired the same dismay as the enormity of the cosmos. Hans Jonas explains that "the time dimension of life's cosmic existence" was "no less demonised" than the space dimension, reflecting the "basic experience of alienness and exile" (53). The Gnostics believed that "whole series of ages stretch between [the pneuma] and its goal" and "escape is only achieved by passing through them all" (Jonas 53). Like Hinduism, Buddhism, and Platonism, some schools of Gnosticism taught the doctrine of reincarnation, claiming that "through chains of unnumbered generations the transcendent Life enters the world, sojourns in it, and endures its seemingly endless duration, and only through this long and laborious way, with memory lost and regained, can it fulfil its destiny" (Jonas 53). Naturally, this doctrine rendered the concept of time all the more terrifying by stretching it well beyond the confines of a single human lifespan.

A Gnostic interpretation of the dream also explains why the man and child continue to journey through the cave instead of making their way out into the sun. Gnosticism teaches that "the world," that is, the entire cosmic system, "vast though it may be, is like a closed cell" (Jonas 55). The unenlightened spirit is imprisoned in the manifest cosmos and "wherever it seeks an escape it only passes from one world into another that is no less world. This multiplication of demonic systems to which unredeemed life is banished is a theme of many Gnostic teachings" (Jonas 52). If the child in *The Road* is indeed a Gnostic savior, then his journey through the cave can also be interpreted in light of what can loosely be referred to as the Gnostic redeemer myth, which teaches that the powers responsible for imprisoning the divine light in the realm of matter "can be overcome only from within. This means that the savior-god must assimilate himself to the forms of cosmic existence and thereby subject himself to its conditions" (Jonas 127). Alex Hunt and Martin Jacobsen interpret this as "an inversion of Platonic thinking," arguing that "McCarthy's allegory of the cave is not about getting out to the sun and to illuminating wisdom but about going in deeper, lost in the darkness with a fading light" (157). I believe that the dream is not so much an inversion of Platonic thinking as a reinterpretation of it, in the same way that Gnosticism itself shares some ideas with Platonism while revising others.

Both Gnosticism and Platonism are based on "ontological or metaphysical dualism," professing "two levels of existence." In Platonism, this dualism consists of "the spiritual eternal ideas and their transitory (spatial) counterparts; the latter do indeed signify a loss of being, but nevertheless belong to the good part of creation." Gnostic dualism is "distinguished" from Platonic dualism "in the one essential point, that it is anti-cosmic; that is, its conception includes an unequivocally negative evaluation of the visible world together with its creator" (Rudolph 60). In other words, while the Platonist can escape out of the cave of ignorance and experience enlightenment at the sight of the visible sun, the Gnostic must step out of manifest creation altogether; complete, permanent liberation can be achieved only through "the Ascent of the Soul," that is, the ascent of the fully enlightened pneuma "after death" (Jonas 165). According to Gnostic teachings, "death is thus very definitely an act of liberation," enabling "escape from the entanglements of earthly existence" and a return to the "true home" (Rudolph 171). Thus, for the Gnostic, the sunlit world outside is just an extension of the cave and therefore still within the walls of the prison; in order to break free from the prison, one has to cease existing in manifest, bodily form.[28]

Furthermore, the voyage the man and the child undertake through the cave is not fruitless from a Gnostic perspective, because their exploration leads them to the discovery of "a great stone room where lay a black and ancient lake" (3). The dark and ancient body of water evokes the dark waters of chaos that precede the creation of the world in numerous mythologies. We encounter these dark waters at the beginning of Genesis: "And the earth was without form, and void; and darkness was upon the face of the deep. And the Spirit of God moved upon the face of the waters" (1:2). In Gnosticism, this is the "turbid water," or the "water of the Abyss," from whence "the original matter of the world of darkness originates" (Jonas 99). The man and the child observe a blind monster drinking from these black waters:

> And on the far shore a creature that raised its dripping mouth from the rimstone pool and stared into the light with eyes dead white and sightless as the eggs of spiders. It swung its head low over the water as if to take the scent of what it could not see. Crouching there pale and naked and translucent, its alabaster bones cast up in shadow on the rocks behind it. Its bowels, its beating heart. The brain that pulsed in a dull glass bell. It swung its head from side to side and then gave out a low moan and turned and lurched away and loped soundlessly into the dark. (3–4)[29]

The creature's appearance and behavior strongly suggest the demiurge as described in Gnostic cosmologies. Although these genesis myths vary between the different schools of Gnosticism, the most common variation follows the story that the demiurge was the end product of the transgression of a divine being named Pistis Sophia, who, horrified by her own creation, cast the "work of fright" into "boundless darkness and bottomless water . . . like an abortion," where she hoped it would remain concealed (Jonas 301). The Gnostic demiurge is androgynous, both "male and female" (Jonas 302), and McCarthy's creature is consistently referred to as the neuter "it." Furthermore, the demiurge is "lion-shaped" (Jonas 302) and McCarthy's creature, albeit pale and transparent, also possess leonine characteristics in the way it laps water, sniffs, swings its head, crouches, moans, lurches, and lopes on soundless paws. Carl James Grindley argues that the creature "is an allusion to . . . Yeats's 'Second Coming'" (12), which refers to "a shape with lion body and the head of a man" (line 14). Most significantly, McCarthy's creature is blind and ignorant, its eyes sightless and its brain encased in dull glass. These are also the main characteristics of the Gnostic demiurge, who, knowing "nothing else except water and darkness . . . thought that he existed alone" and boasted, "I am God." His mother, Sophia, reproaches him with the words "'Thou art mistaken, Samael'—that is, the blind god. 'An immortal Man of Light exists before thee, who will reveal himself in your creation'" (Jonas 304). The arrival of the light-bearing child in *The Road* seems to be a fulfillment of Sophia's prophecy.

In the man's second cave dream, the child is once again the leader, literally lighting the way: "The light was a candle which the boy bore in a ringstick of beaten copper" (280). It has already been established in my discussion of the word "salitter" that McCarthy is familiar with alchemical concepts, and it seems likely that the attention drawn to the copper ringstick also bears some alchemical significance. *Turba Philosophorum*, the oldest known work of Latin alchemy, claims that "copper, like man, has a body and a soul" and gives instructions on how to work with copper in order to achieve "the liquefaction of the body and the separation of the soul from the body" (36, 66). As in all alchemical texts, chemistry is inextricably merged with spiritual doctrine, so that the chemical purification of the copper serves as a metaphor for the spiritual purification of the alchemist: "Therefore, it behoves you, O all ye Sons of the Doctrine, to destroy the body and extract the soul therefrom!" (66). The alchemical significance of the copper reinforces the Gnostic doctrine of salvation, consisting of the permanent separation of the pneuma from the prison of the body.

At the end of the second cave dream, the man senses that "they had reached the point of no return which was measured from the first solely by the light they carried with them" (280). Once again, the light, like the metaphorical fire, symbolizes an indwelling grace that guides the man and the child along a spiritual path. From a Gnostic perspective, the light they carry with them corresponds to the idea that "the psyche bears within itself the potential for liberation or destruction" (Pagels, *Gnostic Gospels* 126). This teaching is expressed in the Gospel of Thomas, which states, "If you bring forth what is within you, what you bring forth will save you. If you do not bring forth what is within you, what you do not bring forth will destroy you" (qtd. in Pagels, *Gnostic Gospels*). The trope of light as the objective correlative of spirituality is also used in Buddhist texts. The sage Nagasena teaches that spiritual insight "is like a lamp which a man would take into a dark house. It would dispel the darkness, would illuminate, shed light, and make the forms in the house stand out clearly" (Conze, *Buddhist Scriptures* 155). If the journey through the cave is a metaphor for spiritual development, then reaching the point of no return suggests the impossibility of regressing or relapsing into the earlier state of ignorance; it does not imply that further progress is no longer possible.

As pilgrims journeying through the cave prison of the manifest world, the man and the child stand in stark contrast to a character they encounter on the road, a purblind old man who calls himself Ely and seems to embody the narrow-minded skepticism of Plato's "cave-dwellers." Ely is a nihilistic, solipsistic materialist, claiming that "when you die it's the same as if everybody else did too" (170). Not only does he actively deny the possibility of any kind of transcendence, but his words reveal an inherent selfishness and lack of empathy; it is safe to conclude that a man who believes such a thing would never sacrifice himself to save anyone else. The child, whose compassion and spirituality place him on the opposite end of the spectrum, convinces his reluctant father to give Ely some of their food. The father instructs the old man to express gratitude to the child: "You should thank him you know. . . . I wouldnt have given you anything." Ely refuses to do so, echoing the father's words in his retort: "I wouldnt have given him mine" (173). Ely's non sequitur shows not only that he is incapable of compassion himself but, worse still, that he does not even value it in others.

Despite Ely's ungracious behavior, the child has no regrets about sharing their meager supplies. The father gently chastises the boy, insisting, "When we're out of food you'll have more time to think about it," but the boy replies, "I know. But I wont remember it the way you do" (174). The father differs from Ely in that even though he is incapable of attaining, or even fully understanding, the child's degree of compassion, he can at least see its worth. When Ely asks if his lack of gratitude will hurt the child's feelings, the father replies, "No. That's not why he did it. . . . You wouldn't understand. . . . I'm not sure I do." Ely suggests that maybe the child "believes in God," but the man replies that he doesn't "know what [the child] believes in" (173). What the man does know is that the child's spirituality is deep and abiding. Ely suggests that the boy will "get over it," referring to his faith, but the man replies, "No he wont" (174). While Ely's rejection of any form of spirituality is already evident in his selfish behavior, he confirms his position as a materialist when he explicitly denies the existence of divinity, claiming, "There is no God and we are his prophets" (170). Ely's oxymoronic words—a direct inversion of the Islamic *shahada*, "There is no God but Allah and Muhammad is his Prophet"—function as a creed professing his nihilism. The father locates the existence of the divine in the figure of his son and he tries to impart this wisdom to Ely:

"What if I said that he's a god?" The old man bluntly rejects such a notion, shaking his head in disagreement and explaining, "I'm past all that now. Have been for years. Where men cant live gods fare no better" (172). Ely's claim that gods can exist only if there are human beings to believe in them is in direct contradiction to the words of the ex-priest in *The Crossing*, who insists that "God needs no witness" (158). Seeing as Ely has been portrayed as an unlikeable and untrustworthy character, while the ex-priest in *The Crossing* is depicted as a wise and compassionate hermit, it is unlikely that Ely's nihilistic pessimism is to be read as the voice of *The Road*.

Although the old man claims that his name is Ely, when questioned, he admits that it is not his "real name" (172). Ely is the only named character within the novel, and this unique position emphasizes the significance of his alias. The name Ely carries various Old Testament connotations, evoking not only the prophet Elijah, whose name means "My God is Yahweh" in Hebrew, but also the Aramaic word "Eli," meaning "my God," and even the lesser known Eli who appears in the Book of Samuel as the high priest of Shiloh, a biblical city where the Ark of the Covenant was located (Coogan 23). Ely's name, however, is false; therefore we may conclude that he is also a false prophet and a false high priest. Furthermore, he is blind, like the pale creature in the father's cave dream. Although in McCarthy's novels blindness is often used to signify spiritual wisdom, Ely and the cave creature seem to be the exception, for they have neither physical sight nor spiritual insight.[30]

The Valentinian Gnostics distinguished between three kinds of people: the spiritual pneumatics, who "immediately grasped the message" of gnosis; the cerebral psychics (in the sense of "psyche"), who "needed some extra guidance"; and the material hylics, who had "no spirituality in them" (Thomassen 111). Judging by the various degrees of spiritual development, or lack thereof, I would tentatively argue that the child represents the pneumatic type, the father the psychic, and Ely the hylic. The Valentinians believed that when the world finally came to an end, the hylics "would go back to what they ultimately came from, and that was matter.... They would go back to the non-existence which they really are" (Thomassen 112). It seems significant, then, that when the father last sees Ely, he is "dwindling on the road behind them . . . dark and bent and spider thin and soon to vanish forever" (174). It is noteworthy that when used as a verb, to "ely" means "to disappear gradually from sight" (*OED*). The fact that the boy "never looked back at all" is unusual in itself, as he insists on looking back at the would-be thief of their shopping cart. From a Gnostic perspective, it would seem that the child has quietly given up on Ely, knowing that he cannot be redeemed.

The narrative development of the novel refutes Ely's pessimistic nihilism, justifying and affirming the protagonists' faith in the symbolic fire of goodness, compassion, and spirituality. As the father nears death, the child grows anxious, but so strong are his empathy and selflessness that he externalizes his personal fears to include the plight of the little boy he glimpsed earlier in the novel: "Do you remember that little boy, Papa? ... Do you think he's all right that little boy? ... Do you think he was lost? ... I'm scared that he was lost." Of course, these are also the child's own fears regarding the life that awaits him after his father's death, but it is nevertheless significant that he never stops thinking about the well-being of others. The father replies, "No. I don't think he was lost. . . . I think he's all right." Once again, these words operate on a dual level, not only referring to the welfare of the little boy, but also serving to reassure the child about his own future. The child persists, "But who will find him if he's lost? Who will find the little boy?" The father utters his final words: "Goodness will find the little boy. It always has. It will again" (281). These dying words are imbued with a visionary, prophetic quality, verified by the fact that goodness does indeed find the little boy in the form of a family of "good guys," a man, a woman, and a little boy and girl who are also "carrying the fire" (282, 283).

Earlier in the novel the disillusioned father had questioned his own quest to preserve the fire: "Do you think that your fathers are watching? That they weigh you in their ledgerbook? Against what? There is no book and your fathers are dead in the ground" (196). These words display the same pessimistic nihilism expressed by Ely, rejecting not only the possibility of life after death and the existence of divine guidance but also the notion that there will be karmic consequences for one's earthly actions. This view fueled much of the father's survivalist tendencies, apparent in his treatment of the would-be thief and his reluctance to share food with Ely or to aid the man who had been struck by lightning. Under the guiding influence of the child's compassion, however, the man comes to suspect that "maybe they are watching. . . . They are watching for a thing that even death cannot undo and if they do not see it they will turn away from us and they will not come back" (210).[31] As Allen Josephs argues, the passage compels the reader to wonder whether "they" are "ghost, angels, archons, aeons," or "gods," but there "is no answer and all that is clear is the quandary itself, yet the very nature of the question, at once rhetorical and pointed, seems to signal some Eliot-like turning, however bleakly."[32] Josephs asks whether it is "some spark of divinity—the 'thing that even death cannot undo'—that they must see in order not to turn away?" (137). Although the nature of the unspecified "they" remains ambiguous, the passage implies that some form of Akashic ledger book does exist and that our actions carry spiritual consequences. Furthermore, it is implied that those who carry the fire will receive some form of otherworldly guidance and protection. This does not necessarily consist of earthly survival; although it manifests itself in that form for the child, it does not do so for the father. Nevertheless, the father dies a peaceful death, secure in the knowledge that "goodness" will find his child.

It is significant that the man refers to the mysterious "they" as "fathers," ancestors who are not "dead in the ground" but who continue to watch over us (196). The man's revelation foreshadows the relationship that the son will continue to have with his dead father. Before the man dies, he tells the child, "If I'm not here you can still talk to me. You can talk to me and I'll talk to you. You'll see.... You have to make it like talk that you imagine. And you'll hear me" (279). When the man dies, the child kneels weeping over his body and promises, "I'll talk to you every day.... And I won't forget. No matter what." The child keeps his promise even after he begins his new life with the family that takes him in as their own: "He tried to talk to God but the best thing was to talk to his father and he did talk to him and he didn't forget" (286).[33] The "thing that even death cannot undo" (210) can be summed up in the metaphor of the divine fire, but it is also apparent in the death-defying power of the selfless, eternal, and sacred bond that we find between the two protagonists.

The woman who becomes the child's new mother figure reassures him "that it was all right" to talk to his father instead of God, because "the breath of God was his breath yet though it pass from man to man through all time" (286). Not only do the woman's words evoke the concept of the pneuma in its dual connotations of "breath" and "spirit," but they simultaneously point to an understanding of the divine that is in accord with the teachings of the Perennial Philosophy, namely that the individual spirit is "identical with the divine Spirit that is the Ground of all being" (Huxley 38). According to the Perennial Philosophy, "the spirit of man, itself essentially divine, is capable of immediate communication with God, the One Reality" (Underhill 24). Gnosticism posits the same unity between the alien God and the pneuma; despite the fact that the alien God "remains transcendent... it is immanent in the form of the divine spark active in creation" (Wagner and Flannery-Dailey 217). In Gnostic thought, "self knowledge is knowledge of God," because "the self and the divine are identical" (Pagels, *Gnostic Gospels* xx). Therefore, when spirit reaches out to spirit, as when the child reaches out to his father, it is a form of divine communion.

The subtle stains of mysticism that have informed much of the novel are brought into sharp relief in the final paragraph. The narrator shifts the perspective away from the personal and immediate to the universal and the timeless: "Once there were brook trout in the streams in the mountains. You could see them standing in the amber current where the white edges of their fins wimpled softly in the flow. They smelled of moss in your hand. Polished and muscular and torsional. On their backs were vermiculate patterns that were maps of the world in its becoming. Maps and mazes. Of a thing which could not be put back. Not be made right again. In the deep glens where they lived all things were older than man and they hummed of mystery" (287). The passage is striking not only for its lyricism and beauty but also for the complex profundity of its message.[34] At first glance this reads like an elegy for the lost world or an ecological warning, a prophetic voice from the future reminding the readers of the present to take care of the environment. Such a reading, however, is hampered by the fact that we are never told that the human race was responsible for the apocalyptic disaster. After all, if the world is to be destroyed by a meteorite, then there is nothing we can do about it. If we read the passage carefully, it becomes apparent that the "thing which could not be put back," that could "not be made right again," is not the destruction of the world but "the world in its becoming," that is, creation itself.

I have thus far come across two other critics who interpret the final paragraph in this manner. Thomas Schaub points out that the "passage has been read to mean that following the devastation of the world, the world could not be made right again"; however, "the grammar of reference and antecedent actually suggests something quite different," namely that "the thing which could not be put back is 'the world in its becoming,' not the world accomplished and destroyed" (165–66). Sean Pryor also argues that the "event which cannot be cancelled or corrected is not that shear of light, but the world itself, its creation. According to some more fundamental fall, the world was always already wrong" (38). Although neither Schaub nor Pryor reads the novel through the lens of Gnosticism, their respective interpretations of the final passage are completely in line with the Gnostic "conviction" that "there is too much evil and pain and death in the world, and so there must have been something wrong with creation" (Barnstone and Meyers 8). The Gnostic Gospel of Philip, for example, teaches that "the world came about through a mistake" (qtd. in Pearson 177). All schools of Gnosticism generally agree that creation was a "process initiated by error" (Jonas 301). This view of things is also apparent in the cosmogony of Jacob Boehme, whose writing, according to Hans Martensen, betrays "the conviction that all this cannot have belonged to God's original creative order; but that it represents a state in which the earth, created of God, became the scene of a catastrophe, a revolt in the spiritual world, which had transplanted itself to nature as an appalling tempest in the morning of time" (138). Nicolas Berdyaev also argues that Boehme "wants to understand the mystery of the creation of the universe as a tragedy not merely human but divine as well" (xv).[35] The final passage of *The Road* is indeed elegiac; however, it is not an elegy for the destroyed world but rather one for some perfected state of being before the fatal flaw of creation.

Despite the anticosmic vision presented in *The Road*, and indeed throughout McCarthy's novels, the image of the brook trout in the mountain stream remains hauntingly beautiful; however, as in *All the Pretty Horses*, where "the world's pain and its beauty" are described as being "in a relationship of diverging equity," this beauty comes at a "terrible cost" (282). This inextricable relationship between beauty and pain finds its objective correlative in the "vermiculate patterns" on the backs of the trout. "Vermiculated" refers to "worm-eaten," that is, "covered with markings resembling those made by the gnawing of worms" (*OED*). There is no doubt that these patterns are aesthetically pleasing, complementing the "white edges of their fins" that "wimpled softly" in the "amber current," but they also evoke disease, devouring, decay, and death, the very things that were initially kept hidden from the young Prince Gautama in a futile attempt to change the destiny that prophesied his becoming the Buddha (Conze, *Buddhist Scriptures* 41). The connotations of vermiculate also evoke the Gnostic imagery of William Blake's "The Sick Rose":

> O Rose thou art sick.
> The invisible worm,
> That flies in the night
> In the howling storm:
> Has found out thy bed

Of crimson joy:
And his dark secret love
Does thy life destroy.
(23)

The "invisible worm" is the fundamental cosmic flaw, burrowed deep into the heart of creation, devouring beauty and joy and bringing sickness and death.

The final passage of the novel suggests that the macrocosmic process of creation is encapsulated in the microcosmic details of created things; the "vermiculate patterns" on the backs of the trout depict "maps of the world in its becoming" (287). These "maps and mazes" (287) suggest a Buddhist mandala, "a diagram which shows deities in their spiritual or cosmic connections, and . . . is used as a basis for winning insight into the spiritual law which is thus represented" (Conze, *Buddhism* 187). Meditating on mandalas facilitates enlightenment and, in this sense, the mandala functions as a map, showing the way out of the maze of saṃsāra. For Buddhists, the very fact that there *is* a way out mitigates the darkness of existence. Huston Smith explains that, "contrary to the opinion of many interpreters, Buddha's philosophy was not ultimately pessimistic," precisely because the "Buddha gave his life to demonstrating how well-being might be attained" (*Religions of Man* 111). It is possible that the reference to "maps and mazes" in the final paragraph of *The Road* serves as a Gnostic reminder that even though creation is fundamentally flawed and "[can]not be made right again" (287), it is nevertheless possible to escape from the cosmic prison of the material world.

The novel ends not with an image of worm-eaten beauty but rather with the humming of mystery.[36] Jay Ellis suggests that this "could be the remembered sound, the vibrations of the smallest strings McCarthy's colleagues at the Santa Fe Institute still imagine might hold the universe together" ("Another Sense of Ending" 36). This concept is by no means solely the invention of modern physics but finds its parallel in the Hindu *Māndūkya Upanishad* as the divine, cosmic "vibration manifesting as the sound 'OM.'" "OM" is "the reflection of absolute reality. OM is 'Ādi Ānadi'—without beginning or end" (Maheshwarananda 15). Swami Krishnananda explains that "OM is not merely a chant or recitation, a word of a part of human language. . . . It is something which exists by its own right. . . . We do not create OM by a chanting of it, but we only produce a vibration sympathetic with the vibration that is already there by its own right and which is called

OM" (17). The humming "of mystery" with which *The Road* concludes is likewise independent of human beings, far "older than man," existing in its own right as a manifestation of the Absolute (287).

The word "mystery" is laden with meaning, suggesting a "mystical presence or nature," "mystical significance," a "religious truth known or understood only by divine revelation," a "doctrine of faith," "an enigma," or a "secret rite" (*OED*). In postclassical Latin, mystery may also refer to the *mysterium iniquitatis* (mystery of iniquity), which, like all of McCarthy's novels, is concerned with "the mystery of the existence of evil," or "any instance of extreme and inexplicable suffering" (*OED*). In a specifically Christian context, mystery refers to "an ordinance, rite, or sacrament," as well as "the consecrated elements used in the Eucharist." Mystery in this context can also refer to "an incident in the life of Christ, or a saint, regarded as a subject for contemplation or as having mystical significance" (*OED*). In *The Road*, these concepts have been removed from the traditional Christian context and applied to the child. As I have already argued, the son in *The Road* is frequently likened to a Christlike savior, albeit in a manner more in line with Gnostic Christianity than traditional doctrine. In this sense, *The Road* can be read as a mystery novel, recounting the mystically significant life of the divine child. "Mystery" is both literally and figuratively the final word of *The Road*; its various connotations embody all of the themes developed throughout the novel and, indeed, the essence of the Perennial Philosophy underlying all of Cormac McCarthy's works.

Notes

INTRODUCTION

1. In *The Varieties of Religious Experience*, William James concludes that the "religious life" can be summed up, "in the broadest possible way," as possessing the following characteristics:

    1. That the visible world is a part of a more spiritual universe from which it draws its chief significance.
    2. That union or harmonious relation with that higher universe is our true end.
    3. That prayer or inner communion with the spirit thereof—be that spirit "God" or "law"—is a process wherein work is really done, and spiritual energy flows in and produces effects, psychological or material, within the phenomenal world. (352)

2. According to Hans Jonas, "the gnostic systems compounded everything—oriental mythologies, astrological doctrines, Iranian theology, elements of Jewish traditions, whether Biblical, rabbinical, or occult, Christian salvation-eschatology, Platonic terms and concepts" (25). Jonas explains, "Since in the material of its representation Gnosticism actually is a product of syncretism, each of these theories can be supported from the sources and none of them is satisfactory alone; but neither is the combination of all of them, which would make Gnosticism out to be a mere mosaic of these elements and so miss its autonomous essence" (33). Karen King writes, "History of religion scholars came to the astonishing conclusion that Gnosticism was an independent religion whose origin lay, not in deviant Christian heresy, but in pre-Christian, Oriental myth and cultic piety" (71). Similarly, Kurt Rudolph argues that "the gnostic documents are often compositions and even compilations from the mythological or religious ideas of the most varied regions of religion and culture: from Greek, Jewish, Iranian, Christian (in Manicheism also Indian and from the Far East)." Rudolph ascribes this to the "Hellenistic syncretism" of "Greek and Oriental traditions and ideas subsequent to the conquests of Alexander the Great" (54).
3. The phrase is a saying of St. Thomas Aquinas (*Summa Theologica* II.2, q. 26, art. 4).
4. Since Dianne Luce has already given us a detailed reading of the Gnostic elements in McCarthy's early novels—most notably *Outer Dark*—in *Reading the World: Cormac McCarthy's Tennessee Period*, it seemed appropriate for me to concentrate on the works not covered in Luce's book. Furthermore, Luce focuses mainly on Gnosticism, Platonism, and existentialism, whereas I wish to expand

this perspective by also drawing on the Eastern and Western traditions of the Perennial Philosophy.
5. For example, the Pūrva Mīmāṃsā school of Indian philosophy was "strongly concerned with textual exegesis, and consequently gave rise to the study of philology and the philosophy of language" (Scharf 195).
6. Medieval theologians read the Old Testament according to the fourfold interpretation: "The commentator can distinguish between the literal (or historical) sense of a text and its spiritual sense, which is subdivided into three: the allegorical (or typological) sense states the Good News prefigured in the sacred history, the tropological (or moral) sense draws a lesson from it for this life, the anagogical sense explains what the letter says about man's last end" (Vauchez and Dobson 43). St. Augustine set forth the fourfold division in *De Genesi ad litteram* (*The Literal Meaning of Genesis*): "In all the sacred books, we should consider eternal truths that are taught, the facts that are narrated, the future events that are predicted, and the precepts or counsels that are given" (19). In the "Epistle to Cangrande della Scala," Dante explains that his own work is informed by the fourfold vision, which he illustrates with an example:

> The meaning of this work is not simple . . . for we obtain one meaning from the letter of it and another from that which the letter signifies; and the first is called the literal, but the other allegorical or mystical. And to make this matter of treatment clearer, it may be studied in the verse: "When Israel came out of Egypt and the House of Jacob from among a strange people, Judah was his sanctuary and Israel his dominion." For if we regard the letter alone, what is set before us is the exodus of the Children of Israel from Egypt in the days of Moses; if the allegory, our redemption wrought by Christ; if the moral sense, we are shown the conversion of the soul from the grief and wretchedness of sin to the state of grace; if the anagogical, we are shown the departure of the holy soul from the thralldom of this corruption to the liberty of eternal glory. (14–15)

CHAPTER 1

1. Other critics have also noted the overwhelming hostility of McCarthy's landscapes. John Beck argues, "One way or another, deserts signal and invite annihilation. The desert is evidence of cosmic indifference or, worse, of an actual hostility toward human life, a mineral disdain for the vulnerability of the organic" (210). John Lewis Longley Jr. writes, "The landscape in *Blood Meridian* is like the landscape on the moon, or like the surface of the earth will be after a prolonged nuclear winter when everything is dead. On the prosaic level of factual realism, this landscape is simply the Great American Desert—desolate, arid,

littered with the bones of animals and men.... At a wider and deeper level, this landscape is the landscape of Hell—the inevitable configuration of a world without Grace" (748). In *Cormac McCarthy's Western Novels*, Barcley Owens concedes that hostile landscapes are a "favourite motif" (5) in McCarthy's writing but points out that nature serves only as a mirror to human depravity, because "man reflects the violent character of a brutal environment" (7). Owens goes on to argue, "As one of the most violent novels in contemporary American literature, *Blood Meridian* parallels its times. The mirror of art that McCarthy holds up to the nineteenth century reflects the ugliness of our time as well" (20). Arguing along the same lines, Edwin Arnold describes *Blood Meridian* as "an extended nightmare of history," adding that to "read it is to enter the darker places of the imagination, to witness the malignity of humankind at its worst" ("Go to Sleep" 44). John Cant writes that while "the postmodern critic ... rejects the essentialist notion of a fixed human nature ... McCarthy's depiction of various of his protagonists 'in extremis' makes it clear that he believes in an all too powerful 'essential' human nature and that violence is inherent to that essence" (5).
2. Dianne Luce also argues that "Gnostic associations of the sun with a malevolent cosmic force dominate the solar imagery of McCarthy's desert novel" (*Reading the World* 78).
3. It is possible that McCarthy picked up this image from Carl Gustav Jung, who in one famous case

> tells of a schizophrenic patient who said "he could see an erect phallus on the sun. When he moved his head from side to side, he said, the sun's phallus moved with it, *and that was where the wind came from.*" Jung found a remarkably similar image in a liturgy of the Mithraic religion, a mystery cult of late antiquity (which he had in a translation by Mead). The Mithraic text reads, "And likewise the so-called tube, the origin of the ministering wind. For you will see hanging down from the disc of the sun something that looks like a tube." (Smoley 161)

The likelihood of the Jungian influence is compounded by the fact that, later in the novel, the narrative voice describes how "a wind was blowing out of the sun where it sat squat and pulsing at the eastern reaches of the earth" (227). The remarkable similarity between these passages in *Blood Meridian* and the Mithraic Phallus Solaris must be deliberate, for McCarthy's usage of the words "squat" and "pulsing" occurs in both instances, thus consciously linking the two passages together. Edwin Arnold also comments on Jung's influence on McCarthy, pointing out that "McCarthy's use of dreams seems closer to the Jungian concept than to the Freudian, for they are often 'mystical' in their manner" ("Go to Sleep" 40).

4. The last pagan emperor of Rome, Flavius Claudius Iulianus, or Julian II (AD 331/2–363) was also a devout Mithraist and Neo-Platonist. In his philosophically and spiritually subtle oration, *Hymn to King Helios*, Julian describes how the visible sun is a symbolic manifestation of "Helios," that is, of Plato's "Good" (Wright 348–435).

5. The vast, indifferent, and often downright malevolent universe is a frequent topic of contemplation in McCarthy's novels. In *Suttree*, we find descriptions of the "cold indifferent dark, the blind stars beaded on their tracks and mitered satellites and geared and pinioned planets all reeling through the black of space" (284). The "enormity of the universe" fills Suttree "with a strange sweet woe" (353). In *All the Pretty Horses*, as John Grady listens "to the wind in the emptiness" and watches "the stars trace the arc of the hemisphere and die in the darkness at the edge of the world," he feels that "the agony in his heart was like a stake" (256). In *The Crossing*, perhaps McCarthy's most mystical novel, Billy Parham looks into the eyes of the she-wolf and sees a "world burning on the shore of an unknowable void" (73–74). In *The Road*, the man sees "the absolute truth of the world. The cold relentless circling of the intestate earth. Darkness implacable. The blind dogs of the sun in their running. The crushing black vacuum of the universe" (130). Later in the same novel, the narrative voice describes how the "earth went trundling past the sun and returned again as trackless and as unremarked as the path of any nameless sisterworld in the ancient dark beyond" (181).

6. John Sepich counts over ninety direct and indirect references to a "hallucinatory void," arguing that "the scale of the landscape often leads into passages in which a greater 'void,' beyond the earth, is the intended allusion" (*Notes* 160). This void beyond the earth is both the void of outer space and the metaphysical void within the human being. Similarly, Sara Spurgeon writes, "McCarthy's earth in *Blood Meridian* and many other works is hollow, full of empty caves and echoing caverns, at once womb and tomb, signifying the hollowness at the heart of all myths" (100).

7. Sproule's predicament echoes Keats's "Ode to a Nightingale": "Through the sad heart of Ruth, when, sick for home, / She stood in tears amid the alien corn" (lines 66–67).

8. In the Egyptian *Book of the Dead*, Anubis "is shown in the vignettes or illustrations attending the weighing of the heart ceremony in the Hall of the Two Truths. Anubis stands next to the scale where the heart of the mummy is weighed to make sure it is as light as the feather of truth" (Remler 17).

9. McCarthy will later develop these ideas in *The Road*, where bands of cannibals roam the apocalyptic wasteland, their "gray and rotting teeth" claggy "with human flesh" (75).

10. The idea that the world has always been an evil place is another of McCarthy's recurring themes. In *Outer Dark*, the tinker tells Rinthy, "I've seen the meanness

of humans till I don't know why God ain't put out the sun and gone away" (192). In *Child of God*, the deputy asks an old man if he thinks "people was meaner then than they are now." The old man replies, "No.... I don't. I think people are the same from the day God first made one" (168). In *Suttree*, the derelict railroader complains that he "never knowed such a place for meanness" as this world, but when Suttree asks if it were "ever any different," the railroader replies, "No. I reckon not" (180). In *All the Pretty Horses*, Alfonsa proclaims, "What is constant in history is greed and foolishness and a love of blood" (239). However, McCarthy subverts this idea in *No Country for Old Men*, making Sheriff Bell wonder if perhaps there is a new breed of evil: "I thought I'd never seen a person like that and it got me to wonderin if maybe he was some new kind" (5).
11. Sigmund Freud (1856–1939) arrived at a similar view of humanity toward the end of his life. In *Civilization and Its Discontents*, he argued,

> The element of truth behind all this, which people are so ready to disavow, is that men are not gentle creatures who want to be loved, and who at the most can defend themselves if they are attacked; they are, on the contrary, creatures among whose instinctual endowements is to be reckoned a powerful share of aggressiveness. As a result, their neighbour is for them not only a potential helper or sexual object, but also someone who tempts them to satisfy their aggressiveness on him, to exploit his capacity for work without compensation, to use him sexually without his consent, to seize his possessions, to humiliate him, to cause him pain, to torture and kill him. *Homo homini lupus*. Who, in the face of all his experience of life and of history, will have the courage to dispute this assertion? (58)

12. This passage echoes a similar theme in McCarthy's *Suttree*, where the protagonist wonders, "Am I a monster, are there monsters in me?" (366). *Blood Meridian*'s reference to the "whited regions of maps where monsters do live" also seems to echo the question put forward by the narrative voice in *Suttree*, "Are there dragons in the wings of the world?" (29). Comparing these two passages, Christopher Campbell argues, "There *are* dragons in the wings of the world, and in *Blood Meridian* they ride upon horses" (47).
13. The quintessentially Gnostic horror felt at the contemplation of the fact that this is a planet on which everything devours everything else is vividly expressed by Ernest Becker in *The Denial of Death*:

> What are we to make of creation in which the routine activity is for organisms to be tearing others apart with teeth of all types—biting, grinding flesh, plant stalks, bones between molars, pushing the pulp greedily down the gullet with delight, incorporating its essence into

one's own organisations, and then excreting with foul stench and gasses the residue. Everyone reaching out to incorporate others who are edible to him.... Creation is a nightmare spectacular taking place on a planet that has been soaked for hundreds of millions of years in the blood of its creatures. The soberest conclusion that we could make about what has actually been taking place on the planet for about three billion years is that it is being turned into a vast pit of fertilizer. (282–83)

14. David Kushner writes, "While [McCarthy] reserves high praises for a few contemporary narratives ('*Fear and Loathing in Las Vegas* is a classic of our time'), his list of great novels stops at four: *Ulysses*, *The Brothers Karamazov*, *The Sound and The Fury* and his favourite, *Moby-Dick*. Like his own work, they explore themes of life and death with both philosophical and artful precision" (44).

15. In *Life and Fate*, one of Grossman's characters contemplates the evil inherent in existence:

> Once, when I lived in the Northern forests, I thought that good was to be found neither in man, nor in the predatory world of animals and insects, but in the silent kingdom of the trees. Far from it! I saw the forest's slow movement, the treacherous way it battled against grass and bushes for each inch of soil.... This is the life of the forest—a constant struggle of everything against everything. Only the blind conceive of the kingdom of the trees and grass as the world of good.... Is it that life itself is evil? (407)

16. The passage evokes the description of the supernatural "grim triune" (129) in *Outer Dark*. The three mysterious figures walk at sunset, "until they had gone on for such a time as saw the sun down altogether and they moved in shadow altogether which suited them very well" (3).

17. McCarthy's novels often call into doubt the nature of the creator of this world. In *Suttree*, for example, the protagonist asks, "What deity in the realms of dementia, what rabid god decocted out of the smoking lobes of hydrophobia could have devised a keeping place for souls so poor as is this flesh. This mawky worm-bent tabernacle" (130). Later, as Suttree contemplates the death of his young son, he asks, "What could a child know of the darkness of God's plan?" (154). Perhaps the ragpicker says it best, telling Suttree, "I always figured they was a God... I just never did like him" (147). In *All the Pretty Horses*, Alfonsa refuses to "believe in a God who could permit such injustice... in a world of his own making" (232). John Grady feels that he has "no reason to be afraid of God," adding that he even has "a bone or two to pick with Him" (272). In *The Crossing*, an ex-priest recalls how he was "seeking evidence for the hand of God in the

world" and that he had "come to believe that hand a wrathful one" (142). Similarly, while recounting the tale of the heretic, he explains, "It was never that this man ceased to believe in God. No. It was rather that he came to believe terrible things of Him" (148). Finally, in *The Road*, the unnamed protagonist cannot bring himself to believe that the world he finds himself in could be the will of a benevolent God: "He raised his face to the paling day. Are you there? he whispered. Will I see you at the last? Have you a neck by which to throttle you? Have you a heart? Damn you eternally have you a soul? Oh God, he whispered. Oh God" (11–12). These inherently Gnostic attacks on the creator of this world constitute a running theme throughout McCarthy's fiction.
18. McCarthy later raises the same idea in *All the Pretty Horses*, where John Grady imagines "the pain of the world to be like some formless parasitic being seeking out the warmth of human souls wherein to incubate" and comes to the realization "that it was mindless and so had no way to know the limits of those souls and what he feared was that there might be no limits" (256–57). Again, the mindlessness here is that of a creature and does not suggest a lack of agency, for this parasitic being actively seeks out "the warmth of human souls" like a larva burrowing into its host. The concept of evil as having a parasitic nature is emphasized within *Blood Meridian* in the image of dead babies hung from the "broken stobs of mesquite." Their bodies are described as "bald and pale and bloated, larval to some unreckonable being" (57). The horror of this image does not rely solely on the portrayal of the slaughter of innocents; the babies themselves are hideous and "larval," as though they were waiting to hatch and spawn further evils.

CHAPTER 2

1. The mystery of the judge continues to be the prime focus of contention among McCarthy's critics, many of whom have commented on the mysterious and paranormal aspect of the judge's nature. Edwin Arnold notes that the judge is no ordinary human being, but rather "of a supernatural kind, like some incubus or terrible force" that "cannot be adequately explained through science or logic" ("Go to Sleep" 45–46). John Sepich writes, "Holden comes out of the archetypes" (*Notes* 141). Barcley Owens credits the judge with "preternatural knowledge and unlimited powers," arguing that there "is no David to stand up to this Goliath" (17, 62).
2. It is interesting that McCarthy has linked the kid's life to his own. The kid's birth in 1833 corresponds to McCarthy's birth in 1933, while the forty-five-year-old "kid's" death in 1878 is linked to the year 1978, in which a forty-five-year-old McCarthy underwent a divorce from his second wife, Anne DeLisle, an event that may well have been traumatic (see "Chronology" in Jarrett xiii–xiv).

3. Chris Dacus interprets the judge's position as the thirteenth member of the gang in light of a Gnostic scripture entitled "The Reality of the Archons." Dacus argues that "there are twelve rulers in addition to Yaldabaoth [the demiurge], making a total of thirteen archons in this Gnostic tract. . . . Given the other Gnostic allusions present in BM, this seems to be a clear reference to this Gnostic text" (13–14).
4. Milton describes the creation of gunpowder in *Paradise Lost*:

> Th' originals of Nature in their crude
> Conception; Sulphurous and Nitrous Foame
> They found, they mingl'd, and with suttle Art,
> Concocted and adusted they reduc'd
> To blackest grain
> (book VI, lines 511–15)

5. Though the judge displays many demonic characteristics, he also transcends the role played by the devil in Judeo-Christian traditions and takes on godlike attributes. Vereen Bell writes that if the judge "is Satan, he may as well be God also, for in this context the two are not conceived as inversions of one another" (*Achievement* 122). Harold Bloom argues that *Blood Meridian* reads like "a post-Homeric quest, where the various heroes (or thugs) have a disguised god among them, which appears to be the Judge's Herculean role" (*How to Read* 260). Barcley Owens identifies the judge with Shiva, as well as with Lucifer and Yahweh, describing Holden as a "mad, murdering god" (62). Christopher Douglas argues that *Blood Meridian* "explores the flaw in the design of the world and implicates the Christian God" and that the judge "works within that flaw and represents it" (17). Douglas's reading places the judge in a sinister alliance with the creator God, rather than in the traditionally satanic role of opposition and rebellion. Though Douglas does not refer to Gnosticism directly, his theory regarding the "flaw in the design of the world" and the judge's position in relation to that flaw nevertheless bears a close resemblance to a Gnostic world view.
6. Chris Dacus argues that "the judge is a kind of prime number (a number divisible by only itself and one). He cannot be 'divided' back into his origins because he does not have an origin but is an aspect of eternity which is always present; he cannot be reduced into something smaller, more manageable" (11).
7. According to Gnostic theology, there is only one demiurge (though he is sometimes given the title of chief archon), and he is the entity responsible for the creation of the manifest world. Though the archons rule over creation, they ultimately answer to the demiurge, as the angelic host answers to the biblical God. Gnostic texts speak of "demons, gods or spirits, who often bear the name 'rulers' or 'commanders' (archons); they sometimes form entire kingdoms with such an

'archon' at the head. The 'chief archon' and real ruler of the world ... is usually identical with the creator of the world (*demiurgeous*)" (Rudolph 67–68).

8. In another sense, the judge's lack of origins does not eliminate the Gnostic interpretation but actually strengthens it, for although there are two schools of Gnostic thought that deal with the origins of evil, the Manichean or dualist school argues that evil always was and always will be, for it too is "without terminus or origin" (*Blood Meridian* 310). The concept of an evil without origins corresponds to the dualistic Iranian school of Gnostic thought, most notably to that of the Manicheans, who believed that good and evil exist as eternally opposed forces of light and darkness that can never be reconciled. Kurt Rudolph explains that, according to the Manichean system, "there are two basic principles existing from the very beginning, mythologically described as the kingdom of light and the kingdom of darkness, which are brought into contact with one another almost by accident and so set the baleful history of the world into motion" (65). After the collapse of the manifest world, "the Archons shall henceforth dwell in their nether regions, but the Father [the alien God] in the upper regions after he has taken back unto himself his own" (qtd. in Jonas 63). Thus, according to the dualist Gnostics, even when the last spirit, or pneuma, returns to its divine origins and the manifest cosmos draws to an end, the eternal forces of evil will continue to exist in a realm of darkness, totally separate from the divine realm of light.

    Opposed to this is the more subtle, monistic Syrian-Egyptian school of Gnostic thought, as typified by the Valentinians, which teaches that evil and darkness emerged out of "the downward movement of the divine: a guilty 'inclination' of the Soul (as a mythical entity) toward the lower realms, with various motivations such as curiosity, vanity, sensual desire," or in some cases, "ignorance" (Jonas 236). In other words, a series of emanations, resulting in "a graduated decline from the highest deity [the alien God] is the cause of the origin of the evil and dark powers" (Rudolph 65). The idea that McCarthy has portrayed the judge from a dualist perspective of eternal evil, rather than from a nondualist position of gradual emanation, has also been put forward by Leo Daugherty, who writes that *Blood Meridian* "exemplifies" the Manichean form of Gnosticism and that what the Manichean Gnostics "saw is what we see in the world of *Blood Meridian*" (162). Dianne Luce also argues that "the Manichean idea of an original principle of darkness, and oppositional force to the Light of the Unknown God seems more consistent with McCarthy's treatment of evil in his novels" (*Reading the World* 68). Thus McCarthy's portrayal of the judge's lack of origins strongly suggests the Manichean, or dualist, perception of evil and strengthens the judge's identification with Gnostic archons.

9. *Blood Meridian* is not the first novel in which McCarthy employs archon-like characters; the three demonic figures in *Outer Dark* have much in common with the judge. When Culla Holme first meets the "grim triune" (130), their leader

seems "to be seated in the fire itself, cradling the flames to his body as if there were something there beyond all warming" (179), prefiguring the judge's own demonic kinship with flames. The demonic associations are further emphasized by the fact that one of the leader's boots is "cleft from tongue to toe like a hoof" (176), suggesting the cloven hooves of the devil. Just as the judge and the Glanton gang in *Blood Meridian* are a dark parody of Jesus and the disciples, the evil trio in *Outer Dark* functions as a dark parody of the Holy Trinity. As William Spencer argues, this "terrible trio, this unholy trinity, parodies the theological concept of a triune God" (69). According to Spencer, the leader of the trio is a "parodic counterpart to Yahweh." Spencer cites examples from the novel in which the leader "manipulates the townspeople" into retributive action or simply deals out punishments himself, arguing that, "like the Father of the Holy Trinity," the leader acts as a judge and as a dispenser of justice" (74). If, however, one reads the work from a Gnostic perspective, then the leader of the trio may be regarded as the demiurge himself.

10. "For we wrestle not against flesh and blood, but against principalities, against powers, against the rulers of the darkness of this world, against spiritual wickedness in high places" (Ephesians 6:12). This biblical reference is often misinterpreted to mean that we struggle against human corruption in high places of church and state. According to the translator's notes in the King James Bible, however, "spiritual" refers to "wicked spirits" and "high places" refers to "heavenly," rather than earthly, positions of power.

11. A Bodhisattva is one who sets out to become a Buddha in order to free all sentient beings from saṃsāra and lead them into Nirvāṇa. Edward Conze writes, "He is a Buddha-to-be, one who wishes to become a Buddha, that is to say, an Enlightened One" (*Buddhism* 125). Even after attaining enlightenment, the Bodhisattva chooses to remain in the world of manifest illusion, reincarnating life after life and refusing to enter the state of Nirvāṇa until every living entity has escaped from the cycle of birth and rebirth.

12. The trope of fetters, tethers, and puppet strings is also frequently employed in *Outer Dark*. The character Rinthy Holme is continually portrayed as a "crippled marionette" (32), pirouetting "like a doll unwinding for just a moment" (53), moving "mute, shuffling, wooden" (210), standing "doll-like, one arm poised" (210), and watching the world with "doll's eyes of painted china" (24). Even her child "dangles" like "a gross eldritch doll" (235). The novel's sinister tinker is also portrayed as "an effigy in rags hung by strings from an indifferent hand" (189), and a "horsefly" follows behind the character Culla Holme's head "as if towed there on a string" (26). All these images of dolls, marionettes, and strings point to the archon puppet masters, manipulating human beings through the forces of heimarmene. The only characters free of such binds are the sinister trio of archons. When the leader of the three is asked, "Where are you bound?," he knowingly distorts the meaning of the question and replies, "I ain't.... By nothing" (233).

13. Chris Dacus interprets the kid's dream in light of "Plato's definition of time as the moving image of eternity," which "is another way of saying that the whole is always present in the part." Dacus argues that in *Blood Meridian* this concept "often manifests itself as one of the judge's discussions of fate and destiny, but also appears in the kid's reported dreams.... This is clearly another reference to time as the moving image of eternity, as a thing already 'accomplished'" (11).
14. In *Reading the World*, Dianne Luce identifies allusions to heimarmene in McCarthy's Southern Gothic novel *Outer Dark*. According to Luce, the character "Harmon," the only member of the novel's demonic triad who possesses a name, is actually a personification of the forces of heimarmene. Citing the work of Hans Jonas, who explains how the Gnostic vision of a cosmos controlled by heimarmene is a negative reevaluation of the classical Greek concept of cosmic harmony, or *harmonia*, Luce argues, "*Outer Dark*'s ominous, smiling enforcer-figure armed with a rifle and ironically named 'Harmon' thus semantically connects the triune with the gnostic concept of *heimarmene*." Luce adds that the novel "develops the malignant, mindless, coercive triune as *heimarmene* ... linking the triune with want and death and with moral law, judgement, and guilt" (89). It is worth noting that, like Harmon, Judge Holden not only represents death and judgement but also carries a rifle with "Et In Arcadia Ego" inscribed upon it. This can be translated either as "I, too, lived in Arcadia," words spoken by the dead reminding the living that they too once enjoyed life's pleasures, or as "Even in Arcadia, there am I," words spoken by Death itself, warning its future victims that there is no place where they may escape their mortal fate. The latter reading ought to be employed for the inscription on the gun, for, like Harmon, the judge symbolizes the inevitable fetters of heimarmene that bind all human beings to their deaths.
15. The judge claims that "each man's destiny is as large as the world he inhabits and contains within it all opposites as well" (330). This description of a system in which each individual destiny already contains all its "opposites" echoes the concept of the "many histories" theory of quantum physics. In *The Fabric of Reality*, David Deutsch explains that "a chain of reasoning based on [photon interference experiments] rules out the possibility that the universe we see around us constitutes the whole of reality. In fact the whole of physical reality, the multiverse, contains vast numbers of parallel universes" (54). Consequently, "what is a rare event in any one universe is a common event in the multiverse as a whole" (52). According to this theory, every possible outcome is realized in a parallel universe. Further references to a quantum view of reality can be found in the judge's claim that the "dance" already "contains complete within itself its own arrangements and history and finale" (329). This idea is akin to the theory that the multiverse "contains all the space and time there is" (Deutsch 279); that is, all past, present, and future events, as well as all the permutations of infinite possibilities. According to the quantum view, time "is not a sequence of

moments, nor does it flow," because "other times" are merely "other universes" (288). Hence our future is not somehow "in the making," because the future already exists, while the past is still in existence. It is quite likely that McCarthy's writing has been influenced by quantum theory as a direct result of his friendship with the scientists of the Santa Fe Institute. David Kushner writes that, "for McCarthy, the scientific life of the Institute plays a fundamental role in his life as a writer, sparking his imagination with 'what if' scenarios while grounding his fiction in a greater reality" (43). Jay Ellis also argues that if we take into account that McCarthy's writing "reflects the influence of his friends and acquaintances at the Santa Fe Institute; more interesting possibilities of interpretation might occur to us than often do in professional reactions to McCarthy's work" ("Do You See" 110).

16. In *The Denial of Death*—a study of humanity's often futile attempts to deal with mortality—Ernest Becker identifies and analyses a character type reminiscent of Glanton. Becker describes this type of individual as "one who asserts himself out of defiance of his own weakness, who tries to be a god unto himself, the master of his fate, a self-created man." However, such "defiant self-creation can become demonic, a passion which Kierkegaard calls 'demoniac rage,' an attack on all of life for what it's dared to do to one, a revolt against existence itself" (84). Then, in a passage that evokes the world depicted in *Blood Meridian*, Becker warns, "Carried to its demonic extreme this defiance gave us Hitler and Vietnam: a rage against our impotence, a defiance of our animal condition, our pathetic creature limitations. If we don't have the omnipotence of gods, we at least can destroy like gods" (85). Robert Jay Lifton also identifies this kind of behavior in Nazi fanaticism, arguing that it "was a religion of the will—the will as 'an all-encompassing metaphysical principle'; and what the Nazis 'willed' was nothing less than the total control over life and death" (197), a statement all too clearly illustrated by the cool efficiency of death camps like Treblinka. Becker's and Lifton's insights shed some light on Glanton's pursuit of violent depravity; his bloodthirsty excesses stem from his subconscious desire to escape the inevitability of death, that most universal and inexorable of fates, behind which the Gnostics saw the machinations of heimarmene.

17. Neil Campbell argues that "McCarthy's 'blood meridian' is the point at which one reaches the fullness of life and simultaneously recognizes the proximity, even the inevitability, of its end. The blood is both life-giving and life-destroying, hence the qualification of the novel's title by 'or the evening redness in the west,' which reminds us of a larger mythic fear about the West as a place where the sun 'dies'" (56).

18. The ubiquitous presence of death permeates the novel, much of the action being set in a barren wilderness where "death" seems "the most prevalent feature of the landscape" (48). Death appears as a character in the form of the "pale sutler" who is the personification of cholera. The description of Death as "a wry and

grinning tradesman" connects him to McCarthy's depictions of the demiurge, who appears as a "weaver" in *Suttree* (5) and *The Crossing* (149), as a metalworker in *All the Pretty Horses* (231), and as a "coldforger" in *Blood Meridian* (310). Death follows "every campaign" and tracks down every human being, hounding out "men from their holes in just those whited regions," or those areas not depicted on maps, "where they've gone to hide from God" (44). When the judge, perhaps in his role as Death, comes to claim the kid's life at the end of the novel, he implies that the kid has been hiding from him: "Was it always your idea . . . that if you did not speak you would not be recognized?" (328).

CHAPTER 3

1. Shane Schimpf offers such a reading of the novel in his introduction to *A Reader's Guide to "Blood Meridian,"* where he argues that *Blood Meridian* "is a meditation on a Nietzschean world where God has died" and that its aim is "to demonstrate how traditional religion, in the form of Christianity, has become stagnant and ineffectual." Schimpf also argues that the "triumph of the scientific paradigm comes at a cost and that cost is nihilism" (3).
2. On the morning of 10 November 1793, the Cathedral of Notre Dame was converted into the Temple of Reason: "Rising up in the nave was an improvised mountain, at the top of which perched a small Greek temple dedicated 'To Philosophy' and adorned on both sides by the busts of philosophers, probably Voltaire, Rousseau, Franklin, and Montesquieu. Halfway down the side of the mountain a torch of Truth burned before an altar to Reason" (Baumer 35).
3. Robert Jarrett writes that the judge is "a nineteenth-century version of Blake's Urizen, a representation of the unrestricted will to power of the transcendental Reason" (*Cormac McCarthy* 79). Shane Schimpf argues that "the transforming power of science and technology" is "embodied in the person of the Judge" (3). According to John Cant, "the judge personifies the extreme of anthropocentrism, of Enlightenment hubris" (170). Steven Frye writes that the judge is "the dark avatar of scientific positivism—in this case the Enlightenment gone horribly astray . . . who espouses a brutish philosophy that McCarthy presents as the ethical outcome of a rigid philosophical materialism" (*Understanding Cormac McCarthy* 69). Frye also states that "the judge can be seen as a potential result of the assertions of a modern science taken to the philosophical extreme, which privileges the phenomenal over the numinous, the material over the transcendent" (78).
4. Other critics have noted the eerily religious connotations of the judge's actions and speeches. Harold Bloom describes the judge as the "spiritual leader of Glanton's filibusters" (*Modern Critical Views* 3). Sara Spurgeon writes, "McCarthy consistently presents the judge as a priest, a mediator between man and nature, shepherding, or more accurately manipulating, the scalphunter's

souls" (88). Shane Schimpf argues that "the Judge is the priest of a new religion and the Glanton gang his disciples" and that this "new religion is science" (22).

5. The judge's words regarding war as a game resonate meaningfully with those of William Broyles, who served as a marine in Vietnam and later became editor in chief at *Newsweek*: "War is a brutal game, but a game, the best there is" (qtd. in Oppenheimer 78). Further similarities are revealed when we compare the judge's words regarding the "man who has offered up himself entire to the blood of war, who has been to the floor of the pit and seen horror in the round and learned at last that it speaks to his inmost heart" (331) with Broyles's description of his own experience of having "explored regions of [his] soul that in most men will always remain unchartered." Broyles writes, "I stood on the edge of my humanity, looked into a pit, and loved what I saw there. I had surrendered to an aesthetic that was divorced from that crucial quality of empathy that lets us feel the sufferings of others. And I saw a terrible beauty there. War is not simply the spirit of ugliness, although it certainly is that, the devil's work. But to give the devil his due, it is also an affair of great and seductive beauty" (qtd. in Oppenheimer 78). Broyles's choice of metaphor, namely, of looking into the pit, is particularly striking in its resemblance to the judge's "floor of the pit."

6. Shane Schimpf writes, "There can be no doubt that this is a reference to Nietzsche," in particular, "his classic text *Beyond Good and Evil*" (7). J. Douglas Canfield also argues that "the judge is not only Nietzschean but social Darwinist," for the "the way that history manifests its 'law' is through the triumph of the strong over the weak" ("Border of Becoming" 43).

7. In *The Crossing*, the ex-priest specifically states that though he originally believed that he could hear the "voice of the Deity in the murmur of the wind in the trees" and thought that "even the stones were sacred," he eventually came to understand that the Absolute does not "whisper through the trees." The ex-priest explains that the call of the divine "voice is not to be mistaken" because "when men hear it they fall to their knees and their souls are riven and they cry out to Him and there is no fear in them but only that wildness of heart that springs from such longing and they cry out to stay his presence for they know at once that while godless men may live well enough in exile those to whom He has spoken can contemplate no life without Him but only darkness and despair." In other words, the ex-priest argues that when one has an experience of the Absolute, one can never again be content with mundane existence but continues to long for another, more lasting experience of the divine. Finally, as though in direct reference to the judge's proclamation, the ex-priest insists that "trees and stones are no part of it" (152). Thus the ex-priest puts forward a vision of an entirely transcendent Godhead that cannot be compared to anything experienced in the manifest realm.

8. When one considers McCarthy's views regarding the mystical experience, it becomes highly unlikely that the judge serves as a mouthpiece for the author's

own beliefs. Shane Schimpf, however, disagrees: "Ultimately, I feel the Judge is expressing McCarthy's worldview" (49). To support his argument, Schimpf quotes an excerpt from an interview with Richard Woodward in which McCarthy states, "There's no such thing as life without bloodshed.... I think the notion that the species can be improved in some way, that everyone could live in harmony, is a really dangerous idea. Those who are afflicted with this notion are the first ones to give up their souls, their freedom. Your desire that it be that way will enslave you and make your life vacuous" (36). Schimpf interprets the comment in the following manner: "Humans live to make war, for war brings us to life. Note McCarthy's disdain for a life without violence in the quote above. He seems to be saying that even if one could live a life without bloodshed, it wouldn't be worth living." Schimpf concludes that "war is the ultimate human endeavor for McCarthy, and this novel is his paean to it" (50–51). There is no reason, however, to read McCarthy's pessimism regarding the potential for the human race as a celebration. Even though he considers a "life without bloodshed" an unattainable and even "dangerous" idea, he still refers to it in terms of improvement. In other words, he suggests that it would be better if the human race were not bloodthirsty, but at the same time he is aware of the impossibility of establishing such a society and discourages any naïve attempts at creating a utopia, for, as history demonstrates, such attempts usually lead to totalitarianism and despotism. Ultimately, the fact that McCarthy continually draws the reader's attention to the judge's lies and contradictions should discourage any conflation between the views of the novelist and his character. Cormac McCarthy is not Judge Holden!

9. William Blake frequently employed metal-forging imagery to evoke the fiery operations of hell. For example, "A Divine Image" contains the lines "The Human Dress is forged Iron, / The Human Form, a fiery Forge" (lines 5–6). The evil within creation is also linked with metalwork in "The Tyger":

> What the hammer? what the chain?
> In what furnace was thy brain?
> What the anvil? what dread grasp
> Dare its deadly terrors clasp?"
> (lines 13–16)

Similarly, Blake writes about the "mind-forg'd manacles" that can be heard in the "cry of every man" ("London," lines 8, 5) evoking spiritual imprisonment and suffering through the image of forged iron.

10. The word was first used in this sense in Plato's *Timaeus* 41.a (ca. 360 BC), where the demiurge was depicted as a benevolent figure necessary for the process of creation.

11. Steven Frye also reads the coldforger passage in a Gnostic light, arguing that the "mysterious coldforger who casts a false coin" suggests the creation of "human

beings themselves who have been cast by the archons." Thus the "coin and by implication the human species are counterfeit currency in the world, a mere collection of husks designed for the malevolent purpose of imprisoning the divine." Frye also comments on the fact that the judge "stands behind the forger, 'enshadowing' him and presiding over his creative activity" and therefore he may be a representation of "the demiurge itself" (*Understanding Cormac McCarthy* 84).

Similarly, Edwin Arnold, while not engaging in a directly Gnostic reading of the coldforger's work, does note that it constitutes "one of McCarthy's more gnostic images." He also argues that the coldforger evokes various mythical and literary characters, "ranging from Pluto, god of the underworld, to Spencer's melancholy gnome-like Mammon, who lives in hell making money." Most significantly, Arnold draws comparisons between McCarthy's "worker in metal" and William Blake's "mythic Los, the smithy who works at the command of Urizen just as the coldforger works to please the judge." Arnold argues that both Urizen and Holden "wish to control the world by denying or obliterating mystery through logic and science." Furthermore, Los assists Urizen, who is essentially Blake's version of the Gnostic demiurge, by forging "the chains that will bind man through the limitations and assumptions of reason alone, which confines and organizes and thus diminishes the world" (Arnold "Go to Sleep" 47). It is also noteworthy that Blake's Urizen is a phonetic pun on "your reason" or "you reason."

Shane Schimpf provides a different reading of the coldforger's task, arguing that the "counterfeit coin is science" and that the "Judge's task is to give men science as a replacement for God and religion both which no longer bear any value" (47). Schimpf adds that the new coinage is counterfeit because "science ... does not ultimately provide any meaning" (48). While I agree that the judge's new doctrine seeks to replace traditional spirituality, I believe that it is essentially a pseudo-religion and therefore cannot be considered "scientific," in the proper sense, but rather "scientistic." In other words, the counterfeit coinage is not strictly "science" but rather materialism, nihilism, reductionism, hence a reversal, parody, or inversion of traditional spiritual values. Furthermore, the concept that the original currency—that is, spirituality—"no longer bears any value" does not fit in with the metaphor of the "false moneyer," who floods the market with counterfeit coins. For in such a situation it is the new, counterfeit currency that bears no real value. The original currency becomes devalued only due to the existence of counterfeit coins. If, as Schimpf argues, neither the original nor the new currency bear any value, than there would be no sense in calling the latter counterfeit; it is counterfeit only in relation to its genuine predecessor. Were it not for the "false moneyer," the genuine coinage would maintain its inherent value in the "markets where men barter."

CHAPTER 4

1. The concept of the "saved savior" or "redeemed redeemer" has been rejected by some contemporary scholars of Gnosticism as the "invention of modern scholarship" (King 138). Karen King argues that while original Gnostic texts "do establish some kind of identity between the Savior and the saved in terms of substance ... the term 'redeemed redeemer' itself never appears in any primary text, and its content was determined only by reference to the Gnostic salvation myth constructed by Reitzenstein, Bultmann, and Jonas—and that myth itself exists nowhere in the idealized form presented by those authors" (143). King concludes that "the concept itself is basically a modern interpretative construct" (144). Kurt Rudolph, on the other hand, does not reject the myth outright, arguing that

   > the precise form given this myth ... can be seen only in Manichean texts and Reitzenstein merely read it into many Gnostic traditions. However the basic idea is not alien to Gnosis, on the contrary Manicheism only drew a consequence from its soteriology, and a whole range of statements only become comprehensible when we start from this, that the idea of a redeemer who sets free the "souls," as particles of light identical with his nature, by means of the knowledge of this identity and thereby suffers the same fate as these souls or particles of light, actually does play a part. (122)

   Rudolph concludes that the "idea of the 'redeemed redeemer' is ... indeed a logical and characteristic formulation of the gnostic redeemer conception, which unites redeemer and redeemed very closely together, but it is only one variation of this. There is no uniform gnostic redeemer myth, such as theologians in particular have imagined" (131). It is important to keep in mind, however, that McCarthy is not a Gnostic scholar who keeps up to date with the latest developments in the field; he is a novelist, and therefore he took from Gnostic writings and commentaries what he needed from what was then available.
2. The kid's words, "I know your kind," suggest the words of Jesus: "I know your works: you are neither cold nor hot. Would that you were cold or hot! So, because you are lukewarm, and neither cold nor hot, I will spew you out of my mouth" (John 3:15–6). The judge also subtly alludes to these words later in the novel, accusing the kid of the sin of lukewarm neutrality: "No assassin, called the judge. And no partisan either. There's a flawed place in the fabric of your heart. Do you think I could not know?" (299).
3. Other critics have commented on the fact that the kid never really seems to be a part of the gang. Brian Evenson, for example, notes that within *Blood Meridian* "there is one who refuses to enter into the spirit of the pack itself—the kid, who seems to remain passive. In the most violent scenes and the most incessant wanderings, his character seems to vanish altogether." Evenson suggests that this

odd absence serves "as if to avoid implicating him in the violence, or as if to imply he is absent in spirit if not in body" (46).

4. Geoffrey Chaucer describes our lives as a pilgrimage in "The Knight's Tale" of *The Canterbury Tales*. "This world is but a thoroughfare full of woe, / And we been pilgrims passing to and fro" (lines 2847–48).

5. The concept of the inordinate day, or of the disrupted rhythms of nature, is a common theme in McCarthy's fiction. In *The Orchard Keeper*, the narrator evokes an image of the planet accelerating in its orbit, "the trees bent as if borne forward on some violent acceleration of the earth's turning" (171). In *Outer Dark*, the river appears to run backward. "He spat. His saliva bloomed palely on the water and wheeled and slid inexplicably upstream, back the way he had come. He turned and watched it in disbelief" (17). In *Child of God*, the protagonist, Lester Ballard, notes, "Disorder in the woods, trees down, new paths needed. Given charge Ballard would have made things more orderly in the woods and in men's souls" (136). In *Suttree*, the world itself seems to be afflicted with a terminal illness: "Everywhere a liquid dripping, something gone awry in the earth's organs to which this measured bleeding clocked a constantly eluded doom" (261). In *All the Pretty Horses*, the protagonists, Rawlins and John Grady, witness a "false blue dawn" in which "the Pleiades seemed to be rising up into the darkness above the world and dragging all the stars away" (60). The vision leads Rawlins to ask, "You think there'll be a day when the sun wont rise?" to which John Grady replies, "Yeah . . . Judgement day" (60). In *The Crossing*, it seems to the protagonist that "the river was running backwards. That or the sun was setting in the east behind him" (130). In *The Road*, the narrative voice describes another instance of the planet's path gone awry: "Something imponderable shifting out there in the dark. The earth itself contracting with the cold" (261). From a Gnostic perspective, such references point to the essentially flawed nature of the created world and, by extension, of its creator.

6. As argued by John Sepich, the kneeling woman evokes the image of Nuestra Señora de Guadalupe (Our Lady of Guadalupe) that allegedly appeared on the cloak of a simple peasant named Juan Diego on 12 December 1531. The mysterious image depicts the Virgin "standing on a crescent moon," clad in a "mantle" that is "sky blue in colour" and "decorated with forty-six stars" (Brading 64). McCarthy's kneeling woman similarly wears a shawl woven with "stars and quartermoons" (315). Further similarities between McCarthy's vignette and the Virgin of Guadalupe abound. For example, the Virgin appears "in an aureoled tabernacle or niche" (Brading 64), just as McCarthy's woman kneels in "a small niche" or "a little cove" (315). The Virgin of Guadalupe has a "face silvery brown in colour" (Brading 64), while the kneeling woman's face is described as "gray and leathery" (315), both women possessing a brown-gray complexion. The Guadalupe image also features "a boyish angel with wings out-stretched" (Brading 64), analogous to the kid, who reaches out to touch the kneeling

penitent. Furthermore, the very subtitle of the chapter—"The Eldress in the Rocks" (305)—calls to mind the two almost identical paintings by Leonardo da Vinci entitled "Virgin of the Rocks," which depict the baby Jesus, John the Baptist, the Madonna, and the angel Gabriel in a barren and rocky wilderness, much like McCarthy's landscape in *Blood Meridian*.

7. Andersen points out that the wedding ceremony is again evoked when the judge finally takes the kid's life. "'Speak or forever,' says the barkeep, asking what he'll have, and this fragment of the wedding ceremony marks the consummation he's about to meet in death (he'll go like a 'bride to the altar' just as Tobin once predicted): when he turns and looks across the room he locks eyes with the judge" (108). It is noteworthy that in *No Country for Old Men*, Carla Jean's death is also marked by an allusion to the wedding ceremony, her final words being essentially "I do" (260).

8. The judge watches and "smiles" at the kid throughout the novel. After their first encounter, the kid rides past and the judge turns to watch him, even turning his horse "as if he'd have the animal watch too. When the kid looked back the judge smiled" (14). When the kid falls asleep riding his horse, he wakes to find that "the judge was there . . . and he looked down upon the refugee with the same smile, as if the world were pleasing even to him alone" (219). The judge's smile of self-satisfaction is all the more disturbing for the fact that it occurs after the Glanton gang has "lost four men" while fleeing from General Elias (218). Even in the midst of delirium, the kid hallucinates about the judge's smile. "In that sleep and in sleeps to follow the judge did visit. . . . The judge smiled" (310). At the end of the novel, when the kid is a forty-five-year-old man and has lived a life of aimless wandering, he encounters his old enemy in a bar. "Watching him across the layered smoke in the yellow light was the judge" (325). The judge smiles—"The judge was standing at the bar looking down at him. He smiled" (326)—and, as always, the smile is an unnervingly sinister one.

9. The Eucharistic sharing of an unidentifiable meat also occurs in McCarthy's *Outer Dark*, where the mysterious leader of the demonic trio invites the protagonist, Culla, to partake in "black and mummified meat," which has been "dusted with ash" and tastes of "sulphur" (171–72). William Spencer argues that the scene represents "a parody of the sacrament of the Holy Eucharist in which Culla takes part with his hellish brethren." Spencer adds that "Culla is being initiated into the religion of evil" and that by accepting the meal "he formally becomes a disciple" (72).

10. In McCarthy's screenplay *The Counselor*, the supremely maleficent Malkina also alludes to this flaw in the human heart: "We would like to draw a veil over all that blood and terror. That have brought us to this place. It is our faintness of heart that would close our eyes to all of that, but in so doing it makes of it our destiny" (184).

11. In "Language and the Dance of Time in Cormac McCarthy's *Blood Meridian*," John Rothfork interprets the judge's accusation in Buddhist terms: "We must be

careful to be consistent here, following something analogous to a Theravada Buddhist line of thinking about how compassion for other beings is ultimately a kind of self-indulgent defense mechanism that serves to reinforce the illusion of possessing a permanent or eternal ego immune from the dance of time. If everything is process, both one's own ego and that of the beloved are illusions of history that must be abandoned, worn out, or lost" (32–33). I disagree with this interpretation for several reasons. First, unlike the practitioners of Theravada Buddhism, the judge shows no interest in extinguishing the ego, whether his own or anyone else's. On the contrary, as I have argued throughout the preceding chapters, the judge's ego is inflated to demonic proportions and he continually encourages others to adopt a similar state of being. Second, in the same speech, the judge chastises the kid for not participating wholeheartedly in the game of war, whereas Theravada Buddhism is primarily concerned with the complete "renunciation of the world" (H. Smith, *Religions of Man* 136); the two positions are incompatible. Third, just because Theravada Buddhism does not regard compassion to be the preeminent virtue, that does not mean it is opposed to compassionate behavior as such. To clarify, the chief difference between Theravada and Mahayana Buddhism lies in their respective attitudes toward wisdom and compassion. Huston Smith explains, "In Theravada the key virtue was *bodhi* wisdom, with the absence of self-seeking emphasized more than the active doing of good. Mahayana moved a different word to the center: *karuna*, compassion. Unless it eventuates in compassion, wisdom is useless" (*Religions of Man* 136). In Theravada Buddhism, compassion is still considered a virtue, even if spiritual wisdom remains the most important goal. In other words, no Theravada Buddhist would ever chastise anyone else for behaving in a compassionate manner. The judge, on the other hand, voices a genuine disapproval of compassionate behavior and shows not the slightest interest in the type of spiritual wisdom sought by the Theravada Buddhists, namely, the egoless pursuit of enlightenment.

12. Kurt Rudolph writes that, for the Manicheans, the "ill-treatment of animals, damage of plants . . . pollution of water, all involved the 'tormenting' of the light enclosed therein," and such acts were considered 'sacrilege'" (340). Hans Jonas explains that the Manichean "abstinence in matters of food" was "ruled by two points of view besides the general ascetic attitude: not unnecessarily to incorporate and thereby bind additional Light-substance; and, as this cannot be wholly avoided (plants also containing it), at least to avoid *hurting* Light in its sentient form in animals" (231).

13. We find a similar reference to Saint Elmo's fire as symbolic of divine fire in McCarthy's favorite novel, *Moby-Dick*. In chapter 119, "The Candles," Captain Ahab addresses the eerie electrical phenomenon with the words "Oh! Thou clear spirit of clear fire, whom on these seas I as Persian once did worship . . . of thy fire thou madest me, and like a true child of fire, I breathe it back to thee"

(Melville 476–77). Ahab not only refers to himself as a "Persian," which clearly identifies him as a Manichean, but acknowledges that his true self is made of the divine fire, in other words, the pneuma, which strives for reunion with the divine, hence the desire to "breathe it back" into its transcendent origins.

14. In the Gospel of Thomas, Jesus tells his disciples, "Whoever is near me is near fire, and whoever is far from me is far from the kingdom" (qtd. in Barnstone and Meyer 64).

15. Shane Schimpf argues that McCarthy's alternate title for *Blood Meridian*, namely *or The Evening Redness in the West*, is "a clever reference" to Jacob Boehme's full title for *Aurora*, which is *Aurora the Day-Spring; or, Dawning of the Day in the East; or, Morning-Redness in the Rising of the Sun. That Is the Root or Mother of Philosophy, Astrology and Theology from the True Ground; or, A Description of Nature* (58).

16. Other critics have also noted the kid's gradual development, whether moral or spiritual. Harold Bloom, for example, argues that the kid undergoes a "moral maturation" and that "McCarthy subtly shows us the long, slow development of the Kid from another mindless scalper of Indians to the courageous confronter of the Judge in their final debate in a saloon" (*How to Read* 257). Steven Frye argues that the kid "stands apart, not because of his purity or separation from the judge's world, but because in the end he responds to circumstances with a moral rectitude and resists the judge's pronouncements even unto death" (*Understanding Cormac McCarthy* 87). Similarly, Dianne Luce argues, "The kid becomes by tiny increments more thoughtful about his violence as his experience with death and suffering grows, and he eventually attempts to break with the judge and atone for his deeds." Luce, however, adds, "Whether these attempts prove effective remains ambiguous even at the end of the novel" ("Ambiguities" 26).

17. Stacey Peebles draws parallels between the Quechan belief system and Gnosticism: "Gnosticism can be seen not only in the basic thematics of the narrative, but also in these Quechan beliefs that parallel the narrative. Gnosticism teaches that the world was created flawed, and thus is filled with suffering.... Again, this is resonant not only with the narrative content of the novel, but also with the Quechan myths, with tales of godly antagonism and corresponding earthly suffering" ("Yuman Belief Systems" 242–43).

18. Andrew Smith writes, "Reincarnation or the transmigration of souls is implied in many Gnostic systems" (211). Similarly, Stephan Hoeller explains, "Reincarnation seems to have been an important feature of the teachings of the school of Carpocrates," adding, "some feel that reincarnation is implicit in the teachings of all Gnostic schools" (103).

19. Another such savior figure seems to be the child in *The Road*. The father announces that if the child "is not the word of God God never spoke" (5). Later the boy is referred to as "God's own firedrake" (26). The choice of the word

"firedrake" is particularly interesting, as the word "dragon" is derived from the Greek δράκων (*drakōn*), which comes from the Greek verb δέρκομαι (*derkomai*), meaning "I see clearly" (Liddell and Scott 370). The Greek δράκων could also mean "snake" or "serpent," a creature that the ancient Gnostics associated with gnosis. Furthermore, the biblical word for "snake" is *nahash*, derived from the root NHSH, meaning "to decipher, to find out" (Bramley 55). Jonas explains, "Since it is the serpent that persuades Adam and Eve to taste of the fruit of knowledge and thereby disobey their Creator, it came in a whole group of systems to represent the 'pneumatic' principle from beyond counteracting the designs of the Demiurge, and thus could become as much a symbol of the powers of redemption as the biblical God had been degraded to a symbol of cosmic oppression" (93). Thus this association with the serpent further identifies the boy as a young incarnation of the pneumatic savior of Gnostic theology.

20. McCarthy also uses "fire" to represent the divine spark in *The Road*. The father reminds the son throughout the journey through the apocalyptic wasteland that they are "the good guys" because they are "carrying the fire" (120). When the son asks, "Where is it? I don't know where it is," the father replies, "Yes you do. It's inside you. It was always there. I can see it" (279). Similarly, in *No Country for Old Men*, Sheriff Bell dreams of his father "carryin fire in a horn. . . . And in the dream I knew that he was goin on ahead and that he was fixin to make a fire somewhere out there in all that dark and all that cold" (309). Here the fire stands in opposition to darkness, a concept frequently associated with spiritual ignorance, evil, and death.

21. I do not agree with the rest of Shane Schimpf's reading of the epilogue. Schimpf argues, "Specifically, if one of McCarthy's intentions is to point out the triumph of science and technology over religion, it can be argued that the man in the epilogue is spreading science. Whether or not this man is the Judge is not that important, although I am inclined to think that it is. . . . Man is altering the landscape to fit his needs via his tools. This is 'progress' but note where the progress takes place—in the barren landscape of the plain" (45). On the contrary, I believe that the figure in the epilogue is spreading spiritual insight, not scientific knowledge, and that he stands in complete opposition to the judge.

22. Mark Busby interprets this passage through the lens of Albert Camus's essay "The Myth of Sisyphus," arguing that "the epilogue is a parable in which the digger is the embodiment of Camus' Sisyphus, who achieves spirit by will in contrast to those around who live inauthentic lives" ("Rolling the Stone" 94). Busby also suggests that his existentialist reading of the epilogue is not entirely removed from my own interpretation of the epilogue in light of Gnosticism, because "Gnosticism and existentialism share a similar view of nature's antagonism to human desire." Busby qualifies this argument by stressing the fact that there remains "one main difference" between the two schools of thought and, citing Edward Moore's *Internet Dictionary of Philosophy*, points out that "nature

is, for modern Existentialism, merely indifferent, while for the Gnostics it was actively hostile toward the human endeavor" ("Rolling the Stone" 91). I agree that existentialism and Gnosticism present similar views of the human condition, especially when one considers the fact that both movements place great emphasis on humanity's alienation; however, an unbridgeable gap remains due to the fact that existentialism is an intellectual philosophy, while Gnosticism is essentially a spiritual practice.

CHAPTER 5

1. The lullaby is traditional to the southern United States and is believed to have been sung by African slaves to their charges. Hence the "poor little lamby" is presumably the child that the mother has to leave behind each day while she takes care of the master's children.
2. In *The Road*, McCarthy depicts the aftermath of an unspecified disaster (possibly a meteorite strike) that seems to have destroyed all life on earth, except for a few human beings who continue to struggle for survival in an apocalyptic landscape.
3. In some ways, the use of blood imagery in the Border Trilogy mirrors McCarthy's use of fire imagery in *Blood Meridian*, *No Country for Old Men*, and *The Road*. In the aforementioned novels, various characters are portrayed as either carrying or liberating "the fire." Fire, in McCarthy's fiction, tends to represent a fragment or spark of the divine trapped in the manifest world. As McCarthy explains in *Blood Meridian*, "Each fire is all fires, the first fire and the last ever to be" (244); thus all living things are held in communion by their common origins in this divine source, to which all life struggles to return.
4. Edgar Allan Poe's "El Dorado" tells the story of a "gallant knight" who rides in "search of Eldorado." As his strength fails him and his life ebbs away, he finds no trace of the fabled city but only death in the form of a "shade" who directs him "Down the Valley of the Shadow" (lines 2, 6, 21).
5. In *Cormac McCarthy's West: The Border Trilogy Annotations*, James Bell points out that Don Héctor attributes this line to Cervantes, despite the fact that "the quotation does not appear in the widely used 1885 John Ormsby translation, or the 1611 Thomas Shelton translation" of *Don Quixote* (110). In fact, the line is spoken by the Duke in a 1973 British made-for-TV BBC production entitled *The Adventures of Don Quixote*, which was later aired in the United States. Despite the fact that Don Héctor quotes this line in the fictional setting of 1950, well before the film aired, it is clear that he is referring to *Don Quixote* because he goes on to say, "That of course is the spanish idea. You see. The idea of Quixote. But even Cervantes could not envision such a country as Mexico" (146).
6. In *Symbols and Their Meanings*, Jack Tresidder explains, "Female emblems such as fountains, lakes, oceans, rivers and the moon . . . all continue to dominate

ancient symbolism of 'Woman' as receptor, carrier, animator, protector and nourisher of life" (12).

7. The entire passage is reminiscent of an eighteenth-century Buddhist haiku by Issa Kobayashi (1763–1828):

> This dewdrop world,
> Is but a dewdrop world,
> And yet . . .
> (157)

8. The concept behind tanha is not unique to Buddhism and can be found in all great mystical and esoteric traditions. Aldous Huxley writes that "all exponents of the Perennial Philosophy have constantly insisted" that "man's obsessive consciousness of, and insistence on being, a separate self is the final and most formidable obstacle to the unitive knowledge of God" (36). It is important to point out that "God" in this instance refers to "the divine Ground of all existence" (21), or the ineffable Absolute, rather than a creator deity.

9. In *The Crossing*, the wolf also sees "man" as a "malignant lesser God come pale and naked and alien to slaughter all his clan and kind and rout them from their house. A God insatiable whom no ceding could appease nor any measure of blood" (17).

10. In *God and Evil: An Introduction to the Issues*, Michael L. Peterson explains,

> Evil, then, from Augustine's perspective, is not a thing, not a being. Although evil in human experience can be very powerful and profound, evil does not, at least metaphysically speaking, represent the positive existence of anything. Evil simply does not exist in its own right; it is not one of the constituents of the universe. Rather, it is the lack of reality and thus the lack of goodness. Put another way, evil enters creation when created beings cease to function as they were created to function by nature. Evil is thus metaphysical deprivation, privation, or degradation. Augustine's term for evil is *privatio boni* (privation of good). (90)

11. The word "homunculous," as used by McCarthy, refers to an "artificial man supposedly made by the alchemists" ("Homunculus"). McCarthy's description of the cuchillero thus evokes clear connotations of an occult and man-made evil.

12. Morse Peckham defines negative romanticism as a "period of doubt, of despair, of religious and social isolation, of the separation of reason and creative power." During such a period, the individual sees "neither beauty nor goodness in the universe, nor any significance, nor any rationality, nor indeed any order at all." Peckham goes on to add that the "typical symbols of Negative Romanticism are individuals who are filled with guilt, despair, and cosmic and social alienation.

... They are often outcasts from men and God, and they are almost always wanderers over the face of the earth" (22). Peckham's definition is directly applicable to many of the characters in McCarthy's fiction.

13. In McCarthy's fiction, the symbol of the coin seems to be inextricably bound with questions of fate and destiny. As previously discussed, the judge in *Blood Meridian* demonstrates the powers of heimarmene by performing an uncanny coin trick by the fire, explaining that the "arc of circling bodies is determined by the length of their tether," whether they are "moons, coins," or "men" (245–46). The same theme is evoked in *No Country for Old Men*, where Anton Chigurh uses coins to determine whether his victims shall live or die. When Chigurh explains the inevitability of fate to Carla Jean, just before he murders her, he seems also to be referring to the powers of heimarmene: "The accounting is scrupulous. The shape is drawn. No line can be erased. I had no belief in your ability to move a coin to your bidding. How could you? A person's path through the world seldom changes and even more seldom will it change abruptly. And the shape of your path was visible from the beginning" (259).

14. Herman Melville's demiurge in *Moby-Dick* is also portrayed as a weaver who has been deafened by his trade: "The weaver-god, he weaves; and by that weaving he is deafened, that he hears no mortal voice; and by that humming, we, too, who look on the loom are deafened; and only when we escape it shall we hear the thousand voices that speak through it" (427).

15. A similar concept is raised in *Blood Meridian* when the deadly "dustspouts" that leave pilgrims "broken and bleeding upon the desert" are described as "mindless coils" (111). The suffering caused by these "mindless coils" suggests the mindless "pain of the world" described in *All the Pretty Horses*.

16. The British philosopher John Stuart Mill (1806–1873) argued that "nearly all the things which men are hanged or imprisoned for doing to one another are nature's everyday performances. Killing, the most criminal act recognized by human laws, nature does once to every being that lives, and in a large proportion of cases after protracted tortures such as only the greatest monsters whom we read of purposely inflict on their fellow living creatures" (qtd. in Peterson 289).

17. The boys' apparent indifference to the suffering of the birds, combined with the words "the horseman rode on," calls to mind the last lines of W. B. Yeats's "Under Ben Bulben," which also serve as the poet's epitaph:

> Cast a cold Eye
> On Life, on Death.
> Horseman, pass by!

Furthermore, the image of the little birds impaled on cactus spines recalls the bush "hung with dead babies" in *Blood Meridian*, on which the infants, like the birds, are impaled on "broken stobs of a mesquite" (57).

18. "Life" never quite manages to "cure" John Grady of his romantic sentiments, which he manages to hold on to despite all the horror and suffering he experiences. Thus his death at the end of *Cities of the Plain* can be understood as the final "cure" of which Alfonsa speaks.
19. It is significant that "Blevins is a patronymic form of the Welsh name Blevin, from the given name Bleiddyn which meant 'Wolf Cub'" ("Blevins"). Thus John Grady's failure to save Jimmy Blevins in *All the Pretty Horses* anticipates Billy Parham's failure to save the wolf in *The Crossing*.
20. Gail Morrison points out that this reference to "the living" and "the dead" recalls the ending of James Joyce's *The Dubliners*: "His soul swooned slowly as he heard the snow falling faintly through the universe and faintly falling, like the descent of their last end, upon all the living and the dead" (288). I believe that the passage also evokes Matthew Arnold's "Dover Beach," which depicts a world that

> Hath really neither joy, nor love, nor light,
> Nor certitude, nor peace, nor help for pain
> And we are here as on a darkling plain;
> Swept with confused alarms of struggle and flight,
> Where ignorant armies clash by night.
> (lines 33–37)

CHAPTER 6

1. The number seven is regarded as "a sacred, mystical and magic number" symbolizing "spiritual order and the completion of a natural cycle" (Tresidder 167). Its significance is "based on early astronomy," in particular on "the seven wandering stars or dynamic celestial bodies (the sun and moon, Mars, Mercury, Jupiter, Venus, and Saturn) after which the days of the week in many cultures were named" (168).
2. This concept recalls the Hindu and Buddhist *kalpas*, or cycles of cosmic creation and destruction. Edward Conze explains, "During the course of one kalpa, a world system completes its evolution, from its initial condensation to the final conflagration. One world system follows the other, without beginning and end, quite interminable" (*Buddhism* 49).
3. This description of the moon echoes the description of the sun in *Blood Meridian*: "The top of the sun rose out of nothing like the head of a great red phallus until it cleared the unseen rim and sat squat and pulsing and malevolent" (44–45).
4. It is interesting that the imagery of Boyd's dream resonates eerily with the descriptions of the burned dead in McCarthy's *The Road*: "Figures half mired in

the blacktop, clutching themselves, mouths howling . . . black skin stretched upon the bones and their faces split and shrunken on their skulls" (190).
5. McCarthy frequently evokes the Akashic ledger books in his fiction. In *Blood Meridian* the judge asks us to consider whether we believe "that gods of vengeance and of compassion alike lie sleeping in their crypt and whether our cries are for an accounting or for the destruction of ledgers altogether they must evoke only the same silence and that it is this silence which will prevail?" (330). In *The Stonemason*, Papaw talks about divine justice as being recorded in these ledgers: "They's a ledger kept that the pages dont never get old nor crumbly nor ink dont never fade" (29). His grandson, Ben, dreams about this ledger but finds that the pages have indeed crumbled and the ink has faded:

> I stood with my job-book beneath my arm in which were logged the hours and the days and the years and wherein was ledgered down each sack of mortar and each perch of stone and I stood alone in that whitened forecourt beyond which waited the God of all being and I stood in the full folly of my own righteousness and I took the book from under my arm and I thumbed it through a final time as if to reassure myself and when I did I saw that the pages were yellowed and crumbling and the ink faded and the accounts no longer clear and suddenly I thought to myself fool do you not see what will be asked of you? (111).

In the first book of *The Crossing*, the narrative voice describes "the earth running under bare poles toward a reckoning whose ledgers would be drawn up and dated only long after all due claims had passed, such is this history" (5). When Billy carries his brother's bones back to American soil in book 4 of *The Crossing*, the "old gods of that country" are described as "tracing his progress over the darkened ground" and "logging his name into their ancient daybook of vanities" (393). In *Cities of the Plain* the narrative voice announces, "The log of the world is composed of its entries, but it cannot be divided back into them" (286). Later in the same novel, we encounter a traveler who narrates his dream vision of "rawhide trunks with latches and corners of hammered copper and these were much scarred from their travels and the years of it and inside of them were old accounts and ledgerbooks and records of the history of that vanished folk, the path they had followed in the world and their reckonings of the cost of that journey" (288). In *The Road* the narrative voice asks, "Do you think that your fathers are watching? That they weigh you in their ledgerbook? Against what? There is no book and your fathers are dead in the ground" (196).
6. Compare this to the passage in *All the Pretty Horses* in which the wild horses stand "waiting for they knew not what with the voice of the breaker still running in their brains like the voice of some god come to inhabit them" (105).

7. The description of the traps alludes to McCarthy's portrayal of the "pain of the world" in *All the Pretty Horses*, which is similarly depicted as a "mindless" and "parasitic being" (257). The blindness of the traps also evokes the blindness of the Gnostic demiurge. Hans Jonas writes that "this perversion of the Divine has retained of it only the power to act, but to act blindly, without knowledge and benevolence. Thus did the demiurge create the world out of ignorance and passion" (327).
8. Jason Ambrosiano also identifies the Gnostic elements in this passage, arguing that while "Arnulfo's admonition utilizes the Catholic Eucharist, it is also somewhat Manichean. He claims that while one can trap the wolf, he or she will only have teeth and skin. The true wolf, its spirit, cannot be known through possession of its body." Ambrosiano then argues that Billy "rejects" Don Arnulfo's ideas and "begins to envision the wolf's connection to the spiritual, to God, as being located in its blood. He sees his own participation in this connection as tied to his own blood" (85). While I agree with Ambrosiano's insight into the Gnostic interpretation of the passage, I do not believe that Billy's fascination with blood is a rejection of Don Arnulfo's ideas. Rather, images of blood within the novel function as symbolic manifestations of that ineffable essence connecting all living beings, which Don Arnulfo refers to as that "unknowable thing" (45).
9. A similar concept is raised in *All the Pretty Horses* when the wild horses are broken: "The animals whinnied to one another in the dark and answered back as if some one among their number were missing, or some thing" (107). This missing "thing" among the horses is the very thing you "lose" when you capture the wolf.
10. In *The Counselor*, Westray also expounds on the transience and insubstantiality of the world: "And everything that exists will one day vanish. Forever. And it will take with it every explanation of it that was ever contrived. From Newton to Einstein to Homer and Shakespeare and Michelangelo. Every timeless creation. Your art and your poetry and your science are not even composed of smoke" (62).
11. Don Arnulfo adds that "it was at such a place that God sits and conspires in the destruction of that which he has been at such pains to create" (47). This description of God suggests the Trimurti (Three Forms) of the Hindu Brahman. According to this system, Brahman possesses a creative function as performed by the God Brahma, a preserving function as performed by the God Vishnu, and a destructive function as performed by the God Shiva (Pereira 32). Don Arnulfo continues to talk in terms that closely resemble Hindu Śaivism, or the worship of the Shiva aspects of the Brahman. As José Pereira explains, "For Śaivism, God is a terrifying, almost consuming, vitality, embodied in libidinousness and destructive power, and expressed through images of poison, fire and death" (32).
12. Aldous Huxley addresses this problem in greater detail, explaining that "so long as the symbol remains, in the worshipper's mind, firmly attached and instrumental to that which is symbolized, the use of such things as white and

variegated vestments can do no harm. But if the symbol breaks loose, as it were, and becomes an end in itself, then we have, at the best, a futile aestheticism and sentimentality, at the worst a form of psychologically effective magic" (246). According to Hans Martensen, Jacob Boehme also protested against the futility of paying mere lip-service to religious ceremonies: "[Boehme] contends so strongly against *Babel*, the existing Church, Protestant and Catholic, in which the Sacraments are only outwardly used, the Word is only outwardly preached and heard, without true dispositions of the heart, without the inward doors being really opened" (164).

13. Don Arnulfo's words about the world lying between the act and the ceremony, along with his insistence that death is the only form of order in the world, echo those of Duena Alfonsa in *All the Pretty Horses*: "In the end we all come to be cured of our sentiments. Those whom life does not cure death will. The world is quite ruthless in selecting between the dream and the reality, even where we will not. Between the wish and the thing the world lies waiting" (238).

14. Dianne Luce quotes a passage from Barry Holstun Lopez's *Of Wolves and Men* to explain why the wolf brutalizes the domestic animals:

> I [call] this exchange in which the animals [predator and prey] appear to lock eyes and make a decision the conversation of death. It is a ceremonial exchange, the flesh of the hunted in exchange for respect for its spirit. In this way both animals, not the predator alone, choose for the encounter to end in death. There is . . . a sacred order in this. . . . And it . . . happens only between the wolf and his major prey species. It produces, for the wolf, sacred meat. . . . Imagine a cow in the place of the moose or white-tailed deer. The conversation of death falters noticeably with domestic stock. . . . They have had the conversation of death bred out of them. They do not know how to encounter wolves. . . . What happens when a wolf wanders into a flock of sheep and kills twenty or thirty of them in apparent compulsion is perhaps not so much slaughter as a failure on the part of the sheep to communicate anything at all—resistance, mutual respect, appropriateness—to the wolf. The wolf has initiated a sacred ritual and met with ignorance" (qtd. in "Vanishing World" 184–85).

McCarthy seems to hint at a similar concept; the wolf understands the sacred aspects of existence in a way that most human beings do not. When humanity fails to apprehend the sacred—when our ceremonies become empty and meaningless—we become ignorant, like the cattle that so infuriate the wolf. This theme is discussed again in *The Counselor*, when Malkina reminisces about her pet cheetahs: "To see quarry killed with elegance is very moving to me. . . . The hunter has a purity of heart that exists nowhere else" (183).

15. The passage recalls the description of the ghostly Comanches in *All the Pretty Horses*, "all of them pledged in blood and redeemable in blood only" (5). Similarly, the judge in *Blood Meridian*, whose dancing at the end of the novel evokes Shiva's dance of destruction, addresses the kid with the following words: "You of all men are no stranger to that feeling, the emptiness and the despair. It is that which we take arms against, is it not? Is not blood the tempering agent in the mortar which bonds?" (329). The judge is a trickster, and his words cannot be taken at face value; however, his pronouncements on the sacred quality of blood resonate meaningfully with the role of blood in the Border Trilogy and indeed with René Girard's theories on the subject. Given the context of the conversation, the judge's words suggest that those who participate in violent bloodshed are forever bound together by the act; however, whether intentionally or not, his words are also a reminder that mankind is united by the fact that the same red blood flows through all human beings.

   We must not suppose, however, that McCarthy condones the redemptive value of bloodshed. In fact, Edwin Arnold's study of McCarthy's unpublished screenplay *Whales and Men* presents an alternate view. Quoting John Western, a character within the screenplay, Arnold writes, "'What is there about our existence that is so fraudulent that only bloodshed can redeem it? Why is torture, God help us, a moral inquiry?' His answer: 'With these howls we hope to provoke the silence of the universe into its own betrayal. For what we require above all else is a witness. Something to say that we are here and justified to be so.... Because deep in our hearts we fear we do not exist.' ... John Western's tortured thoughts might well reflect McCarthy's own bafflement at mankind's capacity for cruelty" ("Cormac McCarthy's *Whales and Men*" 24–25). When reading McCarthy's novels it is necessary, therefore, to distinguish between the destructive, death-seeking act of bloodshed and the symbolic quality of blood as a positive, life-giving, and unifying principle.

16. The knowledge contained within the wolf's eyes is reminiscent of a similar intuition in McCarthy's *Suttree*, where the eponymous protagonist comes to realize that "all souls are one and all souls lonely" (459).

17. McCarthy's treatment of the death of the wolf may be contrasted with Alfred de Vigny's famous poem "La mort du loup" (1843). De Vigny attributes no mystical significance to the wolf he and his fellow hunters kill, admiring only its courage and ability to fight and die in silence (cf. *The Crossing* 114: "The wolf fought in absolute silence"). The poem concludes with an admonition to the reader to emulate the wolf, thus firmly setting the import of the wolf's death in the material, not the spiritual, world:

   > Gémir, pleurer, prier est également lâche.
   > Fais énergiquement ta longue et lourde tache
   > Dans la voie où le Sort a voulu t'appeler,

> Puis après, comme moi, souffre et meurs sans parler.
> (Moaning, weeping, praying is equally cowardly.
> Staunchly carry out your long and heavy task
> In the path to which Fate saw fit to call you,
> Then, later, as I do, suffer and die in silence.)

18. With its references to blood and the terrible beauty of flowers, this passage recalls John Grady's revelation in *All the Pretty Horses*, when the young man similarly envisions that "the world's heart beat at some terrible cost and that the world's pain and its beauty moved in a relationship of diverging equity and that in this headlong deficit the blood of multitudes might ultimately be exacted for the vision of a single flower" (282).
19. Several critics have commented on the importance of this scene. Alex Hunt points out that Billy experiences "a powerful moment of connection with the wolf" and "identifies with the natural world around him" (33). Edwin Arnold also notes that Billy enters into a "borderstate of consciousness" in which "he merges spirits with the wolf," so that when he touches the wolf's lifeless body he is struck by an epiphanic vision of "the magnificence of her final freedom in the ordinate world" ("Go to Sleep" 62). Dianne Luce writes that Billy "responds to the wolf both aesthetically and spiritually" ("Vanishing World" 174).
20. This comparison has also been made by Edwin Arnold, who argues that "Billy's improbable relationship with the wolf is at this point almost mythic and, of the many man-wolf tales we might draw on, the story of Saint Francis of Assisi is the most intriguing" ("McCarthy and the Sacred" 230).
21. Billy's confusion is reminiscent of that experienced in McCarthy's *Outer Dark*, where the similarly guilt-ridden Culla spits in the river and finds that his spittle "slid inexplicably upstream, back the way he had come. He turned and watched it in disbelief" (17). Further comparisons may be drawn between the manifestations of Culla's and Billy's guilt in their postures. When Culla delivers his sister's child, a product of their incest, he sits with his hands "palmupward on his thighs ... watching them as if they were somehow unaccountable" (30). Similarly, after the death of the wolf Billy falls "asleep with his hands palm up before him like some dozing penitent" (126). These outward manifestations of guilt recall the evil omens in Shakespeare's *Macbeth*, where the sun also behaves strangely: "By th' clock 'tis day, / And yet dark night strangles the travelling lamp" (2.4.6–7), and another bird of prey meets an unusual death: "A falcon, tow'ring in her pride of place, / Was by a mousing owl hawked at and killed" (2.4.12–3). John Cant notes that the scene also alludes to the "Rhyme of the Ancient Mariner," arguing that the "reference to Coleridge is obvious" because the shooting of the albatross causes the sun to rise "upon the right" rather than "upon the left." Cant argues that, in both the poem and the novel, "shooting the bird disrupts the natural order" (198).

22. McCarthy often writes about the hidden patterns in things. For example, in *Child of God*, Lester Ballard's remains are dissected by medical students who examine his entrails "like those haruspices of old" and "perhaps [see] monsters worse to come in their configurations" (194). In *Suttree*, the ragman listens to "the sound of morning traffic upon the bridge beat with the dull echo of a dream in his cavern and the ragman would have wanted a sager soul than his to read in their endless advent auguries of things to come, the spectre of mechanical proliferation and universal blight" (256). In *Blood Meridian*, the hooves of the horses stir up the desert floor, creating mysterious patterns in the dust: "The alabaster sand shaped itself in whorls strangely symmetric like iron filings in a field and these shapes flared and drew back again, resonating upon that harmonic ground and then turning to swirl away over the playa. As if the very sediment of things contained yet some residue of sentience" (247). *The Road* also ends with a contemplation of this mysterious pattern: "Once there were brook trout in the streams in the mountains. . . . On their backs were vermiculate patterns that were maps of the world in its becoming. Maps and mazes. Of a thing which could not be put back. Not be made right again" (287).
23. This passage is echoed in the epilogue of *Cities of the Plain*, where a homeless man describes to an aged Billy a similar dream, in which such men sacrifice the dreamer in a strange ritual (272–83). A similar situation is also depicted in *The Road*: "This was the first human being other than the boy that he'd spoken to in more than a year. My brother at last. The reptilian calculations in those cold and shifting eyes. The gray and rotting teeth. Claggy with human flesh" (75).

CHAPTER 7

1. Critics concerned primarily with the concept of "the tale" include Charles Bailey, who writes, "*The Crossing* is about time and storytelling—more specifically, about how human beings exist in a dimension of time, which separates them from God and how that condition influences the art of literature" ("Last Stage" 58). Similarly, Robert Jarrett states, "The long interpolated tales in *The Crossing*, especially the one told by the ex-priest . . . stress that narrative is a means of establishing identity, of lending at least a provisional meaning to one's existence—an existence that is completed only in the listener's reception of the tale" (*Cormac McCarthy* 144). Dianne Luce takes a slightly different approach by focusing on the role of "witnessing" within the matrix of existence, arguing, "The priest comments explicitly on the role of witnessing others' lives as a solution to the problem of living one's own—as a way of breaking out of the relentlessly linear road narrative of one's life and connecting into the larger matrix of the world by witnessing and being witnessed" ("Road and the Matrix" 198). Critics who identify theological concerns in the ex-priest's tale include Florence Stricker, who writes, "*The Crossing*, with all its intertwined narratives, its

alternating of dreams and philosophical dialogues, has all the appearance of a theodicy," adding that "deep down" it "probably . . . poses the questions raised by Leibniz: the goodness of God, the freedom of man, and the origin of evil" (157). Stricker, however, does not go on to explore the ex-priest's specific ideas about the nature of the divine. John Ambrosiano argues that *The Crossing* embodies "a particular postmodernism, a Catholic one" (83). His argument is problematic, because postmodernism necessarily denies the existence of absolute truth, whereas Catholicism is entirely dependent on such a concept, and Ambrosiano offers no satisfactory resolution to these inherent contradictions. Steven Frye also mentions theodicy, arguing, "Since this world of experience is often extremely brutal, *The Crossing* is also related to theodicy, the effort to reconcile God's benevolence with evil." Frye concludes that this paradox can be solved by "an intuitive intimation of a divine source of creation itself, which is revealed in language and finally in narrative," thus shifting the focus onto the importance of storytelling within the novel ("Cormac McCarthy's 'World in its Making'" 55–56). In *Understanding Cormac McCarthy*, Frye engages in a philosophical, specifically Hegelian, reading of the ex-priest's tale.
2. The ex-priest's words recall a scene in McCarthy's *Outer Dark*: "She shook him awake from dark to dark, delivered out of the clamorous rabble under a black sun and into a night more dolorous" (5).
3. The God of the heretic's dream is simultaneously the creator, preserver, and destroyer of the cosmos, echoing the Hindu concept of the Trimurti (Three Forms), in which Brahma functions as the creator, Vishnu as the preserver, and Shiva as the destroyer.
4. McCarthy evokes a similar concept in *Suttree*, where the mysterious demiurgic entity that haunts the novel is described as, among other things, "a weaver, bloody shuttle shot through a timewarp, a carder of souls from the world's nap" (5). The trope of weaving the world into being is also present in *Blood Meridian*, where the cries of the coyotes sounding like the "cries of souls broke through some misweave in the weft of things into the world below" (109) and where "cloudbanks" stand "above the mountains like the dark warp of the very firmament" (154), "warp" and "weft" both suggesting the process of weaving. The image of the world artificer as a skilled worker is further explored in *Blood Meridian*, where the "false moneyer," or "coldforger," also "crouched at his trade," is forever "hammering out like his own conjectural destiny all through the night of his becoming some coinage for a dawn that would not be" (310); and again in *All the Pretty Horses*, where Alfonsa describes how fate lies in the hands of a coiner, "peering with his poor eyes through dingy glasses at the blind tablets of metal before him" (231).
5. Dianne Luce identifies the allusion to Melville's sinister weaver god in McCarthy's screenplay *The Gardener's Son*. Comparing Melville's deafening loom to the deafening mill in McCarthy's screenplay, Luce writes that such noise

"causes human deafness reflecting the deafness of the weaver god, the artificer demiurge who is oblivious to both the true, alien God and the pneumatic spark in humankind" (*Reading the World* 178). Luce also points to a similar reference in McCarthy's *Suttree*, where "a few pieces of Denver silver," inscribed "In God We Trust," are described as "avowing blind faith in deaf deities" (261). Luce, however, does not apply the same interpretation to the heretic's dream in *The Crossing*, arguing that this is a vision of "a more benign weaver-god creating a tapestry . . . for whom the individual is an integral thread of this endless fabric" and that the "weaver-god is reinscribed as a truer god in the heretic's vision" (226, 277).

6. In *The Denial of Death*, Ernest Becker explores humanity's inability to come to terms with this inevitable fate: "Everything that man does in his symbolic world is an attempt to deny and overcome his grotesque fate. He literally drives himself into a blind obliviousness with social games, psychological tricks, and personal preoccupations so far removed from the reality of his situation that they are forms of madness—agreed madness, but madness all the same" (27). The heretic differs only in that he has accepted this state of existence, whereas according to Becker, most of us live under this metaphorical collapsing roof in utter denial of our predicament.

7. In *The Trial of God*, Elie Wiesel depicts a medieval village after a pogrom, where a Jewish man puts Yahweh on trial, accusing him of "hostility, cruelty and indifference" (qtd. in Cohn-Sherbok 128). Wiesel supposedly witnessed such a trial at Auschwitz, where the imprisoned rabbis put God on trial for breaking the covenant, found him guilty, and then went off to pray.

8. It may be necessary at this point to more fully explicate the difference between the ineffable, transcendent Absolute and the lower-order creator deity. Edward Conze explains these two concepts of God in both Buddhist and Gnostic terms:

> As distinct from the theistic religions, both Mahayana and Gnosis differentiate between the still and quiescent *Godhead*, and the active *creator god*, who is placed at a lower level. Of the first, the Hermetists said that "of Him no words can tell, no tongue can speak, silence only can declare Him." And so the Buddhists on countless occasions [speak] about the Absolute which they identified with Nirvana, the Buddha, the Realm of Dharma, Suchness, etc. The demiurge, in his turn, is a secondary divine being who, himself a proud, ambitious and impure spirit, has created this most unsatisfactory world. His Buddhist counterpart is to some extent the Hindu god Brahmā who in his stupidity boasts about having created this cosmos, when in fact it is the automatic product of cycles of evolution and involution going on over the

ages. But, however the world may have come about, at present it is, in any case, the domain of an evil force, of Satan or of Mara the Evil One. (*Further Buddhist Studies* 24–25)

Stephan Hoeller also gives a succinct explanation of "the Gnostic concept of God, which is more subtle than most" (16). According to Hoeller, "The God of the Gnostics is the ultimate reality, beyond and in a sense quite alien to the created universe. Like Kabbalists and most esotericists the world over, Gnostics substitute the idea of the emanation of the Divine in place of the idea of creation. The transcendent God does not create; the divine essence emanates, comes forth, from the unmanifest state into the manifest, making possible further, more specific creation. The original God remains always the first cause, while other entities become subordinate, or secondary, causes of creation" (16–17). This concept also appears in McCarthy's favorite novel, *Moby-Dick*, when Captain Ahab berates the demiurge: "Thou knowest not how came ye, hence callest thyself unbegotten; Certainly knowest not thy beginning, hence callest thyself unbegun. I know that of me, which thou knowest not of thyself, oh, thou omnipotent. There is some unsuffusing thing beyond thee to whom all thy eternity is but time, all thy creativeness mechanical" (Melville 476–77).

9. Although the Buddhists have long maintained that saṃsāra is in fact Nirvāṇa, at the same time they have been careful to point out that this is true only for the enlightened mind. Aldous Huxley writes that "for the fully enlightened, totally liberated person, Samsara and Nirvana, time and eternity, the phenomenal and the Real, are essentially one" (299). Huxley explains, "That Nirvana and Samsara are one is a fact about the nature of the universe, but it is a fact which cannot be fully realized or directly experienced, except by souls far advanced in spirituality. For ordinary, nice, unregenerate people to accept this truth by hearsay, and to act upon it in practice is merely to court disaster" (70). According to this line of thought, to seek, as the priest did, for the divine within the manifest world before one has achieved full enlightenment is to be drawn into the glittering trap of the world. In other words, worshipping this world as though it were the divine itself can only lead to confusion and error and may easily become a hindrance to spiritual growth.

10. Upon psychoanalyzing the behavior of the biblical creator deity, Carl Gustav Jung arrived at a similar conclusion regarding Job's role as witness in the eponymous book of the Old Testament. Jung's diagnosis is as follows: "The character thus revealed fits a personality who can only convince himself that he exists through his relation to an object. Such dependence on the object is absolute when the subject is totally lacking in self-reflection and therefore has no insight into himself. It is as if he existed only by reason of the fact that he has an object which assured him that he is really there" (*Answer to Job* 14). Jung argues that

the book of Job is concerned not with the creator's insecure testing of Job's faith but rather with the creator's insecure testing of his own existence due to a complete lack of personal insight.

11. In the words of Ludwig Wittgenstein, "Wovon man nicht sprechen kann, darüber muß man schweigen" (Whereof one cannot speak, thereof one must be silent) (76).

12. In McCarthy's unpublished screenplay *Whales and Men*, the character Kelly McAmon speaks of the nondual nature of the Absolute. According to Edwin Arnold, "McAmon, in discussing her vision of God, anticipates the priest's tale in *The Crossing* when she says, 'I want a God so large that there's no place to even stand outside of him to say that he's not so.... The problem is that it's so simple we cant see it. It includes everything and everybody so that there's nothing left over outside of it with which to compare it. That's why we cant think our way to God.'" ("Cormac McCarthy's *Whales and Men*" 45). The Perennial Philosophy teaches that we can never think our way to the Absolute, because the Absolute is transrational; while irrational thought precedes reason, transrational thought moves *beyond* it. In Buddhist terms, Nirvāṇa is *attakavacara* (transrational), because it "transcends logic ... and cannot at all be conventionally known" (Nath 622). Similarly, Edward Conze writes that "ultimately, Nirvana is unthinkable and incomprehensible" (*Buddhism* 112).

13. In book 4 of *The Crossing*, a gypsy tells Billy much the same thing, insisting that "the husk is not the thing," because every "representation" is "an idol" and "every likeness a heresy" (413).

CHAPTER 8

1. Tiresias, or Teiresias, is the archetypal blind Theban seer of Greek mythology. Tiresias appears in Sophocles's *Oedipus the King*, where he "knows that Oedipus has killed his father and married his mother, and that the king is himself the polluter of Thebes.... He even tells Oedipus so, but Oedipus is too angry to pay his words serious attention and it is only later that he realises how the prophet, although blind in his eyes, yet saw the truth, while he himself, although his eyes had sight, had nevertheless been blind. In his anguish he puts out his own eyes" (March 368). In *The Crossing*, McCarthy explores these themes of physical and metaphorical blindness through the tale of the blind man.

2. Robert Jarrett also identifies Gnostic elements in the blind man's story, arguing, "While the blind man's vocabulary and imagery allude to Christian discourse, in which the 'light of the world' is associated with Christ, the vision is not Christian.... Historic gnosticism, a version of Christianity that was finally proscribed as heresy, in several points closely resembles the blind man's vision, for gnosticism saw the world as the darkened creation of the flawed demiurge,

preferred mystical interpretations of the parables, and opposed the imagery of light as knowledge to darkness as ignorance" (*Cormac McCarthy* 151).

3. The description of the German officer as an "architect" of "darkness" might also be an allusion to the comment made by the British statesman Sir Edward Grey on the eve of the First World War: "The lamps are going out all over Europe, we shall not see them lit again in our time" (Hynes 3).

4. It is worth noting that the blind man's "deeper fire" is reminiscent of the "inner fire" of the antelopes described in book 1 of *The Crossing*. From a Gnostic perspective, these descriptions serve as a reminder that all living things possess a spark of the divine.

5. The sudden apprehension of the world as a place of darkness and despair is a theme that permeates McCarthy's Border Trilogy. The description of the blind man's anguish is reminiscent of John Grady's experience in *All the Pretty Horses*: "He imagined the pain of the world to be like some formless parasitic being seeking out the warmth of human souls wherein to incubate" (256).

6. The mysterious bell is another common theme in the Border Trilogy. In book 1 of *The Crossing*, Billy wakes from a dream to hear "somewhere a solitary bell that tolled and ceased" (112), and in *All the Pretty Horses* John Grady similarly hears "a bell that tolled and ceased where no bell was" (30).

7. In book 1 of *The Crossing*, Don Arnulfo has already told Billy, "You cannot touch the world. You cannot hold it in your hand for it is made of breath only" (46). In book 2, the ex-priest explains that "this world also which seems to us a thing of stone and flower and blood is not a thing at all but is a tale" (143).

8. Robert Browning expresses much the same idea in "Bishop Blougram's Apology" when he writes, "Some think creation's meant to show him forth / I say it's meant to hide him all it can" (lines 652–53). Such intuitions regarding the deceptive nature of the manifest world recall the words of the ex-priest in book 2 of *The Crossing*, when he tells Billy, "Trees and stones are no part of it" (152).

9. The reference to the "good God" suggests the beliefs of the Cathars, who, like the Gnostics, distinguished between the transcendent "Good God" or "the God of Light," who "reigns over and governs the heavens," and "the God of Evil" or "Satan," who "reigns over and governs the visible world and all other bodies" (Costen 63). The Cathars, whose name translates as the "pure ones," flourished peacefully in the Languedoc region of France in the twelfth and thirteenth centuries before they were brutally massacred by the Crusaders during the Inquisition. Like the Buddhists, the Cathars believed in reincarnation, avoided attachment to the things of this world, followed a largely vegetarian diet, and practiced nonviolent resistance, for "to kill, even in self-defence, was contrary to the dictates of their faith" (Hoeller 149).

10. In an interview with Gary Wallace, McCarthy proclaims "that our inability to see spiritual truth is the greatest mystery." When Wallace asks, "But what exactly is truth?" McCarthy gives him an elegantly laconic reply: "'Truth,' he repeated,

his implications tacit" (138). McCarthy puts his own views regarding truth into the mouth of John Grady in *All the Pretty Horses*. When the captain tells the young man, "We can make the truth here," John Grady replies, "There aint but one truth.... The truth is what happened. It aint what come out of somebody's mouth" (168).

11. Although Jacob Boehme is often mistaken for a Gnostic, his conception of God remains within the boundaries of Lutheran Christianity in that he continues to worship the creator of the cosmos. Nicolas Berdyaev writes, "Boehme's torment over the problem of evil relates him to the ancient gnostics. But his conclusions differ from theirs, by his incomparably more Christian character" (xi).

12. McCarthy depicts a similar situation in *The Road*, where the protagonist also dreams of a lost world no longer accessible to him. In this case, the world of beauty and color has vanished not through the loss of sight but through an unspecified apocalyptic disaster that leaves behind a landscape of darkness and ash. Much like the blind man in *The Crossing*, the man in *The Road* finds that such dreams "torment" him, but unlike the blind man, he *would* "wish them away."

> He mistrusted all of that. He said the right dreams for a man in peril were dreams of peril and all else was the call of languor and death. He slept little and he slept poorly. He dreamt of walking in a flowering wood where birds flew before them he and the child and the sky was aching blue but he was learning how to wake himself from just such siren worlds. Lying there in the dark with the uncanny taste of peach from some phantom orchard fading in his mouth. He thought if he lived long enough the world at last would all be lost. Like the dying world the newly blind inhabit, all of it slowly fading from memory. (18)

The man in *The Road* mistrusts the dreams of the lost world because he feels that they are the deceptively alluring call of death: "And the dreams so rich in color. How else would death call you?" (21).

13. It is precisely such beauty that John Grady contemplates in *All the Pretty Horses*, fearing that "the world's heart beat at some terrible cost and that the world's pain and its beauty moved in a relationship of diverging equity and that in this headlong deficit the blood of multitudes might ultimately be exacted for the vision of a single flower" (282). In other words, the blind man can no longer appreciate the beauty of this "single flower" and, as a result, nothing remains to distract him from the "blood of multitudes" or the "terrible cost" exacted by the world.

14. The blind man's words recall Alfonsa's claim in *All the Pretty Horses*—"What is constant in history is greed and foolishness and a love of blood" (239)—along with the words of Mr. Wade in *Child of God*, who, when asked if "people was meaner then than they are now," replies, "I think people are the same from the day God first made one" (168).

15. Such views were also taught by Śaṅkara, a philosopher of the Advaita school of Hinduism, who explained that Brahman (the Godhead) was essentially nondual and that "the multiplicity of things exists only through 'Maya' (which one usually translates as 'mere appearance')" (Otto 3).
16. As previously mentioned, in McCarthy's *Whales and Men* one of the characters asks, "What is there about our existence that is so fraudulent that only bloodshed can redeem it?" (Arnold, "Cormac McCarthy's *Whales and Men*" 24). The blind man's words address this very problem.
17. In fact, the idea that the blind can see more clearly, or conversely that those who have eyes cannot actually see, is a common theme in McCarthy's fiction. In *Outer Dark*, for example, a preacher tells Culla, "In a world darksome as this'n I believe a blind man ort to be better sighted than most" (226). Later, when Culla insists that his mutilated child "ort to have two" eyes, he is told, "Maybe he ort to have more'n that. Some folks has two and cain't see" (232). At the end of the novel, Culla asks a blind man, "Why don't ye pray back your eyes?" The blind man replies, "I believe it'd be a sin. Them old eyes can only show ye what's done there anyways. If a blind man needed eyes he'd have eyes.... What needs a man to see his way when he's sent there anyhow?" (241). *Cities of the Plain* also features a blind man with insight into the true nature of the world, who frequently imparts words of wisdom to John Grady: "Men speak of blind destiny, a thing without scheme or purpose. But what sort of destiny is that? Each act in this world from which there can be no turning back has before it another, and it another yet. In a vast endless net" (195).
18. The vague, malignant presence "of things disturbed" recalls John Grady's experience of evil in *All the Pretty Horses* as "something imperfect and malformed lodged in the heart of being. A thing smirking deep in the eyes of grace itself like a gorgon in an autumn pool" (71). John Grady also observes the night sky and the dying fire and experiences an apprehension of the enormity of the cosmos: "The fire had burned to coals and he lay looking up at the stars in their places and the hot belt of matter that ran the chord of the dark vault overhead and he put his hands on the ground at either side of him and pressed them against the earth and in that coldly burning canopy of black he slowly turned dead center to the world, all of it taut and trembling and moving enormous and alive under his hands" (119). Barcley Owens identifies this vision of the campfire and the night sky as a common theme in the Border Trilogy, arguing, "The cinematic visual effect, from campfire to stars, emphasizes mankind's primal beginnings and his remote isolation in the vast cosmos" (66).

CHAPTER 9

1. Charles Bailey discusses the role of fate in the novel, arguing that as "Billy's three crossings, despite his courageous efforts, become 'doomed enterprises,' so do all

heroic actions. Those actions rest on the hero's belief that he can control his fate and that belief bears the mark of pride" ("Doomed Enterprises" 64).
2. This sentiment is very much in keeping with the words of the shopkeeper in *All the Pretty Horses*, who claims "that it was good that God kept the truths of life from the young as they were starting out or else they'd have no heart to start at all" (284).
3. In *Cities of the Plain*, Billy carries the dead John Grady, "gathered in his arms" (261), through the streets of Juárez. McCarthy is able to foreshadow the future in this way because the last book of the Border Trilogy, *Cities of the Plain*, was actually written first. After an interview with McCarthy in 1992, soon after the publication of *All the Pretty Horses*, Richard Woodward explains, "The book is, in fact, the first volume of a trilogy; the third part has existed for more than 10 years as a screenplay" (40).
4. Such an unlikely convergence of paths is also discussed in *Blood Meridian*, when the Glanton gang members examine the junction where the path of luckless travelers was crossed by the path of their murderers. "The trail of the Argonauts terminated in ashes as told and in the convergence of such vectors in such a waste" and "the expriest asked if some might not see the hand of a cynical god conducting with what austerity and what mock surprise so lethal a congruence" (153).
5. Similarly, in *All the Pretty Horses* John Grady is visited by the dead Blevins in a dream and when he asks "what it was like to be dead," the latter replies "that it was like nothing at all" (225).
6. An incubus is a "feigned evil spirit or demon . . . supposed to descend upon persons in their sleep, and especially to seek carnal intercourse with women" (*OED*). In *Cities of the Plain*, Tiburcio is referred to as an "incubus of uncertain proclivity" (183). In the same novel, Magdalena suffers an epileptic fit and is described "bowed in the bed and raging as if some incubus were upon her" (72).
7. This idea is also put forward in book 3 of *The Crossing* by the blind man, who tells Billy that the "world was new each day for God so made it daily" (278).
8. Edwin Arnold argues the same point when he writes, "The gypsy attempts to show Billy, through his story of the two airplanes, that the 'vanity' of his need to 'reclaim' his dead brother is as selfish and misguided as the rich man's attempt to recover the plane in which his son died," because "the actual plane and Boyd's desiccated corpse, as physical objects, no longer have any inherent meaning" ("McCarthy and the Sacred" 228).
9. Here the gypsy reiterates the wisdom of Don Arnulfo in book 1 of *The Crossing*, when he tells Billy, "El lobo es una cosa incognoscible. . . . Lo que se tiene en la trampa no es mas que dientes y forro." (The wolf is an unknowable thing. . . . That which one has in the trap is no more than teeth and fur.) (45). This concept is explored at greater length in McCarthy's unpublished screenplay *Whales and Men* through the character of Peter Gregory, who speculates, "More and more

language seemed to me to be an aberration by which we had come to lose the world. Everything that is named is set at one remove from itself. Nomenclature is the very soul of secondhandness" (qtd. in Arnold, "Go to Sleep" 37). Huston Smith is similarly critical of the power of words, arguing that "words can build up a kind of substitute world that dilutes the intensity of direct experience." Smith concludes that "the highest modes of experience transcend the reach of words entirely" (*Religions of Man* 142). McCarthy's gypsy, Don Arnulfo, and Peter Gregory all argue that words are not the same as experiences and that the deepest, or rather highest, realities of existence must be experienced directly, not merely talked or read about.

10. In *The Counselor*, Westray states, "Alles Vergänglich ist nu rein Gleichnis, as Goethe has it. Everything that perishes is but a likeness. That's really Plato on wheels" (62).

11. The concept of such "witnessing" is also raised by the heretic in book 2 of *The Crossing*. "He saw the world pass into nothing in the very multiplicity of its instancing. Only the witness stood firm. And the witness to that witness" (154). The judge in *Blood Meridian* also claims, "Whether in my book or not, every man is tabernacled in every other and he in exchange and so on in an endless complexity of being and witness to the uttermost edge of the world" (141).

12. The gypsy's words echo the words of the shaman in book 1, who also tells Billy that the world, as we know it, exists in "men's hearts" and "while it seemed a place which contained men it was in reality a place contained within them" (134).

13. Dianne Luce interprets the gypsy's words to mean "that we are always alive, that we know nothing but life, because time does not exist outside of ourselves" (*Reading the World* 225). But John Grady's and Billy's meetings with the dead Jimmy Blevins and Boyd, respectively, suggest otherwise; we do not "know nothing but life," because we are painfully aware of the death of others.

14. The image of the "candled skull" is also evoked in *Outer Dark*, when the narrative voice describes Rinthy in the lamplight: "The lamp just at her elbow belaboured by a moth whose dark shape cast upon her face appeared captive within the delicate skull, the thin and roselit bone, like something kept in a china mask" (59). The "something" held "captive" within the "mask" of her face subtly evokes the concept of the trapped pneuma. Dianne Luce also interprets the passage from a Gnostic perspective, arguing, "The visual illusion of this dark moth as captive spirit suggests the pneuma benighted in matter" (*Reading the World* 82).

15. In this struggle, the dream pilgrims recall the epilogue to *Blood Meridian*, in which a solitary man is depicted "progressing over the plain" and "striking the fire out of the rock" (337). Leo Daugherty has identified this highly symbolic image as that of a pneumatic "in possession of gnosis," "working to free spirit from matter" (169). The figure in *Blood Meridian*, however, works "in the dawn," "uses an implement," and "move[s] on again" (337), in contrast to the figures in *The Crossing*, who work in the twilight, carry no tools, and eventually disappear,

suggesting that the latter fail in their Gnostic quest to liberate the spirit from the darkness of the manifest cosmos.

16. The "demented vivisectionists" of *The Crossing* also recall the hallucinated "brainsurgeon" in *Suttree* (188), which Dale Cooper and Ethan Carry have identified as one of the many manifestations of evil within the novel: "The thing, the weaver, the brain-surgeon and the huntsman . . . represent a nightmarish, even ghoulish, force of evil at war in the world with forces of good" (167–68). The demiurgical "surgeon" is evoked again in *Blood Meridian*, where the members of the Glanton gang are described as "tattooed, branded, sutured, the great puckered scars inaugurated God knows where by what barbarous surgeons across chests and abdomens like the tracks of gigantic millipedes" (167). *Blood Meridian* also features a description of the bodies of murdered Mexican soldiers, lying in a common grave "with their wounds like the victims of surgical experimentation" (184).

17. In McCarthy's unpublished screenplay *Whales and Men*, a character named John Western describes a similar vision following the massacre of a pod of whales: "I dont know what it was. A flare. Something. And I thought: What would happen if chaos should come? Would we be worse off? What if this were the sun misrisen at midnight? What if all order were suddenly in abeyance, the skies given over to the access of sudden random moons, everything mindless and migratory? So that all we knew to be so was set aside and we found ourselves dwelling in a silent pandemonium. Would we be worse off?" (qtd. in Arnold, "Cormac McCarthy's *Whales and Men*" 26). Edwin Arnold points out that this moment "clearly anticipates Billy Parham's vision at the end of *The Crossing*, in which 'order' is suddenly in abeyance" ("Cormac McCarthy's *Whales and Men*" 26).

18. Hans Jonas gives an elaborate account of the Manichean system of cosmology, explaining how the "sun and moon are agents of salvation in Manichaean myth," working as "protective escorts" that carry the spirit back to the divine source of Light (127, 225). The "sun transmits the Light to the Light above it in the world of praise, and it goes on in that world until it arrives at the highest and pure Light" (233). Numerous Manichean psalms were composed in praise of the sun's divine function, for example: "Lo, the Darkness I have subdued . . . as the Sphere turns hurrying round, as the sun receives the refined parts of life" (qtd. in Jonas 229). Manichean myths describe how "that part of the devoured Light which is least sullied is extracted from the Hyle (matter), purified to 'light' in the physical sense, and from the purest part are formed sun and moon." This does not hold true for "the planets, which belong to the archons" (Jonas 224).

CHAPTER 10

1. One of the most disturbing instance of animal suffering in *The Orchard Keeper* occurs when the "county humane officer" shoots a couple of dogs in an ironically

inhumane fashion. "Most of the old men had been there the day he shot two dogs behind the store with a .22 rifle, one of them seven times, it screaming and dragging itself along the fence in the field below the forks while a cluster of children stood watching until they too began screaming" (117).
2. The passage also recalls the description in *All the Pretty Horses* of buzzards "feeding on a dead colt" whose "poor form stretched in the tainted grass eyeless and naked" (225).
3. These descriptions of the revolution recall Alfonsa's claim in *All the Pretty Horses*: "What is constant in history is greed and foolishness and a love of blood" (239).
4. This idea is articulated in *Blood Meridian* when Judge Holden states, "All progressions from a higher to a lower order are marked by ruins and mystery and a residue of a nameless rage" (146).
5. The prehistoric past is evoked in *The Orchard Keeper* through passages such as the following: "On a high bluff among trilobites and fishbones, shells of ossified crustaceans from an ancient sea, a great stone tusk jutted" (88). Descriptions of pictographs and the vanished cultures that created them feature in *Blood Meridian*, "pictographs of horse and cougar and turtle and mounted Spaniards helmeted and bucklered and contemptuous of stone and silence and time itself" (138); in *The Crossing*, "along the face of the stone bluffs were old pictographs of men and animals and suns and moons as well as other representations that seemed to have no referent in the world although they once may have" (135); as well as in *No Country for Old Men*: "The rocks there were etched with pictographs perhaps a thousand years old. The men who drew them hunters like himself. Of them there was no other trace" (11). John Cant writes that the pictographs signify "the impermanence and insignificance of human societies and cultures within the timescale of the history of the earth itself" and argues that the "frequent repetition of this image emphasizes the significance it must hold for McCarthy" (228).
6. According to Sara Mosle, the extinction of civilizations and cultures is one of the chief concerns of the Border Trilogy: "That brief moment between a culture's existence and extinction—this is the border that McCarthy's characters keep crossing and recrossing, and the one story, as he's forever writing, that contains all others" (16). Similarly, Jacqueline Scoones points out that the Border Trilogy "portrays a variety of extinctions both past and possible: the extinction of families and homes, customs and beliefs, governments and nations, civilizations, salt seas, the fish that once swam in them, grey wolves and, by inference, all living things" (131). Scoones argues, "One of the predominant Border Trilogy themes is that the human story, our world, is only a fragment of the earth's history—and yet one increasingly influential and dangerous for many of earth's inhabitants" (132).

7. Though I agree with John Scaggs's argument regarding the themes of loss that dominate *Cities of the Plain*, I disagree with his claim that the novel was influenced by Marcel Proust on the grounds that McCarthy explicitly voices his dislike for the French novelist in an interview with Richard Woodward, who writes that for McCarthy, "Proust and Henry James don't make the cut. 'I don't understand them,' he says. 'To me, that's not literature'" (36).
8. *Suttree* is replete with images of urban decay and squalor. Consider, for example, the following description of the river: "Old tins and jars and ruined household artefacts that rear from the fecal mire of the flats like landmarks in the trackless vales of dementia praecox. A world beyond all fantasy, malevolent and tactile and dissociate, the blown lightbulbs like shorn polyps semitranslucent and skullcolored bobbing blindly down and spectral eyes of oil and now and again the beached and stinking forms of foetal humans bloated like young birds mooneyed and bluish or stale gray" (4).
9. The maestro's words echo those of Alfonsa in *All the Pretty Horses*: "For me the world has always been more of a puppet show. But when one looks behind the curtain and traces the strings upward he finds they terminate in the hands of yet other puppets, themselves with their own strings which trace upward in turn, and so on" (231).
10. Judge Holden voices much the same idea in *Blood Meridian* when he states that the "truth about the world" is that it is only "a hat trick in a medicine show," "an itinerant carnival," or "a migratory tentshow" (245).
11. McCarthy's *Suttree* abounds in grotesquely carnivalesque scenes, such as the following:

    > Illbedowered harlots were calling from small porches in the night, in their gaudy rags like dolls panoplied out of a dirty dream. And along the little ways in the rain and lightning came a troupe of squalid merrymakers bearing a caged wivern on shoulderpoles and other alchemical game, chimeras and cacodemons skewered up on boarspears and a pharmacopoeia of hellish condiments adorning a trestle and toted by trolls with an eldern gnome for guidon who shouted foul oaths from his mouthole and a piper who piped a pipe of ploverbone and wore on his hip a glass flasket of some smoking fuel that yawed within viscid as quicksilver. (288)

12. The sacrificial virgin appears again in the epilogue to *Cities of the Plain*, when a mysterious traveler tells the aged Billy about a dream within a dream, in which "a young girl with eyes closed and hands crossed upon her breasts as if in death" is about to be sacrificed on an ancient altar (279).
13. The sinister ticking is reminiscent of a passage in *Suttree* that describes the young protagonist's first realization of mortality: "Lives running out like

something foul, night soil from a cesspipe, a measured dripping in the dark" (136). Later in the same novel, we come across a similar description of "a liquid dripping, something gone awry in the earth's organs to which this measured bleeding clocked a constantly eluded doom" (261). The same theme is evoked in *The Road* when the man dreams of a cave: "Deep stone flues where the water dripped and sang. Tolling in the silence the minutes of the earth and the hours and the days of it and the years without cease" (3).

14. In McCarthy's *The Counselor*, the diamond dealer expresses a similar view: "To partake of the stone's endless destiny. Is not that the meaning of adornment? To enhance the beauty of the beloved is to acknowledge both her frailty and the nobility of that frailty. At our noblest we announce to the darkness that we will not be diminished by the brevity of our lives. That we will not thereby be made less" (20).

CHAPTER 11

1. This is a realization already arrived at in *All the Pretty Horses*, when John Grady muses on the fact that this world seems "to care nothing for the old or the young or rich or dark or pale or he and she. Nothing for their struggles, nothing for their names. Nothing for the living or the dead" (301).
2. In *The Counselor*, a Catholic priest insists that "nothing is unforgivable" (82).
3. In *Civilization and Its Discontents*, Sigmund Freud writes, "Besides the instinct to preserve living substance and to join it into ever larger units, there must exist another, contrary instinct seeking to dissolve those units and to bring them back to their primaeval, inorganic state. That is to say, as well as Eros there was an instinct of death. The phenomena of life could be explained from the concurrent or mutually opposing action of these two instincts" (65–66).
4. John Cant also argues that after the failed romance with Alejandra, John Grady "becomes a divided and self-destructive soul who seeks both love and death in the person of Magdalena, Alejandra's inverse" and that "the balance of the conflict is decided in favor of death" (237, 229).
5. Robert Jarrett similarly argues, "Cole's answer that all sins save suicide may be forgiven reverberates ironically within the narrative, for both Magdalena's return to the White Lake after her subsequent epileptic fit and Cole's return to duel with Eduardo can be constructed as tacit suicides" ("Cormac McCarthy's Sense of an Ending" 328).
6. Dianne Luce mentions Magdalena's essential purity in her analysis of the Gnostic elements in McCarthy's earlier novel *Outer Dark*, with reference to the character of Rinthy:

> Rinthy's position as an essentially innocent woman-child entrapped in "this world" of the flesh is echoed in the child-whore Magdalena kept in

sexual slavery in *Cities of the Plain*.... The innocent held captive in a brothel stands as a gnostic metaphor for the alien spirit imprisoned in the cosmos: Bishop Irenaeus recorded the gnostic conception that the Sophia (wisdom), imprisoned by the world-powers, transmigrates from body to body, suffering repeated indignities and finally becoming a prostitute in a brothel.... And we can back-read the metaphor from *Cities of the Plain* to see its application to Rinthy as well, trapped in a world of sexual assault and harassment, harsh judgement and stunted love. (*Reading the World* 103–4)

7. Similarly, John Cant argues that "the maestro appears as the oracle, the mythic seer, dispensing fatal prophecy, accompanied by his female 'priestess'" (231), that is, the blind man's daughter.
8. The "cold pneuma" that descends upon Magdalena may be compared to John Grady's own experience in *All the Pretty Horses*, when he feels "something cold and soulless enter him like another being" (254).
9. McCarthy also refers to haruspication in *Child of God*, when he describes the dissection of the serial killer Lester Ballard: "His entrails were hauled forth and delineated and the four young students who bent over him like those haruspices of old perhaps saw monsters worse to come in their configurations" (194).
10. Such depictions of evil occur throughout McCarthy's fiction, the most striking instances being the trio of sinister wanderers in *Outer Dark* or Judge Holden in *Blood Meridian*.
11. John Cant argues, "While the sense of realism remains dominant throughout the text there is no mistaking the overall mythic tenor of the tale" (219).
12. A similar scene occurs in *All the Pretty Horses*, when John Grady recounts his misfortunes to a group of children as though he were telling them a story or legend: "I once lived at a great hacienda, he told them, but now I have no place to live.... He told them that he had a novia who was in another town and that he was riding to her to ask her to be his wife" (243).
13. Rosemary Guiley writes, "In folklore, the cat is one of the favoured animal companions of witches.... Cats were familiars; they embodied demons who performed the witches' tasks of *maleficia* against their neighbors.... Black cats were seen to be the devil himself" (53).
14. See Morris Berman, "Introduction."
15. Horses also serve as symbols of redemptive antimodernity in the works of D. H. Lawrence, most notably the stallion in *St. Mawr* and the mare that Gerald cruelly dominates in *Women in Love*.

CHAPTER 12

1. Mary Francis Slattery defines literary realism in the following way: "In literature, realism is reference that gives an illusion of exact correspondence with reality in its limited aspects. It is not unlimited, ultimate reality but the fragmented, flawed world of quotidian experience that literary realism seems to refer to; or, it may be something felt as borrowed from that kind of experience, for instance, fragmentation or flawedness simply as such" (55). Some critics have argued that *Cities of the Plain* belongs to the genre of magical realism. Stacey Peebles examines this theme in "*Lo fantástico*: The Influence of Borges and Crotázar on the Epilogue of *Cities of the Plain*." Similarly, Edwin Arnold writes, "We must also acknowledge the probable literary influence of such dream writers as Borges, Castaneda, and Garcia Marquéz, whose forays into realms of magical realism are surely reflected in McCarthy, most obviously in the Border Trilogy" ("Go to Sleep" 41). I disagree with both Peebles and Arnold on the grounds that Cormac McCarthy has expressed his own distaste for magical realism in an interview: "I'm not a fan of some of the Latin American writers, magical realism. You know, it's hard enough to get people to believe what you're telling them without making it impossible. It has to be vaguely plausible" (qtd. in L. Grossman 61).
2. The idea that human beings construct a false idea of the world is discussed at length by the blind man in *The Crossing*: "He said that the light of the world was in men's eyes only for the world itself moved in eternal darkness and darkness was its true nature and true condition" (283).
3. Billy's words hark back to those uttered by the gypsy in the last book of *The Crossing*: "La cáscara no es la cosa" (The husk is not the thing) (411). The gypsy's statement effectively summarizes McCarthy's own view that a genuine mystical experience consists of "a direct apprehension of reality, unmediated by symbol" (Wallace 138).
4. These questions regarding the nature of time and the way that it manifests itself to human consciousness are, of course, metaphysical, but they also venture into the realm of quantum physics. In *The Fabric of Reality*, quantum physicist David Deutsch writes, "We do not experience time flowing, or passing. What we experience are differences between our present perceptions and our present memories of past perceptions." He explains, "*Nothing* can move from one moment to another. To exist at all at a particular moment means to exist there forever. Our consciousness exists at *all* our (waking) moments" (263). In other words, "It is tempting to suppose that the moment of which we are aware is the only real one, or is at least a little more real than the others. But this is just solipsism. All moments are physically real" (287). If we were to examine a timeline depicting us as observers at various stages of the past, present, and future, we would have to conclude that "they [the observers] are all conscious, and subjectively they are all in the present. Objectively, there is no present" (263).

5. The scepter within a scepter recalls Niels Bohr's model of the atom, in which "the atom is visualized as a nucleus in the center, containing all of the protons and neutrons, with the electrons whirling about it like planets in orbits. Bohr, of course, took his cue for the model from the solar system" (Harkay 388). This now outdated model led some people to speculate whether our solar system is only an atom in a larger solar system and the system extends simultaneously outward and inward, ad infinitum. "Have you ever (late at night, perhaps in an altered state) entertained the hypothesis that our entire universe is just a tiny speck in a giant other universe? And that within each atom of our universe, there exists a whole other tiny universe? And that in each of the 'atoms' of this tiny universe, there is contained yet another universe?" (Conee and Sider 144–45).

6. In *The Crossing*, Don Arnulfo evokes the ancient sacrificial origins of the ceremony of Holy Communion, explaining that "men drink the blood of God yet they do not understand the seriousness of what they do" (45).

7. The traveler's revelation recalls that of the heretic in *The Crossing*, who "had been wrong in his every reckoning of God and yet had come at last to an understanding of Him anyway" (157).

8. Despite the fact that "archatron" is not to be found in the *OED*, the word is strongly suggestive of arch-archon. In the discussion forum on the official Cormac McCarthy website, McCarthy scholar Rick Wallach argues, "Archatron is Greek gnostic for a high archon." (Forum topic: "McCarthy's Western Novels," thread: "Ending COTP," 13 August 1998–19 October 1999, www.cormacmccarthy.com).

9. J. Douglas Canfield argues that "McCarthy presents us with the last parable, a story of sacrificial substitution. As in René Girard's *Violence and the Sacred*, a scapegoat is found, perhaps to point to the ultimate end of our endless reciprocal violence, an Omega to the story that is also its Alpha" ("Crossing" 262). While I agree with Canfield's identification of the Girardian theme, I do not believe that this particular instance of sacrificial substitution is depicted as the final solution to our reciprocal violence. René Girard himself argues that violence is inseparable from human society and that it can never be entirely controlled or contained. According to Girard, "although men cannot live in the midst of violence, neither can they survive very long by ignoring its existence or by deluding themselves into the belief that violence, despite the ritual prohibitions attendant on it, can somehow be put to work as the mere tool or servant of mankind" (268).

10. The traveler's vision recalls that of Lester Ballard in McCarthy's *Child of God*: "He cast about among the stars for some kind of guidance but the heavens wore a different look that Ballard did not trust" (190).

11. The passage evokes *Blood Meridian*, in which the cries of the coyotes sound like the "cries of souls broke through some misweave in the weft of things into the world below" (109). The metaphor of weaving is, of course, evoked at length in

The Crossing when the demiurge weaves a "tapestry that was the world in its making and in its unmaking" (149).

12. The blind man in *The Crossing* arrives at this same anticosmic vision, coming to understand that "the world itself moved in eternal darkness and darkness was its true nature and true condition" (283).
13. We witness much the same transformation in *The Crossing*, when the ex-priest tells Billy about the heretic who arrives at a similar apprehension of reality: "Such a man is like a dreamer who wakes from a dream of grief to a greater sorrow yet" (146).
14. It is noteworthy that in *The Crossing*, the newly awakened heretic feels that "the pin has been pulled from the axis of the universe" (146).
15. Billy hears similar words from the ex-priest in *The Crossing*, who states, "For the path of the world also is one and not many and there is no alter course in any least part of it for that course is fixed by God and contains all consequences in the way of its going and outside of that going there is neither path nor consequence nor anything at all" (158).
16. These words recall those of the ex-priest in *The Crossing*, who also claimed, "Stones themselves are made of air. What they have power to crush never lived. In the end we shall all of us be only what we have made of God. For nothing is real save his grace" (158).
17. The ex-priest in *The Crossing* tells Billy much the same thing when he describes how those who hear the voice of God experience a "wildness of heart that springs from such longing" (152). The ex-priest explains, "It is this which we long for and are afraid to seek and which alone can save us" (153).
18. Edwin Arnold similarly argues that "dreams, [the storyteller] suggests, continue to remind us of what we fail to apprehend in our daily existence, but they cannot and should not 'satisfy' our yearning for that 'other,' else we would cease to strive for it" ("Go to Sleep" 67). The storyteller's words recall the equally paradoxical statement of the blind man in *The Crossing*, who tells Billy, "Ultimamente todo es polvo. . . . En esto vemos la benición más grande de Dios." (Finally everything is dust. . . . In this we see the greatest blessing of God.) (293). Billy, much younger than he is in the Border Trilogy epilogue, asks why this is so and the blind man replies that precisely "because what can be touched falls into dust there can be no mistaking those things for real" (294). In other words, the blind man believes that precisely because all created things are transient and ephemeral there is no mistaking them for the ultimate, eternal Reality of the Absolute.
19. McCarthy alludes to reincarnation, or rather transmigration, in *The Orchard Keeper*, when Arthur Ownby claims, "Lots of times . . . a body dies and their soul takes up in a cat for a spell" (227). The cycles of reincarnation are also hinted at when, after being struck by lightning, Ownby feels "the circle of years closing, the final increment of the curve returning him again to the inchoate, the

prismatic flux of sound and color wherein he had drifted once before and now beyond the world of men" (222).
20. This apocalyptic vision is finally realized in *The Road*: "The bleak and shrouded earth went trundling past the sun and returned again as trackless and as unremarked as the path of any nameless sisterworld in the ancient dark beyond" (181).
21. McCarthy's evocation of the transformations of the ocean in relation to human mortality suggests the following lines from Shakespeare's *The Tempest*:

> Full fathom five thy father lies;
> Of his bones are coral made;
> Those are pearls that were his eyes:
> Nothing of him that doth fade
> But doth suffer a sea-change
> Into something rich and strange. (1.2.396–401)

22. In McCarthy's *Suttree*, the protagonist undergoes various altered states of consciousness brought on by drugs, alcohol, starvation, and feverish delirium, until he finally sees through "the old lie that beholder and beheld are ever more than one" (281), arriving at the spiritual insight that "all souls are one soul" (414) and that a "man is all men" (422). McCarthy addresses this theme again in *The Crossing* when the heretic takes "the priest's hand in his own," bids him to "see the likeness," and makes the pronouncement, "All men are one and there is no other tale to tell" (156–57). In McCarthy's unpublished screenplay *Whales and Men*, Kelly McAmon also utilizes the hand metaphor to illustrate the essential oneness of all human beings: "I see your hand and I see my hand.... And I see that the similarities are so much greater than the differences and I know that there is a connection there that no separation in time or space can ever invalidate. I know that you are my brother and at another level which is harder to reach but just as real I know that you are me. Not figuratively. Not a metaphor. For real. In the flesh" (qtd. in Arnold, "Cormac McCarthy's *Whales and Men*" 25).
23. In *All the Pretty Horses*, John Grady hears "a bell that tolled and ceased where no bell was" (30), and in *The Crossing*, Billy dreams of "a solitary bell that tolled and ceased and then he woke" (112). Similarly, the blind man in *The Crossing* also hears "a bell that tolled slowly three times and ceased," only to learn from a passerby "that there was no church. That there was nothing at all anywhere in sight" (280–81, 282).
24. In McCarthy's *Suttree*, the protagonist experiences a similar sacrament of water when he accepts a drink from a water-bearing child, who comes "up to Suttree where he stood by the roadside and swung the bucket around and brought the dipper up all bright and dripping and offered it." The numinosity of the experiences is conveyed through the description of the child, with his "pale gold hair" like "new wheat" and eyes that are "blue green with no bottoms like the sea"

(470). Edwin Arnold also comments on the similarity between Billy's and Suttree's experiences, arguing that in both novels the act of drinking the water "seems a blessing" ("Last of the Trilogy" 243). An analogous scene occurs in *The Road*, in which another numinous child brings his dying father a cup of water: "There was light all about him. . . . He took the cup and moved away and when he moved the light moved with him" (277).

25. These words are reminiscent of the following passage in *The Road*, not only in its poetic diction but in its evocation of esoteric patterns suggesting the presence of the sacred: "On their backs were vermiculate patterns that were maps of the world in its becoming. Maps and mazes. Of a thing which could not be put back. Not be made right again. In the deep glens where they lived all things were older than man and they hummed of mystery" (287).

26. "How far that little candle throws its beams! So shines a good deed in a naughty world" (Shakespeare, *Merchant of Venice* 5.1.89–90).

CHAPTER 13

1. Dan Flory offers an insightful commentary on Bell's approach to evil:

    > Bell understands neither why nor how someone could knowingly choose to act so evilly. For him, such a decision is incomprehensible. . . . Bell's understanding echoes a dominant position in the history of Western philosophy. Figures such as Augustine, Aquinas, and Kant similarly viewed sin and evil as impossible to choose rationally, a position that reaches back to Socrates and was incorporated into Christian theology. . . . Bell's musings . . . evoke a well-known philosophical position as well as a familiar sense of wonder at the mysterious inexplicability of this kind of evil, its apparently breathtaking, fear-inspiring inscrutability. (119–20)

2. In *Outer Dark*, the tinker proclaims, "I've seen the meanness of humans till I don't know why God ain't put out the sun and gone away" (192). In *Child of God*, the deputy asks an elderly man if he thinks "people was meaner then than they are now," but the man replies, "I think people are the same from the day God first made one" (168). In *Suttree*, the ragman complains that he "never knowed such a place for meanness," but when Suttree asks if it was "ever any different" he concedes, "No. I reckon not" (180). In *Blood Meridian*, Judge Holden compares human beings to wolves, asking, "And is the race of man not more predacious yet?" (147). In *All the Pretty Horses*, Alfonsa insists, "What is constant in history is greed and foolishness and a love of blood" (239). However, in *The Counselor*, the unscrupulous Malkina speculates that "nothing is crueller than a coward, and the slaughter to come is probably beyond our imagining" (184).

3. Bell's reliability as a narrator is somewhat problematized by his reference to the results of some infamous school surveys, which he cites to prove his point that the world is "goin to hell in a handbasket":

> I read in the papers here a while back some teachers come across a survey that was sent out back in the thirties to a number of schools around the country. Had this questionnaire about what was the problems with teachin in the schools. And they come across these forms, they'd been filled out and sent in from around the country answerin these questions. And the biggest problems they could name was things like talkin in class and runnin in the hallways. Chewin gum. Copyin homework. Things of that nature. So they got one of them forms that was blank and printed up a bunch of em and sent em back out to the same schools. Forty years later. Well, here come the answers back. Rape, arson, murder. Drugs. Suicide. So I think about that. (196)

While the results of these surveys were publicised in the real world in 1982, the surveys themselves turned out to be a hoax, uncovered in 1994 by Barry O'Neill, a professor of political science at the University of California, Los Angeles:

> After some research, O'Neill was able to trail this comparison to the year 1982, and managed to find its original author. The creator of the comparison was identified as T. Cullen Davis of Fort Worth, a born-again Christian who devised the lists as a fundamentalist attack on public schools. When O'Neill asked him how he had arrived at his items, Cullen Davis admitted that he had not done so from a scientific survey. O'Neill pursued the questioning one step further and asked Cullen Davis how he knew the top offenses in the schools in the past. "I was there," was Davis' reply. Not surprisingly, O'Neill then asked how he knew the current school problems. Davis' answered: "I read the newspapers."
>
> Although this comparative list of school problems was not based on any research or even on a basic survey, O'Neill points out that many social, educational and political leaders (including senators, mayors, state education officials, journalists, university professors and deans) accepted the lists as factual. Moreover, O'Neill adds, during the late eighties and early nineties the lists became the most quoted "results" of educational research, and possibly the most influential. (Schugurensky)

While *No Country for Old Men* was published in 2005, well after the surveys were exposed as a hoax, the novel is set in the early 1980s, a time when the surveys were frequently cited as a reliable source. Therefore Bell's credibility need not necessarily be called into question. Nevertheless, the question of why McCarthy chose to mention the fraudulent surveys remains a puzzling one. It is, of course, possible that McCarthy is not aware of the hoax himself. After all, the surveys are still frequently cited as fact to this very day. See, for example, an article by Shaun Dolan, "How to Prevent School Violence."

4. There are other instances in which McCarthy and Bell express the same sentiments. In an interview with the *Wall Street Journal*, McCarthy claimed that "people tell me from time to time that my son John is just a wonderful kid. I tell people that he is so morally superior to me that I feel foolish correcting him about things" (Jurgensen 113). Bell makes much the same claim about his wife, Loretta: "She's a better person than me, which I will admit to anybody that cares to listen. Not that that's sayin a whole lot. She's a better person than anybody I know. Period" (90–91). In his televised interview with Oprah Winfrey, McCarthy insisted, "I've been lucky and blessed, one of the luckiest people I've ever know" (qtd. in Lincoln 14); Bell makes the same claim: "Me I was always lucky. My whole life" (91).

5. Significantly, the number 117 is also mentioned in *The Road* as the exact time of the unspecified apocalyptic event: "The clocks stopped at 1:17. A long shear of light and then a series of low concussions" (52).

6. Lydia Cooper argues that "Bell is a rational man and a modern sceptic, but in his mind there is at least a niggling fear that Chigurh just might be a walking, breathing personification of the Prince of Darkness." According to Cooper, *No Country for Old Men* "does not settle for mere symbolism. Chigurh is not 'like' Satan; at some level of the story, he just might *be* Satan" (46). John Cant similarly argues that much of McCarthy's writing "is allegorical in character" and that characters such a Chigurh "are diminished by attempts to read them mimetically" (248). Robert Jarrett argues that although Chigurh is a "signifier of metaphysical evil," the very "banality and flatness of the world represented in the novel exists to erase his metaphysical function. The narrative erasure leaves readers with only the outline of this metaphysical function" ("Genre, Voice, and Ethos" 62).

7. We find this passive approach to evil in *Blood Meridian* when the kid refuses to shoot the judge, much to the latter's disappointment: "No assassin, called the judge. And no partisan either. There's a flawed place in the fabric of your heart" (299). As I have previously argued, the judge's condemnation of the kid's lack of action suggests that this was indeed the most effective form of resistance against the judge's evil. John Vanderheide also comments on this attitude toward evil in McCarthy's fiction, arguing that "in the ideological warfare that McCarthy's novels narrate, the possibility of victory over such nihilism, the possibility of access to the higher forms of power available to humanity, springs from an act of renunciation, in particular a rejection of the temptation to battle nihilism

directly. For in acceding to this temptation, one is immediately constituted as a subject of the nihilism one claims to be fighting" (34).
8. John Cant points out that, "although McCarthy gives Chigurh human form, he denies him human qualities," arguing that "Chigurh is not to be read as a human being" but rather as "death personified" (249). Jim Welsh also argues that Chigurh "is a force and a presence that goes well beyond the banality of an ordinary paid assassin or bounty hunter. Like Death itself, he is larger than life, not merely a stereotype, but an allegorical abstraction" (74).
9. Excerpt from Thomas Hardy's "The Convergence of the Twain":

> Alien they seemed to be;
> No mortal eye could see
> The intimate welding of their later history,
> Or sign that they were bent
> By paths coincident
> On being anon twin halves of one august event,
> Till the Spinner of the Years
> Said "Now!" And each one hears,
> And consummation comes, and jars two hemispheres. (lines 25–33)

10. Bell also muses on the subject of the convergence of two individual destinies: "Here a while back they was two boys run into one another and one of em was from California and one from Florida. And they met somewheres or other in between. And then they set out together travelin around the country killin people. I forget how many they did kill. Now what are the chances of a thing like that?" (40).
11. Chigurh's theory about the destinies of coins and human beings echoes the words of Judge Holden in *Blood Meridian*: "The arc of circling bodies is determined by the length of their tether, said the judge. Moons, coins, men" (246). As I have previously argued, the "tether" refers to the binding law of heimarmene.
12. Jay Ellis argues that "Chigurh must kill her, because he promised he would—but more deeply . . . because she, too, has made choices that brought her to her end at his hands" ("Do You See" 112). Scott Covell points out that "Chigurh reserves the coin for the innocent whom he allows a choice. The guilty have made their choices already, and must die for them" (105).
13. Hanna Boguta-Marchel argues that Chigurh "views reality as a perfectly deterministic system in which one occurrence triggers another, and that one still another, thus forming a meticulously devised sequence of irreplaceable causes and their results which cannot be in any way prevented from being realized" (74). We find a similar view voiced by Alfonsa in *All the Pretty Horses*, who believes that the world is "a puppet show," in which the puppet strings "terminate in the hands of yet other puppets, themselves with their own strings which

trace upward in turn, and so on" (231). In *The Counselor*, the diamond dealer ominously warns the protagonist that "the forms of our undertakings are complete at their beginning. For good or ill" (17). Later in the screenplay, the Jefe tells the Counselor, "I only know that the world in which you seek to undo your mistakes is not the world in which they were made. You are at a cross in the road and here you think to choose. But here there is no choosing. There is only accepting. The choosing was done long ago" (147).

14. "La plus belle des ruses du diable est de vous persuader qu'il n'existe pas" (Baudelaire 29).

15. Jay Ellis points out that, "assuming Chigurh must kill the man he looks at, we must note that he helps him: the man dies with courage, in that he faces . . . his death, and we may imagine that he therefore accepts it" ("Do You See" 112).

16. In *Symbols and their Meanings*, Jack Tresidder explains that "the occult third eye, sometimes called 'the eye of the heart,' symbolizes the eye of spiritual perception, associated with the power of Shiva and the synthesizing element of fire in Hinduism, with inner vision in Buddhism, and with clairvoyance in the Islamic faith" (23).

17. John Vanderheide writes that "the God after which Chigurh models himself approximates the God of orthodox Jewish, Christian, and Islamic theology. He emulates a God who binds himself to His own will . . . a supreme arbiter who subsequently rewards or punishes His subjects—alive or dead—according to what they have done or what they can no longer undo" (42). Steven Frye also argues that "the God [Chigurh] imagines is by no means a deity of benevolence and concern but is instead an abstract and indifferent law giver concerned with balancing the cosmic scales in the interest of principles beyond human understanding" (*Understanding Cormac McCarthy* 163). Although neither Vanderheide nor Frye puts forward a Gnostic reading of Chigurh's statement, both of their descriptions of Chigurh's God call to mind Gnostic portrayals of the demiurge as one who "reigns as king and lord . . . who gives the law and judges those who violate it" (Pagels, *Gnostic Gospels* 37).

18. Following in the footsteps of the ancient Greek philosopher Epicurus (341–270 BCE), the French philosopher Pierre Bayle (1647–1706) summarized the paradox of evil in his *Dictionnaire historique et critque*:

> God is either willing to remove evil and cannot; or he can and is unwilling; or he is neither willing nor able to do so; or else he is both willing and able. If he is willing and not able, he must then be weak, which cannot be affirmed of God. If he is able and not willing, he must be envious, which is also contrary to the nature of God. If he is neither willing nor able, he must be both envious and weak, and consequently not be God. If he is both willing and able—the only possibility that agrees with the

nature of God—then where does evil come from? Or why does he not eliminate it? (qtd. in Neiman 118)

19. Steven Frye argues that in *No Country for Old Men*, "McCarthy makes peace with God, not by embracing a particular orthodoxy or system per se, but by considering seriously and sympathetically a philosophical position that distinguishes God from the created world, thus limiting his capacity to orchestrate the details of its operation" ("Yeats's 'Sailing to Byzantium'" 19). Although Frye doesn't couch this argument in Gnostic terms, such an understanding of God is nevertheless akin to the Gnostic belief in an utterly transcendent alien God that does not participate in creation.
20. The fact that the water trough emerged "out of solid rock" (307) links it to the sacred fire, which is struck "out of the rock" in the epilogue to *Blood Meridian* (337).
21. As I have previously argued, the sacrament of water remains a pervasive theme throughout McCarthy's novels: for example, the numinous "waterbearer" in *Suttree* (410); the spring Billy drinks from in *The Crossing*, which joins him "in sacrament" with all others who had previously drunk there (290); or the sacred child in *The Road*, who brings his dying father a cup of water with otherworldly "light all about him" (277).
22. John Grady makes similar pronouncements regarding the nature of truth in *All the Pretty Horses*. When the captain claims, "We can make the truth here," John Grady replies, "There aint but one truth. . . . The truth is what happened. It aint what come out of somebody's mouth" (168).
23. Robert Jarrett compares Moss's act of compassion to the passages depicting the "clemency" of the kid in *Blood Meridian*, arguing that "these passages provide an intertext within the McCarthy oeuvre for Moss's problematic clemency for the drug runner. . . . Moss's return with water to the wounded drug runner faintly evokes the parables of the Good Samaritan and of Lazarus and Dives, reenacted within the contemporary purgatory of the American Southwest" ("Genre, Voice, and Ethos" 62). Dennis Cutchins also comments on the role of grace and charity in *No Country for Old Men*: "This novel in particular portrays a dangerous world and horrifying evil, but in McCarthy's *No Country*, that evil is always at least somewhat balanced by the rough and imperfect displays of grace and charity that exist along with the novel's violence and destruction. Indeed it may be argued that the acts of grace and charity in McCarthy's novel(s) are more meaningful because they are performed not in a nice world, but in the face of violence and destruction" (164).
24. McCarthy also emphasizes the importance of ordinary human kindness and compassion in *The Counselor*, through the words of a drug dealer, Westray, who has begun to rethink his way of life: "I won't flesh out the argument but the only thing ultimately worth your concern is the anguish of your fellow passengers on

this hellbound train. I have a lot to answer for. I know that. And I may be a motherfucker but I'm not a hypocrite. You have to help Tom Gray up off the barroom floor. It's little enough. But it's not nothing" (62).

25. Other critics have commented on the spiritual significance of Bell's dreams. Steven Frye argues that "hope emerges from Bell's reliance on and reverence for the redemptive power of human relationships and from his vague acknowledgement of mystical transcendence." Frye explains that, in the final dream, "we see him returning to Yeats's image of eternal fire. However, this is not the fire of destruction but purification, creation, and light" ("Yeats's 'Sailing to Byzantium'" 18–19). David Cremean writes that "it is in his final spiritual move into the mystical that Bell reconfigures his 'conservatism,' and it is here that we may find traces of McCarthy's own . . . mystical apprehension of God where truth has its origin, its very being, and endures" (28).

26. Stephen Tatum comments on the connection between Bell's memory of the water trough, his metaphor of the boat, and his dream of the fire carried in a horn: "As a hollow container harboring the promise of new life and light, the animal horn carried here by the father figure resonates too because it symbolically binds together two other important containing shapes that provide material evidence of Bell's ethic of obligation and his emergent 'promise in the heart': the stone water trough he ponders at the beginning of this final monologue; the figure of the boat that he employs to identify his motivation for becoming a lawman" (93).

CHAPTER 14

1. When questioned as to what caused the disaster, McCarthy replied, "A lot of people ask me. I don't have an opinion. At the Santa Fe Institute I'm with scientists of all disciplines, and some of them in geology said it looked like a meteor to them. But it could be anything—volcanic activity or it could be nuclear war. It is not really important. The whole thing now is, what do you do?" (Jurgensen 119–20). Various critics have speculated on the possible nature of the disaster. Paul Patton hypothesizes that it might have been caused by "a large extraterrestrial body that would have exploded on impact, causing a massive dust cloud that would have suddenly cooled the earth. These are not man-made events but rather suggest nature's complete indifference to the conditions of human existence" (132). Steven Frye discusses the implications of a man-made vs. a natural disaster: "The language as articulated seems selected for its ambiguity, allowing for both possibilities, which have vastly different implications. A nuclear holocaust would be the result of human evil, and the meteor or asteroid the outcome of natural evil and the destructive capacity of the universe broadly construed. This blending suggests perhaps that the two are co-implicated and inseparable" (*Understanding Cormac McCarthy* 169).

2. The opening line of Dante's *Inferno*—"Nel mezzo del cammin di nosta vita" (In the midway of this our mortal life) (Alighieri, *Divine Comedy: Inferno*, canto 1, line 1)—is also alluded to by McCarthy's vagrant storyteller in the epilogue to *Cities of the Plain*, who begins his tale with the words "In the middle of my life ..." (268).
3. The number 117 occurs on three different occasions in McCarthy's *No Country for Old Men*. Llewellyn Moss is killed outside his motel room, "standin in front of 117" (237). The number of the room is brought up again when Sheriff Bell returns to the crime scene and walks "up to the door at 117" (243). When Chigurh breaks into the house where Carla Jean is staying, he notes that "the green diode numerals on the radio put the time at 1:17" (202). Several critics have commented on the significance of this number's appearance in *The Road*. For example, Steven Frye writes that, "though the symbolic meaning of the numbers cannot be determined with any certainty, it evokes *Revelation* 1:17 and the dream vision of John the Divine, in which he witnesses the Second Coming of Christ." Frye argues, "It is an image of power and destruction as well as hope and light, and it speaks both comfort and commandment, with Christ demanding that his presence be recorded in words, the allusion suggesting that the novel as parable is a kind of prophesy" (*Understanding Cormac McCarthy* 169). Erik Hage offers a different interpretation, arguing, "If one were to draw a biblical connection, this would place us in Genesis, where God is creating the world and all of life. In 1:17 God places the sun and the stars in the firmament, to light the earth and divide day from night. McCarthy often cuts against the grain of canonical themes and stories and converts them into something that is his own; therefore, it would be just like the author to actually blot out that light in the firmament at 1:17" (143).
4. Various critics have argued for the metaphorical, or even allegorical, nature of the novel. Matthew Mullins goes as far as to argue that "McCarthy's postapocalyptic landscape is not the shade of a prophesied future" but a "rendering of modernity." While I don't subscribe to Mullins's rejection of the literal interpretation of the postapocalyptic setting, I agree with his insistence that, "if we are going to employ the term 'apocalypse' at all, we should think of it in terms of its most literal definition, that is, as a revelation or disclosure first, and as a disaster or global cataclysm second" (76). Carl James Grindley argues along similar terms as Mullins, drawing attention to the "large supply of Judeo-Christian lexical terms (e.g., *God*, thirty-three times and *Christ*, five times)," along with McCarthy's "only published uses of *Christendom, creedless, ensepulchred, enshroud*, and *godspoke*," as well as "some relatively rare items, including *tabernacle* and *chalice*." Grindley points out that, "on the other hand, the novel does not contain any lexical items relating to atomic warfare, nor does McCarthy use forms of *disaster* or *catastrophe* or other related words to describe the novel's central event" (12). John Cant argues that the conditions presented in the novel operate as "a wider metaphor for the condition of man in the realisation of his

cosmic insignificance" (269). Harold Bloom also regards the "literal journey along the ever-dangerous road . . . as an emblem for existence itself" (*Bloom's Guides* 38). Similarly, Thomas Schaub regards the novel as "an allegory of spiritual survival" (154). Steven Frye mitigates this point of view somewhat with the argument that "reading the landscape in *The Road* as simple metaphor appears rather incomplete and limiting, and the wasted world emerges rather as the typological wilderness of the Old and New Testaments, a realm of spiritual quest and striving where the fortitudes of the spirit are put to the test" (*Understanding Cormac McCarthy* 175).

5. Sean Pryor identifies the presence of this terrible cosmic harmony in *The Road*, although he does not place it in a Gnostic context. Pryor engages in a close reading of the sentence "The cold relentless circling of the intestate earth" (*The Road* 130), arguing that, "like clockwork, McCarthy's vowels fall into place to tick the turning earth: *-lent, circ-, -test-, earth*. . . . And the thought of these monotonous, inhuman, celestial rhythms is oppressive. . . . The apocalypse seems then to have altered the meaning of the order of the cosmos, or rather to have exposed its meaning" (Pryor 38). Pryor points out that this "neatly inverts Aristotle's sense of number as the ground of pleasure. It stands in even more stark contradiction to Plato, for whom the order of the cosmos is both beautiful and good" (38).

6. Grace Hellyer also interprets this passage in terms of a cosmic consciousness, arguing, "Here we see that the man's ability to orient himself in relation to the landscape is premised not only on the existence of a universal point of absolute stability, but also on the positing of sentience in the universe—on a transcendent consciousness that confers stability and movement on the heavenly bodies" (53).

7. The image of "coins in the ash" (23) seems significant in light of the fact that coins have played an important role in McCarthy's fiction. As previously discussed, the judge in *Blood Meridian* demonstrates the powers of heimarmene by performing an uncanny coin trick by the fire (245–46). The same theme is evoked throughout *No Country for Old Men*, in which Anton Chigurh uses coins to determine whether his victims shall live or die. In *Blood Meridian* and *All the Pretty Horses*, the demiurge appears as the "false coiner" (310) and the "myopic coiner" (241), respectively. Thus the discarded coins in *The Road* might signify the concept that when the world ends, so will the reign of the demiurge.

8. The idea that photographs are futile attempts to preserve an irretrievable past is also explored in *The Crossing*, when the gypsy tells Billy that every "representation" is "an idol" and "every likeness a heresy." The gypsy explains that people take photographs of themselves and each other because they seek "some small immortality but oblivion cannot be appeased" (413).

9. It is noteworthy that Francisco Collado-Rodríguez draws a parallel between "McCarthy's reiterative motif of ruinous libraries and books" and Jorge Luis Borges's "concern with Gnosticism," specifically in the story "La biblioteca de Babel" (1959), in which Borges conjures up the "image of life as an immense

10. library where we are all trapped" (65n11). Thus McCarthy's image of the man leaving the ruined library is significant from a Gnostic perspective, symbolizing a rejection of the lies and distraction of the manifest world.
10. John Grady arrives at the same understanding in *Cities of the Plain*, experiencing "a knowing deep in the bone that beauty and loss are one" (71).
11. The heretic in *The Crossing* similarly comes to feel that the "pin has been pulled from the axis of the universe" (146), as does the dream traveler in *Cities of the Plain*, who feels that "in their turning things had become uncottered" (285). Both of these apprehensions of the nature of things evoke the definition of duḥkha as "an axle which is off-center with respect to its wheel" (H. Smith, *Religions of Man* 111).
12. Father and son continue to search for the thief in the encroaching darkness: "They went up the road calling out in the empty dusk, their voices lost over the darkening shorelands. They stopped and stood with their hands cupped to their mouths, hallooing mindlessly into the waste" (259–60). This failed attempt to make things right echoes the ending of *The Crossing*, when Billy mistreats a crippled dog and then engages in a similarly futile attempt to call it back: "He walked out on the road and called for the dog. He called and called. Standing in that inexplicable darkness" (425–26). Both scenes depict injustice followed by regret, culminating in an act of compassion that comes too late to help the wronged party.
13. Several critics have framed the difference between father and son in the context of the relationship between the Christian God and Christ. Harold Bloom believes that the "connection between father and son . . . resonates with the Christian notion of the bond between God the Father and Jesus" (*Bloom's Guides* 26). Jay Ellis writes that the father "must move through the burning world like a distrustful Old Testament Yahweh, ready to kill other tribes that threaten him, not really very optimistic about the long-term goals, unable to love the other" ("Another Sense of Ending" 30). Phillip Snyder argues that the "thief and the father both articulate a Law of Moses kind of justice" (82). Snyder adds that although the father initially believes "that 'an eye for an eye' constitutes a negation of a negation and is thus morally valid, the boy's reaction forces upon the father a change of knowledge which leads to remorse" (103). Kenneth Lincoln also argues that "the child faces death with Christ-like pity, the father with Old Testament *lex talionis*" (172). It is noteworthy that the dichotomy between God the Father and Christ the Son is explored in the writings of Jacob Boehme. Nicolas Berdyaev writes that "Boehme opposes the face of the Son which is the face of love, to the face of the Father, which is anger. There is in the Son already no dark principle, he is all light, all love, all goodness. But the Father then takes the form of a divinity of apophatic theology. Gnostic motifs here become discernible" (xxx). We find a similar dichotomy of love and wrath developed throughout *The Road*, apparent in the boy and the

man and their respective attitudes toward the other human beings they encounter on their journey.

14. In the same interview, McCarthy talks about the son to whom *The Road* is dedicated: "But people tell me from time to time that my son John is just a wonderful kid. I tell people that he is so morally superior to me that I feel foolish correcting him about things, but you've got to do something—I'm his father. There's not much you can do to try to make a child into something he's not. But whatever he is, you can sure destroy it. Just be mean and cruel and you can destroy the best person" (Jurgensen 113).

15. The fact that the dead are killed not merely for meat alone but often for some unspecified ritual purpose is suggested by the markings found on decapitated heads: "The crude tattoos etched in some homebrewed woad faded in the beggared sunlight. Spiders, swords, targets. A dragon. Runic slogans, creeds misspelled. Old scars with old motifs stitched along their borders. The heads not truncheoned shapeless had been flayed of their skins and the raw skulls painted and signed across the forehead in a scrawl and one white bone skull had the plate sutures etched carefully in ink like a blueprint for assembly" (90). The reference to "woad," a blue dye produced from the leaves of the plant *Isatis tinctoria*, evokes the Picts, a group of Late Iron Age and Early Medieval Celtic people living in ancient eastern and northern Scotland. The Picts were known for their woad tattoos; the Latin word "Picti" means "painted or tattooed people" (from Latin *pictus*, "painted") (Foster 7). McCarthy's allusion to the distant past suggests that human society has regressed to an earlier mythico-magical state. Furthermore, the image of the "blueprint for assembly" evokes the sinister work of the demiurge.

16. Several critics have commented on the father's ambivalent and, at times, hostile relationship with the God of this world. Rune Graulund points out that, "angry as he is at this absent God, it is obvious that the man is no atheist. The man, who is the very essence of fatherhood, passionately needs to believe in the existence of God, the absent Father" (75). Steven Frye writes that "the man's tortured reflections throughout the novel alternate between a sense that God is wholly absent and a passionate anger that the world is God's creation and thus His ordination and responsibility." Frye adds that the man "rails against a God he sees as active and intimately complicit in their circumstances" (*Understanding Cormac McCarthy* 175). Erik Hage argues that, "the father could be considered a heretic . . . yet even after the very world, its order, and all of its ecclesiastical dimensions have fallen away, he believes in God and carries on a dialogue with that entity, even if it is only, at times, to express his rage and heresy" (87). Jay Ellis claims that *The Road* depicts "McCarthy's sense of god as a kind of absent parent no longer able, or willing, to do anything" ("Another Sense of Ending" 35). Scott Yarbrough argues that, "like Lucifer, like Loki," the man is "at war with God, holding Him accountable for the fallen world which has been laid waste to by

some sort of cataclysm" (51). Allen Josephs adds an interesting dimension to this discussion by tracing the father's attitude to the God of this world in McCarthy's earlier drafts of the novel: "The father thinks of himself as neither believing nor disbelieving in God, then goes on to say that the idea that God had 'looked upon his work' and then 'despaired of it,' abandoning man, did not seem 'unlikely.'" Josephs concludes that "it is clear from the very beginning that ambivalence about God was to form a central theme of *The Road*" (134).

17. Omar Khayyám articulates a similar sentiment in the *Rubáiyát*, as translated by Edward FitzGerald:

> Ah Love! could you and I with Fate conspire
> To grasp this sorry Scheme of Things entire,
> Would we not shatter it to bits—and then
> Re-mould it nearer to the Heart's Desire!
> (108)

18. Thomas Schaub comments on the use of the word *salitter*, arguing, "Here in *The Road*, the odd term certainly signifies the drying up of the divine sap, the invigorating element of natural life that is now turning to ash and dust, blowing in the wind" (161). Allen Josephs writes, "*Salitter*—there could be a dissertation on this usage, as well as a study on the meaning of fire and light as God and Christ in Jacob Boehme and Cormac McCarthy—means divine essence, the stuff of God (not unlike the Tao or Brahman, or in quantum physics the matrix of Max Planck, or even the so-called god-particle of recent physics)" (139). Harold Bloom also notes that "salitter" is "a word borrowed from the seventeenth-century mystic Jakob Boehme that means 'the essence of God.' McCarthy uses the term to suggest the withdrawal of the divine from existence" (*Bloom's Guides* 47).

19. A number of critics have commented on the sentence—"The sacred idiom shorn of its referents and so of its reality" (75)—offering interpretations different from my own. Alex Hunt and Martin Jacobsen claim that, "rather than a higher reality of Platonic forms, in McCarthy's account the loss of the physical world exposes the contingency of the idea—an inversion of Platonic thinking" (157). Thomas Schaub argues that the sentence "poses the question of what access we might have to spirit once those natural signs are obliterated; or, if obliteration itself be our last remaining sign—fire, ash, cannibalized remains—what spirit does it symbolize? What spirit does it summon if not the rough beast slouching toward Bethlehem?" (155). Allen Josephs writes that "sometimes McCarthy reverses the religious reference for negative effect as in this un-writing of *Genesis* by the man. . . . Subtract the idiom and you subtract the referent—the un-reification of God" (134).

20. Steven Frye also argues that the father's words about his son being the word of God are not to be read metaphorically: "The man sees the boy not only as his son but

also as a figure of divine import, and though the boy will display extraordinary qualities of kindness, the man's belief in the boy as the incarnate Word of God could be taken as an expression of mere sentiment, were it not for the many references to divinity, in the context of description and allusion to God" (*Understanding Cormac McCarthy* 172–73). Similarly, Erik Hage claims that *The Road* contains "suggestions that the son of the man is actually a Son of Man and that this road has all of the gravity and importance of the biblical roads to Damascus and Emmaus" (143). Randall Wilhelm offers an interesting interpretation of another scene in the novel in which the father discovers a hidden bunker of provisions and the child is once again referred to as God, albeit in a very subtle way. According to Wilhelm, "When initially seeing the bunker's contents, the father, who is viewing the room as the child holds the lamp above him on the steps, mutters 'Oh my God. . . . Come down. Oh my God. Come down,' (166) but he is talking to the boy. The father says that he has 'found everything,' (117) but the bounty of physical sustenance (which would eventually run out given time) suffers in comparison with the previous statement suggesting incarnate spirituality" (136).

21. McCarthy's working title, "The Grail," indicates that the novel belongs to the tradition of the Grail Quest, most famously depicted in the Arthurian legends. In *The Mystic Grail: The Challenge of the Arthurian Quest*, John Matthews writes,

> The story of the Grail is one of the crowning glories of the Western imagination. No one can say precisely where or when it emerged. Indeed, it seems to have always been present, hidden in the deepest recesses of the human soul. Certainly, it has continued to exert a powerful fascination over all who come in contact with it. This is not surprising, since it deals with themes that are as important today as they have always been—the search for absolutes, the quest for healing, and the unending quest for truth. The Grail has been described as many things: as a stone, fallen from the crown of the Angel of Light during the war in Heaven; as a Cauldron of Celtic antiquity sought after by heroes; as the cup used by Christ to celebrate the Last Supper and the first Eucharist. But, more than the sum of its parts, the Grail is really an idea that represents the presence of a numinous, mystical link between the sacred and the secular. (6–7)

22. The identification of beauty with goodness evokes the Platonic Absolute, which is also the Good and the Beautiful. Martin Lings locates this concept in the traditions that make up the Perennial Philosophy, writing that "beauty provides the intellective soul with the occasional cause for a Platonic 'recollection'—i.e. an objective 'vision'—of the heavenly archetypes; and as 'external goodness.' Beauty provides the contemplative soul with an existential—and not merely mental or conceptual—reminder of its original nature of primordial perfection (i.e. its

pure state of virtue before the fall)" (xvii). This tradition persists even in Gnostic teachings, "the Manichaean view" being "that God is tangible in what is beautiful, is tangible in what affects the senses in a positive way.... God smells sweetly and God is light as opposed to darkness" (BeDuhn 127). Randall Wilhelm also comments on McCarthy's reference to goodness and beauty, arguing that "philosophical conceptions of beauty are historically grounded and ideologically-encoded. Many Classical and Medieval thinkers linked the beautiful with the moral, and its apprehension a strategy for the mind's entrance into a higher consciousness. This position was generally upheld until the twentieth-century, when beauty was exiled from art and considered a charming bourgeois illusion instead of a fundamental element of human consciousness. McCarthy's use of both the beautiful and the sublime in *The Road*, coupled with his emphasis on . . . morality, suggests he is self-consciously working against this dominant discourse and reintroducing beauty as necessary for human goodness" (144n11). The father in *The Road* is once again moved by beauty and goodness when he contemplates "a brass sextant, possibly a hundred years old" and finds himself "struck by the beauty of it. . . . It was the first thing he'd seen in a long time that stirred him" (228).

23. Allen Josephs points out that in an earlier draft of the novel, McCarthy had presented the child's divine nature in more explicit terms:

> It is a longer, more detailed version of the same passage. The boy again has light all about him. But the light does not fall on him—for there is no source of light—but issues from him in a "constant and slow emanation" that spreads from him and from his hand, and "even from" what he touches. The father whispers "Oh blessed child" and goes on to make the comment about all the prophets being so honored here today. Evidently in editing, McCarthy wanted a more subtle rendition of the boy's blessedness, just as he apparently wanted to tone down the title from "The Grail" to *The Road*, but the combination of the *grail* and the *blessed child* in the early drafts clearly conveys McCarthy's sense of the boy's role in unmistakably Christ-like iconography. The fact that he cut it does not mean he changed his mind. It is a Hemingwayesque burying of the all too obvious—the famous iceberg technique—to strengthen the power of the passage. (139)

24. As I have previously argued, another such water sacrament occurs in *Suttree*, where the protagonist encounters a numinous water-bearing child, with "pale gold hair" like "new wheat" and eyes that are "blue green with no bottoms like the sea." The boy approaches "Suttree where he stood by the roadside and swung the bucket around and brought the dipper up all bright and dripping and offered it" (470). In *The Crossing*, Billy also experiences the sacrament of water when he

comes across a "spring beneath a cottonwood," with "a tin cup on a stob." Billy finds himself moved by the experience and takes the cup with something akin to a reverence for the sacred: "He'd not seen a cup at a spring in years and he held it in both hands as had thousands before him unknown to him yet joined in sacrament. He dipped the cup into the water and raised it cool and dripping to his mouth" (290).

25. The metaphor of "carrying the fire" is polysemic, generating various interpretations. Barbara Bennet writes, "Most reviewers have generally agreed that the 'fire' is hope, spiritual belief, or truth, but a closer understanding of Celtic tradition reveals what McCarthy more likely meant. In the Celtic culture, the hearth fire was the center of family activity, providing warmth, light, and food for the family" (75). Leslie Harper Worthington links the carrying of the fire to *No Country for Old Men* as well as to Native American tradition:

> "Carrying the fire" refers to what Sherriff Bell in *No Country for Old Men* remembers his cowboy father doing on the trail and what the Native Americans did before the cowboys. They would carry the embers from the fire of one camp to the next in an animal horn or other fireproof container. The fire carrier was usually a very important member of the tribe and one of the first in the trail procession. He had an extremely important function: to start the fires that they would use for cooking and warmth on the trail. Figuratively in the novel, "carrying the fire" means not only to have hope and continue the quest, but also to maintain their humanity: not to eat people, not to live without conscience or a concern for others. Those carrying the fire hold a special position in the tribe and for their society. (176–77)

Other critics have interpreted the fire in *The Road* as a Promethean motif. Matthew Mullins writes that "the source of the fire carried by the man and the boy lies somewhere beyond themselves, like the fire carried by Prometheus, which was transported from the gods to humans" (90). Scott Yarbrough argues that "the phrase 'carrying the fire'" evokes "Prometheus, the Titan who defied Zeus by giving fire to humankind. . . . Given the meaning of his name, 'forethought,' Prometheus's gift of fire comes to stand for the fire of knowledge, of human intellect and enlightenment" (47–48). Allen Josephs favors a Gnostic reading over a Promethean one, asking, "Is that the figurative fire of civilization? I think it means—textually, in this novel—less something vaguely Promethean than the literal belief in or presence of God or at the very least some entrapped divine spark of the Gnostics" (25).

26. It is noteworthy that *The Crossing* seems to anticipate the apocalypse depicted in *The Road* via Boyd's prophetic dream: "There was a big fire out on the dry lake. . . . These people were burnin. The lake was on fire and they was burnin up. . . . I

had this feelin that somethin bad was goin to happen" (35–36). The judge in *Blood Meridian* also proclaims that the world's "ultimate destination . . . is unspeakable and calamitous beyond reckoning" (245).

27. A description of the dripping of subterranean water, which measures the passage of time and hence serves as a reminder of mortality, also occurs in *Suttree*: "a liquid dripping, something gone awry in the earth's organs to which this measured bleeding clocked a constantly eluded doom" (261).

28. Unlike the Platonists and Neoplatonists, both the Gnostics and the Buddhists insist that existence in the manifest world is wholly undesirable, even in the best possible circumstances. The Buddhists even go as far as to reject rebirth in the heavenly realm of the gods: "Realise that Paradise is only temporary, that it gives no real freedom, holds out no security, cannot be trusted and gives no lasting satisfaction! It is better therefore to strive for final release. Even the dwellers in heaven, with all their might, come to an end. No intelligent man would set his heart on winning the right to a brief stay among them!" (Conze, *Buddhist Scriptures* 224). In *The Road*, the man and the child discover the "tiny paradise" (150) of a bunker stocked with food and supplies but refuse to stay there for more than a few days "because it's dangerous" (139). However, when the boy asks if the danger lies in the possibility that "they," meaning other survivors, will "find us," his father twice reassures him: "No. They wont find us. . . . No they wont. They wont find us" (148). Furthermore, the man has disguised the entrance to the bunker by dragging an old mattress over the hatch. Admittedly, this isn't "much of a ruse" (148–49), but given that the entire quest is fraught with danger, hiding in the bunker does not seem to present more of a risk than journeying out in the open. It is possible, then, that like much of the novel, this passage functions on a symbolic or metaphorical level, urging the spiritual seeker to avoid the deceptive lure of paradise, which distracts from the true goal of the pilgrimage.

29. It is difficult to ignore the similarities, whether intentional or not, between McCarthy's cave-dwelling creature and J. R. R. Tolkien's Gollum, who also has "pale lamp-like eyes," lives underground "by the dark water," and moves soundlessly, "never a ripple did he make" (Tolkien 68).

30. Many critics interpret Ely as a false prophet. Steven Frye writes that "in his playful denial of the divine he implies the figure of Satan, who tempts Christ in the wilderness" (*Understanding Cormac McCarthy* 176). Allen Josephs states that Ely's "pronouncement—a brilliantly succinct Nietzschean-Islamic oxymoron—may be the ultimate expression of atheistically existential angst" (135–36). Francisco Collado-Rodríguez writes that Ely's "message is not about the omnipotence of God as creator of life but about the end of everything, including hope. . . . His prophecy is for total extinction; old religious myths have no room in his understanding of the situation, and he openly scorns the boy's role as mythos" (66). Donovan Gwinner argues that if Ely "is a prophet, a post-apocalyptic

Elijah, he is an anti-prophet . . . one who bears witness to the abyss, to nothingness. . . . Ely's gloominess, mysteriousness, and amorality amount to a troubling, frigid dousing of fire-carrying goodness" (149).

Ely's status as a false prophet is also conveyed through the description of his sitting "like a starved and threadbare buddha, staring into the coals" (168). Ely's Buddha-like pose links him to another sinister depiction of a false Buddha, namely *Blood Meridian*'s Judge Holden, the "great pale deity" (92) who also sits in front of the fire in the lotus position, with "his hands rested palm down upon his knees" and his eyes like "the empty slots" (147). There are further similarities between Ely and the evil bearded leader of the Unholy Trinity in McCarthy's *Outer Dark*. When the man in *The Road* asks Ely about his real name, the latter replies, "I couldnt trust you with it. To do something with it. I dont want anybody talking about me. To say where I was or what I said when I was there. I mean, you could talk about me maybe. But nobody could say it was me. I could be anybody" (172). In *Outer Dark*, the bearded leader gives a similar explanation as to why he would not give a name to one member of the trio: "I wouldn't name him because if you cain't name somethin you cain't claim it. You cain't even talk about it even. You cain't say what it is" (178). Both characters put forward the idea that naming something, or even knowing its name, bestows a certain power of ownership upon the namer or knower. More significantly, the fact that Ely is linked to both Judge Holden and the bearded leader—perhaps two of the most evil characters in McCarthy's fiction—places him squarely in the camp of the maleficent antagonists.

31. It is possible that the child in *The Road* has similar ideas about the unspecified "they" who are "watching." After the man releases a flare on the beach, the boy asks, "They couldnt see it very far, could they, Papa?" When father asks whether he is referring to "the good guys," the boy replies, "Yes. Or anybody that you wanted them to know where you were." The father presses on with his questions, "Like who? . . . Like God?" and the child replies, "Yeah. Maybe somebody like that" (246). There is something rather Manichean about the desire to send a signal to God. After all, the God of the Bible is supposed to be watching over us and ought to know exactly where we are. The child's desire to contact some divine consciousness "out there" suggests that he is searching for something transcendent and wholly other, much like the unknown, hidden, "Alien God" of Gnostic teachings.

32. The "Eliot-like turning" is a reference to T. S. Eliot's "Ash Wednesday":

> Because I do not hope to turn again
> Because I do not hope
> Because I do not hope to turn
> (lines 1–3)

33. The boy's decision to pray to his father recalls a similar scene in *The Crossing*, when Billy finds that he can pray only to his brother: "He tried to think how to pray. Finally he just prayed to Boyd. Dont be dead, he prayed. You're all I got" (274).
34. The epilogue's haunting evocation of the trout that once swam in the mountain streams is preceded by two prior allusions, both in the form of the man's memories of the lost world: "He stood on a stone bridge where the waters slurried into a pool and turned slowly in a gray foam. Where once he'd watched trout swaying in the current, tracking their perfect shadows on the stones beneath" (30). Later the man recalls how he'd "stood at such a river once and watched the flash of trout deep in a pool, invisible to see in the teacolored water except as they turned on their sides to feed. Reflecting back the sun deep in the darkness like a flash of knives in a cave" (42–43). The latter image is particularly striking in that it suggests the Gnostic spark flashing in the darkness of the world while simultaneously evoking the violent and barbaric nature of existence via the reference to "knives in a cave." Thomas Schaub offers a multifaceted interpretation of the significance of the trout imagery, arguing that

> McCarthy taps into a commonplace of American writing, of fishing in America. The association of the fish with the promise of Christian redemption requires no elaboration by me. In American literature this redemptive association plays out in the act of fishing, by which a character communicates with Nature through the natural sign of the fish. Thoreau writes in *A Week on the Concord and Merrimac* of an old man for whom "fishing was not a sport . . . but a sort of solemn sacrament" (152). Here, as later in Thoreau, Melville, and Hemingway, fishing in America is a ritual in which the act of penetrating the water's surface—by eye or hook—connects the fisher with the medium of spirit and its embodiment in the trout. Under the influence of Eliot, of course, this topos takes on an anthropological authority, from Frazer's *The Golden Bough* and Jesse Weston's study of the Grail legend, whose roots she finds in near eastern mythologies of a wasted land and a wounded fisher king. Eliot's poem "The Waste Land" ends with the image of a man fishing "with the arid plain behind," but for our purposes, the story of Nick Adams in "The Big Two-Hearted River" is more apposite. (156)

35. The idea that the world was created in error can also be found in the Hindu mysticism of Śaṅkara, whose writing often implies that "this going forth of God and of the world with God out of the depth of the Godhead" is "an unhappy anomaly, a fate to be redeemed or a great cosmic mistake to be corrected." For Śaṅkara, "the coming forth of God and the world from the primeval oneness of Brahman is the great 'mistake' of Avidya" (Otto 170).

36. Other critics have commented on the numinous mysticism of the novel's epilogue. John Hampsey argues that "the end is mystical and psychological, and nearly outside time itself" (497). Steven Frye points out that, "for all McCarthy's interest in the possibilities of language, perhaps in the mystical content of the Word made Flesh in the figure of the boy, *The Road* ends in silence, with a description of a time before words" (*Understanding Cormac McCarthy* 179). I would add that the epilogue might also point to some ineffable epiphany that exceeds and transcends language, rather than preceding it. Allen Josephs concludes, "It is no coincidence that the final word is 'mystery.' Much of Cormac McCarthy's work hums with mystery, and at the end of *The Road*, or more precisely at the end of the epilogue of *The Road*, we are left with exactly that—with mystery—because McCarthy knows, as Federico García Lorca said, that 'Only mystery makes us live. Only mystery'" (141–42).

Works Cited

Adams, Marilyn McCord, and Robert Merrihew Adams. Introduction. *The Problem of Evil*. Oxford: Oxford UP, 1990. 1–24.

Alighieri, Dante. *The Divine Comedy: Hell, Purgatory, Paradise*. Trans. Henry F. Cary. New York: Collier, 1914.

——. "Epistle to Cangrande della Scala." *Divine Comedy: Hell*. Trans. Dorothy Sayers. London: Penguin Classics, 1949.

Ambrosiano, Jason. "Blood in the Tracks: Catholic Postmodernism in *The Crossing*." *Southwestern American Literature* 25.1 (Fall 1999): 83–91.

Andersen, Elisabeth. *The Mythos of Cormac McCarthy: A String in the Maze*. Saarbrücken, Germany: VDM, 2008.

Aquinas, St. Thomas. *The Summa Theologica*. Trans. Fathers of the English Dominican Province. New York: Benziger, 1947.

Arnold, Edwin T. "Cormac McCarthy's *Whales and Men*." *Cormac McCarthy: Uncharted Territories / Territoires Inconnus*. Ed. Christine Chollier. Reims: UP of Reims, 2003. 17–30.

——. "Go to Sleep: Dreams and Visions in the Border Trilogy." *A Cormac McCarthy Companion: The Border Trilogy*. Ed. Edwin T. Arnold and Dianne C. Luce. Jackson: UP of Mississippi, 2001. 37–47.

——. "The Last of the Trilogy: First Thoughts on *Cities of the Plain*." *Perspectives on Cormac McCarthy*. Rev. ed. Ed. Edwin T. Arnold and Dianne C. Luce. Jackson: UP of Mississippi, 1999. 221–48.

——. "McCarthy and the Sacred: A Reading of *The Crossing*." *Cormac McCarthy: New Directions*. Ed. James D. Lilley. Albuquerque: U of New Mexico P, 2002. 215–38.

——. "The Mosaic of McCarthy's Fiction." *Sacred Violence: A Reader's Companion to Cormac McCarthy*. Ed. Wade Hall and Rick Wallach. El Paso: Texas Western P, 1995. 17–24.

——. "The Mosaic of McCarthy's Fiction, Continued." *Sacred Violence*. Vol. 2, *Cormac McCarthy's Western Novels*. Ed. Wade Hall and Rick Wallach. El Paso: Texas Western P, 2002. 179–88.

——. "Naming, Knowing and Nothingness: McCarthy's Moral Parables." *Perspectives on Cormac McCarthy*. Rev. ed. Ed. Edwin T. Arnold and Dianne C. Luce. Jackson: UP of Mississippi, 1999. 45–70.

Arnold, Matthew. "Dover Beach." *The Norton Anthology of Poetry*. Ed. Margaret Ferguson, Mary Jo Salter, and Jon Stallworthy. 4th ed. New York: Norton, 1970. 999.

Augustine, St. *The Literal Meaning of Genesis*. Trans. John Hammond Taylor. New York: Newman P, 1982. Trans. of *De Genesi ad litteram*.

Bailey, Charles. "'Doomed Enterprises' and Faith: The Structure of Cormac McCarthy's *The Crossing*." *Southwestern American Literature* 20 (Fall 1994): 57–67.

———. "The Last Stage of the Hero's Evolution: Cormac McCarthy's *Cities of the Plain*." *Myth, Legend, Dust: Critical Responses to Cormac McCarthy*. Ed. Rick Wallach. New York: Manchester UP, 2000. 293–302.

Baines, Bill. Rev. of *Blood Meridian; or, The Evening Redness in the West*, by Cormac McCarthy. *Western American Literature* 21.1 (1986): 59–60.

Barnstone, Willis, and Marvin Meyer. *The Gnostic Bible: Gnostic Texts of Mystical Wisdom from the Ancient and Medieval Worlds*. Boston: Shambhala, 2003.

Baudelaire, Charles. "XXIX: Le joueur généreux." *Le spleen de Paris: Petits poèmes en Prose*. 1862. Ed. Yves Florenne. Paris: Le Livre de Poche, 1998.

Baumer, Franklin. *Religion and the Rise of Scepticism*. New York: Harcourt Brace, 1960.

Beck, John. "'A Certain but Fugitive Testimony': Witnessing the Light of Time in Cormac McCarthy's Southwestern Fiction." *Myth, Legend, Dust: Critical Responses to Cormac McCarthy*. Ed. Rick Wallach. New York: Manchester UP, 2000. 209–16.

Becker, Ernest. *The Denial of Death*. New York: Macmillan, 1973.

BeDuhn, Jason. "Jason BeDuhn on Mani and the Manicheans." *The Voices of Gnosticism*. Ed. Miguel Conner. Dublin: Bardic P, 2011. 117–34.

Bell, James. *Cormac McCarthy's West: The Border Trilogy Annotations*. El Paso: Texas Western P, 2002.

Bell, Vereen M. *The Achievement of Cormac McCarthy*. Louisiana: Louisiana State UP, 1988.

———. "Between the Wish and the Thing, the World Lies Waiting." *Southern Review* 28.4 (1992): 37–44.

Bennett, Barbara. "On the Image of Fire and References to Yeats's Poetry." *Bloom's Guides: Cormac McCarthy's "The Road."* Ed. Harold Bloom. New York: Facts on File, 2011. 75–77.

Berdyaev, Nicolas. *Jacob Boehme: Six Theosophic Points and Other Writings*. Michigan: Michigan UP, 1958.

Berman, Marshall. *All That Is Solid Melts into Air: The Experience of Modernity*. New York: Viking Penguin, 1988.

Berman, Morris. "Introduction: The Modern Landscape." *The Re-Enchantment of the World*. Ithaca, NY: Cornell UP, 1981. 15–24.

Bhikkhu, Buddhadasa. *Handbook for Mankind*. Trans. Roderick S. Bucknell. Vipassana Dhura Meditation Society. First electronic edition. December 1996. http://www.vipassanadhura.com/handbook4mankind.html#ch4.

Birkerts, Sven. "The Lone Soul State." *New Republic* 11 July 1994: 38–41.

Bishop, Donald. *Indian Thought: An Introduction*. New Delhi: Wiley Eastern, 1975.

Black, Henry Campbell. *Black's Law Dictionary*. 6th ed. St. Paul, MN: West, 1990.

Blake, William. *The Complete Poetry and Prose of William Blake*. Ed. David V. Erdman. New York: Random House, 1988.

"Blevins Family Name." FamilyTree.com. 25 August 2015. http://www.familytree.com/surnames/Blevins.

Bloom, Harold. *Bloom's Guides: Cormac McCarthy's "The Road."* Ed. Harold Bloom. New York: Facts on File, 2011.

———. *Bloom's Modern Critical Views: Cormac McCarthy*. New York: Infobase, 2009.

———. *How to Read and Why*. New York: Scribner, 2000.

Boehme, Jacob. *Aurora the Day-Spring; or, Dawning of the Day in the East; or, Morning-Redness in the Rising of the Sun. That Is the Root or Mother of Philosophy, Astrology and Theology from the True Ground; or, A Description of Nature*. Trans. Wayne Kraus. Jacob Boehme Online. http://jacobboehmeonline.com/.

———. *Six Theosophic Points: An Open Gate of All the Secrets of Life Wherein the Causes of All Beings Become Known; Six Mystical Points; On the Earthly and Heavenly Mystery; On the Divine Intuition*. Trans. John R. Earle. Kila, MT: Kessinger, 1992.

Boguta-Marchel, Hanna. *The Evil, the Fated, the Biblical: The Latent Metaphysics of Cormac McCarthy*. Newcastle: Cambridge Scholars Publishing, 2012.

Brading, D. A. *Mexican Phoenix: Our Lady of Guadalupe: Image and Tradition Across Five Centuries*. Cambridge: Cambridge UP, 2001.

Bramley, William. *The Gods of Eden*. New York: Avon, 1993.

Brewton, Vince. "The Changing Landscape of Violence in Cormac McCarthy's Early Novels and the Border Trilogy." *Southern Literary Journal* 37.1 (Fall 2004): 121–43.

Browning, Robert. "Bishop Blougram's Apology." *The Poems of Robert Browning*. London: Bibliolife, 2009.

———. "A Grammarian's Funeral." *The Poems of Robert Browning*. London: Bibliolife, 2009.

Buckland, Raymond. *The Fortune Telling Book: The Encyclopedia of Divination and Soothsaying*. Detroit: Visible, 2004.

Busby, Mark. "Into the Darkening Land, the World to Come: Cormac McCarthy's Border Crossings." *Myth, Legend, Dust: Critical Responses to Cormac McCarthy*. Ed. Rick Wallach. New York: Manchester UP, 2000. 227–48.

———. "Rolling the Stone, Sisyphus, and the Epilogue of *Blood Meridian*." *Southwestern American Literature* 36.3 (Summer 2011): 87–95.

Campbell, Christopher D. "Walter De Maria's *Lightning Field* and McCarthy's Enigmatic Epilogue: Y qué clase de lugar es éste?" *The Cormac McCarthy Journal* 2.1 (Spring 2002): 40–55.

Campbell, Neil. "Beyond Reckoning: Cormac McCarthy's Version of the West in *Blood Meridian, or The Evening Redness in the West*." *Critique: Studies in Contemporary Fiction* 39.1 (Fall 1997): 55–64.

Canfield, J. Douglas. "The Border of Becoming: Theodicy in *Blood Meridian*." *Mavericks on the Border: The Early Southwest in Historical Fiction and Film*. Lexington: UP of Kentucky, 2001. 37–48, 214.

———. "Crossing from the Wasteland into the Exotic in McCarthy's Border Trilogy." *A Cormac McCarthy Companion: The Border Trilogy*. Ed. Edwin T. Arnold and Dianne C. Luce. Jackson: UP of Mississippi, 2001. 256–69.

Cant, John. *Cormac McCarthy and the Myth of American Exceptionalism*. New York: Routledge, 2008.

Caron, Timothy P. "'Blood Is Blood': *All the Pretty Horses* in the Multicultural Literature Class." *Cormac McCarthy: New Directions*. Ed. James D. Lilley. Albuquerque: New Mexico UP, 2002. 153–70.

Carragher, Michael. "I Tego Arcana Dei: Aspects of the Demonic in Cormac McCarthy's *Blood Meridian*." *Publications of the Arkansas Philological Association* 23.1 (Spring 1997): 13–21.

Cervantes, Miguel de. *The Ingenious Hidalgo Don Quixote of La Mancha*. Trans. John Rutherford. London: Penguin, 2003.

Chaucer, Geoffrey. *The Canterbury Tales*. New York: Dover, 2004.

Christy, Arthur. *The Orient in American Transcendentalism: A Study of Emerson, Thoreau, and Alcott*. New York: Octagon, 1969.

Cohn-Sherbok, Dan. *Fifty Key Jewish Thinkers*. New York: Routledge, 1997.

Collado-Rodríguez, Francisco. "Trauma and Storytelling in Cormac McCarthy's *No Country for Old Men* and *The Road*." *Papers on Language & Literature* 48.1 (2012): 45–69.

Conee, Earl, and Theodore Sider. *Riddles of Existence: A Guided Tour of Metaphysics*. Oxford: Oxford UP, 2007.

Conze, Edward. *Buddhism: Its Essence and Development*. New York: Harper, 1959.

———. *Buddhist Scriptures*. Maryland: Penguin, 1973.

———. *Buddhist Wisdom Books: The Diamond Sutra and the Heart Sutra*. London: George Allen & Unwin, 1975.

———. *Further Buddhist Studies: Selected Essays*. Oxford: Bruno Cassirer, 1975.

———. *Selected Sayings from the Perfection of Wisdom*. London: Buddhist Society, 1975.

———. *Thirty Years of Buddhist Studies*. Oxford: Bruno Cassirer, 1968.

Coogan, Michael D. *A Brief Introduction to the Old Testament: The Hebrew Bible in Its Context*. Oxford: Oxford UP, 2009.

Cooper, Dale, and Ethan Carry. "*Suttree* and *L'Etranger*: The Hounds of Gnosticism." *Studies on Lucette Desvignes and the Twentieth Century* 6 (1996): 155–76.

Cooper, Lydia R. "He's a Psychopathic Killer, but So What?: Folklore and Morality in Cormac McCarthy's *No Country for Old Men*." *Papers on Language & Literature* 45.1 (2009): 37–59.

Costen, M. D. *The Cathars and the Albigensian Crusade*. Manchester: Manchester UP, 1997.

Covell, Scott. "Devil with a Bad Haircut: Postmodern Villainy Rides the Range in *No Country for Old Men*." *No Country for Old Men: From Novel to Film*. Ed. Lynnea Chapman King, Rick Wallach, and Jim Welsh. Plymouth, UK: Scarecrow, 2009. 95–109.

Cremean, David. "For Whom Bell Tolls: Cormac McCarthy's Sheriff Bell as Spiritual Hero." *No Country for Old Men: From Novel to Film*. Ed. Lynnea Chapman King, Rick Wallach, and Jim Welsh. Plymouth, UK: Scarecrow, 2009. 21–31.

Cutchins, Dennis. "Grace and Moss's End in *No Country for Old Men*." *No Country for Old Men: From Novel to Film*. Ed. Lynnea Chapman King, Rick Wallach, and Jim Welsh. Plymouth, UK: Scarecrow, 2009. 155–72.

Dacus, Chris. "The West as Symbol of the Eschaton in Cormac McCarthy." *Cormac McCarthy Journal* 7.1 (Fall 2009): 7–15.

Daugherty, Leo. "Gravers False and True: *Blood Meridian* as Gnostic Tragedy." *Perspectives on Cormac McCarthy*. Rev. ed. Ed. Edwin T. Arnold and Dianne C. Luce. Jackson: UP of Mississippi, 1999. 159–74.

DeConick, April. "April DeConick on Judas the Demonic Villain and Gnostic Ritual." *The Voices of Gnosticism*. Ed. Miguel Conner. Dublin: Bardic P, 2011. 201–23.

Derrida, Jacques. *Of Grammatology*. Trans. Gayatri Spivak. Baltimore: John Hopkins UP, 1997.

de Silva, Padmasiri. *Tangles and Webs: Comparative Studies in Existentialism, Psychoanalysis and Buddhism*. Colombo, Sri Lanka: Wesley P, 1976.

Deutsch, David. *The Fabric of Reality: The Science of Parallel Universes—and Its Implications*. New York: Penguin, 1997.

De Vigny, Alfred. "La maison du berger." *The French Romanticists: An Anthology of Verse and Prose*. Ed. H. F. Stewart and Arthur Tilley. Cambridge: Cambridge UP, 1917.

———. "La mort du loup." *The French Romanticists: An Anthology of Verse and Prose*. Ed. H. F. Stewart and Arthur Tilley. Cambridge: Cambridge UP, 1917.

Dolan, Shaun. "How to Prevent School Violence." University of Michigan. 31 January 2014. http://sitemaker.umich.edu/356.dolan/how_to_prevent_school_violence.

Donne, John. "Devotions upon Emergent Occasions: Meditation XVII." *John Donne's Sermons on the Psalms and Gospels*. Ed. Evelyn M. Simpson. Berkley: U of California P, 1963.

Douglas, Christopher. "The Flawed Design: American Imperialism in N. Scott Momaday's *House Made of Dawn* and Cormac McCarthy's *Blood Meridian*." *Critique* 45:1 (Fall 2003): 3–24.

Dutt, K. Guru. *Existentialism and Indian Thought*. Bangalore: Basavangudi, 1960.

Eckhart, Meister. "Selected Sermons." *German Mystical Writings: Hildegard of Bingen, Meister Eckhart, Jacob Boehme, and Others*. Ed. Karen J Campbell. New York: Continuum, 1991.

———. *Works of Meister Eckhart*. Ed. Franz Pfeiffer. Montana: Kessinger, 1992.
Elamanamadathil, Francis V. *Emerson and Hindu Scriptures*. Cochin: Academic, 1972.
Eliade, Mircea. *The Sacred and the Profane: The Nature of Religion*. New York: Harcourt, Brace & World, 1959.
Eliot, T. S. "Ash Wednesday." *Collected Poems*. London: Faber & Faber, 1963.
———. "The Hollow Men." *Selected Poems*. London: Faber & Faber, 1961.
———. "Preludes IV." *Selected Poems*. London: Faber & Faber, 1961.
———. "The Waste Land." *Selected Poems*. London: Faber & Faber, 1961.
Ellis, Jay. "Another Sense of Ending: The Keynote Address to the Knoxville Conference." *Cormac McCarthy Journal* 6.1 (Fall 2008): 22–38.
———. "Do You See? Levels of Ellipsis in No Country for Old Men." Ed. Sara Spurgeon. *Cormac McCarthy: "All the Pretty Horses," "No Country for Old Men," "The Road."* New York: Continuum, 2011. 94–116.
———. "Fetish and Collapse in *No Country for Old Men*." *Bloom's Modern Critical Views: Cormac McCarthy*. Ed. Harold Bloom. New York: Infobase, 2009. 133–70.
———. "McCarthy Music." *Myth, Legend, Dust: Critical Responses to Cormac McCarthy*. Ed. Rick Wallach. New York: Manchester UP, 2000. 157–70.
Emerson, Ralph Waldo. "Compensation." *The Complete Prose Works*. New York: Ward, 1891. 26–34.
———. "Experience." *The Complete Prose Works*. New York: Ward, 1891. 102–12.
———. "History." *The Complete Prose Works*. New York: Ward, 1891. 5–14.
———. "Illusions." *The Complete Prose Works*. New York: Ward, 1891. 568–72.
———. "Nature." *The Complete Prose Works*. New York: Ward, 1891. 131–36.
———. "The Over-Soul." *The Complete Prose Works*. New York: Ward, 1891. 67–74.
———. "The Poet." *The Complete Prose Works*. New York: Ward, 1891. 92–101.
Evenson, Brian. "McCarthy's Wanderers: Nomadology, Violence, and Open Country." *Sacred Violence: A Reader's Companion to Cormac McCarthy*. Ed. Wade Hall and Rick Wallach. El Paso: Texas Western P, 1995. 41–48.
FitzGerald, Edward. *Edward FitzGerald's Rubáiyát of Omar Khayyám: A Famous Poem and Its Influence*. Ed. William H. Martin and Sandra Mason. London: Anthem, 2011.
Flory, Dan. "Evil, Mood, and Reflection in the Coen Brothers' No Country for Old Men." *Cormac McCarthy: "All the Pretty Horses," "No Country for Old Men," "The Road."* Ed. Sara Spurgeon. New York: Continuum, 2011. 117–34.
"Form." *The Encyclopedia Britannica*. 11th ed. Vol 10. 1987.
Foster, Sally M. *Picts, Gaels and Scots*. London: B. T. Batsford, 1996.
Francis of Assisi, Saint. "Canticle of the Sun / *Laudes Creaturarum*." *Franciscan Poets*. Ed. Benjamin F. Musser. New York: Books for Libraries, 1967. 95–108.
Freud, Sigmund. *Civilization and Its Discontents*. Trans. James Strachey. New York: Norton, 1962.
Frodsham, J. D. *The Crisis of the Modern World and Traditional Wisdom*. Singapore: Institute of East Asian Philosophies, 1990.

———. *The Murmuring Stream: The Life and Works of Hsieh Ling-Yün*. Kuala Lumpur: University of Malaya P, 1967.
Frye, Steven. "Cormac McCarthy's 'World in Its Making': Romantic Naturalism in *The Crossing*." *Studies in American Naturalism* 2.1 (Summer 2007): 46–65.
———. *Understanding Cormac McCarthy*. Columbia: U of South Carolina P, 2009.
———. "Yeats's 'Sailing to Byzantium' and McCarthy's *No Country for Old Men*: Art and Artifice in the Novel." *No Country for Old Men: From Novel to Film*. Ed. Lynnea Chapman King, Rick Wallach, and Jim Welsh. Plymouth, UK: Scarecrow, 2009. 13–20.
Girard, René. *Violence and the Sacred*. Trans. Patrick Gregory. Baltimore: Johns Hopkins UP, 1979.
Grant, R. M. *Gnosticism and Early Christianity*. New York: Columbia UP, 1959.
Graulund, Rune. "Fulcrums and Borderlands: A Desert Reading of Cormac McCarthy's *The Road*." *Orbis Litterarum* 65.1 (February 2010): 57–78.
Grindley, Carl James. "The Setting of McCarthy's *The Road*." *Explicator* 67.1 (2008): 11–13.
Grossman, Lev. "What Happened When a Very Private Writer Met Two Very Idiosyncratic Filmmaking Brothers." *Time* 29 October 2007, 61.
Grossman, Vasily. *Life and Fate*. Trans. Robert Chandler. New York: Review, 1985.
Guénon, René. *Aperçus sur l'initiation*. Paris: Éditions Traditionnelles, 1946.
———. *The Reign of Quantity and the Signs of the Times*. Trans. Lord Northbourne. Baltimore: Penguin, 1972.
Guiley, Rosemary Ellen. *The Encyclopedia of Witches and Witchcraft*. New York: Facts on File, 1989.
Gwinner, Donovan. "'Everything uncoupled from its shoring': Quandaries of Epistemology and Ethics in *The Road*." *Cormac McCarthy: "All the Pretty Horses," "No Country for Old Men," "The Road."* Ed. Sara Spurgeon. New York: Continuum, 2011. 137–56.
Hage, Erik. *Cormac McCarthy: A Literary Companion*. Jefferson, NC: McFarland, 2010.
Hampsey, John C. "Aestheticizing the Wasteland, Revisioning the Journey: Cormac McCarthy's *The Road*." *Gettysburg Review* 21.3 (August 2008): 495–99.
Hardy, Thomas. "The Convergence of the Twain." *Thomas Hardy: Selected Poems*. Ed. Bob Blaisdell. New York: Dover, 1995.
Harkay, Russel J. *Phenomenal Physics*. Keene, NH: Harkay, 2006.
Harrison, Brady. "That Immense and Bloodslaked Waste: Negation in *Blood Meridian*." *Southwestern American Literature* 25.1 (Fall 1999): 35–42.
Hartmann, Franz. *Jacob Boehme: Life and Doctrines*. New York: Steiner, 1977.
Hellyer, Grace. "Spring Has Lost Its Scent: Allegory, Ruination, and Suicidal Melancholia in *The Road*." *Styles of Extinction: Cormac McCarthy's "The Road."* Ed. Julian Murphet and Mark Steven. New York: Continuum, 2012. 45–62.
Hoeller, Stephan. *Gnosticism: New Light on the Ancient Tradition of Inner Knowing*. Illinois: Quest, 2002.

"Homunculus." *Encyclopedia of Occultism and Parapsychology*. Gale Group, 2001. Answers.com. 23 August 2009. http://www.answers.com/topic/homunculus.

Hontheim, Joseph. "Hell." *The Catholic Encyclopedia*. Vol. 7. New York: Robert Appleton Company. 1910. 14 October 2012. www.newadvent.org/cathen/07207a.htm.

Horace. *Odes and Epodes*. Ed. Niall Rudd. Loeb Classical Library, 33. Cambridge, MA: Harvard UP, 2004.

Hume, David. "Dialogues Concerning Natural Religion." *Reason and Responsibility: Readings in Some Basic Problems of Philosophy*. Ed. Joel Feinberg and Russ Shafer-Landau. Belmont, CA: Cengage Learning, 2008.

Hunt, Alex. "Right and False Suns: Cormac McCarthy's *The Crossing* and the Advent of the Atomic Age." *Southwestern American Literature* 23.2 (April 1998): 31–37.

Hunt, Alex, and Martin M. Jacobsen. "Cormac McCarthy's *The Road* and Plato's Simile of the Sun." *Explicator* 66.3 (2008): 155–58.

Huxley, Aldous. *The Perennial Philosophy*. New York: Harper & Row, 1945.

Hynes, Samuel. *A War Imagined: The First World War and English Culture*. London: Random House, 1990.

James, William. *The Varieties of Religious Experience: A Study in Human Nature*. Rockville, MD: Arc Manor, 2008.

Jarrett, Robert. *Cormac McCarthy*. New York: Twayne, 1997.

———. "Cormac McCarthy's Sense of an Ending: Serialized Narrative and Revision in *Cities of the Plain*." *Myth, Legend, Dust: Critical Responses to Cormac McCarthy*. Ed. Rick Wallach. New York: Manchester UP, 2000. 313–42.

———. "Genre, Voice, and Ethos: McCarthy's Perverse 'Thriller.'" *No Country for Old Men: From Novel to Film*. Ed. Lynnea Chapman King, Rick Wallach, and Jim Welsh. Plymouth, UK: Scarecrow, 2009. 60–72.

Jonas, Hans. *The Gnostic Religion: The Message of the Alien God and the Beginnings of Christianity*. Boston: Beacon, 1958.

Josephs, Allen. "The Quest for God in *The Road*." *The Cambridge Companion to Cormac McCarthy*. Ed. Steven Frye. Cambridge: Cambridge UP, 2013. 133-46.

Josyph, Peter. "Tragic Ecstasy: A Conversation about McCarthy's *Blood Meridian*." *Sacred Violence*. Vol. 2, *McCarthy's Western Novels*. Ed. Wade Hall and Rick Wallach. El Paso: Texas Western P, 2002. 205–22.

Jung, Carl Gustav. *Answer to Job*. Trans. R. F. C. Hull. London: Rutledge & Kegan Paul, 1954.

———. *Man and His Symbols*. London: Aldus, 1979.

Jurgensen, John. "Hollywood's Favorite Cowboy." *Wall Street Journal* 20 November 2009.

Keats, John. "Ode to a Nightingale." *The Norton Anthology of Poetry*. 4th ed. Ed. Margaret Ferguson, Mary Jo Salter, and Jon Stallworthy. New York: Norton, 1970.

King, Karen. *What Is Gnosticism?* Cambridge: Harvard UP, 2003.
Knowles, Elizabeth. "Butterfly Effect." *Oxford Dictionary of Phrase and Fable.* 2nd ed. Oxford: Oxford UP, 2005.
Kobayashi, Issa. *The Year of My Life.* Trans. Nobuyuki Yuasa. Berkley: U of California P, 1972.
Kollin, Susan. "Genre and the Geographies of Violence: Cormac McCarthy and the Contemporary Western." *Contemporary Literature* 42.3 (Fall 2001): 557–88.
Krishnananda, Swami. *The Māndūkya Upanishad.* Rishikesh, India: Divine Life Society Sivananda Ashram, 1996.
Kushner, David. "Cormac McCarthy's Apocalypse." *Rolling Stone* 27 December 2007–10 January 2008: 43–48.
Lawrence, D. H. *The Woman Who Rode Away, St. Mawr, The Princess.* London: Penguin, 2006.
———. *Women in Love.* London: Penguin, 2007.
Lewis, James R. "Akashic Records." *The Dream Encyclopedia.* New York: Visible Ink, 1995.
Liddell, Henry George, and Robert Scott. "δράκων": *A Greek-English Lexicon.* Oxford: Clarendon P, 1940.
Lifton, Robert Jay. "This World Is Not This World." *Holocaust: Religious and Philosophical Implications.* Ed. John K. Roth and Michael Berenbaum. New York: Paragon House, 1989. 191–202.
Lincoln, Kenneth. *Cormac McCarthy: American Canticles.* New York: Palgrave Macmillan, 2009.
Lings, Martin. *The Underlying Religion: An Introduction to the Perennial Philosophy.* Bloomington, IN: World Wisdom, 2007.
Longley, John Lewis, Jr. "The Nuclear Winter of Cormac McCarthy." *Virginia Quarterly Review* 62.4 (1986): 746–50.
Luce, Dianne C. "Ambiguities, Dilemmas, and Double-Binds in Cormac McCarthy's *Blood Meridian*." *Southwestern American Literature* 26.1 (Fall 2000): 21–46.
———. *Reading the World: Cormac McCarthy's Tennessee Period.* Columbia: U South Carolina P, 2009.
———. "The Road and the Matrix: The World as Tale in *The Crossing*." *Perspectives on Cormac McCarthy.* Ed. Edwin T. Arnold and Dianne C. Luce. Jackson: UP of Mississippi, 1999. 195–220.
———. "The Vanishing World of Cormac McCarthy's Border Trilogy." *A Cormac McCarthy Companion: The Border Trilogy.* Ed. Edwin T. Arnold and Dianne C. Luce. Jackson: UP of Mississippi, 2001. 161–97.
———. "When You Wake: John Grady Cole's Heroism in *All the Pretty Horses*." *Sacred Violence: A Reader's Companion to Cormac McCarthy.* Ed. Wade Hall and Rick Wallach. El Paso: Texas Western P, 1995. 57–70.

Maas, Anthony. "Communicatio Idiomatum." *The Catholic Encyclopedia*. Vol. 4. New York: Robert Appleton, 1908.

Maharshi, Sri Ramana. *Be As You Are: The Teachings of Sri Ramana Maharshi*. Ed. David Godman. London: Arkana, 1985.

Maheshwarananda, Paramhans Swami. *The Hidden Power in Humans: Chakras and Kundalini*. Vienna: European UP, 2012.

Manser, A. R. "Existentialism." *Proceedings of the Aristotelian Society*. 37 (1963): 11–50.

March, Jenny. "Teiresias." *Dictionary of Classical Mythology*. London: Cassell, 2000.

Martensen, Hans L. *Jacob Boehme: Studies in His Life and Teachings*. London: Loxley Brothers, 1949.

Matthews, John. *The Mystic Grail: The Challenge of the Arthurian Quest*. New York: Stirling, 1997.

McCarthy, Cormac. *All the Pretty Horses*. New York: Alfred A. Knopf, 1992.

———. *Blood Meridian; or, The Evening Redness in the West*. 1985. New York: Vintage, 1999.

———. *Child of God*. 1973. New York: Vintage, 1993.

———. *Cities of the Plain*. 1998. New York: Vintage, 1999.

———. *The Counselor: A Screenplay*. New York: Vintage, 2013.

———. *The Crossing*. 1994. New York: Vintage, 1995.

———. *The Gardener's Son: A Screenplay*. Hopewell, NJ: Ecco, 1996.

———. *No Country for Old Men*. 2005. New York: Vintage, 2007.

———. *The Orchard Keeper*. 1965. New York: Vintage, 1993.

———. *Outer Dark*. 1968. New York: Vintage, 1993.

———. Papers. Wittliff Collections, Alkek Library. Texas State U, San Marcos. Box 91.

———. *The Road*. New York: Vintage, 2006.

———. *The Stonemason: A Play in Five Acts*. 1994. New York: Vintage, 1995.

———. *The Sunset Limited: A Novel in Dramatic Form*. New York: Vintage, 2006.

———. *Suttree*. 1979. New York: Vintage, 1993.

McMurty, Kim. "Some Improvident God: Metaphysical Explorations in McCarthy's Border Trilogy." *Sacred Violence*. Vol. 2, *Cormac McCarthy's Western Novels*. Ed. Wade Hall and Rick Wallach. El Paso: Texas Western P, 2002. 143–57.

Melville, Herman. "Bartleby the Scrivener." *Billy Bud, and Other Stories*. Hertfordshire, UK: Wordsworth Classics, 1998.

———. *The Enchanted Isles*. 1856. London: Hesperus, 2002.

———. "Fragments of a Lost Gnostic Poem of the 12th Century." *The New Oxford Book of American Verse*. Ed. Richard Ellmann. Oxford: Oxford UP, 1976.

———. *Moby-Dick*. 1851. London: Penguin, 1994.

Meredith, George. "Lucifer in Starlight." *The Norton Anthology of Poetry*. 4th ed. Ed. Margaret Ferguson, Mary Jo Salter, and Jon Stallworthy. New York: Norton, 1970.

Meyer, Marvin. "Marvin Meyer on Judas the Heroic Priest and Gnostic Philosophy." *The Voices of Gnosticism*. Ed. Miguel Conner. Dublin: Bardic P, 2011. 183-200.

Milton, John. *The Poetical Works of John Milton*. London: Watson, 1853.

Monk, Nick. "'An Impulse to Action, an Undefined Want': Modernity, Flight, and Crisis in the Border Trilogy and *Blood Meridian*." *Sacred Violence*. Vol. 2, *Cormac McCarthy's Western Novels*. Ed. Wade Hall and Rick Wallach. El Paso: Texas Western P, 2002. 83-103.

Morrison, Gail Moore. "*All the Pretty Horses*: John Grady Cole's Expulsion from Paradise." *Perspectives on Cormac McCarthy*. Ed. Edwin T. Arnold and Dianne C. Luce. Jackson: UP of Mississippi, 1999. 175-94.

Mosle, Sara. "Don't Let Your Babies Grow Up to Be Cowboys." Rev. of *Cities of the Plain*, by Cormac McCarthy. *New York Times Book Review* 17 May 1998: 16-18.

Mullins, Matthew. "Hunger, Apocalypse, and Modernity in Cormac McCarthy's *The Road*." *Symplokē*. 19.1-2 (2011): 75-93.

Nath, Samir. "Nirvana." *Encyclopaedic Dictionary of Buddhism*. Vol. 3. New Delhi: Sarup & Sons, 1998.

Needham, Joseph, and Wang Ling. *Science and Civilisation in China: History of Scientific Thought*. Cambridge: Cambridge UP, 1956.

Neiman, Susan. *Evil in Modern Thought: An Alternative History of Philosophy*. Princeton, NJ: Princeton UP, 2002.

Nietzsche, Friedrich. *Beyond Good and Evil: Prelude to a Philosophy of the Future*. Trans. Walter Kaufmann. New York: Vintage, 1966.

Nolan, Tom. Rev. of *Blood Meridian; or, The Evening Redness in the West*, by Cormac McCarthy. *Los Angeles Times Book Review* 9 June 1985: 2.

Oppenheimer, Paul. *Evil and the Demonic: A New Theory of Monstrous Behaviour*. New York: New York UP, 1996.

Otto, Rudolph. *Mysticism East and West: A Comparative Analysis of the Nature of Mysticism*. New York: Macmillan, 1957.

Owens, Barcley. *Cormac McCarthy's Western Novels*. Tucson: U of Arizona P, 2000.

Oxford English Dictionary Online (OED). Oxford UP. 2000-.

Pagels, Elaine. "Elaine Pagels on Understanding Gnosticism." *The Voices of Gnosticism*. Ed. Miguel Conner. Dublin: Bardic P, 2011. 135-50.

———. *The Gnostic Gospels*. London: Weidenfeld & Nicolson, 1979.

Parrish, Tim. "The Killer Wears the Halo: Cormac McCarthy, Flannery O'Connor, and the American Religion." *Sacred Violence: A Reader's Companion to Cormac McCarthy*. Ed. Wade Hall and Rick Wallach. El Paso: Texas Western P, 1995. 25-40.

Pascal, Blaise. *Pensées: Notes on Religion and Other Subjects*. Trans. John Warrington. London: Dent, 1973.

Patton, Paul. "McCarthy's Fire." *Styles of Extinction: Cormac McCarthy's "The Road."* Ed. Julian Murphet and Mark Steven. New York: Continuum, 2012. 131–44.

Peach, Emily. *Understanding and Using Tarot Symbolism*. Somerset, UK: Aquarian, 1984.

Pearson, Birger A. *Ancient Gnosticism: Traditions and Literature*. Minneapolis: Fortress, 2007.

Peckham, Morse. *The Triumph of Romanticism*. Columbia: U South Carolina P, 1970.

Peebles, Stacey. "*Lo fantástico*: The Influence of Borges and Cortázar on the Epilogue of *Cities of the Plain*." *Southwestern American Literature* 25.1 (Fall 1999): 105–9.

——. "Yuman Belief Systems and Cormac McCarthy's *Blood Meridian*." *Texas Studies in Literature and Language* 45.2 (Summer 2003): 231–44.

Pereira, José. *Hindu Theology: A Reader*. New York: Image, 1976.

Perry, Whitall N. *A Treasury of Traditional Wisdom*. London: George Allen & Unwin, 1971.

Peterson, Michael L. *God and Evil: An Introduction to the Issues*. Oxford: Westview, 1998.

Pétrement, Simone. *A Separate God: The Christian Origins of Gnosticism*. San Francisco: Harper & Row, 1990.

Phillips, Dana. "History and the Ugly Facts of *Blood Meridian*." *Cormac McCarthy: New Directions*. Ed. James D. Lilley. Albuquerque: U of New Mexico P, 2002. 17–46.

Plautus, Maccius Titus. *Asinaria. Plauti Comoediae*. Ed. F. Leo. Berlin: Weidmann, 1895.

Poe, Edgar Allan. "A Dream Within a Dream." *The Works of Edgar Allan Poe in One Volume*. New York: Walter J. Black, 1927.

——. "El Dorado." *The Works of Edgar Allan Poe in One Volume*. New York: Walter J. Black, 1927.

Pohle, Joseph. "The Real Presence of Christ in the Eucharist." *The Catholic Encyclopedia*. Vol. 5. New York: Robert Appleton, 1909.

Principe, Lawrence M., and Andrew Weeks. "Jacob Boehme's Divine Substance *Salitter*: Its Nature, Origin, and Relationship to Seventeenth Century Scientific Theories." *British Journal for the History of Science* 22.1 (March 1989): 53–61.

Pryor, Sean. "McCarthy's Rhythm." *Styles of Extinction: Cormac McCarthy's "The Road."* Ed. Julian Murphet and Mark Steven. New York: Continuum, 2012. 27–44.

Puckett, N. *Folk Beliefs of the South*. Chapel Hill, U North Carolina P, 1926.

Rai, Supriya. *Spiritual Masters: The Buddha*. Mumbai: Indus Source, 2003.

Rank, Otto. *Will Therapy and Truth and Reality*. New York: Knopf, 1945.

Remler, Pat. *Egyptian Mythology*. Rev. ed. New York: Infobase, 2010.

Reynolds, Michael D. *Falling Stars: A Guide to Meteors and Meteorites*. Mechanicsburg, PA: Stackpole, 2001.

Rotham, G. *The Riddle of Cruelty*. London: Vision P, 1971.
Rothfork, John. "Language and the Dance of Time in Cormac McCarthy's *Blood Meridian*." *Southwestern American Literature* 30.1 (Fall 2004): 23–36.
Rowe, William. "The Problem of Evil and Some Varieties of Atheism." Ed. Marilyn McCord Adams and Robert Merrihew Adams. Oxford Readings in Philosophy. *The Problem of Evil*. Oxford: Oxford UP, 1990. 126–37.
Rudolph, Kurt. *Gnosis: The Nature & History of Gnosticism*. San Francisco: Harper Collins, 1987.
Scaggs, John. "The Search for Lost Time: The Proustian Theme in Cormac McCarthy's *Cities of the Plain*." *Cormac McCarthy: Uncharted Territories / Territoires Inconnus*. Ed. Christine Chollier. Reims: UP of Reims, 2003. 73–82.
Scharf, Peter M. *The Denotation of Generic Terms in Ancient Indian Philosophy*. Philadelphia: American Philosophical Society, 1996.
Schaub, Thomas H. "Secular Scripture and Cormac McCarthy's *The Road*." *Renascence* 61.3 (April 2009): 153–67.
Schimpf, Shane. *A Reader's Guide to "Blood Meridian."* N.p.: Bon Mot, 2006.
Schugurensky, Daniel. "1982: T. Cullen Davis Constructs the School Lists, Giving Life to One of the Most Popular Urban Myths of 20th Century Education." History of Education: Selected Moments of the 20th Century. 31 October 2013. http://schugurensky.faculty.asu.edu/moments/1982davis.html.
Schuon, Frithjof. *Gnosis: Divine Wisdom*. Bedfont, UK: Perennial, 1959.
Scoones, Jacqueline. "The World on Fire: Ethics and Evolution in Cormac McCarthy's Border Trilogy." *A Cormac McCarthy Companion: The Border Trilogy*. Ed. Edwin T. Arnold and Dianne C. Luce. Jackson: UP of Mississippi, 2001. 131–60.
Sepich, John. "'A Bloody Dark Pastryman': Cormac McCarthy's Recipe for Gunpowder and Historical Fiction in *Blood Meridian*." *Mississippi Quarterly* 46.4 (Fall 1993): 547–63.
———. "The Dance of History in Cormac McCarthy's *Blood Meridian*." *Southern Literary Journal* 24.1 (Fall 1991): 16–31.
———. *Notes on "Blood Meridian."* Rev. ed. Austin: U of Texas P, 2008.
Shakespeare, William. *Hamlet*. Ed. Philip Edwards. Cambridge: Cambridge UP, 1985.
———. *Macbeth*. Ed. A. R. Braunmuller. Cambridge: Cambridge UP, 1997.
———. *The Merchant of Venice*. Ed. M. M. Mahood. Cambridge: Cambridge UP, 2000.
———. *The Tempest*. Ed. David Lindley. Cambridge: Cambridge UP, 2002.
Shaviro, Steven. "The Very Life of the Darkness: A Reading of *Blood Meridian*." *Perspectives on Cormac McCarthy*. Rev. ed. Ed. Edwin T. Arnold and Dianne C. Luce. Jackson: UP of Mississippi, 1999. 145–58.
Shaw, Patrick W. "The Kid's Fate, the Judge's Guilt: Ramifications of Closure in Cormac McCarthy's *Blood Meridian*." *Southern Literary Journal* 30.1 (1997): 102–20.
Shy, Todd. Rev. of *The Road*, by Cormac McCarthy. *Christian Century* 124.5 (6 March 2007): 38–41.

Slattery, Mary Francis. "What Is Literary Realism?" *Journal of Aesthetics and Art Criticism* 31.1 (Autumn 1972): 55–62.
Smith, Andrew Phillip. *A Dictionary of Gnosticism*. Wheaton, IL: Quest Books, 2009.
Smith, Huston. *Forgotten Truth: The Primordial Tradition*. New York: Harper Colophon, 1977.
———. *The Religions of Man*. New York: Harper & Row, 1965.
Smith, Margaret. "The Nature and Meaning of Mysticism." *Understanding Mysticism*. Ed. Richard Woods. New York: Image, 1980. 19–25.
Smith, Sam. *The Non-Christian and Anti-cosmic Roots of Amillennialism*. Biblical Reader Communications. 2006. www.BiblicalReader.com.
Smoley, Richard. *Forbidden Faith: The Secret History of Gnosticism*. New York: Harper Collins, 2007.
Snyder, Phillip A. "Hospitality in Cormac McCarthy's *The Road*." *Cormac McCarthy Journal* 6 (Autumn 2008): 69–88.
Soccio, Douglas J. *Archetypes of Wisdom: An Introduction to Philosophy*. Boston: Cengage, 2010.
Somerville, W. B. "The Description of Foucault's Pendulum." *Quarterly Journal of the Royal Astronomical Society* 13 (1972): 40–62.
Spencer, William. "Cormac McCarthy's Unholy Trinity: Biblical Parody in *Outer Dark*." *Sacred Violence: A Reader's Companion to Cormac McCarthy*. Ed. Wade Hall and Rick Wallach. El Paso: Texas Western P, 1995. 69–76.
Spenser, Edmund. *The Faerie Queene*. Ed. Elizabeth Heale. Cambridge: Cambridge UP, 1987.
Spurgeon, Sara L. "Foundation of Empire: The Sacred Hunter and the Eucharist of the Wilderness in Cormac McCarthy's *Blood Meridian*." *Bloom's Modern Critical Views: Cormac McCarthy*. Ed. Harold Bloom. New York: Infobase, 2009. 85–106.
Streng, Frederick J. "Three Approaches to Authentic Existence: Christian, Confucian, and Buddhist." *Philosophy East & West* 32.4 (1982): 371–92.
Stricker, Florence. "'This New Yet Unapproachable America': (For) an Ethical Reading of Cormac McCarthy's Western Novels." *Cormac McCarthy: Uncharted Territories / Territoires Inconnus*. Ed. Christine Chollier. Reims: UP of Reims, 2003. 147–61.
Tatum, Stephen. "'Mercantile Ethics' *No Country for Old Men* and the Narcocorrido." *Cormac McCarthy: "All the Pretty Horses," "No Country for Old Men," "The Road."* Ed. Sara Spurgeon. New York: Continuum, 2011. 77–93.
Teilhard de Chardin, Pierre. *The Phenomenon of Man*. London: Collins. 1959.
Tennyson, Lord Alfred. "In Memoriam A.H.H." *The Norton Anthology of Poetry*. 4th ed. Ed. Margaret Ferguson, Mary Jo Salter, and Jon Stallworthy. New York: Norton,1970.
Thera, Nanavira. *Clearing the Path: Notes on the Dhamma*. New York: Path, 1987.
Thomassen, Einar. "Einar Thomassen on Valentinus and the Valentinians." *The Voices of Gnosticism*. Ed. Miguel Conner. Dublin: Bardic P, 2011. 103–16.

Todorov, Tzvetan. *Facing the Extreme: Moral Life in the Concentration Camps*. New York: Henry Holt, 1996.
Tolkien, J.R.R. *The Hobbit*. 1937. London: Harper Collins, 1997.
Tresidder, Jack. *Symbols and Their Meanings*. London: Duncan Baird, 2000.
Turba Philosophorum. Sioux Falls, SD: NuVision. 2007.
Tyburski, Susan J. "'The Lingering Scent of Divinity' in *The Sunset Limited* and *The Road*." *Cormac McCarthy Journal* 6.1 (Fall 2008): 121–28.
Underhill, Evelyn. *Mysticism*. New York: E. P. Dutton, 1961.
Valéry, Paul. *Collected Works*. Vol. 10. Trans. D. Foliot and J. Matthews. New York: Pantheon, 1962.
Vanderheide, John. "No Allegory for Casual Readers." *No Country for Old Men: From Novel to Film*. Ed. Lynnea Chapman King, Rick Wallach, and Jim Welsh. Plymouth, UK: Scarecrow, 2009. 32–45.
Vauchez, André, and Richard Barrie Dobson. *Encyclopedia of the Middle Ages*. Vol. 1. Cambridge: James Clarke, 2000.
Wagner, Rachel, and Frances Flannery-Dailey. "Wake Up! Worlds of Illusion in Gnosticism, Buddhism, and *The Matrix* Project." *Philosophers Explore "The Matrix."* Ed. Christopher Grau. Oxford: Oxford UP, 2005. 258–87.
Wallace, Gary. "Meeting McCarthy." *Southern Quarterly* 30.4 (1992): 134–39.
Wallach, Rick. "Judge Holden, *Blood Meridian's* Evil Archon." *Sacred Violence: A Reader's Companion to Cormac McCarthy*. Ed. Wade Hall and Rick Wallach. El Paso: Texas Western P, 1995. 125–36.
Wegner, John. "'Wars and Rumors of Wars' in Cormac McCarthy's Border Trilogy." *A Cormac McCarthy Companion: The Border Trilogy*. Ed. Edwin T. Arnold and Dianne C. Luce. Jackson: UP of Mississippi, 2001. 73–91.
Weiss, David W., and Michael Berenbaum. "The Holocaust and the Covenant." *Holocaust: Religious and Philosophical Implications*. Ed. John K. Roth and Michael Berenbaum. New York: Paragon House, 1989. 71–81.
Welsh, Jim. "Borderline Evil: The Dark Side of Byzantium in *No Country for Old Men*, Novel and Film." *No Country for Old Men: From Novel to Film*. Ed. Lynnea Chapman King, Rick Wallach, and Jim Welsh. Plymouth, UK: Scarecrow, 2009. 73–85.
Wesley, John. *Wesley's Notes on the Bible*. Grand Rapids, MI: Christian Classics Ethereal Library. 1818.
Wilber, Ken. *Sex, Ecology, Spirituality: The Spirit of Evolution*. Boston: Shambhala. 1995.
Wilhelm, Randall S. "'Golden chalice, good to house a god': Still Life in *The Road*." *Cormac McCarthy Journal* 6.1 (Autumn 2008): 129–46.
Wittgenstein, Ludwig. *Tractatus Logico-Philosophicus*. Trans. C. K. Ogden. New York: Routledge, 1999.
Woodson, Linda. "Mapping *The Road* in Post-Postmodernism." *Cormac McCarthy Journal* 6.1 (Autumn 2008): 87–97.

———. "You Are the Battleground: Materiality, Moral Responsibility, and Determinism in *No Country for Old Men*." *Cormac McCarthy Journal* 5.1 (Spring 2005): 4–13.

Woodward, Richard. "Cormac McCarthy's Venomous Fiction." *New York Times Magazine* 19 April 1992: 28–31, 36, 40.

Wordsworth, William. "Lines Composed a Few Miles Above Tintern Abbey, on Revisiting the Banks of the Wye During a Tour. July 13, 1798." *The Complete Poetical Works of William Wordsworth*. London: Macmillan, 1888.

———. "My Heart Leaps Up." *The Complete Poetical Works of William Wordsworth*. London: Macmillan, 1888.

———. "Ode: Intimations of Immortality from Recollections of Early Childhood." *The Complete Poetical Works of William Wordsworth*. London: Macmillan, 1888.

Worthington, Leslie Harper. *Cormac McCarthy and the Ghost of Huck Finn*. Jefferson, NC: McFarland. 2012.

Wright, Wilmer Cave. *The Works of the Emperor Julian*. Vol. 3. Cambridge, MA: Harvard UP, 1913.

Yarbrough, Scott D. "Tricksters and Lightbringers in McCarthy's Post-Appalachian Novels." *Cormac McCarthy Journal* 10.1 (Fall 2012): 46–55.

Yeats, W. B. "Byzantium." *The Poems*. Ed. Daniel Albright. London: Everyman, 2001.

———. "A Dialogue of Self and Soul." *The Poems*. Ed. Daniel Albright. London: Everyman, 2001.

———. "Easter, 1916." *The Poems*. Ed. Daniel Albright. London: Everyman, 2001.

———. "Meru." Poem 12 in Twelve Supernatural Songs. *The Poems*. Ed. Daniel Albright. London: Everyman, 2001.

———. "Nineteen Hundred and Nineteen." *The Poems*. Ed. Daniel Albright. London: Everyman, 2001.

———. "Sailing to Byzantium." *The Poems*. Ed. Daniel Albright. London: Everyman, 2001.

———. "The Second Coming." *The Poems*. Ed. Daniel Albright. London: Everyman, 2001.

———. "Two Songs from a Play." *The Poems*. Ed. Daniel Albright. London: Everyman, 2001.

———. "Under Ben Bulben." *The Poems*. Ed. Daniel Albright. London: Everyman, 2001

———. *A Vision: The Collected Works of W. B. Yeats*. Vol 13. Ed. Catherine E. Paul and Margaret Mills Harper. New York: Scribner, 2008.

Index

Title abbreviations are *APH* (*All the Pretty Horses*), *CG* (*Child of God*), *CP* (*Cities of the Plain*), *NCOM* (*No Country for Old Men*), *OD* (*Outer Dark*), *OK* (*The Orchard Keeper*), *TC* (*The Crossing*), *TR* (*The Road*), *WM* (*Whales and Men*)

Absolute: boundaries, 190–91; vs. creator god, 148–49, 360–61n8; form, 308; illusion and impermanence, 131, 150–52; as impersonal, 153; light, 167; longing, 251–52; as other, 251; perception of, 153, 166, 244–45; as Reality, 159, 175, 251; self-knowledge, 314, 323; *TC*, 141, 148–49, 151–55, 159, 198, 199; *TR*, 308; unity with, 157–58, 251, 254–55, 322; as unknowable, 151–52, 155, 158, 188–89, 247, 362nn11–12; witnessing, 157–58; *WM*, 362n12
Adam. *See* Salvator Salvatus
Adam and Eve, 192–93, 300
Ahab, 48, 51, 347n13, 361n9
Akashic ledgers. *See* ledgers, Akashic
alchemy, 301–2, 303, 318, 388n18
alienation: *APH*, 107, 118, 365–66n18; *BM*, 12, 13, 81; *CP*, 226; *TC*, 131, 138–39, 162–63, 176, 196–97; *TR*, 289–90
allegorical interpretation, 6, 328n6
Allegory of the Cave, 22, 314
All the Pretty Horses: alienation, 107, 118, 365–66n18; beauty, 102, 106, 110, 118–19, 357n18, 364–65n13; bell, 122, 138, 363n6, 377n23; blood, 103, 120, 349n3, 356n15, 357n18; coins, 112–13, 359–60n4, 385–86n7; *CP*, 180, 202, 215, 366n3, 369nn2–3; cruelty, 369n3; death, 101–3, 109, 117–18, 137–38, 221–22, 351n12, 355n13; demiurge, 112–15, 330n5, 338–39n18, 354n7, 359–60n4, 385–86n7; dreams, 109–12, 119, 366n5; epigraph, 104; evil, 101, 107–9, 112–15, 330–31n10, 332–33nn17–18, 354nn7–8, 363n5, 365–66n18, 365n14, 378n2; as fairy tale, 372–73n12; fate, 112–16, 209, 210, 370n9, 381n13; ghosts, 102–3, 356n15; illusion and impermanence, 106, 116–18, 122; inordinate day, 344n5; as quest, 103–5, 122; suffering, 101, 105–6, 118, 120–21; title, 101; transience, 102, 106, 215; Truth, 364n10, 366n2, 382n22; unity, 121–23, 233–34

anagogical interpretation, 6, 328n6
anatta, 153, 244–45
animals: kid as savior in *BM*, 78; Manichaeism, 89, 126, 306, 346–47n12; suffering, 202–4, 369n1. *See also* dogs; wolves
anointing, 307–8
anticosmicism: *APH*, 101; *BM*, 7–30, 76, 329nn2–3; *CP*, 208–9, 248–49; cruelty of nature, 20–21; defined, 8; dualism, 316; *TC*, 358–59n1, 375n12; *TR*, 298–99, 324, 385n5
Anubis, 15, 330n8
apocalypse: *BM*, 392n26; *CP*, 208, 252–53; fire, 311; *NCOM*, 263; *TC*, 127, 196–97, 392n26; *TR*, 288, 299, 312–13, 323, 376n20, 379n5, 383–84n1, 384–85n4; as triumph of spirit, 310–12; *WM*, 368n17
archatron, 247, 374n8
archons: *BM*, 35–42, 44, 47, 52, 333–34n3; control of humans, 42–45, 47, 180, 336n12; *CP*, 211; creation of humans, 194; darkness, 162; and demiurge, 3, 35, 334n7; gnosis, 40, 45–46; hierarchy, 38; imprisonment of spirit, 35, 39, 43, 164–65; *NCOM*, 274; *OD*, 335–36n9; planets, 368–69n18. *See also* heimarmene
Arthurian romance, 103, 230. *See also* grail
Ascent of the Soul, 38, 316
atavism, 17, 22, 135, 387n15
atom, 374n5
attachment: *APH*, 105–6; Cathars, 363–64n9; desire, 144–45, 189; to the past, 186–87; *TC*, 173, 190; *TR*, 291, 302–3
St. Augustine, 108, 328n6, 350n10
Aurora (Boehme), 90, 301–2, 347n15
authentic existence, 269, 293
autonomy: *BM*, 40–41; good/evil, 243
avidyā, 191

baptism, 75, 309
Bartleby, the Scrivener (Melville), 86

413

beauty: *APH*, 102, 106, 110, 118–19, 357n18, 364–65n13; *The Counselor*, 371n14; *CP*, 215–16, 386n10; *TC*, 164, 168; *TR*, 118, 292, 307, 324–25, 364n12

bells, 122, 138, 163, 255, 285, 363n6, 377n23

benevolence: evil paradox, 114–16, 141–42, 243, 275–76, 358–59n1, 382n18; *TC*, 176

birds, 55, 115, 352n17

Blake, William, 147, 324–25, 339n3, 341n9, 342–43n11

blindness: ability to see Reality, 165–68, 375–76n18; *CP*, 227, 240, 365n17, 372n7, 375–76n18; demiurge, 113, 185, 354n7; *OD*, 365n17; *TC*, 161–77, 363n2, 373n2; Tiresias, 362–63n1; *TR*, 317, 319, 320; ubiquity of, 173–74

blood: *APH*, 103, 120, 349n3, 356n15, 357n18; *BM*, 356n15; interconnectedness, 103, 133; limits, 135; as sacred, 132; *TC*, 131, 132, 133, 135, 354n8; transubstantiation, 218–19, 245–46, 374n6; *WM*, 356n15

Blood Meridian: anticosmicism, 7–30, 76, 328–29nn1–3, 333n18; apocalypse imagery, 392n26; bridal imagery, 82, 345n7; cruelty of nature, 19–21, 331n12; death, 8–11, 49–51, 329nn2–3, 338n16, 338–39n18; demiurge, 7, 36, 338–39n18, 342–43n11, 359–60n4, 375n11, 385–86n7; destruction, 17, 18, 369n4; dreams, 28–30, 66–69, 112–13, 179–80, 337n13, 342–43n11; epigraphs, 18–19, 21, 32, 50, 53–54; epilogue, 94–99, 348–49nn21–22, 368n15; evil, 7, 12–13, 15–19, 21–24, 40–41, 297, 372n10, 378n2; fate, 42–50, 52, 87–88, 97, 112–13, 274, 337n13, 337–38n15, 366n4, 380n10; fetters, 42, 44, 337n14, 380–81n11; fire, 89–90, 94–96, 99, 349n3, 382n20; Gnostic readings, 4; God, 7, 23–26, 61, 333n18; heimarmene, 41–45, 48–49, 97, 337n14, 351n15, 385–86n7; illusion and impermanence, 27–30, 290–91; interconnectedness, 356n15; ledgers, 353–54n2; metal, 66–69, 179–80, 256–57, 338–39n18, 342–43n11, 359–60n4; modernity, 53, 69, 339n1; parody, 53–69, 339–40nn3–4, 342–43n11; past, 369n5; patterns, 358n22; rationalism, 55–58, 233, 234; representation vs. Reality, 256–57; salvation, 71–99, 343n2; stars and moon, 11, 71–72, 74, 78, 79, 91, 344–45n6; sun, 8–11, 76, 198, 329nn2–3, 353n3; surgeon imagery, 209, 368n16; *TC*

parallels, 182–83; title, 49–50, 53, 338n17, 347n15; *TR* allusion, 290–91; void, 12–13, 330n6; weaving, 359–60n4, 375n11; will, 44, 46–49, 51, 57, 274, 338n16; witnessing, 367n11. *See also* Judge Holden; kid in *BM*

Bodhicitta, 140

Bodhisattvas, 40, 139–40, 336n11

body. *See* corporeality

Boehme, Jacob: *Aurora*, 90, 301–2, 347n15; blindness, 173–74; *BM* epigraph, 32; Christ, 386–87n13; as Christian, 364n11; creation, 324; cruelty of nature, 20–21; devil, 62; fire and divine spark, 96, 283, 302, 305, 310; light/dark, 32, 76, 167, 310; passive resistance, 87; rites, 355n12; salitter, 301–2; science, 58–59; sleep, 52; universal spirit, 90; will, 46, 47, 49

Border Trilogy. *See All the Pretty Horses*; *Cities of the Plain*; *The Crossing*

boundaries, 155, 190–91

Brahma, 354–55n11, 359n3, 360–61n8

Brahman, 354–55n11, 359n3, 365n15. *See also* Absolute

bridal imagery, 82, 273, 345n7

Browning, Robert, 303, 363n8

brutality. *See* cruelty of humans

Buddha, false, 392n30

Buddhism: blindness, 173, 174; body, 186; death, 184, 237, 293, 294, 392n28; dharma, 284–85; fire, 127; gold, 14, 193; heart, 15; influence on Gnosticism, 3; involvement vs. withdrawal, 139–40; *kalpas*, 352–53n2; karma, 272; light, 318; longing, 150; Mahayana, 139, 148–49, 308–9, 346n11, 360–61n8; mandalas, 325; Māra, 40–41, 45, 52, 360–61n8; in McCarthy's works, 5; parody, 66; present, 187; salvation, 26–27; sorrow, 145; symbols vs. reality, 189–90; third eye, 273, 381n16; unity, 308–9; Yogacara, 138, 165, 190. *See also* Absolute; attachment; compassion; enlightenment; illusion and impermanence; separation; suffering

calling, 74, 149–50, 165

Camus, Albert, 348–49n22

cannibalism: *BM*, 17, 92–93; rites, 298, 387n15; *TC*, 136; *TR*, 287, 295–98, 330n9, 358n23

carnival. *See* theater imagery

Cathars, 363–64n9

caves, 22, 314, 315–18, 392–93n29
chance and divine will, 61
charity. *See* compassion
Child of God, 330–31n10, 344n5, 358n22, 365n14, 372n9, 375n10, 378n2
choics. *See* hyle and hylics
Christ: kid in *BM*, 72–73, 85, 94, 343n2; Logos, 304; parody in *BM*, 59–63, 339–40n4; as sacrifice, 218, 248; Second Coming, 288, 384n3; Sermon on the Mount, 199; as serpent, 313; *TR*, 294–97, 300, 305–10, 326, 386–87n13; water, 279. *See also* saviors
churches: *BM*, 53–54; *CP*, 240–41; Gnostic distrust, 129, 305
circle: Absolute, 151; *CP*, 213–14
Cities of the Plain: anticosmicism, 208–9, 248–49; *APH* parallels, 180, 202, 215, 366n3, 369nn2–3; beauty, 215–16, 386n10; blindness, 227, 240, 365n17, 372n7, 375–76n18; compassion, 204, 256, 257; cruelty, 202–4; death, 209, 210–14, 221–22, 235–37, 250, 254, 352n18, 371–72nn4–5; demiurge, 209, 211; destruction, 204–5, 208, 252–53, 369–70nn5–6; dreams, 180, 209, 210–13, 235–36, 238, 240–44, 353–54n4, 358n23; epilogue, 235–57, 371n12, 373n1, 374–75n9; as fairy tale, 229–32, 372n11; fate, 116, 180, 201–16, 244, 246, 249–50; illusion and impermanence, 207, 208, 210–11, 226, 240–44, 248–49, 250–52; incubus, 366n6; ledgers, 353–54n4; magical realism, 235, 373n1; Proust, 370n7; sacrifice, 238, 245, 247–48, 358n23, 371n12, 374–75n9; as screenplay, 201, 366n3; as separate story, 235; sin and forgiveness, 217–34, 372n5; Thanatos, 221–22, 371–72n4; title, 205, 222; unity, 234, 254–56; writing order, 201, 366n3
civilization, destruction of, 17, 18, 204–5, 323–24, 369–70nn4–6
clergy. *See* churches
clocks, 212, 213–14, 246, 371n13, 385n5
coins: *APH*, 112–13, 359–60n4, 385–86n7; *BM*, 41, 66–69, 342–43n11, 351n13, 359–60n4, 380–81n11, 385–86n7; Emerson, 68; fate, 351n13; *NCOM*, 267–68, 270–72, 351n13, 381n12, 385–86n7; *TR*, 291, 385–86n7
coldforger, 66–69, 112–13, 179–80, 256–57, 342–43n11, 359–60n4

collective subconscious, 253
communion. *See* Eucharist; interconnectedness
compassion: as abyss, 139–40; *BM*, 79, 81–83, 88, 346n11, 382–83n23; *CP*, 204, 256, 257; *NCOM*, 277, 278, 280–82, 285, 382–83n23; *TC*, 138–39, 194–95, 197, 386n12; *TR*, 295–96, 319, 321; unity, 295; vs. wisdom, 346n11
"Compensation" (Emerson), 154, 297–98
conspiracy of the world, 246
contracts. *See* covenants
convergence, 267, 268–69, 366n4, 380n10
copper, 318
corporeality: *CP*, 227; darkness, 162, 167; imprisonment, 42, 47, 227; repulsion, 42, 129–30, 186; *TC*, 129–30, 185–86, 354n8
cosmology: Gnosticism, 3–4, 9, 11, 12, 38; malevolence, 8–13, 330n5; salitter, 301–2, 303, 388n18; sceptre, 374n5; *TR*, 289–90, 385nn5–6. *See also* heimarmene
The Counselor: fate, 381n13; forgiveness, 371n2; illusion and impermanence, 354n10; kindness, 383n24; neutrality, 346n10; predators as sacred, 355–56n14; symbols vs. reality, 367n10; transience, 371n14; world as evil, 378n2
counterfeit. *See* coldforger
covenants, 26, 34–35, 39–40, 51, 275, 360n7
creation: Absolute vs. creator god, 148–49, 360–61n8; Brahma, 354–55n11; *CP*, 249; demiurge, 3, 8, 21–22, 35, 127, 141, 302, 360n5; destruction of world, 323–24; dreams, 243; Gnosticism, 21–24, 127, 224, 302, 324, 331–32n13; inordinate day, 344n5; *kalpas*, 352–53n2; of man, 42, 194; *Rubáiyát*, 388n17; Śaṅkara, 395n35; *TC*, 169, 194; *TR*, 299
The Crossing: anticosmicism, 358–59n1, 375n12; apocalypse, 127, 196–97, 392n26; bells, 163, 363n6, 377n23; blindness, 161–77, 363n2, 373n2; blood, 131–33, 135, 354n8; communion, 131, 133–34, 357n19–20, 374n6; compassion, 138–39, 194–95, 197, 386n12; darkness, 126–27, 168, 175–76, 192–93, 195–97, 375n12; death, 137–38, 147, 156, 158, 174, 181–84, 198, 254, 367n13; demiurge, 113, 128, 146–48, 153–54, 168, 179–80, 184–86, 198, 199, 338–39n18, 360n5; direct experience, 367n9; disruption of natural order, 136, 344n5,

The Crossing (continued)
357–58n21; divine spark, 192, 340n7, 363n4; dreams, 127–28, 136–38, 146–47, 167–68, 183–84, 192–93, 360n5; epiphanies, 125–40, 179, 193–97; evil, 141–42, 167–72, 330n5, 358–59n1; fate, 180–84, 210, 366n1, 374n7, 375n15; fire, 126, 127, 136–38, 162, 176, 363n4, 392n26; God, 113, 145–46, 152–53, 169, 176, 332–33n17, 340n7; guilt, 136, 195, 357–58n21, 386n12; heimarmene, 146, 148, 167–68, 180–85, 192–93, 375n15; interconnectedness, 125, 133–35, 139, 140, 143, 154–55, 234, 354n8, 357n19–20; ledgers, 127–28, 353–54n4; longing, 375n17; metal, 179, 180, 338–39n18; past, 186–90, 366–67n8, 369n5, 386n8; pneuma, 134–35, 191–92, 368n15; prayer, 394n33; sacrifice, 131, 254, 374n6; separation, 350n9; storytelling, 141–43, 358–59n1; suffering, 138, 144, 162–63, 168, 174, 175, 177, 180–81, 183, 194; transcendence, 126, 141–59, 185, 340n7; unity, 131, 143, 154–55, 191, 234, 376–77n22; water, 382n21, 391n24; weaving, 113, 146–47, 186, 360n5, 375n11; witnessing, 153, 189, 320, 358–59n1, 367n11; wolves, 125, 128–35, 194, 234, 350n9, 352n19, 354n8, 355–56n14, 357n19–20. *See also* illusion and impermanence in *TC*
cruelty of humans, 15–19, 202–4, 331n11, 369n3
cruelty of nature: *APH*, 369n3; *BM*, 19–21, 331n12; *CP*, 202; Gnosticism, 20, 21, 331–32n13; Grossman on, 21, 332n15; Mill, 351n16; *TC*, 194

Dante Alighieri, 6, 237–38, 288, 328n6, 384n2
dark: as alien, 196; *BM*, 22–23, 69; corporeality, 162, 167; dark night of the soul, 76–77; demiurge and archons, 162, 167, 185; devil, 32; enlightenment, 273–74; evil, 22–23, 167; ignorance, 161, 162, 185, 195–97, 363n2; in man, 16; Manichaeism, 276, 335n8, 368–69n18; *NCOM*, 274; Salvator Salvatus, 94; *TC*, 126–27, 168, 175–76, 192–93, 195–97, 375n12; *TR*, 288, 292, 315, 317; triune in *OD*, 332n16; war, 363n3. *See also* light
deafness, 113
Death: Chigurh as, 266, 269–70, 272–73, 274, 380n8, 381n15; demiurge, 237, 338–39n18;

God as, 237; Judge Holden as, 51–52, 338–39n18. *See also* death
death: *APH*, 101–3, 109, 117–18, 137–38, 221–22, 351n12, 355n13; *BM*, 8–11, 49–51, 329nn2–3, 338n16, 338–39n18; Buddhism, 184, 237, 293, 294, 392n28; *CP*, 209, 210–14, 221–22, 235–37, 250, 254, 352n18, 371–72nn4–5; denial, 50, 360n6; as escape, 156, 158, 237, 302, 316, 392n28; Gnosticism, 184, 237, 316, 392n28; of God, 53, 54, 339n1; heimarmene, 338n16; as illusion, 190, 191; interconnectedness, 254; of kid in *BM*, 51–52, 91–94; killing and fear of, 50, 51; sorrow, 145; *TC*, 137–38, 147, 156, 158, 174, 181–84, 190, 191, 198, 254, 367n13; *TR*, 293–95, 302; West as symbol of, 50; and will, 49, 51. *See also* Death
death wish. *See* Thanatos
demiurge: *APH*, 112–15, 330n5, 338–39n18, 354n7, 359–60n4, 385–86n7; as artisan, 67, 113, 179–80, 341n10, 359–60nn4–5; blindness, 113, 185, 354n7; *BM*, 7, 36, 338–39n18, 342–43n11, 359–60n4, 385–86n7; *CP*, 209, 211; as creator, 3, 8, 21–22, 35, 127, 141, 302, 360–61n8, 360n5; darkness, 162, 167, 185; as Death, 237, 338–39n18; evil paradox, 114–16, 141–42, 243, 275–76, 358–59n1, 382n18; hierarchy, 334n7; lawsuit concerning the world, 147–48; *Moby-Dick*, 113, 146–47, 360n5, 361n9; *NCOM*, 274–75, 381–82n17; *OD*, 335–36n9; order and disorder, 171; origins, 114, 317; *Suttree*, 338–39n18, 359–60nn4–5; *TC*, 113, 128, 146–48, 153–54, 168, 179–80, 184–86, 198, 199, 338–39n18; *TR*, 299–301, 317, 387n15; Yahweh as, 35, 39, 274. *See also* heimarmene
demons: as articulate, 231–32; hierarchy, 334n7; Judge Holden as, 25, 32–35, 49, 52, 84, 85; naming, 231–32; *OD*, 335–36n9; time, 315; *TR*, 297
desire and attachment, 144–45, 189
destiny. *See* fate; heimarmene
destruction: civilization, 17, 18, 204–5, 323–24, 369–70nn4–6; *kalpas*, 352–53n2; Shiva, 354–55n11, 359n3; *TC*, 126; *TR*, 301–3, 308, 310–12, 323–24
determinism. *See* fate; heimarmene
de Vigny, Alfred, 145, 357n17
devil, 32, 33, 49, 62, 64, 85, 373n13. *See also* demiurge; demons; Satan

INDEX ■ 417

Devotions upon Emergent Occasions (Donne), 122, 138, 255, 285
dharma, 284–85
Diamond Sutra, 28–29, 291
direct experience: centrality of, 5, 97, 129; *CP*, 253; vs. faith, 246–47; gnosis, 304, 307; vs. language, 187, 367n9; Perennial Philosophy, 151, 188; Reality, 187–88, 189; Sufism, 189; *TC*, 367n9; *TR*, 307
divination, 51, 87–88, 180–81, 229, 372n9, 381n16
divine spark: Absolute, 154–55; *APH*, 111; *BM*, 74–75, 89–91; Boehme on, 96, 283, 302, 305, 310; *Moby-Dick*, 347n13; *NCOM*, 283; *TC*, 192, 340n7, 363n4; *TR*, 310–11, 314, 348n20, 394–95n34; Valentinians, 95–96. *See also* fire; humanity as divine; pneuma
divine will and war, 61
djinns, 25, 33, 52. *See also* demons
dogs, 194–96, 197, 203–4, 295, 369n1
dolls, 42, 336n12
Donne, John, 122, 138, 255, 285
Don Quixote, 103–5, 349–50n5
dream, world as: *CP*, 212; creation of world, 243; illusion and impermanence, 27–28, 98, 137, 144, 241–42; past as a dream, 186–87; *TR*, 291
dreams: *APH*, 109–12, 110, 119, 366n5; *BM*, 28–30, 66–69, 112–13, 179–80, 337n13, 342–43n11; *CP*, 180, 209, 210–13, 235–36, 238, 240–44, 353–54n4, 358n23; Emerson, 68; Jungian vs. Freudian, 329n3; *NCOM*, 271, 282–84, 287, 382n25; *TC*, 127–28, 136–38, 146–47, 167–68, 183–84, 192–93, 350n9, 360n5; *TR*, 287, 314–18, 353n4, 364n12
dualism: Absolute vs. creator god, 148–49, 360–61n8; as anticosmic, 316; gnosis, 3; Manichaeism, 114, 170, 276, 335n8; *NCOM*, 276–77, 382n19; Valentinians, 114, 170, 335n8
duḥkha. *See* suffering

ego, 107, 128, 148, 158, 159, 244–45, 246, 346n11. *See also* anatta
El Dorado, 103–4
Eliot, T. S., 8, 117, 208, 321–22, 394–95n34, 394n32
Ely in *TR*, 319–21, 392n30
Emerson, Ralph Waldo: "Compensation," 154, 297–98; dream of currency, 68; fire, 96; "History," 154; interconnectedness, 143, 154, 155; "Nature," 143; "The Over-Soul," 154, 309; personal God, 152–53; "The Poet," 96; world as a dream, 241–42
The Encantadas (Melville), 103–5
end of days, 311–12. *See also* destruction
enlightenment: illusion and impermanence, 27, 98; light/dark, 197, 273–74; Māra, 45; as possible for all, 199; suffering, 120, 136; time and space, 191; as waking, 144; and will, 48–49. *See also* gnosis; transcendence
Eucharist: *BM*, 55, 84; *CP*, 245–46; futility of, 355n12; as mystery, 326; *OD*, 345n9; as sacrifice, 218–19; *TC*, 131, 374n6; *TR*, 307
"The Everlasting Gospel" (Blake), 147
evil: as absence, 108, 350n10; *APH*, 101, 107–9, 112–15, 330–31n10, 332–33nn17–18, 354nn7–8, 363n5, 365n14, 365–66n18, 378n2; *BM*, 7, 12–13, 15–19, 21–24, 40–41, 297, 372n10, 378n2; *CG*, 330–31n10, 378n2; *The Counselor*, 378n2; *CP*, 237, 246; creation as, 21–24, 127, 224, 302, 324, 331–32n13; darkness, 22–23, 167; fighting, 87, 264, 281–82, 380n7; ignorance, 159, 171, 313; metal, 66–67, 133; nature of, 7, 21–24, 138, 170, 259–61, 377–78n1; *NCOM*, 259–66, 272–73, 276, 330–31n10, 377–78n1, 379–80n6; *OD*, 330–31n10, 372n10, 378n2; order and disorder, 171; origins of, 4, 114, 167–68, 335n8; paradox, 114–16, 141–42, 243, 275–76, 358–59n1, 382n18; as pervasive theme, 2–3, 330–31n10; *Suttree*, 330–31n10, 332–33n17, 378n2; *TC*, 141–42, 167–72, 330n5, 358–59n1; *TR*, 297, 301, 302, 382n25; void as, 12–13, 16. *See also* God as evil; humanity as evil
exegesis, 6, 328n5
existentialism, 177, 269–71, 293, 348–49n22
extinction, 206, 208, 370n6, 392n30

fairy-tale motif, 229–32, 372–73nn11–12
faith, 129, 246–47
false prophets, 320, 392n30
fate: *APH*, 112–16, 209, 210, 370n9, 381n13; archons, 42–45, 180; *BM*, 42–49, 52, 87–88, 97, 112–13, 274, 337n13, 337–38n15, 366n4, 380n10; *The Counselor*, 381n13; *CP*, 116, 180, 201–16, 244, 246, 249–50; *NCOM*, 267, 268–72, 351n13, 380n10, 381nn12–13; *TC*, 180–84, 210, 366n1,

fate (*continued*)
374n7, 375n15; *TR*, 289. *See also* convergence; heimarmene
father in *The Road*: awareness of mortality, 294; as fire carrier, 310–12; as God, 386–87n13; as Job, 300; relationship with God, 299–301, 387–88n16
Faulkner, William, 4–5, 37, 332n14
fetters, tethers, string motif: *APH*, 116, 370n9, 381n13; *BM*, 42, 44, 337n14, 380–81n11; *CP*, 229; Gnosticism, 41, 42; *OD*, 336n12. *See also* heimarmene
fire: *APH*, 365–66n18; *BM*, 89–90, 94–96, 99, 349n3, 382n20; Christ, 347n14; fire carriers, 310–12, 391–92n25; Gnosticism, 96, 310; *NCOM*, 282–85, 348n20, 349n3, 383n26, 391–92n25; Perennial Philosophy, 283, 310; *TC*, 126, 127, 136–38, 162, 176, 363n4, 392n26; *TR*, 287, 310–14, 321–22, 348n20, 349n3, 353n4
firedrake, 313, 348n19
"Fire Sermon," 127
First Commandment, 39, 274–75
First Noble Truth. *See* suffering
fish, 323–26, 394–95n34
forgery. *See* coldforger
forgiveness: *The Counselor*, 371n2; *CP*, 217–34, 372n5; as divine, 223–24; sacrifice, 217–18; *TR*, 295
fortune-telling. *See* divination
fourfold interpretation, 6, 328n6
"Fragments of a Lost Gnostic Poem of the 12th Century" (Melville), 86
Saint Francis of Assisi, 10–11, 134, 357n20
free will. *See* will
French Revolution, 55, 339n2
Freud, Sigmund, 329n3, 331n11, 371n3

The Gardener's Son, 360n5
Genesis, 300, 313, 317
gnosis: archons, 40, 45–46; *CP*, 239–40, 253; defined, 3–4; direct experience, 304, 307; vs. faith, 129; Gnostic savior, 74; light, 162, 185, 197; Reality, 144, 209, 247; salvation, 4, 5, 26–27, 98, 156–57, 239, 249; *TC*, 142, 156–57; will, 48–49. *See also* enlightenment; illusion and impermanence
Gnostic Apocryphon of John, 41–42, 67, 167–68, 185, 186, 197
Gnosticism: background, 3–5, 327n2; cosmology, 3–4, 9, 11, 12, 38; existentialism, 348–49n22; reincarnation, 93, 315, 348n18; Sethian Gnosticism, 302, 309. *See also* Absolute; alienation; anticosmicism; demiurge; divine spark; dualism; gnosis; God; God as evil; heimarmene; illusion and impermanence; Manichaeism; pneuma; suffering; Valentinians
God: as absent in *TR*, 299–301, 387–88n16; as alien, 3, 321–22, 340n7, 382n19, 393–94n31; as Death, 237; death of, 53, 54, 339n1; father in *TR*, 299–301, 386–87n13, 387–88n16; personal, 152–53; unity of, 190–91; witnessing of, 157–58, 362n10. *See also* Absolute; God as evil; God as good; gods; indifference of God/cosmos
God as evil: *APH*, 332–33nn17–18; *BM*, 23–26, 333n18; Cathars, 363–64n9; *CG*, 365n14; *CP*, 208–9, 238–39, 246; evil paradox, 114–16, 141–42, 243, 275–76, 358–59n1, 382n18; lawsuit concerning the world, 147–48, 155, 360n7; Śaivism, 354–55n11; *Suttree*, 332–33n17; *TC*, 145–46, 169, 176, 332–33n17; *TR*, 332–33n17
God as good: Cathars, 363–64n9; *CP*, 238–39; evil paradox, 114–16, 141–42, 243, 275–76, 358–59n1, 382n18
Godhead. *See* Absolute
God-man myth, 254–55
gods: Chigurh as, 274–75, 381–82n17; Judge Holden as, 35, 36, 39–40, 52, 59–63, 65–66, 91, 274, 334n5, 339–40n4, 392n30; war as, 61–62
gold, 14, 193
Gollum, 392–93n29
good: evil paradox, 114–16, 141–42, 243, 275–76, 358–59n1, 382n18; fire, 2; need for evil, 169–70; Nietzsche, 63, 340n6; sun as, 9, 330n4; *TC*, 170–72; *TR*, 301, 302, 307, 321; vs. will, 62. *See also* God as good
Gospel of Mary, 224
Gospel of Philip, 188, 224, 303, 310, 324
Gospel of Thomas: direct experience, 97; divinity of man, 304, 318; fire, 96; light, 309; Logos, 304, 305; saviors, 306; self-knowledge, 239, 314
grail, 104, 305, 389–90n21, 390–91n23
Grossman, Vasily, 21, 256, 281, 332n15
guilt: *CP*, 222–23; as divine, 222–23, 299; *NCOM*, 282, 381n12; *OD*, 357–58n21;

survivor's, 282; *TC*, 136, 195, 357–58n21, 386n12; *TR*, 295, 299
gunpowder, 34, 334n4
gyre, 283

hand imagery, 254, 255–56, 376–77n22
Hardy, Thomas, 267, 380n9
harmonic vibration, 110
haruspication, 229, 372n9
Heart of Darkness (Conrad), 16
Heart Sutra, 27
heimarmene: *APH*, 113–16; *BM*, 41–45, 48–49, 97, 337n14, 351n15, 385–86n7; *CP*, 209–10, 246, 249–50; death, 338n16; vs. free will, 44, 47, 48–49, 51; gnosis, 209; hylics and psychics, 47; as inexorable, 97–98; as mindless, 113–14, 351n15; *NCOM*, 267, 351n13; *OD*, 337n14; order and disorder, 171; *TC*, 146, 148, 167–68, 180–85, 192–93, 375n15; *TR*, 289
hell: *APH*, 107–9; *BM*, 8, 33, 34, 328–29n1; metal, 341n9; separation, 62; world as, 8, 107–8, 208, 297, 328–29n1
Hermetists, 38, 360–61n8
Hinduism: Brahman, 354–55n11, 359n3, 365n15; influence on Gnostics, 3; *kalpas*, 352–53n2; karma, 272; Śaivism, 354–55n11; third eye, 273, 381n16; unity, 308–9; vibration, 110. *See also* Shiva
"History" (Emerson), 154
Holocaust, 25–26, 338n16
Holy Grail. *See* grail
horn, 282–85, 348n20, 383n26
horses: *APH*, 102, 106, 107, 109–12, 121–22, 233–34, 354n6, 354n9; *BM*, 19–20; modernity, 373n15
humanity as divine: *APH*, 102; *BM*, 74–76, 89–91; Gnosticism, 3, 305, 318; light, 318; Perennial Principle, 15; potential saviors, 306; *The Sunset Limited*, 14; *TR*, 304–11, 313–14, 319–20, 389n20, 390–91n23. *See also* divine spark; pneuma
humanity as evil: *APH*, 108, 354nn7–8, 378n2; *BM*, 15–19, 378n2; body and psyche, 47; *CG*, 378n2; *The Counselor*, 378n2; *OD*, 378n2; *Suttree*, 378n2; *TC*, 128; *TR*, 297–99
Huxley, Aldous. *See* Perennial Philosophy
hyle and hylics, 3, 47, 320

ignorance: blindness, 173, 174; conspiracy of the world, 246; dark, 161, 162, 185, 195–97, 363n2; drunkenness, 211; evil, 159, 171, 313; illusion and impermanence, 159, 161, 211, 212; salvation, 239
illusion and impermanence: Absolute, 131, 150–52; *APH*, 106, 116–18, 122; beauty, 106; *BM*, 27–30, 290–91; cave allegory, 22, 314; compassion, 346n11; *The Counselor*, 354n10; *CP*, 207–11, 226, 240–44, 248–49, 250–52; Diamond Sutra, 28–29; enlightenment, 27, 98; form, 308; haiku, 350n7; ignorance, 159, 161, 211, 212; multiplicity, 365n15; Nirvāṇa, 150–52, 361–62n9; past, 369n5; Perennial Philosophy, 159, 165, 172–73, 215–16; rites, 307–8; "Sailing to Byzantium," 283–84; science, 59; self-knowledge, 240; senses, 165–66, 172–75; sensuality, 233; suffering, 144; theater imagery, 28–29, 210–11; *TR*, 290–93, 303–4, 308, 392n28; will, 146; Yogacarins, 138, 165, 190
illusion and impermanence in *TC*: attachment, 190; Book 1, 127, 130–32, 136–38, 140, 363n7, 367n11; Book 2, 143–44, 150–51, 158–59, 363n8, 367n12; Book 3, 161–77, 363n2, 373n2; Book 4, 190, 191–92; death, 174, 190, 191; fire, 136–38; inscrutability of divine, 191–92; revelation of world, 375nn12–14
immortality, 51–52, 85, 189, 253–54, 281, 308, 309
impermanence. *See* illusion and impermanence
imprisonment: by archons, 35, 39, 43, 164–65; *BM*, 13, 22–23, 39, 40; by body, 42, 47, 227; *CP*, 227; heavenly spheres, 9; revelation, 150; *TR*, 315–16. *See also* heimarmene
incubus, 185, 228, 366n6
indifference of God/cosmos: *APH*, 371n1; *BM*, 7, 10, 23–25, 61; *CP*, 203, 217, 219–21, 222, 228, 248; *NCOM*, 275–76, 382n19; sacrifices, 217–18; *TC*, 183; *TR*, 299–301, 383–84n1, 387–88n16; war, 61
Inferno, 6, 237–38, 288, 328n6, 384n2
inn, world as, 36
inordinate day, 78, 344n5
interconnectedness: *APH*, 107, 121–23, 233–34; blood imagery, 103, 133; *BM*, 356n15; Boehme, 90; *CP*, 215, 234; death, 254; Emerson, 143, 154, 155; nature mystics, 134; *NCOM*, 285; *Suttree*, 356n16; *TC*, 125,

interconnectedness (*continued*)
133–35, 139, 140, 143, 154–55, 354n8, 357nn19–20; *TR*, 323

jackrabbits, 202–3
James, Henry, 370n7
James, William, 1, 187–88, 327n1
jñāna. *See* salvation; wisdom
Job, 25, 153, 217–18, 300, 362n10
Joyce, James, 332n14, 352n20
Judge Holden: as cannibal, 92–93; Chigurh, 274; coins, 41, 66–69, 342–43n11, 351n13, 380–81n11; compared to McCarthy, 340–41n8; as Death, 51–52, 338–39n18; fate, 42–46, 52, 337–38nn14–15; as a god, 35, 36, 39–40, 52, 59–63, 65–66, 91, 274, 334n5, 339–40n4, 342–43n11, 356n15, 392n30; illusion and impermanence, 28–29; judgment, 39, 57, 63; opposition to kid, 83–88, 90–94, 345n8; origins, 37–38, 334n6, 335n8; as other, 31–32; as parody, 55–63, 339–40n4; as prime number, 334n6; Reason, 55–58, 83, 233, 234, 339n3; as Satan, 34, 40–41, 52, 62–66; as scientist, 55–58, 65, 266, 339n3, 348n21; smile, 84, 345n8; as supernatural, 25, 31, 32–42, 44, 47, 49, 52, 84, 85, 333n1, 342–43n11; war, 60–63; will, 48, 57, 61
Jung, Carl Gustav, 142, 217–18, 253, 329n3, 362n10

kalpas, 352–53n2
karma, 272
kid in *BM*: age, 333n2; animals, 78; baptism, 75; as Christ, 72–73, 85, 94, 343n2; compassion, 79, 81–83, 88, 346n11, 382–83n23; covenant, 51; death, 51–52, 91–94; destiny, 87–88; divine spark, 74–75, 89–91; failure, 94, 99; fire, 96; Moses, 77, 78; opposition to Judge Holden, 83–88, 90–94, 345n8; as other, 75–76, 80–81, 344n3, 347n16; pilgrim, 77–78; resurrection, 76–77; sacrifice, 93–94; stars, 71–72, 74, 91; violence, 15, 73, 82–83, 86–88, 344n3, 347n16, 380n7; Virgin Mary, 78–80, 81
killing: fear of death, 50, 51; predator as sacred, 131–35, 355–56n14
kindness, 256, 277, 278, 281–82, 285, 383n24. *See also* compassion

knowledge: vs. faith, 129; fire as, 391–92n25; vs. Reality, 188; vs. spiritual knowledge, 247; water sacrament, 255. *See also* gnosis; self-knowledge
koans, 66

landscape: *BM*, 7–8, 27, 182, 328–29n1; *CP*, 208; *Suttree*, 208, 370n8; *TC*, 176, 182
language. *See* representation vs. Reality
lawsuit concerning the world, 147–48, 155, 360n7
ledgers, Akashic, 127–28, 250, 321–22, 353–54n4
leveling out. *See* optical democracy
libraries, 292, 386n9
lies, 64–66, 68, 186, 292, 297, 386n9
Life and Fate (Grossman), 21, 256, 281, 332n15
light: Absolute, 167; as alien, 196, 297; *BM*, 76, 78; as divine, 228; enlightenment, 273–74; gnosis, 162, 185, 197; in man, 16, 318; Manichaeism, 89, 276, 290, 306, 335n8, 346–47n12, 368–69n18; *TC*, 168, 175–76, 195–97; *TR*, 288, 292, 297, 309, 390–91n23; wisdom as, 161, 162, 195–97
literal interpretation, 6, 328n6
living water, 278
Logos, 304–5, 308
longing, 150, 251–52, 375–76nn17–18
lullabies, 101, 349n1

magical realism, 235, 373n1
Mahayana Buddhism, 139, 148–49, 308–9, 346n11, 360–61n8
mammon, 277
mandalas, 325
Mandean Gnosticism, 309
Manichaeism: animals and plants, 89, 126, 306, 346–47n12; darkness, 16; dualism, 114, 170, 276, 335n8; Genesis, 300; light/dark, 16, 89, 276, 290, 306, 335n8, 346–47n12, 368–69n18; *Moby-Dick*, 347n13; *NCOM*, 276–77; popularity, 198; Salvator Salvatus, 93–94, 343n1; sun/moon, 198–99, 290, 368–69n18
many histories theory, 337–38n15
maps, 237–38, 256, 325, 377n25
Māra, 40–41, 45, 52, 360–61n8. *See also* Satan
Mary Magdalene, 223–24, 372n6
material world: *APH*, 106; *CP*, 242–43; darkness, 164; defined, 27; and Nirvāṇa, 361–62n9; as prison, 40, 45, 164–65, 325; *TC*,

143, 240; *TR*, 319. *See also* illusion and impermanence

māyā. *See* illusion and impermanence

McCarthy, Cormac: age, 333n2; compared to Bell, 262–63, 379n4; compared to Judge Holden, 340–41n8; on family, 379n4, 387n14; on magical realism, 373n1; on morality, 297, 387n14; on Proust and James, 370n7; on spiritual experience, 1, 29–30, 187; on symbols, 187; on truth, 2, 279, 364n10; on violence, 261–62, 340–41n8

medicine show. *See* theater imagery

meditation, 174

Meister Eckhart: God as inexpressible, 247; luminosity of spirit, 309; unity with God, 131, 157–59, 190; will, 49

Melville, Herman: *Bartleby, the Scrivener*, 86; *The Encantadas*, 103–5; "Fragments of a Lost Gnostic Poem . . . ," 86; Gnostic readings, 4–5. *See also Moby-Dick* (Melville)

Merchant of Venice, 257, 377n26

mercy, 219–20

Meredith, George, 170–71

meridian, 49–50, 338n17

"Meru" (Yeats), 15

metal imagery: *APH*, 113, 338–39n18, 359–60n4; Blake, 341n9, 342–43n11; *BM*, 66–69, 179–80, 256–57, 338–39n18, 342–43n11, 359–60n4; as evil, 66–67, 113; *Suttree*, 360n5; *TC*, 179, 180, 338–39n18

Mill, John Stuart, 351n16

Milton, John, 34, 334n4

"Mind-only" teachings, 138, 190

Mithraicism, 329n3

Moby-Dick (Melville): *BM*, 31, 33, 48, 51; cruelty of nature, 20; demiurge, 113, 146–47, 360n5, 361n9; as favorite of McCarthy, 332n14; Saint Elmo's fire, 347n13

modernity: apocalypse in *TR*, 384–85n4; *BM*, 53, 69, 339n1; horses, 373n15; loss of sacred, 232–34; nihilism, 53, 69, 339n1

moon: *APH*, 105; *BM*, 41, 79, 344–45n6; heimarmene, 41; Manichaeism, 368–69n18; *TC*, 127; *TR*, 312; Virgin Mary, 283; women, 105, 350n6

morality: *CP*, 225–26; evil, 169–70; kid in *BM*, 75; McCarthy on, 297, 387n14; Nietzsche, 63, 340n6; order and disorder, 172; *TR*, 295–97

Moses, 77, 78

multiverse, 337–38n15

mystery, 31, 325–26, 333n1, 395n36

mysticism: Absolute as unknowable, 155; certitude vs. articulation, 111; fire, 96; in McCarthy's works, 5; mystics as travelers, 283; parody in *BM*, 66–69, 342–43n11; term, 247; *TR*, 395n36; world as a dream, 241–42. *See also* Boehme, Jacob

names: power of, 231–32, 392n30; vs. thing itself, 129–30, 188, 303–4, 354n8, 354n9

narrator, unreliable, 261, 378–79n3

natural order, disruption, 78, 136, 344n5, 357–58n21

nature: beauty of, 105; divine in, 340n7; as evil, 7, 21–24, 138, 170, 259–61, 377–78n1. *See also* cruelty of nature

"Nature" (Emerson), 143

nature mystics, 134

Nazis, 338n16

negative romanticism, 109, 351n12

negative theology, 188–89

Nietzsche, Friedrich, 46–48, 53, 54, 63, 339n1, 340n6

nihilism: *APH*, 109; *BM*, 69, 99, 233; *CP*, 233; of McCarthy, 3; modernity, 53, 69, 339n1; *TR*, 319–21

Nirvāṇa: Bodhisattvas, 336n11; desire, 144–45; impersonal God, 153; and material world, 150–51, 152, 361–62n9; as transrational, 362n12

No Country for Old Men: bridal imagery, 273, 345n7; Chigurh as supernatural, 263–66, 272, 379–80n6; coins, 267–68, 270–72, 351n13, 381n12, 385–86n7; compassion, 277, 278, 280–82, 285, 382–83n23; demiurge, 274–75, 381–82n17; dharma, 284–85; dreams, 271, 282–84, 287, 382n25; evil, 259–66, 272–73, 276, 330–31n10, 377–78n1, 379–80n6; fate, 267, 268–72, 351n13, 380n10, 381nn12–13; fire, 282–85, 348n20, 349n3, 383n26, 391–92n25; indifference of God, 275–76, 382n19; McCarthy and Bell, 262–63, 379n4; past, 369n5; Revelations, 262–63, 384n3; Satan, 260, 263, 276–77, 379–80n6; Socratic dialogue, 266–72; title, 262, 263; *TR* allusion, 287; transcendence, 273–74, 277–78, 283–85, 382n25; unreliable narrator, 261, 378–79n3;

No Country for Old Men (continued)
water, 277–80, 285, 382n20, 382–83n23, 383n26
no self. See *anatta*

ogdoad, 38
OM, 325
omnipotence/omniscience: evil paradox, 114–16, 141–42, 243, 275–76, 358–59n1, 382n18; *TC*, 176
optical democracy, 13–15
The Orchard Keeper, 202, 344n5, 369n1, 369n5, 376n19
order: and disorder, 170–72, 365n16; disruption of natural, 78, 136, 344n5, 357–58n21
the other: Absolute as, 251; Judge Holden as, 31–32; kid in *BM*, 75–76, 80–81, 344n3, 347n16; Magdalena as, 226–27
Our Lady of Guadalupe, 79, 344–45n6
Outer Dark: blindness, 365n17; Eucharist, 345n9; evil, 330–31n10, 372n10, 378n2; fetters, 336n12; Gnostic readings, 4; guilt, 357–58n21; heimarmene, 337n14; inordinate day, 344n5; Mary Magdalene, 372n6; pneuma, 367–68n14; triune, 332n16, 335–36n9, 337n14, 392n30; waking, 359n2
"The Over-Soul" (Emerson), 154, 309

pacts. See covenants
panentheism and pantheism, 148–49, 150
Paradise Lost (Milton), 34, 334n4
parody in *BM*, 53–69, 339–40nn3–4, 342–43n11
past: *CP*, 206–8; prehistoric imagery, 205, 369n5; quantum physics, 373–74n4; *TC*, 186–90, 366–67n8, 386n8; *TR*, 291–92
patterns, hidden, 136, 358n22
Perennial Philosophy: articulating sacred, 110–11; defined, 2; direct experience, 151, 188; fire, 283, 310; Gnosticism, 5; illusion and impermanence, 159, 165, 172–73, 215–16, 241–42; impersonal God, 153; involvement vs. withdrawal, 139; panentheism vs. pantheism, 149; Reality, 159, 251; rites, 355n12; salvation, 199; self-knowledge, 239–40; separation, 157–58, 190, 350n8; spiritual knowledge vs. knowledge, 247; *The Sunset Limited*, 14; time, 191, 253–54; transcendence, 64; transience, 215–16; unity, 13, 190–91; 308–9, 322; will, 48–49, 62; witnessing, 157–58. See also Absolute
Perennial Principle, 15. See also humanity as divine
personal God, 152–53
phallus, sun as, 9, 329n3
photographs, 291, 386n8
pictographs, 205–6, 369n5
pilgrims, 24–25, 77–78, 192–93, 238, 315, 344n4
Pistis Sophia, 317
planets, 41–42, 127, 289, 300, 368–69n18
plants, 89, 346–47n12
Platonism, 2, 22, 314, 316, 388–89n19
pneuma: in all, 199; *APH*, 372n8; *BM*, 368n15; as breath of God, 308; *CP*, 227–28; defined, 3; end of days, 312; eternity of, 253–54; light, 162; as lost, 78, 81, 188, 290, 315; *NCOM*, 263; *OD*, 367–68n14; *TC*, 129, 134–35, 191–92, 368n15; *TR*, 289, 320, 322. See also divine spark; gnosis
pneumatics: revelation, 27–28; spiritual development, 47, 320; *TC*, 129; *TR*, 320
Poe, Edgar Allan, 104, 349n4
"The Poet" (Emerson), 96
praise, 111
predestination. See fate
preservation by Vishnu, 354–55n11, 359n3
Primal Man. See Salvator Salvatus
prime numbers, 334n6
primitivism. See atavism
procosmic position, 8
Prometheus, 95, 391–92n25
Proust, Marcel, 370n7
psyche and psychics, 3, 47, 320
puppet strings. See fetters, tethers, string motif
Pynchon, Thomas, 4–5, 37

quantum physics, 337–38n15, 373–74n4
Quechas. See Yumas
quests: *APH*, 103–5, 122; *BM*, 79; *TC*, 129; *TR*, 288, 384–85n4, 389–90n21

realism, 235, 373n1
Reality: Absolute as, 159, 175, 251; blindness, 165–68, 375–76n18; direct experience, 187–88, 189; gnosis, 144, 209, 247; Gnosticism, 21–22, 27–30; vs. knowledge, 188; Perennial Philosophy, 159, 251; Platonic, 2, 22, 314; *TC*, 143, 190–92; transience,

215–16. *See also* illusion and impermanence; representation vs. Reality
Reason, 54, 55–58, 83, 233, 234, 339n2, 339n3
rebirth and resurrection, 76–77
redeemed redeemer. *See* Salvator Salvatus
reductionism, 54, 58
regression. *See* atavism
reincarnation, 93, 252, 315, 348n18, 363–64n9, 376n19
renunciation of evil, 380n7
representation vs. Reality: *BM*, 256–57; *The Counselor*, 367n10; *CP*, 242–43, 250–51; direct experience, 187, 367n9; *TC*, 187–88, 189, 256, 362n13, 366–67nn8–9, 373n3, 375n16; *TR*, 303–4
resonance, 110
Revelations, 262–63, 288, 379n5, 384n3
rites: cannibalism, 298, 387n15; futility, 131, 355n12; *TC*, 131, 135; *TR*, 298, 307–8, 387n15
The Road: alienation, 289–90; anticosmicism, 298–99, 324, 385n5; apocalypse, 288, 299, 312–13, 376n20, 379n5, 383–84n1, 384–85n4; atavism, 387n15; attachment, 291, 302–3; beauty, 118, 292, 307, 324–25, 364n12; blindness, 317, 319, 320; cannibalism, 287, 295–98, 330n9, 358n23; cave, 315–18, 392–93n29; celestial bodies, 289, 385nn5–6; clocks, 371n13, 385n5; coins, 291, 385–86n7; compassion, 295–96, 319, 321; cosmology, 289–90, 385nn5–6; death, 293–95, 302; demiurge, 299–301, 317, 387n15; dreams, 287, 314–18, 353n4, 364n12; Ely, 319–21, 392n30; epilogue, 323–26, 394–95n34; evil, 297–99, 301, 302, 332–33n17; fate, 289; fire, 287, 289, 310–14, 321–22, 348n20, 349n3, 353n4; God, 299–301, 321–22, 332–33n17, 387–88n16, 393–94n31; illusion and impermanence, 290–93, 303–4, 308, 392n28; indifference, 330n5, 332–33n17; inordinate day, 344n5; ledgers, 353–54n4; lies, 292, 386n9; light, 288, 292, 297; maps, 325, 377n25; patterns, 358n22; Revelations, 288, 379n5, 384n3; sun, 198, 290, 312; title, 305, 389–90n21, 390–91n23; transcendence, 308–9, 321–22, 393–94n31; transience, 102, 349n2; water, 309–10, 316–17, 377n24, 382n21, 392n27. *See also* son in *The Road*

sacred: as accursed, 126; blood, 132; *The Counselor*, 355–56n14; death of in *TR*, 304–5, 388–89n19; inability to articulate, 110–11; modernity and loss of, 232–34; wolves, 131–35, 355–56n14
sacrifice: *APH*, 120; *BM*, 93–94; Christ as, 218, 248; *CP*, 212, 213, 218–19, 238, 245, 247–48, 358n23, 371n12, 374–75n9; indifference of God, 217–18; Isaac, 300; Salvator Salvatus, 93–94, 218; straw dogs, 194; *TC*, 131, 254, 374n6; *TR*, 300; as violence prevention, 247–48, 374–75n9
Sade, Marquis de, 24, 25
"Sailing to Byzantium" (Yeats), 262, 263, 283–84, 382n25
Saint Elmo's fire, 89–90, 347n13
Śaivism, 354–55n11
salitter, 301–2, 303, 388n18
salvation: *BM*, 71–99, 343n2; darma, 284–85; death, 156; gnosis, 4, 5, 26–27, 98, 156–57, 239, 249; Manichaeism, 93–94, 368–69n18; *NCOM*, 284–85; Perennial Philosophy, 199; Salvator Salvatus, 73–74, 93–96, 218, 254–55, 343n1; self-knowledge, 239; *TC*, 156, 197, 199; *TR*, 287; unity, 254–55. *See also* kid in *BM*; saviors
Salvator Salvatus, 74, 93–96, 218, 254–55, 343n1. *See also* kid in *BM*
Samael, 237, 317. *See also* demiurge
saṃsāra. *See* illusion and impermanence; material world
Śaṅkara, 309, 365n15, 395n35
Santa Fe Institute, 337–38n15, 383–84n1
Satan: as ape, 228; *BM* as parody, 53–69; *CP*, 228–29, 231; creation, 360–61n8; Judge Holden as, 34, 40–41, 52, 62–66; lies, 297; *NCOM*, 260, 263, 276–77, 379–80n6; *TR*, 392n30. *See also* Māra
Saved Savior. *See* Salvator Salvatus
saviors: Gnosticism, 73–74, 306; potential, 306; Salvator Salvatus, 74, 93–96, 218, 254–55, 343n1; son in *TR*, 305–10, 313, 316, 326, 348n19; unity, 254–55. *See also* kid in *BM*
sceptre, 245, 374n5
school surveys, 378–79n3
science: *BM*, 55–63, 65, 266, 339n3, 348n21; *CP*, 233; metal, 67; *NCOM*, 266
scientism, 58
"The Second Coming" (Yeats), 249, 262–63, 283, 317

self-knowledge: Absolute, 314, 323; *anatta*, 244–45; *CP*, 239–40; direct experience, 307; evil and violence, 16; salvation, 239; *TR*, 313–14. *See also* gnosis
senseless kindness, 281
senses, 172–75. *See also* blindness
sensuality, 105–6, 107, 211, 233
separation: ego, 128, 148, 244–45; longing, 150; Perennial Philosophy, 157–58, 190, 350n8; *TC*, 350n9; will to, 62, 107
serpents, 312–13, 348n19
Sethian Gnosticism, 302, 309
seven, 126, 352n1
Shakespeare, William, 249, 253, 257, 357–58n21, 376n21, 377n26
Shiva, 35, 52, 334n5, 354–55n11, 356n15, 359n3, 381n16
"The Sick Rose" (Blake), 324–25
sin: *The Counselor*, 371n2; *CP*, 217–34, 372n5; ego, 158; *TR*, 299, 313. *See also* forgiveness
Sisyphus, 348–49n22
skull imagery, 18–19, 102, 106, 192, 367–68n14
sky motif, 11–12, 202, 365–66n18, 375n10
slave morality, 63, 340n6
sleep: as death, 52; illusion and impermanence, 28, 144, 241–42, 274. *See also* dreams
smile imagery: *BM*, 84, 345n8
snakes, 312–13, 348n19
Socratic dialogue, 266–68, 270–71, 272
son in *The Road*: acceptance of death, 294–95; as alien, 297; compassion, 295–96, 319, 321; as divine, 305–10, 313–14, 319–20, 389n20, 390–91n23; as fire carrier, 310–12; light, 309, 390–91n23; morality, 295–97; relationship with father, 386–87n13; as savior, 305–10, 313, 316, 326, 348n19
Sophia Prunikos, 224–25
soteriology. *See* salvation
soul: Absolute, 131; Ascent of the Soul, 38; dark night of, 76–77; sick soul, 251
Spenser, Edmund, 104
spiritual knowledge. *See* enlightenment; gnosis
stars: *BM*, 11, 71–72, 74, 78, 79, 91, 344–45n6; Gnosticism, 11, 12, 41–42; *Suttree*, 330n5; *TC*, 127, 176; *TR*, 289
The Stonemason, 353–54n4
story: archetypes, 142–43; in *TC*, 141, 358–59n1
straw dogs, 194

strings. *See* fetters, tethers, string motif
suffering: of animals, 202–4, 369n1; *APH*, 101, 105–6, 118, 120–21; beauty, 118–19; *CP*, 202–4, 217, 249; demons, 32; desire, 144–45; enlightenment, 120, 136; fire, 127, 312; *OK*, 202, 369n1; self-suffering, 158; sensuality, 105–6, 107; *TC*, 138, 144, 162–63, 168, 174, 175, 177, 180–81, 183, 194; *TR*, 292, 295, 312; ubiquity of, 120, 144–45, 164
Sufism, 189, 308–9
suicide, 222, 372n5
sun: *APH*, 103; *BM*, 8–11, 76, 198, 329nn2–3, 353n3; Gnosticism, 8, 9, 329n2; as good, 9, 330n4; Manichaeism, 198–99, 290, 368–69n18; *Suttree*, 198; *TC*, 195–99; *TR*, 198, 290, 312; *WM*, 368n17
The Sunset Limited, 14
supernatural: Chigurh in *NCOM*, 263–66, 272, 379–80n6; *CP*, 229–32; evil of, 229–32, 372n10. *See also* Judge Holden
surgeons, 194, 209, 231, 368n16
Suttree: carnival, 211, 370–71n11; clock, 371n13; demiurge, 338–39n18, 359–60nn4–5; evil, 330n5, 330–31n10, 378n2; Gnostic readings, 5; God, 332–33n17; hidden patterns, 358n22; inordinate day, 344n5; interconnectedness, 356n16; landscape, 208, 370n8; monster, 331n12; sun, 198; surgeon, 209, 368n16; unity, 376–77n22; water, 377n24, 382n21, 391n24, 392n27
swallowing metaphor, 315
symbols. *See* representation vs. Reality
syncretism, Gnosticism as, 3, 327n2

tanha, 107. *See also* separation
tarot, 51, 87–88
The Tempest, 253, 376n21
tethers. *See* fetters, tethers, string motif
Thanatos, 109, 221–22, 236, 351n12, 371–72nn3–4
theater imagery, 28–29, 210–11, 370–71n11
Theravada Buddhism, 346n11
third eye, 273, 381n16
thirteen, 34, 333–34n3
time: *BM*, 52, 337n13; *CP*, 214; cycle imagery, 283; as demonic, 315; many histories theory, 337–38n15; Perennial Philosophy, 191, 253–54; quantum physics, 373–74n4; *TC*, 191; *TR*, 308

transcendence: *APH*, 121–22; blocking, 64, 66, 69, 147, 185; *CP*, 251; disassociation with material world, 152, 362–63n9; *NCOM*, 273–74, 277–78, 283–85, 382n25; Perennial Philosophy, 64; *TC*, 126, 141–59, 185, 340n7; *TR*, 308–9, 321–22, 393–94n31; Truth, 279

Transcendentalism. *See* Emerson, Ralph Waldo

transience: *APH*, 102, 106, 215; *The Counselor*, 371n14; *CP*, 201–16, 236–37, 250; lost civilizations, 205–6, 369–70nn5–6; Perennial Philosophy, 215–16; *TC*, 183–84, 215; *TR*, 102, 349n2

transmigration, 376n19

transubstantiation, 218–19, 245–46, 374n6

Trimurti Brahman, 354–55n11, 359n3

triune in *Outer Dark*, 332n16, 335–36n9, 337n14, 392n30

tropological interpretation, 6, 328n6

Truth: *APH*, 364n10, 366n2, 382n22; McCarthy on, 2, 279, 364n10; *NCOM*, 279; *TC*, 166–67; *TR*, 288

"Under Ben Bulben" (Yeats), 352n17

unity: with Absolute, 157–58, 251, 254–55, 322; *APH*, 121–23, 233–34; Buddhism, 308–9; compassion, 295; *CP*, 234, 254–56; of God, 190–91; hand imagery, 255–56, 376–77n22; Hinduism, 308–9; Perennial Philosophy, 13, 190–91, 308–9, 322; salvation, 254–55; *Suttree*, 376–77n22; *TC*, 131, 143, 154–55, 191, 234, 376–77n22; *TR*, 308–9; vs. uniformity, 13–14; *WM*, 376–77n22. *See also* interconnectedness

unknowability: of Absolute, 151–52, 155, 158, 188–89, 247, 362nn11–12; of Chigurh, 265; of world, 130

Urizen, 339n3, 342–43n11

Valentinians: divine spark, 95–96; dualism, 114, 170, 335n8; end of days, 311–12; types of people, 320

Valéry, Paul, 50, 53–54

The Varieties of Religious Experience (James), 1, 187–88, 327n1

vibration, 325

violence: chance and divine will, 61; kid in *BM*, 15, 73, 82–83, 86–88, 344n3, 347n16, 380n7; killing and fear of death, 50, 51; McCarthy on, 261–62, 340–41n8;

prevention through sacrifice, 247–48, 374–75n9; of reductionism, 58; self-knowledge, 16. *See also* war

Virgin Mary, 78–80, 81, 225, 283, 344–45n6

virtue, 169, 170–71

Vishnu, 354–55n11, 359n3

A Vision (Yeats), 283

void, 12–13, 16, 330n6

war: *BM*, 60–64; *CP*, 204–5; dark, 363n3; as game, 60, 340n5; McCarthy on, 340–41n8; metal, 67

The Waste Land (Eliot), 8, 208, 394–95n34

water: *APH*, 105, 111–12; *CP*, 255, 377n24; immortality, 309; living water, 278; *NCOM*, 277–80, 285, 382n20, 382–83n23, 383n26; as pervasive theme, 377n24, 382n21; sacrament of water, 255, 278–79, 309–10, 377n24, 391n24; *Suttree*, 377n24, 382n21, 391n24, 392n27; *TC*, 382n21, 391n24; *TR*, 309–10, 316–17, 377n24, 382n21, 392n27; women, 105, 350n6

weaving: *BM*, 359–60n4, 375n11; *CP*, 231, 248; *Moby-Dick*, 113, 146–47, 360n5; *Suttree*, 338–39n18, 359–60n4; *TC*, 113, 146–47, 186, 360n5, 375n11

West, Nathanael, 4–5, 37

Whales and Men, 356n15, 362n12, 365n16, 367n9, 368n17, 376–77n22

will: *BM*, 44, 46–49, 51, 57, 61, 274, 338n16; *CP*, 209–10, 249–50; vs. fate, 44, 47, 48–49, 51, 180, 182; Free Will Defense, 243; illusion and impermanence, 146; karma, 272; *NCOM*, 270, 271, 272; power, 46, 47–48, 338n16; Sisyphus, 348–49n22; *TC*, 180, 182; war, 61

wisdom: as abyss, 139; vs. compassion, 346n11; as light, 161, 162, 195–97

witches, 229–31, 373n13

witnessing: *BM*, 367n11; Job, 362n10; Perennial Philosophy, 157–58; *TC*, 153, 189, 320, 358–59n1, 367n11

wolves: *BM*, 19; compared to dogs, 194; corporeality, 129–30, 354n8; dreams, 128, 350n9; interconnectedness, 125, 133–34, 234, 357n19–20; as sacred, 131–35, 355–56n14; St. Francis of Assisi, 134, 357n20; *TC*, 125, 128–35, 194, 234, 350n9, 352n19, 354n8, 355–56n14, 357n19–20

Wordsworth, William, 73, 121

world, renewal of, 187, 366n7

Yahweh: Chigurh as, 274–75, 381–82n17; as demiurge, 35–36, 39, 274; Judge Holden as, 36, 39–40, 91, 274
"The Yalu" (Valéry), 50, 53–54
Yeats, W. B., 15, 249, 262–63, 283–84, 317, 352n17, 382n25
Yogacara Buddhism, 138, 165, 190
Yumas, 72, 91, 347n17

www.ingramcontent.com/pod-product-compliance
Lightning Source LLC
Chambersburg PA
CBHW020632230426
43665CB00008B/145